MW01708727

The Nature of the Obligations under the International Covenant on Economic, Social and Cultural Rights

SCHOOL OF HUMAN RIGHTS RESEARCH SERIES, Volume 18

The titles published in this series are listed at the end of this volume.

The Nature of the Obligations under the International Covenant on Economic, Social and Cultural Rights

M. Magdalena Sepúlveda

INTERSENTIA

Antwerpen – Oxford – New York

This Volume is an adapted version of a dissertation defended at Utrecht University on 6 May 2002.

M. Magdalena Sepúlveda
The Nature of the Obligations under the International Covenant on Economic, Social and Cultural Rights

CRC prepared by: G.J. Wiarda Institute, Utrecht University Institute for Legal Studies, Boothstraat 6, 3512 BW Utrecht

ISBN 90-5095-260-7
D/2003/7849/20
NUR 828

PREFACE

Legal scholarship has a vital role to play in developing a better understanding of economic, social and cultural rights as internationally recognized human rights. This has long been a field in relation to which all too few in-depth scholarly inquiries have been undertaken. For these reasons, as well as because of the comprehensiveness and excellence of the analysis, Magdalena Sepulveda's book on the obligations of the State under the International Covenant on Economic, Social and Cultural Rights is to be very warmly welcomed. It makes an outstanding contribution to our understanding of recent developments in this area. It also represents a work of unparalleled depth in analyzing the work of the UN Committee on Economic, Social and Cultural Rights which is the single most important international body whose work is devoted primarily to the promotion of respect for these rights.

One of the book's great strengths is precisely the amount of systematic research and analysis which is devoted to the various outputs achieved by that Committee in the first fifteen or so years of its existence. The meticulous recounting of the approach which the Committee has undertaken in seeking to define and elaborate upon the meaning of the obligations undertaken by States under the Covenant constitutes a vital resource for those wishing to understand the legal nature of the various provisions of the Covenant. Indeed, from the perspective of one who participated actively in the first twelve years of the Committee's life, it is a pleasant surprise to see such a relatively coherent picture emerge on the basis of a heterogeneous array of precedents and practices, often adopted under great time pressure and in response to diverse challenges arising in very different contexts.

Two dimensions of the present work are of particular interest to those seeking to understand the relevant body of law and the monitoring arrangements that have been established to review the compliance of governments with their obligations under the Covenant. The first is the author's very welcome critical scrutiny of the various typologies of states parties obligations which commentators have long urged as the best way to analyze the obligations emerging from the Covenant. The UN Committee had been loathe to adopt this typology until 1999 when it adopted a new approach to its General Comments. This critical analysis is very useful in helping us to understand both the strengths and weaknesses of the new approach.

Equally valuable is the author's attempt to identify a set of criteria against which to measure what she terms the 'legitimacy' of the Committee's work. The assumption is that the higher the degree of legitimacy which is thus achieved, the greater will be the impact of the Committee's work and of the willingness of governments to comply with its exhortations.

In an original and very insightful analysis the author identifies eight different criteria: (a) the independence and expertise of the Committee members; (b) the diversity of their backgrounds and expertise; (c) the continuity and coherence of the membership of the Committee; (d) the efficiency of the Committee's proceedings; (e) the objectivity of the Committee's approach; (f) the reasonableness and practicability of the outcomes endorsed by the Committee; and (h) the support which the Committee succeeds in garnering from other international bodies. Domestic impact, or the resonance of the work of the Committee in the domestic legal and administrative systems of states parties to the Covenant might have been another useful criterion. This innovative framework which the author has developed is a very helpful one and represents an important contribution to the study of the work of the various UN human rights treaty bodies in general.

There are thus many reasons to welcome the publication of an excellent analytical work covering all of the key aspects of the United Nations' efforts to ensure respect for the too often neglected and poorly understood set of rights recognized in the International Covenant on Economic, Social and Cultural Rights and a range of other important international human rights treaties.

Philip Alston[1]

1 Professor of Law, New York University Law School; formerly Chairperson, UN Committee on Economic, Social and Cultural Rights, 1991-1998.

ACKNOWLEDGEMENTS

For the present work I am indebted to the many people and institutions that have supported me over the years.

I wish to express my profound gratitude to my supervisors Professor Cees Flinterman and Professor Fried Van Hoof for their helpful comments and for the great opportunity they gave me to work at SIM. To Professor Van Hoof I owe a particular debt for his unsurpassed guidance and support. I would also like to thank Hans Werdmölder for having trust in me when I requested to come to SIM.

I would like to thank Professor Fernando Mariño Menéndez of Carlos III University in Madrid who was my supervisor there and the members of the reading committee for this dissertation, Professor Bas de Gaay Fortman, Peter Baehr, Ineke Boerefijn, Paul Hunt and Fons Coomans. Special mention should be made of Professor Philip Alston both for his participation in the reading committee and as a source of inspiration over the years.

Several institutions have provided financial support for my studies and Ph.D. research. In this regard I would like to mention the Fundatie van vrij-vrouwe van Renswoude in Utrecht which provided me with a special grant for the book.

I would like to express my thanks to the following persons who provided substantive comments or editorial input on the manuscript: Mark Manly, Ineke Boerefijn, José Antonio Guevara, Juan Amaya-Castro, Saskia Bal, Irnsje Veerman and Peter Morris.

Over the years that it has taken me to complete this study, I have relied greatly on my family and friends and a special word of thanks is owed to Elvira Domínguez, Soledad García, José Antonio Guevara and Sanne Hirs for their friendship and support during the ordeal.

I wish to pay special tribute to my family (Diego, Mona and Diego Andrés) without whom I would never have been in this position, to Marisa Carmona for her support and to my loving husband, Mark, who assisted me with the editing of the book and supported me in countless other ways. His forbearance and understanding were essential, especially during the final months and I am forever indebted to him.

To Diego and Mona with devotion

TABLE OF CONTENTS

PART ONE
THE ROLE OF THE COMMITTEE ON ECONOMIC, SOCIAL AND CULTURAL RIGHTS IN CLARIFYING THE NORMATIVE CONTENT OF THE COVENANT

Selected Abbreviations

ACHR	American Convention on Human Rights
ADHR	American Declaration of the Rights and Duties of Man
AfCHR	African Charter on Human and People's Rights
AIDS	Acquired immunodeficiency syndrome
AJIL	American Journal of International Law
BYIL	British Yearbook of International Law
CAT Committee	Committee against Torture
CAT	Convention against Torture and Other Cruel, Inhuman or Degrading Treatment or Punishment
CEDAW	Convention on the Elimination of All forms of Discriminations against Women
CEDAW Committee	Convention on the Elimination of All forms of Discriminations against Women
CERD Committee	Committee on the Elimination of All forms of Racial Discrimination
CERD	Convention on the Elimination of All forms of Racial Discrimination
CRC Committee	Convention on the Rights of the Child
CRC	Convention on the Rights of the Child
CSR	Convention relating to the Status of Refugee
ECHR	European Convention for the Protection of Human Rights and Fundamental Freedoms
ECOSOC	Economic and Social Council of the United Nations
EJIL	European Journal of International Law
ETS	European Treaty Series (Council of Europe)
FAO	Food and Agriculture Organisation of the United Nations
GA	General Assembly
GDP	Gross domestic product
GNP	Gross national product
HIV	Human immunodeficiency virus
HRC	Human Rights Committee
HRLJ	Human Rights Law Journal
HRQ	Human Rights Quarterly
I/A Court H.R.	Inter-American Court on Human Rights

ICCPR	International Covenant on Civil and Political Rights
ICESCR	International Covenant on Economic, Social and Cultural Rights
ICJ	International Court of Justice
ICJ	Review International Commission of Jurist Review
ICLQ	International and Comparative Law Quarterly
IHRR	International Human Rights Reports
ILC	International Law Commission
ILO	International Labour Organisation
IMF	International Monetary Fund
IOM/FOM	Inter-Office Memorandum/ Field Office Memorandum [UNHCR]
NGO	Non-Governmental Organisation
NILR	Netherlands International Law Review
NQHR	Netherlands Quarterly of Human Rights
OAS	Organisation of American States
OHCHR	Office of the United Nations High Commissioner for Human Rights
OSCE	Organisation for Security and Co-operation in Europe
OUA	Organisation of African Unity
SIM	Netherlands Institute of Human Rights (Studie-en Informatiecentrum Mensenrechten)
UDHR	Universal Declaration of Human Rights
UN	United Nations Organisation
UNAIDS	Joint United Nations Programme on HIV/AIDS
UNDP	United Nations Development Programme
UNESCO	United Nations Educational, Scientific and Cultural Organisation
UNHCR	Office of the United Nations High Commissioner for Refugees
UNICEF	United Nations Children's Fund
VCLT	Vienna Convention on the Law of Treaties 1969
VJIL	Virginia Journal of International Law
WHO	World Health Organisation
World Bank	International Bank for Reconstruction and Development
WTO	World Trade Organisation
Yale Hum. Rts. Dev. L.J.	Yale Human Rights & Development Law Journal

CLARIFICATION CONCERNING THE SOURCES

An explanation of the symbols of the United Nations Documents is in order. Symbols of the United Nations documents are composed of capital letters combined with figures. The letter denotes the main organ to whose body of documentation to which the document and arabic numerals indicate the session or year.

Documents of the ECOSOC begin with:

'E/...'

Due to the fact that the Committee is a subsidiary organ of the ECOSOC, the documents of the Committee begin with:

'E/C.12/...'

The annual reports of the Committee to ECOSOC may be referred to by two symbols:

e.g. E/2001/22

E/C.12/2000/21

[Report on the twenty-second, twenty-third and twenty-fourth sessions (held in the year 2000) of the Committee on Economic, Social and Cultural Rights to the Economic and Social Council]. For reasons of manageability, when referring to the annual reports in the majority of cases, I have used the first of the symbols mentioned.

Another important documentary source for this study are the General Comments adopted by the Committee. At the time of writing the Committee had adopted 14 General Comments. I have referred to them principally with reference to their number. In the bibliography it is possible to find the full reference to each of them.

A word of explanation on the electronic human rights database of the OHCHR is also in order. The database was launched on the Internet in December 1996. Although it is an important source of United Nations documents, there are many documents that it does not include. Older mimeographed documents and printed official record volumes of UN documents are not as accessible as one might expect. Many documents are only available in a limited number of libraries and documentation centres, the majority of which are in 'developed countries.' This factor seriously and dramatically affects researchers and members of human rights organisations in the developing world who cannot afford to travel to the foreign-based institutions which have these documents available.[1]

Therefore, due to the fact that accessibility to the 'hard copies' of some documents is difficult and costly for students, members of human rights organisations and experts based in the developing world, whenever possible I give priority to documents which can be located in the database which is accessible through the world-wide web. For the same reason I have frequently provided Internet addresses in the footnotes.

Finally, it should be noted that throughout the study I illustrate the Committee's approach through its General Comments and Concluding Observations. The Concluding Observations and General Comments quoted are meant to be illustrative of what the Committee has said, but they do not exhaust all instances in which the Committee may have expressed an opinion. In addition, it should be mentioned that the full reference of the General Comments discussed in the text is to be found in the bibliography.

1 For example, the joint library of the Inter-American Court of Human Rights and the Inter-American Institute of Human Rights, which claims to be one of the most complete libraries on the topic of human rights in Latin America, only has a very limited number of published UN documents.

General Introduction

We the peoples of the United Nations
Determined
[...]
To reaffirm faith in fundamental human rights, in the dignity and worth of the human person, in the equal rights of men and women and of nations large and small, and
To establish conditions under which justice and respect for the obligations arising from treaties and other sources of international law can be maintained, and
To promote social progress and better standards of life in larger freedom,
And for these ends
[...]
To employ international machinery for the promotion of the economic and social advancement of all peoples,
have resolved to combine our efforts to accomplish these aims.[1]

1 Introductory remarks: An 'obligations approach'

The International Covenant on Economic, Social and Cultural Rights together with its sister Covenant, the International Covenant on Civil and Political Rights,[2] and the Universal Declaration,[3] form the International Bill of Human Rights which is the pillar for human rights protection within the United Nations.

The Covenant was adopted and opened for signature, ratification or accession by General Assembly Resolution 2200 A (XXI) of 16 December 1966. The Covenant reflects the commitments adopted after World War II to promote social progress and better standards of life, reaffirming faith in human rights and employing the international machinery to that end. The Covenant, in accordance with its article 27, entered into force on January 3, 1976 when thirty-five States had deposited the instrument of ratification or accession with the Secretary-General.

As of February 2002, 145 States had ratified or acceded to the Covenant.[4] Of the different international human rights instruments aimed at the protection of economic, social and cultural rights, the International Covenant on Economic, Social and Cultural

---

1 Charter of the United Nations, signed in San Francisco on 26 June 1945.
2 General Assembly Res. 2200 A (XXI) of 16 December 1966. The ICCPR entered into force on March 23, 1976, in accordance with article 49.
3 Adopted and proclaimed by General Assembly Res. 217 A (III) of December 10, 1948.
4 UN doc. A/56/178.

Rights is both the most universally ratified instrument and the most comprehensive in content.

The Preamble of the Covenant recognises, *inter alia,* that economic, social and cultural rights derive from the 'inherent dignity of the human person' and that 'the ideal of free human beings enjoying freedom of fear and want can only be achieved if conditions are created whereby everyone may enjoy his economic, social and cultural rights, as well as civil and political rights.'[5] The Covenant recognises the right to work (article 6); the right to just and favourable conditions of work (article 7); the right to form and join trade unions and the right to strike (article 8); the right to social security including social insurance (article 9); the right to protection and assistance for the family and the prohibition of child labour (article 10); the right to an adequate standard of living for oneself and one's family, including adequate food, clothing and housing and to the continuos improvement of living conditions (article 11); the right to the highest attainable standard of physical and mental health (article 12); the right to education, the freedom of parents to choose schools other than those established by public authorities (articles 13 and 14) and the right to take part in cultural life and to benefit from scientific progress (article 15).

By ratifying or acceding to the Covenant, States Parties freely assume a wide range of binding obligations. However, the nature of the obligations that it imposes has been the subject of controversy. After the Covenant entered into force, it was interpreted by some government representatives and some scholars as amounting to a mere declaration of 'aspirations' or 'goals to be achieved' rather than imposing binding obligations upon States.[6] The key provision regarding the nature of the obligations imposed by the Covenant, article 2(1) ICESCR, has been at the heart of the debate. Article 2(1) reads as follows:

> 'Each State Party to the present Covenant undertakes to take steps, individually and through international assistance and co-operation, especially economic and technical, to the maximum of its available resources, with a view to achieving progressively the full realization

---

5 Preamble of the ICESCR.

6 See, for example, Cranston, M.: *What are human rights?* The Bodley Head, London/Sydney/Toronto, (1973), Bossuyt, M.: '*La distinction entre les droites civils et politiques et les droits economiques, sociaux et culturels*'. In: *HRLJ*, vol. 8 No. 4, (1975), pp. 783-820 and Vierdag, E.W: 'The legal nature of the Rights granted by the International Covenant on Economic, Social and Cultural Rights.' In: *NYIL vol. IX,* (1978) pp. 69-105. See also the debate in: 'The United Nations human rights covenants: problems of ratification and implementation' contained in: Proceedings of the American Society of International Law, at its sixty-second annual meeting, Washington DC., April 25-27, (1968). See in particular the contribution of Clarence Clyde Ferguson, 'The United Nations human rights covenants: problems of ratification and implementation', pp. 83-96 and George W. Haight, pp. 96-110. In addition, see the description of the position of some US Government officials in Alston, P.: 'U.S. ratification of the Covenant on Economic, Social and Cultural Rights: the need for an entirely new strategy.' In: *AJIL*, vol. 84 No. 2, (1990), pp. 365-393.

> of the rights recognised in the Present Covenant by all appropriate means, including particularly the adoption of legislative measures.'

Certainly, this provision is very complex and it differs significantly from the analogous provision contained in its sister Covenant, the International Covenant on Civil and Political Rights [ICCPR].[7] During the *travaux préparatoires,* the different wording of article 2 of each Covenant was considered to be necessary due to the alleged difference in nature between the obligations imposed by the two sets of rights. It was considered that this alleged difference in nature required different methods of implementation. Traditionally, the difference between the two sets of rights has been presented as a dichotomy where civil and political rights are considered to impose negative obligations which are of an immediate nature, non-resource-dependent and are described in precise terms. Economic, social and cultural rights, on the other hand, are considered to impose only positive obligations and to be of progressive realisation, highly resource-dependent and formulated in vague terms.

From the time of the adoption of the Covenant to the present day, commentators have repeatedly noted the necessity of determining the scope and content of the Covenant obligations in order to enhance the protection of economic, social and cultural rights. In 1984, for example, Alston noted that one of the key obstacles to the overall acceptability of the notion of economic, social, and cultural rights was the vagueness and imprecision of their obligations, and he suggested that the most appropriate manner to overcome the neglect of these rights was to tackle this issue directly.[8] In 1987, co-writing with Quinn, he repeated that a clear understanding of the obligations contained in the Covenant, 'will serve to destroy some of the fallacies and misperceptions which in the past have too often served to distort and obfuscate the debate.'[9] The same view has been held by other commentators. Eide commented in 1989 that '[t]he economic, social and cultural rights are broadly recognised, but the corresponding obligations are not.'[10] In the same line of argument, Craven remarked, 'in the context of obligations, moreover, there has been a tendency either to exaggerate or underplay the precise situation with the effect of preventing a clear and uncontroversial picture from developing.'[11]

The clarification of the normative content of the Covenant is not easily accomplished. However, despite the many obstacles that have hindered the clarification process since the adoption of the Covenant over three decades ago, we now have a deeper

---

7 Article 2(1) ICCPR reads as follows: 'Each State Party to the present Covenant undertakes to respect and to ensure to all individuals within its territory and subject to its jurisdiction the rights recognized in the present Covenant […].'

8 Alston, 1984, p. 54.

9 Alston & Quinn, 1987, p. 158.

10 Eide, 1989*, p. 36.

11 Craven, 1993, p. 369.

understanding of the nature and scope of its obligations. Nevertheless, there is still much room for improvement. Some obligations imposed by the Covenant have not been clearly defined and in respect of those which have been clarified there is still important work to do in the area of promotion. The present study is intended to contribute to the clarification and promotion of the normative content of the Covenant.

The main purpose of the present study is to illustrate that over the years, due to the convergence of a series of factors, we have acquired a deeper understanding of the obligations imposed by human rights treaties. These new circumstances enable us to re-examine the Covenant from the point of view of its obligations. Such a re-appraisal is considered not only possible, but necessary. Many arguments against the 'justiciability' of these rights are still intertwined with considerations as to the 'nature' of the Covenant obligations, yet the Committee on Economic, Social and Cultural Rights considers that these arguments are no longer valid.

For example, while the Covenant's rights have been traditionally considered as imposing merely positive obligations that are highly resource-dependent, the Committee has noted that the Covenant imposes not only positive obligations, but also negative ones. A few of these negative obligations include the prohibition of carrying out forced evictions,[12] the obligation to refrain from taking any measures that result in preventing access to adequate food,[13] the denial of the academic freedom of teachers and students[14] and the deliberate withholding or misrepresentation of information vital to health protection or treatment.[15] The Committee has also made clear that 'while the Covenant provides for progressive realisation and acknowledges the constraints due to the limits of available resources, it also imposes on States Parties various obligations which are of immediate effect.'[16] Consequently, through its work the Committee has noted many immediate obligations in relation to the substantive rights contained in the Covenant.

The present study examines the International Covenant on Economic, Social and Cultural Rights from the perspective of its obligations. It outlines and evaluates the Committee's approach to the nature of the obligations and it identifies the scope of the obligations imposed by articles 2 to 5 of the Covenant as they have been interpreted at the present stage of international human rights law.

Identifying the scope of the obligation imposed by the Covenant is essential in order to strengthen the implementation of the Covenant. States need to know what they are obliged to do in order to comply with the Covenant. Lawyers, advocates, potential victims and all bodies called upon to apply the Covenant need to have a clear understanding of the obligations assumed by the State in order to assess compliance. With

12 General Comment No. 7.
13 General Comment No. 12 para. 15.
14 General Comment No. 13 para. 59.
15 General Comment No. 14 para. 50.
16 General Comment No. 14 para. 30.

a clear understanding of the normative content of the Covenant, violations of its rights are more easily defined and identified.

The necessity to re-examine the obligations imposed by the Covenant in light of the developments that have occurred in human rights law has taken on even greater relevance in the light of the debate over a future optional protocol to the Covenant for the establishment of a petition system.[17] In recent years, we have witnessed important steps toward the adoption of such a protocol to the Covenant. Since 1990, when the Committee began to study the idea of an optional protocol to the Covenant,[18] it has slowly generated a movement in favour of the initiative.[19] Over the years, the initial scepticism of some Committee members,[20] States[21] and some UN organs[22] regarding

---

17 Although throughout the present study the procedure is referred to as a 'complaint procedure' or 'individual complaint procedure', it is important to note that the Committee's draft on an optional protocol does not limit the possibility of submission of communications to individuals.

18 UN doc. E/1991/23 para. 285. See, in addition, the analytical paper adopted by the Committee at its seventh session in December 1992, E/C.12/1992/CRP.2/Add.3.

19 Initially the movement in favour of the adoption of an optional protocol found support principally among experts and academics, for example, through the meeting held in the Netherlands in January 1995 to discuss the draft protocol. See, Coomans, F. & Hoof, G.J.H van (eds.): *The right to complain about economic, social and cultural rights.* Netherlands Institute of Human Rights. SIM Special No. 18, Utrecht, (1995**); Boven, T. van; Flinterman, C. & Westendorp, I. (eds.): *The Maastricht guidelines on violations of economic, social and cultural rights*, Netherlands Institute for Human Rights, SIM Special No. 20, Utrecht, (1998). Nowadays, the increased support in the international community is reflected in the work of some NGOs, such as the International Commission of Jurists, Centre on Housing Rights and Evictions [COHRE], FoodFirst Information & Action Network [FIAN], Habitat International Coalition and Center for Economic and Social Rights.

20 During the early debates regarding the adoption of an optional protocol, some Committee members argued that it was premature to adopt such a protocol. It was considered essential to further develop the normative content of the Covenant before the adoption of an individual complaint procedure. This approach was reflected, for example, in the general discussion held by the Committee on 'The Interpretation and practical application of the obligations incumbent upon States Parties to the International Covenant on Economic, Social and Cultural rights.' According to the summary records of the meeting, Mr. Wimer Zambrano 'was not keen to adopt the draft optional protocol, because a lot of work still needed to be done on the nature of States Parties' commitment to the Covenant [...]. Above all, the Committee itself should have a clearer idea of what was required of States, otherwise it would not perform its function properly.' E/C.12/1995/SR.22 para. 30. This line of argument was common in the early days of the debate on an optional protocol. This is apparent in, for example, the discussion held during the Committee's fourth session when the Committee members examined the organisation of work. See E/C.12/1990/SR.4 of 12 February 1990, particularly the position of Mr. Konate (paras. 19-20), Mr. Fofana (para. 27) and basically along-the same lines, see Mr. Glaiel (paras. 28-30) and Mr. Muterahejuru (paras. 23-26). From this author's point of view, arguments against the adoption of an optional protocol due to the lack of a clear normative content of the Covenant are no longer tenable. Such arguments are insensitive to the developments achieved in the clarification of the normative content of the Covenant during recent years.

21 Many States Parties to the Covenant have stated their positive disposition to the adoption of an optional protocol in their reports or during the constructive dialogue with the Committee. See, for example, Concluding Observations Honduras E/C.12/1/Add.57 para. 4; Concluding Observations Germany E/C.12/1/Add.68 para. 4; Concluding Observations Panama E/C.12/1/Add.64 para. 7; Concluding

the necessity and feasibility of a complaint procedure for the violation of economic, social and cultural rights has slowly but steadily began to dissipate. It seems that there is now an increasing understanding that the adoption of such a procedure is a necessary further step for the protection of economic, social and cultural rights.

Given that the majority of States have not demonstrated the political will to proceed with the adoption of an optional protocol, it is important to create the conditions that would encourage them to do so, as we will see. This study attempts to contribute to this effort by promoting the normative content of the Covenant and demonstrating that many of the Covenant obligations are now clear and concrete.

Moreover, this study attempts to promote the normative content of the Covenant at the present stage of international law as a means of facilitating recourse to a complaint procedure in the event that an optional protocol is finally adopted. This is based on the understanding that greater clarity as to the normative content of the Covenant can assist individuals and lawyers in presenting better arguments in cases before national courts and that the courts, in turn, would be better able to establish what the States must do or not do in order to comply with the Covenant. Nonetheless, it is important to stress that the adoption of a complaint procedure would be the most appropriate way to clarify remaining uncertainties concerning the precise nature of some obligations and new issues that may arise.

1.1 Obstacles to an 'obligations approach'

While the normative clarification of all human rights instruments involves a degree of complexity, many factors have converged to increase the uncertainty with regard to the precise content of the obligations imposed by the Covenant. Among those factors we may note the following:

Observations Portugal E/2001/22 para. 406; Concluding Observations Finland E/2001/22 para. 431; Concluding Observations Belgium E/2001/22 para. 466; Concluding Observations Bulgaria E/2000/22 para. 217; Concluding Observations Mexico E/2000/22 para. 373; Concluding Observations Russian Federation E/1998/22 para. 98; and Concluding Observations Belarus E/1997/22 para. 274. In response to invitations by the Commission on Human Rights to submit their comments on the draft optional protocol, positive support has been expressed, *inter alia,* by the Governments of Georgia [E/CN.4/2000/49 at 4], Lithuania [E/CN.4/2000/49 at 6] and Chile [E/CN.4/2001/62/Add.1 at 1].

22 Initially the Human Rights Commission was sceptical, but in April 2001, eleven years after the Committee began its study of the possibility of an optional protocol, the Commission on Human Rights decided to appoint an independent expert to examine the question of the draft optional protocol to the Covenant. This independent expert must submit a report to the Commission in its 2002 session 'with a view to its consideration of possible follow-up and future actions.' Commission on Human Rights, Res. 2001/30. UN doc. E/CN.4/RES/2001/30, 20 April 2001.

First, the Covenant was drafted with wording that to a greater or lesser degree is general and vague.[23] While such wording is not in itself exceptional given that many international instruments are drafted in general terms, the uncertainty in relation to some of the Covenant's obligations has been excessively prolonged due to the weaknesses of its supervisory system. In fact, in contrast to its sister Covenant, the ICESCR does not establish a special body such as the Human Rights Committee to monitor implementation. The Covenant merely entrusts the Economic and Social Council [ECOSOC] with the responsibility of monitoring implementation by the States Parties, principally through the examination of State reports. However, as we will see, in the years immediately after the entry into force of the Covenant, it became evident that ECOSOC could not perform this function by itself. Therefore, discussions began on the creation of a specific body to assist the ECOSOC in monitoring compliance with the Covenant's obligations. But it was only with the establishment of the Committee on Economic, Social and Cultural Rights in 1987 that proper supervision of the Covenant started.

An additional factor contributing to the undeveloped normative content of the Covenant is the lack of an individual petition procedure. The lack of this implementation procedure has obstructed the task of providing a precise meaning and scope to many of the Covenant's provisions. As is widely recognised, an examination of specific cases is the most appropriate way to determine the scope of the obligations imposed by human rights instruments.[24] Until now, the Committee has been deprived of the possibility of dealing with individual cases, limiting its possibilities for further normative clarification. Fortunately, as we will see, the Committee has been creative in seeking to develop the normative content of the Covenant through other means, such as the General Comments.

Another factor that has obstructed the process of normative clarification is, in Alston's words, that 'the content of the Covenant was not based upon any significant bodies of domestic jurisprudence as was the case with civil and political rights'.[25] As he explains, 'phrases like 'cruel, inhuman and degrading treatment or punishment' had

---

23 See, for example, Craven, 1997, p. 103; Alston, 1991, p. 86 and Eide, 1989, p. 35. Chapter IV section 2.2.4 analyses the vague/precise dichotomy that is alleged to exist between economic, social and cultural rights on the one hand and civil and political rights on the other.

24 For a comprehensive review of the advantages of adopting an optional protocol to the Covenant establishing an individual petition system, see, for example, Alston, *op. cit.* (note 23), pp. 79-100 and Alston, P.: 'Establishing a Right to Petition under the Covenant on Economic, Social and Cultural rights.' In: *Collected Courses of the Academy of European law. The protection of Human Rights in Europe.* Vol. IV, Book 2. European University Institute, Florence (1993), pp. 107-152 and Arambulo, K.: *Strengthening the supervision of the International Covenant on Economic, Social and Cultural Rights: theoretical and procedural aspects*, Intersentia, Antwerp, (1999). For the Committee's approach in this regard see, for example, the analytical paper adopted by the Committee at its seventh session in December 1992, E/C.12/1992/CRP.2/Add.3 paras. 20-28.

25 Alston, 1992, p. 490.

been the subject of in-depth judicial and academic analysis long before their inclusion in the Covenant on Civil and Political Rights. By contrast, the range of rights recognised in the other Covenant was, with the exception of labour-related rights, considerably in advance of most national legislation.'[26] Therefore, the lack of domestic jurisprudence on the topic at the time of the Covenant's adoption meant that the clarification of the Covenant's norms had to begin almost from scratch.

In addition, the practice of giving 'shorthand' titles to economic, social and cultural rights, such as the 'right to work' or the 'right to housing,' has often served to obscure the real meaning of the obligations that these rights impose. Often the neglect or adverse assumptions regarding economic, social and cultural rights derive from the general lack of awareness about the real scope of the obligations. Although the use of short titles is often inevitable,[27] the brevity of these 'shorthand' titles has led to the inaccurate and common belief that economic, social and cultural rights contain extensive obligations which are very difficult to put into practice and this has contributed to the hostile reaction to these rights.[28] Notwithstanding the generosity implied by many of these 'shorthand' titles, the obligations imposed by the Covenant are in most cases not as vast as the 'shorthand' titles might suggest. However, in many cases the obligations imposed by the Covenant's rights are more demanding and substantial than certain government representatives wish to think. Thus, public awareness of the text of the Covenant and the scope of its obligations is essential for its implementation. Without such promotion it is difficult to overcome the misconceptions about the Covenant.

Despite all of the difficulties that have hindered the determination of the obligations imposed by the Covenant, there have been positive steps that have contributed to overcoming these difficulties and to clarifying the normative content of the Covenant.

shorthand titles to rts.

---

26 *Idem.*

27 In fact, for reasons of manageability, this study often refers to the Covenant's rights using their shorthand titles. However, it will indicate the article which contains the right so as to make the reader aware of its full content.

28 The problems arising from the 'shorthand' titles of the Covenant's rights seem to obscure the debate even between the members of the Committee. For example, during a day of general discussion, Mr. Grissa said, 'State legislation on the right to housing would mean, from the people's point of view, the right to be offered housing by the State. That was a situation which was patently untenable from a Government's point of view, particularly in developing countries, such as Algeria […]. It was therefore both inappropriate and undeniable for the Committee to encourage States to legislate on areas in which they would be powerless to act.' (para. 36). This statement provoked the reaction of the Chairperson, Mr. Alston, who responded by emphasising that, '[t]he right to housing was not a matter of a Government providing housing but rather an obligation on the Government to create conditions, policies and programmes conducive to the realisation of the right to housing. Such policies required little in the way of government expenditure, but they frequently required the cessation of the protection of the upper and middle classes' (para. 39). E/C.12/1995/SR.22.

1.2 A new momentum

Over the years many different factors have converged to contribute to creating greater acceptance of the legal character of economic, social and cultural rights and the indivisibility of all human rights. This momentum has favoured the implementation of the Covenant as it has led to the increased acceptance of the instrument and greater clarity as to its content. The factors that have contributed to this momentum are not only external to the Covenant. On the contrary, the work of the Committee has also induced greater State compliance and has thereby created further acceptance of economic, social and cultural rights.

1.2.1 Developments in the field of economic, social and cultural rights

The progress achieved in the clarification of the normative content of the Covenant should be placed within the broader context of the development of international human rights law and in the field of economic, social and cultural rights in particular. As is generally recognised, human rights law has a dynamic character. Human rights are not static but, rather, they evolve over time in order to adapt to new circumstances and strengthen the protection of individuals.

This is also true of economic, social and cultural rights and in the decades since the Covenant entered into force, the mechanisms for the protection of economic, social and cultural rights have significantly increased in number and improved their methods of work. Additionally, human rights instruments have become much more complex, covering components of rights not previously envisaged.

There have been important developments which impact the protection of economic, social and cultural rights at both the universal and regional levels. At the universal level the adoption of an Optional Protocol to the Convention against Discrimination against Women [CEDAW] that provides for a system of individual complaints is particularly worth mentioning.[29] The adoption of this procedure, which recently entered into force,[30] is of great relevance because it allows for the presentation of communications alleging violations of the economic, social and cultural rights contained in the CEDAW. At the European level, we may stress here the Third Additional Protocol to the European Social Charter, which provides for a system of collective complaints alleging violations of the social rights contained therein.[31] In the Americas, it is worth mentioning the Additional Protocol to the American Convention on the Area of Economic, Social and Cultural Rights ('Protocol of San Salvador')[32] which entered into

29 General Assembly Res. A/RES/54/4 of 6 October 1999. It is important to note that the optional protocol establishes not only an individual complaint procedure, but also an inquiry procedure.

30 This Optional Protocol entered into force on 22 December 2000.

31 It was opened for signature on November 9, 1995 and entered into force on September 1, 1998, ETS No. 158.

32 Adopted in San Salvador on 17 November 1988, OAS Treaty Series No. 69.

force in November 1999. The adoption and entry into force of the 'Protocol of San Salvador' constituted a remarkable step forward in the protection of economic, social and cultural rights because it establishes a system of individual complaints for the protection of two of the rights contained therein, trade union rights and the right to education.[33]

It is indisputable that the Covenant has benefited from this evolution as the obligations imposed upon State Parties to the Covenant are now more precise and broader in scope than a decade ago.[34] Over the years, attention to human rights has increased significantly at both the national and international levels and economic, social and cultural rights have been increasingly accepted as an indivisible component of the international human rights regime.[35] The increased attention paid to economic, social and cultural rights significantly benefited the protection afforded by the International Covenant on Economic, Social and Cultural Rights. This is evident from the fact that during recent years the number of States Parties to the Covenant has increased significantly (during the 1990s the number of States Parties to the Covenant increased by nearly 40 percent).[36]

Despite an initial reluctance to deal with economic, social and cultural rights, in recent years a range of international actors, such as the UN treaty bodies, the UN Commission on Human Rights and the Sub-Commission, specialised agencies, NGOs and academic writers have gradually began to pay more attention to these rights. In doing so, they have developed elements for the protection of economic, social and cultural rights that must be taken into account for a contemporary interpretation of the Covenant.

---

33 The rights protected through the individual petitions system are the right to form and join trade unions (Art. 8(a)) and the right to education (Art. 13).

34 As two commentators note, 'the argument for a broader construction of a given right often amounts to the claim that further duties ought to be imposed on the state in order to satisfy the right.' Steiner & Alston, 2000, p. 181.

35 Although the principle of indivisibility and interdependence of all human rights has been repeatedly proclaimed since the 1960s [i.e. Proclamation of Teheran, adopted on May 13, 1968, para. 13; G.A. Res. 32/130 (1977) and 41/117 (1986); Human Rights Commission's Resolutions 1987/19; 1988/22; 1987/20; 1993/22; 1998/33; 2000/9 and 2001/30 and the Declaration on the Right to Development adopted by G.A. Res. 41/128 of 4 of December 1986, Art. 6] it took some time before the principle went beyond the theoretical level. Nonetheless, an import turning point was the Vienna Declaration and Programme of Action that established,
'All human rights are universal, indivisible and interdependent and interrelated. The international community must treat human rights globally in a fair and equal manner, on the same footing, and with the same emphasis. While the significance of national and regional particularities and various historical, cultural and religious backgrounds must be borne in mind, it is the duty of States, regardless of their political, economic and cultural systems, to promote and protect all human rights and fundamental freedoms.' A/CONF.157/23 para. 5

36 As of February 2002, the Covenant had 145 States Parties and of these, fifty States became Parties to the Covenant after 1990.

We will see that in interpreting the Covenant, the Committee has taken into account the developments achieved in human rights law to provide what it has called 'the contemporary interpretation of the Covenant.' As a result, the normative content of the Covenant is now not only more precise, but the scope of the obligations it imposes has also been expanded, providing broader protection to individuals and limiting the discretion of States Parties.

Therefore, the increased attention paid to economic, social and cultural rights by different international actors and the developments achieved in the field will be briefly described in order to illustrate how, through the work of the Committee, they have contributed to clarifying the normative content of the Covenant.

1.2.2 The work of the Committee on Economic, Social and Cultural Rights

One of the most significant steps taken in the process of norm clarification was the decision to establish the Committee on Economic, Social and Cultural Rights.[37] From 1979 to 1986, the supervision of the Covenant was carried out by a Working Group, composed first of government representatives and subsequently of governmental experts, which did not contribute much to the clarification of the normative content of the Covenant. This situation began to shift with the establishment of the Committee.

When the Committee began to function in 1987, it had numerous challenges to overcome[38] and one of the most difficult was precisely the necessity to clarify the normative content of the Covenant. The fact that the precise content of the Covenant obligations had not been seriously developed by its predecessors had further reinforced the assumption by States that the Covenant only imposed vague and general obligations which allowed them a great degree of discretion with respect to its implementation.[39]

At the time the Committee was created, some influential governments and scholars were hostile to economic, social and cultural rights while many UN organs were indifferent and not disposed to collaborate in the implementation of the Covenant. Moreover, NGOs were little involved. The newly established Committee needed to dedicate significant efforts to overcome the relative neglect of the Covenant and to encourage other actors to become involved in the implementation of the Covenant and the clarification of the obligations it imposed. In retrospect, it is possible to say that this goal has since been achieved. There has been increased attention to economic, social and cultural rights from the UN organs such as the Commission on Human Rights and the Sub-Commission on the Promotion and Protection of Human Rights, from UN treaty bodies and from NGOs.

The Committee's work over the years indicates increasing confidence. It has adopted stricter Concluding Observations and more sophisticated and precise General

37 ECOSOC Res. 1985/17. UN doc. E/RES/1985/17, 28 May 1985.

38 For a comprehensive analysis, see Alston, P.: 'Out of the abyss: the challenges confronting the new Committee on Economic, Social and Cultural Rights'. In: *HRQ*, vol. 9 No. 3, (1987), pp. 332-381.

39 See Alston, *op. cit.* (note 8), p. 54.

Comments. By doing so, it has deterred non-compliance and deepened the understanding of the obligations imposed by the Covenant. To the extent that the Committee is able to further define its normative content, the Covenant achieves greater recognition and acceptance and this, in turn, encourages further developments in the protection of economic, social and cultural rights. This is so because the work of the Committee and that of other bodies dealing with economic, social and cultural rights is mutually reinforcing.

1.2.3 The Typologies of States' obligations under human rights treaties

Others' contributions to the clarification of the normative content of the Covenant have come from academic writers. It is particularly worth mentioning the development of a series of 'typologies' to analyse the obligations imposed by human rights treaties. These typologies have contributed to overcoming the simplified view that each set of human rights falls into a neat category. The typologies suggest that each human right imposes a variety of obligations classified in different 'types' or 'levels'. The typologies are analytical tools that explain that the complete fulfilment of each right requires the performance of multiple kinds of duties. Moreover, by analysing the different levels of State duties imposed by each human right (civil, political, economic, social or cultural), it is easier to assess what specific State behaviours are necessary or compulsory for the implementation of a right, thereby increasing the understanding of its content.

The present study seeks to provide a detailed analysis of the different typologies and their importance for the clarification of the normative content of the Covenant. As will be examined in greater detail in Chapter V, the typology that the Committee has chosen is made up of three levels of obligations: 'respect', 'protect' and 'fulfil'. When applying the typology to the right to the highest attainable standard of health, the Committee notes that

> 'The obligation to *respect* requires States to refrain from interfering directly or indirectly with the enjoyment of the right to health. The obligation to *protect* requires States to take measures that prevent third parties from interfering with article 12 guarantees. Finally, the obligation to *fulfil* requires States to adopt appropriate legislative, administrative, budgetary, judicial, promotional and other measures towards the full realisation of the right to health.'[40]

The Committee has illustrated the three levels of obligations by providing precise examples of obligations for each level and this permitted it to clarify the content and scope of the right.

---

40 General Comment No. 14 para. 33.

2 Structure of the study

The study is divided into three Parts. Part One (Chapters I, II and III) examines the role of the Committee on Economic, Social and Cultural Rights in clarifying the normative content of the Covenant. Chapter I begins with a brief overview of the Committee's working methods, stressing how the Committee has developed different means to clarify the normative content of the Covenant. Chapter II paints a broad picture of developments in the field of economic, social and cultural rights and examines how these developments have contributed to the process of clarification of the normative content of the obligations imposed by the Covenant and the consolidation of the principle of the indivisibility of all human rights. Chapter III sets out the rules of interpretation of international human rights norms, emphasising that the specific object and purpose of human rights treaties (the protection of the human person), requires that they be interpreted in a manner which makes the rights effective in the light of present-day circumstances.

As the present study refers basically to the normative content of the Covenant as it has been developed by the Committee on Economic, Social and Cultural Rights, this Chapter also includes a discussion of the 'legitimacy' of the Committee as the interpreter of the Covenant. In other words, I will address the question of why the Committee's interpretation of the Covenant is and should be complied with by States Parties.

In the second part of the study (Chapters IV and V), the focus is on the obligations imposed by the Covenant. Chapter IV analyses the nature of the States Parties' obligations under the Covenant. A preliminary question is to determine if it is possible to examine the nature of the obligations generated by human rights in general or if it is necessary to perform two different analyses, one for the obligations created by civil and political rights and another for those emanating from economic, social and cultural rights. To answer this question we will analyse the alleged difference in nature between the two sets of rights in light of some of the arguments advanced by the drafters of the Covenant to justify the decision to adopt two instruments instead of one.

As is well known, the Universal Declaration on Human Rights guarantees the full range of rights (civil, political, economic, social and cultural), and during the early stages of drafting the Covenants it was envisioned that there would be only one legal instrument containing both categories of rights. However, in the end it was decided that there should be two separate legal instruments, the International Covenant on Civil and Political Rights [ICCPR] and the International Covenant on Economic, Social and Cultural Rights [ICESCR].

The traditional arguments alleging that there is a difference in nature between the two sets of rights were advanced by some of the drafters of the Covenant. In retrospect, we may say that this view is no longer valid. Each of the alleged differences will be analysed in light of present-day circumstances in order to demonstrate that the manner in which the jurisprudence of the two Covenants has evolved now makes the arguments held during the drafting history untenable. While political, ideological and economic circumstances might be invoked to justify the limited view of the nature of human rights and duties held by the majority of the drafters, in our present circumstances, and bearing in mind the significant developments that have occurred in human rights law, we need to adopt a wider perspective.

After examining the alleged differences between the two sets of rights from the point of view of the nature of the obligations that they impose, we will re-examine the meaning of articles 2(1) of each Covenant. The review of articles 2(1) of each Covenant is necessary in this context, because they refer to the general obligations imposed by the Covenant. We will see that, although the wording of article 2 of each Covenant differs significantly, their implications are very similar.

While many authors have addressed the alleged dichotomy between the two sets of rights, in the present study the focus will be on the obligations to which they give rise. The aim of this part is to stress two related points. First, that all human rights, regardless of whether they are civil, political, economic or social, impose a variety of obligations which may be different in nature. Hence, the difference 'in nature' exists between obligations rather than between rights. Secondly, if the differences are between obligations regardless of the rights from which they arise, it is necessary to exercise caution with regard to arguments that courts and quasi-judicial bodies are not suitable to address matters pertaining to economic, social and cultural rights due to the nature of the obligations that these rights impose. If all human rights impose a variety of obligations, some obligations arising from economic, social and cultural rights must have the characteristics 'traditionally' attributed to civil and political rights and the inverse must also be true. Thus, for example, when courts and other quasi-judicial bodies enforce civil and political rights, their decisions often require the compliance by States of positive obligations which may not be very clearly delineated and which may require budgetary allocations.

To explain this point we will introduce the idea that all human rights impose a '*continuum of a variety of duties*' or a '*spectrum of variety of duties*.' At one end of the spectrum there are obligations of no interference by States and towards the other end we find obligations requiring States' positive action. (See figure No. 1).

A specific duty can be located anywhere on the spectrum, regardless of the category from which it springs (civil and political or economic, social and cultural rights). The degree of State involvement, the degree of precision in the delineation of the obligations as well as the resources necessary to comply with a duty do not depend on the Covenant from which the correlative right emerges but, rather, on the specific type of duty in question. We note that a single right may impose a series of duties in order to be effective at a given time and in a given situation and as we move from one end of the spectrum to the other, the duties tend to be of a different nature.

The study attempts to demonstrate this point by examining the evolution in the jurisprudence relating to one of the rights traditionally considered to be 'negative,' the right to life. When examining the jurisprudence on the right to life of the major international human rights supervisory bodies, the European Court of Human Rights, the Inter-American Court on Human Rights and the Human Rights Committee, we will see that over the years this right has been interpreted so as to require States to comply with a number of duties, many of which lie closer to the positive side of the spectrum.

Chapter V focuses on the typologies of States' duties imposed by the Covenant. Academic writers have developed typologies of States' obligations under human rights treaties that have contributed enormously to our understanding of the nature of the obligations imposed by the Covenant. The typologies are analytical tools to examine the obligations imposed by each right and to classify these obligations in different types or levels. First, we will examine the development of the typologies in academic writing, comparing the advantages and shortcomings of each of the proposals. We then proceed to examine the Committee's application of the so-called 'tripartite typology.' This typology considers that all human rights impose three levels of States' obligations: to respect, to protect and to fulfil.

In its most recent General Comments, the Committee has applied the 'tripartite typology' to the rights to adequate food, education and the highest standard of health (General Comment Nos. 12, 13 and 14, respectively). On the basis of the Committee's approach to the 'tripartite typology' in its General Comments, we will examine its Concluding Observations. The idea is to provide concrete examples of the duties imposed by each level of State obligations in order to illustrate the contributions of the Committee in establishing the precise scope and content of the obligations imposed by the Covenant.

The third part of the study (Chapters VI, VII and VIII), focuses on the obligations imposed by Part II of the ICESCR and identifies the normative content of those obligations. It is argued that articles 2 to 5 of the Covenant contain several obligations essential for strengthening the protection of economic, social and cultural rights. Part II imposes obligations with which States Parties must comply with regard to each of the substantive rights contained in Part III of the Covenant (articles 6 to 15 ICESCR.) On the basis of the Committee's work, we will attempt to identify which specific State behaviours are mandatory under Part II of the ICESCR.

3 Preliminary outline of the different categories of State Obligations on the basis of the Covenant's structure

Before embarking on the analysis of the normative content of the Covenant, a preliminary outline of the different categories of States' obligations contained in the Covenant is required. The 31 provisions of the Covenant are divided into five Parts. Part I contains only one provision, article 1, which recognises the right of self-determination. Part II contains articles 2 to 5, which are general provisions applicable to all substantive rights contained in the Covenant.[41] Part III contains the substantive rights in articles 6 to 15. Part IV establishes the supervisory system of the Covenant in articles 16 to 25. Finally, Part V contains miscellaneous provisions relating to such questions as ratification and entry into force. This latter part is composed of articles 26 to 31 whose principal aim is to regulate the ratification, accession and entry into force of the Covenant as well as its amendment. It also provides for the authentic languages and the Covenant's application in federal States. In general, it is possible to conclude that Part V of the Covenant does not impose direct obligations upon States.

In light of the above-mentioned structure of the Covenant, we may classify the obligations imposed by the Covenant into three categories:

(A) *Rights-based obligations*: These are obligations correlative to each of the substantive rights contained in Part III of the Covenant. Each of the rights contained in articles 6 to 15 imposes a complex range of correlative duties, often divided into duties to respect, to protect and to fulfil.[42] For example, article 13 recognises the right of everyone to education. This right imposes a variety of obligations, such as the obligation to respect the freedom of parents to choose their children's school and the obligation to provide compulsory primary education. We may also call these obligations 'correlative obligations' in order to emphasise that they are correlative to the substantive rights or, alternatively, 'rights-based duties'. The Committee has called them 'specific legal obligations.'[43]

It is important to note that, as mentioned, Part I of the Covenant contains only one article, the right of self-determination. Arguably, we might include the obligations derived from this right in the category of Correlative obligations because it also imposes obligations upon States Parties which are correlative to the right.

(B) *General or basic obligations*: These are the obligations imposed by Part II of the Covenant. Part II of the Covenant contains several obligations which do not *directly* concern the enjoyment of specific rights by individuals, but rather the way in which States Parties must behave in order to implement and guarantee the substantive rights contained in the Covenant. The best example is article 2(1) ICESCR, which establishes

---

41 The general application of Part II of both Covenants is beyond doubt. See in this regard, Buergenthal, T.: 'To respect and to ensure: State obligations and permissible derogations.' In: *The International Bill of Rights.* Henkin, L. (ed.), New York, Columbia University Press, (1981), p. 72; Nowak, M.: *U.N. Covenant on Civil and Political Rights Commentary*, N.P. Engel Publisher, Kehl/Strasbourg/Arlington, (1993), p. 27 and McGoldrick, D.: *The Human Rights Committee*, Clarendon Press, Oxford, (1994), p. 269. Although they refer specifically to the rights contained in articles 2 to 5 of the ICCPR, these analyses are still pertinent in the context of the ICESCR. For further analysis see Chapter VI section 1.

42 See the analysis in Chapter V.

43 General Comment No. 13 paras. 49 to 57. This approach was previously used by some academic commentators. See, for example, Alston & Quinn, *loc. cit.* (note 9), p. 158.

the nature of the obligations in the Covenant, but Part II also contains the prohibition of discrimination (article 2(2)), the duty to treat men and women equally in the enjoyment of the rights (article 3), a limitation clause in article 4 and interpretation rules in article 5. The principal difference with the obligations of Part III is that rather than rights-based duties (correlative to the substantive rights), these obligations are legal obligations which regulate the conduct of States Parties with regard to the Covenant as a whole.

(C) *Procedural obligations imposed by Part IV of the Covenant*: The Committee has referred to the obligations contained in Part IV of the Covenant as 'procedural obligations.'[44] Part IV of the Covenant (articles 16 to 25) establishes the supervisory mechanism of the Covenant. The principal obligation for States is contained in Article 16, which establishes the obligation of States Parties to submit a report 'on the measures which they have adopted and the progress made in achieving the observance of the rights recognised in the Covenant.' Article 17 requires States to submit their reports in 'stages' in accordance with the programme established by the UN Economic and Social Council [ECOSOC]. This provision must be seen in conjunction with ECOSOC Resolution 1889/4 which established the reporting cycle[45] and the 'Revised guidelines regarding the form and contents of reports to be submitted by States Parties under articles 16 and 17 of the International Covenant on Economic, Social and Cultural Rights.'[46]

It is apparent from the Committee's work that the non-performance of the reporting obligations contained in articles 16 and 17 of the Covenant is a breach of the Covenant. The Committee has considered that these provisions contain 'obligations' similar in this regard to any other obligation imposed by the Covenant and it does not hesitate to use the term 'violation', if the State does not comply with them by not submitting a report or not submitting it in due time.[47]

The Committee has not only noted that non-reporting by a State Party is a breach of the Covenant, but it has also emphasised that non-compliance with the obligation to report constitutes a severe obstacle to the fulfilment of the Committee's functions.[48] According to the Committee, a situation of persistent non-reporting by State Parties

44 See E/1997/22, Annex IV, para. 19 and Alston, P.: 'Draft optional protocol providing for the consideration of communications', E/C.12/1994/12, report submitted to the Committee on Economic, Social and Cultural Rights. In: *The right to complain about economic, social and cultural rights*. Coomans, F. & Hoof, G.J.H. van (eds.), SIM Special No. 18, Utrecht, (1995), p. 184.

45 E/C.12/1989/4.

46 UN doc. E/C.12/1991/1 of 17 June 1991.

47 See, for example, Concluding Observations Guinea E/1997/22 para. 190; Concluding Observations Saint Vincent and the Grenadines E/1998/22 para. 413; Concluding Observations Solomon Islands E/2000/22 para. 186; and Concluding Observations Congo E/2001/22 para. 188.

48 See, for example, Concluding Observations Solomon Islands E/2000/22 paras. 186 and 207.

risks bringing the entire supervisory procedure into disrepute, undermining one of the foundations of the Covenant.[49]

It is interesting to note that in the debate regarding the adoption of an optional protocol to the Covenant establishing a complaint procedure,[50] the Committee has taken the view that the protocol should establish the possibility of bringing communications alleging violations of articles 1 to 15, but not the obligations contained in Part IV of the Covenant. As a former Chairperson of the Committee, Mr. Alston, explains, 'it is not clear [...] that it is desirable for individuals to be able to bring a communication against a State party on the grounds that it has failed to report in a timely fashion, or at all. While such behaviour clearly constitutes a violation of the State's obligations, there are alternative means by which the Committee has sought to address such problems.'[51]

Although all three categories of obligations are essential for the full protection of the rights contained in the Covenant, the third Part of the present study will only focus on the obligations imposed by Part II of the Covenant (articles 2 to 5 of the Covenant).

4 The importance of focusing on the obligations imposed by Part II of the Covenant

The emphasis on the obligations imposed by Part II of the Covenant is justified by the fact that over the years many national and international bodies as well as commentators have contributed to the clarification of the nature and scope of the obligations imposed by the Covenant. Nevertheless, most of these important contributions refer to obligations correlative to the substantive rights contained in the Covenant (Part III of the Covenant, articles 6 to 15). There has been little analysis of the nature and scope of the obligations imposed by Part II of the Covenant, and particularly of the scope of article 2 of the Covenant.[52]

---

49 E/C.12/1999/11 para. 42.

50 As has been proposed by the Committee, the protocol would allow both individuals and groups to submit complaints. Despite this, for practical reasons, I understand 'individual complaint procedure' as referring to both individuals and groups. (See note 17).

51 Alston, *op. cit.* (note 44), p.184. See also E/CN.4/1997/105, 18 December 1996, para. 18.

52 Of the small body of work directly referring to Part II obligations, it is worth noting the following: Alston & Quinn, *loc. cit.* (note 9), pp. 156-229; Künnemann, R.: 'A coherent approach to human rights.' In: *HRQ*, vol. 17, (1995), pp. 323-342; and Craven, M.: *The International Covenant on Economic, Social and Cultural Rights: a perspective on its development*, Clarendon Press, Oxford, (1995), pp. 106-192. In general, it seems that there has been little work directly addressing the issue of the nature and scope of the equivalent provisions to article 2 ICESCR in all UN human rights treaties. A few exceptions must be mentioned: with regard to Art. 2 of the ICCPR, the work of Schwelb, E.: 'The nature of the obligations of the States Parties to the International Covenant on Civil and Political Rights.' In: *René Cassin Amicorum Discipulorumque Liber*, Pedone, Paris (1969), vol. I, pp. 301-324 and Schachter, O.: 'The obligation to implement the Covenant in domestic law.' In: *The International Bill of Rights*. Henkin, L. (ed.), Columbia University Press, New York, (1981). With

The wording of articles 2 to 5 of the Covenant is complex and to some extent elusive. Unfortunately, over the years these provisions have not generally been given sufficient attention by academic writers. This is not to say that there have not been significant contributions as to the nature and scope of the obligations imposed by the Covenant. In fact, a group of distinguished experts in international law convened by the International Commission of Jurists, the Faculty of Law of the University of Limburg and the Urban Morgan Institute for Human Rights met in 1986 to consider the nature and scope of the obligations of States Parties to the Covenant, as well as the consideration of States Parties' reports and international co-operation under Part IV of the Covenant.[53] They agreed on the so-called 'Limburg Principles on the Implementation of the International Covenant on Economic, Social and Cultural Rights'.[54]

These principles constituted an important step in the process of determining the scope and nature of the Covenant obligations. Moreover, the background papers of the meeting included landmark academic works on the nature and scope of the obligations, such as the article written by Alston and Quinn, 'The nature and scope of States Parties' obligations under the international Covenant on Economic, Social and Cultural Rights.' While the Limburg Principles and the contemporaneous work of commentators provide the foundation for this study, we must keep in mind that the Limburg meeting was held in June 1986 and that in the intervening 15 years or so, there have been numerous developments in international law that have further contributed to the understanding of the Covenant obligations. It is important to bear in mind that the Limburg Principles were adopted before the first session of the Committee on Economic, Social and Cultural Rights and that the Committee's work is essential for the present understanding of the normative content of Part II of the Covenant. Indeed, one of the earliest of the Committee's General Comments, in 1990, refers expressly to 'the nature of States Parties obligations (article 2 para. 1).'[55] Thus, it is important to observe that while contributions such as the Limburg Principles are still relevant and valid, they date from more than a decade ago and many changes have occurred in the meanwhile. The present study attempts to build on these pioneering efforts, but is designed to analyse the Covenant obligations, particularly those imposed by the provisions contained in Part II, at the present stage of international law and to examine how the Committee has supervised and interpreted the obligations of the Covenant in practice.

regard to Art. 2 CAT, Boulesbaa, A.: 'The nature of the obligations incurred by States under article 2 of the UN Convention against Torture.' In: *HRQ*, vol. 12, 1990, pp. 53-93. More recently, the work of Byrnes A. & Connors, J.: 'Enforcing the human rights of women: a complaints procedure for the women's Convention?' In: *Brooklyn Journal of International Law*, vol. XXI No. 3, (1996), pp. 679-798 regarding the obligations imposed by CEDAW.

53 They met in Maastricht from 2 to 6 June 1986.

54 Hereinafter: 'Limburg Principles.' The Limburg Principles are published in: *HRQ*, vol. 9 No. 2, (1987), pp. 122-146.

55 General Comment No. 3. Adopted in the Committee's fifth session in 1990.

While the Committee's interpretations are consistent with the Limburg Principles, it will become apparent that the Committee often goes further. This reflects the dynamic character of international law.

The focus on Part II of the Covenant is further justified by the fact that according to the Draft Optional Protocol proposed by the Committee, individuals would be able to lodge complaints for violations of articles 1 to 15 of the Covenant.[56] While obligations correlative to the rights contained in articles 6 to 15 have been reasonably well developed by the Committee and commentators, there is a lack of substantive work on the present meaning and scope of the obligations imposed by articles 1 to 5. This study aims to contribute to the promotion of the Committee's understanding of the provisions contained in Part II of the Covenant. The importance of the provisions of Part II has been stressed by the Committee which has stated that 'whatever approach is adopted in this regard, given the fundamental importance of articles 2-5 of the Covenant, that they would always be fully applicable in relation to the interpretation of the meaning of any of the specific rights recognised in articles 6-15.'[57]

5 The 'violations' and 'obligations' approaches. The necessity to merge the two approaches

Today it is relatively common to analyse compliance with the Covenant by enumerating acts and omissions which constitute violations (the so-called 'violations approach' to the Covenant). Audrey Chapman first introduced this approach in 1996,[58] and many other commentators have since discussed the Covenant from the point of view of violations.[59] The most important and thorough developments in this regard are to be

violation approach

56 See, Draft Optional Protocol as it was submitted by the Committee to the Commission on Human Rights in 1996, E/1997/22 annex IV. Of course, it could well be that the proposal of the Committee is not adopted.

57 E/C.12/1996/CRP.2/Add.1 para. 32.

58 See, Chapman, A.: 'A 'violation approach' for monitoring the International Covenant on Economic, Social and Cultural Rights'. In: *HRQ*, vol. 18 No. 1, (1996), pp. 23-66; 'A new approach to monitoring the International Covenant on Economic, Social and Cultural Rights,' In: *ICJ* Review No. 55, December 1995, pp. 23-37 and 'Violations of the Right to Health'. In: *The Maastricht guidelines on violations of economic, social and cultural rights*. Boven, T.C. van; Flinterman, C. & Westendorp, I. (eds.), *SIM Special* No. 20, Utrecht, (1998), pp. 87-112 and the background paper submitted to the Committee's Day of General Discussion on the right to education, 'violation of the right to education', UN doc. E/C.12/1998/19 of 14 October 1998.

59 For example, in: *The Maastricht guidelines on violations of economic, social and cultural rights, op. cit. (note 58)* see the following articles: Leckie, S.: 'Another step towards indivisibility: identifying the key features of violations of economic, social and cultural rights', pp.35-86; Leary, V.: 'A violations approach to the right to work (labour rights), pp. 113-123; Coomans, F.: 'Identifying violations of the right to education', pp. 125-146; Westendorp, I.: 'The feasibility of a violations approach of women's economic, social and cultural rights,' pp. 147-163 and Künnemann, R.: 'Violations of the right to food,' pp. 165-190.

found in the 'The Maastricht Guidelines on Violations of Economic, Social and Cultural Rights' which were the result of the unanimous agreement of more than 30 experts in the field of human rights.

While this study will begin by examining these landmark works on violations, the focus will be primarily on the 'obligations' that the Covenant imposes upon States Parties. As is well established, the failure of a State Party to comply with an obligation contained in an international treaty is a violation of that treaty.[60] Rather than identifying 'obligations,' a 'violations approach' directly identifies 'violations' of the rights enumerated in the Covenant. In other words, it identifies the action or omission by which a State fails to comply with the Covenant's obligations, but without first identifying those obligations.

Chapman notes that it is possible to identify violations on the basis of the Committee's work. As she explains, '[t]he work of the Committee attests to the fact that it is possible to identify violations of enumerated rights without first conceptualising their full scope or the States Parties' concomitant obligations with respect to them.'[61]

When Chapman first introduced the 'violation approach' in 1996, she noted that a systematic monitoring of economic, social and cultural rights required five methodological preconditions: '(1) conceptualisation of the specific components of each enumerated right and the concomitant obligations of States Parties; (2) delineation of performance standards related to each of these components, including the identification of potential major violations; (3) collection of relevant data, appropriately disagregated by sex and a variety of other variables; (4) development of an information management system for these data to facilitate analysis of trends over time and comparisons of the status of groups within a country; and (5) the ability to analyse these data in order to determine patterns and trends'.[62] According to Chapman none of these five preconditions was fulfilled at that time and therefore the 'violations approach' was the most feasible and effective alternative to monitor economic, social and cultural rights.[63]

From this author's point of view, Chapman's proposition is both coherent and consistent. However, five years on, it is time to define the obligations. The determina-

60 According to Art. 12 ILC Draft Articles on State Responsibility: 'there is a breach of an international obligation by a State when an act of that State is not in conformity with what is required of it by that obligation [...]'. As adopted by the International Law Commission at its fifty-third session, held in 2001. Report of the International Law Commission on the work of its Fifty-third session, *Official Records of the General Assembly, Fifty-sixth session, Supplement No. 10* (A/56/10), chp.IV.E.1.

61 Chapman, *loc. cit.* (note 58), p. 39. Chapman's approach has not been immune to criticism. For example, S. Leckie indicated in 1998 that '[w]hile in many respects valuable, this approach [Chapman's approach] defines violations very loosely by considering virtually all critical comments by the Committee as *prima facie* violations of the Covenant, whether or not this body (the only authoritative body legally competent to make such pronouncements) viewed a particular act or omission as a violation or not' Leckie, *loc. cit.* (note 59), pp. 53-54.

62 Chapman, *loc. cit.* (note 58), p. 29.

63 *Ibidem:* p. 29 and pp. 36 *et seq.*

tion of the obligations is the first logical first step in determining whether a violation exists. In order to know if certain facts disclose a breach of the State's obligations under the Covenant, it is necessary to first establish with precision the content of those obligations and hence the importance of determining the normative content of the Covenant.[64]

It is worth noting that although the present study focuses on the *obligations* that the Covenant imposes rather than on *violations*, this approach is not presented as an alternative to the 'violations approach' but, rather, it is meant to complement it. From this author's perspective, in order to enhance the protection of the Covenant it is necessary both to clarify the normative content of the Covenant and to continuously identify violations thereof.

A more precise understanding of the obligations imposed by the Covenant will help State Parties, practising lawyers, judges and human rights advocates in general to pursue the implementation of its rights at the international as well as national levels. It will simultaneously facilitate the work of the supervisory bodies.[65]

6 Scope of the Present Study

This study is principally concerned with the obligations imposed by the Covenant upon States Parties. Therefore, it does not examine obligations of actors other than States Parties.

I am perfectly aware that at the current stage of international law development it has been established that States are not the only duty holders. Today it has become clear that private actors may also infringe the enjoyment of human rights. This is a step forward from the traditional view of international human rights law which was defined as a relationship between the State and the individual.[66]

---

64 In Künnemann's view, '[t]he rhetoric of human rights may sometimes lead to thoughtless exaggerations. Unfortunately, on some occasions this gives rise to the somewhat dangerous tendency to term every objectionable social or economic situation a violation of human rights. But human rights must never be separated from the obligations to which they give rise. When speaking of a violation or a breach of human rights, there must be a clear idea of the State obligations involved.' Künnemann, *loc. cit.* (note 52), p. 338.

65 Better knowledge of the obligations would facilitate supervision in the sense that it would be easier to deal with a claim alleging that there is a breach of a precise obligation than with a claim that broadly alleges that some situation is in 'violation' of the Covenant. For example, if a State deliberately and without any justification decided to eliminate a food stamps programme for welfare cases without replacing it with another programme, it would be easier to monitor a claim alleging the breach of the obligations imposed by article 2 ICESCR in conjunction with article 11 ICESCR, than to monitor a claim that the situation (the cut in welfare benefits) is a 'violation of the Covenant' but without providing any precision as to the obligations with which the State has failed to comply.

66 The movement towards the recognition of certain duties for individuals or private bodies was not directly foreseen by the drafters, although the UDHR recognises individual duties in its Preamble and in Art. 29(1). This is also true of the ICESCR in which there are some references to a broader recogniti-

The obligations that the Covenant may impose on other actors are indeed of great importance for the enhancement of the protection of these rights, particularly in the context of globalisation. Nonetheless, in this context we should bear in mind that States retain the primary responsibility for human rights.[67] The present study stresses the duties of States to prevent violations and protect individuals under their jurisdiction against violations of their rights committed by private entities. In this sense, as it has been noted, virtually every claim against private actors can be re-characterised as one against a public actor.[68] Following the developing jurisprudence of the Committee, the implications of the structural adjustment policies of the international financial institutions are analysed in the present study from the point of view of the responsibility of the States Parties.

It should be stressed that the liability of international organisations, especially the international financial institutions has been discussed within the context of the debates on the adoption of a draft optional protocol to the Covenant establishing a complaint procedure.[69] Some NGOs have presented arguments in favour of presenting complaints against transnational corporations and financial institutions.[70] Despite the importance of the points made, the Committee decided not to include them in its draft optional protocol. However, from the Committee's work, it is apparent that obligations exist for

---

on of duty holders, principally in the Preamble and in the suggestion of international obligations of assistance in Art. 2(1), Art. 11 and Art. 23 ICESCR. For the Committee it is beyond doubt that the Covenant imposes obligations upon 'actors other than States Parties' (see note 71).

67 See Rodley, N.: 'Can armed opposition groups violate human rights?' In: *Human rights in the twenty-first century: a global challenge*. Mahoney, K. & Mahoney, P. (eds.), Martinus Nijhoff Publishers, Dordrecht, (1993), pp. 297-318.

68 Forrest *et al.,* 1998, p. 1173. In this regard, I would like to recall the case of A. v. the United Kingdom heard by the European Court of Human Rights [Application No. 25599/94, Judgement of 23 September 1998]. 'A' was a child who was beaten by his stepfather with a garden cane applied with considerable force on a number of occasions. The stepfather was charged with assault, but a jury found him not guilty because it was considered to be 'reasonable chastisement' which was lawful under domestic law. However, in the Court's view, the 'reasonable chastisement' defence to a charge of assault on a child did not provide adequate protection against treatment or punishment contrary to Art. 3 ECHR. Therefore, it concluded that in the circumstances of the case 'the failure to provide adequate protection constitutes a violation of Art. 3 of the Convention.' (para. 24) This failure consisted of the existence of a law according to which deliberate violence against a child is permissible provided that it was 'reasonable' and 'moderate.' Thus, in light of the decision, it would be safe to say that the State was held responsible for its failure to act by amending or repealing a law that does not provide the protection required by the Convention. What an important conclusion! Imagine if we could apply, the same principle to the existence of a law that apparently violates the rights contained in the Covenant. Undoubtedly, this would constitute an important enhancement in the protection of economic, social and cultural rights.

69 See, for example, E/C.12/1996/SR.20.

70 See, for example, the presentation by Mr. Teitelbaum E/C.12/1996/SR.19 paras. 26-27.

actors other than States Parties,[71] while States Parties should provide an environment that facilitates the implementation of these responsibilities.[72]

7 A NOTE ON TERMINOLOGY AND SOURCES

The principal subject of analysis is the International Covenant on Economic, Social and Cultural Rights. I will therefore refer to it by its full title, sometimes merely as the 'Covenant' or with the abbreviation 'ICESCR'. Hence, unless the text clearly indicates a different intention, the term 'Covenant' should be taken as referring to the International Covenant on Economic, Social and Cultural Rights.

When the text refers to 'economic, social and cultural rights', this is limited to the rights imposed by the Covenant, not to any 'moral rights' or rights contained in other human rights instruments, except where specifically noted. Despite the importance that moral duties may have and the fact that the topic under analysis carries important moral weight, the analysis will concentrate on the legal aspects of these rights.[73] Thus, sometimes the obligations under discussion might be seen as somehow softer than those required in the moral realm. Perhaps there are many moral duties that ought to be translated into legal duties in order to achieve full enjoyment of economic, social and cultural rights for all. However, to the extent that those obligations are limited to the moral realm, they are beyond the scope of this work.

It is also important to note that the term 'obligations' should be taken as synonymous with the term 'duties.' In both cases the terms refer to legal obligations which States Parties have assumed by ratifying or acceding to an international instrument.

Among its functions, the Committee is required to submit an annual report on its activities to ECOSOC, and it is to make suggestions and recommendations of a general nature on the basis of its consideration of the State reports and of the reports submitted by the specialised agencies.[74] This report contains the most relevant information on the Committee's work, such as the Concluding Observations, an overview of the Committee's working methods, a summary of the proceedings of the Day of General Discussions, the text of the General Comments adopted as well as information on all organisational matters. The annual reports of the Committee, as well as the summary records of its meetings have been the principal sources for the analysis of the work of the Com-

71 See, for example, General Comment No. 14 paras. 63-65; General Comment No. 13 para. 60; and General Comment No. 12 para. 20.

72 General Comment No. 12 para. 20.

73 As Wellman notes, there is such an important interplay between moral and legal rights that it can be summarised as follows: (1) many basic legal rights recognise and protect fundamental moral rights; (2) moral rights can be the source of new legal rights; (3) the State can, by the exercise of some legal rights, abridge some moral rights; (4) moral rights can, for the most part, morally justify the State in creating and maintaining some analogous legal rights. Wellman, C.: *An approach to Rights: studies in the philosophy of law and morals*, Kluwer Academic Publishers, Dordrecht, (1997), pp. 40 *et seq.*

74 ECOSOC Resolution 1985/17 (f). In: E/C.12/1987/1 of 17 December 1980, p. 11.

mittee on Economic, Social and Cultural Rights. As of December 31, 2001, the Committee had held twenty-seven sessions, and the last Annual Report available was the report of the sessions held in the year 2000 (E/2001/22, Report on the twenty-second, twenty-third and twenty-fourth sessions). Nonetheless, the Concluding Observations of the States examined in the sessions held in the year 2001 have been also taken into account as they have been included in the electronic database of human rights documentation made available on the Internet by the Office of the High Commissioner for Human Rights [OHCHR].[75]

Finally, it is important to stress here that an explanation on the UN documents quoted in the present study may be useful for the reader. Such an explanation has been provided at the end of the work.

75 Available at http://www.unhchr.ch/tbs/doc.nsf (last visited July 2002). The Committee held its 29th session in Geneva from 29 April to 17 May 2002.

Part One: The role of the Committee on Economic, Social and Cultural Rights in clarifying the normative content of the Covenant

Part One of the present study is made up of three chapters and is meant to be a preliminary analysis that will set the stage for an examination of the principal object of the study in Parts Two and Three. The Committee's work is the most obvious source for determining the meaning and scope of the obligations imposed by the Covenant. Thus, Chapter I examines the Committee's origins and its working methods. The emphasis is placed on the manner in which the Committee has used working methods to further develop the normative content of the Covenant. The Committee on Economic, Social and Cultural Rights does not interpret the Covenant in a vacuum and Chapter II paints a broad picture of developments in the field of economic, social and cultural rights and how these developments have contributed to the process of clarifying the normative content of the obligations imposed by the Covenant and the consolidation of the principle of the indivisibility of all human rights. Chapter III sets out the rules of interpretation of international human rights norms, emphasising that the specific object and purpose of human rights treaties (the protection of the human person), requires that they be interpreted in a manner which makes the rights effective in the light of present-day circumstances. This Chapter also includes an excursus on the legitimacy of the Committee and attempts to address the issue of why States comply, or should comply, with the Committee's interpretation of the Covenant.

Chapter I
The Committee on Economic, Social and Cultural Rights

1 Introduction

The Committee on Economic, Social and Cultural Rights is the supervisory body of the International Covenant on Economic, Social and Cultural Rights. Since its first session in 1987, the Committee has achieved significant progress in the clarification of the nature and scope of the Covenant obligations, particularly through its examination of the States' reports and its Concluding Observations, in its ensuring General Comments as well as other activities such as the Days of General Discussion.

The background to the Committee's establishment and its working methods have been analysed in detail elsewhere, and it is not necessary to provide a detailed description here.[1] For our purposes it is sufficient to briefly mention this background information with emphasis on the Committee's role in developing and clarifying the normative content of the Covenant.

2 The establishment of the Committee

As is well known, in contrast to its sister Covenant, the ICESCR does not itself establish a special supervisory body. The supervisory function was entrusted to the Economic and Social Council (ECOSOC).[2] However, in the years immediately after

1 For a general description see 27 ICJ Review, December 1981, pp. 26-39; Alston, P: 'Out of the abyss: the challenges confronting the new UN Committee on Economic, Social and Cultural Rights.' In: *HRQ*, vol. 9 No. 3, (1987), pp. 332-381; Alston, P. & Simma, B.: 'First session of the UN Committee on Economic, Social and Cultural Rights.' In: *AJIL,* vol. 81 No. 3, July (1987), pp. 747-756; Alston, P. & Simma, B.: 'Second session of the UN Committee on Economic, Social and Cultural Rights.' In: *AJIL,* Vol. 82 No. 3, July (1988), pp. 603-615; Alston, P.: 'The Committee on Economic, Social and Cultural Rights.' In: The United Nations and human rights: a critical appraisal. Alston, P. (ed.), Clarendon Press, Oxford, (1992), pp. 473-508; and Craven, M.: The International Covenant on Economic, Social and Cultural Rights: a perspective on its development, Clarendon Press, Oxford, (1995), pp. 35-42.

2 See articles 16 to 21 ICESCR. As two commentators note, '[t]he rationale was that the latter Covenant [ICESCR] was concerned with issues that were essentially the same as those dealt with by the various technical and specialized agencies for which ECOSOC was the established coordinating mechanism. An additional, but unstated, reason was that most states preferred to entrust implementation to a political body over which they could exercise full control, rather than to a specialist body that might

the entry into force of the Covenant, it became evident that ECOSOC could not perform this function by itself. Therefore, discussions were initiated on the creation of a specific body to assist the ECOSOC in monitoring compliance with the Covenant's obligations. By Resolution 1988(LX) of 11 May 1976, ECOSOC established a subsidiary organ for the purpose of assisting it in the consideration of States Parties' reports under the Covenant.[3]

The body established by the ECOSOC was entitled the 'Sessional Working Group on the Implementation of the International Covenant on Economic, Social and Cultural Rights.'[4] It was composed of 15 government representatives of State members of ECOSOC which were also parties to the Covenant, chosen with regard to equitable geographical distribution and appointed for a one-year term.[5] This Working Group held its first session from 17 April to 3 May 1979 and a year later it began its consideration of reports. The work of this body was strongly criticised, *inter alia,* for its political character, its lack of technical expertise, and the short period of membership (1 year) which created constant turnover in membership with devastating consequences for the continuity and consistency of the Group's work.[6]

The deficiencies in the exercise of its work and the low level of confidence in this body generated great criticism and eventually led ECOSOC to take action for improvement.[7] Thus, in 1982, after four sessions of the 'Sessional Working Group', ECOSOC

---

seek to develop either independence or expertise, or worse still, both.' Alston & Simma, 1987, *loc. cit.* (note 1), p. 748.

3 According to the Resolution, 'a sessional working group of the Economic and Social Council, with appropriate representation of States Parties to the Covenant, and with due regard to equitable geographical distribution, shall be established by the Council whenever reports are due for consideration by the Council, for the purpose of assisting it in the consideration of such reports' [para. 9 (a)]. In this Resolution, ECOSOC also established a programme under which the States Parties furnished the reports referred to in article 16 in biennial stages. First stage rights covered by articles 6 to 9, second stage rights covered by articles 10 to 12 and third stage rights covered by articles 13 to 15. Res. 1988 (LX) 'Procedures for the implementation of the International Covenant on Economic, Social and Cultural Rights.' In: UN doc. E/C.12/1987/1 of 17 December 1980, p. 3. (This document contains a selection of resolutions and decisions of relevance for the implementation of the Covenant).

4 ECOSOC Res. 1978/10 'Composition of the sessional working group on the implementation of the International Covenant on Economic, Social and Cultural Rights.' In: E/C.12/1987/1 p. 4.

5 See ECOSOC Res. 1978/10 of 3 May 1978 by which the sessional working group was established. See also Res. 1979/43 of 11 May 1979 and Res. 1981/158 of 8 May 191 by which the ECOSOC incorporated changes and modified the working methods of the sessional working group. In: E/C.12/1987/1 p. 5 and p. 6, respectively.

6 See, 27 *ICJ Review, loc. cit.* (note 1), pp. 26-39; Alston, *loc. cit.* (note 1), pp. 332-381; Alston & Simma, 1987, *loc. cit.* (note 1) pp. 747-756; Alston & Simma, 1988, *loc. cit.* (note 1), pp. 603-615 and Alston, *op. cit.* (note 1), pp. 473-508. After the establishment of the Committee, some members also expressed criticism of the work of its predecessor. See for example, Mr. Alvarez Vita E/C.12/1987/SR.4 para. 14.

7 In its Res. 1980/24 of 2 May 1980 entitled 'Sessional Working Group on the Implementation of the International Covenant on Economic, Social and Cultural rights', the Economic and Social Council noted that the Sessional Working Group 'had encountered certain difficulties in discharging its

decided that specialist expertise was required and by Resolution 1982/33, the Working Group was renamed the 'Sessional Working Group of Governmental Experts on the Implementation of the International Covenant on Economic, Social and Cultural Rights.'

This second working group differed from its predecessor mainly in that the persons designated by governments to represent them were to be experts with recognised competence in the field of human rights. ECOSOC also changed the length of their mandate and the fifteen members of the group were elected for three-year terms (and eligible for re-election).[8] Despite these important changes, the work of the Working Group was still unsatisfactory. In the words of two authoritative commentators, the work of this body was 'totally unproductive.'[9]

In general, there was dissatisfaction with the work of both working groups.[10] Among the shortcomings of the Committee's predecessors, their failure in making any progress in determining the normative content of the Covenant is particularly worth noting here. As one commentator states with relation to the Working Group, 'the most significant shortcomings of the Group's work relate to its output. The Group has failed to include any summary of states' reports, or its deliberations thereon, in its own reports to the Council and has for the most part abstained from making recommendations on other than procedural matters.'[11] Fortunately, in 1985 ECOSOC reviewed the work of the 'Working Group of Governmental Experts' and decided to replace it with the Committee on Economic, Social and Cultural Rights, which held its first session in Geneva from 9 to 27 of March 1987.

The Committee is composed of eighteen independent experts.[12] Members of the Committee are elected by ECOSOC by secret ballot from a list of persons who qualify as 'experts in the field of human rights' and who have been nominated for that purpose

---

responsibilities under the current arrangements,' thus, the Council decided to review the composition, organisation and administrative arrangements of the Sessional Working Group. The formal review began in the ECOSOC organisation session of 1981 and continued in 1982. Nevertheless, as Alston notes, between 1982 and 1985 there was no relevant discussion regarding the possibility of transforming the Working Group into a committee of independent experts, therefore it was a surprise when the Working Group proposed this transformation to ECOSOC in 1985. For an explanation of this change of attitude, see Alston, op. cit. (note 1), p. 484 *et seq.*

8 See ECOSOC Res. 1982/33 of 6 May 1982. In: E/C.12/1987/1 pp. 7-8.

9 Alston & Simma, 1987, *loc. cit.* (note 1), p. 749. For a general analysis of the deficiencies of both working groups see, for example, Alston, *loc. cit.* (note 1), pp. 341-342.

10 For a summary of the 'most commonly cited' criticisms of the work of both working groups, see Alston, loc. cit. (note 1), pp. 341-342 (also in Alston, op. cit. (note 1), pp. 480-481) and Craven, M.: The International Covenant on Economic, Social and Cultural Rights: a perspective on its development, Clarendon Press, Oxford, Paperback edition, with corrections, (1998), pp. 40-41.

11 Alston, *loc. cit.* (note 1), p. 342. Also in Alston, *op. cit.* (note 1), p. 481.

12 ECOSOC Res. 1985/17 of 28 May 1985. In: E/C.12/1987/1 p. 11.

by the States Parties.[13] It is not required that the candidates be nationals of the nominating State.[14] Members are elected for four years and are eligible for re-election.[15]

In formal terms, the Committee's mandate does not derive from the Covenant itself but from ECOSOC and it merely assists ECOSOC in supervising the implementation of the Covenant. The Committee fulfils this supervisory role principally by examining the reports submitted by the States Parties within two years of the entry into force of the Covenant and thereafter every five years.[16]

Although its lack of experience and the vestiges of the past were obstacles in the Committee's early sessions,[17] the Committee quickly overcame these problems and emerged as a unique body, far more capable than those that had preceded it. Over the years it has consolidated its role as the supervisory body of the Covenant.

As early as its second session, commentators noted that the Committee had moved substantially beyond the formal advisory role that was provided for in the text of the ECOSOC Resolution that established it, and 'has begun to emerge as the principal

13 *Idem.*

14 A State Party may nominate a non-national. However, so far, States have always nominated nationals. As Alston notes, if State Parties designate an individual who is not a national 'the chances of election would probably be slight.' Alston, *op. cit.* (note 1), p. 488.

15 One half of the membership of the Committee is renewed every second year, bearing in mind the need to maintain an equitable geographical distribution (paragraphs (i) and (ii)). Only States Parties can nominate persons for the Committee (para. c), but all members of the ECOSOC, whether or not they are Parties to the Covenant, are entitled to take part in the election (para. c). Res. 1985/17 of 28 may 1985. In: E/C.12/1987/1 p. 11.

16 See article 16 ICESCR and ECOSOC Res. 1988/4, 24 May 1988.

17 See E/1987/28. From the description of the first session by Alston and Simma, we find that there were some problems in the consideration of States Parties' reports, e.g. 'the Committee did not succeed in developing a procedure for members to indicate their reaction to the responses provided; patently inadequate responses were therefore acknowledged with the same formal expression of thanks as much more sophisticated and carefully tailored responses.' Alston & Simma, 1987, *loc. cit.* (note 1), p. 754 (footnote omitted). Alston and Simma also described some problems in the Committee's report to the ECOSOC, although they noted that they were an improvement on the equivalent version submitted by the Working Group. In 1988, they noted '[n]evertheless, these observations were based on very little discussion by the Committee and, in most respects, are most unsatisfactory. They treat complex and important matters cursorily and reflect none of the appropriate nuances' (p. 754, footnotes omitted). Additionally, some of the problems reflected the Cold War, and '[p]erhaps the most surprising feature of the session is the extent to which the Eastern European expert members revealed a strong and unequivocal resistance to the adoption of any procedural innovations that would make the Committee more effective and relevant to the problems of the real world' (p. 755). It is interesting to note that a year later, the same commentators writing on the second session of the Committee noted, '[o]n the Soviets' part, the spirit of 'openness' (glasnost) and 'restructuring' (perestroika) led not only to the resignation of the former Soviet expert prior to the session, but also, and more importantly, to a significantly more open and progressive approach to the issues on the part of the other experts from Eastern Europe.' Alston & Simma, 1988, *loc. cit.* (note 1), p. 613. (Footnotes omitted).

forum in which the implications of the concept of economic, social and cultural rights are being explored.'[18]

The Committee is required to submit an annual report on its activities to ECOSOC, and it is to make suggestions and recommendations of a general nature on the basis of its consideration of the State reports and of the reports submitted by the specialised agencies.[19] Its annual report contains the most relevant information on the Committee's work, such as the Concluding Observations, an overview of the Committee's working methods, a summary of the proceedings of the Day of General Discussions, the text of the General Comments adopted as well as information on organisational matters. The Committee's annual reports to the ECOSOC, as well as the summary records of its sessions provide the material sources to identify the normative scope of the Covenant.

3 Brief overview of the Committee's working methods

It is not necessary to describe in great detail the Committee's working methods as detailed and clear analysis may be found elsewhere.[20] Nonetheless, a brief descriptive mention of the Committee's working methods is required because we refer to them in many parts of the study. In the following, the focus will be on the way in which the Committee creatively interprets and develops the provisions of the Covenant, providing a clearer understanding of its normative content.[21]

18 Alston & Simma, 1988, *loc. cit.* (note 1), p. 604. As to the progress made by the Committee during its earlier years see, among others, Craven and Dommen: 'Making room for substance: fifth session of the Committee on Economic, Social and Cultural Rights,' in: *NQHR,* No. 1, (1991), pp. 83-95.

19 ECOSOC Res. 1985/17 (f). In: E/C.12/1987/1 p. 11.

20 See, for example, the description by the Committee of its working methods in the annual reports to the ECOSOC [The last annual report available at the time of writing was E/2001/22, see paras. 26-58] and, among others, Alston, *op. cit.* (note 1), pp. 473-508 and Craven, *op. cit.* (note 1), pp. 30-105. In addition, for the work of the Committee, see 'UN Committee on Economic, Social and Cultural Rights', in: 42 *ICJ Review*, June 1989, pp. 33-39; Leckie: 'An overview and appraisal of the fifth session of the UN Committee on Economic, Social and Cultural Rights,' in: *HRQ,* vol.13, (1991), pp. 545-572; Craven & Dommen, *op. cit.* (note 18), pp. 83-95; O'Flaherty, M; Human Rights and the UN: practice before the treaty bodies. Sweet & Maxwell, London, (1996), pp. 53-81.

21 In any application of the Covenant, an interpretation of the norms is always necessary. As Schwarzenberger has noted, 'Interpretation is the process of establishing the legal character and effects of a consensus achieved by the parties. In contrast, application is the process of determining the consequences of such an interpretation in a concrete case. Thus, interpretation of a treaty is independent of, and need not be followed by, the application of the treaty. Any application of a treaty, including its execution, presupposes, however, a preceding conscious or subconscious interpretation of the treaty.' Schwarzenberger, G.: 'Myths and realities of treaty interpretation.' In: *VJIL,* vol. 9 No. 1, (1968), pp. 7-8 (footnotes omitted).

3.1 Consideration of State Reports

3.1.1 State Reports

In accordance with article 16 ICESCR, States Parties are obliged to submit periodic reports. The reports are to be submitted within two years of the entry into force of the Covenant and thereafter every five years.[22] The reports should reflect the extent to which the rights are being realised in the country concerned, including the 'factors and difficulties affecting the degree of fulfilment of the obligations under the Covenant.'[23]

The State reports provide the basis on which the Committee supervises the implementation of the Covenant by the State Party. The Committee has made important efforts to assist States to comply with their reporting obligations in an adequate manner. For example, in its first General Comment it stresses that reporting is not merely a procedural matter designed to satisfy the formal obligation of article 16 ICESCR but, rather, that the process of preparing and submitting reports should achieve a variety of objectives which the Committee goes on to elaborate upon in the General Comment.[24] Moreover, the Committee has also adopted reporting guidelines to assist States in the preparation of the reports. These reporting guidelines replaced older guidelines prepared by ECOSOC which were of dubious quality. However, in general, State reports have not achieved the level of quality expected by the Committee, which has not infrequently expressed concern regarding the fact that the reports provide insufficiently detailed information, lack statistical data as to the concrete measures and policies adopted and are too focused on information relating to the States' legal system but do not provide sufficient data on its functioning in practice.[25] Fortunately, in recent years, it seems that States have tended to follow the guidelines more closely and have prepared better reports.[26]

---

22 ECOSOC Res. 1988/4 of 24 May 1988.

23 See article 17 ICESCR.

24 See General Comment No. 1 on 'Reporting by States Parties.'

25 See, for example, Concluding Observations Senegal E/C.12/1/Add.62 para. 3; Concluding Observations Syrian Arab Republic E/C.12/1/Add.63 para. 3; Concluding Observations Korea E/C.12/1/Add.59 para. 2; Concluding Observations Bolivia E/C.12/1/Add.60 para. 3; Concluding Observations Nigeria E/1999/22 para. 96; Concluding Observations Cyprus E/1999/22 para. 274; Concluding Observations Zimbabwe E/1998/22 para. 65; Concluding Observations Peru E/1998/22 para. 133; Concluding Observations El Salvador E/1997/22 para. 149; Concluding Observations Portugal [Macau] E/1997/22 para. 245; Concluding Observations Iraq E/1995/22 para. 126; Concluding Observations Kenya E/1995/22 para. 160; and Concluding Observations Argentina E/1995/22 para. 224.

26 The Committee has noted this for example in: Concluding Observations Japan E/C.12/1/Add.67 para. 2; Concluding Observations Nepal E/C.12/1/Add.66 para. 2; Concluding Observations Honduras E/C.12/1/Add.57 para. 2; Concluding Observations Georgia E/2001/22 para. 76; Concluding Observations Australia, E/2001/22 para. 367; Concluding Observations Kyrgyzstan E/2001/22 para. 330; and Concluding Observations Sudan E/2001/22 para. 289.

The reports are potentially important tools through which States contribute to clarify the normative content of the Covenant. After the Committee's fifth session in 1991, Alston wrote,

> 'Clarification of the normative content of the rights recognised in the Covenant has thus been a priority concern for the Committee. In theory this function, in so far as it is to be performed at all, should be achieved through the examination of States parties' reports. In other words, the approaches adopted by States themselves in their internal arrangements (and explained in their reports to the Committee) will shed light upon the norms, while the dialogue between the State and the Committee will contribute further to deepening the understanding of the central issues in that regard.
>
> In practice, however, States' reports have not proven especially enlightening in this respect and States' representatives have manifested a distinct reluctance to engage in any exchange of views with the Committee on these issues.'[27]

Although the quality of State reports improved significantly in the ten years after Alston made this comment, States Parties still do not contribute much through their reports to the clarification of the normative content of the Covenant. Nevertheless, there are some exceptions. For example, some States' reports contribute to clarifying the normative content of article 2(2) (prohibition of discrimination) by incorporating in-depth analysis on the issue.[28]

3.1.2 The pre-sessional working group and the 'list of issues'

Prior to each Committee session, five members of the Committee meet in order to identify in advance the questions which will constitute the principal focus of discussion with State representatives during the constructive dialogue.[29] This 'pre-sessional working group' prepares a list of issues to be taken into consideration when examining the State Party report, which is transmitted to the permanent delegation of the State concerned. The idea is to provide the State with the possibility to prepare answers in advance and thereby to facilitate dialogue with the Committee.

As the Committee notes, the list of issues is not meant to be exhaustive and the dialogue may refer to other points as well.[30] The Committee urges the States to provide written replies to the list of issues well in advance of the session, in order to make these available to the Committee members in the respective working languages. Generally,

---

27 Alston, *op. cit.* (note 1), p. 491.

28 See, for example, Third Periodic Report Mexico E/1994/104/Add.18 paras. 9-48, Fourth Periodic Report Germany E/C.12/4/Add.3 paras. 11-52 and Third Periodic Report Portugal E/1994/104/Add.20 paras. 36-49.

29 The pre-sessional working group was authorised by ECOSOC Res. 1988/4, of 24 May 1988. In: E/C.12/1989/4.

30 E/C.12/2000/21 Chapter II, pp. 29-37.

the 'list of issues' of a given country contains the points which are of concern to the Committee or which have not been properly addressed by the State in its report.

3.1.3 The Constructive Dialogue

The Committee strongly encourages States to be present at the meeting when their reports are examined.[31] The discussion between government representatives and Committee members is called the 'constructive dialogue.'[32] Representatives of specialised agencies concerned such as ILO, WHO and UNICEF and other international bodies may also be invited to contribute at any stage of the dialogue.

The dialogue with State representatives is a valuable opportunity for the Committee to explain the normative content of particular provisions of the Covenant and to comment on difficulties in the implementation of the Covenant. The summary records of such dialogues are made available to the public through printed UN documents and are now also available through the Internet in the database maintained by the OHCHR.[33]

Often, the dialogue is very open and frank and State experts often recognise the failures of the States they represent and the difficulties encountered in the implementation of the Covenant. Committee experts have the opportunity to provide a clear explanation of the scope of the obligations concerned.

3.1.4 The Concluding Observations

The final phase of the examination of State reports is the drafting and adoption of the Committee's Concluding Observations. The Concluding Observations are usually made public only on the last day of the session and are available to all interested parties. Since 1993,[34] the established structure of the 'Concluding Observations' is as follows: 'introduction,' 'positive aspects,' 'factors and difficulties impeding the imple-

---

31 See the Committee's rule of procedure No. 62. In: Rules of Procedure of the Committee, E/C.12/1990/4/Rev.1 of 1 September 1993.

32 As described by a former Chairperson of the Committee, P. Alston, 'the discussion that takes place between the members of the Committee and the representatives of the State Party is designed to achieve a constructive and mutually rewarding dialogue. The process is not in any way an adversarial one and its principal objectives are to assist States Parties in fulfilling their obligations under the Covenant and to create a deeper awareness and understanding of its provisions. Through this dialogue the Committee seeks to obtain a complete picture of the situation in the country concerned, which in turn enables the Committee to make whatever comments they believe appropriate for the most effective implementation of the obligations contained in the Covenant.' Alston, P.: 'The International Covenant on Economic, Social and Cultural Rights.' In: Manual on human rights reporting under six major international human rights instruments. HR/PUB/91/1(Rev.1), United Nations Publications, Geneva, (1997), p. 160.

33 However, not everyone has the opportunity to examine the summary records of the Committee. The summary records are only published in English and French. Moreover, while the 'hard copies' of these documents are not easily accessible to the general public or to many States, the database maintained by the Office of the HCHR does not post them systematically.

34 E/1993/22 para. 265.

mentation of the Covenant,' 'principal subjects of concern,' and 'suggestions and recommendations'. Despite the fact that this structure employs rather diplomatic language, the Committee has become increasingly more adversarial and inquisitive in its work. Nowadays, the Concluding Observations do not merely contain 'suggestions and recommendations' and careful examination reveals that many Concluding Observations are to a greater or lesser extent formal declarations of compliance or non-compliance.[35]

The Concluding Observations increasingly contain strong language that indicates a decision as to whether or not the State has complied with the Covenant. The strong language used by the Committee has provided clearer guidance as to the normative content of the Covenant.

Nowadays, instead of merely 'recommending,' the Committee often *'urges'* the States Parties to do or refrain from a particular act. When the Committee adopts this language it provides a clearer vision of the normative content of the Covenant. For example, article 7 (a)(ii) of the Covenant recognises that the right of everyone to the enjoyment of just and favourable conditions of work entails a remuneration which provides all workers with a 'decent living for themselves and their families.' When the Committee 'urges' a State Party 'to take adequate measures to ensure that the minimum wage is sufficient to meet the basic needs of the wage earner and his or her family,'[36] it clarifies the normative content of article 7 ICESCR, suggesting that a remuneration considered to provide a 'decent living' should be, as a minimum, sufficient to meet the basic needs of the worker and his/her family.

By the same token, the normative content of article 10 ICESCR which requires the adoption of special protection measures for children and young persons was clarified by the Committee when it 'urged' a State Party to 'treat with more concern the growing number of children begging on the street and to take the appropriate measures to solve the problem'[37] and when it 'urges the State Party to take steps towards establishing stronger labour laws in order to protect children from abusive working conditions and to undertake immediate measures towards the eradication of illegal child labour.'[38] In both cases, the Committee's statements suggest that taking actions to combat begging by children and legislative measures to protect against child labour are among the protective measures that States must take in accordance with this article.

35 According to Bruno Simma, a former Committee member, '[t]he Concluding Observations as they stand now, are comprehensive and clear evaluations of a State Party's performance. If necessary, they call a spade a spade and speak of violations of rights protected by the Covenant – a practice that would have met with fierce opposition 10 years ago.' See. Simma, B.: 'The examination of State reports: International Covenant on Economic, Social and Cultural Rights.' In: The monitoring system of human rights treaty obligations. Klein, Eckart (ed.), Colloquium Potsdam, 22/23 November 1996, Berlin Verlag, Berlin, (1998),p. 38.

36 Concluding Observations Georgia E/2001/22 para. 97.

37 Concluding Observations Georgia E/2001/22 para. 102.

38 Concluding Observations Egypt E/2001/22 para. 178.

The prohibition of discrimination under article 2(2) ICESCR is also clearer after the Committee 'urge[d] the State Party to extend the subsidised health-care system to asylum-seekers without discrimination,'[39] because it makes it apparent that the scope of article 2(2) also prohibits discrimination against asylum seekers. The Committee also shed light on the normative content of the right to the highest attainable standard of health (article 12 ICESCR) when it 'strongly urge[d] the State Party to address the problem of female genital mutilation as a matter of high priority with a view to moving actively towards the total eradication of this practice in the country.'[40] This kind of statement makes it clear that this provision protects against the practice of female genital mutilation.

There are numerous occasions in which the Committee has acted to clarify the normative content of the Covenant by 'urging' States to do or to refrain from doing something, particularly in the Concluding Observations.[41] However, it has also occurred with some frequency that the Committee adopts even stronger wording by which it makes clear that some type of State behaviour is either required or prohibited by the Covenant. This approach serves to diminish what Hart has called the 'penumbra of uncertainty' of a given norm.[42]

The Committee has often adopted language that clearly indicates when State behaviours or practices do not comply with the Covenant. For example, when the Committee has qualified certain practices or laws as '*incompatible*' with a concrete article of the Covenant,[43] or when it has expressly declared that a given situation is '*unacceptable*' under the Covenant.[44] The same is true when the Committee has found that some State actions are '*inconsistent*' with the provision of the Covenant,[45] that a practice '*does not*

39 Concluding Observations Italy E/2001/22 para. 138.

40 Concluding Observations Egypt E/2001/22 para. 174.

41 Other examples of Concluding Observations that clarify the normative content of the Covenant provisions by 'urging' the State to do something, include Concluding Observations Egypt E/2001/22 para. 180 (Art. 2(2)); Concluding Observations Republic of Congo E/2001/22 para. 211 (Art. 3); Concluding Observations Portugal E/2001/22 para. 421 (Art. 2(3)); and Concluding Observations Morocco E/2001/22 para. 556 (Art. 10).

42 Hart, H.L.A.: The concept of law, Clarendon Law series, second edition, Oxford, (1994), p. 12.

43 See, for example, Concluding Observations Zimbabwe E/1998/22 para. 73 and Concluding Observations United Kingdom of Great Britain and Northern Ireland E/1998/22 para. 294.

44 Concluding Observations Russian Federation E/1998/22 paras. 106 and 112; Concluding Observations United Kingdom of Great Britain and Northern Ireland E/1998/22 para. 310; and Concluding Observations Dominican Republic E/1997/22 paras. 224 and 230.

45 See, for example, Concluding Observations Libyan Arab Jamahiriya E/1998/22 para. 186, Concluding Observations Azerbaijan E/1998/22 para. 329 and Concluding Observations Ireland E/2000/22 para. 133.

conform' with a certain provision of the Covenant,[46] or that some behaviour is '*contrary to the Covenant.*'[47]

In some situations the Committee has been even more precise and has provided *express verbis* an assessment of non-compliance with the Covenant's obligations. This is so, for example, when the Committee has found that a State is '*not complying*' with its obligations,[48] or when it has indicated that there is a *'breach'* by the State of its obligations under the Covenant.[49] Obviously, the strongest expression of this kind is when the Committee has expressly noted that certain State behaviour is in '*violation*' of the Covenant.[50] When the Committee has used this term, it is even easier to assert the normative content of the Covenant. For example, we may now conclude that, according to the Committee, article 8(1)(d) ICESCR[51] requires States to incorporate the right to strike in domestic law or to repeal legislation that denies this right. Even when the text of an article does not expressly envisage a given obligation, the Committee has sometimes considered States to be 'violating' the right when they do not comply with implicit obligations.[52] For example, it may be concluded that the right to adequate

46 For example, Concluding Observations Iraq E/1998/22 para. 265; Concluding Observations Israel E/1999/22 para. 256; Concluding Observations Egypt E/2001/22 para. 161; and Concluding Observations Morocco E/2001/22 para. 541.

47 See, for example, Concluding Observations El Salvador E/1997/22 para. 165.

48 See, for example, Concluding Observations Sri Lanka E/1999/22 para. 73 and Concluding Observations Syrian Arab Republic E/C.12/1/Add.63 para. 21.

49 See, for example, Concluding Observations Israel E/1999/22 para. 237; Concluding Observations United Kingdom of Great Britain and Northern Ireland E/1998/22 para. 294; Concluding Observations Solomon Islands E/2000/22 para. 186; Concluding Observations Republic of Congo E/2001/22 para. 209; and Concluding Observations Portugal E/2001/22 para. 412.

50 While this kind of statement does not appear as often as one might expect, the Committee has increasingly used this language. See, for example, Concluding Observations Germany E/1999/22 para. 315; Concluding Observations Nigeria E/1999/22 para. 106; Concluding Observations Mexico E/2000/22 para. 382; Concluding Observations Nepal E/C.12/1/Add.66 para. 13; and Concluding Observations Saint Vincent and Grenadines E/1998/22 para. 413. Further, sometimes the Committee indicates that there is a 'clear violation' of the Covenant [*e.g.* Concluding Observations Libyan Arab Jamahiriya E/1998/22 para. 185 and Concluding Observations Canada E/1999/22 para. 406], a 'flagrant violation' [*e.g.* Concluding Observations Cameroon E/2000/22 para. 327] or that the given situation constitutes a 'serious violation' of the State Party's obligation [*e.g.* Concluding Observations Cyprus E/1999/22 para. 288 and Concluding Observations Paraguay E/1997/22 para. 78], that there are 'widespread violations' of the Covenant [*e.g.* Concluding Observations Israel E/1999/22 para. 243] and 'continuing gross violations of economic, social and cultural rights' [*e.g.* Concluding Observations Israel E/C.12/1/Add.69 para. 14].

51 Art. 8(1)(d) ICESCR reads as follows: 'The States Parties to the present Covenant undertake to ensure: […] (d) the right to strike, provided that it is exercised in conformity with the laws of the particular country.'

52 See, for example, Concluding Observations Canada E/1999/22 para. 407, Concluding Observations United Kingdom and Northern Ireland E/1998/22 para. 294 and Concluding Observations Nigeria E/1999/22 para. 111.

housing (article 11(1) ICESCR),[53] entails the obligation to refrain from forced evictions.[54]

Finally, it is important to note that the Committee's interpretation of the normative content of the Covenant through its Concluding Observations seems to enjoy a high degree of acceptance by States Parties. Although States sometimes include reactions to previous Concluding Observations in their periodic reports, such reactions generally attempt to deny the facts on which the Committee has based its assessment rather than to deny the scope of the obligations as set out by the Committee.[55] This tends to reinforce the validity of the Committee's interpretation.

3.2 General Comments

At its third session the Committee began the practice of preparing General Comments on the provisions of the Covenant.[56] As the Committee notes, 'the Committee endeavours, through its general comments, to make the experience gained so far through the examination of States' reports available for the benefit of all States Parties in order to assist and promote their further implementation of the Covenant; to draw the attention of the States Parties to insufficiencies disclosed by a large number of reports; to suggest improvements in the reporting procedures; and to stimulate the activities of the States Parties, international organisations and the specialised agencies concerned in

53 Art. 11(1) ICESCR reads as follow: 'The States Parties to the present Covenant recognise the right of everyone to an adequate standard of living for himself and his family, including adequate food, clothing and housing, and to the continuouos improvement of living conditions [...]'.

54 See, for example, Concluding Observations Dominican Republic E/1997/22 para. 236; Concluding Observations Zimbabwe E/1998/22 para. 84; and Concluding Observations Peru E/1998/22 para. 168. The existence of this obligation is also supported by General Comment No. 7 on 'the right to adequate housing: forced evictions.'

55 For example, the Third Periodic Report of Ukraine notes, 'In its concluding comments, the Committee on Economic, Social and Cultural Rights expressed concerns that the formation of trade unions was prohibited in a number of sectors and areas where wage labour was the norm, for example civil aviation and communications. But no such prohibition is envisaged under Ukrainian law. A number of long-established unions have been operating in these sectors; there are trade unions for aviation workers, civil aviation flight personnel, air traffic controllers, and communications workers' [E/C.12/4/Add.2 para. 177, 21 March 2000.] Similarly, the Fourth Periodic Report of Germany states, 'there is no reason for the Committee to be concerned about the economic rights and the right to health of asylum-seekers during the examination of their applications for asylum. As noted above, their subsistence is ensured during the examination procedure and they are provided with medical assistance' [E/C.12/4/Add.3 para. 202, 10 August 2000.] In both examples, States disagreed with the Committee's assessment of the facts, but they did not oppose the Committee's interpretation of the scope of the given right, specifically that the right to form and join trade unions should be enjoyed by all kinds of workers [Concluding Observations Ukraine E/1996/22 para. 264] and that asylum seekers must enjoy the Covenant's rights [Concluding Observations Germany E/1999/22 para. 316].

56 E/1989/22. The first General Comment issued in the third Committee's session is on 'Reporting by States Parties.'

achieving progressively and effectively the full realisation of the rights recognised in the Covenant.'[57] In this extensive list of endeavours the Committee does not expressly include the clarification of the normative content of the Covenant. However, it is apparent that the General Comments have served this purpose.

The role of the General Comments as instruments for the clarification of the normative content of the Covenant has been clearly set forth by some Committee members. For example, when the Committee was preparing the draft of General Comment No. 13, Mr. Riedel observed: 'general comments placed a greater burden on States Parties and should thus neither be a mere academic exercise nor focus solely on facilitating the Committee's work. Their purpose was, not to dwell on points of policy, *but to clarify the normative issues for the States Parties.*'[58] This statement seems to have found agreement among other Committee members as was evident during subsequent interventions during the same meeting.[59] Particularly important in this regard were the remarks of the Chairperson, Ms. Bonoan-Dandan, who concluded that 'the Committee was currently embarking on a series of comments *designed to define the normative content of the various rights set forth in the Covenant.*'[60]

The General Comments are the most suitable of the Committee's tools to clarify the normative content of the Covenant because they are general in nature and provide an abstract picture of the scope of the obligations. Thus, General Comments provide the most comprehensible and clear survey of the Committee's position. In this connection Buergenthal's view on the HRC's General Comments is of particular relevance as it is also applicable to the General Comments of the Committee:

> 'Over time the general comment has become a distinct juridical instrument, enabling the Committee to announce its interpretations of different provisions of the Covenant in a form that bears some resemblance to the advisory opinion practice of international tribunals [...]. General comments consequently have gradually become important instruments in the lawmaking process of the Committee, independent of the reporting system.'[61]

Two final observations should be made here. First, like the Concluding Observations, General Comments are adopted by consensus and therefore reflect the view of the Committee as a whole. In this regard it is important to note that adoption by consensus

57 E/2001/22, Chapter II, para. 56.

58 Summary Record of the 28th meeting held on 15 November 1999, UN doc. E/C.12/1999/SR.28 para. 41. (Emphasis added).

59 See, in particular, the interventions by Mr. Texier (para. 48) and Mr. Hunt (para. 54). Summary Record of the 28th meeting held on 15 November 1999. UN doc. E/C.12/1999/SR.28.

60 Summary Record of the 28th meting held on 15 November 1999. UN doc. E/C.12/1999/SR.28. Chairperson Mrs. Bonoan-Dandan (para. 52). No Committee member expressed disagreement with these views.

61 Buergenthal, T.: 'The Human Rights Committee.' In: The United Nations and human rights (forthcoming 2000), Chapter 10. As quoted in Steiner and Alston, 2000, p. 732.

might also have an adverse effect on the contents of the General Comments. The consensus rule forces the Committee to find a compromise on controversial issues that may result in a lower standard of protection or a less progressive approach.[62] Second, the interpretations of the normative scope of the Covenant by the Committee through its General Comments have achieved a significant degree of acceptance by States Parties. In fact, to this author's knowledge, States Parties have never formally objected to the General Comments of the Committee. This should be contrasted with the experience of the Human Rights Committee whose General Comments have not enjoyed the same degree of acceptance.[63]

3.3 The days of general discussion

The Committee devotes one day of each session to a general discussion of a particular right or of a particular aspect of the Covenant. As the Committee notes, '[t]he purpose is twofold: the day assists the Committee in developing in greater depth its understanding of the relevant issues; and it enables the Committee to encourage inputs into its work from all interested parties.'[64]

The days of general discussion provide an important opportunity for academics, members of the UN Commission and Sub-Commission, Special Rapporteurs, NGOs with expertise in the field of discussion, as well as specialised agencies to express their views on specific topics. In this regard, background papers submitted within the framework of a day of general discussion are of great value. Here again, the expertise gained by the Committee through these days is made available to all States through the General Comments and Concluding Observations.

So far, the Days of General Discussion have assisted the Committee in developing the normative content of a number of specific rights,[65] as well as in clarifying some other general normative issues under the Covenant.[66] Of particular importance among

62 See Schmidt, M.: 'Treaty-based human rights complaints procedures in the UN: remedy or mirage for victims of human rights violations?' In: *Human Rights/Droits del l'Homme,* No. 2, (1998), pp. 13-18.

63 Some Human Rights Committee General Comments have been considered by some States Parties as *ultra vires* such as General Comment No. 14 and General Comment No. 24. For example, the UK, the US and France made observations with regard to General Comment No. 24 [UN doc. A/40/40 (1985).]

64 E/2001/22, Chapter II, para. 50.

65 The following substantive rights have been the focus of discussion: the right to adequate food (third session); the right to housing (fourth session); the right to take part in cultural life (seventh session); the right to health (ninth session); the role of social safety nets (tenth session); the normative content of the right to food (seventeenth session); the right to education (nineteenth session); and the right of everyone to benefit from the protection of the moral and material interests resulting from any scientific, literary or artistic production of which he is the author (twenty-fourth session). E/2001/22, Chapter II, para. 50.

66 The following general issues have been the focus of discussion: economic and social indicators (sixth session); the rights of the ageing and elderly (eighth session); human rights education and public information activities relating to the Covenant (eleventh session); the interpretation and practical

these was the debate that the Committee devoted in its twelfth session to 'the interpretation and practical application of the obligations incumbent on States Parties to the International Covenant on Economic, Social and Cultural Rights.'[67]

Finally, it should be stated that the Committee's annual reports do not provide detailed information as to the substance of debates held during the days of general discussion and as a result do not give us much insight on the positions adopted by participants. It is therefore necessary to have recourse to the summary records in order to get a more comprehensive overview.

3.4 Follow-up

The Committee has developed various procedures for follow-up on the application of the Covenant, many of which refer to the request for more information.[68] In those cases where States submit additional information as a response to the Committee's request, the information tends, naturally, to have a high degree of specificity.

As a follow-up measure, the Committee may also decide to request a technical assistance mission to the State Party concerned. This is an extraordinary proceeding. As the Committee notes, 'such a decision would be taken only after the Committee had satisfied itself that there was no adequate alternative approach available to it and that the information in its possession warranted such an approach.'[69]

So far, the Committee has sent a technical assistance mission to only two States Parties.[70] In both cases the problems which motivated such extraordinary measures were related to the right to adequate housing and evictions. The Committee's reports on both missions have contributed to clarifying the normative content of the specific right concerned.[71]

---

application of the obligations incumbent on States Parties (twelfth session); a draft optional protocol to the Covenant (thirteenth, fourteenth and fifteenth sessions); revision of the general guidelines for reporting (sixteenth session); and globalisation and its impact on the enjoyment of economic, social and cultural rights (eighteenth session.) E/2001/22, Chapter II, para. 50.

67 Committee's twelfth session, held on May 15, 1995. E/1996/22 Chapter VI paras. 339-344. In addition, see the summary records of the meeting: E/C.12/1995/SR.21 and E/C.12/1995/SR.22.

68 For a description of the procedures adopted by the Committee in relation to follow-up action see E/2001/22 Chapter II paras. 43-46 and Coomans, F.: 'Follow-up action to State reporting on human rights: procedure and practice of the Committee on the Rights of the Child and the Committee on Economic, Social and Cultural Rights.' In: Rendering justice to the vulnerable: Liber Amicorum in honour of Theo van Boven, Kluwer Law International, The Hague, Cambridge, Dordrecht, (2000), pp. 83-98.

69 E/C.12/2000/21, Chapter II para. 44.

70 In both cases the Committee's representatives were Mr. Wimer Zambrano and Mr. Texier. In the case of Panama the visit was from 16 to 22 April 1995. In the case of the Dominican Republic, the visit was from 19 to 27 September 1997.

71 For the report on the technical assistance mission to the Dominican Republic see, E/1998/22 Annex VI. For the report on the technical assistance mission to Panama see, E/1996/22 Annex V.

3.5 Non-submission and considerably overdue reports

As the Committee notes, 'a situation of persistent non-reporting by States Parties risks bringing the entire supervisory procedure into disrepute, thereby undermining one of the foundations of the Covenant.'[72] Therefore, the Committee decided that when a State Party has not submitted the report under article 16 ICESCR or is considerably overdue in the submission of the report, it will examine the implementation of the Covenant by the State concerned in the absence of a State report.

The procedure followed by the Committee is the following: first, it identifies States Parties whose reports are long overdue, then it notifies each State of its intention to consider the situation at a specified future session. In the absence of the report, it considers the status of the economic, social and cultural rights in light of all available information. However, if the State Party concerned indicates that a report will be provided, the Chairperson of the Committee may defer the consideration of the situation for one session.[73]

After an examination of the State's situation, the Committee adopts Concluding Observations which are of a 'preliminary nature', and in a subsequent session the Committee will follow-up these preliminary Concluding Observations. For this purpose the Committee schedules a new meeting to which it invites representatives of the State and experts from the OHCHR, specialised agencies and other UN organs. As is the case during the days of general discussion, the interaction between the Committee and other experts in the follow-up meeting assists the Committee members in developing a common understanding of the normative scope of the Covenant. Unfortunately, the Committee's annual reports contain only very brief summaries of the follow-up meetings and provide little assistance to the general public.[74]

---

72 E/2001/22, Chapter II para. 47.

73 E/2001/22, Chapter II, paras. 47-49. The Committee began this practice during its ninth session.

74 As indicated above, the Committee's annual reports include little information on the days of general discussion.

Chapter II
The Covenant in a Changing International Environment

1 Introduction

During recent decades, international bodies have increasingly paid closer attention to human rights. As a result of this increased attention, we have witnessed, *inter alia*, the drafting and adoption of a number of human rights treaties and a wide range of non-binding instruments, significant improvements in the implementation methods of some existing treaties, as well as the consolidation of the international case law for the protection of these rights.[1]

In recent years there have been various initiatives aimed at furthering the protection of economic, social and cultural rights. This increased interest in economic, social and cultural rights contrasts markedly with the lack of interest in these rights in the past. For many years after the adoption of the Covenant, relevant international actors appeared almost insensitive to the protection of economic, social and cultural rights and to the implementation of the Covenant. The Committee, as well as some commentators, continually denounced the lack of involvement of some international actors such as the UN Commission on Human Rights and the UN Sub-Commission on the Promotion and Protection of Human Rights in the implementation of the Covenant. Similarly, criticism was expressed with regard to the general indifference of international NGOs, and even the academia to the protection of these rights.[2] Fortunately, a positive shift has occurred and, as we will see, many international bodies have increasingly begun to focus on economic, social and cultural rights.

The developments achieved in the field of economic, social and cultural rights have contributed to the consolidation of these rights as an important component of the international human rights protection regime and have been instrumental in putting into practice the principle of the indivisibility of all human rights. Furthermore, the increased interest in economic, social and cultural rights has been accompanied by a series of positive developments in the protection of these rights. As we will see, many

---

1 For a comprehensive analysis of the developments that have occurred in human rights law see, for example, Cassese A.: 'Human rights in a changing world.' Polity, Cambridge, 1990; Buergenthal, T: 'The evolution of international human rights'. In: Héctor Gros Espiell Amicorum Liber, vol. 1, Bruylant, Bruxelles, (1997), pp. 123-147; Higgins, R.: 'International law in a changing international system', *Cambridge Law Journal*, vol. 58 (1), (1999), pp. 78-95; and Cançado Trindade, A.A: 'The current state of international implementation of human rights.' In: *Hague Yearbook of International Law*, vol. 3, (1990), pp. 3-29.

2 See, among others, Steiner & Alston, 1996, p. 316; Chapman, 1996, p. 29; Gomez, 1995; p. 160 and Yokota, 1999, p. 205.

of these new developments or elements have been incorporated by the Committee when it interprets the Covenant.

Before embarking on the analysis of these new developments, two caveats are in order: first, the analysis does not intend to exhaustively cover all of the developments in the field of economic, social and cultural rights, but merely intends to provide a general picture.[3] Second, each international actor examined deals with economic, social and cultural rights in a different way.[4] However, it is important to stress that what these actors have in common is that, according to the Committee, through their different approaches to economic, social and cultural rights they develop elements 'implicit' in the text of the Covenant that must be taken into account in its interpretation.

2 Developments in the field of economic, social and cultural rights

2.1 Increased number of international instruments aimed at the protection of economic, social and cultural rights

Since the adoption of the Covenant in 1966, many other international human rights instruments have been adopted which, to a greater or lesser extent, include the promotion and protection of economic, social and cultural rights.[5] Subsequent to the adoption of the Covenant, instruments which establish legally binding obligations to protect some economic, social and cultural rights have been adopted at the universal level. Of particular note are the Convention on the Elimination of All Forms of Discrimination against Women [CEDAW][6] and the Convention on the Rights of the Child [CRC].[7]

3 The analysis will not cover the developments in the protection of these rights reached under institutional mechanisms of the World Bank. Although we do not deny that some progress has been achieved, this requires a thorough analysis and is beyond the scope of the present study.

4 As we will see, some actors develop standards, others advocate implementation, while still others supervise treaties or analyse economic, social and cultural rights from an academic perspective.

5 As the universal level, after the adoption of the Covenant various relevant legal instruments providing for the protection of some economic, social and cultural rights were adopted. We recall here those instruments adopted under the auspices of some UN specialised agencies such as ILO and UNESCO. Although comprehensive discussion of these instruments is beyond the scope of this study, it is important to mention that some of these instruments provide for individual complaint procedures in the case of a violation of determined economic, social and cultural rights. For further analysis, see, for example, Marks, S.P.: 'The complaint procedure of the United Nations Educational, Scientific and Cultural Organisation, UNESCO' and Swepton, L.: 'Human rights complaint procedures of the International Labour Organisation, ILO.' In: *Guide to international human rights practice.* Hannum, Hurst (ed.), University of Pennsylvania, Philadelphia, (1992). It is also worth mentioning humanitarian law instruments such as the 1977 Additional Protocols to the Geneva Conventions which contain a broad variety of obligations to protect economic, social and cultural rights.

6 Adopted by GA Res. 34/180, December 18, 1979. It entered into force on September 3, 1981. See for example, Arts. 1, 10, 11. It is important to note that an optional protocol establishing an inquiry procedure and an individual complaint procedure have been adopted and opened for signature (General Assembly Res. A/RES/54/4 of 6 October 1999). As the Convention contains economic, social and

Both instruments are aimed primarily at protecting civil and political rights but also contain economic, social and cultural rights and both have recently been enhanced by the adoption of protocols.

With regard to the CEDAW, an important advance was the recent adoption of an Optional Protocol which provides for a system of individual complaints.[8] The adoption of this procedure, which recently entered into force,[9] is of great relevance because it allows for the presentation of communications alleging violations of the economic, social and cultural rights contained in the Convention. New additional protocols have also been adopted with regard to the Convention on the Rights of the Child. One of these covers the involvement of children in armed conflicts,[10] and the other the sale of children, child prostitution and child pornography.[11] These protocols will have an important impact on the enjoyment of the economic, social and cultural rights of children, particularly on the right to education, health and the prohibition of child labour.

Another important instrument for the protection of economic, social and cultural rights was adopted in 1990: the International Convention on the Protection of the Rights of All Migrant Workers and Members of Their Families. Unfortunately, although it would entail a major advance in the protection of economic, social and cultural rights, this instrument has not yet reached the number of ratifications necessary for its entry into force.[12]

Important binding and non-binding instruments aimed at the protection of some economic, social and cultural rights have also been adopted within the framework of UN specialised agencies. By way of example, we may recall here the ILO Conventions, such as the Convention concerning the Prohibition and Immediate Action for the

---

cultural rights, the entry into force of this protocol would significantly enhance the protection of economic, social and cultural rights.

7 Adopted by GA Res. 44/25, November 20, 1989 and which entered into force on 2 September 1990. See, for example, Arts. 24-31.

8 General Assembly Res. A/RES/54/4 of 6 October 1999. It is important to note that the optional protocol also establishes an inquiry procedure.

9 This optional protocol entered into force on 22 December 2000.

10 Adopted and opened for signature, ratification and accession by General Assembly Res. A/RES/54/263 of 25 May 2000. Not yet in force (see article 10).

11 Adopted and opened for signature, ratification and accession by General Assembly Res. A/RES/54/263 of 25 May 2000. The Protocol entered into force on 18 January 2002. (See article 14).

12 Adopted by GA Res. 45/158 of December 1990. As of 1 July 2002, the International Convention on the Protection of the Rights of All Migrant Workers and Members of Their Families had been ratified or acceded to by 19 States, namely, Azerbaijan, Belize, Bolivia, Bosnia and Herzegovina, Cape Verde, Colombia, Ecuador, Egypt, Ghana, Guinea, Mexico, Morocco, the Philippines, Senegal, the Seychelles, Sri Lanka, Tajikistan, Uganda and Uruguay. The Convention will enter into force when 20 States have ratified or acceded to it [UN doc. A/56/179]. It is important to note that this Convention establishes a petitions procedure for the protection of some economic, social and cultural rights.

Elimination of the Worst Forms of Child Labour,[13] the ILO Convention Concerning Indigenous and Tribal Peoples in Independent Countries,[14] as well as the UNESCO Convention against Discrimination in Education[15] and the Convention on Technical and Vocational Education[16] There are also relevant non-binding instruments, such as the Declaration of Alma-Ata on Primary Health Care.[17]

In the more than three decades that have passed since the adoption of the Covenant, there have also been important steps taken towards the protection of economic, social and cultural rights at the regional level. At the European level, the protocols to the European Social Charter and the Revised Social Charter were adopted.[18] Among the protocols, it is particularly worth noting here the Third Additional Protocol to the European Social Charter which provides for a system of collective complaints alleging violations of the social rights contained therein.[19] This procedure has generated important jurisprudence which makes apparent the justiciability of many economic, social and cultural rights. Moreover, the European Convention on Human Rights [ECHR],[20] although principally dedicated to the protection of civil and political rights, has also served to provide a limited degree of protection of some economic, social and cultural rights.[21]

---

13 ILO Convention No. 182 [concerning the prohibition and immediate action for the elimination of the worst forms of child labour], adopted on 17 June 1999, and which entered into force on 19 November 2000.

14 ILO Convention No. 169 [concerning indigenous and tribal peoples in independent countries], adopted on 27 June 1989, entered into force on 5 September 1991.

15 Adopted by the General Conference at its eleventh session, Paris, December 14, 1960.

16 Convention adopted in Paris, November 10, 1989.

17 Declaration of Alma-Ata adopted by the International Conference on Primary Health Care jointly sponsored by WHO and UNICEF in Alma-Ata, USSR, 6-12 September, 1978.

18 Adopted on April 2, 1996, and which entered into force on September 1, 1999. ETS No. 163. The Revised Charter brings together in a single instrument all the rights guaranteed by the 1961 Charter and the 1988 Additional Protocol, along with amendments to these rights and new rights. It was drafted as an autonomous instrument, but with the same supervisory machinery as the Charter.

19 It was opened for signature on November 9, 1995. Entered into force on September 1, 1998. ETS No. 158.

20 Adopted in Rome on November 4, 1950. Entered into force on September 3, 1953. ETS No. 005.

21 It is important to note that the ECHR contains certain rights which are considered as 'social' under the UN Covenant, such as the right to form and join trade unions (Arts. 11 ECHR and 8 ICESCR) and the right to education (Art. 2 Protocol No. 1 ECHR and Art. 13 ICESCR), but in general the protection of economic, social and cultural rights has occurred through an integrated approach (see the text accompanying note 49). For further analysis, see, Berenstein, A.: 'Economic and social rights: their inclusion in the European Convention on Human Rights: problems of formulation and interpretation.' In: *HRLJ*, Vol. 2 Nos. 3-4, (1981), pp. 257-280; Flinterman, C.: 'The protection of economic, social and cultural rights and the European Convention on Human Rights.' In: *The dynamics of the protection of human rights in Europe: essays in honour of Henry G. Schermers.* Lawson, R. and Blois, M. de (eds.), Martinus Nijhoff, vol. III, (1994), pp. 165-174; Scheinin, M: 'Economic and social rights as legal rights.' In: *Economic, social and cultural rights: a textbook.* Eide, A.; Krause, C. & Rosas, A. (eds.), Martinus Nijhoff Publishers, Netherlands, (1995), pp. 41-62 and Krause C. and Scheinin, M.: 'The

Within the framework of the Council of Europe, the attention to economic social and cultural rights has also been evident in a number of other documents which to a greater or lesser extent protect economic, social and cultural rights, such as the European Convention on the Legal Status of Migrant Workers,[22] the Framework Convention for the Protection of National Minorities,[23] and the Convention for the Protection of Human Rights and the Dignity of the Human Being with Regard to the Application of Biology and Medicine.[24] Furthermore, it is important to mention that the recently adopted Charter of Fundamental Rights of the European Union contains an important range of economic, social and cultural rights.[25] [26]

In the Americas, economic, social and cultural rights are promoted and protected within the framework of the Organisation of American States [OAS][27] by the American Declaration of the Rights and Duties of Man [ADHR],[28] the American Convention on Human Rights [ACHR][29] and principally by the Additional Protocol to the American

---

right not to be discriminated against: the case of social security.' In: *The jurisprudence of human rights law: a comparative interpretative approach.* Theodore S.; Rosas, A. & Scheinin, M. (eds.), Institute for Human Rights, Åbo Akademi University, Åbo, Finland (2000), pp. 253-286.

22 Adopted in Strasbourg, France on November 24,1977. ETS No.093.

23 Adopted in Strasbourg, France on February 1, 1995. ETS No.157.

24 Adopted in Oviedo, Spain on April 4, 1997. ETS No. 164.

25 Charter of Fundamental Rights of the European Union. Official Journal of the European Communities, 2000/C 364/01, 18 December 2000. See, among others, Arts. 14, 15, 16, 17, 21, 22, 23, 24 and Chapter IV.

26 For a comprehensive review of the instruments for the protection of economic, social and cultural rights at the European level, see, for example, Eide, A.: 'Future protection of economic and social rights in Europe.' In: *Monitoring human rights in Europe. comparing international procedures and mechanisms.* Bloed, A.; Leicht, L.; Nowak, M. & Rosas, A. (eds.), Martinus Nijhoff Publishers, (1993), pp. 187-219.

27 The OAS Charter was signed in Bogota, Colombia in 1948 and amended by the Protocol of Buenos Aires in 1967, by the Protocol of Cartagena de Indias in 1985, by the Protocol of Washington in 1992 and by the Protocol of Managua in 1993. Various provisions of the OAS Charter refer to human rights but, like the UN Charter, they do so only in vague terms.

28 Adopted in Bogota on May 2, 1948. The protection of economic, social and cultural rights is envisaged in, for example, Arts. VII and XI to XVI. The Declaration was adopted as a non-binding resolution, but gradually its legal status began to change. Today it is deemed to be the normative instrument which embodies the authoritative interpretation of 'the fundamental rights of the individual' which Art. 3(k) of the OAS Charter proclaims as one of the principles to which the Organisation is committed. See I/A Court HR, Interpretation of the American 'Declaration of the Rights and Duties of Man within the Framework of Article 64 of the American Convention on Human Rights', Advisory Opinion No. 10. OC-10/89, July 14, 1989 para. 41.

29 Adopted in San José, Costa Rica, on November 22, 1969. OAS Treaty Series No. 36. See Art. 26 which refers to the progressive achievement of economic, social and cultural rights. In addition it is worth noting that the Convention contains rights that are established under the ICESCR, such as the rights of the family (Art. 17 ACHR) and the rights of the child (Art. 19 ACHR).

Convention on the Area of Economic, Social and Cultural Rights ('Protocol of San Salvador').[30]

Over the years, the supervisory organs of the Inter-American system have paid increasing attention to violations of economic, social and cultural rights included in the ADHR and the ACHR. For example, the Inter-American Commission[31] increasingly addresses the realisation of economic, social and cultural rights in its country reports,[32] and takes into consideration the economic, social and cultural rights contained in the Declaration when dealing with individual cases. [33] Hopefully, the Inter-American Court

30 Adopted in San Salvador on 17 November 1988, and which entered into force on November 16, 1999. OAS Treaty Series No. 69.

31 The Inter-American System is characterised by its wide variety of supervisory mechanism based on the ACHR as well as on the OAS Charter coupled with the ADHR. The Inter-American Commission on Human Rights has a unique 'dual role' within the System. On the one hand, as an OAS Charter organ, the Commission performs functions in relation to all Member States of the OAS, promoting the observance and protection of human rights on the basis of the Declaration. As a Convention organ its functions are only applicable to States Parties to the Convention. For further information about the protection of economic, social and cultural rights within the Inter-American System see, for example: Craven, M.: 'The protection of economic, social and cultural rights in the Inter-American system of human rights.' In: *The Inter-American system of human rights.* Harris, D. and Livingstone, S. (eds.), Clarendon Press, Oxford, (1988).

32 See, for example, Fifth Report on the situation of human rights in Guatemala OEA/Ser.L/V/II.111, doc. 21, 6 April 2001 chapter III; Third Report on the situation of human rights in Paraguay, OEA/Ser.L/V/II.110, doc. 52, 9 March 200, section two; Third Report on the human rights situation in Colombia OEA/Ser.L/V/II.102, doc. 9 rev. 1, 26 February 1999 chapter III and Report on the situation of human rights in Mexico, OEA/Ser.L/V/II.100, doc. 7 rev. 1, September 24, 1998, Chapter VII.

33 By interpreting the Declaration to be incorporated into the general human rights provision of the Charter [see note 28] the Inter-American Commission – an organ established by the OAS Charter to promote and protect human rights – is empowered to hear individual petitions on the basis of the Declaration. With regard to the protection of economic, social and cultural rights contained in the Declaration see, for example, the outstanding resolution in the Yanomani case [Res. 12/85 case 7615 (Brazil), 5 March 1985 in: Inter-American Yearbook on Human Rights 1985, pp. 264-281]. The background of this case is an individual petition against the Government of Brazil alleging violations of the human rights of the Yanomani Indians. The reported violations had their origins in the constructi-on of the Trans-Amazonian highway that crossed the territory where the Indians live, in the failure to establish the Yanomami Park for the protection of the cultural heritage of this Indian group, in the authorisation to exploit the resources of the subsoil of the Indian territories, in permitting the massive penetration into the Indian territory by outsiders carrying various contagious diseases that infected many victims within the Indian community and not providing the essential medical care to those persons affected, and finally in proceeding to displace the Indians from their ancestral lands, with all the negative consequences for their culture, traditions, and customs that this entailed. It is also worth mentioning several more recent admissibility decisions such as Report No. 29/01, case 12.249 Jorge Odir Miranda Cortez *et al.* v. El Salvador, March 7, 2000; Report No. 78/00 case 12.053 Maya Indigenous Communities and their members v. Belize, October 5, 2000; Report No. 03/01, case 11.670 Amilcar Menéndez, Juan Manuel Caride, *et al.* (social security system) v. Argentina, January 19, 2001. In: Annual Report of the Inter-American Commission on Human Rights 2000, OEA/Ser.L/V/II.111, doc. 20 rev., 16 April 2001.

will begin to take into account the protection of economic, social and cultural rights when dealing with the rights under the Convention.[34]

The major development at the Inter-American level has been the adoption and entry into force of the 'Protocol of San Salvador'. The Protocol establishes a system of individual complaints for the protection of trade union rights and the right to education.[35] Unfortunately, although the Protocol has entered into force, at the time of writing there had not yet been a decision of the Inter-American Court on a complaint submitted under the Protocol. Nonetheless, the entry into force of the Protocol has encouraged NGOs to start focusing on these rights at the regional level.[36]

Within this regional framework, other important instruments which provide for the protection of some economic, social and cultural rights are, for example, the Inter-American Convention on International Traffic in Minors,[37] the Inter-American Convention on the Elimination of All Forms of Discrimination against Persons with Disabilities[38] and the Inter-American Convention on the Prevention, Punishment and Eradication of Violence against Women ('Convention of *Belém do Pará*').[39]

At the African level, the African Charter on Human and People's Rights [AfCHR] adopted in 1981[40] contains a full range of economic, social and cultural rights. According to the Charter, the African Commission is empowered to receive individual and non-governmental complaints alleging violations of any right contained therein. Unfortunately, there have been relatively few cases involving economic, social and cultural rights.[41] Furthermore, under the auspices of the Organisation of African Unity,

---

34 The Inter-American Court demonstrated a degree of openness to this approach in the landmark case of Baena Ricardo *et al.* v. Panama [Judgment of February 2, 2001, Series C No. 72] and also in Comunidad Mayagna (Sumo) Awas Tingni v. Nicaragua [Judgement of August 31, 2001, Series C No. 79]. It is to be expected that the Court will maintain this approach.

35 The rights protected through the individual petitions system are the right to form and join trade unions (Art. 8(a)) and the right to education (Art. 13).

36 See, for example, Center for Justice and International Law (CEJIL) Gazette No. 12, 2000 and CEJIL Annual Report 2000. Available at: http://www.cejil.org/trabajo.htm (last visited July 2002).

37 Adopted at Mexico D.F., Mexico, on March 18 1994, at the fifth Inter-American Specialised Conference on Private International Law.

38 Adopted at Guatemala City, on June 7 1999, at the twenty-ninth regular session of the General Assembly.

39 Adopted at Belém do Pará, Brazil on June 9, 1994 at the twenty-fourth regular session of the General Assembly.

40 Adopted at Nairobi on June 26, 1981 and which entered into force on October 21, 1986. OAU doc. CAB/LEG/67/3 rev. 5, 21 I.L.M. 58 (1982).

41 Among the limited number of cases in which the Commission has considered the violation of civil and political rights together with economic, social and cultural rights, it is worth mentioning the decision in a case against Zaire [Communication Nos. 25/89; 47/90; 56/91 and 100/93]. In this case the Commission held that the general situation in Zaire constituted serious and massive violations of the right to life, inhuman or degrading treatment, the right to liberty and security, rights to have one's cause heard, freedom of conscience, the right to enjoy the best attainable physical and mental health, and the right to education, as guaranteed in the Charter. Remarkably, in this case the Commission held that 'the

other instruments have been adopted for the protection of economic, social and cultural rights, such as the African Charter on the Rights and Welfare of the Child.[42] [43]

Under the auspices of other organisations, we find that in 1994 the League of Arab States adopted the Arab Charter on Human Rights,[44] which includes a wide variety of economic, social and cultural rights.[45] Within the framework of the Islamic Conference, 'The Cairo Declaration on Human Rights in Islam'[46] was adopted and also contains some economic, social and cultural rights.[47] Similarly, the enjoyment of economic, social and cultural rights has also been proclaimed within the framework of the Organisation on Security and Co-operation in Europe [OSCE].[48]

All of these instruments adopted at the universal and regional levels have enhanced the attention to economic, social and cultural rights and contributed to putting into practice the principle of indivisibility and the equal status of all human rights.

2.2 The development of economic, social and cultural rights through the work of the UN Treaty bodies

With the exception of the ICESCR, the six major UN treaties for the protection of human rights (CERD, ICESCR, ICCPR, CEDAW, CAT and CRC), are principally focused on the protection of civil and political rights. However, it is important to bear in mind that due to the indivisibility of all human rights, the so-called 'civil and political rights instruments' also provide for a greater or lesser degree of protection of eco-

---

failure of the Government to provide basic services such as drinking water and electricity and the shortage of medicine', constituted a violation of the right to health (Art. 16 AfCHR). In: *IHRR* vol. 4 No. 1 (1997), pp. 89 *et seq.*

42 42 Adopted at Addis Ababa on July 11, 1990. Entered into force November 29, 1999. OAU doc. CAB/LEG/24.9/49 (1990).

43 For further information with regard to the protection of economic, social and cultural rights in the African context, see Oloka-Onyango J.: 'Beyond the rhetoric: reinvigorating the struggle for economic and social rights in Africa.' In: *California Western International Law Journal*, vol. 26, No. 1, (1995), pp. 1-74 and Oloka-Onyango J.: 'Some reflections on the framework of economic social and cultural rights in Africa.' In: *ICJ Review,* No. 55, (1995*), pp. 167-194. See also, Aselm Odinkalu, Chidi: 'Analysis of paralysis or paralysis by analysis? Implementing social, and cultural rights under the African Charter on Human and Peoples' rights.' In: *HRQ,* vol. 23, (2000), pp. 327-369.

44 Adopted on September 15, 1994. The text is reprinted in 18 *HRLJ,* 151 (1997).

45 See, for example, articles 29 to 39 of the Charter.

46 Adopted on August 5, 1990 at the Conference of Foreign Ministers (Session of Peace, Interdependence and Development), held in Cairo, Egypt, (31 July to 5 August 1990).

47 See, for example, articles 9, 10, 13, 16 and 17. The text of the Declaration can be found at: http://www1.umn.edu/humanrts/instree/cairodeclaration.html. (last visited July 2002)

48 In the light of the OSCE commitments in the Human Dimension. See, for example, the Helsinki Final Act [done at Helsinki on 1 August 1975] and the Document of the Stockholm Conference [Stockholm, 19 September 1986]. It is important to stress that as the OSCE is not an exclusively European organisation and we therefore mention it here rather than together with the developments achieved at the European level.

nomic, social and cultural rights or at least for some elements thereof. This has given rise to the so-called 'integrated approach,' defined as the protection afforded by civil and political rights instruments to economic and social rights.[49] This approach was clearly set out by the European Court of Human Rights in the landmark Airey case, where the Court held, 'Whilst the Convention sets forth what are essentially civil and political rights, many of them have implications of a social or economic nature. The Court therefore considers, like the Commission, that the mere fact that an interpretation of the Convention may extend into the sphere of social and economic rights should not be a decisive factor against such an interpretation; there is no water-tight division separating that sphere from the field covered by the Convention.'[50]

Over the years, the supervisory bodies of the UN human rights instruments have demonstrated an increasing openness to addressing the social and economic circumstances that affect individuals when dealing with civil and political rights. This integrated approach has become apparent in the jurisprudence of the treaty bodies, particularly that of the Human Rights Committee.[51]

The advantage of this approach is that it provides for the protection of economic, social and cultural rights in individual cases through quasi-judicial bodies such as the Human Rights Committee. For example, it has been possible to claim the protection of social security benefits through article 26 ICCPR (an autonomous right to non-discrimination).[52] By providing for the justiciability of some elements of economic, social and cultural rights through civil and political rights instruments, the supervisory bodies contribute to clarifying the normative content of economic, social and cultural rights.

The contribution of the treaty monitoring bodies to the protection of economic, social and cultural rights has been accomplished not only through the decisions in

49 One of the first works on an 'integrated approach' was presented by Scott in 1989 and refers to the idea of the 'permeability' of human rights norms. According to Scott, 'permeability' means, 'in broad outline, the openness of a treaty dealing with one category of human rights to having its norms used as vehicles for the direct or indirect protection of norms of another treaty dealing with a different category of human rights.' Scott, 1989, pp. 771.

50 Case of Airey v. Ireland, Application No. 6289/73, Judgement of 9 October 1979, para. 26.

51 An analysis of the application of this approach is beyond the scope of the present study. For a comprehensive study of the 'integrated approach' for the protection of economic, social and cultural rights, see, *inter alia,* Scott, loc. cit. (note 49), pp. 769-878; Scott, C.: 'Reaching beyond (without abandoning) the category of 'economic, social and cultural rights.' In: *HRQ*, vol. 21, (1999), pp. 633-660 and the work co-written with Macklem, Scott, C. & Macklem, P.: 'Constitutional ropes of sand or justiciable guarantee? Social rights in a new South African constitution.' In: *University of Pennsylvania Law Review*, vol. 141, No. 1, November (1992), pp. 1-77.See also Higgins, R.: 'The United Nations: still a force for peace.' In: *The Modern Law Review*, vol. 52, No. 1 January (1989), pp. 1-21; Scheinin, *op. cit.* (note 21), pp. 41-62 and Krause & Scheinin, *op. cit.* (note 21), pp. 253-286.

52 The protection of economic, social and cultural rights or elements thereof through the non-discriminatory provision of article 26 ICCPR is analysed in Chapter VIII section 6.

complaints procedures.[53] By means of their reporting systems and General Comments or Recommendations, the treaty monitoring bodies have developed elements relevant under the ICESCR which have contributed to the clarification of its normative content.[54]

Obviously, all developments achieved by treaty bodies on the same topic can be mutually reinforcing. In the same way that the work of the Human Rights Committee or the Committee on the Rights of the Child may contribute to providing a clearer understanding of some of the Covenant provisions by developing elements implicit in the Covenant's text, the work of the Committee may also assist these other bodies in clarifying the scope of the rights contained in the instruments which they supervise.

Among the emerging topics that have been addressed by different treaty bodies, we find, *inter alia*, gender equality, discipline in schools, traditional practices, domestic violence, the HIV/AIDS pandemic and discrimination against Roma populations. It is beyond the scope of the present study to analyse these cross-cutting developments but some examples are required to illustrate the point.

The Committee has increasingly interpreted the Covenant from a gender perspective. This has become apparent not only in the increasing number of Concluding Observations addressing the issue of gender, but it is also particularly evident in the General Comment issued in April 2000. It is remarkable that General Comment No. 14 on the right to the highest attainable standard of health specifically includes the sections 'gender perspective' and 'women and the right to health.' Obviously the Committee has not been alone in this approach; during recent years the gender perspective has been increasingly integrated into the work of most of the UN organs.[55] In fact, a month before the adoption of General Comment No. 14, the CERD Committee issued General Recommendation XXV on 'Gender Related Dimensions of Racial Discrimination,'[56] and the Human Rights Committee issued a General Comment on article 3 ICCPR dealing with gender equality.

Other issues that have received increasing attention from the Committee during recent years are the problem of discrimination against women reflected in harmful

53 In the case of the CERD Committee, the Human Rights Committee (Optional Protocol to the ICCPR) and the CEDAW Committee (Optional Protocol to CEDAW) which are the instruments which provide for such a procedure.

54 It appears that of the major UN treaty bodies, the only body which does not supervise treaty obligations closely linked with the protection afforded by the Covenant is the Committee against Torture.

55 For a global perspective on how the UN organs have increasingly incorporated the gender perspective into their work, see 'Integrating the human rights of women throughout the United Nations System.' Report of the Secretary-General E/CN.4/2001/71, of 9 January 2000.

56 CERD Committee General Recommendation XXV, of 20 March 2000.

traditional practices,[57] sexual harassment and sexual exploitation,[58] and violence against women.[59] These topics are also among the topics of shared interest with other treaty bodies.

Among these topics, special attention must be paid to the problem of violence against women. In 1993, the World Conference on Human Rights, held in Vienna, condemned violence against women and noted that the equal status of women and human rights should be integrated into the mainstream of the UN System.[60] This conference constituted the driving force for the comprehensive treatment of the problem of domestic violence.[61]

---

57 See, for example, Committee on Economic, Social and Cultural Rights Concluding Observations Guinea E/1997/22 and Concluding Observations Nigeria E/1999/22 and General Comment No. 14 para. 35.

58 See, for example, Concluding Observations Georgia E/2001/22 para. 89 and Concluding Observations Mongolia E/2001/22 paras. 270 and 281.

59 For example, in 1994 the topic of violence against women was considered by the Committee only once in the case of Mauritius [E/1995/22 para. 172.] During the Committee sessions in the following years the topic started to be addressed with regularity. For example, in 1995 [Annual Report E/1996/22] the issue of domestic violence was scrutinised, examining the reports of the Philippines, Sweden, Norway and Mauritius. In 1996 [Annual Report E/1997/22] with regard to Guatemala, Guinea, the Dominican Republic and Finland. In 1997 [Annual Report E/1998/22] with regard to the Russian Federation, the Dominican Republic, the United Kingdom of Great Britain and Northern Ireland, Uruguay and Saint Vincent and Grenadines. In 1998 [Annual Report E/1999/22] with regard to Sri Lanka, Poland, Israel, Cyprus, Switzerland and Canada. In 1999 [Annual Report E/2000/22] with regard to Iceland, Ireland, Tunisia, the Solomon Islands, Bulgaria, Argentina, Cameroon and Mexico. In 2000 [Annual Report E/2001/22], with regard to Italy, Egypt, Republic of Congo, Jordan, Mongolia, Australia and Finland. Furthermore, in 2000 the Committee adopted General Comment No. 14 which explicitly addressees the issue of domestic violence.

60 The Vienna Conference and Plan of Action stated: 'In particular, the World Conference on Human Rights stresses the importance of working towards the elimination of violence against women in public and private life, the elimination of all forms of sexual harassment, exploitation and trafficking in women, the elimination of gender bias in the administration of justice and the eradication of any conflicts which may arise between the rights of women and the harmful effects of certain traditional or customary practices, cultural prejudices and religious extremism. The World Conference on Human Rights calls upon the General Assembly to adopt the draft declaration on violence against women and urges States to combat violence against women in accordance with its provisions. Violations of the human rights of women in situations of armed conflict are violations of the fundamental principles of international human rights and humanitarian law. All violations of this kind, including in particular murder, systematic rape, sexual slavery, and forced pregnancy, require a particularly effective response.' A/CONF.157/23 section B para. 38.

61 This is not to say that UN organs were not aware of the problems before the Conference. In fact, for example, the UN Commission for Human Rights, in Res. 1993/46 of 3 March, condemned all forms of violence and violations of human rights directed specifically against women. But it was not until the Vienna Conference and the subsequent Conference in Beijing in 1995 that the topic attached the relevance that it deserves. In this regard it is worth mentioning the Declaration on the Elimination of Violence against Women [adopted by the UN General Assembly in December 1993], the appointment of a Special Rapporteur on violence against women [UN Commission Res. 1994/45 of 4 March 1994]

As a result of the great emphasis placed on the issue of domestic violence at the Vienna Conference, the UN treaty bodies began to consider the issue of domestic violence more frequently and consistently in their work. An examination of the Committee's work indicates that the problem of violence against women has increasingly been perceived as a priority since 1993.[62] In recent years the Committee has often made reference in its Concluding Observations to the problem of violence against women in general and particularly violence through traditional practices, such as female genital mutilation (FGM).[63] This increased level of concern is also recognisable in the work of other treaty bodies, where the problem is frequently addressed in the Concluding Observations, as well as in General Comments and Recommendations.[64]

Another cross-cutting theme that the treaty bodies have dealt with from their different perspectives, is the HIV/AIDS pandemic. Since the pandemic begun in the early 1980s, the international community has began to mobilise against the disease and the UN organs and treaty bodies have not remained indifferent.[65] The treaty bodies have progressively developed the application of their respective instruments to respond to the pandemic and its consequences. Today it is not rare to find that many of the Concluding Observations of these bodies contain assessments, recommendations and

---

and the Fourth World Conference on Women held in Beijing in September 1995, where the importance of the topic was again emphasised.

62 After 1993 the number of Concluding Observations referring to the issue of violence against women increased significantly. Nowadays, the problem of violence against women is addressed in the great majority of Concluding Observations. Just to give an example, in the annual report of the Committee in the year 2000 [Report on the twenty-second, twenty-third and twenty-fourth sessions E/2001/22] the Committee addressed the issue of domestic violence in all States Parties. It expressly referred to the problem in the Concluding Observations of: Georgia (para. 89); Italy (para. 112); Egypt (para. 162); Republic of Congo (para. 202); Jordan (para. 270); Mongolia (para. 281); Kyrgzstan (para. 345); Australia (para. 377); Portugal (para. 414); and Finland (para. 443). In the remaining States it referred to the issue indirectly. See Concluding Observations Sudan (by addressing the issue of the abduction of women and harmful traditional practices, *e.g.* paras. 297 and 311); Concluding Observations Belgium (by addressing the problem of discrimination against women and violence against children, *e.g.* paras. 475 and 487); Concluding Observations Yugoslavia (by addressing the issue of trafficking in women, *e.g.* para. 507); and Concluding Observations Morocco (by addressing the issue of traditional practices, discrimination and ill-treatment of women workers by their employers, *e.g.* paras. 520 and 532).

63 See, for example, Concluding Observations Iceland E/2000/22 para. 74; Concluding Observations Ireland E/2000/22 para. 128; Concluding Observations Tunisia E/2000/22 paras. 165 and 174; Concluding Observations Solomon Islands E/2000/22 para. 202; Concluding Observations Bulgaria E/2000/22 para. 243; Concluding Observations Argentina E/2000/22 para. 273; and Concluding Observations Cameroon E/2000/22 para. 330. For further analysis see Chapter VIII section 4.

64 See, for example, CEDAW General Recommendation No. 19 on violence against women, adopted on January 30, 1992 and General Recommendation No. 21 on equality in marriage and family relations adopted on February 4, 1994.

65 The pandemic is addressed consistently by some UN specialised agencies such as the Joint United Nations Programme on HIV/AIDS [UNAIDS]; the United Nations Population Fund [UNFPA] and the World Health Organisation [WHO].

suggestions as to how to deal with the pandemic from the human rights point of view.[66] The issues involved are addressed not only through the Concluding Observations, but also through General Comments or Recommendations.[67] While, obviously, the problem of the HIV/AIDS pandemic may be approached from different perspectives, it goes without saying that it is relevant to focus on this disease from the point of view of economic, social and cultural rights.

The protection of the Roma is also a topic that has increasingly been addressed by different treaty bodies. It is beyond doubt that the Committee pays particular attention to the protection of the Roma,[68] and that the same trend is recognisable in the work of other treaty bodies. For example, the CERD Committee has more frequently dealt with the topic, as is underlined by the adoption in August 2000 of a General Recommendation on 'Discrimination against Roma.'[69] The increased focus on the topic is also reflected by the fact that in the same month (August 2000), the Sub-Commission appointed a Special Rapporteur with the task of preparing a comprehensive study on the human rights problems and protection of the Roma.[70]

Although the above-mentioned examples are only some of the many topics in which the work of the different treaty bodies converges, they are sufficient to show that the treaty bodies have developed themes of interest which are of great relevance under the Covenant. This is principally due to the fact that many provisions of the major UN treaty monitoring bodies overlap. This overlap may be seen as an advantage. Each treaty monitoring body has the opportunity to develop elements of economic, social and cultural rights from their own standpoint and specific expertise. For example, the CEDAW Committee develops issues from a women's rights perspective, the Committee on the Rights of the Child focuses on developments related to the special needs of children and CERD Committee on the special needs of different minority groups. This convergence of different perspectives is certainly an advantage because all the developments achieved by treaty bodies on the same topic are mutually reinforcing. Therefore,

---

66 With regard to the Committee on Economic, Social and Cultural Rights, see for example, Concluding Observations Argentina E/2000/22 para. 286; Concluding Observations Cameroon E/2000/22 para. 359; Concluding Observations Egypt E/2001/22 para. 180; Concluding Observations Republic of Congo E/2001/22 paras. 206 and 213; and Concluding Observations Sudan E/2001/22 para. 314.

67 See, for example, CEDAW General Recommendation No. 15 on the avoidance of discrimination against women in national strategies for the prevention and control of acquired immunodeficiency syndrome (AIDS), adopted on February 2, 1990.

68 See, for example, Concluding Observations Bulgaria E/2000/22 para. 223; Concluding Observations Italy E/2001/22 paras. 116 and 129; Concluding Observations Portugal E/2001/22 paras. 413 and 420; and Concluding Observations Finland E/2001/22 para. 452.

69 CERD Committee General Recommendation XXVII, of 16 August 2000. It is important to note that this document specifically addresses the issue of 'measures in the field of education' (paras. 17-26) and 'measures to improve living conditions' (paras. 27-35).

70 Sub-Commission decision 2000/109 of 17 August 2000.

elements developed by other treaty monitoring bodies serve to enrich the Committee's interpretation of the Covenant.

2.3 The increased attention paid by UN Charter bodies, specialised agencies and UN Conferences

2.3.1 The UN Commission on Human Rights and the Sub-Commission on the Promotion and Protection of Human Rights

Although their recent records are still far from perfect, the interest of the Commission on Human Rights[71] and the Sub-Commission on the Promotion and Protection of Human Rights[72] in the field of economic, social and cultural rights has increased dramatically.[73] These two organs have focused greater attention on these rights and this is reflected by the increased number of resolutions adopted on topics related to economic, social and cultural rights in recent years.

This increased interest is also reflected in the recent establishment of special rapporteurs (thematic mandates) on economic, social and cultural rights issues by the Commission.[74] Of particular relevance was the appointment in April 2000 of two special rapporteurs on the right to housing and the right to food, respectively.[75] These two new appointments, together with the special rapporteur on the right to education established

---

71 Hereinafter referred to as 'UN Commission' or merely 'Commission.'

72 Hereafter referred to as 'UN Sub-Commission' or merely 'Sub-Commission.'

73 For example, in 1996 two distinguished commentators stated that 'neither the UN Commission nor its Sub-Commission has been very active in relation to the implementation of economic, social and cultural rights' [Steiner & Alston, *op. cit.* (note 2), p. 316]. For an evaluation of the participation of the UN organs with regard to economic, social and cultural rights, see for example, Economic, Social and Cultural Rights, Advisory Committee on Human Rights and Foreign Policy Advisory Report No. 18, the Netherlands, (1994), p. 13; Castermans-Holleman, M.: 'The protection of economic, social and cultural rights within the UN framework.' In: *NILR,* vol. XLII, (1995), pp. 353-373; and Coomans, F.: 'Economic, social and cultural.' In: Economic, social and cultural rights and collective rights. Coomans, F. & Galenkamp, M., Netherlands Institute of Human Rights, *SIM Special* No 16, Utrecht, (1995).

74 In 1996, during its fifteenth session, the Committee recommended that the Commission on Human Rights give consideration to the appointment of a special rapporteur on economic, social and cultural rights. At the time, the Committee noted 'while there are a large number of thematic and related mechanisms dealing with different aspects of civil and political rights, there is none dealing solely with the economic, social and cultural rights recognised in the Universal Declaration of Human Rights and the International Covenant on Economic, Social and Cultural Rights, despite the acknowledged interdependence, indivisibility and interrelatedness of the two sets of rights.' E/1997/22 Chapter VI para. 390. As of July 2002 the Commission had not yet designated a 'special rapporteur on economic social and cultural rights', although in 1998 it had designated the first special rapporteur directly concerned with one of the Covenant's rights.

75 Both rapporteurs were appointed with a three-year mandate by the Commission on Human Rights Res. 2000/9 (E/CN.4/RES/2000/9, 17 April 2000) and Res. 2000/10 (E/CN.4/RES/2000/10, 17 April 2000) respectively. The appointment of both special rapporteurs was endorsed by the ECOSOC during its 10th meeting held on 16 June 2000.

in 1998,[76] bring to three the total number of rapporteurs whose mandates directly relate to economic, social and cultural rights.[77] The work of these special rapporteurs undoubtedly contributes to the development of those rights under their mandates by bringing new elements and perspectives that must be taken into account when interpreting the Covenant.

Another step taken by the Commission was the decision to appoint an independent expert to examine the question of the draft optional protocol to the Covenant and to submit a report to the Commission in its 2002 session 'with a view to its consideration of possible follow-up and future actions.'[78] Although this decision was taken many years after the Committee initiated discussions on the adoption of an optional protocol,[79] it is still an important step towards greater effectiveness in the supervision of the Covenant.

At the level of the Sub-Commission, economic, social and cultural rights have generally been subject to greater attention than in the Commission. Of particular note are several landmark reports prepared by the Sub-Commission's special rapporteurs, for example, A. Eide on the right to food;[80] D. Türk on the enjoyment of economic, social and cultural rights;[81] H. Guisse on the impunity of violations of economic, social and cultural rights;[82] and R. Sachar on the right to housing.[83] In addition to these well-known reports, there have also been significant recent contributions,[84] as well as new

76 Commission on Human Rights Res. 1998/33. UN doc. E/CN.4/RES/1998/33, 17 April 1998.

77 Although there are other thematic mandates related to the enjoyment of economic, social and cultural rights, the three thematic mandates mentioned above are the only ones aimed at dealing directly with rights contained in the Covenant. The other thematic mandates which also have significance for these rights are, among others, the Commission on Human Rights' independent expert on human rights and extreme poverty, established in 1998 [E/CN.4/RES/1998/25, 17 April 1998], the independent expert on structural adjustment policies and foreign debt, since 2000, which was the result of the Commission's decision to merge the mandates on foreign debt and structural adjustment policies [E/CN.4/DEC/2000/109, 27 April 2000], and the Special Rapporteur of the Commission on the adverse effects of the illicit movement and dumping of toxic and dangerous products and wastes on the enjoyment of human rights, established in 1995 [E/CN.4/RES/1995/81, 8 March 1995].

78 Commission on Human Rights Res. 2001/30. UN doc. E/CN.4/RES/2001/30, 20 April 2001.

79 The Committee began to study an optional protocol to the Covenant in its fifth session held in 1991. UN doc. E/1991/23, para. 25. It has also devoted days of general discussion on the draft optional protocol in three sessions (the thirteenth, fourteenth and fifteenth session).

80 Eide, A: 'Report on the right to adequate food as a human rights', E/CN.4/Sub.2/1987/23, of July 7 1987.

81 Türk, D: 'The realisation of economic, social and cultural rights', E/CN.4/Sub.2/1992/16, of July 3, 1992. [Final report].

82 Guissé, H.: 'Second interim report on the question of the impunity of perpetrators of human rights violations', E/CN.4/Sub.2/1996/15 of July 3 1996.

83 Sachar, R.: 'The right to adequate housing', E/CN.4/Sub.2/1993/15, of June 22, 1993 and E/CN.4/Sub.2/1995/12 of July 12 1995 [final report].

84 For example, in 1998 the Sub-Commission requested that Mr. Eide review and update his study on the right to food submitted in 1987. Sub-Commission Decision 1998/106, 20 August 1998. Accordingly, he presented an up dated report on 'The right to adequate food and to be free from hunger' E/CN.4/

special rapporteurs and working groups that, to a greater or lesser extent, have mandates on economic, social and cultural rights.

There is a wide range of topics relevant to the work of the Committee that have been discussed and developed by the Commission and Sub-Commission. As is evident from the General Comments, the Committee takes into account the work of these bodies when interpreting the normative content of the Covenant.[85] For example, in General Comment No. 4 on the right to adequate housing, the Committee expressly noted that among other documents, the Committee had reviewed the relevant documentation of the Commission and Sub-Commission.[86] In General Comment No. 13, the Committee noted that it took into account the analytical framework of the Special Rapporteur on the right to education when developing its interpretation. The same is true of General Comment No. 12 in which the Committee incorporated the tripartite typology of obligations that had previously been developed by the Sub-Commission Special Rapporteur on the right to food.[87]

We should also note that there is an increasing correlation between the topics addressed by the Commission and Sub-Commission, and the Committee. Emerging topics such as intellectual property rights and the right to drinking-water and sanitation have been subject to intense attention not only from the Committee,[88] but also from the Commission and the Sub-Commission.[89]

Sub.2/1999/12 of 28 June 1999. Other more recent reports are, for example, 'The realisation of the right to education, including education in human rights' presented by M. Mehedi E/CN.4/Sub.2/1999/10 of July 8, 1999.

85 See for example, General Comment No. 13 para. 6 and footnote 3; General Comment No. 12 para. 3; and General Comment No. 4 paras. 2 and 4.

86 General Comment No. 4 para. 2.

87 General Comment No. 12 para. 15. For an in-depth analysis of the tripartite typology see Chapter V, Section 2.

88 At its twenty-first session the Committee decided that it was time to provide 'an authoritative interpretation [...] to the provisions in article 15, para. 1(c) of the Covenant' through a General Comment. [E/2000/22, Chapter VII, paras. 440-443]. The Sub-Commission in its Res. 2000/7 adopted in August 2000 encouraged the Committee to clarify the relationship between intellectual property rights and human rights including through the drafting of a General Comment. During its twenty-fourth session in November 2000, the Committee devoted a day of general discussion to the topic 'The right of everyone to benefit from the protection of moral and material interests resulting from any scientific literary or artistic production of which he is the author.' The Committee decided that as a follow up to the discussion to begin preparing the drafting of a general comment on article 15 (1)(c) [E/2001/22, Chapter VII, para. 641].
Another cross-cutting topic is the issue of safe drinking-water. This topic is often analysed by the Committee when examining State Parties' reports [see, for example, Concluding Observations Morocco E/2001/22 para. 537; Concluding Observations Solomon Islands E/2000/22 para. 205; and Concluding Observations Cameroon E/2000/22 para. 354]. Various Committee's General Comments deal with the issue of safe drinking-water. [See, for example, General Comment Nos. 14, 12, 8 and 6].

89 See, for example, Commission Res. 1998/8 and 1998/12 of 20 August 1998, 1999/8 of 25 August 1999, 1999/30 of 26 August 1999 and 1999/59 of 28 April 1999. Sub-Commission Res. 2000/7, 17 August 2000 and the appointment in 2000 of Mr. Guissé as a Special Rapporteur for the topic.

Finally, we would be amiss if we were not to mention that despite the fact that the Commission and particularly the Sub-Commission have increasingly contributed to clarifying the scope of economic, social and cultural rights and their concomitant obligations, there is still a certain disparity between the time and resources allocated by these organs to civil and political rights on the one hand, and economic, social and cultural rights on the other. It would advance the implementation of the Covenant if these two bodies further increased the attention paid to economic, social and cultural rights issues.

2.3.2 Specialised Agencies

The Covenant expressly provides for a mechanism for the contribution of specialised agencies in the supervision of the Covenant.[90] However, during the early years of the Covenant, commentators noted a lack of interest and participation on the part of some of the relevant specialised agencies in the implementation of the Covenant (with the exception of the ILO which has been reported to have a notable level of involvement in the application of the Covenant).[91] Fortunately, the early apathy towards the implementation of the Covenant among the specialised agencies has dissipated. Recently, specialised agencies have made significant contributions to the Committee's work. In fact, the Committee itself has acknowledged with appreciation the more active participation of some specialised agencies involved in the matters covered by the Covenant, and even of the multilateral financial institutions (Work Bank and IMF).[92]

The more serious involvement of the specialised agencies in the implementation of the Covenant is particularly evident from their active participation in the constructive dialogue with Government representatives, in the days of general discussion and in the

Additionally we need to recall here that the decade (1981-1990) had been declared 'The International Drinking Water Supply and Sanitation Decade.'

90 See articles 18 to 22 ICESCR.

91 See, for example, Craven, M.: *The International Covenant on Economic, Social and Cultural Rights: a perspective on its development*, Clarendon Press, Oxford, Paperback edition, with corrections, (1998) p. 79. The Committee noted at its fourth session that although the interest of the specialised agencies in the Committee's work 'can be demonstrated in a variety of ways, the Committee observes that the attendance by representatives of the appropriate United Nations bodies at its four sessions has, with the exceptions of the ILO, UNESCO and WHO, been very low. Similarly, pertinent materials and written information had been received from only a very limited number of agencies. The Committee considers that a deeper understanding of the relevance of economic, social and cultural rights in the context of international development co-operation activities would be considerably facilitated through greater interaction between the Committee and the appropriate agencies' [General Comment No. 2 para. 4]. For a comprehensive review of the contribution of the ILO see, for example, Leary, V.: 'Lessons from the experience of the International Labour Organisation.' In: *The United Nations and human rights: a critical appraisal.* Clarendon Press, Oxford, (1992), pp. 580-619.

92 See E/2001/22 paras. 648-649. It is relevant to note that in General Comment No. 2 the Committee considered the World Bank and the IMF as specialised agencies. See General Comment No. 2 para. 2.

drafting process of General Comments.[93] However, the contribution of the specialised agencies is not limited to their participation in the implementation of the Covenant itself. Rather, under their own mandates, many of the specialised agencies develop elements closely related to the Covenant which the Committee then takes into account when interpreting the Covenant.

Moreover, it is worth mentioning that the work of some specialised agencies such as the ILO, WHO and UNICEF converges with the work of the human rights treaty monitoring bodies in some topics which are of particular concern to the Committee, such as, the problem of domestic violence, FGM, the HIV/AIDS, the protection of Roma and child labour. The increased concern expressed by some specialised agencies on these topics is visible in some of their reports.[94]

2.3.3 The UN Conferences

The increased attention paid to economic, social and cultural rights has also been reflected in the significant number of UN Conferences held on topics explicitly or implicitly addressed in the Covenant. They include, for example, the World Conference against Racism, Racial Discrimination, Xenophobia and Related Intolerance;[95] the World Conference on Education for All;[96] the Second UN Conference on Human Settlements Habitat II;[97] the World Summit for Social Development;[98] the UN Conference on Human Rights;[99] the UN Conference on Environment and Development;[100] the

93 See the Committee's rule of procedure No. 68. In: Rules of Procedure of the Committee, E/C.12/1990/4/Rev.1.

94 See, for example, reports from WHO, UNICEF, ILO and UNHCR, such as, 'Action for Children affected by AIDS: programme profiles and lessons learnt', WHO/UNICEF, Sales No. 94.XX.USA.8, USA, 1994; Finney R.: 'Breaking the Earthenware Jar: Lessons from South Asia to End Violence against Women and Girls', UNICEF Regional Office for South Asia, Sales No. E.OO.XX.4, 2000; UNHCR's 'Women Victims of Violence Project in Kenya: an Evaluation', UN doc. EC/1995/SC.2/CRP.22; 'Note on certain aspects of sexual violence against refugee women', UN doc. A/AC.96/822; 'Note on International Protection' A/AC.96/951 paras. 63 *et seq.* (HIV/AIDS) and 70 *et seq.* (women and domestic violence); 'Note on International Protection' A/AC.96/914, section IV, paras. 27 *et seq.*; and ILO Report of the Director-General: 'Activities of the ILO, 1996-1997', Report I part 3.

95 Durban, South Africa, 31 August-7 September 2001. The resulting document is the 'Declaration and Programme of Action' adopted on 8, September 2001 A/CONF.189/5.

96 Jomtien, Thailand, 5-9 March 1990. The resulting document is the 'Final report of the World Conference on Education for All Meeting Basic Learning Needs.'

97 Istanbul, Turkey, 3-14 June 1996. Report of the United Nations Conference on Settlements (Habitat II) A/CONF.165/14.

98 Copenhagen, Denmark, 6-12 March 1995. The report of the World Summit for Social Development, A/CONF.166/9.

99 Vienna, Austria, 14-25 June 1993. The resulting document is the Vienna Declaration and Programme of Action. A/CONF.157/23.

100 Rio de Janeiro, Brazil, 3-14 June 1992. The resulting documents are: Agenda 21, the Rio Declaration on Environment and Development, the Statement of Forest Principles, the United Nations Framework Convention on Climate Change and the United Nations Convention on Biological Diversity. A/CONF.151/26/Rev.1.

Fourth World Conference in Women;[101] and the World Summit for Children (WSC).[102] All of these conferences brought together different actors who agreed on shared values, goals and strategies on issues closely linked with the protection afforded by the Covenant. These Conferences have undoubtedly contributed to the development of a common understanding on many issues. The conferences have also been particularly important for raising awareness and public concern with regard to some socio-economic topics.[103] In fact, many conferences have acted as catalysts, encouraging different actors to address problems from their own perspectives.

It is important to stress that UN Conferences have adopted a multidisciplinary approach to their subjects. Participants coming from different fields and areas of expertise are brought together with policy makers, diplomats, academics, NGO representatives and civil society leaders. All of these actors contribute to the final outcome of each Conference and their different inputs are a positive contribution to the conceptual development of economic, social and cultural rights. Moreover, such conferences also open the door to debate, and always attract a great deal of attention from the media, improving general awareness of issues related to the Covenant as well as acknowledging the existence of problems that otherwise would not have received such attention.

Finally, it is important to sound a note of caution. The UN Conference (as well as some NGOs) sometimes deal with the Covenant's rights from a narrow perspective and tend not to use human rights language. For example, the final texts produced by some UN Conferences and the public campaigns of NGOs have sometimes avoided reference to the existence of 'binding obligations,' such as those imposed by the Covenant.[104] These kinds of situations have been criticised by Committee members and

---

101 Beijing, China, 4-15 September 1995. The resulting document is the Beijing Declaration and Platform for Action. A/CONF.177/20.

102 United Nations, New York, 29-30 September 1990. The resulting document is the World Declaration and Plan of Action on the Survival, Protection and Development of Children.

103 Some of these Conferences have also had follow-up review through special sessions of the General Assembly, such as, Implementation of the outcome of the UN Conference on Human Settlements (Habitat II, 6-8 June 2001); and Special Session on the International Conference on Population and Development (30 June-2 July 1999).

104 I would like to illustrate this point with an example: OXFAM International, a network of organisations working in the field of poverty eradication and development co-operation has adopted what they call a 'rights-based' approach, in which five rights are emphasised: '(1) the right to sustainable livelihood (2) the right to basic social services (3) the right to life and security (4) the right to be heard (social and political citizenship) and (5) the right to equity (gender and diversity).' [See SIM Special No. 27 on the Workshop and Conference Organised and hosted by NOVIB and SIM in The Hague, the Netherlands, 2-5 October 2000, p. 4]. From this author's perspective, this rather peculiar approach should be reconsidered as it would be advisable for OXFAM to adopt accepted international human rights terminology so that they would be in a better position to use international standards and mechanisms to implement their strategy.

experts.[105] It would be desirable for the implementation of the Covenant if future UN Conferences dealing with issues regulated under the Covenant did not neglect the fact that there are *legal obligations* which are binding for more than 140 States. The Covenant's normative language clearly establishes individuals' 'rights' and States' 'obligations' and the implementation of those rights and obligations would be enhanced if relevant international actors made efforts to use the normative language contained in the Covenant. The Committee itself has noted that the adoption of a 'human rights-based approach' by different international actors would greatly facilitate the implementation of the Covenant's rights.[106]

2.4 The contribution of scholarly writers

In the process of the consolidation of economic, social and cultural rights and in the clarification of the normative content of the Covenant, scholarly writing has played a significant role. Through their writings, experts promote these rights, advance new ideas, and on that basis present a clearer explanation of the nature and scope of the obligations.

In this regard, it is important to highlight the contributions of several key meetings of experts in economic, social and cultural rights in which agreements have been reached on relevant aspects of the Covenant. We may recall here, for example, the symposium held in the Netherlands in June 1986 where a group of distinguished experts in international law agreed on 'The Limburg Principles on the Implementation

105 See, for example, the Committee's statement on the World Summit for Social Development where it noted that the neglect of the Covenant in the final document of the Summit 'will have significant adverse consequences both from the viewpoint of the international human rights regime and of that of the evolving approach to social development. The exclusion or marginalization of the Covenant will signal the continuing separation of human rights and social development issues, in complete contradiction to the recognised need for an integrated approach. Similarly, neglecting the implementation and monitoring mechanism established under the Covenant will risk a futile proliferation of ineffectual approaches to implementation at the expense of working towards ensuring the effectiveness of those that already exist' [E/1995/22, Annex V, para. 7]. Years later the Final Report of the World Conference of Education for All Meeting Basic Learning Needs, celebrated in Jomtien, Thailand on 5-9 March 1990, did not adopt human rights wording. This fact was questioned by the Chairperson of the Committee and the Special Rapporteur on the right to education during the day of general discussion on the right to education. According to the then Chairperson, Mr. Alston, the Declaration 'could not be qualified as a human rights approach.' See, Day of General Discussion held during the nineteenth session on the 30th November 1998, E/1998/22, Chapter V, paras. 488-489. For an in-depth analysis of the lack of human rights wording in the work of international bodies, see Alston, P.: 'What's in a name: does it really matter if development policies refer to goals, ideals or human rights?' In: *SIM Special* No. 22, (1998), pp. 95-106 and Steiner, H.: 'Social rights and economic development: converging discourses*?' Buffalo Human Rights Law Review*, vol. 4, (1998), pp. 25- 42.

106 The Committee referred to this issue in General Comment No. 14, para. 64, but it is certainly relevant with regard to all Covenant rights.

of the International Covenant on Economic, Social and Cultural Rights.'[107] During the symposium, the experts explicitly stated that they believed that the principles that they had unanimously agreed upon reflected 'the present state of international law' with regard to the protection of economic, social and cultural rights.[108]

Another important expert contribution was the 1995 'Bangalore Declaration and Plan of Action' on the realisation of economic, social and cultural rights. This Declaration specifically examined the role of lawyers regarding economic, social and cultural rights and was agreed upon by more than one hundred jurists from all continents at a conference organised by the International Commission of Jurists in Bangalore, India.[109] In 1997 another important event was held in the Netherlands, where a group of more than thirty experts in the field of human rights, and in particular in economic, social and cultural rights, adopted 'The Maastricht Guidelines on Violations of Economic, Social and Cultural Rights.'[110]

At the Latin American level, it is important to recall the 'Quito Declaration on the Enforcement and Realisation of Economic, Social, and Cultural Rights in Latin America and the Caribbean' adopted in July 1998 at a conference organised in Quito, Ecuador that brought together an important number of experts and activists from Latin America.[111] This Declaration claims to be more comprehensive than its precursors, such as the Limburg Principles and the Maastricht Guidelines, because, according to the text itself, its aim is both legal and political.[112]

Finally, it should be stressed, that although there can be no doubt that the number of academic studies on economic, social and cultural rights has increased in recent years, there are still far fewer works in this area than there are dedicated to 'civil and political rights.' In fact, it is still easy to agree with a current member of the Committee, who opined in 1996 that economic, social and cultural rights, 'have yet to become equal subjects for serious research and discussion.'[113]

107 The Limburg Principles are to be found in 'The Limburg Principles on the Implementation of the International Covenant on Economic, Social and Cultural Rights.' In: *HRQ,* vol. 9 No. 2, (1987), pp. 122-146.

108 *Ibidem:* p. 121.

109 The Bangalore Declaration and Plan of Action is contained in the Special Issue of *ICJ Review* No. 55, (1995), pp. 219- 227.

110 The Maastricht Guidelines are contained in SIM Special No. 20.

111 The Quito Declaration and Programme of Action was adopted on July 24, 1998. Available at: 2 *Yale Hum. Rts. Dev. L.J.* 6 (1999). http://www.yale.edu/yhrdlj/index_enhanced.htm (last visited July 2002).

112 See, the 'Preface to the Quito Declaration on the Enforcement and Realisation of Economic, Social, and Cultural Rights in Latin America and the Caribbean.' Jochnick, C. and Mujica Petit, J. In: 2 *Yale Hum. Rts. Dev. L.J.* 5 (1999). See at: http://www.yale.edu/yhrdlj/index_enhanced.htm (last visited July 2002)

113 Hunt, 1996, p. 69.

2.5 The contribution of NGOs

As many commentators have noted, during the first years after the Covenant entered into force, there was a certain reluctance on the part of NGOs to focus on economic, social and cultural rights.[114] This fact was reflected in the poor participation of NGOs in the Committee sessions during the early years. Fortunately, their participation has steadily increased since that time.[115]

It is interesting to note that the increased NGO participation in the implementation of the Covenant is not only due to the increased interest among NGOs,[116] but also because the Committee itself has actively encouraged NGO participation. Specifically, in 1993 the Committee adopted a procedure designed to enhance the participation of NGOs.[117] The procedure for NGO participation has been further improved over the years and the Committee now provides one of the most developed opportunities for NGO participation in any treaty body supervisory proceeding. NGOs can participate at different stages of the Covenant's supervision process.[118] Within the framework of the Covenant's supervision, their contributions include oral and written information submitted to the Committee, including alternative reports and working papers prepared for the days of general discussion on topics relating to their interest.[119]

The increased interest of NGOs in the field of economic, social and cultural rights is not only reflected in their participation in the supervisory mechanisms of the Covenant. NGOs have also significantly enhanced their work with the general public and their public information campaigns in the field of economic, social and cultural rights have improved considerably. To illustrate this, there are now numerous bulletins and

114 See, among others, Alston, 1997, p. 372; Eide, 1989, p. 49; Gomez, *loc. cit.* (note 2), p. 161; Chapman, *loc. cit.* (note 2), p. 41; Steiner & Alston, *op. cit.* (note 2), p. 369 and Yokota, *op. cit.* (note 2), p. 205. Some members have also acknowledged the lack of attention by NGOs to the Committee during the Committee's sessions. See, for example, Mr. Wimer Zambrano E/C.12/1990/SR.4 para. 39 of 12 February 1990.

115 As an example, during the tenth session of the Committee in 1995, only two NGOs with consultative status were represented by observers at the session [Habitat International Coalition and International Service for Human Rights, E/1995/22 chapter I, para. 6]. In contrast, at the twentieth session, four years later, the number of NGOs represented had increased to twelve (the number of NGOs represented by observers rose to nineteen considering, in addition, NGOs with no consultative status) [E/C.12/1999/11, Chapter II, paras. 6-7].

116 As an example, we may recall the new statute of Amnesty International [AI] as amended by the 25th International Council, meeting in Dakar, Senegal, 17 to 25 August 2001. The new statute expands its mission and has come closer to the protection of economic, social and cultural rights through its work against discrimination. The new statute is available at: http://www.web.amnesty.org/web/aboutai.nsf (last visited July 2002).

117 See E/C.12/1993/WP.14, of 12 May 1993.

118 For a review of the procedure see, 'Non-governmental organisation participation in the activities of the Committee on Economic, Social and Cultural Rights.' E/2001/22, Annex V, pp. 149 *et seq.*

119 See, for example, the written statement submitted by the Netherlands section of the International Committee of Jurists in the Committee's eighteenth session. UN doc. E/C.12/1988/NGO/1.

newsletters published by NGOs, such as, 'Basic Rights,'[120] 'COHRE Newsletter'[121] and 'Hungry for what is right,'[122] which principally focus on economic, social and cultural rights.

The work of NGOs has significantly contributed to clarifying the normative content of the Covenant[123] and to promoting awareness of its content through their public information campaigns. In this way, they have assisted enormously in the consolidation of the Covenant as a key international human rights instrument.

In addition, we should not forget that, at least at the regional level, the contributions of some NGOs have been extremely important for enhancing the justiciability of economic, social and cultural rights, particularly through the submissions of claims alleging the violation of these rights under procedures which allow for collective or individual complaints, as is the case of the Additional Protocol to the European Social Charter and the American Convention of Human Rights, respectively.[124]

3 The role of the Committee in light of new developments

As the supervisory body of the Covenant the Committee has gradually incorporated the developments achieved in the field of economic, social and cultural rights in its interpretation of the Covenant. By doing so, the Committee maintains the validity and currency of the Covenant in the light of changing circumstances and simultaneously clarifies the Covenant's normative content.[125]

The Committee has expressly noted that it takes into account new elements developed by other bodies which are 'implicit' in the text of the Covenant and uses them to provide 'a contemporary interpretation' of it. As the Committee notes in General Comment No. 13,

---

120 Bulletin published by the Center for Economic and Social Rights.

121 Bulletin published by the Centre on Housing Rights and Evictions [COHRE].

122 Magazine published by FoodFirst Information & Action Network [FIAN].

123 To illustrate this point with one example, we may recall here the 'Thesaurus of Economic, Social and Cultural Rights.' The Thesaurus was the result of a project launched in 1996, by the Science and Human Rights Program of the American Association for the Advancement of Science (AAAS) and Human Rights Information and Documentation Systems, International (HURIDOCS) and it is certainly an important tool to promote a clear understanding of the Covenant within the general public.

124 In this regard, it is important to mention the contribution of the International Commission of Jurists, which has been very active not only in studies and publications on the topic of economic, social and cultural rights, but also in submitting complaints under the collective complaints procedure of the European Social Charter. In fact, the ICJ submitted the first complaint [complaint No. 1/1998] against Portugal for a violation of the prohibition of child labour. At the Inter-American level, the Center for Justice and International Law [CEJIL] has presented several cases alleging violation of economic, social and cultural rights to the Inter-American Commission on Human Rights. (See note 36).

125 See the statement of the Committee in, for example, General Comment No. 13 para. 5; General Comment No. 14 para. 27; General Comment No. 12 para. 3; General Comment No. 4 para. 2; and General Comment No. 4 para. 7.

> 'The Committee notes that since the General Assembly adopted the Covenant in 1966, other international instruments have further elaborated the objectives to which education should be directed. Accordingly, the Committee takes the view that States parties are required to ensure that education conforms to the aims and objectives identified in article 13(1), as interpreted in the light of the World Declaration on Education for All [...], the Convention on the Rights of the Child [...], the Vienna Declaration and Programme of Action [...], and the Plan of Action for the United Nations Decade for Human Rights Education [...]. While all these texts closely correspond to article 13(1) of the Covenant, they also *include elements which are not expressly provided* for in article 13(1), such as specific references to gender equality and respect for the environment. These new elements are *implicit in*, and reflect a *contemporary interpretation* of article 13(1).'[126]

It is beyond the scope of the present study to refer to each of the elements which are 'implicit' in the Covenant's text and that the Committee takes into account in order to interpret the Covenant. However, I will illustrate this point with some examples.

While article 12 ICESC protects the 'right to the highest attainable standard of health,' this provision does not specify any special needs of the beneficiaries. Obviously, indigenous peoples are among the beneficiaries but the effective protection of indigenous peoples' right to health requires that their specific needs be taken into account. As the Committee notes, 'emerging international law and practice' have developed some of these specific elements that must be taken into account to effectively protect the right to health of indigenous peoples.[127] Among the emerging international norms that the Committee considers relevant are the Convention on Biological Diversity,[128] the United Nations Framework Convention on Climate Change[129] and the United Nations Convention to Combat Desertification in Countries Experiencing Serious Drought and/or Desertification,[130] as well as Agenda 21 of the World Conference on Environment and Development and the Vienna Declaration and Programme of Action. As suggested by the Committee, all of these instruments develop elements not expressly mentioned in article 12 ICESCR such as, *inter alia,* the cultural acceptability of the health services provided and the protection of medicinal plants, animals and minerals which are vital to indigenous communities. According to the Committee,

---

126 General Comment No. 13 para. 5 (footnote omitted and emphasis added.)

127 According to General Comment No. 14, 'In the light of emerging international law and practice and the recent measures taken by States in relation to indigenous peoples, the Committee deems it useful to identify elements that would help to define indigenous peoples' right to health in order to better enable States with indigenous peoples to implement the provisions contained in Article 12 of the Covenant' (para. 27).

128 The Convention was adopted in 1992 at the UN Conference on Environment and Development, the so-called 'the Earth Summit', held in Rio de Janeiro, Brazil. It entered into force on 29 December 1993. Additional information is available at: http://www.biodiv.org (last visited July 2002).

129 Adopted in New York on May 9, 1992. Entered into force on March 21, 1994.

130 Adopted in Paris on October 14, 1994. Entered into force on December 26, 1996.

these new elements must be taken into account in implementing the right to health of indigenous populations at the present state of development of human rights law.[131]

Another example of how the Committee incorporates developments in the field into the Covenant may be found in General Comment No. 5 on persons with disabilities and in General Comment No. 6 on the economic, social and cultural rights of older persons. Although the Covenant, in contrast to other instruments aimed at the protection of economic, social and cultural rights, does not expressly refer to these groups of beneficiaries, it is understood that they are protected under the Covenant. However, the effective protection of both persons with disabilities and older persons requires special measures and these are outlined by the Committee in these General Comments. In doing so, the Committee makes use of the standards developed by other bodies such as the General Assembly, the Commission and the Sub-Commission and the ILO. As one commentator has noted, these two General Comments 'are not so much concerned with the Committee's own experience, but make extensive reference to norms established in other fora.'[132]

According to the Committee, new elements which are implicit in the Covenant and which must thus be taken into account may be found in legally binding instruments such as the ILO Conventions and the Additional Protocols to the Geneva Conventions,[133] but also in non-binding instruments. In this regard the Committee has expressly stated that it also 'obtains guidance on the proper interpretation'[134] of the Covenant from non-binding instruments such as the 1993 Vienna Declaration and Programme of Action or the 1978 Alma-Ata Declaration on Primary Health Care.[135]

In addition, the Committee has expressly noted that it takes into account the practice of other treaty bodies. For example, it has noted in a General Comment,

> 'In formulating this paragraph, the *Committee has taken note of the practice evolving elsewhere* in the international human rights system, such as the interpretation given by the Committee on the Rights of the Child [...], as well as the Human Rights Committee's interpretation of article [..].'[136]

The Committee is certainly well aware of the contribution of scholarly writers and it is fair to say that it makes efforts to incorporate, to the maximum extent possible, an academic perspective when it interprets the Covenant. It is now general practice to

131 General Comment No. 14 para. 27 and footnote No. 19.
132 Craven, 1998, p. XII.
133 See, for example, General Comment No. 13 para. 31; General Comment No. 14, footnote 4; and General Comment No. 6 para. 27.
134 General Comment No. 13 para. 9.
135 See, for example, General Comment No. 13 paras. 5 and 9; General Comment No. 12 para. 43; General Comment No. 14 footnote 4; General Comment No. 14 para. 34; General Comment No. 5 para. 17; and General Comment No. 5 para. 34 and footnote 32.
136 General Comment No. 13, footnote No. 18. (Emphasis added).

invite experts and scholars to participate in the Committee's Day of General Discussions on the topic of their expertise, as well to request their contributions during the drafting process of the General Comments.[137]

In sum, following the Committee's reasoning, new international binding and non-binding instruments as well as the work of other treaty bodies may contain elements which, although not expressly provided for in the Covenant's text, are implicit in it. These new elements must be taken into account as required by a contemporary interpretation of the Covenant.[138]

4 Concluding Comments

Since the adoption of the Covenant, many developments have occurred in the field of economic, social and cultural rights. The pace of developments has intensified in recent years and has contributed to the consolidation of economic, social and cultural rights as an important component of the international human rights regime. This circumstance has enormously benefited the development of the normative content of the Covenant. The obligations imposed by the Covenant are now much more precise than a decade ago.

When the Committee draws on the work of different international actors such as treaty bodies, UN organs, specialised agencies, NGOs and scholarly writers, and incorporates these new developments into its interpretation of the Covenant, it extends the application of the Covenant into these new areas and at the same time it clarifies the normative content of the provisions of the Covenant. This becomes clear if we bear in mind that the Covenant covers a broad range of themes but does not provide much guidance with regard to the specific requirements of some of the beneficiaries (*e.g.* children, women, the female child, Roma communities), or the way in which States should tackle specific problems such as trafficking in human beings, domestic violence and third party violations of the rights. When the Committee takes into account the elements developed by other international actors to provide a 'contemporary interpretation' of the Covenant, it extends the protection afforded by the Covenant to some specific aspects that may have passed unnoticed to the Committee but not to other specialised bodies.

---

137 See, for example, the background papers submitted by experts for the Day of General Discussion on the right to education (Committee's nineteenth session), such as, 'State obligations, indicators, benchmarks and the right to education', paper submitted by P. Hunt E/C.12/1998/11; 'The right to education as a human right: an analysis of key aspects', background paper submitted by F. Coomans UN doc. E/C.12/1998/16; and 'Violations of the right to education', submitted by A. Chapman UN doc. E/C.12/1998/19. UN experts also contributed to the day of general discussion organised by the Committee. See, for example, Background paper submitted by Katarina Tomaševski, Special Rapporteur of the Commission on Human Rights on the right to education. UN doc. E/C.12/1998/18.

138 The principles of interpretation employed by the Committee are examined in Chapter III, section 2.

The Committee should not incorporate all the emerging trends in the field of economic, social and cultural rights, but certainly it should gradually draw on the work of other actors to address matters which are found explicitly and implicitly in the text of the Covenant. To do otherwise could well mean that the Covenant becomes obsolete.

CHAPTER III
THE COMMITTEE'S INTERPRETATION OF THE OBLIGATIONS IMPOSED BY THE COVENANT

1 INTRODUCTION

In subsequent chapters we will examine the normative content of the Covenant as interpreted by the Committee on Economic, Social and Cultural Rights. We will see that over the years the obligations imposed by the Covenant have broadened in scope. This has occurred because the Committee not only clarifies the normative content of the Covenant, but its interpretation also has the effect of extending the scope of protection afforded.

In the present Chapter, however, we shall embark upon some preliminary analysis in order to set the stage for our examination of the normative content of the Covenant. First, we will demonstrate that the Committee's dynamic interpretation of the Covenant is consistent with the rules of interpretation of international treaties and with the specific object and purpose of the Covenant. Secondly, we will evaluate the legitimacy of the Committee's interpretation of the Covenant. In other words, we will examine the factors that bring pressure upon States for voluntary compliance with the Committee's interpretation and inquire whether or not the Committee complies with those factors.

2 THE COMMITTEE'S INTERPRETATION OF THE COVENANT UNDER THE GENERAL RULES OF INTERPRETATION OF HUMAN RIGHTS TREATIES

2.1 Introduction

Human rights law is embedded in the broader discipline of international law, and therefore, in general, the rules for interpretation which are applicable under international law are also applicable to human rights treaties. In general, the principles of interpretation of international treaties are contained in the Vienna Convention of the Law of Treaties [VCLT] which are considered to be the customary international law principles of treaty interpretation.[1]

1 It is worth stressing here the case of Golder v. the United Kingdom, where the European Court of Human Rights held, in 1975 when the VCLT had not yet entered into force, that articles 31 to 33 of the VCLT 'enunciate in essence generally accepted principles of international law to which the Court has already referred on occasion.' Golder v. United Kingdom, Application No. 4451/70, Judgement of 21 February 1975, para. 29. See also note 17.

Therefore, the rules set out in the VCLT should be considered to be the relevant international law principles for the interpretation of human rights instruments. However, as has been stated, they are not the '*alpha* and *omega*' of the rules of interpretation.[2] The interpretation of human rights treaties requires that we take into account the specific characteristics of human rights treaties.[3]

This section contains a brief overview of, first, the rules of interpretation contained in the VCLT, second, the principles applicable to human rights treaties due to their specific object and purpose, and finally, the Committee's approach to interpretation.[4] The aim of the section is to show that when interpreting the Covenant, the Committee follows the general rules of treaty interpretation.

2.2 General overview of the rules of interpretation of international treaties

The rules for treaty interpretation are contained in articles 31 to 33 of the Vienna Convention on the Law of Treaties [VCLT]. It is not our intention to study these rules in detail, but rather to provide a brief overview emphasising those aspects relevant to our topic.[5]

---

2 Dijk, P. van & Hoof, G.J.H. van: Theory and practice of the European Convention on Human Rights, Kluwer Law International, third edition, The Hague/ London/Boston, (1998), p. 72.

3 In Bernhardt's words, 'the general rules of treaty interpretation are in principle also applicable to human-rights treaties, but the object and purpose of these treaties are different and, therefore, the traditional rules need some adjustment.' Bernhardt, 1988, pp. 70-71. See also Dijk, P. van and Hoof, G.J.H. van, *op. cit.* (note 2), pp. 72-82. As we will see in the analysis that follows, there is an important body of international jurisprudence that provides support for this view.

4 It is beyond the scope of the present study to address the debate concerning the question of whether or not the specific features of human rights law create a special regime, different from the rules of general international law, or if these features merely require the adaptation of the general rules to the special object and purpose of the human rights treaties. For a comprehensive analysis of the topic see Craven, M.: 'Legal differentiation and the concept of human rights treaty in international law'. In: *EJIL,* vol. 11, (2000), pp. 489-519. For a different view see, Vierdag, E.W.: 'Some remarks about features of human rights treaties'. In: *NYIL*, vol. XXV, (1994), pp. 119-142.

5 For a comprehensive study of the rules of interpretation of the VCLT and its application to human rights treaties, see, among others, Harris, D.J.: Cases and materials on international law. Sweet & Maxwell, fifth edition, London, (1998), pp. 810-822; Brownlie, I.: Principles of public international law, Oxford University Press, fifth edition, (1998), pp. 631-638; Bernhardt, R.: 'Interpretation in international law,' in: Encyclopaedia of public international law, (1984), pp. 1416-1426; Bernhardt, *op. cit.* (note 3), pp. 65-71; Dijk P. van & Hoof, G.J.H. van, *op. cit.* (note 2), Chapter II, pp. 71-95; Newman, F. & Weissbrodt, D.: International human rights: law, policy and process, Anderson Publishing, Cincinnati Ohio, Second edition, (1996), pp. 423 *et seq.*; Steiner, H. & Alston, P.: International human rights in context: law, politics, morals. Oxford University Press, second edition, Oxford, (2000), pp. 109-110; Mahoney, P.: 'Judicial activism and judicial self-restraint in the European Court of Human Rights: two sides of the same coin', in: *HRLJ,* vol. 11 No. 1-2, (1990), pp. 57-88; Golsong, H: ' Interpreting the European Convention on Human Rights beyond the confines of the Vienna Convention on the Law of Treaties? in The European system for the protection of human rights, Macdonald, Matscher, Petzold (eds.), Martinus Nijhoff Publishers, (1993), pp. 147-162;

The principal provision for treaty interpretation is article 31 VCLT.[6] The first rule established by this provision is that 'a treaty shall be interpreted in good faith' (article 31(1) VCLT). This rule stresses the importance of the principle of good faith contained in article 26 VCLT and applies it to the problem of treaty interpretation.[7] By virtue of this rule, States are bound by what they have agreed to observe as is reflected in the ordinary meaning of the terms of the treaty (literal interpretation).[8]

However, the literal interpretation is not sufficient in itself, and we are required to take into account the *context* in which the treaty is applied. This is to say, that we must take a systematic view of the whole treaty (systematic interpretation), as well as taking into account the *object and purpose* of the treaty (teleological interpretation).

The second and third paragraphs of article 31 stress the importance of the systematic method of interpretation by clarifying the concept of 'context'.[9] For the purpose

---

Prebensen, S.: 'Evolutive interpretation of the European Convention on Human Rights', in Protecting human rights: the European perspective: studies in memory of Rolv Ryssdal. Mahoney, Matsher, Petzold and Wildhaber (eds.), Verlag, Köln, Berlin, Bonn, München, (2000), pp. 1123-1137; Bos, M.: 'Theory and practice of treaty interpretation,' in *NILR,* vol. XXVII (1980), pp. 3-38 and pp. 135-170; Schwarzenberger, G.: 'Myths and realities of treaty Interpretation', in *VJIL,* vol. 9 No. 1, (1968), pp. 1-19; Dijk, P. van: 'A common standard of achievement about universal validity and uniform interpretation of international human rights norms', in *NQHR*, vol.13 No. 2, (1995), pp. 105-121; Hassan, P.: 'The International Covenants on Human Rights: an approach to interpretation', *Buffalo Law Review*, vol. 19 No. 3, (1970), pp. 35-50; and Falk, R.: 'On treaty interpretation and the New Haven approach: achievements and prospects,' in *VJIL*, vol. 8 No. 2 (1968), pp. 323-355.

6 Art. 31 VCLT: 'General rule of interpretation':
'1. A treaty shall be interpreted in good faith in accordance with the ordinary meaning to be given to the terms of the treaty in their context and in the light of its object and purpose.
2. The context for the purpose of the interpretation of a treaty shall comprise in addition to the text, including its preamble and annexes:
(a) any agreement relating to the treaty which was made between all the parties in connection with the conclusion of the treaty;
(b) any instrument which was made by one or more parties in connection with the conclusion of the treaty and accepted by the other parties as an instrument related to the treaty.
3. There shall be taken into account, together with the context:
(a) any subsequent agreement between the parties regarding the interpretation of the treaty or the application of its provisions;
(b) any subsequent practice in the application of the treaty which establishes the agreement of the parties regarding its interpretation;
(c) any relevant rules of international law applicable in the relations between the parties.'
It is important to stress that the interpretation process is a single combined operation and therefore that the various means of interpretation of this provision interact. That is why, as Brownlie notes, that the heading is 'General rule', in the singular. Brownlie, *op. cit.* (note 5), p. 633.

7 According to the basic rule of good faith or the principle of *pacta sunt servanda,* established in article 26 VCLT, treaties 'must be performed in good faith.'

8 See text of article 31(1) VCLT in note 6.

9 I here follow M. Bos, who considered that the words 'together with the context' in paragraph 3 are not an impediment to viewing all the aspects enumerated in this paragraph as part of that context, and therefore a further form of 'systematic interpretation.' Bos, *loc. cit.* (note 5), p. 145.

of interpreting a treaty, the 'context' of a treaty entails 'in addition to the text, including its preamble and annexes': (i) any agreement or instrument in connection with the conclusion of the treaty and related to it (article 31(2) VCLT); (ii) any subsequent agreement and practice regarding the interpretation of the treaty (article 31(3)(a)(b)); (iii) any relevant rules of international law applicable in relations between the parties (article 31(3)(c)). Finally, the last paragraph of Article 31 stresses that if States agree to give a special meaning to a term, that meaning shall prevail.[10]

It is worth stressing that in applying the rules of interpretation, due respect must be paid to the principle of 'good faith.' As O'Connor notes, 'the principle of good faith may be invoked to ensure that any of the positive rules of the law of treaties are applied honestly, fairly and reasonably.'[11]

The supplementary means of interpretation are contained in article 32 VCLT.[12] According to this provision, the supplementary means of interpretation are, among others, the intention of the parties at the time of drafting, as reflected by the *travaux préparatoires*, and the circumstances of the treaty's conclusion. As indicated by the provision, recourse to these methods should be had to confirm the meaning resulting from the application of the methods established in article 31, or to determine from the meaning when the interpretation according to article 31 still 'leaves the meaning ambiguous or obscure' or 'leads to a result which is manifestly absurd or unreasonable.' The final provision regarding treaty interpretation is article 33 VCLT, which contains the rule for the interpretation of treaties in two or more languages.

It is of particular importance that under the VCLT, the *travaux préparatoires* are only a supplementary means of interpretation. As has been established by the International Court of Justice, treaties should be interpreted and applied within the framework of the legal system prevailing at the time of the interpretation, rather than at the time of the drafting or adoption of the text.[13] As we will see, in the interpretation of human rights treaties, the intention of the drafters does not generally play a major

10 Art. 31(4) VCLT: 'A special meaning shall be given to a term if it is established that the parties so intended.'

11 O'Connor, 1991, p. 110.

12 Art. 32 VCLT reads as follows:
'Recourse may be had to supplementary means of interpretation, including the preparatory work of the treaty and the circumstances of its conclusion, in order to confirm the meaning resulting from the application of Article 31, or to determine the meaning when the interpretation according to Article 31:
(a) leaves the meaning ambiguous or obscure; or
(b) leads to a result which is manifestly absurd or unreasonable.'

13 I.C.J. Advisory Opinion on the Legal Consequences for States of the Continued Presence of South Africa in Namibia (South West Africa) notwithstanding Security Council Resolution 276 (1970). Advisory Opinion of 21 June 1971. (ICJ Reports 1971, p. 31).

role.[14] It is necessary to replace the search for the historic intention of the drafters with an analysis of subsequent developments in domestic and international law.[15]

2.3 The specific object and purpose of human rights treaties

It is well established that the rules for treaty interpretation provide the framework for interpreting human rights treaties. This is apparent in the jurisprudence of the major human rights supervisory bodies. The Human Rights Committee[16] as well as the two regional human rights Courts have expressly noted that the rules of interpretation set out in the VCLT contain the relevant international law principles for interpretation.[17]

However, as stated above, the application of these rules does not resolve all the problems of treaty interpretation because the rules of the VCLT are not unequivocal.[18] Moreover, the interpretation of human rights treaties requires that we take into account the specific characteristics of human rights treaties. Already in 1951, the International Court of Justice noted the special character of human rights treaties. In its Advisory Opinion on Reservations to the Convention on the Prevention and Punishment of the Crime of Genocide, the Court stated that the contracting States to such instruments do not have any individual advantages or disadvantages nor interests of their own, but merely a common interest.[19]

---

14 For example, it is not rare to find decisions of the European Court of Human Rights that are contrary to the express intentions of the drafters. See, Mahoney, *loc. cit.* (note 5), 1990, p. 62 and Prebensen, *op. cit.* (note 5), pp. 1132-1136. The Inter-American Court also seems to follow this approach, see, for example, the separate opinion of Judge Rodolfo E. Piza Escalante in I/A Court HR, Advisory Opinion on 'Proposed amendments to the naturalization provisions of the Constitution of Costa Rica,' OC-4/84 of 19 January 1984, paras. 2-3.

15 See the Case of Dudgeon v. the United Kingdom, Application No. 7525/76, Judgement of 22 October 1981 and Marckx v. Belgium, Application No. 6833/74, Judgement of 13 June 1979.

16 See, for example, Alberta Union v. Canada, Communication No. 118/1982, inadmissibility decision of 18 July 1986, para. 6.3.

17 With regard to the Inter-American Court, see its Advisory Opinion OC-4/84, loc. cit. (note 14), paras. 21-23; Advisory Opinion OC-3/83 '*Restrictions to the death penalty* (Arts. 4(2) and 4(4) American Convention on Human Rights)', of September 8, 1983, Series A No. 3 and Advisory Opinion OC-7/86, '*Enforceability of the right to reply or correction* (Arts. 14(1), 1(1) and 2 American Convention on Human Rights)', of August 29, 1986, para 21. At the European level see, for example, Golder v. the United Kingdom, loc. cit. (note 1), para. 29 and Loizidou v. Turkey, Application No. 1531/89, Judgement of 18 December 1996, para. 43.

18 As has been indicated: '[t]he rules of the Vienna Convention do not provide a clear-cut solution to all problems of treaty interpretation. In fact, those rules themselves are not unequivocal.' Dijk, P. van & Hoof, G.J.H. van, *op. cit.* (note 2), p. 72.

19 See International Court of Justice in its Advisory Opinion on Reservations to the Convention on the Prevention and Punishment of the Crime of Genocide. 'In such a Convention, the contracting States do not have any interests of their own; they merely have, one and all, a common interest, namely, the accomplishment of those high purposes which are the raison d'être of the convention. Consequently in a convention of this type one cannot speak of individual advantages or disadvantages to States, or

From the point of view of State duties, what distinguishes human rights treaties from other international treaties is that the former are agreements between States which grant specific rights to individuals who are not themselves parties to the instruments, and in which the correlative duties fall primarily on States. As Sieghart points out, in human rights treaties there is an asymmetry: 'those whose rights are being protected are not themselves parties to the treaties, while those whom the treaties oblige to protect these rights do not obtain an obvious correlative benefit from the assumption of that obligation.'[20]

The Inter-American Court has explained this special feature of the human rights instruments with clarity, emphasising that,

> 'Modern human rights treaties in general, and the American Convention in particular, are not multilateral treaties of the traditional type concluded to accomplish the reciprocal exchange of rights for the mutual benefit of the contracting States. Their object and purpose is the protection of the basic rights of individual human beings irrespective of their nationality, both against the State of their nationality and all other contracting States. In concluding these human rights treaties, the States can be deemed to submit themselves to a legal order within which they, for the common good, assume various obligations, not in relation to other States, but towards all individuals within their jurisdiction [...].'[21]

The European Commission of Human Rights applied the same approach in the case of Austria v. Italy when it held that 'the obligations undertaken by the High Contracting Parties in the European Convention are essentially of an objective character, being designed rather to protect the fundamental rights of individual human beings from infringements by any of the High Contracting Parties than to create subjective and reciprocal rights for the High Contracting Parties themselves.'[22]

This approach is also apparent in the jurisprudence of the European Court of Human Rights. In the *Wemhoff Case*, the Court noted that because the Convention is a 'law-making treaty, it is [...] necessary to seek the interpretation that is most appropriate in order to realise the aim and achieve the object of the treaty, not that

---

of the maintenance of a perfect contractual balance between rights and duties.' Advisory Opinion of 28 May 1951 (ICJ Report 1951, p. 23).

20 Sieghart, P.: The international law of human rights, Clarendon Press, Oxford, (1983), pp. 20-21.

21 I/A Court HR, Advisory Opinion OC-2/82 'The effect of reservations on the entry into force of the American Convention on Human Rights (Arts. 74 and 75)', of 24 September 1982, para. 29. Reference to the specific object and purpose of the Convention as a human rights treaty are also found in contentious cases, such as Velásquez Rodríguez v. Honduras, Preliminary Objections, Judgement of 26 June 1987, Series C No. 1, para. 30; Fairén Garbi and Solís Corrales v. Honduras, Preliminary Objections, Judgment of 26 June 1987, Series C No. 2, para. 35 and Cayara v. Peru, Preliminary Objections, Judgment of 3 February 1993, Series C No. 14, para. 37.

22 Austria v. Italy, Application No. 788/60, 4 Yearbook of the European Convention on Human Rights, 1961, pp. 116 *et seq.*

which would restrict to the greatest possible degree the obligations undertaken by the parties.'[23]

In sum, the object and purpose of human rights treaties play a central and crucial role in the interpretation of human rights treaties. The specific object and purpose of human rights treaties is the protection of the individual human person. This not only justifies but compels interpretation and application of the provisions of human rights instruments in a consistent manner. This object and purpose requires that we take into account, at a minimum, the two following principles:[24]

2.3.1 The effectiveness rule[25]

Due to the fact that the overriding function of human rights treaties is the protection of individuals' rights, it seems clear that their interpretation should make that protection effective.[26] As the Inter-American Court has noted, '[t]he object and purpose of the American Convention is the effective protection of human rights. The Convention must, therefore, be interpreted so as to give it its full meaning and to enable the system for the protection of human rights entrusted to the Commission and the Court to attain its '*appropriate effects*'.'[27]

The application of this principle is evident in the case law of the European Court. According to the European Court,

> 'In interpreting the Convention, regard must be had to its special character as a treaty for the collective enforcement of human rights and fundamental freedoms [...] thus the *object and purpose* of the Convention as an instrument for the protection of individual human beings *require that its provisions be interpreted and applied so as to make its safeguards practical and effective.*'[28]

---

23 Wemhoff v. Germany, Application No. 2122/64, Judgement of 27 June 1968 para. 8.

24 It is important to mention that there are other principles for interpretation that should also be considered, such as the interpretative principle that limitation provisions shall be construed and applied in a restrictive way. Nevertheless, because other principles do not directly result from the special object and purpose of human rights treaties, their analysis is beyond the scope of the present study.

25 For a deeper analysis of the effectiveness principle, see Dijk, P. van & Hoof, G.J.H. van, *op. cit.* (note 2), p. 74 *et seq.* and Merrills, J.G.: 'The effectiveness principle' in: The development of international law by the European Court of Human Rights, Manchester University Press, New York, (1988), Chapter 5.

26 As Brownlie notes, the International Law Commission did not provide a separate formulation of this principle considering that it was reflected sufficiently in the doctrines of interpretation in good faith in accordance with the ordinary meaning (Art. 31(1) VCLT). Brownlie, *op. cit.* (note 5), p. 636.

27 Velásquez Rodríguez v. Honduras, *loc. cit.* (note 21), para. 30 (emphasis added).

28 Case of Soering v. the United Kingdom, Application No. 14038/88, Judgement 7 July 1989, para. 87. See also, for example, Airey v. Ireland, Application No. 6289/73, Judgement of 9 October 1979 para. 24; Artico v. Italy, Application No. 6694/1980, Judgement of 13 May 1980, para. 33; McCann and others v. the United Kingdom, Application No. 18984/91, Judgement of 27 September 1995, paras.

The European Court has applied this principle on many occasions and in doing so has extensively interpreted the duties imposed upon States by the Convention.[29]

To recapitulate: the special object and purpose of human rights treaties requires that their provisions be made practical and effective. This is valid even if such an interpretation implies a major burden for States Parties. However, it is important to keep in mind that the effectiveness principle has limits. As the International Court of

146-147; Yasa v. Turkey, Application No. 2249/93, Judgement of 2 September 1998, para. 64; and Hugh Jordan v. the United Kingdom, Application No. 24746/94, Judgement 4 May 2001, para. 102.

29 Among the different cases in which the European Court has applied this principle, it is interesting to recall here two cases relating to article 6 ECHR (fair trial clause). The first of these cases is the *Golder Case*. In this case, taking into account the ordinary meaning of the terms used in article 6(1) ECHR and the object and purpose of the Convention as a law-making treaty, the Court ruled that article 6(1) gave rise to implicit obligations. In their separate opinions, Judge Sir Gerald Fitzmaurice and Judge Verdross criticised the Court ruling, considering that it was an illegitimately extensive interpretation which exceeded the original intention of the drafters. However, the Court itself justified its decision in the text of the ruling, saying that '[…] the right to access constitutes an element which is inherent in the right stated by Article 6 para. 1. This is not an extensive interpretation forcing new obligations on the Contracting States: it is based on the very terms of the first sentence of Article 6 para. 1 read in its context and having regard to the object and purpose of the Convention, a lawmaking treaty.' Golder v. the United Kingdom, *loc. cit.* (note 1), para. 36. (Emphasis added).
Another landmark case in that of Airey v. Ireland. In this case, Mrs. Airey needed to obtain a decree of judicial separation from her allegedly violent and alcoholic husband. Mr. Airey had abandoned the matrimonial home but Mrs. Airey feared that he might seek to return. The decree of judicial separation was obtainable only in the High Court. Although at that time there was no legal aid available in Ireland for the purpose of seeking a judicial separation, according to domestic law the parties were able to bring their cases in person. The applicant complained that the prohibitive cost of litigation prevented her from bringing proceedings before the High Court for the purpose of petitioning for judicial separation and she therefore argued that her right of access to a court was effectively being denied. The Government of Ireland contended that Ms. Airey enjoyed the protection of Art. 6(1) of the Convention since she was free to appear before the High Court without the assistance of a lawyer. The Court rejected the government's submission because it did not take account of the principle of effectiveness, holding that the 'Convention is intended to guarantee not rights that are theoretical or illusory but rights that are practical and effective.' The Court considered that under the circumstances of the case it was not realistic to suppose that Mrs. Airey could effectively conduct her own case. The Court decided that for that reason, she did not enjoy an effective right of access to the High Court. Therefore it concluded that Ireland was in breach of Art. 6(1) ECHR. During the proceedings before the Court, the Government of Ireland also argued that as Art. 6(1) did not guarantee any right to free legal aid, that the Convention should not be interpreted so as to achieve social and economic developments in a Contracting State and that such developments can only be progressive. But again the Court emphasised the principle of effectiveness stating that although the 'further realisation of social and economic rights is largely dependent on the situation – notably financial – reigning in the State in question [...] the Convention must be interpreted in the light of present-day conditions and it is designed to safeguard the individual in a real and practical way as regards those areas with which it deals. Whilst the Convention sets forth what are essentially civil and political rights, many of them have implications of a social or economic nature.' Consistently, the Court considered 'that the mere fact that an interpretation of the Convention may extend into the sphere of social and economic rights should not be a decisive factor against such an interpretation; there is no water-tight division separating that sphere from the field covered by the Convention.' Airey v. Ireland, *loc. cit.* (note 28), para. 26.

Justice has highlighted, the rule of effectiveness cannot justify attributing a meaning to a provision that is contrary to the letter and spirit of the instrument.[30]

2.3.2 The evolutive interpretation[31]

The protection of individuals also requires an evolutive interpretation of human rights treaties. Human rights are not static and therefore effective protection of these rights involves taking into account developments in law and society.[32]

The necessity of taking into account the changes occurring in society and in law is often emphasised by the European Court of Human Rights which has frequently underlined that the Convention is a 'living instrument which must be interpreted in the light of present-day conditions.'[33]

It is again worth noting that, as with the effectiveness principle, the importance of the evolutive interpretation is the consequence of the overriding object and purpose of human rights treaties. The interpretation of the text in light of the object and purpose (article 31 VCLT) is required to make human rights provisions 'practical and effective' and to take into account 'present-day conditions' for the protection of the individual. This is clear, for example, in the *Loizidou Case* where the European Court held,

> 'That the Convention is a living instrument which must be interpreted in the light of present-day conditions is firmly rooted in the Court's case-law […]. It follows that these provisions cannot be interpreted solely in accordance with the intentions of their authors as expressed more than forty years ago.'

Subsequently the Court added,

---

30 See ICJ, Advisory Opinion on the Interpretation of Peace Treaties with Bulgaria, Hungary and Romania (1949-1950) Advisory Opinion of 18 July 1950. (ICJ Reports 1950, p. 229).

31 For a deeper analysis of the evolutive interpretation of human rights treaties see, *inter alia*, Mahoney, *loc. cit.* (note 5), pp. 57-88; Bernhardt, *op. cit.* (note 3), pp. 65-71; Dijk, P. van & Hoof, G.J.H. van, *op. cit.* (note 2), pp. 71-95; Prebensen, op. cit. (note 5), pp. 1123-1137.

32 As the International Court of Justice has held, '[T]he Court take into consideration the changes which have occurred in the supervening half-century, and its interpretation cannot remain unaffected by the subsequent development of law […]. Moreover, an international instrument has to be interpreted and applied within the framework of the entire legal system prevailing at the time of the interpretation. In the domain to which the present proceedings relate, the last fifty years […] have brought important developments […] In this domain, as elsewhere, the corpus iuris gentium has been considerably enriched, and this the Court, if it is faithfully to discharge its functions, may not ignore.' Advisory Opinion on the 'Legal Consequences for States of the Continued Presence of South Africa in Namibia (South West Africa), notwithstanding Security Council Resolution 276 (1970)', loc. cit. (note 14), p. 16, para. 31.

33 See, for example, the Case of Tyrer v. the United Kingdom, Application No. 5856/72, Judgement of 25 April 1978, para. 15 where the Court noted, 'the Convention is a living instrument which […] must be interpreted in the light of the present-day conditions'; Marckx v. Belgium, *loc. cit.* (note 15), para. 41; Airey v. Ireland, *loc. cit.* (note 28), para. 26; and Loizidou v. Turkey, Preliminary objections, Application No. 15318/89, Judgement of 23 March 1995 para. 71.

> 'In addition, the object and purpose of the Convention as an instrument for the protection of individual human beings requires that its provisions be interpreted and applied so as to make its safeguards practical and effective [...].'[34]

The Inter-American Court also applies the principle of evolutive interpretation.[35] The Court itself has explained that due to the evolution of international human rights law, in the interpretation process

> 'It is appropriate to look to the Inter-American system of today in the light of the evolution it has undergone since the adoption of the Declaration, rather than to examine the normative value and significance which that instrument was believed to have had in 1948.'[36]

More recently, the Inter-American Court has made express mention of the jurisprudence of the European Court of Human Rights and indicated that 'human rights treaties are living instruments, the interpretation of which must evolve over time in view of existing circumstances.'[37]

As Bernhardt notes, 'human rights treaties must be interpreted in an objective and dynamic manner, by taking into account social conditions and developments; the ideas and conditions prevailing at the time when the treaties were drafted retain hardly any continuing validity.'[38] As he emphasises, present-day conditions are more important for the interpretation of human rights treaties than 'ideas, convictions and circumstances at the time when the provisions were drafted and came into force.'[39] Obviously this principle has limits. It is well established that the interpretation of a treaty cannot lead to the creation of new rights.[40] As Mahoney states 'the only matter which can be

---

34 Loizidou v. Turkey, *loc. cit.* (note 33), paras. 71-72.

35 See for example: I/A Court HR Paniagua Morales et al. v. Guatemala [Preliminary Objections, Judgement of 25 January 1996, Series C No. 23, paras. 40-42] and Advisory Opinion on 'The right to information on consular assistance in the framework of the guarantees of the due process of law' [OC-16/99 of 1 October 1999, paras. 114-115]. It is interesting to note that in the latter advisory opinion, the Inter-American Court expressly notes that 'international human rights law has made great headway thanks to an evolutive interpretation of international instruments of protection.'

36 Advisory Opinion OC-10/90 'Interpretation of the American Declaration of the Rights and Duties of Man within the framework of article 64 of the American Convention on Human Rights', of July 14, 1989, para. 37.

37 It quotes specifically the jurisprudence of its European counterpart in the cases of Tyrer [*loc. cit.* (note 33)], Marckx [*loc. cit.* (note 15)] and Loizidou [*loc. cit.* (note 33)]. See, I/A Court HR, Advisory Opinion OC-16/99, *loc. cit.* (note 35), para. 114. See, also I/A Court HR, Villagrán Morales *et al.* v. Guatemala, Judgement of 19 November 1999, Series C No. 77, para. 193.

38 Bernhardt, op. cit. (note 3), p. 71.

39 Bernhardt, *op. cit.* (note 3), p. 70.

40 See, for example, the joint dissenting opinion of Judges Ryssdal, Bindschedler-Robert, Lagergren, Matscher, Sir Vincent Evans, Bernhardt and Gersing, 'An evolutive interpretation allows variable and changing concepts already contained in the Convention to be construed in the light of modern-day conditions [...], but it does not allow entirely new concepts or spheres of application to be introduced

evolutively interpreted – and perhaps thereby expanded into unforeseen fields of application – is a matter which is already explicit or implicit in the wording of the text.'[41]

Finally, it is worth stressing that although the interpretation 'in the light of present-day conditions' is of importance to all human rights instruments in order that they should not become obsolete. Arguably the very subject matter of the Covenant (economic, social and cultural rights), makes such an interpretation even more compelling. An instrument aimed at the protection of economic, social and cultural rights is more exposed to changes in perception in society and economic, social and political conditions than are civil and political rights instruments. Even without a sociological analysis, which is beyond the scope of this study, it is evident that there have been many changes that have influenced the protection afforded by the Covenant. Among these changes is, for example, the perception of equality between the sexes. Today there is more awareness that situations such as domestic violence, sexual abuse, and sexual harassment are forms of discrimination against women. New, evolving perceptions as to what forms of treatment are acceptable must be taken into account for a proper interpretation of the Covenant. The Committee has an important role, not only in promoting such changes in perception, but also in creatively interpreting the Covenant by incorporating such changes in perception into the protection afforded by the Covenant.[42]

In addition, there are some notions contained in the Covenant whose meaning is very sensitive to developments occurring, not only in law, but also in society as a whole. Let us examine, for example, the concept of 'family' (article 10 and article 7(a)(ii) ICESCR). In different parts of the world today, domestic legislation recognises

---

into the Convention: that is a legislative function that belongs to the member States of the Council of Europe. The desirability of affording proper safeguards for the adjudication of claims in the ever-increasing field of social security is evident. There are, however, limits to evolutive interpretation and the facts of the present case go beyond those limits as far as Article 6 para. 1 is concerned.' Feldbrugge v. the Netherlands, Application No. 8562/79, Judgement of 23 April 1986, para. 24. Nevertheless, the majority decision took the opposite point of view as regards the specifics of the case.

41 Mahoney, *loc. cit.* (note 5), p. 66.

42 That the Committee has expressly assumed this role is evident, for example, in the joint statement adopted by the Committee on Economic, Social and Cultural Rights, the Human Rights Committee and the Committee on the Elimination of Discrimination against Women at the fiftieth anniversary of the Universal Declaration on Human Rights where they stated, 'The Human Rights Committee, the Committee on Economic, Social and Cultural Rights, and the Committee on the Elimination of Discrimination against Women recognise their critical role in increasing the understanding of gender factors in the enjoyment of human rights. They are conscious of the need to interpret creatively the human rights norms they monitor so that they can be applied to those experiences of women which differ from those of men. The Committees underline that a broader, inclusive understanding of such rights brings with it an international legal obligation for States Parties to ensure to women the full enjoyment of all their human rights.' E/1999/22 Chapter VI, decisions adopted by the Committee at its ninth session (para. 6).

the existence of many different forms of family not accepted even a few years ago.[43] We may notice this, for example, in relation to the evolution in the protection of children born out of wedlock, homosexual couples and single parent families. In many countries these different forms of family are now provided with protection and the Committee needs to take into account this evolution when interpreting the Covenant.[44]

2.4 The Committee's approach to the rules of interpretation

To illustrate the methods for interpretation used by the Committee, we may focus on the General Comments, which provide clear and straightforward examples of how the Committee interprets the Covenant.

From the General Comments, it is easy to deduce that the Committee has applied the rules of interpretation set forth in the VCLT. For example, the Committee has interpreted the specific wording of the Covenant (literal interpretation), taking into account other provisions of the Covenant (systematic interpretation).[45] The Committee has also referred to the legislative history of the Covenant (supplementary means of interpretation), although such references are basically to reinforce an interpretation achieved by other methods.[46]

It is worth stressing here that the interpretation process is a single combined operation where all methods of interpretation interact and it is the interpreter who is called upon to find an appropriate balance amongst them. A careful examination of the

---

43 I am not suggesting that there is one form and concept of family. Obviously, the concept varies from State to State, and even within a State over time. The point stressed here is that the notion is susceptible to evolution over the years and that the Committee, as the supervisory body of the Covenant, is required to take this evolution into account.

44 It is interesting to recall here the Fourth Periodic Report of Germany. The Report, dealing with Art. 10, refers to the concept of family and stated, '[t]he forms of families have changed and will continue to change. Therefore we encounter very different family forms today. This is not surprising against the background of the economic, cultural and political changes, but rather a normal part of the continuous change of society in general. Today families comprise married and unmarried parents who raise their children together or alone including stepparents, adoptive parents and foster-parents. One feature which all these long-term relationships have in common is the reliable relationship between the children and their parents. They all have the same right to protection and assistance even if they do not succeed in living together as a family.' E/C.12/4/Add.3, 10 August 2000, para. 122.

45 See, for example, General Comment No. 13 para. 51. 'As already observed, the obligations of States Parties in relation to primary, secondary, higher and fundamental education are not identical. Given the wording of article 13(2), States Parties are obliged to prioritise the introduction of compulsory, free primary education. This interpretation of article 13(2) is reinforced by the priority accorded to primary education in article 14. The obligation to provide primary education for all is an immediate duty of all States Parties.'

46 For example, in General Comment No. 9 the Committee notes that 'The Covenant does not negate the possibility that the rights it contains may be considered self-executing in systems where that option is provided for. Indeed, when it was being drafted, attempts to include a specific provision in the Covenant to the effect that it be considered 'non-self-executing' were strongly rejected' (para. 11).

Committee's work clearly indicates that the Committee is not only guided by the rules of interpretation set forth in the VCLT but also gives due priority to the object and purpose of the Covenant.[47]

Thus, with more or less success, the Committee attempts to interpret the Covenant in a manner which gives the fullest effect to its provisions in the light of contemporary circumstances, notwithstanding that sometimes such interpretations may entail broad or extensive obligations for States. The Committee has repeatedly noted that 'the Covenant's rights should not be misinterpreted as depriving its correlative obligation of all meaningful content.'[48] On the contrary, according to the Committee, in the light of the object and purpose of the Covenant, an extensive or inclusive interpretation of the rights is required.[49]

The Committee has made express mention of the necessity that States should interpret the Covenant so as to produce an 'effective' result. In General Comment No. 9, for example, the Committee notes,

> '[I]n most States, the determination of whether or not a treaty provision is self-executing will be a matter for the courts, not the executive or the legislature. In order to perform that function effectively, the relevant courts and tribunals must be made aware of the nature and implications of the Covenant and of the important role of judicial remedies in its implementation. Thus, for example, when Governments are involved in court proceedings, *they should promote interpretations of domestic laws which give effect to their Covenant obligations.*'[50]

Furthermore the Committee mentions,

> 'It is generally accepted that domestic law should be interpreted as far as possible in a way which conforms to a State's international legal obligations. Thus, when a domestic decision maker is faced with a choice between an interpretation of domestic law that would place the State in breach of the Covenant and one that would enable the State to comply with the

47 For example, General Comment No. 4 states, 'In the Committee's view, the right to housing should not be interpreted in a narrow or restrictive sense which equates it with, for example, the shelter provided by merely having a roof over one's head or views shelter exclusively as a commodity. Rather it should be seen as the right to live somewhere in security, peace and dignity. This is appropriate for at least two reasons. In the first place, the right to housing is integrally linked to other human rights [author's note: systematic interpretation] and to the fundamental principles upon which the Covenant is premised [*a.n.*: teleological interpretation]. This 'the inherent dignity of the human person' from which the rights in the Covenant are said to derive requires that the term 'housing' be interpreted so as to take account of a variety of other considerations, most importantly that the right to housing should be ensured to all persons irrespective of income or access to economic resources.' General Comment No. 4 para. 7. See, also, General Comment No. 3 para. 9.

48 General Comment No. 14 para. 31; General Comment No. 13 para. 44; General Comment No. 9 para. 11; and General Comment No. 3 para. 9.

49 See, for example, General Comment No. 12 para. 6 and General Comment No. 14 para. 11.

50 General Comment No. 9 para. 11. (Emphasis added).

> Covenant, international law requires the choice of the latter. Guarantees of equality and non-discrimination *should be interpreted, to the greatest extent possible, in ways which facilitate the full protection of economic, social and cultural rights*.'[51]

It is well established that the overriding object and purpose of human rights treaties also requires that developments that have occurred in international law be take into account, the so-called 'evolutive interpretation.' In Chapter Two, we analysed the developments that have occurred in the field of economic, social and cultural rights and how the Committee has incorporated these developments in its interpretation of the Covenant, providing a 'contemporary interpretation' of the treaty.[52] Here, it is important to stress that this approach is the application of the rule of 'evolutive interpretation' of human rights treaties.

As reflected in the General Comments, in attempting to make the rights contained in the Covenant effective in present-day conditions, the Committee also takes into account changes in perceptions as well as new obstacles to the implementation of the Covenant. This is plainly the Committee's approach to some 'evolving notions' contained in the Covenant.[53] For example, article 11 of the Covenant refers to the right of a person to an adequate standard of living for '*himself and his family*.' The Committee, referring to the right to adequate housing, explains that,

> 'While the reference to 'himself and his family' reflects assumptions as to gender roles and economic activity patterns commonly accepted in 1966 when the Covenant was adopted, the phrase cannot be read today as implying any limitations upon the applicability of the right to individuals or to female-headed households or other such groups. Thus, the concept of 'family' must be understood in a wide sense. Further, individuals, as well as families, are entitled to adequate housing regardless of age, economic status, group or other affiliation or status and other such factors. In particular, enjoyment of this right must, in accordance with article 2(2) of the Covenant, not be subject to any form of discrimination.'[54]

The same evolution occurs with notions such as 'health'. As the Committee has explicitly stated in General Comment No. 14,

> 'Since the adoption in 1966 of the International Covenant on Economic, Social and Cultural Rights and the International Covenant on Civil and Political Rights, the world health situation has changed dramatically and the notion of health has undergone substantial changes and has also widened in scope. More determinants of health are being taken into

---

51 General Comment No. 9 para. 15. (Emphasis added).

52 See Chapter II section 3.

53 As described by Prebensen, 'evolving notions,' are 'terms which are susceptible to evolve depending on changes in perceptions in society and on economic, social and political conditions.' And he adds, 'the open-ended wording gives ample reasons for assuming that the [...] States could not have expected the Convention to be interpreted as a fossilised instrument.' Prebensen, *op. cit.* (note 5), p. 1125.

54 General Comment No. 4 para. 6. See, also General Comment No. 12 para. 1.

> consideration, such as resource distribution and gender differences. A wider definition of health also takes into account such socially-related concerns as violence and armed conflict. Moreover, formerly unknown diseases, such as human immunodeficiency virus (HIV) and acquired immunodeficiency syndrome (AIDS) and others that have become more wide-spread, such as cancer, as well as the rapid growth of the world population, have created new obstacles for the realisation of the right to health which need to be taken into account when interpreting article 12.'[55]

In sum, the Committee is guided by rules of interpretation contained in the VCLT, but these are not the only rules considered by the Committee. According to the Committee, the object and purpose of the Covenant, which is the protection of the human person, requires that rights be interpreted in a manner that gives them full effect in the light of present-day conditions. In practice, this means that over the years, in light of the developments achieved in human rights law as well as changes in social perceptions, the Committee has provided a broader interpretation of the Covenant's rights, which implies more burdensome obligations for States. In light of the rules for the interpretation of human rights treaties analysed above, it is possible to conclude that this approach is absolutely in line with the rules for the interpretation of treaties in general international law as well as with the work of other human rights supervisory bodies.

3 The legitimacy of the Committee's interpretation of the Covenant

3.1 Introduction

At the domestic level, the process of determining the scope of a given norm is usually carried out by the courts, and to a lesser extent by the legislative and executive powers. Due to the special characteristics of international law, the process of determining the scope and content of the obligations imposed by an international treaty differs significantly from the process which operates at the domestic level.[56]

At the international level, the possibility of recourse to a court for a legally binding decision, such as in the case of the European Court of Human Rights and the Inter-American Court,[57] is exceptional. Human rights treaties typically do not provide for a judicial body. Rather, they usually envisage special bodies composed of independent experts entrusted with the task of monitoring compliance with the treaty provisions.

According to the traditional rules of general international law, the observations, views or comments of all UN treaty-monitoring bodies do not have the same legal

55 General Comment No. 14 para. 10.

56 See Steiner & Alston, *op. cit.* (note 5), pp. 108-110.

57 At the African level there is an Optional Protocol for the establishment of a Court, not yet into force. See Protocol to the African Charter on the Establishment of the African Court on Human and Peoples' Rights. OUA doc. OAU/LEG/MIN/AFCHPR/PROT.1 rev.2 (1997).

status as court decisions because they are not legally binding upon States.[58] However, today it is well established that although the interpretations of treaty-monitoring bodies may not have legally binding status, it is beyond doubt that they do carry considerable legal weight.[59]

While the competencies of these bodies vary, as some of them are competent to receive individual complaints,[60] they are the most authoritative bodies for determining the scope of the obligations imposed by the treaty they are called upon to monitor.[61] As has been indicated with regard to the Committee's Concluding Observations, '[w]hile the Committee's concluding observations, in particular suggestions and recommendations, may not carry legally binding status, they are indicative of the opinion of the only expert body entrusted with and capable of making such pronouncements. Consequently, for States parties to ignore or not act on such views would be to show bad faith in implementing their Covenant-based obligations.'[62]

The present analysis focuses on the work of the Committee on Economic, Social and Cultural Rights. The Committee interprets the Covenant, principally through its Concluding Observations, General Comments and through some statements adopted during its sessions. As noted, the Committee's interpretations of the Covenant are not binding as such upon States Parties to the Covenant. However, the Committee's interpretations seem to be widely accepted by the States Parties.

As a preliminary issue, it is important to examine why States comply (or should comply), with the Committee's interpretation of the Covenant. It is also important to identify the factors that bring pressure upon States to voluntarily comply with the Committee's interpretation. In order to analyse this question, we will introduce the concept of legitimacy adapted by Franck to the international system. As he defines it,

58 In contrast, the judgements of the two existing human rights court are legally binding upon States. See Art. 68 ACHR and Art. 46 ECHR.

59 With regard to the Committee's work see Craven, M.: The International Covenant on Economic, Social and Cultural Rights: a perspective on its development. Clarendon Press, Oxford, (1995), p. 91. Although it is beyond the scope of the present study, it is worth noting that in regard to the 'views' of the Human Rights Committee, some authors, such as Pocar have argued that the views are indirectly binding through the medium of article 2(3) ICCPR (the obligations to remedy the violations). See, Pocar, F.: 'Legal value of the Human Rights Committee's views.' In: *Canadian Human Rights Yearbook* (1991-1992), pp. 119-123.

60 Of the six major international human rights treaties, the supervisory bodies of the ICCPR, CERD, CAT and, recently, CEDAW are competent to clarify norms through individual complaints.

61 The Committee itself considers that, through its General Comments, it makes an 'authoritative interpretation' of the Covenant's provisions. For example, when referring to the Draft General Comment on Intellectual Property Rights, the Committee emphasised 'the timeliness and appropriateness of providing an authoritative interpretation – through its general comments – to the provisions in article 15, paragraph 1(c) of the Covenant.' E/C.12/1999/11 para. 441. See, also E/C.12/1999/11 para. 53.

62 UN Fact Sheet No. 16 (Rev. 1) on the Committee on Economic, Social and Cultural Rights. Available at: http://www.unhchr.ch/html/menu6/2/fs16.htm (last visited July 2002).

> 'Legitimacy is a property of a rule or rulemaking institution which itself exerts a pull toward compliance on those addressed normatively because those addressed believed that the rule or institutions has come into being and operates in accordance with generally accepted principles of right process.'[63]

This notion of 'legitimacy' suggests that there are a couple of factors, one related to the 'rule-making' and the other to the 'rule', that predispose those addressed by the rule toward voluntary obedience. In our analysis, the 'ruler' is the Committee, the 'rules' would be the Committee's interpretations of the Covenant in the form of Concluding Observations, General Comments or specific Committee statements and, finally, those addressed by the rule are the States Parties to the Covenant.

As the analysis of the 'legitimacy' of the Committee is intimately related to the 'role of the Committee in clarifying the normative content of the Covenant', I have chosen to include it as an excursus in the present chapter. Therefore, in this section we will try to identify the factors that attribute 'legitimacy' to the Committee's work, or in other words, which predispose States to comply with the Committee's interpretation of the Covenant. The extent to which States Parties view the Committee's interpretation as having 'legitimacy' will determine both how inclined they are to comply and the cost of non-compliance (in terms of the 'mobilisation of shame'). Thus, when States do not perceive that the Committee and its work have a high degree of 'legitimacy', the degree of compliance will be lower and it will be less costly to ignore the Committee's interpretation.[64]

3.2 The Committee's legal standing

Before embarking on an examination of the 'legitimacy' of the Committee's interpretation of the Covenant, it is necessary to briefly assess the legal standing of the Committee.

As analysed earlier,[65] the Covenant does not establish a special body to monitor implementation. It merely entrusts the Economic and Social Council (ECOSOC) with the responsibility of monitoring implementation by the States Parties, principally through the examination of States' reports. From 1979 to 1986, a Working Group composed first of government representatives and subsequently of governmental experts, supervised the Covenant. In 1985 the Committee on Economic, Social and Cultural Rights was created by ECOSOC Resolution 1985/17.[66] This makes the Committee a peculiar UN treaty-monitoring body because, rather than being established by the

---

63 Franck, T.M.: The power of legitimacy among nations. Oxford University Press, New York, Oxford, (1990), p. 24.
64 *Ibidem*: p. 49.
65 See Chapter I section 2.
66 UN doc. E/RES/1985/17, 28 May 1985.

Covenant, it is a subsidiary organ of ECOSOC. Formally speaking, the Committee's mandate is merely to 'assist' ECOSOC, rather than being directly responsible for the supervision of the Covenant. [67]

Admittedly, to some extent, the special status of the Committee places it in a vulnerable situation, because a decision by ECOSOC could terminate the Committee's existence. Although it would be highly desirable to put an end to this uncertainty by bringing the Committee into line with other human rights supervisory bodies, to do so would require an amendment of the text of the Covenant, a procedure that is burdensome and only binding on those States Parties that accept it.[68]

Fortunately, until now the legal standing of the Committee has been more of an advantage rather than an obstacle to its work. The ECOSOC has allowed the Committee to act with independence, it has enjoyed broad discretion to develop its working methods and it has had some degree of financial stability.[69] In practice, although the Committee is not a 'treaty body' *per se*, over more than fifteen years it has performed its tasks on an equal footing with the treaty bodies and has achieved recognition and respect.

It is therefore important to emphasise that it seems unnecessary to differentiate the Committee from other UN treaty monitoring bodies because of its peculiar legal standing. In examining the Committee's 'legitimacy' (that is to say, the factors that bring pressure upon States to comply with its work), it is appropriate to treat the Committee as we would any other treaty-monitoring body. The *sui generis* legal standing of the Committee differentiates it in only a very formal manner from the other bodies and has no direct consequence on the factors that bring pressure upon States Parties to comply with its pronouncements. It seems unlikely that a State Party to the Covenant will consider the legal standing of the Committee as an element weighing in favour of non-compliance.

Arguably, the fact that the legal status of the Committee is somewhat uncertain, makes it even more crucial for the Committee to act in a manner that leads to the recognition of its work by States Parties, NGOs and individuals. As long as the Committee's interpretations of the Covenant are perceived as enjoying a high degree of 'legitimacy' it will be more costly for States Parties not to comply with them.

---

67 As the respective mandates of other human rights supervisory bodies come from the treaties that establish them, they are directly responsible for their supervisory activities before the States Parties to that Covenant.

68 See Art. 29 of the Covenant and Art. 40 VCLT. For a comprehensive review of the legal procedures available to bring the Committee's mandate into line with those of other human rights treaty bodies, see the report submitted by the Secretary-General in response to the ECOSOC Res. E/1996/38 of 26 July 1996. E/1996/101 of 30 September 1996.

69 See, Alston, 1992, pp. 488-489 and Craven, 1998, p. 51.

3.3 The 'legitimacy' of the Committee's work

Although the Committee's interpretations of the Covenant (principally through its Concluding Observations and General Comments), are not legally binding, there is a bundle of factors that brings pressure upon States to comply with its interpretation. As long as the Committee satisfies the factors that give rise to 'legitimacy,' it will be costly for State Parties to reject the Committee's interpretations to satisfy other perceived interests.

In examining the 'legitimacy' of the Committee's interpretative function as regards the Covenant, I propose to analyse the following indicators:[70]

(a) Independence and expertise; (b) diversity; (c) continuity and coherence; (d) predictability; (e) efficiency; (f) objectivity; (g) reasonableness and practicability; and (h) support in the work of other international bodies.[71]

This bundle of factors compels States Parties to comply with the Committee's interpretation of the Covenant. These factors should be seriously analysed and taken into account by the Committee (and in general by all treaty-monitoring bodies), if it expects its pronouncements to enjoy a high level of compliance by States Parties. As is clearly explained elsewhere, legitimacy is a matter of degree[72] and therefore the 'legitimacy' of the Committee depends on the level of fulfilment of these indicators.

The following analysis first briefly explains each factor and subsequently examines whether the Committee satisfies it in practice. It is important to bear in mind that the fulfilment by the Committee of each of the factors is a matter of degree,[73] hence there will always be room for improvement.

3.3.1 Independence and expertise of members

The independence and expertise of the members is without doubt one of the central factors determining the legitimacy of the Committee's work. If there is no confidence in the Committee as a body of independent experts, States would not feel bound to comply with its views and the cost of non-compliance in terms of the mobilisation of shame would be low.

In contrast to the members of the first working group on the implementation of the Covenant who were government representatives, Committee members must be 'experts

70 Note that I have not employed the specific factors analysed by Frank. Examining the 'rule-legitimacy in the community of States', the factors Frank uses are: 'determinacy', 'symbolic validation', 'coherence' and 'adherence.'

71 These factors are indicative only, it is no doubt possible to identify other indicators of legitimacy for the Committee's work.

72 See, Franck, *op. cit.* (note 63), particularly Chapter 3, pp. 41-49.

73 Franck, *op. cit.* (note 63), pp. 3-26

with recognised competence in the field of human rights, serving in their personal capacity.'[74] Therefore, Committee members do not represent the States of which they are nationals and/or which have nominated them,[75] and they may not receive directions from governments.

In order to stress the independence of Committee members, it is required that, before assuming their duties, Committee members must make the following solemn declaration: 'I solemnly undertake to discharge my duties as a member of the Committee on Economic, Social and Cultural Rights impartially and conscientiously.'[76] The independence of the Committee members is further strengthened by the fact that the expenses of the Committee members are paid by the United Nations and not by Governments.

However, Committee membership is part-time (*ad honorem*), and Committee members certainly have to earn their living fulfilling others functions and they may (and in fact some of them do) occupy government positions. Obviously, this is not the ideal situation, and some scholars have expressed criticism in this regard.[77] However, the fact that some Committee members hold government positions should not necessarily lead to the conclusion that the Committee as a whole is not truly independent.

In the case of the members who occupy, or have occupied, governmental positions,[78] their independence should be analysed on a case by case basis. It will depend

74 ECOSOC Res. 1985/17 (b). It is interesting to note that the formal requirements for the Committee members seem to be less demanding than those for membership of the Human Rights Committee, in the sense that the latter requires not only 'recognised competence in the field of human rights' but also 'high moral character' (Art. 28 ICCPR).

75 As was analysed in Chapter I, States Parties may nominate non-nationals (see the text accompanying note 14).

76 As established by the 'Rules of Procedure of the Committee', contained in: E/C.12/1990/Rev.1 of 1 September 1993 (Rule 13).

77 See, for example, the criticisms by Robertson, with regard to the members of the HRC. Robertson, A.: 'The implementation system: international measures'. In: Henkin L. (ed.), The International Bill of Rights, Columbia University Press, New York, (1981), p. 338.

78 A survey of the present Committee's composition reveals that there are eight Committee members who are diplomats or who hold governmental positions: Mr. Ahmed (Diplomat, Egypt), Mr. Ceausu (Diplomat, Romania), Mr. Kouznetsov (Diplomat, Russian Federation; he is also an academic in the field of international law), Mr. Martynov (Diplomat, Belarus), Marchan Romero (Diplomat, Ecuador), Mr. Rattray (Adviser to the Government of Jamaica, Jamaica), Mr. Sadi (Diplomat, Jordan) and Mr. Wimer Zambrano (Diplomat, Mexico). The information on the Committee's members has been obtained from the contact list of the Committee's members which is available at the Secretariat of the Committee, on file with the author, from the curricula vitae of the members of the Committee [UN doc. CESCR/Members of July 4, 2001] as well as from information made available by the Commonwealth of Australia. Available at: http://www.dfat.gov.au/qwon/1999_2001/001101_a.html (last visited July 2002). It is important to note that in the exercise of their functions, Committee members should also be immune to influence from any non-governmental organisations with which they might have relations. Due to the fact that there is no information available on the affiliation of Committee members to NGOs, this issue is not analysed here. However, it would be convenient for the Committee to follow Guidelines Nos. 7 and 8 of the 'Guidelines for the exercise of their functions by members of the Human

on many factors such as the specific position, their level of expertise and commitment to the Committee's work,[79] as well as the practice of their governments (some Governments would be more inclined than others to exert political pressure).[80] Nonetheless, it is certainly up to each Committee member to make the utmost effort to be, and to appear to be, independent from his or her government.[81]

The Committee as a whole seems to attach a high degree of importance to this factor, and as one commentator recognises, 'members of the Committee have consistently stressed their independence before State representatives and there is little evidence of them allowing political affiliations to compromise their role in examining State reports.'[82] The Committee has also developed some practices aimed at ensuring the independence of its members. For example, it is established practice that each Committee member does not generally participate in the examination of the report presented by the country of which they are a national.

From this author's perspective, although it is not the ideal situation, the fact that some members of the Committee hold governmental positions does not undermine *per se* the independence of the whole body. It does not follow that holding a government position necessarily affects a member's independence. However, this is a delicate situation because any serious questioning of the independence of its members would negatively affect the legitimacy of the Committee as a whole.

It is relevant to note here the 'guidelines for the exercise of their functions by members of the Human Rights Committee.' This document, developed by the Human Rights Committee, stresses the importance of the independence of the members of the Committee, and sets out detailed guidelines for the application of this principle with regard to the participation of the members in considering State reports and in communications, as well as in their relationships with non-governmental organisations and their Governments.[83] It would be desirable for the Committee to adopt similar guidelines or adhere to those of the Human Rights Committee as a way to strengthen its commitment to the maintenance of the independence of its members. This kind of guideline should most certainly be instituted in the event of the adoption of an optional protocol establishing a petition procedure.

With regard to the expertise required, it would be fair to say that despite the fact

Rights Committee'. See note 83.

79 Reflected, for example, in their record of attendance at the Committee's sessions.

80 It would be reasonable to conclude, for example, that a State with strong democratic institutions and a tradition of respect for human rights would be less inclined to give instructions to their national experts than a State with a newly established democracy or with weak democratic institutions.

81 As the Human Rights Committee has noted, the Committee members 'should not only be impartial, but should also appear to be so.' Guidelines for the exercise of their functions by members of the Human Rights Committee, Report of the Human Rights Committee, A/53/40 vol. 1, Annex 3, para. 2.

82 Craven, *op. cit.* (note 59), p. 48. (Footnote omitted).

83 'Guidelines for the exercise of their functions by members of the Human Rights Committee', Report of the Human Rights Committee, A/53/40 vol. 1, Annex 3, para. 5.

that one might question the 'genuine' expertise of some members of the Committee over the years, the expertise of the Committee as a whole has been reflected in its work. It goes without saying that many recognised experts in the field of economic, social and cultural rights are and have been members of the Committee. However, as Craven correctly noted in 1995, 'it is apparent that the Committee does not possess expertise in all the subject areas encompassed by the Covenant.'[84] This statement is probably true not only of the composition of the Committee in the past, but also of the current composition. While the supervision of the Covenant requires expertise in a variety of fields, including public health, macroeconomic policies, education, housing and so forth, in practice there seems to be a limited range of expertise, as reflected by the overrepresentation of the legal profession. In fact, 14 of the 18 current Committee members have a legal background.[85] It appears that only four of them come from other academic disciplines, specifically, fine arts, economics and international affairs.[86]

The limited range of specialities within the Committee is certainly a significant deficiency of the Committee's current composition. As Scott notes, 'whatever necessary skills they bring to the interpretative enterprise, lawyers cannot claim a monopoly of knowledge of the interpretative *content* to be given to human rights.'[87] Certainly, greater 'diversity of knowledge' would be necessary to enhance the legitimacy of the Committee charged with supervising compliance with economic, social and cultural rights.

3.3.2 Diversity of membership

Another important indicator of legitimacy is the diversity of the Committee's members. The crucial value of the diversity factor in all treaty bodies, including the Committee, has been clearly discussed elsewhere and it is not necessary to analyse it in any detail here.[88]

---

84 Craven, *op. cit.* (note 59), p. 45.

85 They are Mr. Atangana (Judge, Supreme Court, Cameroon); Ms. Barahona Riera (Academic, Law, Costa Rica); Mr. Hunt (Academic, Law, New Zealand); Mr. Kouznetsov (Academic, International Law, and Diplomat, Russian Federation); Mr. Malinverni (Academic, Constitutional Law, Switzerland); Mr. Pillay (Chief Justice, Supreme Court, Mauritius); Mr. Riedel (Academic, Law, Germany); Mr. Sadi (Diplomat, Attorney at Law, Jordan); Mr. Texier (Judge, Conseiller à la Cour de Cassation, France); Mr. Thapalia (Academic, Law/Political Science, Nepal); Mr. Ceausu (Diplomat, Romania); Mr. Marchan Romero (Diplomat, Ecuador); Mr. Rattray (Adviser to the Government, Jamaica); and Mr. Wimer Zambrano (Diplomat, Mexico).

86 Ms. Bonoan-Dandan (Academic in Fine Arts, Philippines); Mr. Grissa (Academic, Economics, Tunisia); Mr. Ahmed (Diplomat, Egypt, with a background in International Affairs); and Mr. Martynov (Diplomat, Belarus, with a background in International Affairs).

87 Scott, 2000, p. 403.

88 See in particular the comprehensive analysis by C. Scott. *Ibidem*: pp. 411-417. The author analyses the value of 'diversity of knowledge' in two components: 'diversity of disciplinary expertise' and 'diversity of social experience.' The analysis here corresponds to the latter.

The ECOSOC Resolution that established the Committee prescribes that the election of its members shall be made with 'due consideration being given to equitable geographical distribution and to the representation of different forms of social and legal systems; to this end, fifteen seats will be equally distributed among the regional groups, while the additional three seats will be allocated in accordance with the increase in the total number of States Parties per regional group.'[89] In practice, this means that each geopolitical group[90] has three members and that the Latin American, African, and Western European and Other groups each have one extra seat.[91]

This rule is designed to ensure that the Committee is composed of individuals belonging to different cultures and social realities. Diversity is an important factor for legitimacy. Here again Scott provides the explanation:

> 'It seems evident enough that these bodies [treaty bodies] need to be diversity-sensitive in a strong sense, given that one of the central normative functions of international human rights supervision is to understand, reveal and help counteract exercises of power that produce oppression for dominated social groups. This function will be undermined without the insight of lived experience being part of the international institutional dialogue. As such, the judgement exercised by the institution risks being systematically impaired if the perspectives of such groups are not adequately represented.'[92]

With regard to the Committee's composition, it has been reported that 'the range of legal systems found on the international plane are generally well represented with a mixture of common law and civil systems and a variety of constitutional forms with different philosophies. Similarly, there is a fairly wide representation of differing social structures.'[93] As to the variety of legal systems represented, this statement remains valid with regard to the present composition of the Committee. Nevertheless, one significant deficiency of the Committee's composition is the gender inequality among its members. Women have been underrepresented among the Committee members and, in fact, at present only two of eighteen members are women.[94]

---

89 ECOSOC Res. 1985/17, XXIIth plenary meeting, 28 May 1985 para. b.

90 The geopolitical regions are the following: African, Asian, Latin American and Caribbean, Central and Eastern European, and Western European and Others.

91 The nominating countries of the present Committee member are as follows, Mr. Ahmed (Egypt); Mr. Atangana (Cameroon); Ms. Barahona Riera (Costa Rica); Ms. Bonoan-Dandan (Philippines); Mr. Ceausu (Romania); Mr. Grissa (Tunisia); Mr. Hunt (New Zealand); Mr. Kouznetsov (Russian Federation); Mr. Malinverni (Switzerland); Mr. Martynov (Belarus); Mr. Marchan Romero (Ecuador); Mr. Pillay (Mauritius); Mr.Riedel (Germany); Mr. Rattray (Jamaica); Mr. Sadi (Jordan); Mr. Texier (France); Mr. Thapalia (Nepal); and Mr. Wimer Zambrano (Mexico).

92 Scott, *op. cit.* (note 87), p. 403.

93 Craven, *op. cit.* (note 59), p. 44.

94 Ms. Barahona Riera (Costa Rica) and Ms. Bonoan-Dandan (Philippines).

3.3.3 Continuity and coherence

Frequent changes in the Committee's composition, as was the case in the working group that preceded the Committee, have proven to be disruptive and may lead to work that lacks coherence or consistency. For the Committee to maintain a set of core principles and a determined course of action, it is important that its members serve for a reasonable period of time. Moreover, the longer members are able to serve, the greater the confidence and expertise they are able to develop within the context of the Committee and its relations with the Secretariat and States Parties.[95] The continuity of membership has also had positive consequences in terms of the independence of the members.

In an attempt to overcome the problems faced by the first working group due to the one-year mandate of its members,[96] it was decided that the mandate would have to be longer. According to the ECOSOC Resolution that established the Committee, members are to be elected for 4 years and are eligible for re-election, with the election of half of the membership every two years.

In general, the Committee has enjoyed a high degree of continuity. In fact, many Committee members have been re-elected, serving for eight years and some for even longer.[97] Certainly, this factor has been an advantage because it has allowed the Committee to maintain a core position on many topics, such as in the distribution of wealth, poverty, discrimination and forced evictions.

A careful analysis of the Committee's work also suggests that, over the years, some Committee members have consistently pursued specific thematic areas of expertise in the dialogue with State representatives. The principal advantages of this are that it has enabled them to be very specific in their questioning and has meant that certain subjects have become *de rigueur* in the dialogue.[98]

---

95 According to Craven, for example, the continuity of Committee membership has the advantage that it 'promotes stability through allowing the development of inter-personal relationships which can help to avoid unnecessary friction.' Craven, *op. cit.* (note 69), p. 43.

96 See the overview of the Committee's establishment in Chapter I section 2.

97 For example, Ms. Jiménez Butragueño, who was first a member of the Sessional Working Group on Independent Experts, then a Committee member for 8 years. Mr. Alston was Rapporteur from 1987-1990 and Chairperson from 1991-1998.

98 For example, Ms. Jiménez Butragueño consistently stressed the importance of the protection of the rights of elderly persons. This is evident from the fact that she was the rapporteur for the draft General Comment No. 6 regarding older persons, but moreover, because over the years, she tirelessly put questions to State representatives on the topic. See, for example, E/C.12/1996/SR.37 para. 43; E/C.12/1997/SR.38, E/C.12/1998/SR.48 para. 65 and E/C.12/2000/SR.4 para. 42. It is also possible to link other topics to specific members. For example, Mr. Hunt is actively interested in questions relating to the effects of the policies implemented by States with the support of international financial institutions, such as the World Bank and the IMF. See, for example, E/C.12/2000/SR.6 para. 49 and E/C.12/2000/SR.11 para.15.

3.3.4 Predictability

Linked with the consistency of the Committee is the predictability of some responses. To the degree that the Committee maintains an identifiable line of reasoning and course of action, States Parties are able to expect that some types of behaviour will be subject to strong condemnation by the Committee. Therefore, they will have the opportunity to weigh their options and may realise that sometimes it is preferable to act in conformity with the Committee's views in order to avoid strong condemnation, if this is likely to occur.

Nonetheless, the Committee must be very cautious in this regard. It must act with rigour, marking a pattern in its responses to States, but in a constructive way, in order not to provide a disincentive to co-operation.

The predictability of a strict response by the Committee to some forms of behaviour could occur in relation to procedural as well as substantive issues. In other words, the Committee may establish a strict line in the way that it assesses some States' behaviour in relation to the application of substantive rights, as well as in the procedural matters related to the supervision of the Covenant.

The Committee has developed predictability in both of these respects. Informed States should be aware of the way that the Committee will react to given forms of State behaviour. For example, in the past, the Committee allowed some States to postpone the examination of their reports, even though this practice was extremely disruptive.[99] At its eighth session in 1993, the Committee decided to amend its rules of procedure and established that once a State Party has agreed to the scheduling of its reports, the Committee will proceed with the examination of the report even in the absence of a representative of the State Party.[100]

Certainly, this decision requires that the Committee should strike a tactful balance. On the one hand, if the Committee were to accept a postponement, it would send the wrong signal to States that have made a great effort to submit their reports on time and it might lead them to take their obligations less seriously in future. On the other hand, the Committee must be very cautious in order not to undermine the participation of the State in the supervision. The Committee must act with severity, but in a constructive way, a balance that is certainly difficult to achieve in practice.

With regard to requests for postponement, the Committee has managed to keep to a recognisable course of action. So far, States Parties seem to understand that even if they request a postponement, the Committee will examine the report anyway. Since the Committee adopted this policy, the number of requests for postponement has decreased significantly. While five States requested postponements in the first eight sessions,

99 E/2001/22, Chapter II, para. 42.
100 E/1994/22 para. 347. Rules of Procedures No. 62(3).

nowadays such requests are very exceptional and the Committee does not usually grant them.[101]

A continuous, strict response by the Committee on substantive issues may also positively influence States to take measures at the domestic level in order to avoid strong criticism from the Committee. For example, if a State Party does not incorporate the right to strike in its legislation, it is likely that the Committee will consider this as a violation of the Covenant (article 8 ICESCR) and state as much in its Concluding Observations.

If States receive more signals of the Committee's strict approach to some forms of behaviour, in most cases they would take greater care to avoid conduct that could lead to censure by the Committee.

3.3.5 Efficiency

The legitimacy of the Committee's work also depends on the effective use of the limited time and resources at its disposal. The Committee has to perform its function within a limited time[102] and with extremely limited resources including limited assistance from the Secretariat and a lack of appropriate technological support, such as

---

101 There are some exceptions. For example, during its tenth session the Committee considered the request of the Dominican Republic and postponed the examination of the report to the next session in 'view of exceptional circumstances' [E/1994/22 para. 207]. During its twenty-second session in May 2000 the Committee agreed to postpone the examination of the Third Periodic Report of Portugal, which was scheduled for that session but was finally examined during the twenty-fourth session in November 2000. Nonetheless, in the case of Portugal, during the twenty-second session representatives of the State appeared before the Committee to offer a detailed apology which was accepted by the Committee which seemed convinced that Portugal had taken its commitment under the Covenant seriously [See E/C.12/2000/SR.10]. In recent years, the Committee has become more rigorous, for example, in November 2000, the Permanent Mission of Yugoslavia to the United Nations Office at Geneva requested the Committee to postpone the examination of the Third Periodic Report of the Federal Republic of Yugoslavia and to prepare a new report. Having considered the request, and despite the truly exceptional circumstances pertaining to the country, the Committee decided to proceed with the scheduled consideration of the report but in a preliminary discussion. Thus, the Committee agreed on a number of preliminary recommendations aimed to assist the State to prepare the new report. Additionally, the Committee fixed a date for the submission of the new report by the State. See E/2001/22, Chapter II, para. 72 and Preliminary Recommendations Yugoslavia E/2001/22 paras. 496-511.

102 The Committee has very limited time to examine State Party reports. Since 1997 it generally has two ordinary sessions of three weeks each per year [E/RES/1995/39 of 25 July 1995]. In 1999 the Committee requested ECOSOC to authorise the holding of additional extraordinary sessions. The ECOSOC approved the holding of two additional three-week extraordinary sessions during 2000 and 2001 respectively. The sessions were used to reduce the backlog of reports. Accordingly, in 2000 the Committee held its twenty-third (extraordinary) session from 14 August to 1 September 2000 and during 2001 it held its twenty-sixth (extraordinary) session from 13 to 31 August 2001. At each session, the Committee has devoted three meetings of three hours each to the public examination of a State report and generally between two and three hours to discussing each set of Concluding Observations in private. E/2001/22, Chapter I, para. 4.

laptops and Internet access. Due to the budgetary crisis at the UN, these problems seem to be structural and it is not foreseen that they will change in the short term. Given these circumstances, the legitimacy of the Committee will depend on its ability to deal with these constraints in an efficient manner.

It goes without saying that the improvement of this situation is a matter of urgency, not only in regard to supervision of the Covenant, but in general in relation to all treaty bodies. As commentators have noted, without major improvements, the effectiveness of the UN human rights treaty monitoring system will be under threat.[103]

If supervision is to be effective, an optimal use of limited resources is required of the Committee. Only by carefully allocating its time and resources will the Committee be able to examine the State reports with the efficiency required.

The Committee is characterised by an ability to innovate and is continuously reviewing its working methods to improve the efficiency and effectiveness of its supervision. Examples of good practices in this respect are the procedure developed by the Committee to deal with the following issues:

(i) *The non-submission of or excessively overdue State reports*

The backlog in the submission and examination of State reports is one of the most serious problems that undermine the efficacy of the system and could be said to be of such gravity that it affects the legitimacy of the Committee.[104] Faced with this serious threat, during its ninth session the Committee began to examine the implementation of the Covenant in persistent non-reporting States without the benefit of the relevant reports, instead making use of all the information which was available.[105] Again, this decision required a sensitive approach. If the Committee would not have taken any measures against the non-submission of or excessively overdue reports, it would have sent the wrong signal to those States that have made a great effort to submit their reports on time and this might lead them to take their obligations less seriously. On the other hand, the Committee must be very cautious in order not to undermine the

103 See generally, Alston, P. & Crawford, J.: The future of human rights treaty monitoring. Cambridge University Press, Cambridge, (2000). In addition see: 'Final report on enhancing the long-term effectiveness of the United Nations Systems', prepared by P. Alston, UN doc. E/CN.4/1997/74.

104 In 1997, the Committee considered the backlog of reports as one of the two major challenges facing it. In its analysis, it is apparent how the problem of this backlog negatively affects the legitimacy of the system. As the Committee notes, 'the backlog of State Parties' reports to be considered is unacceptable for several reasons: (a) with the existing backlog, the possibility of examining reports, inasmuch as they are considered in chronological order, is delayed by two years or more; (b) as more reports are submitted the backlog will get much worse; (c) this situation causes significant inconvenience to States Parties; (d) by the time the pending reports are finally considered they may require considerable updating; (e) Specialised agencies, non-governmental organisations and others with an interest in the reports cannot plan properly under such circumstances.' E/1998/22, Chapter VII para. 505.

105 See in E/1998/22, Chapter III, section D: 'Procedures in response to non-submission and considerably overdue reports.'

participation of States in the supervisory process and to be able to perform the task with seriousness. In the event that the State does not provide any information, it is doubly important for the Committee to have a range of sources of information which will provide it with a clear impression of the situation in the country concerned.

On the whole, the Committee has been relatively successful in the application of this policy. For example, during its twentieth session, the Committee considered the situation of the Solomon Islands without a report and in the absence of any representative from the State concerned and adopted its preliminary Concluding Observations.[106] At its twenty-first session, the Committee reconsidered the situation of the country with the aim of determining the possible actions by the Committee, the OHCHR, specialised agencies and other UN organs that could assist the Government in complying with its obligations.[107] At this follow-up meeting, a representative of the State was present and expressed the willingness of the Government of the Solomon Islands to co-operate with the Committee in order to finalise the drafting of the report as soon as possible and to submit it to the Committee.[108]

With such clear practice by the Committee, States will be aware that if they are long overdue in their reporting obligations, the Committee will sooner or later schedule the examination of the Covenant's implementation even in the absence of a report. Therefore it is in the interest of the State to submit a report.

(ii) *Unfocused dialogue with State representatives*
Another problem that the Committee needs to tackle is the tendency of unfocused dialogue with Government representatives. Vague and repeated questions from Committee members lead to irrelevant answers from Government representatives.

The Committee itself has recognised this fact, acknowledging that the dialogue with States is 'often too diffuse and untargeted making it difficult for representatives who wish to answer constructively to do so adequately and making it very easy for representatives who prefer to keep the dialogue at the level of generality and abstraction.'[109] The Committee has taken this problem seriously, considering the advantages that a more focused dialogue may have.[110]

---

106 E/2000/22, paras. 184-212.
107 E/2000/22, Chapter VI, paras. 410-416.
108 E/2000/22, Chapter VI, para. 415.
109 E/1998/22, Chapter VII, para. 507.
110 According to the Committee, in the event of a better focused dialogue, '(a) it would provide, in advance, a better indication of the principal issues; (b) it would demonstrate the Committee's knowledge of the situation and its desire and capacity to go into selected issues in depth; (c) it would facilitate requests to specialised agencies and NGOs for targeted and up to date information on specific issues; (d) it would enhance the prospect that genuine experts would be sent by the reporting State; (e) it would facilitate the preparation of clearer and more precise concluding observations, thus enabling the State Party, NGOs and the media to know precisely how things stood and providing a much stronger basis for follow-up measures by the Committee.' E/1998/22, Chapter VII, para. 508.

The Committee has made important efforts to impose discipline and time-limits in order to structure the dialogue.[111]

Moreover, the aim of establishing a pre-sessional working group was precisely to focus the dialogue by identifying in advance questions which are likely to be the principal focus of the dialogue, enabling State representatives to prepare their answers in advance.

Nonetheless, the Committee still has a way to go in making meaningful dialogue the general rule. We often still find vague dialogue and the Chairperson calling upon State representatives as well as Committee members to be more precise and targeted.[112] Members have to make efforts to target their questions.

The necessity of a focused dialogue is not only for its own sake. Rather, it is a means to an end because the more focused and precise the dialogue with the Government representatives, the easier it is to measure the difficulties faced by the State in the implementation of the Covenant as well as to draft more precise and targeted Concluding Observations. To the extent that the Committee's interpretations of the obligations imposed by the Covenant contained in the General Comments and Concluding Observations are more precise, the easier it is for States Parties to comply with them and for the Committee to assess State compliance.[113]

(iii) *Compliance with the Concluding Observations and with follow-up measures*

In December 1999, the Committee decided to include in all of its Concluding Observations a request to each State Party to inform the Committee in its next periodic report the steps it has taken to implement the recommendations. If States were to seriously comply with this request, it would certainly facilitate the accountability of States. However, the Committee will need to take a series of measures to ensure that States comply, otherwise it may damage its own legitimacy. Specifically, it is necessary for the Committee to achieve more precision in its Concluding Observations, because the more precise, clear and specific these are, the easier it is to follow them up.

So far, the Committee has not been very successful in achieving compliance with follow-up requests to States Parties. When the Committee requests that States take measures in response to specific recommendations made at a previous session, these

---

111 As has been established, during the presentation of the State reports the Committee has urged members not to '(a) raise issues outside the scope of the Covenant; (b) repeat questions already posed or answered; (c) add unduly to an already long list on a particular issue; or (d) speak more than five minutes in any intervention. The Chairperson and/or individual members may, if necessary, intervene concisely to indicate whenever the dialogue seems to be going off on a tangent, when responses seem to be taking an unduly long time, or when answers lack the necessary focus and precision.' E/2001/22, Chapter II, para. 38.

112 See, for example, E/C.12/2000/SR.11 para. 66 [Egypt] and E/C.12/2001/SR.35 para. 33 [Syrian Arab Republic].

113 This latter factor is more related to the legitimacy of the rule rather than the legitimacy of the body called upon to interpret it.

recommendations generally require the provision of additional information in the next periodic report or, on occasion, on a given date before the report is presented.[114] However, there is poor compliance with the Committee's requests. As indicated by the Committee, up to January 2002, of the fifteen cases in which the Committee had required specific follow-up measures, the States in question had taken action in less than half of these cases.[115]

This is a very delicate issue, particularly bearing in mind that on some occasions the Committee has asked States to provide information in specific individual cases. For example, in 1996 the Committee requested that the United Kingdom should provide information on the case of three Vietnamese refugees in Hong Kong who had been denied medical and dental treatment mainly for refusing to return voluntarily to Vietnam. Fortunately, in this case the State replied before the deadline imposed by the Committee. However, this case was exceptional. There have been other situations in which the Committee has requested follow-up measures in the protection of specific individuals and not achieved the expected result. For example, in 1998 the Committee urged the Government of Nigeria to release two trade union leaders who had been imprisoned for four and two years, respectively, without being charged or tried. The Nigerian Delegation could not explain why they had not been tried or charged. Although the measures requested were urgent, up to January 2002 there was no indication in the records of the Committee of any action taken by Nigeria in response to its request.[116] While it is important that the Committee should, at the very least, try to provide protection in the individual cases that come to its attention, the Committee needs to be very careful in formulating its requests in order not to threaten its legitimacy. It would be desirable for the Committee to respond in a rigorous and strict manner when States do not comply with its requests for follow-up measures, otherwise it might encourage further transgressions in the future because States do not feel bound to comply.

(iv) *Flexibility in the face of obstacles*

The effectiveness of the Committee's work also depends on its capacity to react with creativity to the problems it encounters in carrying out its functions. Throughout its existence there have been many instances in which the Committee has increased the effectiveness of its work by reacting to problems with pragmatism. Perhaps, the most far-reaching were the decisions to request that the Dominican Republic and Panama

114 Unfortunately, the Committee does not make public the additional information provided by States in response to a request for follow-up measures, therefore it is not possible to assess whether or not the responses have been satisfactory.

115 See: 'Follow-up to the consideration of reports under articles 16 and 17 of the Covenant', E/C.12/2002/3 of 10 January 2001.

116 E/C.12/2002/3 of 10 January 2002, pp. 10-11.

should accept on-site missions after it became apparent that these two States would not provide the Committee with all the additional information requested of them.

The Committee has also demonstrated flexibility with regard to the periodic nature of the State reports. According to the Committee's rules of procedure (rule 58),[117] after the initial report, subsequent reports are to be submitted at five-year intervals. However, due to the backlog in the examination of reports, the Committee noted that 'a strict interpretation of the five-year rule may lead to the situation where a State Party's next periodic report is due the same year as the Committee's consideration of the State's preceding report.' In the face of this problem, the Committee decided during its twenty-fourth session to follow a more flexible rule. Thus 'as a general rule, a State Party's next periodic report should be submitted five years after the Committee's consideration of the State's preceding report.' However, the Committee may reduce this five-year period on the basis of criteria such as the quality of the information submitted by the State and the constructive dialogue, the adequacy of the State Party's response to the Concluding Observations and the State Party's record of compliance with the Covenant at the domestic level.[118]

Nonetheless, this reaction provides evidence of a more serious and structural problem, which is the delay between the submission and the examination of reports. The Committee has attempted to resolve the problem through additional extraordinary sessions.[119] Although these sessions were only aimed at the examination of State reports, the backlog remains. If no additional extraordinary sessions are allowed, the Committee would need to identify the means to respond to the delays without undermining the quality of its work. In this regard, the option of examining a large number of reports, without an increase in the length of sessions and/or secretariat assistance, might lead to superficial examination which would negatively affect the Committee's legitimacy.

(v) *Professional Secretariat*

Finally, the support that the Committee may receive from the Secretariat is also a relevant factor for improving the efficiency and quality of the Committee's work. A dedicated, specialised Secretariat would facilitate the work of the Committee, as well as assist in retaining the 'institutional memory.'

The support that the Committee has received from the Secretariat over the years has proved to be insufficient. In 1995, the Committee expressed its dissatisfaction because,

---

117 The 'Rules of procedure of the Committee' are contained in UN doc. E/C.12/1990/4/Rev.1 of September 1, 1993.

118 E/2001/22, Chapter VII, 'Review of the methods of work of the Committee,' para. 637.

119 In 1999, ECOSOC [decision 199/287] and the General Assembly [Res. 54/251 (Part IV, of 23 December 1999] approved two additional extraordinary sessions of three weeks which were held from 14 August to 1 September (twenty-third session) and from 13-31 August 2001 (twenty-sixth session). E/2001/22, Chapter I, paras. 4-5. (See note 102)

for a number of years, it had requested, without success, that the Secretary-General provide adequate secretariat support and the services of a full-time expert in the field.[120] The situation at this point was serious and the Committee felt obliged to draw attention to the fact that 'there is not a single specialist in these rights within the Centre for Human Rights [...]. It considers this situation to be a negation of the off-proclaimed equality of the two sets of rights.'[121] The following year, the Committee emphasised that the necessity of expert Secretariat support was even more pressing due the fact 'that economic, social and cultural rights differed significantly from the issues generally dealt with by the Secretariat.'[122]

In the 'Plan of Action to Strengthen the Implementation of the International Covenant on Economic, Social and Cultural Rights'[123] the necessity for the Committee to receive greater support was strongly emphasised. It indicated that,

> 'The Committee has been the most innovative of all treaty bodies [...]. Many of its procedural and other innovations have been adopted by the other treaty bodies and have been warmly welcomed by the Commission on Human Rights, the Economic and Social Council and the General Assembly. Nevertheless, the Committee has been unable to take full advantage of its own efforts because of a lack of expert staff assistance. To a greater extent than other treaty bodies, the Committee on Economic, Social and Cultural Rights is called upon to deal with issues that are particularly complex and receive very little attention from the perspective of particular rights elsewhere within the international system.'[124]

The situation seems to have improved in recent years. At least in its Annual Report for the year 2000, the Committee noted with appreciation the increasing flow of public information that it is receiving from the Secretariat which has led to greater efficiency and quality in its work.[125]

Recapitulating, to the extent that the Committee uses its staff and available time with greater efficiency and creativity, it increases the 'legitimacy' of its work in the eyes of States Parties, favouring compliance by States. In contrast, however, if the Committee exposes itself to public criticism in regard to the way that it uses its limited time and resources, it will negatively affect the level of compliance. Therefore, the Committee needs to continuously re-examine its working methods in order to identify the most appropriate means to perform its functions with efficiency.

---

120 E/1996/22, Chapter VII, para. 393.
121 E/1996/22, Chapter VII, para. 350.
122 E/1997/22, Chapter VI, paras. 374-377.
123 The Plan of Action is contained in E/1997/22, Annex VII, p. 112 *et seq.*
124 E/1997/22 , Annex VII, para. 8.
125 E/2001/22, Chapter VII, para. 653.

3.3.6 Objectivity

Another factor which is important for assessing the degree of legitimacy of the Committee's interpretation of the Covenant is its capacity to perform an objective assessment of the accuracy of the information submitted by the State Party. It is of great relevance that the Committee receives information from a variety of reliable sources which allows it to compare and to evaluate the information received from States. If the Committee bases its work primarily or exclusively on information from States, it may undermine the objectivity of its conclusions. Moreover, being open to a variety of sources is relevant not only for achieving objectivity but also for improving the performance of its supervisory role.

In the reporting system, States Parties must provide the Committee with the necessary information through their reports and it is expected that the information is as objective as possible. However, although we cannot say that States are untruthful in their reports, it would be fair to say that States tend to be at least 'overoptimistic' in assessing their achievements, slightly benevolent in relation to their failures and forgetful of their mistakes. Therefore, the supervision of the Covenant requires that the Committee has recourse to other sources of information in order to contrast divergences and similarities and thus to obtain a clearer picture of the situation in the State Party.[126]

In this regard, the Committee should make better use of the information produced by specialised agencies, which have developed a great deal of expertise in many areas covered by the Covenant. But these sources of information are somewhat 'official' and UN agencies are sometimes overly cautious for fear of endangering relations with governments. Therefore, the Committee should be open to a wider variety of sources, particularly non-governmental sources.

The objectivity on the Committee's work does not depend solely on the variety and reliability of the information received by Committee members. Obviously it will also depend on the capacity of the Committee to process and evaluate this information, attaching to each source the relevance that it deserves. This is certainly a complex task. In order to avoid undermining the persuasiveness of its conclusions, the Committee must analyse the information received and evaluate it, assigning to each source a different level of importance depending on factors such as reliability, impartiality of the organisation and the technical methods used for the collection of information. For example, if the Committee places excessive importance on information received from

126 An interesting example is when the Committee reviewed the Third Periodic Report of Colombia [E/1994/104/Add.2]. The Committee also received three 'alternative' reports from NGOs as well as a report from the Colombian Ombudsman ('*Defensor del Pueblo*'). The many discrepancies between these reports and the State Report allowed the Committee constructively to undertake an in-depth analysis of the different positions during the dialogue. See E/C.12/1995/SR.32 particularly the interventions by Mr. Texier (para. 19), Mr. Thapalia (para. 23), Ms. Jiménez Butragueño (para. 26), Mr. Ahmed (para. 31) and Mr. Gonzalez (Colombia) (para. 44).

NGO sources, it may undermine its legitimacy in the eyes of States and therefore it must strike a proper balance.

There have been important developments in relation to the Committee's access to information over the years. While in the beginning the Committee was not open to information from different sources,[127] this situation has improved significantly as now the Committee welcomes information from a wide spectrum of sources.[128] In fact, Committee members now receive a significant amount of information from NGOs, interested individuals and specialised agencies, but they also receive a wide range of information collected by the Secretariat.[129]

From the summary records of the Committee, it is not rare to find that Committee members have taken information from a variety of sources, such as the national and international press,[130] NGO reports,[131] from the United States Department of State,[132] from the Concluding Observations of others treaty bodies,[133] the reports of specialised agencies, such as the UNDP Report[134] and even from television coverage.[135] The Committee has yet to make effective use of the information contained in reports by special rapporteurs and thematic mechanisms, as well as the information available from some specialised agencies and academic institutions. While we may not say that all sources provide objective information, we may at least agree that to the extent that Committee members are open to a variety of sources of information, there are greater guarantees that it will perform its work more objectively.

Finally, it is worth stressing that recourse to a wide range of reliable sources of information by the Committee is also essential for increasing the legitimacy of the Committee by improving its efficiency and the quality of its work. With more and better information, the Committee is in a better position to make incisive, precise and useful comments.

---

127 See, Alston, *op. cit.* (note 69), p. 503.

128 As the director of a leading NGO in the field of housing rights has noted, '[t]he Committee has gained growing support due to its openness to alternative information sources and its willingness, on occasion, to accept the credibility and reliability of this information, even when it contradicts reports or other representations by States Parties.' Leckie, S.: 'The Committee on Economic, Social and Cultural Rights: catalyst for change in a system needing reform.' In: The future of human rights treaty monitoring, *op. cit.* (note 103), p. 130.

129 E/2001/22, Chapter VII, para. 653.

130 See, for example, Ms. Jiménez Butragueño's intervention in E/C.12/1998/SR. 47 para. 27 and that of Mr. Riedel in E/C.12/1997/SR 38 para. 14.

131 See, for example, Mr. Thapalia E/C.12/2000/SR.6 para. 55.

132 See, for example, Mr. Pillay E/C.12/1998/SR.47 para. 62 and Mr. Rattray E/C.12/1997/SR.38 para. 12.

133 See, for example, Mr. Ahmed E/C.12/2000/SR.6 para. 42; List of Issues Italy 21/05/99 E/C.12/Q/ITA/1 para. 6 that mention the Concluding Observations of CERD and CEDAW with regard to Italy.

134 See, for example, Mr. Texier E/C.12/2000/SR.13.

135 See Mr. Ahmed E/C.12/1998/SR.33 para. 63.

3.3.7 Reasonableness and practicability

Another factor that influences the 'legitimacy' of the Committee is that it acts reasonably in its dealings with States Parties and requires from them the adoption of measures with which they might feasibly comply. This requires that the Committee demonstrate sound judgement, clarity and precision in its recommendations and that these clearly address the actual situation of the State.

States perceive that the Committee has a good understanding of their situations when it requests that they adopt measures with which they are able to comply. In this regard, it is crucial for the Committee to be able to differentiate the 'unwillingness' from the 'inability' of the State to comply with the Covenant's obligations.[136] Obviously, this is not an easy task and it requires a great deal of expertise and information.

The reasonableness of the Committee's pronouncements is very important because if the Committee requires the adoption of measures which are beyond the real possibilities of States they will simply not comply and the non-compliance by States Parties, in turn, will gravely threaten the legitimacy of the Committee.

In general, the Committee seems to act with common sense. The fact that it often provides for different treatment between developed and developing countries reflects this, because the standard of what is 'reasonable' for each category of States is in many cases different, particularly in relation to obligations to fulfil.[137] Nonetheless, in its recommendations the Committee is sometimes unnecessarily vague and needs to address some situations in a more precise manner.

On the whole, the Committee only makes requests which States can be reasonably expected to implement. In fact, the Committee might be criticised for being too cautious in this respect as it errs on the side of caution rather than making far-reaching or progressive requests to States.

3.3.8 Support received from other international bodies

The legitimacy of the Committee is enhanced when other international bodies support its work. Undoubtedly, the support of the UN political organs, such as the General Assembly and the Human Rights Commission, is of particular importance. When these bodies adopt resolutions reaffirming the work of the Committee, these resolutions undoubtedly act as legitimating factors that cannot be ignored.

---

136 According to the Maastricht Guidelines No. 13: '[i]n determining which actions or omissions amount to a violation of an economic, social or cultural right, it is important to distinguish the inability from the unwillingness of a State to comply with its treaty obligations.'

137 The obligation to respect (refrain from doing something), as well as the obligation to protect from third party violations are equal for developed and developing States in the vast majority of cases. However, when the Committee refers to obligations to fulfil, it differentiates between developed and developing States. See, for example, Concluding Observations Republic of Korea E/1996/22 para. 76 in comparison with Concluding Observations Colombia E/1996/22 para. 198. For an explanation of the typology of obligations see Chapter V sections 1 and 2.

In this regard, it is worth mentioning that the General Assembly has provided support for the Committee's work through a significant numbers of resolutions, recognising its work as well as calling upon States Parties to comply with its recommendations and views. For example, through its resolutions, the General Assembly has recognised the importance of the work performed by the Committee's examination of reports and the provision of recommendations. It has noted with appreciation the General Comments adopted, as well as the continuing efforts of the Committee to strive for uniform standards in the implementation of the provisions of the Covenant. It has also appealed to other bodies dealing with similar human rights questions to respect the standards expressed in the General Comments of the Committee. The General Assembly has also urged States Parties to the Covenant to make every effort to meet their reporting obligations, to take into account the Concluding Observations, emphasising the importance of their strict compliance with their obligations under the Covenant, and urging all States Parties whose reports have been examined by human rights treaty bodies to provide adequate follow-up to the observations and final comments of the treaty bodies. The General Assembly has also welcomed the contribution to the work of the human rights treaty bodies made by specialised agencies and other United Nations bodies and has invited them to continue to pursue further co-operation.[138]

This kind of support is also provided by the Commission of Human Rights, which has routinely noted with interest the work carried out by the Committee and has called upon States Parties to submit their reports in a regular and timely manner. The Commission has provided important support to the legitimacy of General Comments, noting with interest the 'the assistance given to States Parties in the fulfilment of their obligations through its general comments' and encouraging the Committee 'to continue its efforts towards the promotion and protection of human rights at national and international levels and the full realisation of specific rights, notably through the drafting of further general comments.'[139] In this regard, it is interesting to note that the Commission has repeatedly invited the Committee to draft and adopt a General Comment on the right to food as a 'contribution to the clarification of the content' of that right.[140] Consequently, after the adoption of General Comment No. 12, the Commission welcomed the work of the Committee.[141] On some occasions, the Commission has also taken note, with interest, of the day of general discussion held by the Committee.[142]

---

138 See, for example, A/RES/54/157 of 8 February 2000; A/RES/53/138 of 1 March 1999; A/RES/52/116 of 19 February 1998; A/RES/52/118 of 23 February 1998; A/RES/50/170 of 26 February 1996; A/RES/50/171 of 26 February 1996; A/RES/49/178 of 23 December 1994; and A/RES/48/119 of 11 March 1994.

139 See, for example, E/CN.4/RES/2000/9 of 11 April 2000.

140 See, for example, E/CN.4/RES/1999/24 of 23 April 1999 and E/CN.4/RES/1998/23 of 17 April 1998.

141 E/CN.4/RES/2000/10 of 17 April 2000.

142 See, for example, E/CN.4/RES/1999/25 of 23 April 1999.

The Commission has also called upon UN bodies, States and civil society in general, to take actions to confront some problems that hinder the effectiveness of the work of the treaty-monitoring bodies. This occurred, for example, with respect to the budgetary constraints of the treaty monitoring bodies. In this regard, the Commission has requested that the Secretary-General should provide adequate resources for each treaty body and make the most efficient use of existing resources in order to give the human rights treaty bodies adequate administrative support and better access to technical expertise and relevant information. It has also encouraged all Governments, United Nations bodies and specialised agencies, non-governmental organisations and interested persons to consider contributing to the appeal for extra budgetary resources for the treaty bodies.

Another obstacle to the effectiveness of the work of the treaty bodies that the Commission has considered is the backlog of reports, urging States Parties to make every effort to submit their reports to the Committee in a regular and timely manner. But it has also urged States Parties to take other actions such as contributing, individually and collectively, to the identification of practical proposals and ideas for improving the functioning of the treaty bodies, to carefully consider the Concluding Observations of the treaty bodies in identifying their needs for technical assistance and to promote a concerted effort to ensure the participation of representatives of all sectors of civil society in the process of preparation of their reports and to withdraw reservations.[143] The continuing efforts of the treaty-monitoring bodies to improve the reporting procedures have not passed without notice by the Commission. The Commission has welcomed and supported improvements made by the treaty bodies as reflected in their respective annual reports.[144]

The legitimacy of the Committee is also bolstered when different treaty bodies share a common approach on a variety of issues covered by the Covenant. As more international bodies provide support, for example in the fight against domestic violence, for gender equality, for protecting the Roma community, for condemning human trafficking, and so forth, the more positive the reception by States Parties of the measures adopted by the Committee on these related issues.

As we have analysed, the Committee's interpretations of the Covenant also finds support in the work of expert bodies, such as other UN treaty bodies and the UN Sub-Commission, as well as in the work of some specialised agencies which deal with economic, social and cultural rights under their mandates. It is relevant to note that co-ordination through formal (*e.g.* the Chairperson's meetings), and informal arrangements with other treaty monitoring bodies, as well as specialised agencies which deal with issues of interest under the Covenant, is essential to achieve broad support and a

143 See, for example, E/CN.4/RES/2000/75 of 26 April 2000, E/CN.4/RES/1999/25 of 23 April 1999 and E/CN.4/RES/1998/33 of 17 April 1998.

144 E/CN.4/RES/2000/75 of 26 April 2000.

common pattern of development, taking into account the need to avoid unnecessary duplication, and rationalising the limited time and resources.

3.4 Concluding Comments on the legitimacy of the Committee

Given the absence of an express provision establishing the Committee's interpretation as being binding, the will of States Parties to comply depends on the 'legitimacy' of the Committee's work which is built upon the factors discussed. To the extent to which the Committee (as well as any other treaty-monitoring body) improves its work in relation to the factors mentioned above, it increases its 'legitimacy' and the pressure on States to comply will be higher because any non-compliance will be received with greater public condemnation. Hence, the greater fulfilment of these factors leads to greater legitimacy which in turn brings about greater compliance.

From the analysis above, it is fair to conclude that the Committee meets many of the factors that provide legitimacy. This statement is supported by the fact that there is a significant level of acceptance of the Covenant's interpretation among States, as is reflected in their practice before the Committee, as well as by a plethora of resolutions and decisions adopted by States in international fora.[145]

Nevertheless, as has been mentioned, legitimacy is a matter of degree.[146] The Committee still needs to make improvements in relation to many of the factors analysed. The number of Committee members who hold government positions is very high. While a government position is not incompatible with membership in the Committee *per se* and the independence of Committee members needs to be analysed on a case by case basis, the Human Rights Committee has correctly stressed that members should not only be independent but should also 'appear to be' independent.[147] Certainly, the fact that 8 of 18 of the current members of the Committee hold government positions would tend to undermine the appearance of independence.

---

145 As we have analysed, in many cases the Committee's interpretation has found support in the work of international bodies composed of State representatives, such as the General Assembly and the Human Rights Commission. The resolutions of these organs may be adduced as subsequent evidence of the interpretation of the Covenant as well as evidence of State practice in the sense of indicating State understanding of the obligations by which they are bound. In fact, these organs sometimes call upon States to comply with the obligations imposed by the Covenant, or, on some other occasions, they merely restate the existence of such obligations, although not always expressly referring to the Covenant.

146 See, Franck, *op. cit.* (note 63), particularly Chapter III, pp. 41-49.

147 According to the Human Rights Committee: 'The appearance of impartiality of members of the Committee should not be affected by their connection with Governments. They should abstain from engaging in any functions or activities which may appear to be not readily reconcilable with the obligations of an independent expert under the Covenant [...].'Guidelines for the exercise of their functions by members of the Human Rights Committee, *loc. cit.* (note 83), Guideline No. 9.

In addition, a disproportionate number of the current (and past) members of the Committee are from the legal profession and it is necessary to include a greater number of persons with expertise in others fields such as public health, macroeconomic policy and education. Another striking feature of the Committee's composition is the gender balance: only 2 of 18 members are women. This is a serious deficiency of the Committee and should be addressed through the nomination of greater numbers of non-lawyers and women in the future.

Over the years the Committee has improved its working methods, demonstrated increased openness to external sources of information and has acted in a flexible manner in the face of new challenges. The Committee's efforts in this regard are laudable. However, the Committee must undertake continuous efforts to increase its level of legitimacy. Only to the extent that the Committee improves upon these factors does it make it more difficult for recalcitrant States not to comply with its views.

If the Committee suffers a crisis of confidence in the eyes of States, its role as the principal interpreter of the Covenant, as well as the outcome of its supervisory work, would cease to carry important legal weight and States would not be likely to respect it. On the contrary, the more serious the efforts of the Committee to fulfil each of the factors, the more likely its interpretations of the Covenant would be considered in practice as being legally binding in the sense that States Parties would find it difficult to ignore them. The cost of non-compliance in terms of 'public shame' would be high.

Finally, it is important to stress that we have referred here to the legitimacy of the Committee as an interpreter of the Covenant. However, there are some other factors that also influence the way in which States comply with the Committee's interpretations that do not depend on the Committee to a great extent, such as the dissemination of the Committee's work. To the extent that the Committee's Concluding Observations, General Comments and Summary Records are made available to the general public, the easier it is for the general public to have a better understanding of the Covenant and to put pressure on their governments to comply. The 'mobilisation of shame' is probably one of the more effective means to put pressure upon States to comply with the Covenant's interpretations, but to achieve this result it is necessary that the general public be more aware of the Committee's work. However, the Committee certainly cannot accomplish this task on its own. While the Committee continuously stresses the importance of dissemination in most of its Concluding Observations, it is up to States Parties and NGOs to achieve better results. NGOs in particular have an important role to play in achieving this task.

4 Concluding Comments

In interpreting the Covenant, the Committee attempts to make its provisions completely effective in the light of present-day circumstances. By doing so, the Committee extends the protection afforded by the Covenant, enhancing the protection it provides.

The Committee's approach to interpretation is in line with the general principles of treaty interpretation and its work enjoys an acceptable degree of legitimacy. Compliance in good faith with the obligations imposed by the Covenant (article 26 VCLT) requires States to comply with the normative content of the Covenant as the Committee interprets it.

PART TWO:
THE OBLIGATIONS IMPOSED BY THE COVENANT

Part Two of this study includes Chapters IV and V and analyses the nature of the obligations imposed by the Covenant. Chapter IV includes a comparative analysis of the obligations imposed by the Covenant on Economic, Social and Cultural Rights and those imposed by the Covenant on Civil and Political Rights. It demonstrates that there is no difference in nature between economic, social and cultural rights on the one hand, and civil and political rights on the other, but, rather, that each set of rights imposes a spectrum of State obligations. Chapter V discusses the typologies of state duties that have been developed by scholars. It goes on to analyse the manner in which the Committee has classified the obligations imposed by the Covenant and applied the tripartite typology of respect/protect/fulfil in its General Comments. The Committee's Concluding Observations are then examined in the light of this typology.

CHAPTER IV
THE NATURE OF STATE PARTY OBLIGATIONS UNDER THE INTERNATIONAL COVENANT ON ECONOMIC, SOCIAL AND CULTURAL RIGHTS

1 INTRODUCTION

This chapter will analyse the legal nature of States Parties' obligations under the International Covenant on Economic, Social and Cultural Rights. The analysis will focus on the nature of these rights as legally binding obligations arising from a determined conventional source of international law. It is outside the scope of this study to deal with the nature of these rights from the philosophical and ideological perspectives.[1]

As is well known, the Universal Declaration of Human Rights[2] guarantees the full range of rights, civil, political, economic, social and cultural and during the early stages of drafting the Covenants it was envisioned that there would be only one legal instrument containing both categories of rights. However, in the end it was decided that there would be two separate legal instruments, the International Covenant on Civil and Political Rights [ICCPR][3] and the International Covenant on Economic, Social and Cultural Rights [ICESCR].[4]

As we will see, in retrospect we may argue that the majority of the Covenants' drafters were mistaken in their belief that the two clusters of rights and the obligations that they impose were different in nature. While political, ideological and economic circumstances might be invoked to justify their limited view of the nature of human rights and duties, in our present circumstances,[5] and bearing in mind the significant

---

1 For a defence of these rights from a philosophical perspective see, for example: *Law, rights and the welfare state*. Sampford & Galligan, D.J. (eds.), Croom Helm, London/Sydney/Wolfeboro, New Hampshire (1986); Plant, R.: 'A defence of welfare rights.' In: *Economic, social and cultural rights: progress and achievement*. Beddart, R. & Hill, D. (eds.), Macmillan, London, (1992), pp. 22-46; and Wellman, C.: *An approach to rights: studies in the philosophy of law and morals*, Kluwer Academic Publishers, Dordrecht, (1997).

2 Adopted and proclaimed by General Assembly Res. 217 A (III) of 10 December 1948.

3 General Assembly Res. 2200 A (XXI) of 16 December 1966. The ICCPR entered into force on 23 March 1976, in accordance with article 49.

4 General Assembly Res. 2200 A (XXI) of December 16, 1966. The Covenant entered into force on 3 January 1976, in accordance with article 27.

5 As we will see, the post-War period, the Cold War and the existence of a socialist bloc influenced the drafting of the Covenants. While today the economic and political context is totally different, there are new obstacles to the enjoyment of these rights, such as those arising from globalisation, structural adjustment programmes, the foreign debt of developing countries and the enormous inequalities in the distribution of wealth. The UN Sub-Commission on the Promotion and Protection of Human Rights has analysed these topics in depth. See, for example, the final reports of the Special Rapporteurs Mr. D. Türk on 'The realisation of economic, social and cultural rights', in particular Part II: 'Ongoing

developments that have occurred in human rights law, we need to adopt a wider perspective.

With the aim of making the protection of individuals' human rights effective, supervisory bodies have provided a better and broader understanding of all human rights and their correlative obligations. Human rights law has developed in a way which was hardly imaginable for those involved in the drafting process. In retrospect, it is fair to argue that the two sets of rights are not different in nature. The developments achieved in human rights law render many of the drafters' arguments with respect to the nature of these rights unsustainable.

This Chapter will attempt to demonstrate that from the point of view of States' duties, there are no sharp distinctions between civil and political rights on the one hand, and economic, social and cultural rights on the other. Both kinds of rights impose multiple obligations of different types.

To explain this point, I will introduce the idea that all human rights impose a 'continuum' or 'spectrum' of duties. At one end of the spectrum there are obligations of non-interference by States and at the other end there are obligations requiring positive actions by States (see figure 1). While the drafters basically focused on the two extremes, identifying each with a category of rights, the case-law of the major human rights monitoring bodies as well as the work of academics have made apparent that all human rights impose different kinds of duties which cover the whole spectrum from the negative extreme to the positive one.

2 The Drafting History of the Covenants and the Alleged Difference in Nature of the Rights and Obligations

2.1 The adoption of two separate Covenants and the different wording used in articles 2(1) of each Covenant

The adoption of the Covenants was the result of a lengthy process lasting nearly twenty years[6] which cannot be isolated from its political context.[7] During the drafting, the decision to adopt two separate Covenants generated extensive and complex debate.[8]

Barriers: The main challenges of our time'. E/CN.4/Sub.2/1992/16, of 3 July 1992, paras 38-138 and Mr. J. Bengoa on 'The relationship between the enjoyment of human rights, in particular economic, social and cultural rights and income distribution.' E/CN.4/Sub.2/1997/9, of 30 June 1997.

6 The drafting started in 1947 with the first session of the Drafting Committee of the Commission on Human Rights and was finalised on 16 December 1966 when the General Assembly adopted the two Covenants.

7 See Donnelly, 1998, pp. 7-17 and 149 *et.seq*.

8 For an analysis of the approach of the United Nations in this regard, see Jhabvala, F.: 'On human rights and the socio-economic context.' In: *NILR*, vol. XXXI, (1984), pp. 149-182; Bossuyt, M.: *Guide to the 'travaux préparatoires' of the International Covenant on Civil and Political Rights*. Martinus Nijhoff Publisher, Dordrecht, (1987); Scott, C.: 'The interdependence and permeability of human rights

The initial decision to deal with all human rights in a single instrument was discarded in favour of the adoption of two separate treaties in a movement heavily influenced by political factors.[9]

The reasons given for this separation have been analysed elsewhere[10] and it is outside the scope of this study to examine the topic in detail. Nonetheless, we will mention those reasons that directly concern the issue under discussion. For this purpose, it is useful to refer to the analysis carried out by C. Scott who classified the arguments in favour of having two separate instruments in three broad categories: (a) 'implementation-based reasons'; (b) 'ideological or political reasons'; and (c) 'pragmatic reasons'.[11]

The most relevant category here is that of 'implementation-based reasons' because this category covers arguments claiming that there are two distinguishable categories of rights of different natures. Furthermore, the two other categories have been superseded.[12] On the one hand, the ideological or political context has changed dramatically with the end of the Cold War. The Cold War was one critical obstacle to the development of economic, social and cultural rights[13] and its end encouraged, at least under the framework of the UN, the protection of human rights in general,[14] but particularly that

norms: towards a partial fusion of the International Covenants on Human Rights.' In: *Osgoode Hall Law Journal,* vol. 27, Ottawa, Canada (1989), pp. 791 *et seq.*; and Nowak, M.: 'The effectiveness of the International Covenant on Civil and Political Rights: stocktaking after the first eleven sessions of the Human Rights Committee.' In: *HRLJ*, vol. 1, Nos. 1-4, (1980), pp. 136 *et seq.*

9 In 1950, by Res. 421 E(V) of December 4, 1950, the General Assembly decided (35 votes to 9, with 7 abstentions) to adopt one single Covenant [5 GAOR, Plenary Meetings, at p. 564 para. 162, UN doc. A/PV.317 (1950)]. Two years later, the General Assembly reversed this decision (by 27 votes to 20, with three abstentions) by Res. 543 (VI) (1952) of February 5, 1952 [GAOR, 6th Session, UN doc. A/2119 (1952), p. 36]. See, also, Jhabvala, *loc. cit.* (note 8), p. 156.

10 For a more detailed analysis of the drafting history of the Covenants, see *inter alia,* Bossuyt, op. cit. (note 8); Jhabvala, loc. cit. (note 8); Scott, loc. cit. (note 8), pp. 791 *et seq.*; McGoldrick, D.: 'Sustainable development and human rights: an integrated conceptions.' In: *International and Comparative Law Quarterly,* vol. No. 45, October (1996), pp. 796-818; and *Morphet*, 1992, pp. 74-92.

11 Scott, *loc. cit.* (note 8), pp. 794-5.

12 As Scott notes, although the three categories of reasons are not watertight and were often invoked at the same time, after the Cold War, the so-called 'political and ideological' reasons are no longer valid and the 'pragmatic reasons' can also be factored out because, for the most part, those reasons were subordinated to the 'implementation' arguments and were coloured by politics. *Ibidem*: p. 811.

13 According to the Committee, the Cold War was one of the reasons why the Covenant has been neglected. In its words, 'the Cold War [...] situated much of the general human rights debate in a context of ideological controversy. This affected economic, social and cultural rights in particular, since these were often portrayed falsely as being solely the concern of either the Communist countries or a handful of developing countries.' Statement of the Committee to the World Summit for Social Development adopted during the tenth session. E/1995/22, Annex V, para. 7.

14 For a view on how the end of the Cold War permitted some obstacles to the implementation of human rights to be overcome, see Buergenthal, T.: 'The evolution of international human rights'. In: *Héctor Gros Espiell Amicorum Liber*, vol. 1, Bruylant, Brussels, (1997), pp. 123-147.

of economic, social and cultural rights.[15] This is not to say that there are no longer ideological obstacles to the implementation of economic, social and cultural rights, but, rather, that there are now different obstacles. After the Covenant entered into force, the ideological concerns shifted toward the North-South dimension,[16] and away from the confrontation between East and West (the socialist bloc versus the Western countries).[17] On the other hand, developments after the adoption of the Covenants have demonstrated that many of the so-called 'pragmatic reasons'[18] advanced by government representatives in favour of separation into two Covenants were incorrect assessments or merely based on short-term political considerations.[19]

As Scott notes, the core of the 'implementation-based reasons' were that the two categories of rights were different in nature, and therefore that each required different methods of implementation.[20] This assumption was clearly expressed in the texts of both Covenants, particularly in the wording used in the general provisions regarding obligations (article 2(1) of each Covenant), which were intended to reflect the alleged difference in nature among the obligations imposed by two categories of rights.[21]

---

15 For a view of how the end of the Cold War fostered more effective supervision of the Covenant see, Simma, B.: 'The examination of State reports: International Covenant on Economic, Social and Cultural Rights.' In: *The monitoring system of human rights treaty obligations*. Klein E. (ed.), Colloquium Potsdam, 22-23 November 1996, Berlin Verlag, Berlin, (1998), p. 47. See, also, Alston, P. & Simma, B.: 'Second session of the UN Committee on Economic, Social and Cultural Rights.' In: *AJIL,* vol. 82 No. 3, July (1988), pp. 603-615 and Alston, P.: 'The interplay between rights: denial and neglect.' In: *Human rights: the new consensus*, Regency Press, (1994*), p. 113.

16 Steiner & Alston, 2000, p. 238.

17 Scott, *loc. cit.* (note 8), p. 795. However, it is important to stress, as Scott correctly mentions, that during the drafting process, some developing countries did not follow the East-West pattern. *Idem.*

18 Scott recognises five 'pragmatic reasons': '(i) the concern that the world community was expecting quick results and that devoting the requisite attention to economic rights would produce too great a delay; (ii) the related concern that the articles on economic rights drafted to that point needed considerable reworking, whereas the political rights were, for the most part, already expressed satisfactorily; (iii) the reminder that any covenant had to be generally acceptable to the large majority of the UN members, so it could be ratified and enter into force; (iv) the concern that the work of specialised agencies, notably the International Labour Organisation, might be overlapped and duplicated if economic rights were included; and (v) the view that two instruments were desirable because virtually all states would be willing to sign at least one.' *Ibidem*: pp. 795-6.

19 The limited relevance of the practical arguments advanced during the drafting process is indicated by the fact that both Covenants were adopted at the same time, and that the great majority of States are now party to both Covenants, with the exception of Belize, Haiti, Mozambique, South Africa and the United States, which have ratified the ICCPR but not the ICESCR, and China, Eritrea, the Solomon Islands and Guinea-Bissau which have ratified the ICESCR but not the ICCPR. Information as of July 2002.

20 Scott, *loc. cit.* (note 8), p. 794.

21 UN doc. A/2929 (1955) p. 7 para. 9. It is important to stress that the difference in formulation in the general obligation provisions of the two sets of rights started very early in the drafting process. In 1954 the drafts already used different wording. See UN doc. E/2573, Report of the tenth session of the Commission on Human Rights (1954). Annex I, Sections A and B.

Both articles 2(1) differ significantly. While article 2(1) ICCPR establishes the obligation 'to respect and to ensure,'[22] the corresponding provision of the sister Covenant (article 2(1) ICESCR) requires a State Party to 'undertake to take steps [...] to the maximum of its available resources, with a view to achieving progressively the full realisation of the rights' recognised in the Covenant.

The different terminology is of great relevance, particularly when we bear in mind that article 2 of both Covenants specifies the general obligations assumed by the States Parties in relation to each of the substantive rights protected therein. As explained earlier,[23] both articles 2 are contained in Part II of each Covenant which establishes general obligations applicable to all of the rights contained in Part III of each Covenant (articles 6 to 27 ICCPR and 6 to 15 ICESCR).[24]

The differences in the wording of the general obligation provisions of the Covenants reflect the different implementation methods that it was assumed that the two sets of rights required due to their different nature. Since the majority position during the drafting considered that civil and political rights required merely non-interference by the State, the adoption of legislative and administrative measures was believed to be sufficient to achieve this non-interference. These measures were considered as non-resource dependent and of an immediate nature, and, as a result, every State was considered to be able to undertake them regardless of their level of resources.[25] In

22 Article 2 ICCPR states: 'Each State Party to the present Covenant undertakes to respect and to ensure to all individuals within its territory and subject to its jurisdiction the rights recognised in the present Covenant, without distinction of any kind, such as race, colour, sex, language, religion, political or other opinion, national or social origin, property, birth or other status.
Where not already provided for by existing legislative or other measures, each State Party to the present Covenant undertakes to take the necessary steps, in accordance with its constitutional process and with the provisions of the present Covenant, to adopt such legislative or other measures as may be necessary to give effect to the rights recognised in the present Covenant.
Each State Party to the present Covenant undertakes: (a) To ensure that any person whose rights or freedoms as herein recognised are violated shall have an effective remedy, notwithstanding that the violation has been committed by persons acting in an official capacity; (b) To ensure that any person claiming such a remedy shall have his right thereto determined by competent judicial, administrative or legislative authorities, or by any other competent judicial, administrative or legislative authorities, or by any other competent authority provided for by the legal system of the State, and to develop the possibilities of judicial remedy; (c) To ensure that the competent authorities shall enforce such remedies when granted.'

23 See Introduction section 3. In addition: Chapter VI, Section 1.

24 See, for example, Nowak, M.: *U.N. Covenant on Civil and Political Rights Commentary*, N.P. Engel Publisher, Khel/Strasbourg/Arlington, (1993), p. 33 and McGoldrick, D.: *The Human Rights Committee*, Clarendon Press, Oxford, (1994), p. 269.

25 This generalised but limited approach in regard to human rights is reflected in the words of one commentator who noted in 1967, 'It is in fact known that, for the realisation of civil and political rights, it is generally sufficient that the law recognise them and the State administration observe them; while the realisation of the economic, social and cultural rights, all those financial and technical means are needed which make economic development and social progress practically possible.' Capotorti, 1968, p. 132.

contrast, since the drafters generally saw economic, social and cultural rights as requiring merely positive State actions they assumed that they were dependent on socio-economic conditions and therefore that their implementation was necessarily gradual.[26]

The drawbacks of such a limited approach to the implementation requirements with regard to civil and political rights became apparent after the ICCPR entered into force. According to Schachter, the assumption that civil and political rights merely required the adoption of legislative and administrative measures for their implementation, led many States to report[27] during the first years of the functioning of the Human Rights Committee that their countries did not require any additional measures for the implementation of the ICCPR's rights, because all of its rights were 'enshrined' in their constitutions and/or legislative texts. As he explicitly notes, 'to a man from Mars, a large part of the world would seem safe for human rights and the Covenant virtually redundant.'[28]

As Jhabvala mentions, such an approach by States Parties could be attributed to naivety or to the introduction of double standards.[29] As he explains, it would be naïve to think that civil and political rights only call for relatively simple legislative and administrative measures, because in reality the establishment of the necessary administrative and judicial machinery to implement the Covenant is a long and costly process, particularly in developing countries.[30] On the other hand, such an approach may also have flowed from the use of double standards. In his words, 'for while the 'implementation' of civil and political rights was considered as having been accomplished once they had been established on paper, a very different standard – real enjoyment – was set up for the evaluation of the implementation of economic, social and cultural rights [...] If however, the real enjoyment, or, at least the real availability of rights, was taken as the test of implementation then it could not be held that civil and political rights had been, or could be, implemented through their mere establishment on paper.'[31]

The simplicity of some of the early assumptions of States in regard to the implementation requirements of the civil and political rights have been overcome by reality. Nowadays it is well established that the implementation of these rights requires much more than mere legislative and administrative measures. However, the limited approach to the implementation of economic, social and cultural rights has yet to be clearly left behind. Despite the important developments in international law and the significant contributions of scholars who have emphasised the similarities between the two clus-

26 See, for example, Commission on Human Rights, Report of the thirty-fourth Session. ECOSOC Official Records 1978. E/1978/38.

27 In accordance with Art. 40 ICCPR.

28 Schachter, 1979, p. 463. Also in Schachter, 1981, p. 320.

29 Jhabvala, *loc. cit.* (note 8), p. 163.

30 *Ibidem*: pp. 163-165.

31 *Ibidem*: p. 165.

ters of rights, the view that economic, social and cultural rights can only be implemented progressively in a costly process is still being put forward in some quarters.[32]

At the same time, the supervisory mechanisms for the protection of the rights contained in the two Covenants differ significantly, principally due the lack of an individual complaint procedure under the ICESCR. Notwithstanding the important steps taken to adopt an optional protocol establishing an individual complaint procedure for violations of economic, social and cultural rights, such a mechanism remains an aspiration.[33] It might be fair to say that among the reasons for the slow movement on this issue is the traditional, well-rooted view with respect to the difference in nature among the two clusters of rights.

It is interesting to note that during the negotiation of the Optional Protocol to the Convention on the Elimination of All Forms of Discrimination against Women [CEDAW], the debate regarding the justiciability of economic, social and cultural rights contained in the Convention made even more apparent the prevalence of the assumption of the different nature of the two sets of rights. In fact, the nature of these rights was one of the most hotly debated topics in the negotiating process and some government representatives seemed to revert to the old arguments against economic,

---

32 Some influential studies employing this line of thinking were written during the 1970s and early 1980s [for example, Cranston, M.: *What are human rights?* The Bodley Head, London/ Sydney/ Toronto, (1973); Bossuyt, M.: 'La distinction entre les droites civils et politiques et les droits economiques, sociaux et culturels.' In: *Revue des Droits de l'Homme* (Human Rights Law Journal), vol. 8 No.4, (1975); Vierdag, E.W: 'The legal nature of the rights granted by the International Covenant on Economic, Social and Cultural Rights.' In: *NYIL,* vol. IX (1978)] but these views have arguably been surpassed by recent developments in human rights law. In recent years, scholars seem to have taken greater care not to question the legal nature of economic, social and cultural rights. Nevertheless, it is unfortunate that every now and then some scholars stress the immediacy of the obligations arising from the ICCPR by contrasting the wording of each article 2 of the Covenants and emphasising the notion of the 'progressive realisation' of the rights contained in the ICESCR without noting the existence of immediate obligations. From this author's perspective, such an approach does not assist us to overcome the well-rooted assumption that economic, social and cultural rights are of a secondary status.

33 The Committee began to study the possibility of an optional protocol during its fifth session held in 1990 [E/1991/23 para. 25]. Since then important steps have been taken, among them a series of studies carried out under the auspices of the Committee, particularly the reports presented by P. Alston [*e.g.* E/C.12/1991/WP.2, E/C.12/1992/WP.9 and E/C.12/1994/12], as well as studies carried out independently by experts and scholars. With regard to the latter, the expert meeting organised by SIM in January 1995 and the comprehensive study carried out by K. Arambulo deserve special attention [Arambulo, K.: *Strengthening the supervision of the International Covenant on Economic, Social and Cultural Rights: theoretical and procedural aspects*, Intersentia, Antwerp, (1999)]. More than a decade has passed since an optional protocol was first proposed and it is not rare that States Parties to the Covenant express their support for the adoption of a protocol in their reports or during the constructive dialogue with the Committee. But still, one might be sceptical as to the existence of the political will to adopt it.

social and cultural rights. Fortunately, the indivisibility of all human rights has prevailed as of late.[34]

Moreover, on occasion during the constructive dialogue with the Committee[35] and before UN political organs,[36] government representatives still occasionally suggest that the two sets of rights are of a different nature and that they require different methods of implementation. Therefore, it is important to examine the alleged differences between the two sets of rights in the light of the developments achieved in international human rights law in recent years.

2.2 Re-examining the alleged difference in nature among States' obligations

In the following analysis we will briefly re-examine some of the arguments used by those drafters who were in favour of adopting two different Covenants due to the alleged difference in the nature of the two sorts of rights which led to a different formulation of articles 2 of each Covenant.[37] For reasons of manageability, we will analyse the arguments of the alleged different nature through the following dichoto-

34 It will be interesting to see how the CEDAW Committee deals with Communications regarding the violation of economic, social and cultural rights of women. The Optional Protocol entered into force on 22 December 2000. Up to February 2002, there had not been any jurisprudence relating to economic, social and cultural rights. Thus far, one may agree that the final adoption of the Protocol to CEDAW is one step forward in the protection of economic, social and cultural rights. For an elaborate view of the drafting history of the Optional Protocol to CEDAW see Byrnes A. & Connors, J.: 'Enforcing the human rights of women: a complaints procedure for the women's Convention?' In: *Brooklyn Journal of International Law*, vol. XXI No. 3, (1996), pp. 679-798.

35 See, for example, Mr. Wyss (Switzerland) E/C.12/1998/SR.38 para. 2, Mr. Potman (the Netherlands) E/C.12/1998/SR.13 para. 11 and Mr. Fifoot (United Kingdom of Great Britain and Northern Ireland) E/C.12/1997/SR.36 para. 45. In the last case, the Committee in its 1997 Concluding Observations explicitly remarked, 'The Committee [...] finds disturbing the position of the State party that provisions of the Covenant, with certain minor exceptions, constitute principles and programme objectives rather than legal obligations, and that consequently the provisions of the Covenant cannot be given legislative effect' [Concluding Observations United Kingdom of Great Britain and Northern Ireland E/1998/22 para. 293]. Three years previously the Committee had noted, 'the Committee finds unacceptable the view expressed by the Government that the rights enshrined in the [ICESCR] are 'different in nature' from civil and political rights and therefore not capable of being the subject of an enforcement procedure under domestic law.' [Concluding Observations United Kingdom of Great Britain and Northern Ireland and its Dependent Territories [with the exception of Hong Kong] E/1995/22 para. 285].

36 For example, when the UN Economic and Social Council endorsed the Commission's decision to appoint an independent expert to examine the question of a draft optional protocol to the Covenant (Commission Res. 2001/30 adopted on 20 April 2001, E/CN.4/RES/2001/30), the representative of the United States, explaining his position, said 'that while his country had joined consensus on the decision, it did not support the draft optional protocol, as it confused economic, social and cultural rights, which should be realised progressively, with legally enforceable entitlements.' ECOSOC, 9th meeting of 4 June 2001. UN Press Release, 5 June 2001. Available at: http://www.unhchr.ch/huricane/huricane.nsf/newsroom (last visited July 2002).

37 See UN doc. A/2929, Report of the tenth session of the General Assembly (1955) and UN doc. A/5655.

mies: (1) positive/negative; (2) progressive/immediate; (3) expensive/cost-free; and (4) vague/precise.

Nonetheless, some preliminary considerations are necessary. First, it is important to note that the arguments of States' delegations in the various phases of the drafting process were not always consistent. Those drafters who were in favour of two different Covenants on the basis of 'implementation reasons' did not always present their arguments in the manner that they are summarised below; however, we have attempted to capture the underlying reasoning rather than the form of their arguments. Secondly, since many commentators have analysed the distinction between the two categories of rights from the point of view of these dichotomies,[38] the following analysis will examine only those aspects that directly concern the discussion of the obligations. The emphasis will be placed on how new developments in international human rights law have made apparent the simplicity of the dichotomies.

As will be seen, the assumption that civil and political rights only require state abstention (negative obligations) and that economic, social and cultural rights require States to take action (positive obligations), forms the basis of the other assumptions.[39] It is now well established that a positive/negative distinction between the two sorts of rights cannot be made, and, as a result, the alleged difference in nature between them needs to be reappraised.

2.2.1 Positive/negative obligations

Some delegations opposed to a single instrument containing the full range of rights considered that civil and political rights merely required the non-intervention of the State (negative obligation), and viewed economic, social and cultural rights as requiring active intervention on the part of the State (positive obligations).[40] This approach

---

38 See, for example, Bossuyt, *loc. cit.* (note 32); Vierdag, *loc. cit.* (note 32); Hoof, G.J.H. van: Legal nature of economic, social and cultural rights: a rebuttal of some traditional views. In: *The right to food.* Alston, Philip & Tomaševski, Katarina (eds.), Martinus Nijhoff Publishers, Utrecht, (1984); Matas, D.: Economic, social and cultural rights and the role of lawyers: North American perspectives. In: *I.C.J. Review*, No. 55, (1985) pp.123-140; Scott, *loc. cit.* (note 8); Hunt, P.:. Dartmouth, Aldershot, (1996); Robertson, B.: *'Economic, social and cultur Reclaiming social rights: international and comparative perspective al rights: time for a reappraisal,'* New Zealand Business Roundtable, New Zealand, September (1997); O'Regan, K.: 'Introducing socio-economic rights.' In: *ESR Review*, vol. 1 No. 4, (1999), pp. 71-72; and Pease, K.: Economic globalisation and American society. In: *The United States and human rights: looking inward and outward.* Forsythe, D. (ed.), University of Nebraska Press, Lincoln, (2000).

39 In a lucid analysis, Scott and Macklem note that the alleged 'positive nature' of economic, social and cultural rights stands as an 'umbrella category', which entails arguments against those rights which tend to consider that they are not capable of being made subject to judicial review (what the authors called 'institutional legitimacy'). Scott & Macklem, 1992, p. 44.

40 UN doc. A/2929 (1955) p. 7 para. 9. It is important to emphasise that some substantive rights contained in both Covenants do not fit the simplistic scheme according to which civil and political rights merely establish negative obligations and economic, social and cultural ones, merely positive obligations.

has since found support in some academic writings, principally during the 1970s,[41] and it is now often considered as a general characterisation of these rights.[42]

Admittedly, there is some merit to the distinction between civil and political rights and economic, social and cultural rights as being, respectively, negative and positive in character. However, this assumption is no longer tenable. The academic literature[43] as well as the jurisprudence of the major human rights supervisory bodies[44] shows that positive and negative duties are part of the normative requirement of both sorts of rights. As Shue notes, attempting to classify every right as either flatly negative or positive, is an 'artificial, simplistic and arid exercise.'[45]

Today it is beyond doubt that civil and political rights instruments, such as the European Convention on Human Rights, or the Inter-American Convention, although drafted basically in terms of obligations not to interfere in the exercise of individuals' rights, also impose 'positive obligations' on the part of the States Parties which are

---

There are some civil and political rights that directly require positive actions on the part of the duty-holder. For instance, the right to be informed at the time of arrest or detention (Art. 9(2) ICCPR), the right to compensation when someone has been the victim of an unlawful arrest or detention (Art. 9(5) ICCPR), the right to legal assistance when an individual does not have sufficient means to pay (Art. 14(3)(d)) or the right to have the free assistance of an interpreter when this is necessary (Art. 14(3)(f)). On the other hand, economic, social and cultural rights may directly impose a negative obligation (duty of non-interference) upon the State. The negative component of the rights contained in the ICESCR is even implied in the terminology used as in the case of those substantive rights which use the wording to 'respect', to 'guarantee' and to 'ensure'. For example, the obligation 'to respect' (non-interference) the right of parents to choose the schools of their children (Art. 13(3)), the obligation not to interfere with the liberty of individuals to establish and direct educational institutions (Art. 13(4) ICESCR) and to respect scientific freedom and creative activity (Art. 15(3)). Obligations to 'guarantee' are found in the non-discrimination provision (Art. 2(2) ICESCR) and the prohibition of gender discrimination with respect to remuneration for employment (Art. 7(a)(1)). Finally, there are obligations 'to ensure' concerning equal treatment for men and women (Art. 3 ICESCR), the obligation 'to ensure' the right to form and join trade unions and 'to ensure' the right to strike (Art. 8 ICESCR).

41 See, for example, Vierdag, *loc. cit.* (note 32), pp. 80-81 and Bossuyt, *loc. cit.* (note 32), p. 790.

42 Scott & Macklem, *loc. cit.* (note 39), p. 24.

43 See, for example, Shue, H.: *Basic rights: subsistence, affluence and U.S. foreign policy*, Princeton University Press, first edition, New Jersey, (1980), p. 84; Hoof, G.J.H. van, *op. cit.* (note 38), p. 26; Scott and Macklem, *loc. cit.* (Note 39), pp. 48-71; Viljanen, V.: 'Abstention or involvement? The nature of State obligations under different categories of rights.' In: *Social rights as human rights: a European challenge*, Institute for Human Rights, Åbo Akademi University, Åbo, Finland, (1994), p. 52; Stammers, N.: 'A critique of social approaches to human rights.' In: *HRQ*, vol. 17, No. 3 (1995), p. 488; Donnelly, *op. cit.* (note 7); and Dijk, P. van: ''Positive obligations' implied in the European Convention on Human Rights: are the States still the 'masters' of the Convention?' In: *The role of the nation-State in the 21st century. Human rights, international organisations and foreign policy: essays in honour of Peter Baehr*. Castermans-Holleman, M., Hoof, G.J.H van & Smith, J. (eds.), Kluwer, The Hague, (1998), pp. 17-33.

44 See note 46.

45 Shue, 1984, p. 84.

often not explicitly contained in the text.[46] Conversely, most economic, social and cultural rights have been interpreted as containing elements that require the State to abstain from interfering with the individual's exercise of the right. As several commentators note, the right to food includes the right for everyone to procure their own food supply without interference;[47] the right to housing implies the right not to be a victim of forced eviction;[48] the right to work encompasses the individual's right to choose his/her own work and also requires the State not to hinder a person from working and to abstain from measures that would increase unemployment;[49] the right to education implies the freedom to establish and direct educational establishments;[50] and the right

46 At the international level, there are many well-known cases at the European Court of Human Rights, such as Marckx v. Belgium, Application No. 6833/74, Judgement of June 13 1979; Airey v. Ireland, Application No. 6289/73, Judgement of 9 October 1979; X and Y v. The Netherlands, Application No. 8978/80, Judgement of 26 March 1985; Plattform 'Ärzte für Das Leben' v. Austria, Application No. 21/6/1998, Judgement of 21June 1988, para. 32; National Union of Belgian Police v. Belgium, Application No. 4464, Judgement of 27 October 1975; Swedish Engine Drivers' Union v. Sweden, Application No. 5614/72, Judgement of 6 February 1976; Young, James and Webster v. the United Kingdom, Application Nos. 7601/76 and 1806/77, Judgement of 13 August 1981; Gustafsson v. Sweden, Application No. 15573/89, Judgement of 25 April 1996; McCann and Others v. the United Kingdom, Application No. 1898/91, Judgement of 27 September 1995; and Osman v. the United Kingdom, Application No. 23452/94, Judgement of 28 October 1998. At the Inter-American level, see, for example, Velásquez Rodríguez v. Honduras, Judgement of 29 July 1988, Series C No. 4, para. 166; Godínez Cruz v. Honduras, Judgement of 20 January 1989, Series C No. 5, para. 175; and Advisory Opinion No. 11 'Exceptions to the exhaustion of domestic remedies (Arts. 46(1), 46(2)(a) and 46(2)(b) of the American Convention on Human Rights', OC-11/90 of 10 August 1990, Series A No. 11, paras. 22-23.

47 For a comprehensive review of the negative duties implicit in the right to adequate food, see, for example, Report of UN Sub-Commission Special Rapporteur, Mr. Eide E/CN.4/Sub.2/1999/12, of 28 June 1999 and Eide, A.: 'The right to an adequate standard of living including the right to food.' In: *Economic, social and cultural rights: a textbook.* Eide, A.; Krause, C. & Rosas, A. (eds.), Martinus Nijhoff Publishers, first edition, Dordrecht, (1995*).

48 For a comprehensive review of the negative duties implied in the right to adequate housing, see, for example, Report of UN Sub-Commission Special Rapporteur, Mr. R. Sachar E/CN.4/Sub.2/1993/15, of 22 June 1993, paras. 66-68; Leckie, S.: 'The justiciability of housing rights.' In: *The right to complain about economic, social and cultural rights*. Coomans, F. & Hoof, G.J.H. van (eds.), Netherlands Institute of Human Rights, SIM Special No.18, Utrecht (1995); and Leckie, S.: 'The Committee on Economic, Social and Cultural Rights: catalyst for change in a system needing reform.' In: *The future of UN human rights treaty monitoring*. Alston, P. & Crawford, J. (eds.), Cambridge University Press, Cambridge, (2000).

49 For a comprehensive review of the negative duties implicit in the right to work, see, for example, Drzewicki, K.; Krause, C. & Rosas, A. (eds.): *Social rights as human rights: a European challenge*, Institute for Human Rights, Åbo Akademi University, Åbo, Finland (1994).

50 For a comprehensive review of the negative duties implicit in the right to education, see, for example, Report of UN Sub-Commission Special Rapporteur, Mr. Mehedi E/CN.4/Sub.2/1999/10, of 8 July 1999, paras. 61-73; Coomans, F.: 'Clarifying the core elements of the right to education.' In: *The right to complain about economic, social and cultural rights*. Coomans, F & Hoof, G.J.H. van (eds.), SIM Special, No.18, Utrecht, (1995); and Nowak, M.: 'The right to education.' In: *Economic, social and*

to adequate health implies the obligation not to interfere with the provision of health care.[51]

The supervisory bodies of both Covenants clarified that positive and negative obligations arise from both categories of rights. We frequently find mention of positive obligations in regard to civil and political rights, as well as negative obligations regarding economic, social and cultural rights in the General Comments of both Committees, as well as when they examinine State Parties' reports. For example, when interpreting article 2 of the ICCPR, the Human Rights Committee has clearly stated that the obligations under this Covenant require States to take specific activities to enable individuals to enjoy their rights. As it stresses, '[t]his is obvious in a number of articles [...] but *in principle this undertaking relates to all rights set forth in the Covenant*.'[52] The fact that the Human Rights Committee specifically addressed the existence of positive obligations when dealing with article 2 is particularly relevant, because, as previously stated, this article specifies the obligations of the States with regard to all substantive rights contained in the Covenant. This means that States Parties must take positive action with respect to such diverse areas as, for example, the right to life;[53] the prohibition of torture;[54] the right to humane treatment;[55] the protection of children;[56] and the protection of minorities.[57] The Committee on Economic, Social and Cultural Rights has also stated very clearly in its Concluding Observations and General Comments that economic, social and cultural rights carry negative obligations.[58]

2.2.2 Cost-free obligations/expensive obligations

Another argument for the alleged difference in nature among the obligations imposed by the two Covenants was that civil and political rights imposed obligations that are

---

cultural rights: a textbook. Eide, A.; Krause, C. & Rosas, A. (eds.), Martinus Nijhoff Publishers, Dordrecht, (1995).

51 For a comprehensive review of the negative duties implied in the right to health, see, for example, Toebes, B.: *The right to health as a human right in international law*, Intersentia, Antwerp, (1998), pp. 312-325.

52 HRC General Comment No. 3 para. 1.

53 HRC General Comment No. 6 para. 5.

54 HRC General Comment No. 20 para. 10.

55 HRC General Comment No. 21 paras. 3 and 11.

56 HRC General Comment No. 17 para. 3.

57 HRC General Comment No. 23 para. 6.1.

58 For example, General Comment No. 7 is dedicated exclusively to forced evictions, which clearly entail a negative obligation for States. Negative obligations to respect economic, social and cultural rights are also stated in General Comment No. 2 para. 6; General Comment No. 12 para. 15 (right to adequate food); General Comment No. 13 para. 47 (right to education); and General Comment No. 14 paras. 33-34 (the right to the highest attainable standard of health).

cost-free while the obligations imposed by economic, social and cultural rights required government expenditure. This argument has also been echoed in scholarly discussion.[59]

Today, this view seems to be very simplistic and is apparently 'counter-factual' because it is well known that all human rights require that States, at the very least, establish an institutional structure to secure an appropriate degree of compliance with these rights and this will always entail expenditure of resources.[60]

The argument can be restated as follows: In general the implementation of civil and political rights requires fewer resources than some economic, social and cultural rights. In these terms, the argument is more difficult to dispute. However, assuming that all rights involve cost, any difference between the rights would be quantitative (more or less resources required), rather than flowing from a difference in the nature of the obligation.[61]

What is important to emphasise here is that, in the way that it has been presented, the cost-free/expensive dichotomy is not really different from the negative/positive obligation. Due to the fact that civil and political rights were considered to impose merely negative obligations upon States, it was concluded that their implementation did not require any resources, or more precisely, only a relatively small amount. In contrast, as economic, social and cultural rights were said to require positive actions, they were viewed as being very costly.

Once we accept that the realisation of both clusters of rights entails positive and negative obligations, the alleged difference in nature as to the resources required for their realisation is rendered untenable. This is not to say that there is no difference in the level of resources required for the realisation of specific obligations. While the realisation of different obligations may well require different levels of resources, in practice such differences in the resources required may exist independenthy of whether the obligations originate in one cluster of rights or the other.

All human rights impose a plurality of duties and each of those duties potentially requires different degrees of State involvement as well as different levels of resources. In this sense, it would not be accurate to qualify as 'cost-free' (implying a minimum level of resources) or 'expensive' one or the other category of rights as a whole, nor

---

59 See, for example, Bossuyt, *loc. cit.* (note 32), pp. 783-820. While the author advances several differences, the financial implications for the State seems to be the most important.

60 A clear example of how civil and political rights are not cost-free and may require a large amount of resources is provided by Hunt who analyses the expenditure of the Government of New Zealand on the domestic realisation of civil and political rights. See Hunt, *op. cit.* (note 37), pp. 57-60.

61 Bossuyt and Vierdag have been recognised as representatives of the school of thought which differentiates between the nature of the two categories of rights (as well as between the obligations arising form their respective instruments). Vierdag differentiates his position from Bossuyt, stating that the observations of the latter are based entirely on the financial element, and argues that the financial element alone is not the most appropriate key to determining the nature of economic, social and cultural rights because, as he recognises, some of the rights contained in the ICCPR require considerable expenditure as well. See Vierdag, loc. cit. (note 32), p. 82.

to attribute such a character to a single right. The differences are not with regard to the rights but rather with regard to the duties that they impose. For example, the duty not to interfere with the freedom of expression by refraining from censorship may be cheaper than the duty to take positive measures to create conditions which are favourable to pluralism in the media. By the same token, the duty not to carry out forced evictions[62] may be cheaper than the duty to provide housing to those in need.

In sum, the point here is that depending on whether a given duty is placed near either the negative or the positive end of the spectrum, the level of resources required for its implementation will vary. If it falls closer to the negative end of the spectrum, less resources will be required, while closer to the positive end of the spectrum signifies that a higher level of resources will be required for its implementation. However, this is not a distinction between rights, but, rather, one between the different duties that each right may impose.

2.2.3 Progressive/immediate obligations

The alleged positive and negative dichotomy between the two clusters of rights also influenced the debate as to the progressive or immediate character of the obligations.[63] It was considered that only obligations of non-interference (attributable to civil and political rights)[64] were amenable to immediate application, while positive duties (attributable to economic, social and cultural rights) were necessarily of gradual implementation.[65]

It is now well established that the notion of progressive realisation contained in article 2(1) of the ICESCR does not detract from the fact that the ICESCR also imposes obligations of immediate effect. As one commentator notes, a contrary interpretation

62 The term 'forced evictions' is used as defined in General Comment No. 7 paras. 3-4.

63 This approach was clear during the debate on article 2(2) and article 40(1) of the ICCPR. These provisions were criticised because they were considered to introduce the notion of progressiveness, which was viewed as 'inappropriate' for those civil and political rights considered capable of immediate implementation due to their requirement of negative action by the State. In contrast the obligations of the ICESCR were viewed as subjects of progressive realisation because they required positive action by the State. See, UN doc. A/2929 (1955), Chapter V, para. 10 and Chapter VII para. 162, Third Committee Report para. 20.

64 Article 23(4) ICCPR, which provides that States Parties 'shall take appropriate steps to ensure equality of rights and responsibilities of spouses', is a probable exception. The preparatory work seems to suggest that this provision might be interpreted as permitting States Parties to take progressive measures. See Schwelb, E.: 'Some aspects of the International Covenants on Human Rights of December 1966'. In: *International protection of human rights: proceedings of the seventh Nobel symposium.* Eide, A. & Schou A. (eds), Interscience Publishers, Stockholm, (1968), p. 125; Statement on behalf of the sponsor in GAOR A/C.3/SR.1094; 16th Session (1961-1962), Annexes, Agenda Item 35; Report of the Third Committee, A/5000, para. 84. For a current interpretation of this provision see, HRC General Comment No. 19 'Protection of the family, the right to marriage and equality of spouses (Art. 23), adopted at the thirty-ninth session, on 27 July 1990.

65 Some scholars have also held this view, see, for example, Robertson, A.H. & Merrills, J.G.: *Human rights in the world*, Manchester University Press, Manchester, Fourth edition, (1996), p. 276.

would be contrary to the object and purpose of the Covenant.[66] The Committee on Economic, Social and Cultural Rights has often emphasised that while the Covenant provides for progressive realisation, it also imposes various obligations which are of immediate effect.[67] The existence of immediate obligations with respect to economic, social and cultural rights is also established under regional human rights treaties aimed at the protection of economic, social and cultural rights.[68]

According to the Committee, '[t]he concept of progressive realisation constitutes a recognition of the fact *that full realisation of all economic, social and cultural rights* will generally not be able to be achieved in a short period of time.'[69] Arguably, this would be true of the realisation of both categories of rights. Admittedly, some dimensions of economic, social and cultural rights may involve progressive realisation to a greater extent than some civil and political rights, but it would be difficult to dispute that the full realisation of all human rights requires States to develop progressive policies.[70] It is difficult to deny that the implementation of rights contained in the ICCPR, such as article 14 (equality before the courts and tribunal), article 25 (right to

---

66 As Alston notes, describing the provisions of the Covenant as goals to be achieved progressively rather than through immediate implementation is manifestly incompatible with the object and purpose of the Covenant. See Alston, P.: 'U.S. ratification of the Covenant on Economic, Social and Cultural Rights: the need for an entirely new strategy.' In: *AJIL*, vol. 84, (1990), pp. 365-392.

67 See, for example, General Comment No. 3 para. 1, General Comment No. 11 para. 10 and General Comment No. 12 para. 16. The Committee has also stressed the existence of immediate obligation in its Concluding Observations, see, for example, Concluding Observations Zimbabwe E/1998/22 para. 79 and Concluding Observations Sri Lanka E/1999/22 para. 90.

68 In the Americas, the Inter-American Commission on Human Rights notes,'[t]he principle that economic, social and cultural rights are to be achieved progressively does not mean that the governments do not have the immediate obligation to make efforts to attain the full realisation of these rights […]'. Inter-American Commission Annual Report 1993, OEA/Ser.L/V/ii.85, February 1, 1993. At the European level, the European Social Charter generally requires that States Parties uphold the Charter standards, irrespective of their national resources, and that they do so immediately upon ratification. Gomien, D.; Harris, D. & Zwaak, L.: *Law and practice of the European Convention on Human Rights and the European Social Charter*, Council of Europe Publishing, Strasbourg, (1996), p. 381.

69 General Comment No. 3 para. 9 (emphasis added).

70 As Matas notes, the dichotomy between both categories of rights in terms of immediate and progressive obligations stems from confusion between 'rights' and 'goals'. As he explains, '[t]here is a difference between respect for the right to food and no one starving, respect for the right to shelter and no one homeless, and so on. […] If, for economic, social and cultural rights, rights and goals were the same, then for political and civil rights, they would also be the same. If respect for the right to food meant achievement of the ultimate goal of no one starving, then respect for the right to vote would mean achievement of the ultimate goal of everyone voting. Respect for the right to life would mean achievement of the ultimate goal of no one dying. But, clearly, respect for the right to vote does not mean everyone voting. Respect for the right to life does not mean no one dying.
The equation of economic, social and cultural rights with their related goals is more than just harmless confusion. The equation makes the achievement of respect for the rights seem unrealistic, a pious hope rather than something that can actually be accomplished. Equation of rights with goals ends up undermining efforts to respect the rights.' Matas, *op. cit.* (note 38), pp. 125-126.

vote, to be elected and equal access to public service) and article 23(2) (the right to marry), require the gradual removal of obstacles to their full implementation.

The immediate character of the obligations arising from the ICCPR was subject to debate during the drafting of the Covenant as well as in contemporaneous academic writing.[71] Further analysis with respect to obligations arising from the ICCPR is outside of the scope of this study, but it is, however, important to note that it has been established that the obligations imposed by the ICCPR are of immediate nature and that States cannot justify their failure to protect these rights by invoking a lack of resources. As McGoldrick notes, the Human Rights Committee seems not to accept the lack of resources as an excuse for non-compliance with the obligations imposed by the ICCPR, even when such an obligation may require significant resourcce levels for its implementation.[72] This position is also clear in some of its General Comments.[73]

The fact that civil and political rights are interpreted as being of immediate implementation, irrespective of the level of resources necessary for such implementation, suggests that, from the fact that rights require positive state action involving the use of resources, we need not jump to the conclusion that they are of a progressive nature. The distinction between immediate and progressive obligations seems not to be

---

71 For a further analysis of the issue of the progressive/immediate character of the obligations arising from the ICCPR see Schwelb, E.: 'The nature of the obligations of the States Parties to the International Covenant on Civil and Political Rights.' In: *René Cassin Amicorum Discipulorumque Liber*, Pedone, Paris (1969), vol. I, pp. 301- 324; Schwelb, op. cit. (note 64), pp. 839-842; Nowak, *op. cit.* (note 24), pp. 56 *et seq.*; McGoldrick, *op. cit.* (note 24), pp. 12 *et seq.*; and Boerefijn, I.: *The reporting procedure under the Covenant on Civil and Political Rights: practice and procedure of the Human Rights Committee.* Intersentia, Antwerp, (1999), pp. 20 *et seq.* The discussion has primarily focused on the specific formulation of some articles of the ICCPR such as Arts. 2(2) and 40 ICCPR, which seem to reveal a tendency for progressive implementation. It is important to note that Art. 2(2) requires States Parties to 'undertake to take the necessary steps' in order to adopt legislative or other measures. Some commentators have noted that this provision seems to recognise the principle of progressive application. In their view, the fact that a proposal to set a time-limit for taking 'the necessary steps' was not accepted, means that 'the immediate nature of the obligation is therefore somewhat weakened.' Robertson & Merrills, *op. cit.* (note 65), p. 35. The immediate or progressive character of other provisions has also been discussed. This is true with regard to, for example, Art. 23(1) ICCPR which states that the family is the natural and fundamental unit of society and is entitled to protection by society and the State, Art. 24(1) which determines the right of every child to measures of protection on the part of his family, society and the State and Art. 10(3) which provides that the essential aim of the penitentiary system shall be the reformation and social rehabilitation of prisoners, as well as the obligation to segregate juvenile offenders from adults. For a discussion of these three articles, see Caportorti, Francesco, *Patti internazionali sui diritti dell'uomo*, Cedam, Padova, (1967), pp. 30-31. For a rebuttal of this view, see Schwelb, *op. cit.* (note 71), p. 304.

72 See McGoldrick, *op. cit.* (note 24), pp. 273-274. The author provides clear examples, with cases before the HRC regarding prison conditions.

73 See, for example, the HRC's General Comment No. 21 para. 4. 'Treating all persons deprived of their liberty with humanity and with respect for their dignity is a fundamental and universally applicable rule. Consequently, the application of this rule, as a minimum, cannot be dependent on the material resources available in the State party.' (Emphasis added).

completely dependent on the level of resources required for the realisation of such rights. The ICCPR imposes positive obligations with financial consequences and it is clear that these obligations are of immediate effect, regardless of any financial or other considerations.[74]

2.2.4 Vague/precise obligations

Another argument held by some of the drafters was that civil and political rights had to be drafted in precise terms, whereas economic, social and cultural rights could 'by their very nature' be drafted only in general terms. Thus, a Covenant containing both sets of rights would 'lack equilibrium'.[75]

An alleged dichotomy between the two categories of rights in terms of their preciseness or vagueness is also linked to the alleged dichotomy between positive and negative duties. As Scott and Macklem explain, '[a]lthough the argument about imprecision is, in theory, independent of whether or not the right is felt to be negative or positive, this probably concedes too much, at least in respect of the strongest critics of social rights, who have difficulty conceptualising social rights as being anything but positive. Thus the imprecision argument is often bound up in the overall claim that social rights are positive.'[76]

Before embarking on an examination of this dichotomy, it is important to note that at the time of the drafting there were two schools of thought regarding the manner in which the substantive rights should be drafted. One school held that it was impossible in general instruments, such as the Covenants, to define the scope and the substance of each right in detail. According to this position that task should be left to national legislation. The other school of thought was of the opinion that substantive rights should be drafted with the greatest possible precision.[77]

The final result was a compromise between these two schools of thought which led to some inconsistencies in the way that the substantive rights were formulated in both Covenants. Some rights were drafted in general terms while others were more specifically described.[78] Thus, both the ICESCR and ICCPR contain rights described in

---

74 See McGoldrick, *op. cit.* (note 24), p. 275 and Nowak, *op. cit.* (note 24), p. 56.

75 See, for example, Mrs Mehta (India) and Ms. Roosevelt (United States of America) E/CN.4/SR.248 p. 8, of 10 July 1951. In addition see, UN doc. E/2573 (E/CN.4/705), Report of the tenth session of the Commission on Human Rights (1954), para. 173, p. 17.

76 Scott & Macklem, *loc. cit.* (note 39), p. 45.

77 UN doc. A/2929 (1955).

78 See Arambulo, *op. cit.* (note 33), p. 20.

general terms.[79] However, it is fair to say that circumstantial factors during the drafting process seem to have affected the ICESCR to a greater extent.[80]

Nevertheless, even if we assume that clarifications are required with respect to both Covenants due to the vagueness of some provisions, we must admit when comparing the scope of the obligations arising from the ICCPR with those emanating from the ICESCR, that the latter are more imprecise in scope. As we will try to demonstrate, the vagueness of the formulation of some economic, social and cultural rights provisions is the consequence of external circumstances rather than of the 'inherent' nature of economic, social and cultural rights.

The shape and contour of a right, or more precisely, of the obligations that it imposes, are the result of years of repeated application.[81] In this regard, economic, social and cultural rights suffer an enormous disadvantage. The vagueness of many of these rights is a consequence of the lack of attention. Civil and political rights have received far more attention than economic, social and cultural rights and, consequently, the former are now more precisely defined than the latter.[82]

The fact that some of the norms contained in the Covenant have maintained a degree of imprecision for so long has been the consequence of the implementation measures adopted for the Covenant. The lack of an individual compliant procedure has hindered the clarification process.[83] It is well known that individual complaints procedures, such as those established under the First Additional Protocol to the ICCPR, the European Convention on Human Rights and the American Convention, contribute significantly to the clarification of the content and scope of the obligations. Addition-

---

79 See Robertson & Merrills, *op. cit.* (note 65), p. 38. These commentators refer to some provisions in the ICCPR which 'are so general or imprecise as to make their interpretation a task of some difficulty.'

80 For clear examples of the different factors that were completely external to the 'inherent' nature of the rights that influenced the wording in which human rights were adopted in the Covenants, see the autobiographical account of John Humphrey, the first Director of the UN Division of Human Rights, 'Human rights & the United Nations: a great adventure'. Transnational Publishers, New York, (1984). As an example of how positions that changed over the years had a marked influence on the drafting, he points out that the ILO was opposed to the inclusion of economic, social and cultural rights, 'presumably because that they felt that this would impinge on their jurisdiction; but realising that their inclusion was now [1951] probably inevitable, they wanted the articles to be as general and as weak as possible.' In contrast, the author describes UNESCO and WHO as wanting 'detailed provisions stipulating explicit obligations'. See, Humphrey, *Ibidem:* pp. 141 and 143.

81 Matas, *op. cit.* (note 38), p. 125.

82 Chapter IV, section 2.2.4.

83 As Alston notes, if an individual complaint procedure is not adopted under the ICESCR, 'the result will be that the obligations flowing from the Covenant will continue to be stated only in the most general terms and will rarely be subject to the type of detailed judicial analysis that can help immeasurably in facilitating a clearer, more precise and more nunced understanding of the implications of international human rights norms'. Alston, P.: No right to complain about being poor: the need for an optional protocol to the economic rights Covenant, In: *The future of human rights protection in a changing world: fifty years since the four freedoms address. Essays in honour of Torkel Opsahl.* Eide, A. & Helgesen, J. (eds.), Norwegian University Press, Oslo, (1991), p. 88.

ally, the fact that the Covenant did not establish an independent expert body to supervise its implementation has negatively affected the degree of precision of these rights. As indicated earlier, serious efforts to clarify the normative content of the Covenant only began with the Committee which is a relatively new body.[84] Nonetheless, over the years the Committee has contributed significantly to establishing the meaning and scope of the obligations that the ICESCR imposes upon States Parties.

However, even admitting that nowadays, due to external reasons, civil and political rights are generally more precise than economic, social and cultural rights, this is not an 'inherent' characteristic of the obligations. The ICCPR has been interpreted as containing obligations that were not previously clear and in the near future their precision might be in dispute due to new circumstances not anticipated at the time of the drafting.[85] It is far from clear how far the duties imposed by civil and political rights will evolve in the future.[86] As we will see, the degree of protection needed to secure such rights varies according to changing circumstances.[87]

2.3 The present significance of the differences in wording of articles 2(1) of each Covenant

2.3.1 The meaning of article 2(1) ICESCR

The wording of article 2 of each Covenant was meant to reflect the alleged difference in nature between the two clusters of rights.[88] Since the dominant position among the drafters was that economic, social and cultural rights entailed highly resource-dependent positive obligations, the formulation finally adopted in article 2(1) of the ICESCR requires a State Party 'to take steps […] to the maximum of its available resources, with a view to achieve progressively the full realisation of the rights' recognised in the Covenant.

The wording of article 2(1) ICESCR differs significantly from the wording adopted in article 2(1) of the ICCPR, which establishes the obligation of each State Party 'to respect and to ensure' the rights recognised therein. This difference in wording is found in the UN Covenants but it is also *generally* the case that instruments aimed at protect-

84 Although both Covenants (the ICESCR and the ICCPR), entered into force in 1976, the first session of the Human Rights Committee, the monitoring body of the ICCPR, was held in March 1977, while the first session of the Committee on Economic, Social and Cultural Rights was ten years later in March 1987.

85 See, Federick Schauer: 'Authority and indeterminacy.' In: *Authority*. Pennock, Roland J. and Chapman, John W. (eds.), Nomos XXIX, New York University Press, New York, (1987), pp. 28 *et seq.*

86 This is evident, for example with regard to the protection afforded by the right to privacy. According to Plant, '[c]omputers and information technology pose a range of threats to privacy which could not have been foreseen two or three decades ago, and the degree of protection needed to secure such rights will therefore vary with technological advance.' Plant, 1986, p. 37.

87 See section 3.3.

88 See UN doc. A/2929, Report of the tenth session of the General Assembly (1955) and UN doc. A/5655.

ing civil and political rights adopt different wording regarding the obligations they impose than those aimed at the protection of economic, social and cultural rights.[89]

Despite the significant differences in the wording of the general obligations of article 2 of each Covenant, developments in international human rights law have rendered many of the drafters' assumptions untenable. It is therefore necessary to inquire into the present meaning of these articles.

The Committee on Economic, Social and Cultural rights expressly denies any sharp distinction between article 2(1) of each Covenant. As it notes,

> 'While great emphasis has sometimes been placed on the difference between the formulations used in this provision [art. 2(1)ICESCR] and that contained in the equivalent article 2 of the International Covenant on Civil and Political Rights, it is not always recognised that there are also significant similarities. In particular, while the Covenant provides for a progressive realisation and acknowledges the constraints due to the limits of available resources, it also imposes various obligations which are of immediate effect.'[90]

In other words, the Committee notes that the Covenant also imposes obligations with which States must comply immediately, regardless of their state of development. The immediate nature of some obligations arising from the Covenant is often repeated by the Committee[91] and this interpretation has been echoed by academic writers.[92] The immediate nature of some of the obligations of the Covenant is dealt with below.[93]

In sum, although many provisions of the Covenant are to be implemented progressively and in accordance with the maximum of the State Party's available resources, there are other rights that must be ensured immediately, without delay, upon the Covenant's entry into force.

2.3.2 The meaning of the State obligation to 'respect and ensure'

At the present stage of development of international law, the scope of the phrase 'respect and ensure' contained in article 2 ICCPR has a broader meaning than the drafting history of the Covenants suggests. It now seems clear that although the drafters principally envisaged the imposition of negative obligations upon States (abstention), article 2(1) of the Civil and Political Rights Covenant not only requires States to refrain

---

89 For example, Art. 1 ACHR (obligation to respect and ensure), Art. 1 Protocol of San Salvador (obligation to adopt measures), Art. 1 ECHR (obligation to secure) and Art. 1 ESC (obligation to pursue).

90 General Comment No. 3 para. 1.

91 See, for example, General Comment No. 4 para. 10; General Comment No. 11 para. 10; General Comment No. 12 para. 16; General Comment No. 13 para. 3 1; General Comment No. 14 para. 30; and Concluding Observations Zimbabwe E/1998/22 para. 79.

92 See, for example, Limburg Principle No. 22.

93 For an analysis of the immediate nature of some obligations of Part III, see Chapter V section 2.3 and Chapter VII section 2 *et seq.* for the immediate nature of the obligations contained in Part II of the Covenant.

from interfering in individuals' freedoms, but also imposes positive obligations upon States.

It is well established that while the duty 'to respect' entails negative obligations of non-interference by the State, the duty 'to ensure' is identified with the requirement of positive obligations upon States. This is the interpretation of the Human Rights Committee[94] as well as of commentators.[95]

Interpreting article 2(1) ICCPR, the Human Rights Committee expressly notes,

> 'The obligation under the Covenant is not confined to the respect of human rights, but that States Parties have also undertaken to ensure the enjoyment of these rights to all individuals under their jurisdiction. This aspect calls for specific activities by the States Parties to enable individuals to enjoy their rights. This is obvious in a number of articles (e.g. art. 3 which is dealt with in General Comment 4), but in principle this undertaking relates to all rights set forth in the Covenant.'[96]

Thus, despite the limited approach taken by the Covenants' drafters, today it is apparent that obligations to take measures are not confined merely to economic, social and cultural rights. It is possible to arrive at the same conclusion through an analysis of regional human rights treaties directed primarily at the protection of civil and political rights, such as the American Convention on Human Rights (ACHR) and the European Convention on Human Rights (ECHR).

Article 1 of the ACHR also uses the wording 'respect' and 'ensure'.[97] The Inter-American Court of Human Rights has interpreted this wording as linking the 'obligation to respect' with a negative undertaking and the obligation to 'ensure' with a posi-

---

94 The HRC has unambiguously endorsed this interpretation in several General Comments. See, for example, General Comment No. 4, para. 3, General Comment No. 17 paras. 18 and 10 and General Comment No. 28 para. 3.

95 Buergenthal, T.: 'To respect and to ensure: State obligations and permissible derogations.' In: *The International Bill of Rights*. Henkin, Louis (ed.), New York, Columbia University Press, (1981), p. 77; Shelton, D.: 'State responsibility for covert and indirect forms of violence.' In: *Human rights in the twenty-first century: a global challenge*. Mahoney, K. & Mahoney, P. (eds.), Martinus Nijhoff Publishers, Dordrecht, (1993), p. 267; O'Flaherty, M. & Heffernan L.: *International Covenant on Civil and Political Rights: international human rights law in Ireland*, Brehon Publishing, Dublin, (1995), p. 5; Harris, D. & Joseph, S.: *The International Covenant on Civil and Political Rights and United Kingdom Law*, Clarendon Press, Oxford, (1995), pp. 2-3; Klein, E.: The duty to protect and to ensure human rights under the International Covenant on Civil and Political Rights. Unpublished document on file with the author, (1999), p. 303; and Nowak, *op. cit.* (note 24), p. 36.

96 HRC General Comment No. 3 para. 1.

97 Article 1(1) ACHR reads: 'The States Parties to this Convention undertake to respect the rights and freedoms recognised herein and to ensure to all persons subject to their jurisdiction the free and full exercise of those rights and freedoms, without any discrimination for reasons of race, colour, sex, language, religion, political or other opinion, national or social origin, economic status, birth, or any other social condition.'

tive one. The Court has held this view in several judgements,[98] as well as in several advisory opinions.[99] Scholars adopt the same interpretation.[100]

At the European level, the wording varies from that of the ICCPR and ACHR as article 1 of the ECHR uses the wording 'to secure' for the general obligation of a contracting party. However, the term 'secure' has been interpreted to encompass both terms used in the ICCPR.[101] Furthermore, the duty 'to respect' is contained in the European Convention in some substantive rights.[102] In this regard, it is interesting to note that while the notion of 'respect' is generally interpreted as an obligation of a negative character, at the European level it is wellestablished that the meaning of the word 'respect' as it is contained in certain provisions is not clear-cut and its requirements vary considerably from case to case.[103] Today it is clear that it entails not only obligations upon States to refrain from acting (negative undertaking), but also some positive obligations on the part of the State.[104]

In conclusion, under contemporary international law, the duties to 'respect' and to 'ensure' under article 2(1) ICCPR imply not only the obligation to abstain from interfering in the individual's freedoms, but also the duty to take the positive actions necessary to ensure those rights. This is clearly the interpretation adopted by the HRC and it is supported by the practice of other international supervisory bodies for the protection of human rights.

---

98 See, for example, Velásquez Rodríguez, *loc. cit.* (note 46), paras. 166-168 and Godínez Cruz, *loc. cit.* (note 46), paras. 175-177.

99 See, for example, I/A Court H.R. Advisory Opinion No. 7 'Enforceability of the right to reply or correction (Arts. 14.1 and 2 ACHR)', OC-7/86 of 29 August 1986 paras. 28-33 and Advisory Opinion No. 11 'Exceptions to the exhaustion of domestic remedies (Arts. 46(1), 46(2)(a) and 46(2)(b) of the American Convention on Human Rights', *loc. cit.* (note 46), paras. 22-23.

100 See, for example, Buergenthal, T. & Shelton, D.: *Protecting human rights in the Americas: Cases and material*, Engel, Kehl, fourth revised edition, (1995), p. 431 and Faúndez Ledesma, H.: *El sistema interamericano de protección de los derechos humanos*. Inter-American Institute for Human Rights, Costa Rica, (1996), pp. 64-67.

101 See, for example, Viljanen, *op. cit.* (note 43), p. 52.

102 See article 8 ECHR and Art. 2 Protocol 1 of the ECHR.

103 See, for example, Abdulaziz, Cabales and Balkandaly v. the United Kingdom, Application Nos. 9214/80, 9473/81 and 9474/81, Judgement of 28 May 1985, para. 67; Cossey v. the United Kingdom, Application No. 10843/84, Judgement of 27 September 1990, para. 36; and B. v. France, Application No.13343/87, Judgement of 25 March 1992, para. 44.

104 See, for example, in regard to the obligation to 'respect' for family life and 'private life': Marckx, *loc. cit.* (note 46), para. 37; Abdulaziz, Cabales and Balkandaly, *loc. cit.* (note 103), para. 67; Rees v. the United Kingdom, Application No. 9532/81, Judgement of 17 October 1986, para. 35; López Ostra v. Spain, Application No. 16798/90, Judgement of 9 December 1994, para. 51; Cossey, *loc. cit.* (note 103), para. 36; and B. v. France, Application No. 13343/87, Judgement of 25 March 1992, para. 44. With regard to the duty to 'respect' the right to education, see Campbell and Cosans v. the United Kingdom, Application Nos. 7511/76 and 7743/76, Judgement of 25 February 1982, para. 37.

3 The spectrum of State obligations

3.1 Introduction

As we have seen, the assumption that civil and political rights impose merely negative obligations and economic, social and cultural rights solely positive obligations, may be considered as the source of the other alleged dichotomies among the two sorts of rights.

Nowadays it is well established that all human rights impose a variety of obligations, which have been identified as different levels or layers in the 'tripartite typology' of States' obligations.[105] For the sake of the analysis here, we shall refer to this as a 'continuum of a variety of duties' or a 'spectrum of a variety of duties.'[106] The idea is to stress that all human rights impose a variety of different obligations. Each obligation may require different levels of State interference, different levels of resources and may be established with greater or lesser precision. The discretion of the State as regards each of the obligations that a single human right may impose may vary depending on their different levels of precision.

The starting point of the analysis here is the jurisprudence of the major human rights supervisory bodies, such as the European Court of Human Rights, the Inter-American Court and the Human Rights Committee. These bodies have increasingly developed the positive component of the duties under civil and political rights. Today even those civil and political rights considered as the most classical negative rights, such as the right to life and the prohibition of torture and ill-treatment, are interpreted as imposing a spectrum of duties with different levels of State involvement.

Evolution in this area of the law has come from the necessity to provide effective protection for such rights and from interpreting the human rights instruments taking into account their specific object and purpose.[107] As a result of this evolution, the differences between civil and political rights and economic, social and cultural rights have blurred considerably.

---

105 While the 'tripartite typology' of State obligations developed by academia and openly accepted by the Committee is the most accurate analytical tool for assessing the existence of the different levels of obligations that all human rights impose, we are not using it at this stage of the analysis for reasons of manageability, as well as for substantive reasons. It will be discussed below when we examine the issue of the typologies of obligations. See Chapter V.

106 It is worth mentioning that the idea of a continuum of obligations is suggested in the 'tripartite typology' of States' duties as it was first developed by Henry Shue in 1980. Moreover, the expression 'continuum of a variety of duties' is used by Judge Kate O'Reagan, *loc. cit.* (note 38), p. 71 and a 'spectrum of obligations' has also been used by Künnemann in regard to the 'tripartite typology'. See Künnemann, 1995, pp. 323-342.

107 See the analysis on treaty interpretation in Chapter III section 2.

3.2 The concept of a spectrum of State obligations

According to the idea that all human rights impose a '*continuum of a variety of duties*' or a '*spectrum of a variety of duties*,' at one end of the spectrum there are obligations of non-interference by States and towards the other we find obligations requiring States' positive action (See figure 1). A specific duty can be located anywhere on the spectrum, notwithstanding from which category it springs (civil and political or economic, social and cultural rights). The degree of State involvement as well as the resources necessary to comply with the duties emanating from a specific right do not depend on the Covenant from which that right emerges but, rather, on the specific type of duty in question. We note that a single right may imposes different duties in order to be effective at a given time and in a given situation.

3.3 A concrete example: the right to life and State obligations

Even though the issue of positive obligations arising from civil and political rights will not figure prominently in this study, the issue is still relevant and it serves to illustrate the idea of the 'continuum of a variety of duties' imposed by each human right.

The significance of the 'continuum of obligations' is best seen in concrete cases. The following discussion will therefore analyse case law relating to the right to life and attempt to determine the different types of obligations arising from it. In the following analysis, the different obligations that the right to life imposes on States will be characterised as a sequence or spectrum of obligations. First, however, some preliminary considerations are necessary:

(a) The analysis is limited to the case law of the Inter-American Court of Human Rights, the European Court of Human Rights and the Human Rights Committee and focuses principally on their supervision of the implementation of the right to life contained in article 4 ACHR, article 2 ECHR and article 6 ICCPR respectively.[108]

(b) The following list of obligations is not intended to be an exhaustive description of all the obligations that the right to life may impose at the international level but is merely intended to illustrate the notion of a 'spectrum of State obligations'. The analysis will deal with the case law of different supervisory bodies together and focuses on topics in which they seem to converge. The case law cited is merely exemplary as a full discussion of the case law on the right to life would of course be a major undertaking and would lead us rather far afield. The analysis intends to focus on the more

108 The provisions in the three conventions employ different wording. The ICCPR and the ECHR use the phrase 'the right to life' while the ACHR refers to the right to respect for life. Nevertheless, this difference does not affect our analysis.

recent cases, although reference to some older landmark decisions is sometimes necessary.

(c) At the two ends of the spectrum we place the most negative and positive obligations, respectively. For the sake of illustration, we will say that on the left extreme of the spectrum we find the most negative obligation, which we identify as the duty to refrain from killing someone. At the other end (the right extreme of the spectrum), we find the duty to satisfy the basic needs necessary to keep someone alive, which we identify as the most positive component of the right to life.

(d) At the current stage of development of international human rights law, both extremes are merely abstractions because existing obligations fall somewhere in between the two extremes, but without extending to either extreme. This is particularly true of what we have identified as the most negative component (to refrain from killing someone), because the prohibition of the death penalty is not established in the instruments under analysis,[109] as well as because there are circumstances in which state agents may legitimately kill someone *i.e.* self-defence. With regard to the most positive component we have to recognise that when dealing with individuals' complaints, international human rights supervisory bodies seem reluctant to interpret the right to life as imposing, in all circumstances, the duty to provide for the commodities necessary to keep someone alive.

(e) As we move from the negative end of the spectrum to the positive one, the obligations require more resources for their implementation and their scope becomes increasingly more imprecise.

(f) All of the duties within the spectrum are essential components of the right to life. The right cannot be secured through the fulfilment of only one duty and the State violates the right to life if it fails to comply with any one of its corresponding duties. Consequently, it is possible to violate the right to life on different grounds. In practice, it is not rare to find that human rights' supervisory bodies deal with different grounds separately before ruling on whether there has been a violation of the right to life.

---

109 See article 6(2) ICCPR, article 2(2) ECHR and article 4(2) ACHR. It is worth noting that under general international law the abolition of the death penalty is not expressly required. Nonetheless, there are some instruments which do commit State Parties to abolition. The prohibition of the death penalty is established under Protocol No. 6 ECHR [adopted by the Committee of Ministers of the Council of Europe in December 1982], Second Optional Protocol to the ICCPR aiming at the abolition of the death penalty [adopted by General Assembly Res. 44/128 of 15 December 1989] and Second Protocol to the American Convention on Human Rights to Abolish the Death Penalty [adopted at Asunción, Paraguay on 8 June 1990, 20th Regular Session of the General Assembly, OAS Treaty Series No. 73]. For a comprehensive analysis of the death penalty see, Rodley, N.: *The treatment of prisoners under international law*. Clarendon Press, Oxford, second edition, (1999), pp. 204-242.

Negative extreme of the spectrum: the duty to refrain from killing someone

A. *The duty to refrain from intentional and unlawful taking of life*

This duty requires States to abstain from *arbitrarily* killing individuals under their jurisdiction.[110] This is a minimum that entails that the State cannot take someone's life. Nevertheless, this is not an absolute prohibition of taking life by the State, because there are some circumstances when the deprivation of life may be justified.[111] This is true, for example, in the case of self-defence by law enforcement officials or in the implementation of a death sentence ordered by a court following conviction for a crime for which that penalty is provided by law (in countries that still retain it). Nevertheless, in the latter case, the death penalty cannot be imposed except for the most serious crimes and following proceedings which strictly respect all the procedural safeguards of fair trial.

Under this duty we would also consider the obligation of States to refrain from extraditing individuals if there is a real risk of a violation of the right to life in the requesting State.[112] This latter obligation entails a more positive requirement than the mere abstention from arbitrarily killing someone, because it would entail positive

110 The ICCPR and the ACHR forbid any 'arbitrary deprivation' of life, while the ECHR refers to any 'intentional deprivation'. The analysis here intends to cover both wordings.

111 Article 2(2) ECHR establishes that, '[d]eprivation of life shall not be regarded as inflicted in contravention of this article when it results from the use of force which is no more than absolutely necessary: (a) in defence of any person from unlawful violence; (b) in order to effect a lawful arrest or to prevent the escape of a person lawfully detained; (c) in action lawfully taken for the purpose of quelling a riot or insurrection.'

112 See, for example, Kindler v. Canada, Communication No. 470/91, views of 30 July 1993, para. 9.4 and Soering v. the United Kingdom, Application No. 14038/88, Judgement of 7 July 1989. In the latter case, the European Court expressly stated the obligation of State 'not to surrender an individual unless satisfied that the conditions awaiting him in the country of destination are in full accord with each of the safeguards of the Convention.' (para. 86). It is interesting to note that in the case of Ng v. Canada, Communication No. 469/1991, views of 5 November 1993), the HRC took a limited view of the positive measures that States must take to determine whether or not there is a real risk of a violation of the right to life in the requesting country. According to the Committee, if Canada extradited Mr. Ng it would expose him to a real risk of a violation of his rights under article 6(2) in the USA [which was not party to the Optional Protocol], and Canada itself may thereby be in violation of the Covenant [paras. 14.1 and 14.2]. However, considering the facts of the case, the HRC concluded that there was no indication in the files that the trial in the USA would not meet the requirements of due process (Art. 14 ICCPR). In an unfortunate decision it was held that 'the Committee does not find that the terms of article 6 of the Covenant necessarily require Canada to refuse to extradite or to seek assurances. The Committee notes that the extradition of Mr. Ng would have violated Canada's obligations under article 6 of the Covenant if the decision to extradite without assurances had been taken summarily or arbitrarily. The evidence before the Committee reveals, however, that the Minister of Justice reached his decision [not to seek assurances] after hearing extensive arguments in favour of seeking assurances' [para. 15.6 (emphasis added)].

measures for the State to ensure that there is no risk of the arbitrary imposition of the death penalty in the requesting country.

B. *The duty to take positive measures to protect individuals under the jurisdiction of the State from being killed*

This is a step further along the continuum from duty [A]. Here the right to life encompasses not only the obligation of the State to refrain from arbitrarily or intentionally killing individuals or to refrain from extraditing individuals if their lives would be at risk. This duty requires States to take positive measures to protect the lives of individuals. The Inter-American Court and the European Court have held that the protection of the right to life requires States to take appropriate steps to safeguard the lives of those within their jurisdictions.[113] These measures include the establishment of criminal penalties, civil remedies and compensatory proceedings to prevent arbitrary killings in the State concerned and go as far as the duty to take specific preventive measures to protect an individual whose life is at risk from the criminal acts of another individual or group. Certainly all these measures involve the diversion of State resources.

B.1. *To protect individuals from being killed by State agents*

States not only have to refrain from intentional deprivation of life, but must also take appropriate steps to safeguard the lives of those within their jurisdiction from wrongdoing by the State's agents that may result in an unintended deprivation of life. The measures required are wide-ranging, from establishing legislative measures aimed at controlling and limiting the circumstances in which firearms may be used by State agents to providing appropriate training for law enforcement personnel in the use of force and firearms.[114]

When planning and conducting an operation where individuals' lives are at risk,[115] States are required to take precautions in the choice of means and methods employed by State officials. The planning and conduct of an operation must be carried out and controlled by the authorities in a manner which minimises, to the greatest extent

113 See, for example, L.C.B. v. the United Kingdom, Application No. 2341/94, Judgement of 9 June 1998, para. 36; Osman, *loc. cit.* (note 46), para. 115; Kaya v. Turkey, Application No. 22535/93, Judgement 28 March 2000, para. 101; Kiliç v. Turkey, Application No. 22492/93, Judgement of 28 March 2000, para. 62; and Velokova v. Bulgaria, Application No. 41488/98, Judgement of 18 May 2000, para. 75.

114 See, for example, McCann and others, *loc. cit.* (note 46), para. 151, Hugh Jordan v. the United Kingdom, Application No. 24746/94, Judgement 4 May 2001, para. 102 and Guerrero v. Colombia, Communication No. 45/1979, views of 31 March 1982 para. 13.I.

115 Individuals' lives may be put at risk when the State decides to carry out a security operation which may involve the use of force or firearms [McCann and others, *loc. cit.* (note 46)], but also when the State carries out nuclear testing [L.C.B., loc. cit. (note 112), paras. 38-40]. In general, States must prevent putting individuals' lives at risk when this is avoidable.

possible, any risk to life.[116] Among other measures, States are required to take into account different contingencies in planning, to adopt provisions for a margin of error, to consider sufficient alternative possibilities and to establish procedures to review the lawfulness of the use of force in specific cases.[117] In general, States have the duty to 'take appropriate care' in the control and organisation of an operation in which there is a risk to life.[118]

Therefore, for example, if in carrying out a police operation, a State fails to take the precautions required by the circumstances of the case and someone is killed as a result, it would likely be regarded as a failure to protect the right to life. In such a case the violation of the right to life would be due to an omission on the part of the State.

B.2. *To protect individuals from being killed by third parties*

States are required to take 'reasonable' protective measures to protect an individual whose life is at risk from the criminal acts of other individuals. A State's obligations in this respect extend beyond the duty to establish effective criminal law provisions to deter the commission of offences and may imply the duty to take preventive operational measures to protect an individual whose life is at risk.

If a State fails to protect the right to life by, for example, failing to penalise dangerous behaviour or, if in well defined circumstances, it fails to provide security to protect an individual at risk, this gives rise to State responsibility even though the damaging action may have been committed by private individuals.[119] In the case of Osman v. the United Kingdom, the test that the European Court established to find a violation of the positive obligation to protect the right to life from the criminal acts of another individual was that the 'authorities knew or ought to have know at the time of the existence of a real risk to the life of an identified individual from the criminal acts of a third party and that they failed to take measures within the scope of their powers.'[120] In other words, if in the above-mentioned circumstances the State fails to take positive measures to prevent and suppress offences against the person at risk, it would be a violation of the right to life. Again, here it would be the consequence of the State having omitted

116 McCann and others, *loc. cit.* (note 46); Ergi v. Turkey, Application No. 23818/94, Judgement 28 July 1998, paras. 79-81; I/A Court H.R. Neira Alegría *et al.* v. Peru, Judgement of 19 January 1995, Series C No. 20, paras. 74-76; and Guerrero, *loc. cit.* (nota 114), paras. 13.2 and 13.3.

117 As the European Court emphasises, 'a general legal prohibition of arbitrary killing by the agents of the State would be ineffective, in practice, if there existed no procedure for reviewing the lawfulness of the use of lethal force by State authorities.' McCann and others, *loc. cit.* (note 46), para. 161.

118 McCann and others, *loc. cit.* (note 46), para. 213 and Güleç v. Turkey, Application No. 21593/93, Judgement of 27 July 1998, para. 73.

119 See, for example, Delgado v. Colombia, Communication No. 195/1985, views of 12 July 1990, paras. 5.5-5.10, Osman, *loc. cit.* (note 46), para. 115 and Kaya, loc. cit. (note 113) para. 101.

120 Osman, *loc. cit.* (note 46), para. 116.

to take positive measures which might be very costly, such as the cost of surveillance and protection for the individual at risk.

C. *The duty to carry out an effective official investigation when individuals have been killed or have disappeared*

Respecting the right to life, in conjunction with the general duties to 'ensure' (article 1(1) ACHR and article 2(1) ICCPR) or 'to secure' in the case of the ECHR (article 1 ECHR), requires States to carry out an 'effective' official investigation by an appropriate and impartial body (a) when individuals have been killed as a result of the use of force[121] and (b) when there is a case of the 'disappearance' of a person in circumstances that may involve a violation of the right to life.[122] Very graphically, the European Court tends to call these obligations the 'State's procedural obligations to protect the right to life',[123] because they refer to the way in which the State must 'proceed' after a deprivation of life has occurred under its jurisdiction or after someone has disappeared.

The responsibility of the State to proceed with an 'effective' investigation is engaged even when there is no evidence that agents of the State have been implicated in the killing or disappearance and even if members of the victim's family or others have not lodged a formal complaint about the killing with the authorities.[124] This duty is more stringent when the disappeared person was last held in State custody. In such circumstances it is incumbent upon the State to provide a plausible explanation as to the detainee's fate, as well as to ensure some form of independent monitoring.[125]

---

121 See, for example, Hugh Jordan, *loc. cit.* (note 114), para. 105; Kaya, loc. cit. (note 113), para. 108; Velásquez Rodríguez, *loc. cit.* (note 46), para. 177; Neira Alegría *et al.*, *loc. cit.* (note 116), paras. 74-76; and Ana Rosario Celis Laureano v. Peru, Communication No. 540/1993, views of 25 March 1996, para. 8.2.

122 See, for example, Ana Rosario Celis Laureano, *loc. cit.* (note 121), para. 8.2; Bleier v. Uruguay, Communication No.30/1978, views of 29 March 1982, para. 14; Joaquín and José Herrera Rubio and Ema Rubio de Herrera v. Colombia, Communication No. 161/1983, views of 2 November 1987, para. 10.3; Nydia Erika Bautista de Arellana, v. Colombia, Communication No. 563/1993, views of 27 October 1995, para. 10; and Cyprus v. Turkey, Application No. 25781/94, Judgement of 10 May 2001, para. 136 (as to Greek–Cypriot missing persons).

123 See, for example, Timurtas v. Turkey, Application No. 23531/94, Judgement of 13 June 2000, para. 90; Ergi, *loc. cit.* (note 116), para. 82; Kaya, *loc. cit.* (note 113), para. 96; Kiliç, *loc. cit.* (note 113), para. 78; Case of Ta* v. Turkey, Application No. 24396/94, Judgement of 14 November 2000, para. 72; and the case of Cyprus, *loc. cit.* (note 122), para. 131.

124 See, for example, Velásquez Rodríguez, *loc. cit.* (note 46); I/A Court H.R. Fairén Garbi and Solís Corrales, Judgement of 15 March, 1989, Series C No. 6 paras. 157-161; Ergi, *loc. cit.* (note 116), para. 82; Yasa v. Turkey, Application No. 22495/93, Judgement of 2 September 1998, para. 100; Tanrikulu v. Turkey, Application No. 23763/94, Judgement of 8 July 1999, para. 103; and Velokova, *loc. cit.* (note 113), para. 74.

125 See, Case of Ta*, *loc. cit.* (note 123), para. 63. The Court held that the detainee must be presumed to have died in custody. Also, Satik and others v. Turkey, Application No. 31866/96, Judgement of 10

If the State fails to undertake an official investigation it would be in breach of the right to life.[126] However, it would also entail a breach of the obligation if, after having investigated, the investigation is considered by the supervisory organs to be 'ineffective'. The human rights monitoring organs have referred to various reasons for considering an investigation 'ineffective', including, for example, because it was not initiated promptly and immediately after someone's death; because it was short in length and limited in scope; because it contained unexplained failures to take obvious steps; or due to the lack of independence of the organs entrusted to investigate.[127]

Particularly worthy of mention is the position of the European Court regarding the requirements for an 'effective investigation'. According to the European Court the investigation must also be effective in the sense that it is capable of leading to the identification and punishment of those responsible.[128] Otherwise, according to the Court, the investigation would be 'ineffective in practice and it would be possible in some cases for agents of the State to abuse the rights of those within their control with virtual impunity.'[129]

In general, the form of an 'effective' investigation will vary according to the circumstances of the case. Nonetheless, in all cases an effective investigation will entail the allocation of resources.

October 2000, paras. 55-56 (as to the violation of Art. 3 ECHR). As for the Americas see, for example, Velásquez Rodríguez, *loc. cit.* (note 46) para. 188.

126 Within the European Court's case law, this is apparent in Tanli v. Turkey, Application No. 26129/95, Judgement of 10 April 2001, para. 154; the case of Cyprus, *loc. cit.* (note 122), para. 136; and Timurtas, *loc. cit.* (note 123), para. 90. The same reasoning has been adopted by the Human Rights Committee [*e.g.* Herrera Rubio, *loc. cit.* (note 122), para. 11]. However, in the Americas, in light of the Court's statement in the Fairén Garbi and Solís Corrales case [Fairén Garbi and Solís Corrales, *loc. cit.* (note 124), para. 159], it is not quite clear that a lack of investigation in itself constitutes a violation of the State's' duties.

127 Kiliç, *loc. cit.* (note 113), para. 83, Velokova, *loc. cit.* (note 113), paras. 78 and 82 and Kaya, *loc. cit.* (note 113), para. 109.

128 However, as the Court notes, 'this is not an obligation of result but of means.' Hugh Jordan, *loc. cit.* (note 114), para. 107. See also Assenov and others v. Bulgaria, Application No. 24760/94 of 28 October 1998, para. 102. Although the latter case deals with a violation of Art. 3 ECHR, the statements regarding the necessary investigation may reasonably be extended to the protection of the right to life. The Inter-American Court seems to adopt the same approach when it says, 'the duty to investigate [...] is not breached merely because the investigation does not produce a satisfactory result.' See, *Velásquez Rodríguez, loc. cit.* (note 46),para. 177 and *Godínez Cruz, loc. cit.* (note 46), para. 188 In addition, Caballero Delgado and Santana v. Colombia, Judgement of 8 December 1995, Series C No. 17, para. 58.

129 Assenov and others, *loc. cit.* (note 128), para. 102.

D. *The duty to provide an effective remedy (duty to take measures as a consequence of a previous failure to protect the right to life)*

So far, we have examined the responsibility of States when there is an arbitrary deprivation of life by State agents (duty [A]), when they fail to protect the right to life (duty [B]), even when private persons have committed the deprivation of life (duty [B.2]), when they fail to carry out an 'effective' official investigation after individuals have been killed or have disappeared and even when there is no evidence to implicate State agents in the facts (duty [C.2]). Here we will examine the measures that States must take after a failure to prevent the deprivation of/protect the right to life in any of the above mentioned cases.

The important point here is that every time that State responsibility is engaged, new positive obligations may arise. According to the supervisory bodies whose decisions are analysed here, these obligations arise from article 1(1) ACHR (to ensure rights),[130] article 2(3) ICCPR (to ensure an effective remedy in case of violation)[131] and article 13 ECHR (effective remedy).[132]

While the obligations that we will examine here arise when substantive rules have already been violated, they nonetheless entail positive actions with clear financial implications for the State. These obligations may arise not only when State agents have committed the violation of the right to life, but also when there is no evidence that State agents have been involved in the killing or disappearance of a person.[133]

Given the jurisprudence of the major human rights supervisory bodies, it is safe to say that when there has been a violation of the right to life, States are required to take the following actions:[134]

130 In a seminal case, the Inter-American Court gave a very broad interpretation to the duty to 'ensure' contained in Art. 1(1) ACHR. It indicates that 'As a consequence of this obligation, [obligation to ensure] the State must prevent, investigate and punish any violation of the rights recognised by the Convention and, moreover, if possible attempt to restore the right violated and provide compensation as warranted for damages resulting from the violation'. Velásquez Rodríguez, *loc. cit.* (note 46), para. 166.

131 Art. 2(3)(a) ICCPR reads as follows: 'Each State party to the present Covenant undertakes: to ensure that any persons whose rights or freedoms as herein recognised are violated shall have an effective remedy, notwithstanding that the violation has been committed by persons acting in an official capacity.'

132 Article 13 ECHR states, ' Everyone whose rights and freedoms as set forth in [the] Convention are violated shall have an effective remedy before a national authority notwithstanding that the violation has been committed by persons acting in an official capacity.'

133 See, for example, Kaya, *loc. cit.* (note 113), para. 125.

134 See, for example, Kaya, *loc. cit.* (note 113), para. 124; Tanrikulu, *loc. cit.* (note 124), para. 117; Velásquez Rodríguez, *loc. cit.* (note 46), para. 166; Caballero Delgado and Santana, *loc. cit.* (note 128), para. 58; Bleier, *loc. cit.* (note 122) para. 15; Herrera Rubio, *loc. cit.* (note 122), paras. 12 and 15; and Ana Rosario Celis Laureano, *loc. cit.* (note 121), para. 10.

(a) To provide compensation where appropriate. After someone has been deprived of life, it is not possible to restore it. Nevertheless, the State may be required to make payment to the victim's family.

(b) To undertake a thorough and effective investigation capable of leading to the identification and punishment of those responsible for the deprivation of life or the disappearance of a person in circumstances that may involve the violation of the right to life. According to the ECHR, the complainant must have effective access to the investigation procedure.[135]

(c) To prosecute perpetrators and bring to justice those found responsible. According the Human Rights Committee, some form of criminal proceeding is necessary. As it notes, in the event of a violation of the right to life, disciplinary and administrative measures against those responsible might not fully discharge the State's international responsibility. It may be obligated to resort to criminal proceedings.[136]

It is worth noting that the Human Rights Committee interprets the obligation to provide an appropriate remedy (article 2(3) ICCPR) as imposing a variety of positive obligations upon the State. In addition to those mentioned above, it has interpreted the provision as creating an obligation to provide appropriate protection for members of the victims' family against possible harassment,[137] and the broad obligation to take measures to ensure that similar events do not occur in the future.[138]

E. *The duty to satisfy the basic needs necessary for sustaining the lives of those persons who cannot do so themselves*

The protection of the right to life sometimes requires States to provide assistance or commodities to those deprived of the means to protect their lives through their own efforts. In light of the case law, it is possible to distinguish two different kinds of duty-holders: (a) individuals who cannot satisfy their basic needs through their own efforts because they are held in State custody and (b) individuals who cannot satisfy

---

135 See, for example, Kaya, *loc. cit.* (note 113), para. 124 and Tanrikulu, *loc. cit.* (note 124), para. 117.

136 See, for example, Nydia Erika Bautista de Arellana, *loc. cit.* (note 122), where the HRC held, 'purely disciplinary and administrative remedies cannot be deemed to constitute adequate and effective remedies within the meaning of article 2, paragraph 3 of the Covenant, in the event of particularly serious violations of human rights, notably in the event of an alleged violation of the right to life' [para. 8.2]. In Ana Rosario Celis Laureano, *loc. cit.* (note 121), the HRC laid down the obligation to bring to justice those responsible for the disappearance 'notwithstanding any domestic amnesty legislation to the contrary' [para. 10].

137 Nydia Erika Bautista de Arellana, loc. cit. (note 121), para. 10.

138 The reference to an 'obligation to take measures to prevent similar violations in the future', is a general statement common to every case in which the HRC has found a violation. With regard to the right to life, see, for example, note 137.

their basic needs because they are in a vulnerable and disadvantaged position in society.

E.1. *For individuals held in State custod*

Following the use of the term by the HRC when referring to 'individuals held under State custody', we speak of anyone deprived of liberty under the laws and authority of the State in an institution or establishment within the jurisdiction of the State, such as prisons, psychiatric hospitals and detention centres.[139]

States are required to take adequate measures to protect the lives of individuals held in their custody. These obligations include the duty to provide proper medical care when someone in State custody requires it and to make available adequate food and water in order to sustain life.[140] It is important to note here that the duty to provide medical treatment as well as the duty to meet survival requirements to allow individuals to sustain life with dignity while they are being held under State custody has also been analysed under the prohibition of inhuman and degrading treatment.

At the universal level, article 10(1) ICCPR stipulates that 'all persons deprived of their liberty shall be treated with humanity and with respect for the inherent dignity of the human person.' As the Human Rights Committee observes, when liberty is constrained other rights should not be limited any more than required by this deprivation of liberty.[141] Therefore, when individuals are deprived of their liberty they retain the right to enjoy economic, social and cultural rights which should be provided by the State in a way that allows them to live in dignity. It is worth stressing that according to the HRC, '[t]reating all persons deprived of their liberty with humanity and with respect for their dignity is a fundamental and universally applicable rule. Consequently, the application of this rule, as a minimum, cannot be dependent on the material resources available in the State party.'[142]

Additionally, the Human Rights Committee has emphasised that article 10(1) ICCPR must be applied in accordance with the relevant UN standards applicable to the treatment of prisoners,[143] and in most of those instruments there are express provisions concerning economic, social and cultural rights.[144]

---

139 See HRC General Comment No. 21 para. 2.

140 See, for example, Barbato v. Uruguay, Communication No. 84/1981, views of 21 October 1982, para. 9.2 Neira Alegría *et al.*, *loc. cit.* (note 116), para. 60 and Velokova, *loc. cit.* (note 113), para. 75.

141 As it notes in HRC General Comment No. 21 'Persons deprived of their liberty enjoy all the rights set forth in the Covenant, subject to the restrictions that are unavoidable in a closed environment' [para. 3].

142 HRC General Comment No. 21 para. 4.

143 HRC General Comment No. 21 para. 4.

144 See: Standard Minimum Rules for the Treatment of Prisoners (1957); the Body of Principles for the Protection of All Persons under Any Form of Detention or Imprisonment (1988); the Code of Conduct for Law Enforcement Officials (1979); and the Principles of Medical Ethics relevant to the Role of

Detention conditions that have been considered by the Human Rights Committee as violating article 10(1) ICCPR include the following: (1) the lack of a mattress or other bedding; (2) inadequate hygienic or sanitary conditions; (3) no ventilation or electric lighting; (4) denial of exercise; (5) denial of medical treatment or inadequate medical attention; (6) denial of food, or inadequate quality and quantity of food; (7) the lack of clean drinking water; and (8) the lack of necessary measures to accommodate a disabled person.[145] Although each of these conditions taken individually may not be considered as a violation of article 10(1) (with the exception of a denial of medical treatment),[146] the combination of two or more has been consistently considered as a breach of article 10(1) ICCPR.[147]

At the European level, the European Court has also consistently held that conditions of persons in a place of detention may amount to inhumane treatment.[148] Violations of article 3 of the European Convention have been found for conditions such as: overcrowding; inadequate heating or toilets; sleeping arrangements, food; inadequate recreation; and provision for contact to the outside world.[149]

Once again, in order to assess conditions of detention, account should be taken of the cumulative effect of the conditions as well as the specific allegations. It is also important to stress that even when the State has left the administration of prisons or psychiatric hospitals in the hands of private companies or corporations, it retains

---

Health Personnel, particularly Physicians, in the Protection of Prisoners and Detainees against Torture and Other Cruel, Inhuman or Degrading Treatment or Punishment (1982).

145 See, for example, Christopher Brown v. Jamaica, Communication No. 775/1997, views of 23 March 1999; Errol Smith and Oval Stewart v. Jamaica, Communication No. 668/1995, views of 8 April 1999; and Lancy Gallimore v. Jamaica, Communication No. 680/1996, views of 23 July 1999.

146 See, note 145 and General Comment No. 20 'concerning the prohibition of torture and cruel treatment or punishment' (Art. 7) which stated: 'the protection of the detainee also requires that prompt and regular access be given to doctors […]' (para. 11). In addition see, for example, Trevor Bennett v. Jamaica, Communication No. 590/1994, views of 25 March 1999.

147 In order to succeed in a petition, the complainant should make a specific allegation. It is not sufficient merely to refer to the general conditions of the place of detention. After receiving the complaint, the Committee requests the State to investigate the matter. If the State does not do so, or is unable to contest the facts, the Committee finds a violation. Additionally, as the Committee has emphasised, the State Party is under the obligation to ensure that all individuals within its territory and subject to its jurisdiction enjoy the rights recognised in the Covenant and to provide an effective remedy in case a violation has been found. In this kind of case the State is always requested to compensate the victim and to ensure that similar violations do not occur in the future.

148 For example, in Hurtado v. Switzerland, Application No. 17549/90, Judgement of 28 January 1994, the European Commission held unanimously that article 3 ECHR had been violated because Mr. Hurtado was not given immediate medical treatment for the fracture of one of his ribs that he had suffered during his arrest. Finally, the case was resolved by a friendly settlement.

149 See, for example, Harris, D.; O'Boyle, M. & Wabrick, C.: *Law of the European Convention on Human Rights*. Butterworths, London, (1995), pp. 55 *et seq*. and Dijk, P. van & Hoof, G.J.H. van: *Theory and practice of the European Convention on Human Rights*, Kluwer Law International, The Hague, third edition, (1998), pp. 317 *et seq*.

ultimate responsibility for the protection of human rights. Thus, the State is still responsible for any mistreatment suffered by individuals in those kinds of institutions.[150]

In sum, States are not only prohibited from intentionally killing individuals, but they are also obliged to take measures to fulfil the survival requirements of those individuals who cannot satisfy their survival requirements by their own means because they are being held in custody. While not yet generally regarded as a violation of the right to life *per se*, the denial of access to adequate health treatment, food or water to a prisoner or individuals being held under State custody may entail a violation of the prohibition against inhuman or degrading treatment. Indeed, the right to be treated with dignity has been interpreted as requiring States to provide certain commodities for the satisfaction of the basic needs of those individuals in their custody.

E.2. *For deprived individuals under the jurisdiction of the State*

While there is consistent case law establishing the duty of States to ensure the satisfaction of the requirements necessary for sustaining life (such as food, water and health), for individuals being held in custody, the obligation to ensure access to the means of survival for deprived people under the jurisdiction of the State is not yet clearly established in the case law of the international supervisory bodies. Nevertheless, this approach has been adopted by academic writers[151] and by the Human Rights Committee.

As the Human Rights Committee stated almost a decade ago, the right to life cannot be interpreted in a narrow sense. In its well-known General Comment on the right to life, the Committee suggested that the right to life entails the adoption of positive measures to protect life through the elimination of malnutrition and epidemics. In the HRC's words,

---

150 See General Comment No. 20 on article 7 where it stated that 'it is the duty of the State party to afford everyone protection through legislative and other measures as may be necessary against the acts prohibited by article 7 whether inflicted by people acting in their official capacity, outside their official capacity or in a private capacity' (para. 2). At the European level, the Judgement of the ECHR in A. v. the United Kingdom [Application No. 25599/94, Judgement of 23 September 1998] is of great relevance. The Court found the UK responsible under Art. 3 for the beating of a child by his stepfather. The Court considered that the 'obligation on the High Contracting Parties under Art. 1 of the Convention to secure to everyone within their jurisdiction the rights and freedoms defined in the Convention, taken together with Art. 3, requires States to take measures designed to ensure that individuals within their jurisdiction are not subjected to torture or inhuman or degrading treatment or punishment, including such ill-treatment administered by private individuals. Children and other vulnerable individuals, in particular, are entitled to State protection, in the form of effective deterrence, against such serious breaches of personal integrity' (para. 22).

151 Ramcharan, B.G.: The concept and dimensions of the right to life. In: *The right to life in international law*. Ramcharan, B.G. (ed.), Martinus Nijhoff Publishers, Dordrecht, (1985), pp. 6-10. See also, Ramcharan, B.G.: 'The right to life.' In: *NILR*, (1983), p. 314.

'The Committee has noted that the right to life has been too often narrowly interpreted. The expression 'inherent right to life' cannot properly be understood in a restrictive manner, and the protection of this right requires that States adopt positive measures. In this connection, the Committee considers that it would be desirable for States parties to take all possible measures to reduce infant mortality and to increase life expectancy, especially in adopting measures to eliminate malnutrition and epidemics.'[152]

The Committee has been consistent in this position. For example, in General Comment No. 28 the Human Rights Committee again clearly establishes that according to article 6 ICCPR, States Parties are obliged to take positive measures to protect life and among the measures it suggests is the necessity to provide health care and family planning programes for women. Moreover, it expressly requires that when reporting on article 6, States should provide information 'on the impact on women of poverty and deprivation that may pose a threat to their lives.'[153]

The same line of argument has been held by the HRC when examining States' party reports. The Committee often recommends that States take positive measures for the satisfaction of certain basic needs as a requirement for compliance with the right to life. For example, when examining the Fourth Periodic Report of Canada, the HRC stated, '[t]he Committee is concerned that homelessness has led to serious health problems and even to death. The Committee recommends that the State party take positive measures required by article 6 to address this serious problem.'[154]

Despite the consistent position of the HRC in relation to the necessity to adopt positive measures to protect the right to life in its Concluding Observations as well as General Comments, it is noteworthy that when it has dealt with individual complaints, the HRC has seemed rather reluctant to apply the same approach.[155]

---

152 HRC General Comment No. 6 para. 5.

153 HRC General Comment No. 28 para. 10 reads as follows: 'When reporting on the right to life protected by article 6, States Parties should provide data on birth rates and on pregnancy- and childbirth-related deaths of women. Gender-desegregated data should be provided on infant mortality rates. States Parties should give information on any measures taken by the State to help women prevent unwanted pregnancies, and to ensure that they do not have to undergo life-threatening clandestine abortions. States Parties should also report on measures to protect women from practices that violate their right to life, such as female infanticide, the burning of widows and dowry killings. The Committee also wishes to have information on the particular impact on women of poverty and deprivation that may pose a threat to their lives.'

154 Concluding Observations Canada CCPR/C/79/Add.105 para. 12, of 7 April 1999. In addition, see, for example, in GAOR Official Records Fifty-fourth session, Supplement No. 40 A/54/40 (I), Concluding Observations Lesotho (para. 255) and Poland (para. 349) and in GAOR Official Records, Fifty-third Session, Supplement No. 40 A/53/40 (I) the Concluding Observations Ecuador (para. 284).

155 See, for example, Plotnikov v. Russian Federation, Communication No. 784/1997, inadmissibility decision of 25 March 1999. In a nutshell, the case refers to the complaint lodged by a Russian national who suffered from a grave disease for which it is necessary to take expensive medicines. The applicant argued that his life was threatened because of the lack of money for medicine caused by an inadequate index law regarding savings accounts coupled with hyperinflation which reduced his ability to pay for

The European Court has discussed the lack of financial assistance by the State and the provision of certain commodities necessary for survival in the light of the prohibition of torture and inhuman treatment.[156] In this regard it is worth noting that the Court has suggested that in circumstances where an 'abrupt withdrawal of facilities will entail the most dramatic consequences for an individual,' such action would amount to inhuman treatment. In the case of D. v. the United Kingdom, the applicant, a national of Saint Kitts and Nevis who was in an advanced stage of AIDS, was threatened with deportation from the UK. The applicant was in prison and was receiving medical assistance for his disease. The applicant argued that his removal to Saint Kitts and Nevis would entail aviolation by the UK of the right to life (article 2 ECHR) because he was terminally ill and the medical evidence confirmed that his reduced life expectancy would be further shortened if we were to be suddenly deprived of the medical treatment that he was receiving in the UK. It was established in the case that the applicant would not receive adequate treatment for his disease in the receiving country.

The Court found that the UK Government could not be considered responsible for the individual's limited life expectancy which was the result of his fatal illness and the lack of medical treatment in his own country and therefore that article 2 was not applicable in the circumstances. However, the Court made clear that the complaint of the applicant under article 2 (right to life) was 'indissociable from the substance of his complaint under article 3 (prohibition of torture and ill-treatment) in respect of the consequences of the impugned decision for his life, health and welfare.'[157]

Finally, the Court concluded that the removal of the applicant to his own country where there were no facilities to treat his illness 'would amount to inhuman treatment by the respondent State in violation of article 3.'[158] It is remarkable that the Court made clear that the UK had assumed responsibility for treating the applicant's condition and that he had become reliant on the medical treatment he was receiving. Thus, his removal would expose him 'to a real risk of dying under most distressing circumstances and would thus amount to inhuman treatment.'[159] Furthermore, it should be pointed out that this case suggests that there is an obligation to refrain from expelling an individual when the risk of a violation of the right to life in a third country is not due to possible State actions, but rather, due to the lack of material resources to meet survival requirements.

More recently, the European Court has expressly stated that,

---

the necessary medicine and medical treatment. The Committee decided that the Communication was inadmissible without further explanation.

156 For further analysis see, Cassese, A.: 'Can the notion of inhuman and degrading treatment be applied to socio-economic conditions?' In: *EJIL*, vol. 2, (1991), pp. 141-145.

157 D. v. the United Kingdom, Application No. 146/1996, Judgement of 2 May 1997, para. 59.

158 *Ibidem:* para. 54.

159 *Ibidem:* para. 53.

'An issue may arise under Article 2 of the Convention [right to life] where it is shown that the authorities of a Contracting State put an individual's life at risk through the denial of health care which they have undertaken to make available to the population generally.'[160]

In a recent case the Inter-American Court has gone beyond the approach of its European counterpart. In the 'street children' case, which refers to the murder by agents of the State of five children 'who lived on the streets in a risk situation'[161] the Court held,

'The right to life is a fundamental human right, and the exercise of this right is essential for the exercise of all other human rights. If it is not respected, all rights lack meaning. Owing to the fundamental nature of the right to life, restrictive approaches to it are inadmissible. In essence, the right to life includes, not only the right of every human being not to be deprived of his life arbitrarily, but also the right that he will not be prevented from having access to the conditions that guarantee a dignified existence [...].'[162]

Furthermore, when the Court examined the alleged violation of article 19 ACHR (rights of the child), it held,

'The Court wishes to record the particular gravity of the fact that a State Party to this Convention can be charged with having applied or tolerated a systematic practice of violence against at-risk children in its territory. When States violate the rights of at-risk children, such as 'street children', in this way, it makes them victims of a double aggression. First, such States do not prevent them from living in misery, thus depriving them of the minimum conditions for a dignified life and preventing them from the 'full and harmonious development of their personality,' even though every child has the right to harbour a project of life that should be tended and encouraged by the public authorities so that it may develop this project for its personal benefit and that of the society to which it belongs. Second, they violate their physical, mental and moral integrity and even their lives.'[163]

In sum, we must recognise that at the current stage of development of international human rights law, when examining individual petitions, international supervisory bodies do not generally interpret the right to life as imposing a duty to provide assistance for preserving human life. However, it is entirely possible that such a development may come in the near future, taking into account developments in recent years and the fact that such interpretations are not rare at the national level.[164] Nonetheless,

---

160 Cyprus, *loc. cit.* (note 122), para. 219.

161 Villagrán Morales *et al.* v. Guatemala, Judgement of 19 November 1999, Series C No. 77, para. 188.

162 *Ibidem*: para. 144.

163 Villagrán Morales *et al., loc. cit.* (note 163), para. 191.

164 See, for example, relevant cases of the Supreme Court of India, such as Paschim Banga Khet Mazdoor Samity v. State of West Bengal [(1996) AIR SC 2426 at 2429] and Olga Tellis and others v Bombay Municipal Corporation [AIR 1986 SUPREME COURT 180]. Along the same line, see the Judgement

supervisory organs have established the existence of significant positive obligations which demonstrate that the obligations arising from traditional negative rights, such as the right to life and freedom from inhuman treatment, are getting progressively closer to the positive extreme of the spectrum. The lack of international case law interpreting the right to life as imposing a duty upon States to satisfy the basic needs necessary for sustaining life, seems to be more related to the very cautious attitude of the international supervisory bodies and the limited scope of individual complaint procedures with regard to economic, social and cultural rights rather than to any 'inherent' limitation preventing such an approach.

Positive extreme of the spectrum: Obligation to satisfy the basic needs necessary for sustaining life

3.4 Concluding comments on the spectrum of obligations arising from the right to life

An examination of the jurisprudence related to the right to life clearly demonstrates that the right entails a broad range of obligations which go beyond the negative obligation to refrain from arbitrary or intentional deprivation of life. The analysis of the spectrum of States' duties imposed by the right to life shows us:

(a) That the right to life imposes negative, as well as positive obligations. States are not only required to abstain from killing, but must also take positive measures that involve the expenditure of a considerable amount of resources. Admittedly, on the whole, the majority of the obligations may be placed closer to the negative extreme of the spectrum. Nonetheless, there is a tendency to interpret the right to life as imposing an increasing number of positive obligations.

(b) As we move away from the negative end of the spectrum, the obligations are less precise and States enjoy more discretion in the fulfilment of their obligations. For example, the prohibition of arbitrarily depriving someone of the right to life is more precise and does not allow as much discretion for States as the obligation to take measures to protect the lives of individuals under their jurisdiction. In general, it is possible to say that not only are the obligations to take positive measures to protect

of the Swiss Federal Court of 27 October 1995 on the right to minimum subsistence conditions, CDDH (97) 19 and Cruz del Valle Bermúdez *et al.* v. MSAS, Case No. 15.789, Judgement of the Political and Administrative Chamber of the Venezuelan Supreme Court, Judgement No. 916 [*Sentencia de la Sala Político – Administrativa de fecha 15 de julio de 1999, Cruz del Valle Bermúdez y otros v. MSAS, Expediente No. 15.789, Sentencia No. 916*].

individuals' lives implicit in the wording of the different provisions on the right to life, but also that supervisory bodies have tended to formulate these obligations in vague terms.

(c) Each duty imposed by the right to life is of a different nature to the others. This conclusion derives from the fact that some duties require State abstention, while others require taking positive measures and some are described in precise terms by the treaty provisions or by the supervisory bodies, while others are vague and imprecise in scope. However, all of these obligations can, and indeed are, subject to scrutiny by judicial and quasi-judicial organs.

(d) All States' duties with regard to the right to life are considered as being of an immediate nature, regardless of the fact that some of them are highly resource-dependent. States are required to immediately comply, even with the most expensive obligations arising from the right to life. The immediate nature of such positive obligations exists irrespective of the State's level of resources.

In this regard, it is interesting to note the approach of the European Court in relation to the resources required by the positive obligation imposed by the right to life. According to the Court,

> 'Bearing in mind the difficulties in policing modern societies, the unpredictability of human conduct and the operational choices which must be made in terms of priorities and resources, the scope of the positive obligation must be interpreted in a way which does not impose an impossible or disproportionate burden on the authorities.'[165]

This approach recognises that the adoption of the positive measures required by the right to life may impose a considerable economic burden upon States, as is also the case with the positive obligations imposed by economic, social and cultural rights. However, the Court has established that the State must take measures that are 'reasonable' and 'proportionate.' Such a limit or test is perfectly applicable to positive obligations arising from economic, social and cultural rights. This shows us that judicial and quasi-judicial bodies may perfectly well decide on issues regarding the implementation of economic, social and cultural rights by applying the same test.

(e) The case law examined indicates that while it is easier to assess the existence of a violation of a right when the State has acted in contravention of a specific prohibition than when the responsibility of the State is engaged as the result of an omission, the latter type of assessment is certainly not impossible. Indeed, judicial and quasi-judicial

165 See, for example, Osman, *loc. cit.* (note 46), para. 116 and Kaya, *loc. cit.* (note 113), para. 86.

supervisory bodies often find a violation of certain civil and political right because the State has failed to act.[166]

In sum, human rights impose a spectrum of different obligations which may be of different types. The right to life, one of the rights considered to be the most negative in character, also imposes positive obligations, whose meaning is not always clear and precise and which may require a significant allocation of resources.

4 Concluding Comments

Many of the arguments used by the drafters who where in favour of adopting two different Covenants due to the alleged difference in nature of the two sorts of rights, are no longer tenable. Despite the different wording of articles 2(1) of each Covenant, the jurisprudence of human rights supervisory bodies has demonstrated that there is no difference in the nature of the obligations that the two Covenants impose. When interpreting rights in accordance with the object and purpose of international human rights instruments and in accordance with the principle of effectiveness, traditional negative human rights have been interpreted by international human bodies as entailing a broad range of positive State obligations.

The existence of positive obligations is apparent not only in relation to the right to life, but also in other civil and political rights, such as, the prohibition of torture and ill-treatment, the right to privacy and the right of peaceful assembly. It is now clearly established that purely negative duties would not provide effective protection for the individual and therefore an interpretation that civil and political rights only impose negative duties would not be compatible with the object and purpose of the treaties which protect them.[167]

The examination of the jurisprudence with regard to the right to life clearly shows that the right to life entails positive obligations, albeit ones that allow States a broad margin of discretion. Such positive obligations require the expenditure of considerable resources and they are less precise than the mere prohibition of arbitrarily depriving someone of the right to life. They are not only implicit in the text, but also vaguely

---

166 See, in addition to the above mentioned cases as regard the right to life, the following examples where the HRC has found a violation of another different right contained in the ICCPR by the failure of the Government to act, as in Wright v. Jamaica, Communication No. 459/1991, views of 27 October 1995, violation Art. 6 ICCPR; Ximena Vicario v. Argentina, Communication No. 400/1990, views of 3 April 1995, violation Art. 24; Sandra Frei v. Colombia, Communication No. 514/1992, views of 4 April 1995, violation of Arts. 14(1), 23(4) and 17(1); and Coeriel and Aurik v. the Netherlands, Communication No. 453/1991, views of 31 October 1994, violation of Art. 17. At the European level, the Court has found a violation of Conventional rights by the Government's failure to act in many cases. See note 46.

167 See in Chapter III section 2.3.

formulated by supervisory bodies. Nevertheless, they can be, and indeed are, subject to scrutiny by judicial and quasi-judicial organs.

The rights contained in human rights instruments are subject to the dynamic evolution of international human rights law. At the present stage of development of international law, it is clear that the right to life, like all traditional civil and political rights, does not entail merely the obligation to refrain from acting. Negative undertakings are not the only duties imposed by these rights and the same is true with regard to economic, social and cultural rights, which may entail different kinds of obligations (positive actions as well as State abstention).

This means that there is no watertight division between the obligations imposed by the two categories of rights. All human rights impose a continuum or spectrum of obligations of different types. Each obligation may require a different level of State involvement and a different level of resources for its implementation. The closer the obligation is to one or the other end of the spectrum affects the amount of resources and State involvement required and the degree of discretion allowed to the State in fulfilling the obligation.

At the present stage of development of international law, the content of the obligations, this is to say, the form that they take and the way in which they impose their requirements upon States, are similar in regard to both categories of human rights. This is not to say that they are identical, however. If we analyse the rights as imposing a continuous spectrum of obligations with the most negative obligation at the one end and the most positive at the other, it would be fair to say that, in general, civil and political rights tend to be interpreted so as to require less intervention by States (obligations closer to the negative component), and that economic, social and cultural rights tend to be interpreted as imposing obligations closer to the positive extreme of the spectrum. Nevertheless, such differences are not due to the 'nature' of the obligations. They merely demonstrate a tendency which has been remarkably influenced by the international implementation mechanisms which are undoubtedly much more developed with respect to the former group of rights.

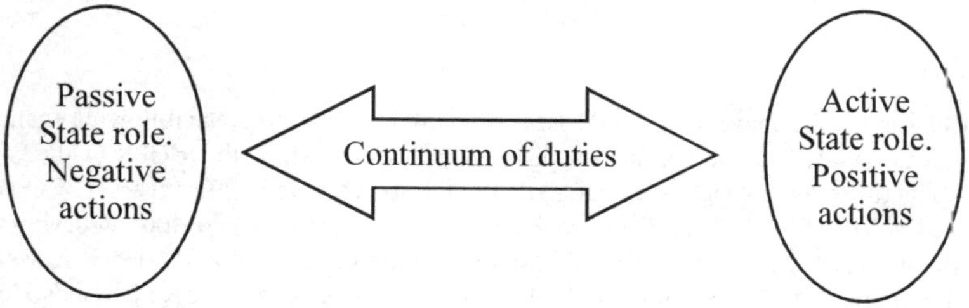

Figure 1

CHAPTER V
THE TYPOLOGIES OF STATE DUTIES IMPOSED BY THE COVENANT

1 TYPES OF STATE DUTIES IMPOSED BY HUMAN RIGHTS TREATIES

1.1 Introduction

The preceding Chapter analysed the nature of the obligations imposed by the UN Covenants. It concluded that there is no difference in the nature of civil and political rights on the one hand and economic, social and cultural rights on the other. All human rights impose a spectrum of different types of duties. Therefore, useful distinctions are not to be made between rights but, rather, between different kinds of duties.[1]

Various scholars have commented on the types of State duties imposed by human rights treaties. This Chapter will examine different typologies of States' duties imposed by human rights treaties as scholars have defined them. Afterwards, the focus will shift to the typology used by the Committee on Economic, Social and Cultural Rights and the Chapter finishes with an analysis of the obligations imposed by the Covenant, as interpreted by the Committee in its General Comment and Concluding Observations in the light of the typologies. The point here is to show that an analysis based on typologies of States' duties under human rights treaties provides a better understanding of the scope of the rights and helps to illustrate that all human rights are equal in nature.

1.2 The tripartite typology: its evolution

The early 1980s gave rise to a useful distinction between the obligations imposed by human rights treaties. Specifically, in 1980, H. Shue proposed that for every basic right there are three types of correlative obligations: 'to avoid depriving', 'to protect from deprivation' and 'to aid the deprived.' The proposal of what he called 'a very simple tripartite typology of duties' has been widely discussed and applied by scholars.

Since Shue's proposal was published, the 'tripartite typology' has evolved and scholars have developed typologies containing more than three levels. While there is no consensus about the precise meaning of the different levels, essentially the same 'tripartite typology' presented by Shue is better known today in more concise terms, specifically, the obligations 'to respect', 'to protect', and 'to fulfil'. This distinction is

1 See Shue, H.: *Basic rights: subsistence, affluence and U.S. foreign policy*, Princeton University Press, second edition, New Jersey (1996), p. 52.

well established and is regularly used by the Committee on Economic, Social and Cultural Rights. Below I will analyse different propositions regarding the typology of States' duties.[2] In the examination of the different typologies that follows, I use the wording used by the original authors themselves, but with some changes for editorial reasons. In all cases the relevant reference is found in the corresponding footnote.

1.2.1 Shue's tripartite typology: Duties of avoidance, protection and aid

In 1980, H. Shue[3] identified three categories of basic rights: (1) Security rights; (2) Subsistence rights; and (3) Liberty. According to Shue, each of these basic rights, as well as many others, can be analysed by a 'very simple tripartite typology of interdependent duties.'[4] His proposal was remarkable in that it went beyond the traditional assumption that there was a single correlative duty for each right, and argued that for every right there were three types of duties. This analysis is very significant because it notes that the dichotomy of 'negative' and 'positive' rights is mistaken. As Shue explains 'it is impossible for any basic right – however 'negative' it has come to seem – to be fully guaranteed unless all three types of duties are fulfilled.'[5]

According to Shue, the fulfilment of a basic right involves the following kinds of duties:

'I. To avoid depriving
II. To protect from deprivation
   1. By enforcing duty (I) and
   2. By designing institutions that avoid the creation of strong incentives to violate duty (I)

---

2 I have chosen those typologies that are in line with the typology used by the Committee. However, I do not mean to suggest that they are the only typologies developed so far. In fact, Charles Sampford has developed an interesting but different approach. He analyses human rights in what he calls 'the fourth dimension of rights'. These four dimensions of rights are: (1) negative rights, (2) protective rights, (3) positive rights and (4) psychological rights. According to the author, a 'human right in its full sense requires this fourth dimension for its realisation. It is only this fourth-dimensional conception that fully respects the ultimate value to which conceptions of human rights are directed.' See, Sampford, C.: 'The four dimensions of rights.' In Sampford, C.J.G. & Galligan, D.J. (eds.): *Law, rights and the welfare State*. Croom Helm, London/Sydney/Wolfeboro, New Hampshire, (1986) and Galligan, B. & Sampford, C. (eds.): *Rethinking human rights*, Federation Press, Sydney, (1997), pp. 50-71.

3 Shue, H.: *Basic rights: subsistence, affluence and U.S. foreign policy*. Princeton University Press, first edition, New Jersey, (1980) pp. 52 *et seq.* and Shue, H.: 'The interdependence of duties'. In: *The right to food*. Alston, P. & Tomaševski, K. (eds.), Martinus Nijhoff Publishers, Utrecht, (1984), p. 85.

4 Although he focused the analysis on the correlative duties of the three basic rights that he examined (right to subsistence, security and liberty), as he notes these rights are not the only basic rights and the 'tripartite typology' is applicable to many other rights. Shue, *op. cit.* (note 1), pp. 52 and 157.

5 Shue, *op. cit.* (note 1), p. 53.

III. To aid the deprived
1. Who are one's special responsibility,
2. Who are victims of social failures in the performance of duties (I), (II-1), (II-2) and
3. Who are victims of natural disasters.'

It is important to note that Shue's analysis was not restricted to the State as a duty bearer. He analysed duties in general, developing a classification of all duties imposed by basic rights which should be performed by States, individuals and institutions.[6] The present study is limited to an analysis of the duties imposed upon States by human rights treaties and therefore only describes duties from the States' perspective.

(1) *Duties to avoid depriving*: This level requires States not to eliminate a person's only available means of subsistence. This duty is the traditional duty to abstain from interfering. As the author explains, 'a duty simply not to take actions that deprive others of a means that, but for one's own harmful actions, would have satisfied their subsistence rights or enabled them to satisfy their own subsistence right, where the actions are not necessary to the satisfaction of one's own basic rights and where the threatened means is the only realistic one. Duties to avoid depriving require merely that one refrain from making an unnecessary gain for oneself by a means that is destructive for others.'[7]

(2) *Duties to protect from deprivation*: This level requires States to protect people against the deprivation of the only available means of subsistence by other people. According to Shue, the duties to protect encompasses two kinds of duties. Some duties to protect are secondary duties of enforcing the duty of avoiding the destruction of people's means of subsistence while others encompass the design of laws and institutions to avoid the creation of strong incentives to deprive individuals of their means of subsistence.[8]

(3) *Duties to aid the deprived*: This level requires States to provide for the subsistence of those unable to provide for themselves. Shue recognises three sub-categories. First are duties to aid those who are one's particular responsibility. Shue gives the example of the duties of parents towards their own young children. Arguably, from the perspective of the State as a duty bearer we might think of the duties to provide for the survival requirements of those held in State custody (*e.g.* in prisons or mental hospitals.) The second and third sub-categories refer to the duties to aid those in need of assistance due

---

6 Although Shue considers that all three types of duties must be performed if the basic rights are to be fully honoured, he notes that the same individual or institution need not necessarily perform all three. Shue, *op. cit.* (note 1), p. 52.
7 Shue, *op. cit.* (note 1), p. 55. Footnote omitted.
8 *Ibidem*: p. 57.

to the failure to fulfil the duty to avoid depriving and duties to protect from deprivation and because they are victims of natural disasters.[9]

The author explains that there is a systematic interdependence of duties.[10] As he notes, 'if everyone who ought to fulfil duties to avoid did so, performance of duties to protect might not be necessary.'[11] As the author mentions, duties to aid become relevant only after failures to perform the first two kinds of duties. To the extent that the duties to avoid and to protect are fulfilled, the duty to assist will be less burdensome. In his words 'if either duties to avoid or duties to protect are construed too narrowly, the other duty then becomes unrealistically broad.'[12]

In 1984, Shue suggested an additional duty, 'the responsibility to take due care', that entails the duties to 'foresee and prevent serious harms to some degrees and in some cases[13] The rationale for the addition is that people are responsible for the harms to which they contribute not only unintentionally but also unknowingly.[14] In terms of his original typology, he placed this duty near the duty to protect by designing institutions (type II-2,), but, as he notes '[t]hese institutions would, however, not only reduce the incentives to deprive people of their rights, but positively inhibit such deprivation, even unintended deprivation.'[15]

Shue has also confronted his own typology to self-criticism. While in 1980 he concentrated principally on the duty to aid, sixteen years later Shue emphasised the importance of the duty to protect people through design of better institutions to ensure that rights are respected in the first place (duty II-2). In hindsight, he considered that devoting too much attention to duties to aid was 'unfortunate above all because it obscured the importance of the second general kind of duty, the duty to protect.'[16] In retrospect, the author admits, 'I gave the creation of better institutions designed to ensure that rights are respected in the first place less attention than I now believe it deserves' and he continues '[w]orse, I conceived of duty II-2 [the duty to protect people from a violation of their rights by designing better institutions] much too negatively and much too narrowly.'[17] Therefore, in the second edition of his landmark book he agrees to give a broader and more positive content to the second duty to protect as a way to prevent violations.[18]

---

9 *Ibidem*: pp. 56-59.
10 *Ibidem*: pp. 60 *et seq*.
11 Shue, *op. cit.* (note 1), p. 61.
12 Shue, *op. cit.* (note 1), p. 61.
13 Shue, *op. cit.* (note 1), pp. 89-91.
14 *Idem.*
15 *Idem.*
16 Shue, *op. cit.* (note 1), p. 159.
17 *Idem.*
18 *Ibidem*: pp. 153-173.

1.2.2 Eide's analysis: Obligations to respect, protect and fulfil

In 1987, A. Eide proposed a tripartite typology with more concise names which differed from Shue's typology in some aspects, specifically with regard to the second and third levels.[19] Over the years Eide has further developed his proposal.[20] The first version of Eide's typology refers to three levels of States' obligations: Obligations to respect, protect and fulfil. In recent studies Eide has modified his approach and added a fourth level: the obligation to facilitate. Using the author's own words, we may describe the typology as follows:[21]

(1) *Obligation to respect*: It requires a State 'to respect the resources owned by the individual, her or his freedom to find a job of preference, to make the optimal use of one's own knowledge and the freedom to take the necessary actions and use the necessary resources – alone or in association with others – to satisfy his or her own needs […]. Consequently, as part of the obligation to respect these resources the State should take steps to recognise and register the land rights of indigenous peoples and land tenure of small-holders whose title is uncertain.'[22]

(2) *Obligation to protect*: This level requires 'active protection against other, more assertive or aggressive subjects – more powerful economic interests, such as protection against fraud, against unethical behaviour in trade and contractual relations, against the marketing and dumping of hazardous or dangerous products.'[23] According to Eide, the adoption of legislation based on the specific requirements in the country concerned is important at this level.

---

19 E/CN.4/Sub.2/1987/23, 7 July 1987. I refer here to the final report by Mr. Eide as Special Rapporteur of the Sub-Commission. Nevertheless, there are two previous reports: Eide 1983, E/CN.4/Sub.2/1983/25 and Eide 1984, E/CN.4/Sub.2/1984/25. Eide's approach to typologies was first presented in: *Food as a human right*. Eide, A.; Eide B.W.; Goonatilake, S.; Gussow, J. & Omawale (eds.), United Nations University, Tokyo, (1984*), p. 154.

20 Over the years Eide has further developed his approach in various documents, *inter alia*, (1987) E/CN.4/Sub.2/1987/23, 7 July 1987; (1989) 'The right to adequate food as a human right', UN Sales No. S.89.XIV.2, New York, 1989, p. 19; 'Realisation of social and economic rights – the minimum threshold approach.' In: *The Review of the ICJ*, No. *43,* December, (1989**), pp. 40-52 reprinted in *HRLJ*, vol. 10, (1989*), pp. 35-50; (1999) E/CN.4/Sub.2/1999/12, 28, June 1999; and (2000) 'Universalisation of human rights versus globalisation of economic power'. In: *Rendering justice to the vulnerable: liber amicorum in honour of Theo van Boven*. Coomans, F.; Grünfeld, F.; Westendorp, I. & Willems, J. (eds.), Kluwer Law International, The Hague, (2000), pp. 99-120.

21 See, Eide 1999, E/CN.4/Sub.2/1999/12, 28 June 1999, paras. 51-57. In the present definition we follow specifically Eide, 2000, *op. cit.* (note 20), pp. 110-111.

22 *Idem.*

23 *Idem.*

(3) *Obligation to facilitate (assist)*: it requires States 'to facilitate opportunities by which the rights listed can be enjoyed. It takes many forms, some of which are spelled out in the relevant instruments.' As an example Eide mentions article 11.2 ICESCR.[24]

(4) *Obligation to fulfil*: This fourth level requires States to fulfil the rights of everyone who could otherwise not enjoy their economic, social and cultural rights. 'This level of obligation is important in an emergency when conditions for survival are temporarily disrupted (severe draught or flood, armed conflict, or the collapse of economic activities within a particular region of the country). As a more permanent feature, fourth level obligations increase in importance with increasing rates of urbanisation and the decline of groups or family responsibilities.'[25] As the author notes, the obligation to fulfil 'could consist of the direct *provision* of basic needs, such as food or resources which can be used for food (direct food aid, or social security) when no other possibility exists.'[26]

Finally, it is worth mentioning that in a more recent publication,[27] Eide employs the 'tripartite typology' as it had been used by the Committee in General Comment No. 12. This typology contains three levels: 'obligation to respect', 'to protect' and 'to fulfil'. The tertiary level (obligation to fulfil) entails two sub-categories, the 'obligation to facilitate' and the 'obligation to provide'. The Committee's approach will be further examined below, however here we note that, as explained by Eide, the last two obligations basically correspond to his previous third and fourth levels, respectively.

---

24 Article 11(2) reads as follows,
'The States Parties to the present Covenant, recognizing the fundamental right of everyone to be free from hunger, shall take, individually and through international co-operation, the measures, including specific programmes, which are needed:
(a) To improve methods of production, conservation and distribution of food by making full use of technical and scientific knowledge, by disseminating knowledge of the principles of nutrition and by developing or reforming agrarian systems in such a way as to achieve the most efficient development and utilization of natural resources;
(b) Taking into account the problems of both food-importing and food-exporting countries, to ensure an equitable distribution of world food supplies in relation to need.'

25 Eide, 2000, *op. cit.* (note 20), p. 111.

26 *Idem*. (Emphasis in the original).

27 Eide, A.: 'Economic, social and cultural rights as human rights.' In: *Economic, social and cultural rights: a textbook*. Eide, A.; Krause, C. & Rosas, A. (eds.), Martinus Nijhoff, second revised edition, Dordrecht, (2001), pp. 9-28.

1.2.3 Van Hoof's analysis: Additional obligation to promote

In 1984, responding to the tripartite typology suggested by Shue, F. van Hoof referred to the categories of obligations to respect, protect and ensure, but he added a new category of duties: the obligation to promote.[28]

According to van Hoof the types of obligations can be defined as follows:[29]

(1) *Obligation to respect*: It 'forbids the State itself to act in any way which would directly encroach upon recognised rights or freedoms.'

(2) *Obligation to protect*: 'It forces the State to take steps, through legislation or otherwise, which prevent or prohibit others (third persons) from violating recognised rights and freedoms.'

(3) *Obligation to ensure*: It 'requires more far-reaching measures on the part of the government in that it has to actively create conditions aimed at the achievement of certain results in the form of a (more) effective realisation of recognised rights and freedoms.'

The significant innovation of van Hoof's typology was the fourth level:

(4) *Obligation to promote*. 'This type of obligation encompasses measures aimed at long-term goals', for example, 'the duty on the part of the government to set training programmes.' According to van Hoof, this obligation can only be achieved progressively or over the long term.[30]

1.2.4 Steiner and Alston's proposal of five levels of obligations

More recently, Steiner and Alston have developed a scheme of five types of State duties which they state derives from the proposals by Shue and van Hoof.[31]

They identified the following five types of State duties:

(1) *Duty to 'respect [the] rights of others'*: 'This duty requires the state to treat persons equally, to respect their individual dignity and worth, and hence not to interfere with or impair their declared rights, whether physical security rights or rights to fair process, equal protection, speech or political participation […]. The broad idea is to not

---

28 Hoof, G.J.H. van: 'Legal nature of economic, social and cultural rights: a rebuttal of some traditional views'. In: *The right to food*. Alston, P. & Tomaševski, K. (eds.), Martinus Nijhoff Publishers, Utrecht, (1984), pp. 106-108.

29 *Idem*.

30 Hoof, G.J.H. van, *op. cit.* (note 28), pp. 106 and 108.

31 Steiner & Alston, 2000, pp. 180-185.

worsen an individual's situation by depriving that person of the enjoyment of a declared right.'[32]

(2) *Duty to 'create institutional machinery essential to [the] realisation of rights'*: As the authors note, the duty here is not simple non-interference, but rather, that 'public funds must be expended to create the infrastructure on which the practical realisation of the rights depends.'[33]

(3) *Duty to 'protect rights/prevent violations'*: Here again, institutional machinery is required, but in this case 'to comply with a specific command of the treaties.' For example, the command expressed in article 2 ICCPR to 'ensure to all individuals' the recognised rights. States must then take the necessary measures to ensure the right. This State duty also involves State expenditure.[34]

(4) *Duty to 'provide goods and services to satisfy rights'*: It primarily requires the provision of 'material resources to the rights-bearer, like housing, of food or health care, matters associated with the ICESCR [...]. Resources provided by the State may go directly from it to the individual rights bearer, as by providing food stamps or subsidised public housing, or it may go indirectly to the ultimate beneficiary through, say, subsidies to construction firms that will then offer low-rent housing. Unlike the duty of respect (do not worsen the situation of the rights-bearer), this duty to provide generally is meant to improve the situation of the rights-bearer.'[35] As the authors explain, although categories (2) and (3) above also involve State expenditures, at this level the expenditures are at the core of and are the very essence of the individual right.

(5) *Duty to 'promote rights'*: As the authors mention, 'this state duty refers to bringing about changes in public consciousness or perception or understanding about a given problem or issue, with the purpose of alleviating the problem [...]. Like the duty of protection, it generally requires the state to expend funds and create the institutions that are necessary to promoting acceptance of the right. Thus, a state's duty to promote often involves public education.'[36]

32 *Ibidem*: 182.
33 *Idem.*
34 *Ibidem*: 183
35 *Idem.*
36 Steiner & Alston, *op. cit.* (note 31), p. 184.

1.3 Evaluation of the different typologies of State obligations imposed by human rights norms

1.3.1 Comparative commentary

We have analysed four different approaches to the categorisation of the duties imposed by human rights obligations. The typologies which followed Shue's proposal might be considered as evolving from it. The typologies presented renamed his proposed categories and introduced some innovations.

We find that the first level, the duty to respect, understood as the traditional negative duty of non-interference, is basically the same in all four typologies. Although it is true that Shue named it the 'duty to avoid,' he was pleased with the change from 'duty to avoid depriving' to 'duty to respect', because in his opinion the new name was more accurate.[37]

The second level, the duty to protect, is also common to all categories. While there is no consensus about its precise scope, the core meaning of the duty is that the State must take positive action to safeguard against intrusive and harmful action by third parties. Differences might exist regarding the extent of the actions required by States to comply with this duty, but it is clear that as presented by all authors, it entails an important preventive function.

One of the differences among the typologies is to be found in the fact that the 'duty to aid' presented by Shue is not present in the other proposals which put forward two other duties in its place: the 'duty to fulfil' and the 'duty to promote.' Shue disagreed with this change, and in 1984 he defended the merits of the so-called 'duty to aid' over other terms.[38] As he explained, the 'duty to aid' better described the notion that the duty is a response to failure in the performance of the duties 'to respect and protect'. He noted that what they have in common is the requirement that resources be transferred to those who cannot provide for their own survival.[39] However, he considered that '[t]he description in terms of fulfilment and promotion suggests that the rest of us would be going beyond duties to respect and to protect if we acted upon duties to fulfil and promote. The rights of some people need to be 'fulfilled' or 'promoted', however, because other people have already failed to perform duties to respect and protect. Rather than going beyond respect and protection, we are having to go back and make up for failures in respect and protection.'[40]

However, the essence of the 'duty to aid', which is 'the duty to provide the subsistence of those unable to provide for their own', is to be found in all four categories, albeit with differences in the labels. Eide named it the 'duty to fulfil', van Hoof

37 Shue, 1984, *op. cit.* (note 3), p. 85.
38 *Ibidem*: p. 86.
39 *Ibidem*: p. 56.
40 Shue, 1984, *op. cit.* (note 3), p. 86.

included it in the 'duty to ensure' and Steiner and Alston called it the 'duty to provide goods and services to satisfy rights.'

Another important difference is to be found in relation to the 'duty to promote' which is proposed by van Hoof and is also included by Steiner and Alston. While Shue and Eide's proposals do not explicitly contain this duty, it could be considered that its inclusion as an independent duty is an improvement over the original typology. While the 'duty to promote' requires positive actions of a long-term character and may therefore be considered to be included in the 'duty to fulfil' and even in the 'duty to protect', it can be viewed as distinct in nature from these other duties which also entail positive actions.

Admittedly, when States take measures to comply with one level of duty, these measures might at the same time serve to comply with the duty to promote. For example, in aiming to comply with the duty to protect the right to adequate housing, States might promote the rights of tenants, or in attempting to protect the right to the highest attainable standard of health they may promote consumers' rights. While such promotional activities are only one of the ways that States have to comply with their duties, it is possible to say that the requirement to 'promote' human rights is not solely an ancillary obligation. The promotion of human rights has taken on an independent character and all human rights should be viewed as imposing this level of obligation. Certainly, individuals would be better protected if States were to take active measures to promote human rights. It is not possible to have effective protection of human rights if individuals are unaware of their rights and the mechanisms available to protect them.

Nowadays, human rights supervisory bodies stress the importance of the promotion of human rights,[41] and seem to impose the duty to promote by requiring States to encourage citizens to respect and protect all human rights, through education, training and public information.

As affirmed by the Committee on Economic, Social and Cultural Rights, 'human rights education is itself a human right.'[42] The Covenant contains specific provisions relating to the promotion of human rights. Of particular importance are the requirement to promote rights established in the Preamble;[43] article 2(1)[44] and article 13(1).[45] In

41 For an examination of the importance attributed by the UN treaty bodies to promotion and human rights education, see the Document prepared by the Office of the High Commissioner for Human Rights under the framework of the implementation of the Plan of Action for the Decade for Human Rights Education. Presented to the eighth meeting of Chairpersons of the human rights treaty bodies in September 1997 (HRI/MC/1997/Misc.3).

42 As stated in the Day of General Discussion on human rights education and public information activities relating to the International Covenant on Economic, Social and Cultural Rights, held on 5 December 1994. E/1996/2 para. 324.

43 The Preamble of the Covenant establishes:
'The States Parties to the present Covenant, [...] Considering the obligation of States under the Charter of the United Nations to promote universal respect for, and observance of, human rights and freedoms, Realising that the individual, having duties to other individuals and to the community to which he

addition, the Committee often recommends that State take action to promote human rights and to provide training and information, for example, in General Comment No. 3 paragraph 7[46] and in the Revised Guidelines regarding the form and contents of reports to be submitted by States Parties.[47]

The obligation to promote rights is essential for all human rights. Nevertheless, it is important to highlight that to a greater extent than other human rights, all economic, social and cultural rights are intertwined in such a manner that the implementation of an appropriate educational programme may benefit various rights. For instance, in many cases, specific educational information focused on women could have a positive effect on the enjoyment of the economic, social and cultural rights and the well-being of children and the family as a whole. For example, if women receive information about safe food supplies and hygiene it might lead to healthier conditions within their families.

In Steiner and Alston's proposal we also find a new level, the 'duty to create institutional machinery essential to realisation of rights'. Although they present it as an independent level, this duty seems to be considered in the other typologies as part of other levels. In fact, Shue emphasises the importance of the duty to design, build and maintain institutions as part of the 'duty to protect.' Eide considers that the 'duty to respect' entails to some extent the establishment of institutions, as for example, those necessary to recognise and register the rights of indigenous people.[48] In more general

---

belongs, is under a responsibility to strive for the promotion and observance of the rights recognised in the present Covenant,

Agree upon the following articles: [...]'.

44 Article 2 para. 1 reads as follows:
'Each State Party to the present Covenant undertakes to take steps, individually and through international assistance and co-operation, especially economic and technical, to the maximum to its available resources, with a view to achieving progressively the full realisation of the rights recognised in the present Covenant by all appropriate means, including particularly the adoption of legislative measures [...]'.

45 Article 13 para. 1 reads as follows:
'The States Parties to the present Covenant recognise the rights of everyone to education. They agree that education shall be directed to the full development of the human personality and the sense of its dignity, and shall strengthen the respect for human rights and fundamental freedoms. They further agree that education shall enable all persons to participate effectively in a free society, promote understanding, tolerance and friendship among all nations and all racial, ethnic or religious groups, and further the activities of the United Nations for the maintenance of peace [...]'.

46 General Comment No. 3 para. 7. Other measures which may also be considered 'appropriate' for the purposes of article 2(1) include, but are not limited to, administrative, financial, educational and social measures.

47 Revised guidelines regarding the form and contents of reports to be submitted by States Parties under articles 16 and 17 of the International Covenant on Economic, Social and Political Rights (E/C.12/1991/1): '3. What difficulties have you encountered in the realisation of the right to education, as spelt out in paragraph 1? What time-related goals and benchmarks has your Government set in this respect? [...]'.

48 Eide, 2000, *op. cit.* (note 20), p. 110.

terms this duty may also arise from Eide's secondary level (the 'duty to protect'), which entails the adoption of legislation.

Again, although the 'duty to create institutional machinery essential to the realisation of rights' might be considered to be included in the other levels of State duties, at the present stage of development of human rights law, it is necessary to consider it as an independent level of obligation. Steiner and Alston's approach is consistent with recent developments in human rights law which have made it clear that human rights require States to create and establish institutional machinery.[49] Identifying this obligation as a separate independent level may help to assess its compliance in regard to each human right.

Eide added to his original tripartite proposal of respect, protect and fulfil, the 'duty to facilitate,' which requires States to 'facilitate opportunities by which the rights listed can be enjoyed'. Eide mentions article 11(2) ICESCR as an example of this duty as it relates to the right to food. Article 11(2) ICESCR provides that States shall take steps to 'improve measures of production, conservation and distribution of foods by making full use of technical and scientific knowledge and by developing or reforming systems.'[50] Steiner and Alston's proposal is that this is part of the duty to 'provide goods and services.' As they explain, the realisation of economic, social and cultural rights need not depend on 'direct' provision by States (*e.g.* resources provided by the State to the duty bearer) or 'indirect' provision (*e.g.* food stamps), and that other, radically different policies may also achieve the goal of satisfying a right. As an example of satisfying the right to food, they mention the option of undertaking a programme of expropriation and land reform.[51]

In sum, despite the differences between the labels and the numbers of levels, all four of the above-mentioned categories are essentially the same. With the exception of the 'duty to promote' (proposed by van Hoof and also contained in Steiner and Alston's proposal), which has an independent nature, separate from the other levels, the additional levels proposed by Eide and Steiner and Alston, such as the 'duty to assist' and the 'duty to create institutional machinery essential for the realisation of rights', may to some extent be considered implicit in the scope of the original levels. Nevertheless, from our perspective, it is advantageous to consider these new levels separately.

---

49 In civil and political rights instruments, this obligation arises from the 'duty to ensure' (Art. 1 ACHR and Art. 2 ICCPR) and 'to secure' (Art. 1 ECHR). See the analysis in Chapter IV section 2.3.2. Clear evidence of the existence of this duty was provided by the Inter-American Court in the Velásquez Rodríguez Case where it held, '[t]he second obligation of States Parties is to 'ensure' the free and full exercise of the rights recognised by the Convention to every person subject to its jurisdiction. This obligation implies the duty of States Parties to organise the governmental apparatus and, in general, all the structures through which public power is exercised, so that they are capable of juridically ensuring the free and full enjoyment of human rights.' Velásquez Rodríguez v. Honduras, Judgement of 29 July 1988, Series C No. 4, para. 166.

50 Eide, 1999, *op. cit.* (note 20), para. 52.

51 Steiner & Alston, *op. cit.* (note 31), p. 184.

Nevertheless, the delineation of States' obligations as obligations to respect, protect, fulfil and promote has the advantage that it has received widespread support and is frequently applied to the different economic, social and cultural rights.[52] In fact, the Maastricht Guidelines on Violations of Economic, Social and Cultural rights employ these notions. With respect to the tripartite typology the Guidelines state the following:[53]

> '(1) Obligation to respect: requires States to refrain from interfering with the enjoyment of economic, social and cultural rights.
> (2) Obligation to protect: requires States to prevent violations of such rights by third parties.
> (3) Obligation to fulfil: requires States to take appropriate legislative, administrative, budgetary, judicial and other measures towards the full realisation of such rights.'

In the Guidelines, the meaning of the first and second levels is basically the same as that developed by the authors mentioned above while the third has been envisaged in broad terms which might encompass Eide's 'duty to assist' and 'duty to fulfil,' as well as the 'duty to provide goods and services to satisfy the rights' as developed by Steiner and Alston.[54] However, the Guidelines do not contemplate the 'duty to promote' as developed by van Hoof and included by Steiner and Alston and this lacuna is a significant deficiency.

1.3.2 The advantage of the use of typologies

If one were to choose which of the proposed typologies was the most accurate or appropriate to analyse the duties imposed by the Covenant, Steiner and Alston's proposal might prove to be the most convincing because it is systematic, comprehen-

52 Today many commentators in economic, social and cultural rights use this method of analysis when examining specific substantive rights. For example, Tomaševski, K.: 'Human rights indicators: the right to food as a test case.' In: *The right to food*. Alston, P. & Tomaševski, K. (eds.), Martinus Nijhoff Publishers, Utrecht (1984), p. 154; Coomans, F.: 'Clarifying the core elements of the right to education.' In: *The right to complain about economic, social and cultural rights*. Coomans, F. & Hoof, G.J.H. van (eds.), SIM Special, No. 18, Utrecht, (1995), pp. 11-26; Eide, A.: 'Economic, social and cultural rights as human rights.' In: *Economic, social and cultural rights: a textbook*. Eide, A.; Krause, C. & Rosas, A. (eds.), Martinus Nijhoff Publishers, Dordrecht, (1995), pp. 78-81; and Toebes, B.C.A.: *The right to health as a human right in international law*, Intersentia, Antwerp, (1998), pp. 312 *et seq*.

53 Maastricht Guideline No. 6.

54 It is important to note that the Utrecht Draft Optional Protocol to the Covenant also includes the tripartite typology in the levels: respect, protect and fulfil. (See article III). In the Explanatory note on the Utrecht Draft, the obligation to fulfil is more clearly explained than in the Maastricht Guidelines. It states that the obligation to fulfil, 'requires more far-reaching (positive) measures on the part of the Government in that it has to actively create conditions aimed at achieving a certain result in the form of a (more) effective realisation of recognised rights and obligations' [See Hoof, G.J.H. van, 1995, p. 162]. In light of this explanation it is clear why the obligation to fulfil may entail both an obligation to 'facilitate' and an 'obligation to provide.' See the analysis of the Committee's General Comments below.

sive and elaborates on the other typologies. Nonetheless, Eide's typology has the advantage of being widely applied and because it uses concise terms. In any case, it is important to bear in mind that typologies are merely analytical tools in the sense that they help to translate the complexities of reality into simpler academic notions. According to Shue,

> 'Typologies are at best abstract instruments for temporarily fending off the complexities of concrete reality that threaten to overwhelm our circuits. Be they dichotomous or trichotomous, typologies are ladders to be climbed and left behind, not monuments to be caressed or polished.'[55]

As analytical tools, all of the typologies mentioned above provide us with a better understanding of the complexities of reality. They are guidelines that assist us to approach the complex interconnection and interdependencies of the duties that must be honoured in order to achieve the full protection of human rights.

The advantage of an analysis based on types of State duties imposed by human rights is that it serves to illustrate the significance and implications of (a) the interdependency of all duties, (b) the equal nature of all human rights and (c) the scope of the obligations.

A. *The interdependency of all duties*

Even from the earliest studies of the typologies of States' duties, it was clear that there is, in Shue's words, a 'systematic interdependence of duties' which signifies that the full protection of a right requires compliance with different duties.

Typologies of State duties imposed by human rights make apparent that human rights cannot be fully realised by performing merely one of the variety of types of duties that they impose. All duties imposed by human rights treaties are interrelated and must be performed if the rights contained in those instruments are to be fully guaranteed.

Therefore, in all of the typologies we have discussed, the different layers or levels of duties cannot be analysed in isolation. All levels interrelate in a complex manner and the full protection of a given right contained in a human rights treaty cannot be achieved by relying merely on one or two of them but must involve the performance of all levels of duties.

As all duties are interdependent, States must observe all of them. If States concentrate their efforts on only one type of duty, the protection of a given right becomes more difficult to achieve. For example, if a government focuses only on the duty to respect, but does not protect individuals from third party infringements, there is a greater chance that some individuals will be deprived of the enjoyment of the right. Hence, the

55 Shue, 1996, *op. cit.* (note 1), p. 160.

duty to fulfil would be more burdensome for the State. However, if States make efforts to comply with each level, the full protection of the rights becomes more feasible.[56]

B. *The equal nature of all human rights*

An analysis based on types of State duties assists us to understand that there is no difference in the nature of the obligations imposed by civil and political rights and economic, social and cultural rights. The typologies mentioned above apply to all kinds of human rights instruments whether they contain civil and political rights, solely economic, social and cultural rights, or both categories of rights.

All human rights impose a variety of obligations that may be classified as obligations to respect, protect, fulfil and promote. As Eide notes, most of the time, when it is argued that sharp differences exist between civil and political rights and economic, social and cultural rights, the argument relies upon situations where the focus on economic, social and cultural rights is on this tertiary level (obligation to fulfil), while civil and political rights are observed on the primary level (obligation to respect). This approach is arbitrary, as he observes.[57]

As analysed in Chapter IV,[58] all human rights impose a continuum or spectrum of multiple types of obligations which entail a complex relation among acts and omissions (positive and negative actions). The tripartite typology in all of its variations is the best interpretative tool to describe these obligations. It expands the very simplistic view of merely two types of obligations (negative/positive), which implicitly places civil and political rights in a position of superiority over economic, social and cultural rights. It also clearly suggests that there are some kinds of obligations that cannot properly be described in terms of acts (positive obligation) and omissions (negative obligation), because they impose a complex mix of both.

Admittedly, if one wishes to apply the negative/positive distinction to the tripartite typology, we might consider that duties to avoid depriving or the so-called *obligations to respect*, would resemble the traditional 'negative obligations,' while the *obligations to assist or* the *obligations to provide goods and services* would resemble 'positive obligations.'[59] But all of the other levels of obligations would be placed in an interme

56 Shue, 1996, *op. cit.* (note 1), p. 61.

57 Eide, 1989*, *loc. cit.* (note 20), p. 40.

58 See Chapter IV section 3: 'Spectrum of State obligations.'

59 However, the negative/positive analysis of the level of State duties is very simplistic. On the one hand, a given level or type of obligation may require both acts and omissions for its fulfilment. For example, the obligation to respect might entail a positive component *e.g.* the obligation to take legislative actions prohibiting certain State behaviour. On the other hand, the decision to place certain obligations in the positive or negative compartment rests on the point of view of the analyst. If we take, for example, the duty to protect, we may find that from the point of view of the individual, the obligation to protect takes the same form as negative rights (the right not to be affected in the enjoyment of the right), but from the point of view of the State, these obligations do not entail negative duties of non-interference but,

diate position between these extremes. The duties to protect (prevent), to create institutional machinery, and even the duty to promote, are difficult to classify as 'positive' or 'negative'. It would therefore be much more appropriate to use the tripartite typology and avoid the positive/negative distinction, because the latter is not appropriate to describe all of the State duties imposed by human rights treaties.

C. *The scope of the obligations*

The typologies of obligations reflect the manner in which the State must behave in order to discharge its commitments. Hence, they assist us to assess the compliance of a State Party with its commitments under human rights instruments, and, in particular, under the Covenant. To the extent that there is a more precise picture of what behaviours are required by the State, the scope and content of each of the variety of the obligations imposed by a human right will be clearer and it will be easier to assess when the State has violated the Covenant.[60]

The typologies of States' duties analysed above demonstrate that establishing accountability for economic, social and cultural rights is as complex as establishing accountability for civil and political rights. In fact, for an international body there is little difference between evaluating whether the State Party has complied with its obligation to respect, protect, and fulfil civil and political rights and conducting the same evaluation of compliance with economic, social and cultural rights. This is not to say that this is an easy task. On the contrary, such assessments involve many complexities, but they are not reasons to argue that courts or quasi-judicial bodies cannot perform such analysis with respect to both categories of rights. The level of complexity involved in the identification of non-compliance by the State with human rights obligations may be the same in regard to civil and political rights or economic, social and cultural rights, depending on the level of obligation involved. For example, identifying a violation of the right to life when the State has arbitrarily killed someone may be as complex as determining a violation of the right to housing when the State has carried out a forced eviction.[61] The process is more complex when supervisory bodies have to evaluate whether a State has taken all the necessary measures to comply

---

rather, they provide the basis for a positive duty for the State to prevent that interference by third parties.

60 There is a breach of an international obligation when the act of the State is not in conformity with what is required of it by the relevant obligation. Art. 12 ILC Draft Articles on Responsibility of States for Internationally Wrongful Acts [as included in the final text adopted on 9 August 2001]. See, also, Limburg Principle No. 70: 'A Failure by a State party to comply with an obligation contained in the Covenant is, under international law, a violation of the Covenant.'

61 The term 'forced evictions' is used as defined by General Comment No. 7 paras. 3-4. Therefore, it does not apply to 'evictions carried out by force in accordance with the law and in conformity with the provisions of the International Covenants on Human Rights' (para. 4).

with its positive obligations to protect the lives of those under its jurisdiction[62] or to avoid the destruction of individuals' houses by non-State actors.

In sum, although the four above-mentioned typologies differ in regard to names and the number of levels, they are in essence the same. All are tools that provide a clearer understanding of the scope and nature of the State obligations imposed by human rights treaties. An analysis based on typologies shows us that the correct distinction is between obligations, not between rights. Each human right imposes a variety of different types of obligations, all of which must be performed to fully implement the right.

2 The approach of the Committee on Economic, Social and Cultural Rights to typologies of State Party obligations

2.1 Introduction

The Committee has not been indifferent to the typologies on State obligations developed by scholars. In fact, it has referred to typologies in its statements, General Comments and Concluding Observations.

The approach of the Committee to different typologies will be examined in the following sections. We will start by analysing the typologies that the Committee has expressly chosen to apply to the Covenant's rights. Due to the importance of its analysis, the Committee's approach to the tripartite typology will be analysed in greater detail.

The analysis of the Committee's approach to the tripartite typology will be divided between the approach of the Committee in its General Comments and statements, and its approach in the Concluding Observations. The different objectives and context of these Committee activities justify separate treatment.

The General Comments and Committee statements adopt an abstract approach aimed at all States Parties to the Covenant. The Committee employs General Comments to assist States to comply with their obligations under the Covenant and therefore it is appropriate that they contain analytical tools such as typologies. Concluding Observations are adopted after the examination of State Parties' reports. They relate to the specific circumstances of the State concerned and provide the Committee's view on the implementation of the Covenant in that State. The Committee does not usually include an express mention of the typologies in its Concluding Observations. Nevertheless, as we will see, Concluding Observations provide us with an accurate, practical view of the Committee's approach to the typologies.

62 See the analysis on 'Spectrum of States' obligations', in Chapter IV section 3.

2.2 The typologies referred to by the Committee

The most explicit statement with regard to the typologies of State duties made by the Committee is found in the 'Outline for drafting general comments on specific rights of the International Covenant on Economic, Social and Cultural Rights' which was adopted by the Committee during its twenty-first session in 1999.[63] The Outline suggests dividing the texts of General Comments into six sections: 'introduction', 'normative contents of the right', 'State party's obligations', 'obligations of other relevant actors', 'violations' and 'recommendations for States Parties.'

The third section on 'State party's obligations' refers to the application by the Committee of three categorisations or typologies of State obligations:

> 'A. Obligations of immediacy; obligations of progressive realisation
> B. Obligations of conduct; obligation of result
> C. Obligation to respect, to protect and to fulfil, and obligation to promote.'

As the Committee states, the Outline was not intended to be strictly adhered to. Its aim is to provide a signpost and checklist of issues to be considered in the process of drafting general comments.[64] Despite the fact that the Outline may not always be followed by the Committee in its General Comments, it provides us with a clear insight into the Committee's approach to the typologies on State obligations.

In the following sections we shall analyse the typologies chosen by the Committee in the Outline. We will first address the first two categories: (A) obligations of immediacy and obligations of progressive realisation and (B) obligations of conduct and result. Subsequently, we will analyse in greater length the third typology chosen by the Committee, 'obligation to respect, protect and fulfil and promote'. More detailed analysis of this typology is justified by the fact that it is the only one specifically geared to State duties imposed by human rights, is widely applied by scholars and has been employed by the Committee in its General Comments since 1999.

2.3 Obligations of immediacy and obligations of progressive realisation

The Committee applies this typology in its General Comments and Concluding Observations, emphasising that the Covenant imposes obligations of progressive realisation but also of immediate effect.[65] The recognition of these two kinds of obligations is extremely important for the implementation of the Covenant.

---

63 E/C.12/1999/11, Annex IX, pp. 135-136. Adopted at the 37th meeting on 19 November 1999.
64 E/C.12/1999/11 para. 53.
65 Limburg Principles Nos. 16 and 21.

2.3.1 Immediate/progressive obligations in the Committee's General Comments

The Committee often refers to the immediate/progressive typology in the General Comments. In General Comment No. 3 on 'the nature of States Parties obligations,' the Committee explicitly states that, 'while the Covenant provides for a progressive realisation and acknowledges the constraints due to the limits of available resources, it also imposes various obligations which are of immediate effect.'[66] The existence of immediate obligations arising from the Covenant has often been stated by the Committee in subsequent General Comments.[67] For example, General Comment No. 9 establishes that, '[t]he Committee has already made clear that it considers many of the provisions in the Covenant to be capable of immediate implementation.'[68] Subsequently, the General Comment mentions the Covenant's rights previously enumerated in General Comment No. 3.[69]

The rights that the Committee mentions in both General Comments as examples of immediate obligations are the following: (i) article 3 (equal right of men and women); (ii) article 7(a)(i) (equal remuneration for work of equal value); (iii) article 8 (right to form and join trade unions and the right to strike); (iv) article 10(3) (protection of children and young persons, particularly their protection against economic and social exploitation); (v) article 13(2)(a) (compulsory primary education); (vi) article 13(3) (liberty of parents to choose the school of their children); (vii) article 13(4) (freedom to establish educational institutions); and (viii) article15(3) (freedom for scientific research and creativity activity.) The above-mentioned inventory helps to clarify that immediate obligations exist under the Covenant and that States Parties must comply with them regardless of their stage of development. As one may note, the compliance of the obligations mentioned by the Committee requires principally the non-interference of States. However, the Committee has emphasised that those provisions enumerated in General Comment Nos. 3 and 9 are not the only rights which impose immediate obligations. In fact, the Committee has suggested that immediate obligations are also inherent in rights traditionally considered to impose merely obligations of a progressive character, such as the right to adequate housing,[70] the right to education,[71] the right to

---

66 General Comment No. 3 para. 1.

67 See General Comment No. 4 para. 8; General Comment No. 9 para.10; General Comment No. 11 para. 10; General Comment No. 12 para. 16; General Comment No. 13 paras. 31 and 43; and General Comment No. 14 para. 30.

68 General Comment No. 9 para. 10.

69 However, we have to recognise that the wording used in General Comment No. 3 to refer to the immediate character of these provisions is much weaker than in General Comment No. 9. In fact, in General Comment No. 3 the Committee merely says that the rights mentioned, 'would seem to be capable of immediate application by judicial and other organs in many national legal systems.' General Comment No. 3 para. 5.

70 For example, in General Comment No. 4 the Committee notes 'States parties should consequently take immediate measures aimed at conferring legal security of tenure upon those persons and households currently lacking such protection [...]' [para. 8]. Moreover, it notes that 'effective monitoring of the

food[72] and the right to the highest attainable standards of health.[73] However, as we will see, in these statements the Committee has been very general. It would have further contributed to the clarification of the normative content of the Covenant if the Committee had addressed the immediate aspects of these provisions in more detail.

Among the obligations that the Committee specifically indicates as being of an immediate nature are the 'obligation to take steps'[74] and the 'obligation to guarantee the rights without discrimination.'[75] However, it does not provide any further guidance. The obligation 'to take steps' (article 2(1)) and the obligation to guarantee the rights without discrimination (article 2(2)) are both obligations contained in Part II of the Covenant and are analysed in detail below in Chapters VII and VIII respectively. However, here it is important to stress that these obligations apply to all substantive rights contained in Part III of the Covenant.

In its General Comments the Committee has also referred to the immediate nature of some specific obligations arising from the substantive rights contained in Part III of the Covenant. While these obligations are not the primary focus of the present study, it is important to observe here that the Committee considers the following obligations to be immediate in character:

1. *Immediate obligations arising from the right to adequate housing*: In General Comment Nos. 4 and 7, the Committee notes that regardless of the state of development of any country, there are certain steps which must be taken immediately. However, in its General Comments the Committee has specifically mentioned only three: the duty to provide legal security of tenure, which includes legal protection against

situation with respect to housing is another obligation of immediate effect' [para. 13]. (Emphasis added).

71 For example, in General Comment No. 11 on 'plans of action for primary education' the Committee states '[…] it needs to be stressed in this regard that the State party's other obligations, such as non-discrimination, are required to be implemented fully and immediately' [para. 11].

72 For example in General Comment No. 12 on 'the right to adequate food' the Committee held, 'some measures at these different levels of obligations of States Parties are of a more immediate nature, while other measures are more of a long-term character, to achieve progressively the full realisation of the right to food.' [para. 16].

73 For example, in General Comment No. 14 on 'the right to the highest attainable standard of health' the Committee stressed that, 'while the Covenant provides for progressive realisation and acknowledges the constraints due to the limits of available resources, it also imposes on States Parties various obligations which are of immediate effect. States Parties have immediate obligations in relation to the right to health, such as the guarantee that the right will be exercised without discrimination of any kind (article 2(2)) and the obligation to take steps (Art. 2(1)) towards the full realisation of article 12' [para. 30]. (Emphasis added).

74 See General Comment No. 3 para. 2, General Comment No. 13 para. 43 and General Comment No. 14 para. 30.

75 General Comment No. 3 para. 1, General Comment No. 11 para. 10, General Comment No. 13 paras. 31 and 43 and General Comment No. 14 para. 30.

forced evictions,[76] the obligation to provide effective monitoring of the housing situation in the State concerned[77] and the duty to refrain from forced evictions.[78] Additionally, in its statements regarding the UN Conference on Human Settlements (Habitat II), the Committee also mentions that the ratification of the Covenant obliges States 'to take immediate measures to promote the right to housing and, where necessary, to seek international co-operation, in accordance with articles 11, 22 and 23 of the Covenant.'[79]

2. *Immediate obligations arising from the right to education*: The Committee dedicates two General Comments to the right to education, General Comment Nos. 11 and 13.[80] However, despite indicating once again that the obligation of 'non-discrimination' and the 'obligation to take steps'[81] are of an immediate nature, it is not clear which other obligations imposed by this right are of an immediate nature.

The only other obligation that the Committee has referred to as being of an immediate nature is the obligation to provide compulsory primary education free of charge (articles 13 and 14 of the ICESCR). However, it has not been absolutely clear in establishing its immediate character. The wording of article 13(2)(a) of the ICESCR suggests that the obligation to ensure compulsory primary education free of charge is immediate for all countries.[82] This seems to be the interpretation given by commenta-

76 General Comment No. 4 para. 8 and General Comment No. 7 para. 9.

77 General Comment No. 4 para. 11. From this author's point of view, the obligation to monitor the national situation is a general obligation arising from the Covenant with respect to the enjoyment of all substantive rights contained therein. Therefore, it is analysed in Chapter VII section 6.

78 General Comment No. 7 para. 9 states, '[...] in view of the nature of the practice of forced evictions, the reference in article 2(1) to progressive achievement based on the availability of resources will rarely be relevant. The State itself must refrain from forced evictions and ensure that the law is enforced against its agents or third parties who carry out forced evictions.'

79 E/1996/22, Annex VII, para. 10.

80 The right to education, as well as the right to adequate housing are the rights most frequently addressed by the Committee in the General Comments. In fact, it has dedicated two General Comments to each. See General Comment Nos. 11 and 13 regarding the right to education and General Comment Nos. 4 and 7 regarding the right to adequate housing.

81 It is noted that, 'While the Covenant provides for progressive realisation and acknowledges the constraints due to the limits of available resources, it also imposes on States Parties *various obligations which are of immediate effect*. States Parties have immediate obligations in relation to the right to education, *such as* the 'guarantee' that the right 'will be exercised without discrimination of any kind' (Art. 2 (2)) and the obligation 'to take steps' (Art. 2 (1)) towards the full realisation of Art. 13. Such steps must be 'deliberate, concrete and targeted' towards the full realisation of the right to education.' [General Comment No. 13 para. 43, emphasis added]. The expression 'such as' implies that the obligations mentioned are not the only obligations of an immediate nature that the right to education imposes.

82 Art.13 (2)(a) reads as follows: 'The States Parties to the present Covenant recognise that, with a view to achieving the full realisation of this right: (a) Primary education shall be compulsory and available to all.'

tors[83] and it is clearly the interpretation given by the Committee in its General Comment on the right to education, which states, '[t]he obligation to provide primary education for all is an *immediate duty* of all States Parties.'[84]

Nonetheless, according to article 14 ICESCR, if at the time of becoming a Party to the Covenant, a State has not been able to secure compulsory primary education free of charge, it has an alternate obligation to submit, within two years, a detailed plan of action for the progressive implementation of the compulsory primary education free of charge.[85] According to the General Comment, the requirement to adopt a plan of action within two years must be interpreted as meaning two years from the Covenant's entry into force in the State concerned or within two years of a subsequent change in circumstances which led to the non-observance of the obligation.[86]

Therefore, reading articles 13 and 14 of the ICESCR together, we may conclude that the obligation to provide free primary education is an immediate one for States Parties with the necessary means to implement it, but that States without the necessary resources are allowed to ensure it progressively.[87] Nevertheless, in the latter case, States are obliged to adopt a plan of action within two years, in which they have to fix a reasonable number of years for the implementation of the obligation of compulsory primary education free of charge. Therefore, the obligation is different from other progressive obligations contained in the Covenant because there is a fixed period of time within which States Parties have to comply and resource constraints cannot relieve States Parties of this obligation.[88]

As the Committee stresses,

> '[t]he plan of action must be aimed at securing the progressive implementation of the right to compulsory primary education, free of charge, under article 14. Unlike the provision in article 2(1), however, article 14 specifies that the target date must be 'within a reasonable number of years' and moreover, that the time frame must 'be fixed in the plan'. In other words, the plan must specifically set out a series of targeted implementation dates for each

83 Alston, P. & Quinn, G.: 'The nature and scope of States Parties' obligations under the International Covenant on Economic, Social and Cultural Rights.' In: *HRQ,* vol. 9 No. 2, (1987), p. 186.

84 General Comment No. 13 para. 51. (Emphasis added).

85 Art. 14 ICESCR establishes, 'Each State Party to the present Covenant which, at the time of becoming a Party, has not been able to secure in its metropolitan territory or other territories under its jurisdiction compulsory primary education, free of charge, undertakes, within two years, to work out and adopt a detailed plan of action for the progressive implementation, within a reasonable number of years, to be fixed in the plan, of the principle of compulsory education free of charge for all.'

86 General Comment No. 11 para. 8.

87 This approach would find support in the position of some Committee members who have indeed expressed their views that 'developing countries deserved special treatment when they appeared before the Committee.' See in E/C.12/1995/SR.22 the statement of Mr. Ahmed (para. 42) and Mr. Texier (para. 48).

88 General Comment No. 11 paras. 3 and 9.

stage of the progressive implementation of the plan. This underscores both the importance and the relative inflexibility of the obligation in question.'[89]

However, the Committee seems not to be very demanding in relation to the implementation of this obligation, For example, when analysing the second periodic report of Aruba in 1999, the Committee 'recommends that a plan of action be adopted urgently to move towards the provision of free compulsory primary education as required by article 14 of the Covenant.'[90] This is a very weak statement from the Committee, considering that at that time such a Plan had not been adopted after more than 10 years [the Kingdom of the Netherlands adopted the Covenant in 1979].

3. *Immediate obligations arising from the right to food*: In General Comment No. 12, the Committee is again rather laconic in assessing which obligations are of an immediate character and which are more progressive. In fact, after the Committee indicates that the right to adequate food imposes three types of obligations on States Parties (obligation to respect, to protect and to fulfil), it merely notes that, '[so]me measures at these different levels of obligations of States Parties are of a more immediate nature, while other measures are more of a long-term character, to achieve progressively the full realisation of the right to food.'[91]

4. *Immediate obligations arising from the right to the highest attainable standard of health*: In General Comment No. 14, the Committee merely states that, '[w]hile the Covenant provides for progressive realisation and acknowledges the constraints due to the limits of available resources, it also imposes on States Parties various obligations which are of immediate effect. States Parties have immediate obligations in relation to the right to health, such as the guarantee that the right will be exercised without discrimination of any kind (article 2(2)) and the obligation to take steps (article 2(1)) towards the full realisation of article 12. Such steps must be deliberate, concrete and targeted towards the full realisation of the right to health.'[92] Again, it says that there are many ('various') obligations of an immediate character, but it does not provide any further guidance as to what they are.

2.3.2 Immediate/progressive obligations in the Committee's Concluding Observations

Through its General Comments, the Committee has explicitly noted that the Covenant imposes progressive as well as immediate obligations. While the Committee has mentioned some rights which impose immediate obligations, it has not used the General Comments to fully develop their scope. Nonetheless, further guidance as to the exis-

89 General Comment No. 11 para. 10.
90 E/1999/22 para. 207.
91 General Comment No. 12 para. 16.
92 General Comment No. 14 para. 30.

tence of immediate obligations imposed by the Covenant rights is provided by the Concluding Observations. For instance, while General Comment Nos. 3 and 9 merely enumerate rights which can be of immediate application, through its Concluding Observations the Committee provides more guidance as to the scope of the obligations imposed by those provisions that are of immediate character. This is true, for example, of the duty to eradicate illegal child labour and to establish a legal minimum age for work (article 10(3) ICESCR),[93] the duty to take legislative measures to protect the right to form and join trade unions and the right to strike (article 8 ICESCR)[94] and the duty to introduce anti-discrimination legislation to protect women (articles 2(2) and 3 ICESC).[95] In the same vein, through the Concluding Observations, the Committee has emphasised the immediate character of the duty to refrain from forced evictions.[96]

In its Concluding Observations, the Committee has gone further than in its General Comments and has suggested the existence of obligations of an immediate character not mentioned by the General Comments, for example, the obligation to improve health and social conditions in prisons and detention centres[97] and the duty to protect the cultural rights of minorities.[98] Although the Committee has stated that these duties must be implemented immediately, notwithstanding the States Parties' level of development, it is interesting to note that the Committee has been rather cautious when addressing these issues. In fact, the immediate character of the obligation to improve health and social conditions in detention centres and of the duty to protect the cultural rights of minorities is well established by other human rights monitoring bodies, principally those established by civil and political rights instruments. This is so because civil and political rights instruments contain norms that may also provide protection in the socio-economic sphere. For example, the obligation to protect the 'cultural rights of minori-

93 See, for example, Concluding Observations Sri Lanka E/1999/22 para. 90; Concluding Observations Egypt E/2001/22 para. 178; Concluding Observations Kyrgyzstan E/2001/22 para. 359; and Concluding Observations Morocco E/2001/22 para. 556.

94 See, for example, Concluding Observations United Kingdom of Great Britain and Northern Ireland E/1998/22 para. 294 and Concluding Observations Republic of Korea E/1996/22 para. 80.

95 See, for example, Concluding Observations United Kingdom of Great Britain and Northern Ireland E/1995/22 para. 298. For further analysis on the duties imposed by the prohibition of discrimination against women see Chapter VIII section 4.

96 The immediate character of the duty to refrain from forced evictions has been expressly noted by the Committee in General Comment No. 7 para. 8 and it has constantly emphasised this through Concluding Observations, for example, Concluding Observations Peru E/1998/22 para. 168 and Concluding Observations Nigeria E/1999/22 para. 136.

97 See, for example, Concluding Observations Russian Federation E/1998/22 para. 168 and Concluding Observations Cyprus E/1999/22 para. 288.

98 Analysing the report of Zimbabwe, the Committee stated that, '[a]lthough many provisions of the Covenant are to be implemented progressively and in accordance with the maximum of State party's resources, *there are other rights that must be ensured immediately,* such as *de jure* non-discrimination and *protection of the cultural rights of minorities*.' Concluding Observations Zimbabwe E/C.12/1997/10 para. 79. (Emphasis added).

ties' found in article 15(1) ICESCR may also be protected by some civil and political rights that are considered to be of an immediate nature. This is true of, for example, article 26 ICCPR (non-discrimination provision); article 27 ICCPR (the protection of minorities);[99] and of specific rights such as the freedom of religion (article 18 ICCPR), expression (article 19 ICCPR) and association (article 22 ICCPR).[100]

Regarding the immediate effect of the obligation to provide minimum material conditions in prisons or detention centres, we also find that its immediate character is well established in the case-law of human rights treaty monitoring bodies. At the universal level, article 10, paragraph 1 of the ICCPR stipulates that 'all persons deprived of their liberty shall be treated with humanity and with respect for the inherent dignity of the human person'. As the Human Rights Committee observes, when liberty is constrained, other rights should not be limited any more than required by this deprivation of liberty.[101] Therefore, when individuals are deprived of their liberty, they retain the right to enjoy economic, social and cultural rights which should be provided by the State in a way that allows them to live in dignity.[102] States must comply with this

---

99 It is interesting to note that under article 27 ICCPR, States are required to respect, protect and fulfil the right of members of a minority to enjoy their culture. Under this instrument it is well established that the obligations are of an immediate nature. Just to give some examples, an obligation to respect was envisaged by the Human Rights Committee when it stated, 'Article 27 requires that a member of a minority shall not be denied his right to enjoy his own culture. Thus, measures whose impact amount to a denial of the right will not be compatible with the obligations under article 27[...]' [Lansmann *et al.* v. Finland, Communication No. 511/1992, views of 26 October 1994, para. 9.4]. An obligation to protect under Art. 27 ICCPR has been clearly established. In this regard the HRC has held 'As the earlier case law by the Committee illustrates, the right of members of a minority to enjoy their culture under article 27 includes protection to a particular way of life associated with the use of land resources through economic activities, such as hunting and fishing, especially in the case of indigenous people.' J.G.A. Diergaardt v. Namibia (late Captain of the Rehoboth Baster Community) *et al.* v. Namibia [Communication No. 760/1997, views of 20 July 2000, para. 10.6]. The existence of obligations to fulfil has been established by General Comment No. 23 [CCPR/C/21/Rev.1/Add.5] as well as in its case law. For example, in deciding a case in 1990, submitted by the Chief of an indigenous band in Canada, the Human Rights Committee held, '[h]istorical inequities, [...] and certain more recent developments threaten the way of life and culture of the Lubicon Lake Band, and constitute a violation of article 27 so long as they continue' [Communication No. 167/1984, views of 26 March 1990]. In the later judgement of Mahuika *et al.* v. New Zealand, the HRC emphasised, 'the Committee recalls its general comment on article 27, according to which, especially in the case of indigenous peoples, the enjoyment of the right to one's own culture may require positive legal measures of protection by a State party and measures to ensure the effective participation of members of minority communities in decisions which affect them.' [Mahuika *et al.* v. New Zealand, Communication No. 547/1993, views of 27 October 2000, para. 9.5].

100 See: Rodley, N.: 'Conceptual problems in the protection of minorities: international legal developments.' In: *HRQ* vol. 17 No. 1, (1995), pp. 48-71 and Scheinin, M.: 'The right to enjoy a distinct culture: indigenous and competing uses of land.' In: *The jurisprudence of human rights law: a comparative interpretative approach*. Orlin, T.S.; Rosas, A. & Scheinin, M. (eds.), Institute for Human Rights, Åbo Akademi University, Åbo, Finland (2000), pp. 159-222.

101 HRC General Comment No. 21 para. 3.

102 See below the analysis in the 'obligation to fulfil', when dealing with the 'tripartite typology.'

obligation notwithstanding their level of resources. As the Human Rights Committee notes, '[t]reating all persons deprived of their liberty with humanity and with respect for their dignity is a fundamental and universally applicable rule. Consequently, *the application of this rule, as a minimum, cannot be dependent on the material resources available in the State party.*'[103]

In examining State Parties' reports, the HRC has expressed its concern about the material conditions in detention centres[104] and when dealing with individual cases the HRC has often found a violation of article 10(1) ICCPR when States do not provide conditions of dignity in detention centres.[105] It has also found a violation of article 7 (the prohibition of torture and cruel, inhuman and degrading treatment) in individual cases. For example, in the case of Mukong v. Cameroon the Committee held,

> 'As to the conditions of detention in general, the Committee observes that certain minimum standards regarding the conditions of detention must be observed *regardless of a State party's level of development*. These include, in accordance with [...] the U.N. Standard Minimum Rules for the Treatment of Prisoners [...], minimum floor space and cubic content of air for each prisoner, adequate sanitary facilities, clothing which shall be in no manner degrading or humiliating, provision of a separate bed, and provision of food of nutritional value adequate for health and strength. It should be noted that *these are minimum requirements which the Committee considers should always be observed, even if economic or budgetary considerations may make compliance with these obligations difficult.*'[106]

The material conditions in prisons are also a subject of concern for the Committee against Torture [CAT]. The CAT requires States to take immediate measures to improve conditions in prisons.[107] This Committee has also paid attention to education and training activities for prison staff[108] and it has clearly noted that respect for persons detained in prisons '*must* be in keeping with the Standard Minimum Rules for the Treatment of Prisoners.'[109] This strong requirement regarding the application of the

103 General Comment No. 21, para. 4. (Emphasis added). See Chapter IV, section 3.3, the text accompanying notes 143 *et seq.*

104 See, for example, HRC Concluding Observations Gabon CCPR/CO/70/GAB para. 14 and HRC Concluding Observations Morocco CCPR/C/79/Add.44 para. 12.

105 See in Chapter 4, section 3.3, the text accompanying notes 145-146.

106 Albert Womah Mukong v. Cameroon, Communication No. 458/1991, views of 21 July 1994, para. 9.3. (Emphasis added and footnote omitted).

107 CAT Conclusions and Recommendations Greece CAT/C/XXVI/Concl.2/Rev.1 paras. 5 and 6, Bolivia CAT/C/XXVI/Concl.3 para.11 and Egypt A/54/44 para. 203.

108 See, for example, Conclusions and Recommendations Georgia CAT/C/XXVI/Concl.1/Rev.2 paras. 5(g) and 6(i).

109 CAT Conclusions and Recommendations Guatemala CAT/C/XXV/Concl.6 para. 7(f). (Emphasis added).

Standard Minimum Rules for the Treatment of Prisoners[110] is of particular relevance here given that the Rules contain a range of economic, social and cultural rights provisions.[111]

At the European level, the case law also suggests the existence of immediate State obligations to provide for a certain level of socio-economic conditions in places of detention. It is important to note in this regard that violations of article 3 of the European Convention have been found where there were conditions such as: overcrowding, inadequate heating or toilets, sleeping arrangements, food and inadequate recreation and provision for contact to the outside world.[112] At the American level, the requirement of the immediate provision of a certain minimum level of socio–economic conditions to persons deprived of their liberty is to be found in article 5(2) ACHR, which states that 'all persons deprived of their liberty shall be treated with respect for the inherent dignity of the human person.' The Inter-American Court has clearly stated that detention conditions must be compatible with personal dignity and as the State is the institution responsible for detention establishments, it is the guarantor of these rights of prisoners.[113]

Recapitulating, it is clear that the Covenant contains rights which impose obligations of an immediate nature. To some extent the Committee has gone further in its Concluding Observations than through its General Comments in indicating the immediate nature of some obligations such as, the protection of the cultural rights of minorities and the fulfilment of material conditions in detention centres. Nonetheless, here again the Committee has not been explicit enough and at the same time it has been overly cautious. It has principally mentioned obligations with a well-established immediate character in the light of the case law of other human rights monitoring bodies. It would be desirable for the Committee to make further efforts to develop the immediate obligations imposed by the Covenant through its Concluding Observations

2.3.3 Concluding comments on the immediate/progressive typology

This typology is useful in that it illustrates that the Covenant imposes obligations of both immediate and progressive character. However, the Committee is still too broad and generic in its statements. It often merely indicates the existence of some obligations which are of an immediate character but without specifying to which obligations it refers. It would be appropriate if, in future, the Committee used the General Comments

110 Adopted by the First United Nations Congress on the Prevention of Crime and the Treatment of Offenders, held in Geneva in 1955, and approved by ECOSOC Res. 663(XXIV) of 31 July 1957 and 2076 (LXII) of 13 May 1977.

111 See, for example, rule Nos. 9, 10, 11, 15, 17, 20 and 22.

112 See: Harris, D.; O'Boyle, M. & Warbrick, C.: *Law of the European Convention on Human Rights*. Butterworths, London, (1995), pp. 55 *et seq*.

113 See, for example, I/A Court H.R. Neira Alegría *et al.* v. Peru, Judgement of 19 January 1995, Series C No. 20, para. 60.

and Concluding Observations to both identify those obligations which are of an immediate character and define their scope.

Furthermore, the Committee should pay greater attention to the negative obligations imposed by the Covenant. In General Comment Nos. 3 and 9, the Committee enumerates those provisions that it considers susceptible of immediate application, most of which require abstention. By doing so, the Committee suggests that all negative obligations imposed by the rights set forth in the Covenant are of immediate application. Nonetheless, it has not clearly specified which negative obligations are imposed by each substantive right. To the extent that the Committee provides clear guidance as to the immediate obligations imposed by each substantive right, the easier it would be to assess whether or not States Parties are in compliance with the Covenant.

2.4 Obligations of conduct and obligations of result

In General Comment No. 3 on the nature of States Parties' obligations under the Covenant, the Committee indicates that the Covenant includes both obligations of conduct and obligations of result.[114] Nevertheless, the Committee has not developed this typology any further. Despite having included the typology in the 'Outline for drafting general comments on specific rights of the International Covenant on Economic, Social and Cultural Rights'[115] the Committee has not incorporated it in its subsequent General Comments.

From the present author's point of view, the non-application of the typology conduct/result in the work of the Committee is an advantage. Admittedly, by mentioning the conduct/result typology in General Comment No. 3 and in the 'Outline for drafting general comments', the Committee has followed an approach commonly adopted in international law. In fact, in discussions on the nature of the obligations arising from international treaties, a distinction is usually made between obligations of conduct and obligations of result. However, as we will see, there are strong arguments for not using this typology when referring to the obligations imposed by the Covenant.

As this section will attempt to demonstrate, although international human rights law is embedded in the general regime of public international law, the conduct/result typology commonly applied in international law is not appropriate to characterise the duties imposed by the Covenant nor, more generally, to characterise the State duties imposed by human rights treaties. Although the Committee on Economic, Social and Cultural Rights, as well as some scholars sometimes use the conduct/result typology,[116] it is

114 General Comment No. 3 para. 1.

115 Adopted by the Committee during the twenty-first session in the 37th meeting on 19 November E/C.12/1999/11, Annex IX, pp. 135-136.

116 See, for example, Goodwin-Gill, G.S.: 'Obligations of conduct and result.' In: *The right to food.* Alston, P. & Tomaševski, K. (eds.), Martinus Nijhoff Publishers, Utrecht (1984), pp. 111-118; Eide, 1987, *op. cit.* (note 20), para. 71, p. 15; Leckie, S.: 'Another step towards indivisibility: identifying

confusing and especially so when applied to State duties imposed by human rights treaties. Therefore, it is suggested that it is better not to use the conduct/result typology when referring to States' duties imposed by the Covenant.

2.4.1 The meaning of 'obligations of conduct' and 'obligations of result' in international law

In 1977, within the framework of the International Law Commission's (ILC) studies on State responsibility,[117] Special Rapporteur Roberto Ago presented a report which contained the notions of 'obligations of specific conduct' and 'obligations requiring to achieve a particular result.' Since the ILC introduced these notions in articles 20 and 21 of the Draft Articles on State Responsibility, they have become common terms in international law.[118]

While the obligations of conduct and result have a clear and well-established meaning in civil law systems, particularly in the French system, the use of these notions at the international level is much less clear than one might hope.[119] Hence, a brief analysis of both terms at the international level is necessary.

From the text of the Draft Articles on State Responsibility provisionally adopted by the Commission on first reading in 1996, and the Commentary on those articles, these two terms may be described as follows:[120]

a. *International obligations of conduct (or obligations of means)*: These obligations require the State to adopt a particular course of conduct (active or passive). In other

---

the key features of violations of economic, social and cultural rights.' In: *HRQ,* vol. 20, No. 1, (1998), p. 92; Meron, T.: *Human rights and humanitarian norms as customary law*, Oxford University Press, Oxford, (1989), pp. 182 *et seq*.; and Craven, M.: *The International Covenant on Economic, Social and Cultural Rights: a perspective on its development*, Clarendon Press, Oxford, (1995), pp. 107-109. See in addition, The Maastricht Guideline No. 7.

117 The topic of State responsibility was selected at the ILC's first session in 1949 as one of the topics suitable for codification. Over the years, the issue was extensively discussed by the ILC and a series of ILC Special Rapporteurs analysed the topic, Mr. F.V. Garcia Amador 1955-1961; Mr. R. Ago 1963-1979; Mr. W. Riphagen 1979-1987, Mr. G. Arangio Ruiz 1987-1996 and Mr. J. Crawford 1997-2001. The Draft Articles on Responsibility of States for Internationally Wrongful Acts were finally adopted by the ILC on 9 August 2001.

118 Articles 20 and 21 of the Draft Articles on State Responsibility were provisionally adopted by the ILC at its twenty-ninth session in 1977 [see Yearbook of the International Law Commission, 1977, vol. II (Part Two), report of the Commission to the General Assembly on the work of its twenty-ninth session, pp. 10 *et seq.*] and on first reading at its forty-eighth session in 1996 [see, Report of the ILC on the work of its forty-eighth session. General Assembly Official records fifty-first Session, Supplement No. 10 (A/51/10), Chapter III].

119 For a comprehensive analysis of differences between the meaning at the domestic and the international levels, see, Dupuy, P.M.: 'Reviewing the difficulties of codification: on Ago's classification of obligations of means and obligations of result in relation to state responsibility.' In: *EJIL*, No. 10 vol. 2, (1999), pp. 371-385.

120 ILC Yearbook,1977, vol. II (Part Two), pp. 11-30.

words, these obligations require States to take or refrain from taking certain legislative, executive or judicial measures.[121]

b. *International obligations of result*: These obligations require States to achieve a specified result, but they are free to use the means they choose to fulfil the obligations. The key element of these obligations is that they leave the State discretion in the choice of the means necessary to achieve the required result.[122]

As may be deduced from the Commentary on the Draft Articles, the distinction between 'obligations of conduct' and 'obligations of result' was adopted because it was considered essential for determining the existence of a breach of an international obligation and when that breach has occurred. In this regard, it was said that there is a breach of an international obligation of conduct whenever the act or omission of the State is not in conformity with a specifically determined conduct required of it by that obligation, independent of whether that action or omission had harmful consequences.[123] In contrast, there is a breach of result when the conduct adopted does not achieve the result required of it by those obligations. In this case, it is not the conduct or the means adopted by the State that matter, but, rather, the final result achieved. As set out in the 1977 Commentary of the Draft Articles on State Responsibility, obligations of conduct are more onerous than obligations of result. This is so, because in the case of an obligation of conduct, the State is obliged to engage in a given conduct

121 Art. 20 reads as follows:
'Breach of an international obligation requiring the adoption of a particular course of conduct.
There is a breach by a State of an international obligation requiring it to adopt a particular course of conduct when the conduct of that State is not in conformity with that required of it by that obligation.'
Art. 20 Text of the Draft Articles provisionally adopted by the Commission on first reading. Report of the ILC on the work of its forty-eighth session (6 May-26 July 1996). General Assembly Official Records fifty-first Session. Supplement No. 10 A/51/10 Chapter III.

122 Art. 21 reads as follows:
'Breach of an international obligation requiring the achievement of a specified result.
There is a breach by a State of an international obligation requiring it to achieve, by means of its own choice, a specified result if, by the conduct adopted, the State does not achieve the result required of it by that obligation.
When the conduct of the State has created a situation not in conformity with the result required of it by an international obligation, but the obligation allows that this or an equivalent result may nevertheless be achieved by subsequent conduct of the State, there is a breach of the obligation only if the State also fails by its subsequent conduct to achieve the result required of it by that obligation.'
Art. 21 Text of the Draft Articles provisionally adopted by the Commission on first reading. Report of the ILC on the work of its forty-eighth session (6 May-26 July 1996). General Assembly Official Records fifty-first Session. Supplement No. 10 A/51/10 Chapter III.

123 See Yearbook of the ILC 1977, Summary Records of the twenty-ninth session, vol. I, p. 217. As Goodwin-Gill notes, 'ascertaining that the obligation [of conduct] has been fulfilled turns on the simple question, whether the State's act or omission is or is not in fact in conformity with the internationally required conduct, the sufficient injury being the breach of legal duty'. Goodwin-Gill, *op. cit.* (note 116), p. 112.

(an act or omission), and there would be a violation if the State does not comply. In contrast, in the case of an obligation of result, the State is not obliged to comply with a precise conduct, but, rather, has discretion as to the choice of means.

Moreover, according to Ago, obligations of result may take an even more permissive form than that of leaving the State a free initial choice of the means of achieving the required result. The discretion of the State in choosing the means sometimes extends to allowing the State to apply a remedy *a posteriori,* meaning that if the State has not achieved the result by the first means chosen, it has the opportunity to resort to other means to achieve this result. As he points out, although in some cases the means chosen do not lead to the required result, the State can still discharge its obligation by offering compensation for the damage suffered.[124]

Therefore, the assessment of a breach of an obligation of conduct entails relatively little difficulty. According to the Commentary, it requires a mere comparison between the conduct and the norm's prescription and if the required act has not been performed there is a breach of the obligation of conduct. However, determining a definitive breach of an obligation of result is much more complex. It is necessary to assert that *in concreto* the result has not been achieved or that there is no further possibility of using other means to achieve the result, when the means used have proved to be inadequate and the international obligation permits action to rectify the resulting situation.[125]

2.4.2 State obligations imposed by human rights and the conduct/result typology

Having defined the meaning of obligations of conduct and result under international law as defined in the 1997 Report of the International Law Commission, the following will be demonstrated: first, that the notions have not been properly used to categorise economic, social and cultural rights on the one hand and civil and political rights on the other, suggesting that the former have a character which is somehow 'less binding'; second, that the conduct/result scheme is very confusing and should be avoided when referring to States' duties imposed by human rights norms.

---

124 ILC Yearbook, 1977, vol. II (Part Two), paras. 18-30. As an example of this kind of obligation of result he cites Art. 9 ICCPR, because it was considered that reading it in conjunction paragraphs 1, 4 and 5 shows 'that the State can consider that it has acted in conformity with its international duties even when, having failed to achieved the main result required by the obligation stated in article 9, it has nevertheless achieved the alternative result of making reparation for the injury unlawfully caused to the person who suffered an arrest or detention which should not have taken place.' ILC Yearbook, 1977, vol. II (Part One), para. 23.

125 ILC Yearbook, 1977, vol. II (Part Two), para. 14. As explained by Ago, 'the initial conduct of a State organ which has created a situation incompatible with the internationally required result becomes a complete breach of the international obligation only if the State refrains, despite the possibility open to it, from eliminating this situation or confirms it by further action. It will be as a result of this later action or omission that the existence of the breach will be definitely established and that the responsibility of the State will be directly engaged.' ILC Yearbook, 1977, vol. II (Part One), para. 44.

A. *Overview of the traditional assumption*
Traditionally it has been argued that economic, social and cultural rights impose obligations of result in contrast to civil and political rights which are said to impose obligations of conduct. According to one author, this assumption is one of the 'myths' that have hindered the protection of economic, social and cultural rights.[126] The reasoning behind this dichotomy is that economic, social and cultural rights allow a wide margin of discretion to States and that this flexibility results in these rights being somehow 'less binding' or 'less rights' than civil and political rights which are said to require more concrete steps.

According to the international notion of obligations of conduct and result, such general statements are untenable. Indeed, it is striking that the very examples given by the former Special Rapporteur Mr. Ago in his commentary to articles 20 and 21 of the Draft Articles on State Responsibility indicate precisely the opposite. He mentioned a provision of the ICESCR as an example of an obligation of conduct,[127] and obligations of civil and political rights contained in the ICCPR and some provisions of the ECHR as obligations of result.[128]

The traditional assumption that economic, social and cultural rights impose obligations of result and civil and political rights obligations of conduct is a consequence of exclusively attributing obligations of non-interference to civil and political rights which are considered to have been secured by the mere adoption of legislation. In contrast, this traditional approach attributes to economic, social and cultural rights merely positive obligations as it considers that such obligations cannot be complied with immediately due to their dependence on economic resources.

Today, the assumption that economic, social and cultural rights only impose obligations of result and civil and political rights obligations of conduct is very simplistic and inaccurate. Obligations arising from one or the other sort of rights cannot be classified as carrying exclusively obligations of conduct or obligations of result. In general, we

126 See, Matas, 1985, p. 124. As Matas notes this 'myth' has led to the belief that 'as long as the State is taking steps to achieve the result, it does not matter if the result is achieved. Political and civil rights are, on the other hand, obligations of conduct pointing to a certain measure that a State must adopt.'

127 In giving examples of obligations of conduct, Mr. Ago mentions obligations arising from labour conventions and from some international agreements in matters of health and education and Art. 10(3) ICESCR which imposes the obligation to punish by law the harmful labour of children and young persons ('harmful to their morals or health or dangerous to life or likely to hamper their normal development'). As he explains, 'this obligation is breached simply by the fact that the law providing for the punishment of such practices has not been enacted, even if no specific instance of employment of children in such work has been found in the country concerned.' ILC Yearbook, 1977, vol. II (Part One), paras. 5-7.

128 Ago indicates as examples of obligations of result, among others, the obligations arising from: the right to leave a country, freedom of association obligations, prohibition of slavery and servitude, and the right to liberty and the security of the person. As he notes, in all of these cases the State is free to choose whatever means it deems most appropriate in each particular case, to ensure these freedoms and rights to individuals. ILC Yearbook, 1977, vol. II (Part One), paras. 17 and 20.

may say that human rights instruments do not impose merely one type of obligation. Scholars[129] and the Committee itself have clearly established that the Covenant and international human rights instruments in general impose both types of obligations.

The Committee has noted that the obligations undertaken by States Parties '*include both* what may be termed (following the work of the International Law Commission) obligations of conduct and obligations of result.'[130] There are strong reasons to interpret this paragraph as indicating that the Covenant imposes a 'hybrid' of both kinds of obligations considering, for example, that the draft of General Comment No. 3 was prepared by P. Alston[131] who had co-written an article in 1987 clearly indicating that, 'the relevant obligations [of the Covenant] can best be understood as hybrids between obligations of result and obligations of conduct.'[132,133] Nevertheless, it would have been appropriate for the Committee to expressly indicated this. From this author's perspective it is not the same to say that the Covenant contains 'both' kinds of obligations, as it is to say that the obligations imposed are a 'hybrid' of both.

Nevertheless, what we want to emphasise here is that while it is well established that the Covenant does not exclusively contain obligations of result, but 'both' kinds of obligations (or a mixture of both), it may be more appropriate for the Committee to avoid applying the conduct/result typology because, as we will see, it is not accurate to define obligations imposed by human rights treaties.

B. *The drawbacks of the conduct/result schema*

The Committee has appropriately rejected the approach which attributes to economic, social and cultural rights merely obligations of result. Nonetheless, the Committee's assertion that the Covenant imposes both obligations of conduct and obligations of result might not be entirely appropriate.

Nowadays scholars have manifested their scepticism as to the utility of applying the conduct/result typology to State duties. Although it is beyond the scope of this study to discuss in detail all of the inconveniences of the international notions of conduct/result, some comments are required.[134] Principally, we will focus on two problems that

---

129 See, for example, Meron, *op. cit.* (note 116), p. 184 and the Maastricht Guideline No. 7.

130 General Comment No. 3 para. 1. (Emphasis added).

131 See, for example, E/C.12/1990/SR.46 and E/C.12/1990/SR.48 which contain the debate held by the Committee members on the draft general comment concerning the nature of State Parties' obligations (under Agenda item 4).

132 Alston & Quinn, *loc. cit.* (note 83), p. 185.

133 The analysis of Craven is that in paragraph 1 of General Comment No. 3 the Committee is essentially stating that the Covenant incorporates a 'mixture of the two types of obligations'. Craven, *op. cit.* (note 116), p. 107.

134 For a reasoned analysis of the inconvenience in codifying the notions of obligations of conduct and result see, Dupuy, *loc. cit.* (note 119), pp. 371-385; Crawford, J.: 'Revising the draft articles on state responsibility.' In: *EJIL*, No. 10 vol. 2, (1999), pp. 435-460; and the Second Report on State Responsibility. Special Rapporteur Mr. James Crawford. UN doc. A/CN.4/498 of 17 March 1999. For a specific

the application of this typology to human rights instruments may cause. First, we will address the difficulty in asserting the conduct/result nature of some obligations and, second, the difficulty in identifying when a breach of an obligation has occurred.

As presented by the 1977 Draft Articles and the Commentaries to articles 20 and 21, identifying whether a specific treaty provision entails an obligation of conduct or an obligation of result is an easy task. If it is left to the State to choose the means of achieving the purpose it would be an obligation of result. In contrast, if the norm envisages a specific conduct to be followed by the State, it would be an obligation of conduct. However, what seems at first to be an easy task becomes much more complex in practice when we are dealing with human rights norms.

In practice, it may be very difficult to determine whether an obligation imposed by human rights treaties is an obligation of conduct or an obligation of result because there is no clear dividing line between the two. The two types of obligations sometimes overlap.[135] As Tomuschat correctly notes,

> 'It is perhaps the most serious objection against the ILC's classification scheme that [...] not infrequently obligations of conduct and obligations of result are intertwined to such a degree that the different components can hardly be separated from one another.'[136]

The complexity of applying the conduct/result schema to human rights norms is well illustrated by Tomuschat with the prohibition of torture.

> 'The prohibition of torture may be characterised as an obligation of conduct, i.e. as a ban to inflict specific treatment on individuals. However, the substance of the obligation has a more comprehensive scope. To make the prohibition fully effective, it is necessary to establish appropriate monitoring mechanisms to control the discharge of their functions by the police and prison officers. In that regard, States have a wide margin of discretion (obligation of result). Again, it may well be that under special circumstances there exists just one remedy that can be considered suitable to avert the danger of torture being practised (obligations of means [conduct]). Thus, the basic obligation, by meandering through different stages of elaboration and implementation, can take different substantive forms.'[137]

In regard to obligations imposed by the Covenant, scholars have repeatedly noted the same difficulty in assessing whether an obligation is that of conduct or result. Just to give some examples, we find that in 1994 Goodwin-Gill already noted that the con-

---

reference to the inconvenience of their application to the European Convention on Human Rights, see Tomuschat, C.: 'What is a 'breach' of the European Convention on Human Rights?' In: *The dynamics of the protection of human rights in Europe: essays in honour of Henry G. Schermers*. Lawson, R. & Blois, M. de (eds.), Martinus Nijhoff Publishers, Dordrecht, vol. III, (1994), pp. 315-335.

135 Report of the International Law Commission on the work of its fifty-first session (3 May- 23 July 1999). General Assembly Official Records Supplement No. 10 (A/54/10 and Corr.1 & 2 para. 158).

136 Tomuschat, *op. cit.* (note 134), p. 324.

137 *Ibid.* (Footnote omitted).

duct/result distinction sometimes becomes blurred.[138] Later, Alston and Quinn explicitly presented the idea of a 'hybrid' of obligations of conduct and result.[139]

This difficulty is apparent in the example given by Craven on the right to work. As he notes,

> 'Article 6 [ICESCR], which provides for the right to work, requires steps to be taken towards the achievement of full employment (an obligation of result), but also prohibits forced labour (an obligation of conduct). Additionally, to the extent that the rights within the Covenant are not capable of immediate fulfilment, States are required to undertake certain obligations of conduct with a view to their progressive achievement [...].'

> '[t]he distinction between obligations of conduct and result is complicated by the fact that some of the specified 'steps' may also be seen to be independent norms imposing separate obligations of result. Article 6(2), for example, provides that the steps to be taken in the realisation of the right to work 'shall include technical and vocational guidance and training programmes'. It would not be distorting the sense of the Covenant to suggest that vocational guidance should be provided as of right as a partial definition of the right to work.'[140]

Admittedly, the notion of 'progressiveness' enshrined in article 2(1) of the ICESCR suggests that the Covenant imposes 'obligations of result', with a wide margin of discretion for States Parties to choose the means for implementing the Covenant. However, today it is apparent from the work of the Committee, as well as from the relevant academic writing, that States Parties to the Covenant have a more limited discretion as to the means to implement the Covenant than what article 2 ICESCR may suggest at first glance. Indeed, substantive provisions of the Covenant already specify certain steps that States Parties must take to implement the rights (*e.g.* article 11(2) ICESCR).[141] Furthermore, over the years the Committee has identified means which

---

138 Referring specifically to Arts. 2 and 11 of the ICESCR Goodwin-Gill notes that, '[...] the freedom of choice may be confined by reference to specific objectives, and further structured in the light of declared methods proposed and preferred in terms of the particular instrument.' Goodwin-Gill, *op. cit.* (note 116), pp. 111-118, at 115.

139 As Alston and Quinn explain, '[t]hey are obligations of result in the sense that states must match their performance with their objective capabilities. They are loose obligations of conduct in the sense that states are obliged to take active, though largely unspecified, steps toward their satisfaction. This hybrid mixture of obligation types is due to the fact that the concept of 'progressive achievement' mandates the existence of an ongoing process of development the adequacy of which is loosely controlled by norms deduced from a state's objective capabilities. The existence of such a process or course of conduct is, in other words, a necessary but a sufficient element of the full satisfaction of state obligations under the Covenant.' Alston & Quinn, *loc. cit.* (note 83), p. 185.

140 Craven, *op. cit.* (note 116), p. 108. (Footnote omitted).

141 As Alston and Quinn note, 'where the text of the various 'recognised' rights specify the 'steps' to be taken for their achievement then the obligations so created can truly be said to be obligations of conduct.' Alston & Quinn, *loc. cit.* (note 83), p. 185.

are necessary or indispensable for the full protection of the rights.[142] In fact, it is not rare that the Committee indicates that certain measures are 'necessary' or that a certain conduct is 'prohibited' and the distinction between obligations of conduct and result is therefore blurred.[143]

While we might still recognise some obligations imposed by the Covenant as being obligations of conduct or result, often these obligations will overlap and it becomes impossible to differentiate between them.[144] Therefore, it might be better not to classify the obligations in watertight compartments. As noted by Mr. Crawford in the 1999 Report, 'the two types of obligations [conduct and result] constituted a continuum and the decision to place certain obligations in one compartment and not the other rested on a subjective notion of the probability of achieving the intended outcome in a particular field.'[145]

The second drawback of the conduct/result typology is that it makes it difficult to identify when there is a breach of a human rights obligation. As discussed above, the aim of the conduct/result typology as presented by Ago was to facilitate finding whether there has been a breach of an international obligation and when that breach has taken place. However, as the present ILC Special Rapporteur J. Crawford has indicated, an abstract categorisation of obligations of conduct and result does not allow for the fact that the moment at which a breach occurs might differ, depending on whether the rule is one in the field of human rights or in another domain.[146]

This issue is of particular relevance in relation to the obligations of result. As Ago points out, the majority of the obligations pertaining to human rights protection are obligations of result.[147] Obligations of result are said to enjoy a greater degree of permissiveness than obligations of conduct. However, this degree of permissiveness is nonetheless variable depending on whether the obligation entailed a freedom to choose between various means of achieving the required result[148] or if, in addition to

142 As we have analysed in Chapter 1, rights and obligations evolve over time. In Steiner and Alston's words, '[r]ights are not static. They evolve. They broaden or contract over time. One way of understanding an expansion of the content of a given right [...] is to examine the duties related to that right, and to inquire whether and how they have expanded. The argument for a broader construction of a given right often amounts to the claim that further duties ought to be imposed on the State in order to satisfy the right'. Steiner & Alston, *op. cit.* (note 31), p. 181.

143 See, Goodwiln-Gill, *op. cit.* (note 116), p. 113.

144 Report of the International Law Commission on the work of its fifty-first session (3 May-23 July 1999). General Assembly Official Records Supplement No. 10 (A/54/10 and Corr. 1 & 2 para. 158).

145 *Ibidem*: para. 150.

146 *Ibidem*: para. 158.

147 ILC Yearbook, 1977, vol. II (Part One), para. 20.

148 It was considered that this freedom of choice was present both where the international obligation was completely neutral as to the choice, and where the instrument in which the obligation was embodied expresses a simple preference for one means over another. Cited examples of the latter were article 2(1) ICESCR and article 2(2) ICCPR. As indicated, 'there can be no doubt that, in these cases, the legislative means is expressly indicated at the international level as the most normal and most appropri-

this freedom of choice, it also includes the possibility that the State considers itself discharged of its obligations by achieving an alternative result.[149] In the case of both kinds of obligation of result, it was considered that the only criterion for establishing whether or not the obligation had been breached was the result actually achieved. As indicated in the commentary, 'the breach can consist only in the fact that the State has not in practice succeeded in achieving the result internationally required by one or other of the means available to it for doing so.'[150]

According to the 1977 Commentary, so long as there has been no concrete failure by the State in achieving the result required of it by an international obligation, no one can claim that it has committed a breach of the obligation on the grounds that it has not taken the measures most appropriate to achieve the required result or if it has taken a measure susceptible in principle to frustrating the achievement of that result.[151]

This approach is not completely compatible with human rights duties as they have evolved as a result of the interpretations of human rights supervisory bodies. Today some human rights may be breached by the mere existence of a law which contradicts a human right norm, even when it cannot be established *in concreto* that the State has failed in its task as regards the result required. In other words, the mere fact that the State has not taken the most appropriate measure to achieve a required result may give rise to a breach of the international obligation.

As mentioned by Crawford, 'the international community attaches such value to certain rights like the right to life, to physical and moral integrity, to non-discrimination and to recognition as a person before the law that the mere enactment of legislation contrary to those rights entails international responsibility.'[152] As he notes, the findings of the International Criminal Tribunal for the Former Yugoslavia concerning torture bear out this point. In this context it is worth mentioning the case of Prosecutor v. Anto Furundzija. In this case, the Trial Chamber held,

> '149. Firstly, given the importance that the international community attaches to the protection of individuals from torture, the prohibition against torture is particularly stringent and sweeping. States are obliged not only to prohibit and punish torture, but also to forestall its occurrence: it is insufficient merely to intervene after the infliction of torture, when the physical or moral integrity of human beings has already been irremediably harmed. Conse-

---

ate means of achieving the purposes of the Covenant in question. But recourse to such means is not specifically required; it is not made an exclusive condition.' ILC Yearbook, 1977, vol. II (Part One), para. 18.

149 In other words, a State can be considered to have acted in conformity with its international obligations even if, having failed to achieve the main result, it has nevertheless achieved the alternative result of making reparation for the injury caused to the person. See the text accompanying note 124.

150 ILC Yearbook, 1977, vol. II (Part One), para. 27.

151 ILC Yearbook, 1977, vol. II (Part One), para. 27.

152 Report of the International Law Commission on the work of its fifty-first session (3 May-23 July 1999). General Assembly Official Records Supplement No. 10 (A/54/10 and Corr. 1 &2 para. 158).

> quently, States are bound to put in place all those measures that may pre-empt the perpetration of torture. As was authoritatively held by the European Court of Human Rights in Soering, international law intends to ban not only actual breaches but also potential breaches of the prohibition against torture (as well as any inhuman and degrading treatment. It follows that international rules prohibit not only torture but also (i) the failure to adopt the national measures necessary for implementing the prohibition and (ii) the maintenance in force or passage of laws which are contrary to the prohibition.'
>
> '150. [...]Normally, the maintenance or passage of national legislation inconsistent with international rules generates State responsibility and consequently gives rise to a corresponding claim for cessation and reparation (*lato sensu*) only when such legislation is concretely applied. By contrast, in the case of torture, the mere fact of keeping in force or passing legislation contrary to the international prohibition of torture generates international State responsibility. The value of freedom from torture is so great that it becomes imperative to preclude any national legislative act authorising or condoning torture or at any rate capable of bringing about this effect.'[153]

In the Americas, it is well established that the Inter-American Commission on Human Rights is competent to find any norm of the internal law of a State to be in violation of the obligations which the latter has assumed, whether or not that norm has been applied to a concrete case.[154] In its Advisory Opinion No. 14/94 the Inter-American Court expressly stated that in the case of 'self-executing legislation' incompatible with a human right, the violation of the human right is incurred by its promulgation alone.[155]

In sum, the dynamic evolution of human rights law has restricted the sphere in which States are free to choose the means of fulfilling their international obligations,[156] blurring the distinction between obligations of conduct and result. Thus, this typology does not allow us to determine with precision when there has been a breach of an international human rights obligation.

153 Prosecutor v. Anto Furundzija, Judgement of 10 December 1998. Available at: http://www.un.org/icty/furundzija/trialc2/judgement/index.htm (last visited July 2002).

154 See I/A Court HR, Advisory Opinion OC-14/1994 of December 9, 1994, paras. 37-38. In addition see, Inter-American Commission on Human Rights case No. 11.625, María Eugenia Morales de Sierra v. Guatemala, Report No. 4/01, 19 January 2001.

155 As indicated by the Court 'In the case of self-executing laws [...] the violation of human rights, whether individual or collective, occurs upon their promulgation hence, a norm that deprives a portion of the population of some of its rights –for example, because of race– automatically injures all the members of that race' [para. 43]. Earlier in the same Opinion, the Court defines the term 'self-executing norms' ('*leyes de aplicación immediata*') as those which affect the legal sphere of the individual from the moment it enters into force (see para. 41). I/A Court HR, Advisory Opinion on 'International Responsibility for the promulgation and enforcement of laws in violation of the Convention', OC-14/94 of 9 December 1994.

156 Report of the International Law Commission on the work of its fifty-first session (3 May-23 July 1999). General Assembly Official Records Supplement No. 10 (A/54/10 and Corr. 1 & 2 para. 160.

2.4.3 Concluding comments on the conduct/result typology

The Committee has clearly stated that the Covenant imposes both obligations of conduct and obligations of result. Furthermore, the Committee has suggested that when drafting General Comments it should explicitly identify therein obligations of conduct and obligations of result.

Despite the importance that the Committee seems to attribute to this typology in General Comment No. 3 adopted in 1990, it would appear that the Committee has forgotten to apply it since that time. The non-application of the conduct/result typology by the Committee may however be considered as an advantage because of numerous drawbacks of the typology. Hence, it is rather surprising that the Committee referred to this typology again in 1999 when it adopted the 'Outline for drafting general comments'.[157]

The appropriate approach is to consider that the obligations of the Covenant are 'hybrids' of both kinds of obligations.[158] Thus, it may make little sense to determine whether they are obligations of conduct or obligations of result and categorising them in this manner would be little more than a futile, if complex, exercise. During the second reading of the Draft Articles on State Responsibility there was a debate within the ILC regarding the usefulness of the conduct/result typology. The ILC Special Rapporteur on State Responsibility, J. Crawford, was sceptical about the value of the distinction between obligations of conduct and result, notably due to the complexity of their application in the field of human rights law.[159] When the ILC adopted the Draft Articles on Responsibility of States for Internationally Wrongful Acts without a vote on 9 August 2001 during its fifty-fifth session, the distinction between obligation of conduct and obligation of result had been eliminated.

The Committee and human rights scholars also should avoid applying this typology to human rights norms. At the international level, human rights courts, with few exceptions, tend not to use the typology.[160] It is particularly important to avoid applying this

157 E/C.12/1999/11, Annex IX, pp. 135-136. Adopted at the 37th meeting on 19 November 1999.

158 Alston & Quinn, *loc. cit.* (note 83), p. 185.

159 Special Rapporteur, Mr. James Crawford, Second Report on State Responsibility. UN doc. A/CN.4/498, para. 56. He presents more arguments than those mentioned above. In a nutshell, Crawford states that the distinction seems to have no consequences in terms of the remainder of the draft articles and it is not clear if the existence of a breach is determined by reference to whether the breach was of an obligation of conduct or result. Furthermore, he stresses the complexities arising in light of article 23 of the Draft Articles on State Responsibility. This article covers a breach of an obligation to prevent a given effect, which although it has been codified separately, is a sub-category of the obligations of result. Therefore he considers that there is a case for deleting articles 20, 21 and 23 of the Draft Articles, which have been considered extremely confusing. See, also, GA Official Records, fifty-fourth session Supplement No. 10 A/54/10 and Corr. 1 & 2 paras. 132 *et seq.* and Crawford, *loc. cit.* (note 134) pp. 435-460.

160 In the European and Inter-American human rights systems, the Courts do not refer to this typology except in a very limited number of cases. According to Dupuy, the ECHR has considered this typology only three times in a 'more or less direct way.' The cases that he refers to are Colozza v. Italy [Applica-

typology to economic, social and cultural rights. In addition to all of the general inconveniences analysed above, the use of this typology evokes the traditional misleading assumption that economic, social and cultural rights impose merely loose obligations of result and that they are therefore 'less binding' than civil and political rights. As Scheinin notes, 'it might, however, be worth considering whether it would not be more justified in the context of economic and social rights to use another distinction between different State obligations emanating from the treaty provision than that of the conduct/result scheme.'[161]

The reference to the conduct/result typology in General Comment No. 3 and in the 'Outline for drafting general comments' may be understood as attempts by the Committee to reject the traditional assumption that economic, social and cultural rights only impose obligations of result. However, if the Committee applies the conduct/result typology in future General Comments, as is suggested by the Outline, this would ignore the debate on the utility of these notions and the negative consequences that their strict application might entail for the protection of human rights. It would be appropriate for the Committee to review its 'Outline for drafting general comments' and eliminate the reference to the conduct/result typology.

2.5 The application of the tripartite typology by the Committee in its General Comments

2.5.1 The Committee's understanding of the tripartite typology

The first explicit explanation of the Committee's approach to the tripartite typology is found in General Comment No. 12 on the right to adequate food. Although the Committee suggested an approach influenced by tripartite typology in previous General Comments, it only made explicit its application in 1999 and since then it has explicitly incorporated the tripartite typology in its General Comments (Nos. 13 and 14).[162] However, the Committee has approached the typology of State duties in a rather confusing way.

In General Comment No. 12, the Committee indicates that all human rights impose three types or levels of obligations:

---

tion No. 9317/81, Judgement of 22 January 1985] and De Cubber v. Belgium [Application No. 9186/80, Judgement of 26 October 1984]. Dupuy, *loc. cit.* (note 119), p. 377. At the Inter-American level, the typology is even more rarely applied. Nonetheless, it has been mentioned by Judge A.A. Cançado Trindade in his separate opinion in Olmedo Bustos *et. al.* v. Chile, ('The last temptation of Christ Case'), Judgement of 5 February 2001, Series C No. 73, , para. 26.

161 Scheinin, M.: 'International human rights in national law.' In: *An introduction to the international protection of human rights: a textbook*. Hanski, R. & Suksi, M. (eds.), Institute for Human Rights, Åbo Akademi University, second revised edition, Åbo, Finland (1999), p. 14.

162 The category may be inferred in other previous General Comments, as for example, General Comment No. 8 para. 7 and General Comment No. 7 para. 8.

1. Obligations to respect
2. Obligations to protect
3. Obligations to fulfil
   According to the Committee this level incorporates both:
   3.a. Obligation to facilitate
   3.b. Obligation to provide

The Committee noted that originally Eide proposed three levels of obligations: the obligations to respect, protect and assist/fulfil. But it emphasised that 'the intermediate level of 'to facilitate' has been proposed as a Committee category, but the Committee decided to maintain the three levels of obligations.'[163]

This approach was maintained in General Comment No. 13, but a year later in General Comment No. 14, the Committee indicated that the obligation to fulfil, not only incorporated an 'obligation to facilitate' and an 'obligation to provide', but also an 'obligation to promote.'[164]

According to the General Comments, each level of State duties entails:[165]

1. *Obligation to respect*: This duty requires States Parties not to take any measures that result in denying or limiting access to the enjoyment of the Covenant's rights. It includes abstaining from enforcing discriminatory practices as a State policy.

The actions or policies that contravene this level include the adoption of laws or policies manifestly incompatible with the standards set forth in the Covenant or other international legal obligations or in pre-existing domestic law and the repeal or suspension of legislation necessary for the continued enjoyment of the Covenant's rights.[166]

2. *Obligation to protect*: This obligation requires States to take all necessary measures to ensure that individuals under their jurisdiction are protected from infringements of the Covenant's rights by third parties (individuals, groups or corporations). States are required to adequately regulate the action of other entities, preventing them from denying or limiting the enjoyment of these rights. In addition, States are to protect individuals under their jurisdiction when third parties engage in practices which are harmful to the enjoyment of these rights.

163 General Comment No. 12 para. 15.
164 General Comment No. 14 para. 33.
165 See General Comment No. 12 para. 15; General Comment No. 13 para. 46; and General Comment No. 14 paras. 34-37.
166 See General Comment No. 14 para. 50; General Comment No. 13 para. 59; and General Comment No. 12 para. 19.

As the Committee understands it, this obligation entails the duty to uphold the principle of non-discrimination in legislation or to take other measures ensuring equal access to the enjoyment of the Covenant's rights provided by third parties, the obligation to discourage practices against these rights by penalising harmful behaviours and the adoption of measures to prosecute perpetrators. It is also under the obligation to protect that States must take measures to protect all vulnerable and marginalized groups in society.[167]

It is important to emphasise here the position of the Committee with regard to discrimination by third parties as set out in General Comment No. 5. Although this General Comment refers specifically to persons with disabilities and was drafted without using the terminology of the tripartite typology, the content is very clear as regards the 'obligation to protect.' The approach of the Committee in this General Comment could be seen as being applicable to the Covenant as a whole.

As the Committee states in General Comment No. 5,

> 'Given the increasing commitment of Governments around the world to market-based policies, it is appropriate in that context to emphasise certain aspects of States parties' obligations. One is the need to ensure that not only the public sphere, but also the private sphere, are, within appropriate limits, subject to regulation to ensure the equitable treatment of persons with disabilities. In a context in which arrangements for the provision of public services are increasingly being privatised and in which the free market is being relied on to an ever greater extent, it is essential that private employers, private suppliers of goods and services, and other non-public entities be subject to both non-discrimination and equality norms in relation to persons with disabilities. In circumstances where such protection does not extend beyond the public domain, the ability of persons with disabilities to participate in the mainstream of community activities and to realise their full potential as active members of society will be severely and often arbitrarily constrained. This is not to imply that legislative measures will always be the most effective means of seeking to eliminate discrimination within the private sphere. Thus, for example, the Standard Rules place particular emphasis on the need for States to 'take action to raise awareness in society about persons with disabilities, their rights, their needs, their potential and their contribution.'
>
> In the absence of government intervention there will always be instances in which the operation of the free market will produce unsatisfactory results for persons with disabilities, either individually or as a group, and in such circumstances it is incumbent on Governments to step in and take appropriate measures to temper, complement, compensate for, or override the results produced by market forces. Similarly, while it is appropriate for Governments to rely on private, voluntary groups to assist persons with disabilities in various ways, such arrangements can never absolve Governments from their duty to ensure full compliance with their obligations under the Covenant.'[168]

167 See General Comment No. 14 para. 51.
168 General Comment No. 5 paras. 11 and 12.

3. *Obligation to fulfil*: According to the Committee's General Comment No. 14, this duty includes the obligations to: facilitate, to provide and to promote.[169]

3.A. *Obligation to fulfil (facilitate)*: This duty requires States to pro-actively engage in activities intended to enable and assist individuals and communities to enjoy the Covenant's rights.

3.B. *Obligation to fulfil (provide)*: This duty requires States to provide a specific right contained in the Covenant when individuals or groups are unable, for reasons beyond their control, to realise that right themselves by the means at their disposal. In such cases, States have the obligation to provide that right directly. However, the Committee mentions that the extent of this obligation is always subject to the text of the Covenant. Therefore, sometimes there is an obligation to provide even when people might have the means to satisfy the obligation by their own efforts (*e.g.* compulsory primary education).[170] According to the Committee, the obligation to provide also applies to persons who are victims of natural disasters.[171] It is worth stressing that General Comment No. 13 suggests that it is under the duty to fulfil that States Parties are required to give recognition to the Covenant's rights in national legal systems and in national policies.[172]

3.C. *Obligation to fulfil (promote)*: According to General Comment No. 14, this duty requires States to undertake a variety of different actions, such as: research on the Covenant's rights; the provision of information to individuals under their jurisdiction; to provide training; to ensure the dissemination of appropriate information relating to the Covenant's rights; and to support people in making informed choices about their enjoyment of these rights.

As the Committee mentions, there are many ways by which States may violate the duty to fulfil, as for example, when they fail to adopt or implement national policies designed to ensure the enjoyment of the Covenant's rights; through insufficient expenditure or a misallocation of public resources which results in the non-enjoyment of these rights; the failure to monitor the realisation of the rights at the national level; the failure to take measures to reduce the inequitable distribution of wealth and the enjoyment of the rights.[173]

It is worth noting that in its General Comments, the Committee has also developed the tripartite typology with regard to the international obligations of States in relation

169 General Comment No. 14 para. 33.

170 This seems to be the only exception, as is mentioned in General Comment No.13 paras. 47-48.

171 General Comment No. 12 para. 15.

172 General Comment No. 13 para. 37.

173 See, for example, General Comment No. 14 para. 52.

to other States, as opposed to obligations towards individuals under their jurisdiction.[174] In the light of the General Comments, it is possible to define each level as follows:

1. *Obligation to respect*: This duty requires States Parties to abstain from interfering with the enjoyment of economic, social and cultural rights in other countries. States violate this obligation if they fail to take into account the obligations imposed by the Covenant when entering into bilateral or multilateral agreements with other States, international organisations and other entities, such as multinational corporations.[175]

2. *Obligation to protect*: In the Committee's words, States must prevent third parties from violating these rights in other countries if they are able to influence these third parties by way of legal or political means in accordance with the Charter of the United Nations and applicable international law.[176]

3. *Obligation to fulfil*: When referring to these international obligations, the Committee has stressed that the obligations that this level entails depend on the availability of resources.

3.A. *Obligation to fulfil (facilitate)*: According to the Committee, this duty is conditional on the availability of resources. Therefore, if States have resources, they must assist access to the enjoyment of these rights in other States to the extent of their possibilities.

3.B. *Obligation to fulfil (provide)*: States must provide the necessary aid when required, depending on the availability of resources.

3.C. *Obligation to fulfil (promote)*: In the light of General Comment No. 14, we may conclude that this level requires States to ensure that the Covenant's rights are given due attention in international agreements and, to that end, should consider the development of further legal instruments. When new agreements are being studied, States should take steps to ensure that these instruments do not adversely impact upon the Covenant's rights. Accordingly, States Parties which are members of international financial institutions, such as the International Monetary Fund, the World Bank, and regional development banks, should pay greater attention to the protection of the

174 See General Comment No. 12 para. 36 and General Comment No. 14 para. 38.

175 General Comment No. 14 para. 49. From this author's perspective, the obligation to take into account the Covenant's rights when negotiating with international organisations or other States seems to be an obligation 'to protect' rather than an obligation to 'respect.' See Chapter V section 3.3.

176 General Comment No. 14 para. 39.

Covenant's rights in influencing the lending policies, credit agreements and other international measures taken by these institutions.[177]

2.5.2 The application of the tripartite typology to specific rights

As already mentioned, the Committee began to expressly apply the 'tripartite typology' in its General Comment No. 12 on 'The right to adequate food (article 11)' in 1999. Thereafter, apparently pursuant to the 'Outline for drafting general comments', it has applied the typology in General Comment No. 13 on 'the right to education' and No. 14 on 'The right to the highest attainable standard of health.'

From these three General Comments, it is possible to infer the Committee's abstract understanding of the typologies, as analysed in the prior section. Nevertheless, it is important not to lose sight of the fact that the General Comments in which the Committee has applied the tripartite typology are focused on the specific substantive rights of the Covenant. In these General Comments, the Committee has given examples of the obligations that the different levels entail as regards these specific rights.

A. *The tripartite typology and the right to food*

As indicated in General Comment No. 12 on the right to adequate food, this right imposes the following duties:[178]

A.1. *Obligations to respect*: This duty requires States Parties not to take any measures that result in preventing access to adequate food.

A.2. *Obligation to protect*: This duty requires measures by the State to ensure that enterprises or individuals do not deprive individuals of their access to adequate food.

A.3. *Obligation to fulfil*:

A.3.1. *Obligation to facilitate*: This requires States to proactively engage in measures intended to strengthen people's access to and utilisation of resources and means to ensure their own livelihood, including food security.

A.3.2. *Obligation to provide*: This requires States to fulfil (provide) the food directly, whenever an individual or group is unable, for reasons beyond their control, to enjoy the right to adequate food by the means at their disposal. This obligation also applies to persons who are victims of natural or other disasters.

---

177 See General Comment No. 14 para. 39.

178 See General Comment No. 12 para. 15.

B. *The tripartite typology and the right to education*

Following the structure of article 13 of the Covenant, which is divided into two paragraphs,[179] General Comment No. 13 analyses the tripartite typology in two steps. First, it applies it to the right to education in general in a broad and summarised manner. Subsequently, it gives specific examples of the duties that each level entails with regard to article 13(2) ICESCR.[180]

B.1. *Obligation to respect*: This duty requires States Parties to avoid measures that hinder or prevent the enjoyment of the right to education.

B.2. *Obligation to protect*: This duty requires States Parties to take measures that prevent third Parties from interfering with the enjoyment of the right to education.

B.3. *Obligation to fulfil*:

B.3.1. *Obligation to fulfil (facilitate)*: This duty requires States to take positive measures that enable and assist individuals and communities to enjoy the right to education.

B.3.2. *Obligation to fulfil (provide)*: In relation to this level, the Committee makes an important remark. According to the Committee, as a general rule, States Parties are obliged to provide a specific right in the Covenant when an individual or group is unable, for reasons beyond their control, to realise the right themselves by the means at their disposal. However, as it mentions, the extent of this obligation is always subject to the text of the Covenant. The Committee notes that in the light of the Covenant, States Parties have an enhanced obligation to fulfil (provide) regarding the right to education, but the extent of this obligation is not uniform for all levels of education. It varies depending, for example, on whether it is primary, secondary or higher education.[181]

Subsequently, the Committee provides specific examples of the duties entailed by each level with regard to article 13(2) ICESCR. By way of illustration the Committee notes,

(i) *Obligation to respect*: It requires States to respect the availability of education by not closing private schools.

---

179 The first paragraph of Art. 13 establishes the aims and objectives of education, while the second paragraph contains an enumeration and description of the specific rights and obligations, *inter alia*, the right to receive education; the right to primary education; the right to secondary education; technical and vocational education; the right to higher education; the right to fundamental education, regulation of the school system, the fellowship system and material conditions of teaching staff; and the right to educational freedom.

180 See, General Comments No. 13 paras. 46-57.

181 General Comment No. 13 paras. 47-48.

(ii) *Obligation to protect*: It requires States to protect the accessibility of education by ensuring that third parties, including parents and employers, do not stop girls from going to school.

It is interesting to note that the Committee includes in this General Comment its approach to some aspects of school discipline such as 'corporal punishment' and 'public humiliation.' The important aspect to stress under the analysis of the obligation to protect is that, according to the Committee, States Parties are required to take measures to ensure that disciplinary regimes are consistent with the Covenant, not only in public schools but also in private educational institutions within its jurisdiction.[182]

(iii) *Obligation to fulfil*:
Obligation to fulfil (facilitate): It requires States to take positive measures to ensure that education is culturally appropriate for minorities and indigenous peoples, and of good quality for all.
Obligation to fulfil (provide): It requires States to design and provide resources for curricula which reflect the contemporary needs of students in a changing world. States are to fulfil (provide) the availability of education by actively developing a system of schools, including building classrooms, delivering programmes, providing teaching materials, training teachers and paying them domestically competitive salaries.

C. *The tripartite typology and the right to the highest attainable standard of health*
The General Comment No. 14 is remarkable due to its elaborate content and clear academic language. This General Comment developed the tripartite typology in general, giving examples not only of the duties that each level entails, but also providing examples of the violation of the duties to respect, protect and fulfil.[183] As previously mentioned, in this General Comment, the Committee introduces a new level of State duties, the 'duty to fulfil (promote)'. This duty was not employed in the previous General Comments.

According to General Comment No. 14, among the duties required by each level are the following:[184]

---

182 General Comment No. 13 para. 41. See in addition Art. 28(2) CRC and the well-known ECHR case: Costello-Roberts v. the United Kingdom [Application No. 13134/87, Judgement of 25 March 1993]. Unfortunately in the Concluding Observations, the Committee addresses the issue of corporal punishment in private schools only very exceptionally, as in the case of the Concluding Observations on the Third Periodic Report of the United Kingdom of Great Britain and Northern Ireland E/1998/22 paras. 299 and 311.

183 General Comment No. 14 paras. 50-52.

184 See, General Comment No. 14 paras. 34-37 and 50-52.

C.1. *Obligation to respect*: This duty requires States (i) to refrain from denying or limiting equal access for all persons, including prisoners or detainees, minorities, asylum seekers and illegal immigrants, to preventive, curative and palliative health services; (ii) to abstain from enforcing discriminatory practices as a State policy; and to abstain from imposing discriminatory practices relating to women's health status and needs; (iii) to refrain from prohibiting or impeding traditional preventive care, healing practices and medicines, from marketing unsafe drugs and from applying coercive medical treatments.[185]

Curiously, after mentioning the above 'obligations', the Committee suddenly adopts different language and indicates other forms of non-intervention but refers to them as behaviours that States merely 'should' follow. This use of language suggests that either the Committee did not consider these abstentions as obligations (although the whole paragraph is under the topic 'specific legal obligations'), or that the Committee did not agree unanimously on their inclusion, but considered that there was a strong basis for considering them as 'obligations.' In fact, as we will see, some of these specific forms of non-interference seem to be considered as mandatory by the Committee in the Concluding Observations.

The General Comment notes that, 'in addition' States 'should': (a) refrain from limiting access to contraceptives and other means of maintaining sexual and reproductive health, from censoring, withholding or intentionally misrepresenting health-related information, including sexual education and information, as well as from preventing people's participation in health-related matters; (b) refrain from unlawfully polluting air, water and soil, *e.g.* through industrial waste from State-owned facilities, from using or testing nuclear, biological or chemical weapons if such testing results in the release of substances harmful to human health; and (c) refraining from limiting access to health services as a punitive measure, *e.g.* during armed conflicts in violation of international humanitarian law.[186]

C.2. *Obligations to protect*: The Committee mentions the following duties required by this level: (i) to adopt legislation or to take other measures ensuring equal access to health care and health-related services provided by third parties; (ii) to ensure that privatisation of the health sector does not constitute a threat to the availability, accessibility, acceptability and quality of health facilities, goods and services; (iii) to control the marketing of medical equipment and medicines by third parties; (iv) to ensure that medical practitioners and other health professionals meet appropriate standards of

---

185 As the Committee mentions, this may be permitted 'on an exceptional basis for the treatment of mental illness or the prevention and control of communicable diseases. Such exceptional cases should be subject to specific and restrictive conditions, respecting best practices and applicable international standards, including the Principles for the Protection of Persons with Mental Illness and the Improvement of Mental Health Care'. General Comment No. 14 para. 34.

186 General Comment No. 14 para. 38.

education, skill and ethical codes of conduct; (v) to ensure that harmful social or traditional practices do not interfere with access to pre- and post-natal care and family planning; (vi) to prevent third parties from coercing women to undergo harmful traditional practices, *e.g.* female genital mutilation; and (vii) to take measures to protect all vulnerable or marginalized groups of society, in particular women, children, adolescents and older persons, in the light of gender-based expressions of violence.[187]

C.3. *Obligation to fulfil*: When analysing the duties entailed by this level, the Committee is not as rigorous as in previous paragraphs of the General Comment. The Committee expressly mentions that the obligation to fulfil contains obligations to 'facilitate', 'provide' and 'promote.'[188] However, when it provides examples of the duties required by this level, it first mentions a variety of specific obligations but does not classify them into the three sub-categories mentioned, and then proceeds to give generic examples of duties without stating to which category each belongs.[189]

We might interpret this approach as a recognition of the fact that all duties are interrelated, and that, therefore, it is sometimes very difficult to classify them as 'facilitate', 'provide' and 'promote'. And to a certain extent that might be a futile exercise here. Nevertheless, it would have been more appropriate for the Committee to provide an explanation of the reasons for this approach. Moreover, once again, when the Committee spells out which duties are required of States, it abruptly changes the wording from the mandatory 'must' to 'should' without providing further explanation.[190]

Among the duties that this level entails, the Committee mentions, but does not classify them into the three subcategories, the following: (i) to give sufficient recognition to the right to health in the national political and legal systems, preferably by way of legislative implementation, and to adopt a national health policy with a detailed plan for realising the right to health; (ii) to ensure the provision of health care, including immunisation programmes against the major infectious diseases, and to ensure equal access for all to the underlying determinants of health, such as nutritiously safe food and potable drinking-water, basic sanitation and adequate housing and living conditions; public health infrastructures should provide for sexual and reproductive health services, including safe motherhood, particularly in rural areas; (iii) to ensure the appropriate training of doctors and other medical personnel, the provision of a sufficient number of hospitals, clinics and other health-related facilities, and the promotion

---

187 As with the obligation imposed by the primary level to respect, when the Committee enumerates the obligations entailed by the secondary level to protect, it adopts two sets of strikingly different language. Instead of referring to what States are 'obliged' to do, it uses the non-mandatory term 'should' [General Comment No. 14 para. 35]. It would have been more appropriate for the Committee to provide an explanation with regard to this change of language.

188 General Comment No. 14 para. 33.

189 General Comment No. 14 paras. 36 and 37.

190 General Comment No. 14 para. 36.

and support of the establishment of institutions providing counselling and mental health services, with due regard to equitable distribution throughout the country; (iv) to provide a public, private or mixed health insurance system which is affordable for all; (vi) to promote medical research and health education, as well as information campaigns, in particular with respect to HIV/AIDS, sexual and reproductive health, traditional practices, domestic violence, the abuse of alcohol and the use of cigarettes, drugs and other harmful substances; (vii) to adopt measures against environmental and occupational health hazards and against any other threat as demonstrated by epidemiological data. For this purpose they should formulate and implement national policies aimed at reducing and eliminating pollution of air, water and soil, including pollution by heavy metals such as lead from gasoline; and (vii) to formulate, implement and periodically review a coherent national policy to minimise the risk of occupational accidents and diseases, as well as to provide a coherent national policy on occupational safety and health services.

When the Committee differentiates between the three sub-levels of the duty to fulfil it mentions the following examples:[191]

C.3. *Obligation to fulfil*:
C.3.1. *Obligation to fulfil (facilitate)*: This duty requires States, *inter alia,* to take positive measures that enable and assist individuals and communities to enjoy the right to health.
C.3.2. *Obligation to fulfil (provide)*: This duty requires States to provide a specific right contained in the Covenant when individuals or a group are unable, for reasons beyond their control, to realise that right themselves by the means at their disposal.
C.3.3. *Obligation to fulfil (promote)*: This duty requires States to undertake actions that create, maintain and restore the health of the population. Such obligations include: (i) fostering recognition of factors favouring positive health results, *e.g.* research and provision of information; (ii) ensuring that health services are culturally appropriate and that health care staff are trained to recognise and respond to the specific needs of vulnerable or marginalized groups; (iii) ensuring that the State meets its obligations in the dissemination of appropriate information relating to healthy lifestyles and nutrition, harmful traditional practices and the availability of services; and (iv) supporting people in making informed choices about their health.

2.5.3 Comments on the approach of the Committee to the tripartite typology in the General Comments

The Committee's decision to employ the 'tripartite typology' to analyse the duties imposed by the Covenant would appear to be appropriate. If, as many think, it is correct to categorise obligations imposed by human rights instruments and particularly

191 General Comment No. 14 para. 37.

by the Covenant, the tripartite typology (in all of its variations, including that of the Committee), is the most appropriate means to describe those obligations.

The tripartite typology illustrates that bipolar approaches to typologies of States' duties such as positive/negative or conduct/result are both simplistic and misleading. The 'tripartite typology' clearly highlights that all human rights (civil and political as well as economic, social and cultural) entail multiple types of duties.

As analysed above, there is no general agreement regarding the content (number and scope of the levels) of the different typologies of States' duties.[192] Therefore, it is appropriate that the Committee has developed its own understanding of the 'tripartite typology.' However, the Committee has not been very consistent in its approach to the tripartite typology. As was mentioned,[193] the Committee included in a General Comment an analysis of the obligations of States Parties in three types of levels (respect, protect and fulfil) for the first time in 1999. But it also incorporated 'intermediate categories'. Therefore, although it states that it has decided to maintain the three-level terminology, in practice its typology entails five levels: respect, protect, facilitate, provide and promote.

According to General Comment Nos. 12 and 13 the levels are as follows:

1. Obligation to respect
2. Obligation to protect
3. Obligation to fulfil
   - 3.1 Obligation to fulfil (facilitate)
   - 3.2 Obligation to fulfil (provide)

However, in General Comment No. 14 on the right to the highest attainable standard of health, the Committee incorporates a new sub-level in the 'obligation to fulfil': the 'obligation to promote'(3.3).

As recognised by the Committee, 'according to General Comments No. 12 and 13, the obligation to fulfil incorporates an obligation to *facilitate* and an obligation to *provide*. In the present General Comment, the obligation to fulfil also incorporates an obligation to *promote* because of the critical importance of health promotion in the work of WHO and elsewhere.'[194]

This explanation is deficient. From this statement it is not clear if the Committee considers that all substantive rights impose 'obligations to promote' or if it considers it important only with regard to the right to health. Moreover, the incorporation of the 'obligation to promote' as a sub-level or 'intermediate category' of the obligation to fulfil does not take into account relevant academic approaches which consider the

192 See section 1.2.

193 See section 2.5.1.

194 General Comment No. 14, footnote No. 23.

'obligation to promote' as an independent level which exists in regard to all human rights.[195] [See figure 2].

According to some scholars, all human rights impose the 'obligations to promote' and thus the right to food and the right to education also incorporate the duty to promote. Therefore, it is a failure of the Committee not to incorporate this level (or sub-level in the Committee's approach) in General Comments No. 12 and 13. The lack of attention that the Committee gives to the 'duty to promote' in these General Comments is not consistent with the Committee's approach in the Concluding Observations. As we will see, in the Concluding Observations, the Committee makes systematic reference to the 'duty to promote', emphasising its importance in regard to all substantive rights contained in the Covenant.[196]

Although the tripartite typology of respect, protect and fulfil has the advantage that it is widely used by scholars,[197] the incorporation under the duty to fulfil of three sub-levels – fulfil (facilitate), fulfil (provide) and fulfil (promote) – gives the impression that in order to keep the terminology 'tripartite' the Committee has given an extremely broad scope to the 'duty to fulfil'. Although all of these sub-categories require positive actions on the part of States, from this author's perspective the duties to 'facilitate', 'provide' and 'promote' are of a different nature and it might be more appropriate to consider them as independent categories.[198] The importance of amending to typology

195 See above the approach of Hoof, G.J.H. van, *op. cit.* (note 28), pp.106-108 and Steiner & Alston, *op. cit.* (note 31), p. 184. In addition, see, for example, Leckie, S.: 'The right to housing.' In: *Economic, social and cultural rights: a textbook.* Eide, A.; Krause, C. & Rosas, A. (eds.), Martinus Nijhoff Publishers, Dordrecht, (1995), p. 51 and Leckie, 2001, p. 156.

196 See section 3.4.3.

197 See the application of the typology 'respect, protect and fulfil' to: the right to education [*e.g.* Coomans, *op. cit.* (note 52), pp. 23-26, Chapman A. and Rusell S.: Background paper submitted to the day of general discussion on the right to education UN doc. E/C.12/1998/19]; the right to health [*e.g.* Toebes, *op. cit.* (note 52), pp. 312-332]; the right to housing [*e.g.* Leckie, 1995, *op. cit.* (note 195), pp. 50-51 and Leckie, 2001, *op. cit.* (note 195), p. 156; and the right to food [*e.g.* Künnemann, R.: 'A coherent approach to human rights.' In: *HRQ*, vol. 17, (1995), pp. 131-137].

198 It is possible to consider that the three kinds of obligations to facilitate, provide and promote have in common the requirement of positive action by the State. In this regard, it is interesting to take into account Robert Alexy's analysis of the structure of rights. According to Alexy, rights to positive actions (*sentido amplio)* may be divided into three groups: (a) protection rights, (b) procedural and organisatory rights and (c) positive rights in a limited sense (a right to claim from the state a positive factual action). In light of Alexy's analysis, the obligation to fulfil (facilitate) would be considered as (b), and the obligation of fulfil (provide) as (c). However, the obligation to (facilitate) promote, would be under (c) and in that case it would need to be analysed as an obligation to facilitate, or, as I believe, it would require consideration as a completely separate level. [Author's translation from the Spanish. In Alexy's words: *'Los derechos a prestaciones en (sentido amplio) pueden ser divididos en tres grupos: (1) derechos a la proteción, (2) derechos de organización y procedimiento y (3) derechos a prestaciones en sentido estricto.'* For a comprehensive analysis on the issue, see Alexy, R.: *Teoría de los derechos fundamentales*, Centro de Estudios Constitucionales, Madrid, (1993), pp. 430 *et seq.*].

to accommodate these duties in separate categories is perhaps most pressing with regard to the 'duty to fulfil (promote).'[199]

Finally, it is worth mentioning that the Committee's typology lacks a specific obligation 'to create institutions and machinery necessary for the enjoyment of rights' as proposed by Steiner and Alston.[200] Although the Committee suggests that this duty is already included in the second level, the 'duty to protect', and in the third level the 'duty to fulfil,'[201] the lack of an independent level may be a disadvantage. Consideration of the duty to 'create institutional machinery necessary for the enjoyment of rights' as a separate level would assist us to understand and assess the existence of such obligations.

In sum, General Comments are key instruments for the development of a theoretical approach to the obligations imposed by the Covenant. The Committee has made a laudable effort and significant contribution by incorporating the tripartite typology into its Concluding Observations. However, the Committee needs to be yet more consistent and precise in its approach. It seems that the Committee itself does not possess a clear understanding of the levels of duties imposed by the Covenant. It would be appropriate for the Committee to develop a precise and comprehensive typology of State duties imposed by the Covenant that is applicable to all substantive rights. The final result should be typology with clearly defined and coherent levels, even if this requires abandoning the label 'tripartite'.

3 The Tripartite Typology in the Concluding Observations

3.1 Introduction

Through the General Comments, the Committee has defined its understanding of the tripartite typology of State duties and applied it to some specific rights. As mentioned above, General Comments are the most suitable tools for the Committee to develop a theoretical approach to the tripartite typology.[202] However, the Committee only began applying the tripartite typology in 1999 and has only done so in a limited number of General Comments.

In contrast to the abstract approach of General Comments, the Committee's Concluding Observations relate to specific countries and the particular circumstances of

199 See the analysis in section 3.4.3.
200 See section 1.2.4.
201 As we might infer from the examples given in General Comment No. 14 on the right to health. See General Comment No. 14 paras. 35 and 36.
202 For an analysis on the Committee's working methods, particularly the 'General Comments' and 'Concluding Observations', see Chapter I section 2.

each and aim to address problems of implementation at the domestic level.[203] Despite this more casuistic approach, it is beyond doubt that over the years the Committee has discussed a wider range of issues in the Concluding Observations than in the General Comments.[204] Moreover, although the Concluding Observations do not allow for much abstract analysis of the scope and content of the 'tripartite typology,' they are in fact where the Committee applies its approach in concrete cases.

Unfortunately, the Committee does not use the terminology of the tripartite typology (respect/protect/fulfil) with great frequency in its Concluding Observations. In the few cases that the Committee explicitly refers to the tripartite typology it does so in broad terms and particularly in regard to the States' obligations relating to international financial institutions.[205] Nonetheless, a comprehensive analysis of all of the Concluding Observations enables us to identify the Committee's approach regarding States' duties imposed by the Covenant.

This section will analyse the Committee's Concluding Observations in the light of the tripartite typology developed by the Committee through the General Comments. In order to do so, I have focused on those Concluding Observations in which the Committee uses imperative language. By 'imperative language' we refer to those situations in which the language used by the Committee makes it apparent that it is not merely suggesting that the State should do or refrain from doing something, but that it is indicating what is required of the State under the Covenant. The ways in which the Committee does so are diverse. For example, to indicate what States are required not to do, the Committee may state that a given behaviour is a 'violation' of, a 'breach' of or is 'incompatible' with the Covenant. In the same vein, to indicate what States must do, the Committee may 'urge' or 'call upon' the State to do something.

---

203 It is important to note, however, that the General Comments are the result of the experience gained by the Committee in the examination of the States Parties' reports. Therefore, to a certain extent, they should reflect the work of the Committee in the Concluding Observations. As it has been noted, the objectives of the General Comments are 'to make the experience gained so far through the examination of these reports available for the benefit of all States Parties in order to assist and promote their further implementation of the Covenant; to draw the attention of the States Parties to insufficiencies disclosed by a large number of reports; to assist States Parties, the international organisations and the specialised agencies concerned in achieving progressively and effectively the full realisation of the rights recognised in the Covenant'. Alston, P.: 'The International Covenant on Economic, Social and Cultural Rights.' In: *Manual on human rights reporting under six major international human rights instruments*, United Nations, second edition, Geneva, HR/PUB/91/1 (Rev.1), (1997), p. 163.

204 As to July 2002, there had only been fourteen General Comments and of these only three rights had been analysed in the light of the tripartite typology (right to food, education, and heath). In contrast, since 1990 (when the Committee issued its first General Comments) the Committee has issued more than one 100 Concluding Observations on specific countries.

205 See, for example, Concluding Observations Bulgaria E/C.12/1999/11 para. 236. 'The Committee recommends that in negotiations with international financial institutions, the State party take into account its obligations to respect, protect and fulfil all of the rights enshrined in the Covenant'. The same in Concluding Observations Argentina E/C.12/1999/11 para. 276 and Concluding Observations Cameroon E/C.12/1999/11 para. 352. See the analysis in section 3.3.

To understand this approach, it is important to bear in mind that the Concluding Observations are the result of a 'constructive dialogue' between the Committee and Government representatives. For the most part this dialogue is not adversarial or confrontational. The aim of the 'constructive dialogue' is to try to assist States Parties to fulfil their obligations under the Covenant and to create a deeper awareness and understanding of its provisions.[206] Therefore, the wording used by the Committee in its Concluding Observations in general is rather diplomatic and soft. This approach is reflected in the structure of the Concluding Observations in which the Committee often expresses its views in 'principal subjects of concern' and 'suggestions and recommendations'.[207]

Nevertheless, over the years the Committee has gradually began to take a more adversarial position. Nowadays, it is not rare for the Committee to explicitly state that there has been a 'violation'[208] or a 'breach'[209] of the Covenant or that a given action or omission is 'incompatible' with the Covenant. More frequently, the Committee comes close to stating that a violation has occurred by using the terms 'urge', 'calls upon States' to do or not to do something,[210] or expresses 'concern' or 'grave concern' with respect to specific State actions or omissions. When we consider that the Concluding Observations generally adopt cautions, diplomatic wording and that the Committee usually only 'recommends' that States Parties should adopt or abstain from a given course of action, these expressions indeed constitute 'imperative language.' As they emanate from an authoritative body[211] they allows us to identify the obligations of the Covenant without great speculation.[212]

---

206 See Alston, *op. cit.* (note 203), p. 160.

207 Concluding Observations are structured in five sections: Introduction; Positive aspects; Factors and difficulties impeding the implementation of the Covenant; Principal subjects of concern; and Suggestions and recommendations.

208 See, for example, Concluding Observations Libyan Arab Jamahiriya ('clear violation) E/C.12/1997/10 para. 185; Concluding Observations Sri Lanka E/1999/22 para. 74; Concluding Observations Nigeria E/1999/22 para. 111; Concluding Observations Israel ('widespread violation') E/1999/22 para. 234; Concluding Observations Canada ('clear violation') E/1999/22 para. 406; Concluding Observations Cyprus ('serious violation') E/C.12/1999/11 para. 288; Concluding Observations Cameroon ('flagrant violation') E/C.12/1999/11 para. 377; and Concluding Observations Mexico E/C.12/1999/11 para. 382.

209 See, for example, Concluding Observations United Kingdom of Great Britain and Northern Ireland E/C.12/1997/10 para. 294 and Concluding Observations Israel E/1999/22 para. 237.

210 In regard to 'Concluding Observations' see the analysis in Chapter I section 2.2.

211 See the analysis concerning the 'legitimacy' of the Committee in Chapter III section 3.3.

212 If someone tells us: 'I recommend that you do not drive through a red light because it is not in conformity with the traffic law', we might infer that in accordance with the traffic law it is prohibited to drive through a red light. When such statements come from the police or a law enforcement official, it is much more probable that it is an obligation imposed by road traffic law. Furthermore, if the supervisor of the traffic law (the law enforcement official) tells us: 'I urge you not to drive through a red light' or 'I call on you not to do so', it is very difficult to deny that there is an obligation. When the Committee expresses its view with 'strong language,' it is exercising its authority as the supervisory body of the Covenant. In this sense, the statements of the Committee might be interpreted as 'commands' in

Having identified those obligations imposed by the Covenant which are more precise, I classify them into each level of State duties (respect, protect and fulfil), in order to give examples of the duties imposed by each level. However, we must bear in mind that States' duties are interrelated. That which is relatively clear in abstract blurs considerably in reality where there may not be sharp distinctions between the different levels of States' duties. Hence, the following analysis should be understood as an interpretative analysis of the Committee's Concluding Observations. This means that it is entirely possible that a duty that is placed, for example, under the obligation to respect might also be considered as an obligation to protect or vice versa. The following is my interpretation of the Committee's Concluding Observations but there may well be different approaches.

Finally, it is important to stress that the following inventory of duties does not intend to be exhaustive as regards all the obligations that each level may entail. The aim is merely to show that by analysing the Concluding Observations in the light of the tripartite typology, it is possible to identify a list of concrete duties derived from each level.

3.2 Obligation to respect

By applying the Committee's understanding of the tripartite typology to the Concluding Observations, it is possible to arrive at the following list of duties which can be derived from this obligation.

1. *The duty to avoid depriving individuals of the possibility to be self-supporting on the basis of their own work*

States must refrain from interfering with individuals who by their own efforts are earning their living in a legal way. According to the Committee, this duty also has a positive component, in the sense that States are not only required to refrain from interfering, but that they must also provide opportunities to individuals to be self-supporting by encouraging self-sufficiency strategies within their territory.[213]

In the case of Azerbaijan, for example, the Committee noted that a large proportion of unemployed persons had found a means of subsistence in the informal sector which appeared to have surpassed the formal economy in size. The Committee found it regrettable that there appeared to be attempts on the part of the Government to eradicate the informal sector. Consequently, the Committee urged the Government 'to work with the

---

the sense in which this term is understood by H.L.A. Hart. See, Hart, H.L.A: *The concept of law*, Clarendon Law Series, second edition, Oxford, (1994), pp. 18 *et seq*.

213 The Committee emphasises that States must support self-sufficiency strategies. A clear example is to be found in the Statement of the Committee on Economic, Social and Cultural Rights to the UN Conference on Human Settlements (Habitat II) adopted at the thirteenth session, 55th meeting 6 December 1995 para. 12.

informal sector and seek to regulate it, rather than eliminate it, as it serves as a means of sustenance for a large number of persons.' It then went further, recommending to the State that those engaged in the informal sector should be able to benefit from low interest loans and credit incentives such as those provided to small businesses in the formal economy.[214]

Examining the initial report of Israel, in particular the policy of 'general closures,'[215] by which the movement of people and goods is restricted between certain areas, the Committee expressed its concern that Palestinian workers from the occupied territories were prevented from reaching their workplaces, thereby depriving them of their livelihood.[216] The Committee considered that this practice resulted 'in widespread violations'[217] of the economic, social and cultural rights of Palestinians. Consequently, the Committee urged Israel to cease this practice.[218]

In the case of the Dominican Republic, the Committee manifested its concern about the militarisation of some communities (*La Ciénaga* and *Los Guandules*). In the Committee's view the military presence in those communities interfered with the self-sufficiency strategies that the residents were able to undertake to improve their housing conditions. Consequently, the Committee recommended that the Government 'fully withdraw the military from these two areas so that improvements can be made in these communities' living conditions.'[219]

2. *The duty to abstain from depriving individuals of the means of subsistence, particularly their land*

The Committee has further strengthened the duty to refrain from hindering individuals in their possibilities to be self-supporting on the basis of their own work. It also includes in this level the duty to respect the resources owned by individuals, particularly their land. States must refrain from the illegal confiscation of lands. Any expropriation of individual land must be subject to due process (in accordance with the law and with due respect to all procedural guarantees), and be duly compensated.

The issue has been analysed by the Committee in the light of article 1(2) of the ICESCR which contains the right to self-determination and expressly states that 'in no case may a people be deprived of its own means of subsistence'.[220] For example, examining the initial report of Israel, the Committee expressed concern over the expro-

---

214 Concluding Observations Azerbaijan E/C.12/1997/10 paras. 336 and 348.

215 Concluding Observations Israel E/1999/22 paras. 243-245.

216 Concluding Observations Israel E/1999/22 para. 244.

217 Concluding Observations Israel E/1999/22 para. 243.

218 Concluding Observations Israel E/1999/22 para. 265.

219 See, Report on the technical assistance mission to the Dominican Republic of the Committee on Economic, Social and Cultural rights 19-27 September 1997 [E/C.12/1997/10, Annex VI, para. 94] and Concluding Observations Dominican Republic E/1998/22, Appendix II, para. 329.

220 Art. 1(2) ICESCR.

priation by the Government of Israel of Palestinian lands and resources for the expansion of Israeli settlements.[221] The Committee urged Israel to respect the right to self-determination as recognised in article 1 paragraph 2.[222]

The duty to refrain from depriving individuals of their means of subsistence is often stressed by the Committee in relation to the resources of indigenous populations. The Committee not only embraces measures taken by States which entail the restitution to indigenous populations of their lands,[223] but also indicates its concern when States do not comply with this kind of duty. For example, the Committee expressed its concern that the Government of Cameroon had adversely affected the rights of the *Baka Pygmies*, in particular their right to an adequate standard of living 'by the compulsory acquisition by the Government of their land.'[224]

3. *The duty to abstain from interfering with the enjoyment of the Covenant's rights*
From the Concluding Observations it is apparent that States are not only required to refrain from denying individuals the enjoyment of the rights, but also that they must avoid obstructing or hindering the enjoyment of the rights. For example, States must avoid interfering with the exercise of the right to strike by completely denying by law the exercise of this right or by imposing excessive requirements for the exercise of the right (not justified by reasons of national security or public order).[225] Moreover, according to the Committee, States must avoid not only direct interference in the enjoyment of the right, but also avoid taking measures that may indirectly have the same result. This occurs, for example, if the legislation of a State allows the right to strike, but this right cannot be enjoyed because the Government intimidates and arrests strikers.[226]

---

221 Concluding Observations Israel E/1999/22 paras. 250 and 254 (the last paragraph refers to confiscation of Bedouin Palestinian land).

222 Concluding Observations Israel E/1999/22 para. 265.

223 For example, the Committee has commended Argentina for the restitution to the indigenous peoples of some of their lands. Concluding Observations Argentina E/C.12/1999/11 para. 252. See also Concluding Observations Norway E/1996/22 para. 211 and Concluding Observations Finland E/2001/22 para. 451.

224 Concluding Observations Cameroon E/2000/22 para. 337. In addition see, Concluding Observations Paraguay E/1997/22 para. 83 and Concluding Observations Panama E/C.12/1/Add.64 para. 28.

225 See, for example, Concluding Observations Colombia E/1996/22 para. 188; Concluding Observations United Kingdom of Great Britain and Northern Ireland [Hong Kong] E/1997/22 para. 358; Concluding Observations Egypt E/C.12/1/Add.44 para. 34; and Concluding Observations Jordan E/C.12/1/Add.46 para. 35.

226 See, for example, Concluding Observations Guinea E/1997/22 para. 201; Concluding Observations Nigeria E/1999/22 para. 111; Concluding Observations Republic of Korea E/C.12/1/Add.59 para. 20; and Concluding Observations Ukraine E/C.12/1/Add.65 para. 27. When the Committee examined the report of Tunisia it addressed another kind of indirect limitation. The Committee noted with concern the existence of only one confederation of trade unions which was required to authorise all strikes. According to the Committee such regulation 'severely curtails the right to strike and to freedom of association'. Concluding Observations Tunisia E/2000/22 para. 167.

States are also required to avoid interference in the enjoyment of economic, social and cultural rights of specified groups of individuals. For example, States must abstain from measures that obstruct (make more difficult) the enjoyment of the economic, social and cultural rights of women, such as the requirement of spousal authorisation for access to health care or to purchase or build a house. This is equally applicable to limits on inheritance by women, their access to property[227] and enjoyment of their civil and political rights such as the freedom of movement or expression.[228]

States must abstain not only from interfering through legislative actions but through any action whatsoever. Through its Concluding Observations, the Committee has addressed a variety of State actions that interfere with the enjoyment of economic, social and cultural rights. For example, the right to take part in cultural life (article 15(a) ICESCR) has been considered by the Committee to be affected by banning plays, prohibiting books or cultural practices, imposing censorship, maintaining a high price on publications, and even by military or police presence on university campuses.[229]

The Concluding Observations have stressed that the enjoyment of the right to education can be adversely affected when States impose certain conditions on the

---

227 For example, when examining the report of Tunisia the Committee was particularly concerned that according to the laws on inheritance, females were entitled to receive only half of the inheritance of males. Therefore, it strongly recommended that everyone should enjoy the right to inherit on a basis of equality. Concluding Observations Tunisia E/C.12/1999/11 paras. 165 and 173.

228 In the case of Sudan, the Committee was gravely concerned about the occurrence of flagellation or the lashing of women for wearing allegedly indecent dress or for being out on the streets after dusk on the basis of the Public Order Act of 1996 which has seriously limited the freedom of movement and of expression for women in Sudan. The Committee expressed its concerned about the fact that some restrictions on the freedoms of religion, expression and association and peaceful assembly still exist, thereby hampering the enjoyment of economic, social and cultural rights. Concluding Observations Sudan E/C.12/1/Add.48 paras. 23 and 24.

229 For example, when examining the report of the Dominican Republic, the Committee expressed its concern about a claim made by a group representing black Dominicans that the State violates their cultural rights by allowing the police and the local communities to suppress Afro-American or Africa-identified cultural practices [Concluding Observations Dominican Republic E/1997/22 para. 226]. In regard to Tunisia the Committee expressed its concern over the censorship exercised on cultural productions recommending the State to establish transparent criteria for censorship in law and in practice and to make it fully compatible with the right of all persons to take part in cultural life [Concluding Observations Tunisia E/C.12/1999/11 paras. 171 and 181]. In the case of Guinea, the Committee found that the Government was not implementing article 15 ICESCR satisfactorily on the basis that access to culture remains difficult as demonstrated for example by the high price of publications. [Concluding Observations Guinea E/1997/22 para. 209]. Examining the report of Tunisia the Committee manifested serious concern that the police presence on university campuses may infringe the freedoms necessary for academic and cultural expression, which the State Party is obliged to respect under article 15 of the Covenant. [Concluding Observations Tunisia E/C.12/1999/11 para. 170]. In the case of Egypt the Committee was gravely concerned over the official censorship imposed on the media as well as literary and artistic works and called upon the Government to respect the freedom which is indispensable for creative activity, including in the media as provided for under article 15(3) of the Covenant. [Concluding Observations Egypt E/C.12/1/Add.44 paras. 25 and 41].

enjoyment of the right, such as the payment of compulsory fees. Examining the report of Cameroon, the Committee regretted 'the requirement of a parental contribution in the form of compulsory fees levied by primary schools which, in view of high levels of poverty, greatly restricts access to primary education, particularly for girls.'[230]

It is apparent from the work of the Committee that State interference with the enjoyment of economic social and cultural rights may occur not only when the rights are enshrined as negative freedoms such as the right to join and form trade unions (article 8(1)(a)), to choose the school of one's children (article 13(3)) or to carry out a scientific or research and creativity activity (article 15), but in general with regard to all the Covenant's rights. All the rights contained in the Covenant impose upon the State the duty of non-interference. For example, in accordance with the General Comments on the right to housing[231] and in the Concluding Observations, the Committee has emphasised the duty to refrain from arbitrary evictions.[232] The uniformity of approach in the General Comments and Concluding Observations is also manifested regarding the right to health, which has been interpreted as imposing a negative obligation of non-interference.[233] In this regard, the Committee pays particular attention to the duty to refrain from carrying out the practice of female genital mutilation, which has serious consequences for the physical, psychological and social health of women.[234]

In sum, restrictions to the enjoyment of the economic, social and cultural rights may be of very different types. They may range from clear intervention or acts of force by the State to the imposition of requirements such as compulsory fees for education. In all such cases the Committee urges States to refrain from interfering or to eliminate excessive restrictions.

4. *The duty to abstain from enforcing any discriminatory law, policies or practice*

In the General Comments the Committee has clearly and explicitly stated that any discrimination in access to Covenant rights constitutes a 'violation' of the Covenant.[235] While such language is not often used in the Concluding Observations, it is still clear that States are required to abstain from enforcing discriminatory laws, policies or practices. If a State has discriminatory legislation in place, the Committee requires its repeal or amendment so that it is consistent with the prohibition of discrimination. For

230 Concluding Observations Cameroon E/C.12/1999/11 para. 341.

231 General Comment No. 4 and No. 7.

232 See, for example, Observations and recommendations adopted by the Committee in the Report on the technical assistance mission to Panama. E/1996/22, Annex V, para. 72, Concluding Observations Nigeria E/1999/22 para. 136 and Concluding Observations Saint Vincent and the Grenadines E/1998/22 para. 431.

233 See General Comment No. 14 para. 34.

234 See, for example, Concluding Observations Nigeria E/1999/22 para. 133 and Concluding Observations Guinea E1997/22 para. 207.

235 See, for example, General Comment No. 12 para. 18 and General Comment No. 14 para. 50.

example, the Committee has placed particular emphasis on the elimination of discriminatory legislation against women[236] and against children born out of wedlock.[237]

Despite the positive component involved in the obligation to amend or abolish discriminatory legislation, at this level the emphasis is on the negative requirement of refraining from denying or limiting equal access for all persons to the rights guaranteed by the Covenant.[238] This obligation does not depend on the availability of resources because it is not a progressive obligation.[239] Although what may be available for individuals in an affluent country can be far removed from the reality of a poorer one, all States, notwithstanding their level of resources, must ensure equal access to available resources. It is important to note, that the issue at this level of State responsibility is not that the State must provide a good, but, rather, that individuals have to be treated in a non-arbitrary way.

5. *The duty to abstain from interfering with the provision of services (or direct satisfaction of these rights) provided by others*

When actors other than the State are providing for the satisfaction of the Covenant's rights, States have the duty not to obstruct such actions. For example, in the case of Mexico, the Committee was concerned about the heavy presence of military forces within the indigenous communities of Chiapas and other states in the region because that presence interfered with the supervision and implementation of development programmes and the distribution of economic and social assistance provided by non-governmental and intergovernmental entities.[240] Therefore, according to the Committee

---

236 See, for example, Concluding Observations Surinam E/1996/22 para. 164; Concluding Observations Paraguay E/1997/22 para. 84; Concluding Observations Guatemala E/1997/22 paras. 126 and 14; Concluding Observations El Salvador E/1997/22 para. 161; Concluding Observations Peru E/1998/22 para. 136; Concluding Observations Dominican Republic E/1998/22 para. 231; Concluding Observations Iraq E/1998/22 para. 274; Concluding Observations Poland E/1999/22 para. 160; Concluding Observations the Netherlands E/1999/22 para. 206; Concluding Observations Cameroon E/2000/22 para. 246; Concluding Observations Egypt E/2001/22 para. 175; Concluding Observations Sudan E/2001/22 para. 321; Concluding Observations Belgium E/2001/22 para. 484; and Concluding Observations Morocco E/2001/22 para. 551.

237 See, for example, Concluding Observations Algeria E/1996/22 para. 296; Concluding Observations Uruguay E/1998/22 para. 377; Concluding Observations Luxembourg E/1998/22 para. 403; Concluding Observations Sri Lanka E/1999/22 paras. 74 and 88; and Concluding Observations Morocco E/2001/22 para. 558.

238 See, for example, Concluding Observations Sri Lanka E/1999/22 paras. 73 and 74; Concluding Observations Nigeria E/1999/22 para. 108; Concluding Observations Israel E/1999/22 para. 238; Concluding Observations Italy E/2001/22 para. 141; Concluding Observations Egypt E/2001/22 para. 180; and Concluding Observations Portugal E/2001/22 para. 413.

239 For a more comprehensive analysis of the duties imposed by the principle of non-discrimination see Chapter VIII.

240 Concluding Observations Mexico E/2000/22 para. 387.

States parties should guarantee that development and social assistance programmes be implemented without the interference of the armed forces.[241]

6. *The duty to refrain from implementing public policies that affect the enjoyment of economic, social and cultural rights, particularly of the more vulnerable groups within society*

All States Parties to the Covenant have the obligation to respect the rights contained therein in any public policy that they may implement. The duty to refrain from implementing public policies that affect the enjoyment of the Covenant rights has been specifically developed by the Committee with regard to the implementation of structural adjustment programmes [SAPs] of the World Bank and the International Monetary Fund [IMF][242] by developing States.

Before embarking on the analysis of the duty of developing States to refrain from implementing SAPs that may violate the Covenant, it is important to note that when the Committee makes reference in its Concluding Observations to international financial institutions and their relations with States Parties to the Covenant, it distinguishes between two categories of States. On the one hand, the Committee places States Parties to the Covenant which receive loans or grants from financial institutions (principally developing States) and on the other, States Parties to the Covenant that are seen to influence the policies of international financial institutions through their participation in the decision-making organs (developed States). Although all States Parties to the Covenant must respect the three levels of States' duties (respect, protect and fulfil), when the Committee refers to the relationships between States Parties and international financial institutions in its Concluding Observations, it emphasises different levels of obligations for each category of States.

In regard to developing States, the Committee has developed duties on the first and second levels (the obligation to respect and protect) and in regard to developed States it has further developed duties on the second level (the obligation to protect). Therefore, the analysis first refers to the duty to respect pertaining to developing States implementing SAPs negotiated with international financial institutions. Later, it

241 Concluding Observations Mexico E/2000/22 para. 393. See, also, Concluding Observations Sri Lanka E/1999/22 para. 86.

242 It is beyond the scope of the present study to analyse in any detail the 'structural adjustment programmes' of both institutions. Suffice it to note here that although the 'structural adjustment programmes' of the two institutions are not identical, as has been noted, most of the following elements are present in both: 'trade liberalisation, abolishment of subsidies, devaluation of local currency, privatisation and reduced public expenditure in general.' See Skogly, S.: *From human capital to human rights: the human rights obligations of the World Bank and the International Monetary Fund.* Dissertation presented to the University of Oslo Faculty of Law for the Degree of Doctor of law, Unpublished, Oslo, May (2000), p. 32. On file with the author.

addresses the obligations to protect of States Parties to the Covenant (developing and developed) which are members of international financial institutions.[243]

It is interesting to note that when examining the reports of developing States that have implemented structural adjustment programmes, the Committee has expressly used in its Concluding Observations the terminology of the tripartite typology: respect, protect and fulfil. For example, after examining the Third Periodic Report of Bulgaria, the Committee recommended that 'in negotiations with international financial institutions, the State party take into account its obligations *to respect, protect and fulfil* all the rights enshrined in the Covenant.'[244] The same was established in the Concluding Observations of Argentina.[245] Therefore, according to the Committee, States Parties to the Covenant must take into account the three levels of State obligations when negotiating with international financial institutions. At this point we will refer to the duties derived from the first level of obligations.[246]

The first level of obligations would impose the duty of developing States to avoid implementing SAPs that may affect the enjoyment of the Covenant's rights, particularly by the more vulnerable groups within society. Initially, the Committee did not address the issue in its examination of the reports of developing States that had implemented SAPs. Although the Committee has increasingly examined this obligation and in recent years has adopted a stricter approach, it has not developed this duty with great precision.

While the Committee has consistently developed the second level of obligations (duty to protect), stressing that States Parties must take all necessary measures to ensure that the SAPs will not adversely affect the most vulnerable groups within society,[247] it only began to develop the duty to respect (the duty to refrain from implementing policies that may violate the Covenant) much later. For years the Committee had avoided expressly indicating in its Concluding Observations when the SAPs had had a negative impact on the enjoyment of the Covenant. Instead, sometimes it merely included a 'soft warning' in the Concluding Observations, but without any assessment

243 See section 3.3.

244 Concluding Observations Bulgaria E/2000/22 para. 236 (emphasis added).

245 Concluding Observations Argentina E/2000/22 para. 276. Nonetheless, the Committee has not been very consistent. For example, examining the report of Cameroon the Committee recommended that 'in negotiations with international financial institutions, the State party take into account its international legal obligations to protect, promote and fulfil economic, social and cultural rights.' Concluding Observations Cameroon E/2000/22 para. 352. There was no apparent reason for the Committee not to mention the duty 'to respect' which was mentioned with regard to Bulgaria and Argentina.

246 The obligations to protect pertaining to developing States implementing SAPs is examined below in section 3.3. It is important to stress here that all States Parties to the Covenant which are members of financial institutions would be under an obligation to respect the Covenant's rights. Nonetheless, the Committee has particularly developed the obligation to respect only with respect to States Parties to the Covenant receiving assistance from international financial institutions.

247 See, for example, Concluding Observations Mali E/1995/22 para. 353 and Concluding Observations Philippines E/1996/22 para. 124.

or a direct recommendation. For example, in the Concluding Observations on the second periodic report of Romania it was stated that '[t]he Committee notes that the structural adjustment programme now being implemented by Romania, *may have adverse consequences* for the implementation of economic, social and cultural rights [...]'.[248]

At its twenty-first session[249] the Committee began to directly indicate in the Concluding Observations when the implementation of the structural adjustment programmes 'has hampered' or 'negatively affected' the enjoyment of economic, social and cultural rights.[250] For example, when examining the Second Periodic Report of Argentina in 1999, the Committee noted that '[w]hile the Government has succeeded in stabilising the value of the currency, the implementation of the structural adjustment programme *has hampered* the enjoyment of economic, social and cultural rights, in particular by the disadvantaged groups in society.'[251]

However, it is interesting to note that the assessment of the effects of the SAPs on the enjoyment of the Covenant's rights is generally included in the Concluding Observations under the section 'factors and difficulties impeding the implementation of the Covenant' rather than in the section 'principal subjects of concern.'[252] This fact is relevant when we bear in mind that, in general, the Committee includes in the section 'factors and difficulties' a broad description of the socio-economic conditions of the State concerned as well as external factors, such as natural disasters that have affected the ability of the State to comply. Typically, this section is a description of the State's situation and does not provide an assessment of State responsibility giving the impression that such factors are beyond the sphere of the Committee's supervision.[253]

---

248 Concluding Observations Romania E/1995/22 para. 90. See also Concluding Observations Argentina E/1995/22 para. 231.

249 Held in Geneva from November 15 to December 3, 1999.

250 See, for example, Concluding Observations Argentina E/2000/22 para. 258; Concluding Observations Cameroon E/2000/22 para. 324; Concluding Observations Bulgaria E/2000/22 para. 221; and Concluding Observations Nepal E/C.12/1/Add.66 para. 11. See also Concluding Observations Venezuela E/C.12/1/Add.56 para. 8.

251 Concluding Observations Argentina E/2000/22 para. 258 (emphasis added). This statement is a remarkable contrast to the Concluding Observations on the First Periodic Report of Argentina in 1994, when the Committee referred to the same issue in softer language: '[t]he Government has succeeded in stabilising the value of the currency but the implementation of the structural adjustment programme may harm certain social groups.' Concluding Observations Argentina E/1995/22 para. 231 (emphasis added).

252 For an analysis of the structure of the Committee's Concluding Observations see Chapter I section 3.1.4.

253 As Boerefijn indicates, '"factors and difficulties"' as identified by the Committee relate to conditions affecting the human rights situation in general. The factors have not as such been regularly the subject of the Committee's suggestions and recommendations, which gives the impression that the Committee found that it could not play a role in solving all of them.' Boerefijn, I.: *The Reporting procedure under the Covenant on Civil and Political Rights: practice and procedure of the Human Rights Committee.* Intersentia, Antwerp, (1999), p. 308. Although she is here referring to the section 'factors and difficul-

The fact that the Committee tends not to directly condemn the implementation of SAPs may be a consequence of the fact that it is very difficult for the Committee to fully assess the responsibility of the State in the implementation of the SAPs. In order to do so, the Committee would require information, for example, on the potential results of alternative policies or to what extent the State has 'freely' consented to a given policy. However, such comparisons are difficult and the Committee generally lacks the necessary information.[254] Therefore, it is understandable that the Committee has generally only stated the facts without providing any evaluation.

Nonetheless, it appears that recently the Committee has reconsidered its approach. Recently it has not only acknowledged the negative effect of SAPs as 'factors affecting the implementation of the Covenant', but it has also required States Parties to review their policies and to adjust them to the requirements of the Covenant. For example, in the case of Cameroon, the Committee indicated under 'factors and difficulties' that 'the Government's economic reform programme for the period 1998-1999, which implemented the structural adjustment programme in Cameroon approved by the IMF, the World Bank and the *Agence française de développment* [...], while increasing the real GDP growth rate has impacted negatively on the enjoyment of economic, social and cultural rights by increasing poverty and unemployment, worsening income distribution and causing the collapse of social services.'[255] Subsequently, it recommended that the State 'review its macroeconomic reform programmes with respect to their impact on the standard of living of vulnerable groups [...], and to make efforts to adjust these reforms in a way that better responds to the current needs of such groups.'[256]

In the case of Egypt, it indicated as 'factors and difficulties impeding the implementation of the Covenant' that 'some aspects of structural adjustment programmes and economic liberalisation policies introduced by the Government of Egypt, in concert with international financial institutions, have impeded the implementation of the Covenant's provisions, particularly with regard to the most vulnerable groups of Egyptian society.' This is a mere recognition of the facts and not an assessment. However, the Committee also incorporated as a 'principal subject of concern' its regret that 'the State party does not take its obligations under the Covenant into account in its negotiations with international financial institutions.' The latter statement implies the disapproval of the Committee.[257] A statement of disapproval was also included in the Con-

ties' contained in the HRC's Concluding Observations, the remark is plainly applicable to the section contained in the Committee's Concluding Observations.

254 As Skogly notes, the SAPs implemented by States 'are "joint ventures", where not only finance, but also planning of the measures to be taken are done in partnership. Due to the secrecy with which the SAPs are negotiated, it is difficult to say exactly who is responsible for what.' Skogly, *loc. cit.* (note 242), p. 243.

255 Concluding Observations Cameroon E/C.12/1999/11 para. 324.

256 Concluding Observations Cameroon E/C.12/1999/11 para. 352.

257 Concluding Observations Egypt E/C.12/1/Add 44 paras.10 and 14.

cluding Observations of the Republic of Korea, which stated that 'the Committee is concerned that the State party did not take into account its Covenant obligations when negotiating with international financial institutions to overcome its financial crisis and restructure its economy. The over-reliance on macro-economic policies has had profound negative effects on the enjoyment of economic, social and cultural rights in that there have been large-scale employee dismissals and lay-offs, significant deterioration in the employment stability, growing income inequalities, an increasing number of broken families and marginalization of a large number of persons.'[258]

In sum, according to the approach followed by the Committee, particularly since 1999, it is possible to conclude that developing States must refrain from implementing structural adjustment policies that adversely affect the enjoyment of the Covenant rights. In order to do so, States are required to take into account their obligations under the Covenant when negotiating with international financial institutions.

Finally, it is important to stress that 'the duty to refrain from implementing public policies that affect the enjoyment of economic, social and cultural rights, particularly of the more vulnerable groups' does not only refer to SAPs. There are other policies implemented by States that may violate the Covenant. In the case of Israel, for example, the Committee noted that the policy of 'general closures', by which Israel restricted and controlled the movement of people and goods between some regions, hampered the realisation of economic, social and cultural rights, especially of Palestinians.[259]

In this case, the Committee explicitly stated that those policies resulted 'in widespread violation' of the Palestinians' economic, social and cultural rights.[260]

3.3 Obligation to protect

The protection of the Covenant's rights against third party interference has been clearly stated in the Committee's Concluding Observations. This obligation is extremely important in regard to economic, social and cultural rights because it expands the responsibility of States. The obligation to protect does not refer to State responsibility for non-State actions, but, rather, to State responsibility for its own failure to prevent and protect against human right violation committed by private entities.

It is apparent that the Committee considers that this level requires States to enact legislation to regulate the conduct of any individuals, groups or entities within its jurisdiction whose activities have or may have an impact on the enjoyment of the Covenant's rights. Through such regulation, States must prevent such actors from violating

258 Concluding Observations Republic of Korea E/C.12/1/Add.59 para. 12.

259 The Committee expressly mentioned the 'general closures' between Israel and the West Bank and the Gaza Strip, between Jerusalem and the West Bank and between the West Bank and the Gaza Strip. The restrictions apply only to Palestinians and not to Jewish Israeli citizens. Concluding Observations Israel E/1999/22 para. 243. See the text accompanying note 215.

260 Concluding Observations Israel E/1999/22 para. 243.

economic, social and cultural rights. Sometimes the legislation required must be of a penal nature, meaning that States must penalise certain abusive behaviours that may adversely affect the enjoyment of economic, social and cultural rights, particularly of vulnerable groups, such as women, children and indigenous populations.[261]

It is important to note that the obligation to protect through legislation, although insufficient on its own, may play an important role as an instrument of mobilisation to change perceptions within society which may accelerate the implementation of the rights. These duties are intertwined with the duties to promote, although the latter basically attempt to change behaviour through education.

The emphasis that the Committee has placed on the obligation to protect is most appropriate. There cannot be effective protection of economic, social and cultural rights without an acceptance of the relevance of the protection of these rights in the private sphere. Increasingly, private actors are the sources of threats to rights guaranteed by the Covenant, as well as obstacles to their implementation. In the era of globalisation, the role of Governments as direct violators or providers of these rights is becoming less important. Yet there is still much room for improvement in the protection of these rights by holding States responsible for violations of economic, social and cultural rights where the actor involved is a private individual or group. We must not forget that from the victim's point of view, it is the same whether it is the State, a private individual or an enterprise which committed the violation of his/her economic, social and cultural rights.

As the Committee notes, legislative measures taken by States Parties to protect the rights of individuals from third party violations must be effective. This means that it is not sufficient that States merely adopt legislation if they do not take the necessary measures to effectively enforce it,[262] for example, when the State enacts legislative measures protecting labour rights but does not allocate sufficient resources for labour inspections.[263]

From the Concluding Observations it is possible to identify the following list of duties derived from this level:

261 See, for example, Concluding Observations Jordan E/2001/22 para. 250; Concluding Observations Portugal E/2001/22 paras. 423 and 424; Concluding Observations Morocco E/2001/22 paras. 531 and 555; Concluding Observations Dominican Republic E/1998/22 para. 230; Concluding Observations Spain E/1997/22 para. 111; Concluding Observations Finland E/1997/22 para. 318; and Concluding Observations Sweden E/1996/22 para. 146.

262 See, Concluding Observation Sri Lanka E/1999/22 para. 76; Concluding Observations Poland E/1999/22 para. 156; Concluding Observations Australia E/2001/22 para. 391; Concluding Observations Finland E/2001/22 para. 454; and Concluding Observation Georgia E/2001/22 para. 82.

263 See Concluding Observation Peru E/1998/22 paras. 148 and 161.

1. *The duty to take measures to prevent third parties from interfering with the enjoyment of the Covenant's rights*

The Concluding Observations have addressed a variety of situations in which the Committee has considered that there are duties to take measures to prevent third parties interfering with the enjoyment of the Covenant's rights. For example, in accordance with its General Comment Nos. 4 and 7 on the right to adequate housing,[264] through the Concluding Observations the Committee has required States to take measures to protect populations from forced evictions by private actors.[265] Already in 1995 when examining the report of the Philippines, it was noted that 'the Committee is unable to accept statements made by the Government to the effect that the Covenant provides no protection from forced eviction. The right to housing cannot be interpreted as being silent in relation to such an issue and the Committee has consistently drawn the attention of other States Parties to this matter.'[266] With regard to the right to housing, it is important to stress that States are also required to protect individuals from the abusive behaviour of landlords, such as arbitrary rent increases. For example, in the case of Australia, the Committee 'strongly recommended' that the State develop a housing strategy at the federal level including provisions not only to protect tenants from forced evictions but also from arbitrary rent increases.[267]

2. *The duty to uphold the principle of non-discrimination in legislation*

According to the Committee, States are required to introduce legislation providing protection against discrimination on all the grounds contained in the Covenant. The Committee has stressed this duty with particular concern in regard to gender discrimination,[268] protection of ethnic minorities,[269] protection of Roma populations[270] and pro-

264 General Comment No. 4 concerning the right to adequate housing (Art. 11(1) of the Covenant) and General Comment No. 7 concerning forced evictions.

265 See, for example, Concluding Observations Jordan E/2001/22 para. 256; Concluding Observations Argentina E/2000/22 para. 284; Concluding Observations Cameroon E/2000/22 para. 355; Concluding Observations Mexico E/2000/22 para. 389; Concluding Observations Dominican Republic E/1998/22 para. 225; and Concluding Observations United Kingdom of Great Britain and Northern Ireland E/1995/22 para. 274.

266 Concluding Observations Philippines E/1996/22 para. 117. See, also, paras. 131-132.

267 Concluding Observations Australia E/2001/22 paras. 386 and 399.

268 See, for example, Concluding Observations Austria E/1995/22 para. 246; Concluding Observations United Kingdom of Great Britain and Northern Ireland E/1995/22 para. 298; Concluding Observations Guatemala E/1997/22 para. 141; Concluding Observations El Salvador E/1996/22 para. 161; Concluding Observations Dominican Republic E/1998/22 para. 231; Concluding Observations Switzerland E/1999/22 para. 354; and Concluding Observations Republic of Congo E/2001/22 para. 211.

269 See, for example, Concluding Observations Belgium E/1995/22 para. 157; Concluding Observations Iraq E/1998/22 para. 273; Concluding Observations United Kingdom of Great Britain and Northern Ireland E/1998/22 paras. 295 and 307; and Concluding Observations Sri Lanka E/1999/22 para. 89.

270 See, for example, Concluding Observations Spain E/1997/22 para. 104; Concluding Observations Germany E/1999/22 para. 317; Concluding Observations Bulgaria E/2000/22 para. 223; Concluding Observations Italy E/2001/22 para. 129; and Concluding Observations Portugal E/2001/22 para. 413.

tection of persons with HIV/AIDS.[271] Another important issue increasingly addressed by the Committee is the obligation of States to protect against any discriminatory or xenophobic behaviour, particularly against foreigners, immigrants and refugees.[272] The Committee has urged States Parties to take all appropriate preventive and penal measures to combat effectively all forms of racial discrimination[273] and has welcomed the adoption of plans of actions to combat intolerance and violence.[274]

3 *The duty to take measures to protect vulnerable groups within society*

The duty to protect is particularly important in relation to vulnerable groups within society, such as women, children and indigenous populations. From the Concluding Observations, it is apparent that the Committee requires States to intervene in private relations so as to ensure the protection of vulnerable groups. A brief analysis of the measures required to protect women and children is therefore pertinent.

A. *Protection of women*

Consistent with its position that the economic, social and cultural rights of women are a 'critical concern', the Committee[275] often emphasises the duty to protect women from third party violations.

The principal focus of the Committee's attention is the duty to protect the equal enjoyment of economic, social and cultural rights by women, requiring States to interfere in private relations so as to make equal enjoyment of human rights possible. As a result, the Committee has addressed many aspects of this level of obligation, principally those which focus on the protection of women against different forms of discrimination.[276] Special attention has been paid to the following issues:

(a) *Duty to protect women workers from discrimination at work*:

The Covenant requires States to take a variety of measures to protect women workers against discriminatory acts at work such as, arbitrary dismissal related with pregnancy, pregnancy testing and sexual harassment. The principal obligation of States is the

---

271 See, for example, Concluding Observations Russian Federation E/1998/22 para. 126; Concluding Observations Germany E/1999/22 para. 334; and Concluding Observations Egypt E/2001/22 para. 180.

272 See, for example, Concluding Observations Belgium E/1995/22 para. 157; Concluding Observations Spain E/1997/22 para. 104; Concluding Observations Denmark E/2000/22 paras. 105 and 113; Concluding Observations Italy E/2001/22 para. 138; and Concluding Observations Portugal E/2001/22 para. 413.

273 See, for example, Concluding Observations Spain E/C.12/Add.2 para. 17 and Concluding Observations Denmark E/C.12/1999/11 para. 112.

274 Concluding Observations Norway E/C.12/1995/13 para. 8.

275 Statement of the Committee on Economic, Social and Cultural Rights to the Fourth Conference on Women. E/1996/22, Annex VI, para.9.

276 For a comprehensive analysis of the principle of non-discrimination under the Covenant see Chapter VIII, in particular section 4 on article 3 of the Covenant.

adoption of regulatory legislation to discourage employers from such practices. However, legislative measures are not sufficient: States are also responsible for implementing the law.[277]

One of the issues frequently addressed by the Committee is the practice of pregnancy testing. According to the Committee, States parties are required to prohibit dismissal on the ground of pregnancy.[278] In the case of Mexico, for example, the Committee was 'deeply concerned' about the situation of women workers in the *maquiladoras* (assembly plants), because some of them were subject to pregnancy tests upon recruitment and at regular intervals thereafter and were dismissed if found to be pregnant. Consequently, the Committee 'urged' the State 'to adopt immediate steps towards the protection of women workers in the *maquiladoras*, including prohibiting the practice of demanding medical certification that prospective workers are not pregnant and taking legal action against employers who fail to comply.'[279]

(b) *Duty to ensure that harmful social or traditional practices do not interfere with the enjoyment of economic, social and cultural rights of women*:

States are required to implement laws and to adopt or repeal legislation to discourage practices which violate the rights of women such as, bride kidnapping, polygamy, and the penal punishment of lesbianism.[280] It is important to stress that concerns regarding the elimination of social or traditional practices which interfere with the equality between sexes is common to several of the human rights treaty bodies. For example, the HRC frequently addressed the issue,[281] as have CEDAW[282] and CRC.[283]

In this regard it is important to mention that, in line with General Comment No. 14, it is clear from the Concluding Observations that States must prevent third parties from

---

277 See, for example, Concluding Observations Poland E/1999/22 para. 152 and Concluding Observations Mongolia E/C.12/1/Add.47 para. 23.

278 See, for example, Concluding Observations Dominican Republic E/1997/22 para.233; Concluding Observations Poland /1999/22 para. 152; and Concluding Observations Bulgaria E/C.12/1999/11 para. 242.

279 Concluding Observations Mexico E/C.12/1999/11 paras. 383 and 399. With regard to the working conditions for women in the '*maquilas*' (assembly plants) see also, Concluding Observations Honduras E/C.12/1/Add.57 para. 15.

280 See, for example, Concluding Observations Nepal E/C.12/1/Add.66 para. 13; Concluding Observations Kyrgyzstan E/C.12/1/Add.49 paras. 16 and 30; Concluding Observations Morocco E/2001/22 para. 520; Concluding Observations Cameroon E/C.12/1999/11 para. 347; and Concluding Observations Zimbabwe E/1998/22 para. 73.

281 See, for example, HRC Concluding Comments Sudan CCPR/C/79/Add.85 para. 11 and HRC Concluding Comments Tanzania CCPR/C/79/Add.97 para. 12. For further information on the HRC approach to customs and traditions in its Concluding Observations, see Boerefijn, *op. cit.* (note 253), pp. 319 *et seq.*

282 See, for example, CEDAW Concluding Observations Guinea CEDAW/C/2001/II/Add.2 and Indonesia in A/53/38, part I, paras. 262-311.

283 See, for example, CRC Concluding Observations Kuwait CRC/C/15/Add.96 para. 28 and Concluding Observations Iraq CRC/C.15/Add.94 para. 21.

coercing women to undergo female genital mutilation [FGM].[284] Although States are required to combat adverse practices by all means at their disposal, in relation to FGM there is a strong basis for considering that the Committee requires States to consider the practice as a criminal offence. For example, in the case of Egypt, the Committee noted with concern that although the State had undertaken initial steps against the practice of FGM by criminalizing FGM outside of hospitals by persons without a medical qualification, this measure did not make the practice of FGM by medical practitioners a criminal offence.[285]

(c) *Duty to protect women against domestic violence*:
This is an obligation that has taken on increasing importance in the Committee's work. States are required to take immediate action to combat and prevent domestic violence.[286] In the case of Egypt, for example, the Concluding Observations state that '[t]he State party *must* enhance its strategies and programmes aimed at combating domestic violence. In this regard the Committee *urges* the State party to criminalize marital rape and also to combat this problem through information campaigns and educational programmes.'[287] It is apparent from the Committee's work that States are required to adopt specific legislation and policies to prohibit domestic violence, and, in general, all forms of discriminatory behaviour against women.[288] Examining the report of the Russian Federation, the Committee expressed its concern regarding the hesitation of the police to intervene to protect women or to bring charges against their aggressors in cases of violence against women. The Committee subsequently recommended that 'legislation be adopted to protect women victims of domestic violence,

284 See, for example, Concluding Observations Sudan E/C.12/1/Add.48 para. 39; Concluding Observations Guinea E/1997/22 para. 207; Concluding Observations Nigeria E/1999/22 para. 133; and Concluding Observations Senegal E/C.12/1/Add.62 para. 24. See, in addition, General Comment No. 14 para. 35 and CEDAW Recommendation No. 14 on female circumcision. It is important to stress that there is an obligation to protect women from female genital mutilation when private individuals carry out the practice. However there is also an obligation to respect, this is to say to cease the practice if it is undertaken by State agents *e.g.* in public hospitals.

285 Concluding Observations Egypt E/C.12/1/Add.44 para. 16. Some States seem to recognise the existence of the obligation to criminalize FGM [*e.g.* Fourth Periodic Report of Sweden E/C.12/4/Add.4 para. 22]. The CEDAW and the HRC have adopted the same approach, requiring that the practice be made punishable under law. See, for example, CEDAW Concluding Observations Cameroon in A/55/38, paras. 30-66 at 54; CEDAW Concluding Observation Burkina Faso in A/55/38, paras. 239-286 at 262; HRC Concluding Comments Lesotho CCPR/C/79/Add.106 para. 12; and HRC Concluding Comments Sudan CCPR/C/79/Add.85 para. 10.

286 See, for example, Concluding Observations Georgia E/2001/22 para. 101; Concluding Observations Italy E/2001/22 para. 133; and Concluding Observations Republic of Congo E/2001/22 para. 202. Domestic violence will be analysed later. See Chapter VIII section 4.4.

287 Concluding Observations Egypt E/C.12/1/Add.44 para. 35.

288 See, for example, Concluding Observations Cameroon E/C.12/1999/11 para. 348. See in Chapter VIII section 3.3 the analysis of the obligation to take legislative measures against discrimination.

that specific programmes be put in place to assist such victims and that perpetrators of such acts be brought to justice.'[289]

B. *Protection of Children*

States are required to take measures to protect children and prevent third parties from interfering in the enjoyment of their rights. The Committee gives special attention to the following issues:

(a) *Duty to prevent and protect children against economic exploitation*:

States are required to regulate child labour and in particular to adopt and enforce legislation establishing a minimum working age.[290] Moreover, States are required to impose penalties on those who economically exploit children. According to the Committee, States must adopt legislation imposing 'severe penalties' on employers in case of infringements.[291]

Examining the report of Morocco, it was held that 'the Committee urges the State party to take remedial action, including the imposition of appropriately severe penalties, in order to ensure that employers [...] are prevented from resorting to child labour under the legal minimum working age.'[292] The strong language used by the Committee in the case of Morocco contrasts with the milder language used by the Committee after examining the Third Periodic Report of Portugal. Although the Committee noted that the occurrence of child labour in Portugal was 'in breach of the State party's international obligations, in particular its obligations under the Covenant,'[293] it merely 'suggested' that the State 'strictly implement the measures at its disposal to monitor and impose the appropriate penalties on persons or companies using child labour.'[294] The Committee's statement in the case of Portugal is especially weak if we take into account that a year before the Committee's examination of Portugal's report, another

289 Concluding Observations Russian Federation E/1998/22 paras. 102 and 118.

290 See, for example, Concluding Observations Morocco E/C.12/1/Add.55 para. 44; Concluding Observations Egypt E/2001/22 para. 163; Concluding Observations Republic of Congo E/2001/22 para. 204; Concluding Observations Sri Lanka E/1999/22 para. 90; Concluding Observations Nigeria E/1999/22 para. 134; and Concluding Observations Germany E/1999/22 para. 332. As it is possible to deduce from the Concluding Observations, according to the Committee the minimum working age is 15 years old. This is in line with ILO standards (ILO Conventions, No. 138 (1973) concerning the minimum age for admission to employment and No. 182 (1999) concerning the abolition of the worst forms of child labour and immediate measures for their prohibition) and with article 7 of the European Social Charter.

291 See, for example, Concluding Observations Morocco E/C.12/1/Add.55 paras. 20 and 44; Concluding Observations Portugal E/2001/22 para. 423; Concluding Observations Russian Federation E/1998/22 paras. 119 and 129; and Concluding Observations Zimbabwe E/1998/22 para. 75.

292 Concluding Observations Morocco E/C.12/1/Add.55 para. 44.

293 Concluding Observations Portugal E/C.12/Add.53 para. 10.

294 Concluding Observations Portugal E/C.12/Add.53 para. 21.

human right supervisory body had found Portugal to be in violation of the provision of the European Social Charter which prohibits child labour.[295]

(b) *Duty to take measures to protect children against sexual exploitation*:
The Committee has given particular attention to this topic. It has emphasised the responsibility of States to take all necessary measures to prevent and protect children against prostitution, 'sex tourism' and paedophilia.[296] The Committee has stressed the need to ensure that specific and appropriate penal legislation is enacted and enforced to combat such situations. The Committee has also called upon States to take remedial actions against sexual abuse.[297] In the case of Sri Lanka, for example, the Committee 'strongly' recommended 'that Sri Lankan authorities renew their efforts to seek out those who are responsible for the exploitation of children and to prosecute them to the full extent of the law. The Committee encouraged the Government to seek the co-operation of other Governments in bringing to justice all those who engage in the sexual exploitation of children, and international assistance to establish rehabilitation programmes to facilitate the reintegration into society of children who have been victimised.'[298]

It is noteworthy that the Committee's approach with regard to economic and sexual exploitation in the Concluding Observations is consistent with its approach in the General Comments. As mentioned earlier, the protection of children from economic and social exploitation (article 10(3) ICESCR) is expressly considered as an obligation of an immediate character (*e.g.* General Comment Nos. 3 and 9).[299]

4. *The duty to ensure that enterprises (national and transnational) do not deprive individuals of their enjoyment of economic, social and cultural rights*

From the Concluding Observations, it is possible to conclude that States Parties must take measures to protect the economic, social and cultural rights of individuals under their jurisdiction against abusive behaviour on the part of the private business sector (national and transnational corporations).

295 See the decision of the supervisory body of the European Social Charter in the collective complaint procedure, Communication No. 1/1998 International Commission of Jurists v. Portugal. In the decision on the merits, the Committee of Ministers found a violation of Article 7(1) of the Charter (prohibition of work by children under fifteen years). [Committee of Ministers Resolution ChS (99) 4, adopted on 15 December 1999].

296 See, for example, Concluding Observations Finland E/1997/22 para. 318; Concluding Observations Germany E/1999/22 para. 320; Concluding Observations Belgium E/2001/22 para. 487; and Concluding Observations Dominican Republic E/1997/22 para. 232.

297 See, for example, Concluding Observations Panama E/C.12/1/Add.64 para. 34.

298 Concluding Observations Sri Lanka E/1999/22 para. 90. See, also, for example, Concluding Observations Panama E/C.12/1/Add.4 para. 34.

299 See the previous discussion on the issue, in Chapter IV section 2.2.3.

In examining the Third Periodic Report of the Russian Federation, the Committee expressed its 'serious concern' about the level of contamination of both domestically produced and imported foodstuffs. The Committee observed that the contamination was apparently caused in 'domestic production by the improper use of pesticides and environmental pollution [...], and for imported food by the illegal practices of some food importers'. Subsequently, the Committee noted that 'it is the responsibility of the Government to ensure that such food-stuff does not reach the market.'[300] It further recommended that 'vigorous action be taken against enterprises which have been found to import contaminated food.'[301] In the case of Morocco, the Committee expressed concern 'that the State party does not exercise sufficient control, by means of legislative and administrative measures, over factories manufacturing foodstuffs which do not conform to international standards and cause death or constitute a health hazard to the population of Morocco.'[302] Consequently, the Committee 'urged' Morocco 'to take the appropriate legislative and administrative measures to ensure that sufficient control is exercised on factories manufacturing foodstuffs so that the products manufactured conform to international standards and do not constitute any health hazard.'[303]

The Committee has paid special attention to situations in which corporations negatively affect the environment by interfering with the enjoyment of economic, social and cultural rights, such as the right to food and health,[304] and when they have imposed abusive working conditions on individuals under State jurisdiction.[305]

A. *The protection of the environment*

Over the years the Committee has gradually developed the duty to protect the environment against the negative actions of private enterprises. As the Committee stresses, the damage to the environment may negatively impact the enjoyment of economic, social and cultural rights of individuals, particularly their rights to food and health.

Examining the report of the Russian Federation, the Committee linked the questions of contaminated food to questions relating to a seriously polluted environment and the lack of investment in infrastructure for the maintenance and improvement of the water supply. It recommended that the State Party 'examine these linkages and take appropriate action to clean up the environment and prevent enterprises from engaging in further pollution, especially that which contaminates the food chain.' The Committee also

300 Concluding Observations Russian Federation E/1998/22 para. 110.
301 Concluding Observations Russian Federation E/1998/22 para. 124.
302 Concluding Observations Morocco E/2001/22 para. 541.
303 Concluding Observations Morocco E/2001/22 para. 565.
304 See, for example, Concluding Observations Russian Federation E/1998/22 para. 100; Concluding Observations Azerbaijan E/1998/22 para. 345; Concluding Observations Nigeria E/1999/22 para. 123; Concluding Observations Cameroon E/2000/22 para. 337; and Concluding Observations Solomon Islands E/2000/22 paras. 204 and 209.
305 See, for example, Concluding Observations Russian Federation E/1998/22 para. 104 and Concluding Observations Mexico E/2000/22 para. 399.

recommended that the maintenance and improvement of the water supply system be undertaken 'as a matter of priority'.[306] In the case of Honduras, the Committee stated that it was 'particularly concerned about the extremely negative effects of the use of pollutants and toxic substances in specific agricultural and industrial sectors, such as banana growing and gold-mining, on the environment, thereby putting at risk the health and lives of workers and those living in the vicinity of the affected areas. In this regard, the Committee is also concerned that Environmental Studies are conducted by or on behalf of those sectors without effective review by independent bodies.'[307] Consequently, the Committee 'strongly' recommended Honduras to 'implement the existing legislative and administrative measures to avoid violations of environmental [...] laws by transnational companies.'[308]

The Committee pays special attention when the degradation of the environment affects the living conditions of indigenous peoples requiring the adoption of measures to prevent the depletion of the natural resources on which they depend for their livelihood. In the Concluding Observations of the Russian Federation mentioned above the Committee also expressed concern about the destruction of the environment by widespread pollution that especially affected the means of subsistence of indigenous populations whose food supply is based on fishing and reindeer herding.[309] The Committee stated that it was 'alarmed' at reports that the pollution was caused by oil and gas companies which signed agreements 'under circumstances which were clearly illegal' and that the State had not taken adequate steps to protect the indigenous peoples from such exploitation, allowing the companies to violate the economic, social and cultural rights of indigenous people with impunity.[310] Subsequently, the Committee recommended 'that action be taken to protect the indigenous peoples from exploitation by oil and gas companies and more generally that action be taken to ensure their access to traditional and other sources of food.'[311]

Examining the initial report of Nigeria, the Committee noted 'with alarm' the extent of devastation that oil exploration has caused to the environment and the quality of life in some regions particularly those of Ogoniland where oil had been discovered and extracted without due regard to the health and well-being of the people and the environment.[312] Consequently, the Committee noted that: 'the rights of minority and ethnic

306 Concluding Observations Russian Federation E/1998/22 para. 124.

307 Concluding Observations Honduras E/C.12/1/Add.57 para. 24.

308 Concluding Observations Honduras E/C.12/1/Add.57 para. 36. See, in addition, Concluding Observations Azerbaijan E/1998/22 paras. 331 and 345 and Concluding Observations Solomon Islands E//2000/22 paras. 204 and 209.

309 See, for example, Concluding Observations Russian Federation E/1998/22 paras. 100 and 116; Concluding Observations Honduras E/C.12/1/Add.57 para. 25; Concluding Observations Venezuela E/C.12/1/Add.58 para. 12; and Concluding Observations Panama E/C.12/1/Add.64 para. 28.

310 Concluding Observations Russian Federation E/1998/22 para. 100.

311 Concluding Observations Russian Federation E/1998/22 para. 116.

312 Concluding Observations Nigeria E/1999/22 para. 123.

communities – including the Ogoni people – should be respected and full redress should be provided for the violations that they have suffered of the rights set forth in the Covenant.'[313] In the case of Cameroon, the Committee expressed concern that the resources of the rainforest upon which the Baka Pygmies depend for subsistence had deteriorated and 'urged' Cameroon to take effective measures to protect the rights of the Baka Pygmies to an adequate standard of living, in particular their right to food, when negotiating contracts for projects which have a negative on their lives.[314]

B. *The protection of workers*

The issue most frequently addressed by the Committee with regard to this level of State responsibility is the duty to take measures to ensure that enterprises do not deprive workers of their rights. The Committee requires States to intervene in private labour relations so as to ensure that enterprises will not take advantage of workers' vulnerability. Special attention is paid by the Committee to the duty to ensure the protection of women workers. States are required to protect them, in particular, from discrimination and arbitrary dismissal related to pregnancy and from sexual harassment in the workplace.[315]

The principal obligation on the part of States is to provide a legal framework to protect the rights of workers and to ensure that companies comply with it. The Committee has expressed 'deep concern' when workers are left free to negotiate the conditions of their employment without a legal framework to protect their rights as it considers that Governments are obliged under the Covenant to ensure that all workers enjoy favourable conditions of employment.[316] When examining the initial report of Honduras, for example, the Committee expressed concern 'about the lack of legislative and administrative measures by the State party to control the negative effects of transnational companies' activities on the employment and working conditions of Honduran workers and to ensure compliance with national labour legislation. Examples of such negative impacts are the low-level of wages and the sub-standard working conditions in the *maquilas* (assembly plants), and particularly those employing primarily women workers.'[317]

In general, in light of articles 7 and 8 of the Covenant, the Committee has addressed a variety of situations in which States are required to ensure the protection of workers. Particular importance has been paid to: (a) The duty to ensure just and fair conditions of work, such as fair wages, safe conditions of work and reasonable limits to working

313 Concluding Observations Nigeria E/1999/22 para. 132.

314 Concluding Observations Cameroon E/2000/22 para. 352.

315 See the analysis below, in Chapter VIII section 4.

316 See, for example, Observations Cameroon E/2000/22 paras. 331 and 349 and Concluding Observations Dominican Republic E/1997/22 para. 214.

317 Concluding Observations Honduras E/C.12/Add.57 para. 15.

hours,[318] (b) The duty to ensure the right to form and join trade unions and the right to strike.[319]

In the case of Kyrgyzstan, the Committee was 'disturbed' to learn that some employers had hampered the activities of trade unions and that trade union rights in general were not protected by law 'as vigorously as they should be'. Therefore, it urged the State 'to apply all legal means to put an end to the interference of employers with the freedom of trade union activity by discouraging workers from forming trade unions.'[320]

According to the Concluding Observations, States must take measures to prevent violations of labour-related rights by enterprises. In this regard, States must establish sufficient labour inspections to ensure that there is no impunity for violations of these rights.[321] In the case of Morocco, for example, the Committee expressed its concern that the State Party did not provide 'for appropriately severe and enforceable penalties' to prevent employers from violating rights and subsequently it 'urged' the State Party 'to take remedial action, including the imposition of appropriately severe penalties'.[322]

Sometimes the Committee has gone further, indicating the measures which are 'necessary' to remedy the negative impact on the enjoyment of the Covenant's rights as the result of acts committed by enterprises. A good example is the case of the exploitation of Haitians in the Dominican Republic. The Committee acknowledged the extremely difficult and 'unacceptable' living conditions of the workers in the *bateyes* (sugar cane plantations). The Committee criticised the State's inaction to protect Haitian workers by allowing employers to exploit their vulnerability and explicitly noted that legislative measures were 'necessary'. The Committee then went further and specifically indicated which legislative actions appeared to be necessary. Unfortunately, the Government did not take the appropriate actions required, but a year later the Committee reiterated its concern over the inadequacy of the measures taken by the authorities

---

318 See, for example, Concluding Observations Bolivia E/C.12/1/Add.60 para. 33; Concluding Observations Georgia E/2001/22 para. 97; Concluding Observations Australia E/2001/22 para. 392; Concluding Observations Finland E/2001/22 para. 455; Concluding Observations Russian Federation E/1998/22 para. 104; Concluding Observations Honduras E/C.12/1/Add.57 para. 38; and Concluding Observations Cameroon E/2000/22 para. 331.

319 See, for example, Concluding Observations Canada E/1999/22 para. 406; Concluding Observations Sri Lanka E/1999/22 para. 81; Concluding Observations Zimbabwe E/1998/22 para. 83; Concluding Observations Peru E/1998/22 para. 148; Concluding Observations Libyan Arab Jamahiriya E/1998/22 para. 183; and Concluding Observations Republic of Korea E/1996/22 para. 80.

320 Concluding Observations Kyrgyzstan E/C.12/1/Add.49 paras.15 and 28.

321 See, for example, Concluding Observations El Salvador E/1997/22 paras. 162 and 165; Concluding Observations Guatemala E/1997/22 para. 131; Concluding Observations Russian Federation E/1998/22 paras. 104 and 119; and Concluding Observations Poland E/1999/22 para. 162.

322 Concluding Observations Morocco E/C.12/1/Add.55 para. 20.

and urged the Government to adopt positive measures to improve living conditions in the *bateyes*.[323]

5. *Obligations to protect in regard to international financial institutions*
As mentioned above,[324] when the Committee makes reference in its Concluding Observations to international financial institutions and their relationship with States Parties to the Covenant, it distinguishes between two categories of States: States Parties to the Covenant receiving loans or grants from financial institutions (principally developing States), and States Parties to the Covenant that are seen to influence the policies of international financial institutions through their participation in the decision-making organs (developed States). Here we will address the duties to protect established for each category of States as derived from the Concluding Observations.[325]

A. *States receiving funds or grants from international financial organisations*
The Committee notes that when States Parties to the Covenant negotiate with international financial institutions, they must take into account the three levels of State obligations (respect, protect and fulfil).[326] The second level of obligations (duty to protect) has received the greatest attention from the Committee and is analysed below.[327]

The Committee has stressed the important role of developing States as 'protectors' of economic, social and cultural rights, particularly of the most vulnerable groups within society, when they negotiate with financial institutions (*i.e.* the International Monetary Fund and the World Bank) and international organisations (*i.e.* the World

323 Concluding Observations Dominican Republic E/1997/22 paras. 224-225; Concluding Observations Dominican Republic E/1998/22 paras. 216 and 233–234; and Report on the technical assistance mission to the Dominican Republic of the Committee on Economic, Social and Cultural Rights, 19-27 September 1997, E/C.12/1997/10, Annex VI, paras. 73-103.

324 See the text accompanying notes 242-243.

325 It is important to stress that the analysis is from the point of view of the obligations upon States Parties to the Covenant which are members of financial institutions. The obligations that the institutions (as legal persons) may have in regard to the Covenant are beyond the scope of the present study. For a comprehensive analysis of the human rights obligations of the World Bank and the IMF, see: Skogly, *loc. cit.* (note 242). For a different approach in regard to the relationship between the IMF and the Covenant, see the working paper submitted by F. Gianviti (General Counsel of the IMF) to the Committee, 'Economic, social and cultural human rights and the International Monetary Fund'. UN doc. E/C.12/2001/WP.5.

326 In the Concluding Observations of Bulgaria, the Committee recommended 'that in negotiations with international financial institutions, the State party take into account its obligations to respect, protect and fulfil all the rights enshrined in the Covenant.' Concluding Observations Bulgaria E/2000/22 para. 236. In the same vein, see, for example, Concluding Observations Cameroon E/2000/22 para. 352 and Concluding Observations Argentina E/2000/22 para. 276. See, also, for example, Concluding Observations Georgia E/2001/22 para. 96; Concluding Observations Egypt E/2001/22 para. 170; and Concluding Observations Senegal E/C.12/1/Add.62 para. 60.

327 In the text accompanying notes No. 242-243 the first level of obligations (duties to respect) pertaining to developing States and their relationship with international financial institutions have been analysed.

Trade Organisation).[328] For example, in the Concluding Observations of Nepal, 'the Committee strongly recommends that Nepal's obligations under the Covenant should be taken into account in all aspects of its negotiations with international financial institutions, like the International Monetary Fund, World Bank and the World Trade Organisation, to ensure that economic, social and cultural rights, particularly of the most vulnerable groups, are duly protected.'[329] Since the Committee's twenty-first session held in 1999, it has incorporated this statement in most Concluding Observations of developing States which have negotiated with international financial institutions.[330]

Therefore, States Parties to the Covenant have the 'duty to take into account the obligations under the Covenant' in all negotiations with financial institutions with the aim being to ensure that any programme undertaken in agreement with these institutions is consistent with their obligations under the Covenant. This means that States Parties are not only obliged to avoid implementing policies that may negatively affect the enjoyment of the Covenant's rights, but also that they must comply with the duty to protect.

According to the Committee, the second level (to protect) implies that States Parties must take measures to protect vulnerable groups in society from any adverse effects that they may have suffered due to the measures adopted as a consequence of an agreement with an international financial institution or international organisation. The Committee's approach in this regard has developed consistently over the years. In 1996, for example, the Concluding Observations of Philippines stated that '[t]he Committee recalls that every effort must be made in times of structural adjustment to ensure that the basic economic social and cultural rights of the poorest and most disadvantaged sectors of the population are protected to the greatest extent possible.'[331] In 1997, when examining the report of Guinea, the Committee noted that the Government had negotiated an agreement with the World Bank and the IMF and stressed that '[i]n this regard, the Committee emphasises, [...], that from the point of view of the Covenant and its interpretation by the Committee, any reform measures must be accompanied by

328 In regard to States' obligations as members of the WTO see the 'statement of the CESCR to the Third Ministerial Conference of the World Trade Organisation. Adopted at its twenty-first session, 47th meeting held on 26 November 1999. E/C.12/1999/11, Annex VII, para. 8.

329 Concluding Observations Nepal E/C.12/Add.66 para. 8.

330 See, for example, Concluding Observations Mexico E/2000/22 para. 396; Concluding Observations Egypt E/2001/22 para. 170; Concluding Observations Senegal E/C.12/1/Add.62 para. 60; Concluding Observations Syrian Arab Republic E/C.12/1/Add.63 para. 29; and Concluding Observations Ukraine E/C.12/1/Add.65 para. 20. In the case of Cameroon, Bulgaria and Argentina which were examined during the twenty-first session in 1999, although the Committee did not include the same wording it expressly indicated the duties of the State to respect, protect and fulfil all rights enshrined in the Covenant when negotiating with international financial institutions. See section 3.2.

331 Concluding Observations Philippines E/1996/22 para. 124.

the adoption of targeted programmes designed to protect the vulnerable groups and members of society.'[332]

The Committee has paid particular attention to the requirement that the State must establish social safety nets to protect the economic, social and cultural rights of the most vulnerable groups of society in times of structural adjustment measures.[333] For example, in the Concluding Observations on the first report of Morocco the Committee stated that it 'wishes to bring to the attention of the State party the need to adopt further measures to provide adequate safety nets for the vulnerable sectors of society affected by structural adjustment programmes.'[334]

In recent years, when the Committee has found that the policies and programmes undertaken by States Parties in agreements with financial institutions have negatively affected the enjoyment of the Covenant, it has expressly noted this in the Concluding Observations and subsequently recommended that States re-evaluate and adjust them in accordance with the requirements of the Covenant.[335] It is interesting to note that General Comment No. 14 is very strong in this regard and considers that there is a 'violation' of the Covenant in the event that the State fails 'to take into account its legal obligations regarding the right to health when entering into bilateral or multilateral agreements with other States, international organisations and other entities, such as multinational corporations.'[336]

In sum, from the Committee's Concluding Observations, it is possible to conclude that developing States must take into account their obligations under the Covenant in relation to the design and implementation of programmes that specifically target the protection of the most vulnerable groups within society when negotiating with international financial institutions. It is the responsibility of the States Parties to the Covenant to take the necessary preventive measures to ensure that vulnerable groups do not suffer adverse effects when they implement plans and policies negotiated with international financial institutions.

---

332 Concluding Observations Guinea E/1997/22 para. 194. See, in addition, Concluding Observations Mali E/1995/22 para. 353.

333 During its tenth session, on May 16,1994 the Committee held a day of general discussion on 'The role of social safety nets as a means of protecting economic, social and cultural rights, with particular reference to situations involving major structural adjustment and/or transition to a free market economy.' E/1995/22, Chapter VI, paras. 363–390.

334 Concluding Observations Morocco E/1995/22 para. 119. See, in addition, Concluding Observations Surinam E/1996/22 para. 154 and Concluding Observations Algeria E/1996/22 paras. 284 and 300.

335 See, for example, Concluding Observations Bulgaria E/2000/22 paras. 221 and 236; Concluding Observations Argentina E/2000/22 paras. 258 and 276; and Concluding Observations Cameroon E/2000/22 para. 352.

336 General Comment No. 14 para. 50. The Committee classifies this obligation under the 'obligation to respect.' In the present study this obligation has been classified as an 'obligation to protect', because in the light of the Concluding Observations, the emphasis is on the positive actions that States are required to undertake rather than on the duty to refrain from intervening.

B. *Developed States*

Given the character of international human rights obligations and the principle of good faith, it is to be expected that States Parties to the Covenant comply with their obligations in all their spheres of activity, at the national and international levels. Therefore, when States Parties take actions through international organisations of which they are members, they are expected to take into account the duties to respect, protect and fulfil the rights enshrined in the Covenant.

Already in 1990, the Committee addressed (in a General Comment) the role that international organisations, such as the World Bank and the IMF, should play in the implementation of the Covenant.[337] However, it was not until nearly ten years later that the Committee began to clarify the responsibility of the States Parties to the Covenant who are also members of those organisations. In recent years, the Committee has suggested that the States Parties to the Covenant must seek the implementation of the Covenant through their actions within international financial institutions such as the World Bank and the IMF. Thus far, the Committee has stressed this duty in regard to States Parties which are viewed as having an influence in the decision-making organs of the international financial institutions.

At its twenty-second Session,[338] when examining the report of Italy the Committee 'encouraged' the Government 'as a member of international organisations, in particular IMF and the World Bank, to do all it can to ensure that the policies and decisions of those organisations are in conformity with the obligations of States Parties to the Covenant, in particular the obligations contained in article 2, paragraph 1, concerning international assistance and co-operation.'[339] The Committee repeated the same statement at its twenty-fourth session in regard to Belgium.[340] In the Concluding Observations adopted at the twenty-sixth extraordinary session,[341] the Committee again included the same statement in the Concluding Observations of Japan[342] and Germany.[343] Moreover, the Committee has indicated with more precision some of the provisions of the Covenant which contain the obligations that States are required to take into account. Thus, according to the Committee, as members of international financial institutions, in particular the IMF and the World Bank, States are required to do 'all they can' to ensure that the policies and decisions of those organisations are in conformity with the obligations of States Parties to the Covenant, in particular the obligations contained in article 2(1),[344] article 11 (the right to adequate standard of living including

337 General Comment No. 2 on 'International technical assistance measures (article 22)'.

338 Held in Geneva from 25 April to 12 May 2000.

339 Concluding Observations Italy E/2001/22 para. 126.

340 Concluding Observations Belgium E/2001/22 para. 493.

341 Held in Geneva from 13 to 31August 2001.

342 Concluding Observations Japan E/C.12/1/Add.67 para. 37.

343 Concluding Observations Germany E/C.12/1/Add.68 para. 31.

344 The obligations imposed by article 2(1) ICESCR are analysed in Chapter VII.

food, clothing and housing), article 15 (the right of everyone to take part in cultural life and to enjoy the benefits of scientific progress), article 22 (technical assistance measures of all United Nations Organs and the specialised agencies concerned),[345] and article 23 ICESCR.[346]

With this statement, the Committee suggests that States Parties to the Covenant have the duty to ensure that the policies and decisions of the international financial institutions of which they are members are in conformity with the obligations imposed by the Covenant. By encouraging States to 'do all they can' it is apparent that the Committee implies more than merely a negative obligation to refrain from designing or supporting policies or programmes that would violate the Covenant's rights but, rather, a much more active role aimed at the implementation of the Covenant, particularly the obligation to assist and co-operate with other States. However, the Committee's approach is still too broad. It would be appropriate for the Committee to develop further the obligations of States Parties in this regard.

6. *Duty to regulate the provision of public services provided by private entities*

In the Concluding Observations, the Committee notes the importance of the duty to protect against third party violations in the context of the privatisation of public services. From a close reading of the Concluding Observations, it is possible to conclude that when States Parties privatise the provision of public goods, they remain responsible for regulating the activities of the providers so as to prevent them from violating the Covenant's rights.[347] This in apparent in the Concluding Observations in which the Committee has stressed that States must take measures to regulate services provided

345 See General Comment No. 2, particularly para. 2.

346 Article 23 ICESCR reads as follows, 'The States Parties to the present Covenant agree that international action for the achievement of the rights recognised in the present Covenant includes such methods as the conclusion of conventions, the adoption of recommendations, the furnishing of technical assistance and the holding of regional meetings and technical meetings for the purpose of consultations and study organised in conjunction with the Governments concerned.'

347 It is interesting to note that when dealing with individual complaints, the Human Rights Committee has also stressed that States Parties are not relieved from their obligations under the Covenant due to the delegation of functions. See, for example, Lindgren *et al.* v. Sweden (Communication Nos. 298-9/88, views of 9 November 1990, para. 6.6) and B.d.B. *et al.* v. the Netherlands, (Communication No. 273/88, inadmissibility decision of 30 March 1989, para. 6.5).

by third parties, for example, in private hospitals,[348] private schools,[349] private prisons,[350] or with regard to the water supply.[351]

In the case of the Philippines, after acknowledging the Government's plan to privatise and decentralise health programmes the Committee stated that, 'while there is no reason that the private sector should not be fully involved in the provision of health services, the Committee emphasises that such an approach does not in any way relieve the Government of its Covenant-based obligation to use all available means to promote adequate access to health-care services, particularly for the poorer segments of the population.'[352] As the Committee has mentioned, States are required to ensure that private health remains affordable to all sectors of society.[353]

With regard to private schools, the Committee has established that States Parties must monitor and guarantee the quality of education provided by private schools,[354] as well as to ensure that their students are not subject to corporal punishment.[355] In the case of private prisons in Australia, the Committee stressed the duty to ensure that labour in these private prisons is voluntarily undertaken and is properly remunerated in conformity with the Covenant.[356]

3.4 Obligations to fulfil

The Committee has indicated that the duty to fulfil incorporates three sub-categories: (a) obligation to facilitate, (b) obligation to provide and (c) obligation to promote. The duties that fall under each of these sub-levels will be analysed separately.

3.4.1 Obligation to fulfil (facilitate)

According to the Committee's approach in its General Comments, the obligation to facilitate implies that the State must take positive measures aimed at enabling and assisting individuals to enjoy the Covenant's rights. Through the Concluding Observations, the Committee refers to this level in broad terms, mainly indicating the necessity

348 It is relevant to recall here General Comment No. 14 which states, 'Obligations to protect include [...] the duties of States [...] to ensure that privatisation of the health sector does not constitute a threat to the availability, accessibility, acceptability and quality of health facilities, goods and services' General Comment No. 14 para. 35. See also, for example, Concluding Observations Italy E/2001/22 para. 237.

349 See, for example, Concluding Observations United Kingdom of Great Britain and Northern Ireland E/1998/22 paras. 299 and 311 and Concluding Observations Armenia E/2000/22 para. 310.

350 See, for example, Concluding Observations Australia (third periodic report) E/C.12/1/Add.50 para. 30.

351 See, for example, Concluding Observations Nepal E/C.12/1/Add.66 para. 30.

352 Concluding Observations Philippines E/1996/22 para. 120.

353 Concluding Observations Finland E/2001/22 para. 457.

354 See, for example, Concluding Observations Armenia E/2000/22 para. 310.

355 See Concluding Observations United Kingdom of Great Britain and Northern Ireland E/1998/22 paras. 299 and 311. In addition, see General Comment No. 13 para. 41.

356 Concluding Observations Australia (Third Periodic Report) E/C.12/1/Add.50 para. 30.

to adopt reforms to combat poverty, to achieve better wealth distribution or to overcome obstacles to the enjoyment of the rights. Through its Concluding Observations the Committee tends not to develop the precise content of this level of obligation. But the precise measures required must be determined by each State. This is in fact an appropriate approach, because the precise measures necessary to facilitate the enjoyment of rights within the territory must be determined by each State and will depend on the particular circumstances of each State Party.

Taking into account the circumstances of the State, the Committee has demonstrated a preference for the adoption of measures that would permit the enjoyment of economic, social and cultural rights in general. For example, when States Parties demonstrate a high degree of concentration of land ownership, the Committee encourages the adoption of agrarian reforms, particularly when they may provide for the distribution of land to peasants, indigenous peoples and rural women.[357]

Despite the fact that the precise duties to facilitate will depend on the specific circumstances of the State, the Committee has provided good examples of how the creation of institutional machinery is an essential component of the obligations that States Parties must comply with in order to implement given rights, such as the right to adequate housing or the right to take part in cultural life.

The Committee has placed particular importance on the duty to facilitate with regard to the right to adequate housing. A good example is provided by the Committee's report on its technical assistance mission to Panama.[358] In this report the Committee members who made an *in loco* visit to Panama gave 'specific examples of housing problems' that they witnessed while they were there. It is interesting to see that many of the 'essential' problems were caused by the lack of institutional machinery to enable individuals to enjoy the right to adequate housing. For example, they observed deficiencies in the legalisation relating to the ownership of the land (non-existence of titles of ownership), the lack of urban development planning in certain zones and a lack of an adequate national housing plan. In other States Parties the Committee has identified the same kinds of problems in the enjoyment of the right to adequate housing.[359] In the light of the recommendations provided by the Committee when facing housing problems, it is possible to conclude that to enable individuals to enjoy the right to adequate housing, States Parties must establish institutional mechanisms for the regularisation

357 See, for example, Concluding Observations Paraguay E/1997/22 paras. 71 and 82; Concluding Observations Peru E/1998/22 para. 141; Concluding Observations Dominican Republic E/1998/22 paras. 204 and 224; Concluding Observations Saint Vincent and the Grenadines E/1998/22 para. 418; Concluding Observations Philippines E/1995/22 para. 119; and Concluding Observations Guatemala E/1997/22 para. 136.

358 Report on the Technical Assistance Mission to Panama of the Committee on Economic, Social and Cultural Rights (16-22 April 1995). E/1996/22, Annex V, pp. 78 *et seq*.

359 See, for example, Concluding Observations Dominican Republic E/1995/22 para. 331; Concluding Observations Canada E/1999/22 para. 421; and Concluding Observations Philippines E/1996/22 paras. 131 and 132.

of property ownership, the protection of security of tenure, and in general they must adopt a national social housing plan to ensure the necessary conditions for the enjoyment of housing rights by individuals.[360] It is interesting to note that the Committee also considers it necessary that States provide incentives to the private sector to participate in the enjoyment of these rights by permitting, for example, the private sector to build or finance housing. But it stresses that this approach does not relieve the government of its Covenant-based obligations to use all available resources.[361]

The establishment of institutional machinery is essential for the protection of many other substantive rights. For example, in order to take part in cultural life (article 15 ICESCR), States must establish certain institutional machinery, such as, declaring the indigenous languages as official languages, allowing them to be used in contacts with public organs and administrative or judicial bodies.[362]

With regard to the duty to facilitate, it is interesting to stress the suggestion of the Committee that States Parties introduce institutional arrangements, within the government administration, to ensure that its obligations under the Covenant are taken into account at an early stage in the Government's formulation of national policies on issues such as social welfare, housing, health and education.[363]

3.4.2 Obligation to fulfil (provide)

The duty to provide a specific right contained in the Covenant when individuals are unable, for reasons beyond their control, to realise that right themselves by the means at their disposal is not addressed by the Committee with great frequency in the Concluding Observations.

The Committee has not frequently required States to directly provide commodities of services for the satisfaction of rights, and when it has done so, it has used 'soft' language (*i.e.* it provides recommendations). Among the situations in which the Committee has recognised that individuals are unable to enjoy rights for reasons beyond their control are cases of persons under detention and mentally ill persons in State institutions, low-income groups and victims of natural disasters.

With regard to prisoners and persons in mental institutions, the Committee requires States to satisfy their basic needs with dignity.[364] For those who live in poverty,

---

360 Report on the Technical Assistance Mission to the Dominican Republic of the Committee on Economic, Social and Cultural Rights (19-27 September 1997). E/C.12/1997/10, Annex VI, para. 91.

361 See, for example, Concluding Observations United Kingdom of Great Britain and Northern Ireland [Hong Kong] E/1997/22 para. 329 and Concluding Observations Philippines E/1996/22 para. 118.

362 See, for example, Concluding Observations Denmark E/C.12/1999/11 para. 95 and Concluding Observations Peru E/1998/22 para. 139.

363 See, for example, Concluding Observations Argentina E/2000/22 para. 275 and Concluding Observations Iceland E/2000/22 para. 85.

364 See, for example, Concluding Observations Dominican Republic E/1997/22 para. 231; Concluding Observations Russian Federation E/1998/22 para. 125; and Concluding Observations Cyprus E/1999/22 para. 288.

although the whole philosophy of the Committee is oriented towards their protection, when it comes to the Concluding Observations, the Committee is very cautious and it does not often require States to directly provide assistance for the enjoyment of the Covenant's rights. In the majority of cases, the Committee only 'recommends' that States provide such assistance.[365] Nonetheless, more recently, the Committee seems to have adopted a stricter approach. In the Concluding Observations of Nepal adopted in the 2001 it stated, '[t]he Committee *urges* the State party to continue to direct resources to those most in need and to report to the Committee on the result of its efforts [...]. In this regard the Committee would like to remind the State party of its obligations, even under severe resource constraints, to protect the vulnerable groups of society, as stated in paragraph 12 of the Committee's General Comment No. 3 (1990) on the nature of States parties' obligations (art. 2, paragraph 1 of the Covenant).' This approach is certainly more in line with the Committee's approach in its General Comment in which it uses stricter language than in the majority of the Concluding Observations.

In order to understand the approach of the Committee to this level of duty in the Concluding Observations, we must bear in mind that the Covenant does not require States to provide for all rights. The provider function of the State only comes into play when people have failed to satisfy their own needs due to circumstances beyond their control. Obviously, the possibilities for States to provide for the satisfaction of rights depend on the availability of resources. Nonetheless, as the Committee has mentioned, even in times of severe resources constraints, States must adopt 'relatively low-cost targeted programmes' for the protection of the most vulnerable members of society[366] and to seek assistance in order to comply with this obligation if necessary.[367] However, in the Concluding Observations, the Committee does not frequently remind States of these duties.[368]

Of the few occasions when the Committee has referred to the duty to directly satisfy the rights in the Concluding Observations, it has perhaps most frequently analysed the right to adequate housing. According to the Concluding Observations, States are required to allocate resources for the construction of low-cost housing or to provide low-

365 For example, the Concluding Observations of the Russian Federation reads, 'the Committee recommends that assistance to those who live in poverty be increased and that adequate financial resources be made available to them so that they can live in dignity. Similar efforts should be undertaken on behalf of pensioners, many of who live in serious financial difficulty.' [Concluding Observations Russian Federation E/1998/22 para. 122]. In the case of Italy, 'The Committee recommends that the State party set up its efforts to assist those living under the poverty line.' [Concluding Observations Italy E/2001/22 para. 136].

366 According to General Comment No. 3 'even in times of severe resources constraints the vulnerable members of society can and indeed must be protected by the adoption of relatively low-cost targeted programmes.' General Comment No. 3 para. 11.

367 See the analysis of the obligations imposed by article 2(1) ICESCR in Chapter VII.

368 See, for exceptions, Concluding Observations Colombia E/1996/22 para. 194 and Concluding Observations Philippines E/1996/22 para. 124.

cost rental housing units for those vulnerable and disadvantaged groups within society.[369]

On occasion, the Committee has also required that States provide sanitation and drinking-water to deprived areas and rural populations.[370] Sometimes the Committee has also required States to make available medicines and medical attention for those who cannot afford it.[371] In this regard it is interesting to note that, exceptionally, the Committee has required States to provide assistance to persons with HIV/AIDS. For example, in the Concluding Observations of Germany it was stated that, 'the Committee urges the State party to provide more adequate assistance to persons with HIV/AIDS, without any discrimination on the basis of race, origin, nationality or gender.'[372]

Through the Concluding Observations, the Committee has noted that the duty to provide also arises in favour of persons who are victims of natural or other disasters, although it has paid little attention to this issue. Examples of this obligation are to be found in the Concluding Observations of Ukraine where the Committee urged the State to provide special assistance and medical care to the victims of Chernobyl[373] and in the Concluding Observations of Japan, where the State was encouraged to speedily assist the poorer victims of an earthquake.[374]

3.4.3 Obligation to fulfil (promote)

Although from the text of the General Comment No. 14 it is not clear whether the Committee only envisaged an obligation to promote with regard to the right to the highest standard of health or, rather with regard to all substantive rights,[375] in the Concluding Observations the obligation to promote has been analysed by the Committee as part of many substantive rights. Therefore, from the Concluding Observations it is apparent that the 'duty to fulfil (promote)' may arise with regard to all substantive rights. The importance that the Committee lays on to the duty to promote in the

369 See, for example, Concluding Observations Panama E/1996/22 para. 311; Concluding Observations Egypt E/2001/22 para. 179; Concluding Observations Nigeria E/1999/22 para. 136; Concluding Observations El Salvador E/1997/22 para. 179; Concluding Observations Philippines E/1996/22 para. 118; Concluding Observations Colombia E/1996/22 para. 198; Concluding Observations United Kingdom of Great Britain and Northern Ireland [Hong Kong] E/1997/22 para. 361; Concluding Observations Mexico E/2000/22 para. 403; and Concluding Observations Italy E/2001/22 para. 129.

370 370 See, for example, Concluding Observations El Salvador E/1997/22 para. 179 and Concluding Observations Dominican Republic E/1998/22 para. 239.

371 See, for example, Concluding Observations Russian Federation E/1998/22 para. 127; Concluding Observations Italy E/2001/22 para. 138; and Concluding Observations Finland E/1997/22 para. 32.

372 Concluding Observations Germany E/1999/22 para. 334. See, also, Concluding Observations Honduras E/C.12/1/Add.57 para. 47.

373 Concluding Observations Ukraine E/1996/22 para. 275.

374 Concluding Observations Japan E/C.12/1/Add.67 paras. 27 and 55.

375 See the analysis of the Committee's approach to the tripartite typology in section 2.

Concluding Observations is in accordance with the Covenant's preamble and the Charter of the United Nations.[376]

In 1995, the Committee noted that 'the exercise of and strengthening of respect for human rights can take place only when there exist awareness of those rights by both the authorities and individuals.'[377] Consequently it decided to undertake the following measures: 'the Committee will regularly consider the efforts made by States Parties to translate into all local languages the texts of international human rights norms and instruments, general comments and concluding observations by the treaty bodies, and reports of any national institutions or government organs entrusted with the promotion and protection of human rights.'[378]

Through its Concluding Observations the Committee has been consistent in this approach. If when examining the report of a State, the Committee observes that the State has not done enough to promote awareness of the rights set forth in the Covenant, it duly demonstrates its concern.[379] The Committee has often required States to undertake training programmes to increase the awareness of the Covenant's rights. In relation to most States the Committee has mentioned which groups within society must be targeted by educational and training programmes in human rights. In many cases it has required States specifically to target parliamentarians, local government officials,

376 Article 1 of the United Nations Charter establishes among the purposes of the organisation, '[t]o achieve international co-operation in solving international problems of an economic, social, cultural or humanitarian character, and in promoting and encouraging respect for human rights and for fundamental freedoms for all without distinction as to race, sex, language, or religion' (Art. 1 No. 3 UN Charter). In the same vein, Art. 55 of the Charter reads, 'with a view to the creation of conditions of stability and well-being which are necessary for peaceful and friendly relations among nations based on respect for the principle of equal rights and self-determination of peoples, the United Nations shall promote: […] universal respect for, and observance of, human rights and fundamental freedoms for all without distinction as to race, sex, language, or religion.' See in addition the Preamble of the Covenant, particularly paragraphs 5 and 6.

377 Conclusions and decisions adopted by the CESCR in the Day of General Discussion 11th Session, 5 December 1994, 'Human Rights education and public information activities relating to the ICESCR'. E/1996/22, Chapter VI, para. 324.

378 Conclusions and decisions adopted by the CESCR in the Day of General Discussion 11th Session, 5 December 1994, 'Human Rights education and public information activities relating to the ICESCR' [E/1996/22, Chapter VI, para. 331]. It is worth noting that the General Assembly has also stressed the importance to the dissemination at the national level of the reports of the Committee, the summary records and the Concluding Observations in several resolutions. See, for example, A/RES/54/157 para. 13 of 8 February 2000, A/RES/54/176 para. 7 of 15 February 2000, A/RES/53/138 para. 24 of 1 March 1999 and A/RES/52/116 para. 15 of 19 February 1998.

379 See, for example, Concluding Observations Dominican Republic E/1997/22 paras. 222 and 242; Concluding Observations Paraguay E/1997/22 paras. 80 and 87; Concluding Observations Spain E/1997/22 para. 106; Concluding Observations Mauritius E/1996/22 paras. 241 and 246; and Concluding Observations Denmark E/2000/22 para. 103.

judges, lawyers, students, teachers, the police and other law enforcement agents.[380] But, curiously enough, it has rarely mentioned other professionals involved in matters relating to economic, social and cultural rights such as social workers, medical personnel and government officials dealing with development or economic planning. Increasingly, however, it has started to mention other groups. For example, in the case of Jordan, the Committee explicitly mentioned care workers and health professionals as target groups for training.[381]

As may be deduced from the Concluding Observations, there is a strong basis for suggesting that States are required to widely disseminate the Concluding Observations adopted by the Committee following the examination of States Parties' reports.[382] The Committee not only requires States to widely disseminate the Concluding Observations adopted but has also paid particular attention to the obligations to promote each substantive right. The enjoyment of many economic, social and cultural rights depends to a great extent on the information level of the individuals in question. The rights cannot be exercised without access to a minimum level of information.

In this regard, special attention has been paid by the Committee to the duty to promote arising from the right to the highest attainable standard of health. For example, the Committee has required States to promote healthy lifestyles among people to improve the quality of their nutrition, to combat alcoholism and smoking and to reduce the risk of cardiovascular disease and cancer.[383] In light of the HIV/AIDS pandemic, the Committee has paid special attention to the importance of a public campaign

---

380 See, for example, Concluding Observations Belarus E/1997/22 para. 293; Concluding Observations Poland E/1999/22 para. 164; Concluding Observations Jordan E/C.12/1/Add.46 para. 338; Concluding Observations Finland E/1997/22 para. 295; Concluding Observations Azerbaijan E/1998/22 para. 358; Concluding Observations Canada E/1999/22 paras. 433 and 434; Concluding Observations Belarus E/1997/22 para. 293; Concluding Observations Portugal [Macao] E/1997/22 para. 265; and Concluding Observations Denmark E/2000/22 para. 119.

381 See Concluding Observations Jordan E/C.12/1/Add.46 paras. 31 and 32. Additionally, in the case of Cyprus, for example, it expressly mentioned trade unions, women's organisations and communities. Concluding Observations Cyprus E/1999/22 para. 291.

382 See, for example, Concluding Observations Australia E/2001/22 para. 402; Concluding Observations Kyrgyzstan E/2001/22 para. 363; Concluding Observations Egypt E/2001/22 para. 185; Concluding Observations Morocco E/C.12/1/Add.55 para. 60; Concluding Observations Jordan E/C.12/1/Add.46 para. 39; Concluding Observations Portugal E/C.12/Add.53 para. 24; Concluding Observations Dominican Republic E/1997/22 para. 242; Concluding Observations Portugal [Macao] E/1997/22 para. 267; Concluding Observations Finland E/1997/22 para. 321; Concluding Observations Zimbabwe E/1998/22 para. 81; Concluding Observations Iraq E/1998/22 para. 283; Concluding Observations the Netherlands E/1999/22 para. 226; Concluding Observations Nigeria E/1999/22 para. 138; and Concluding Observations Iceland E/2000/22 para. 89.

383 See, Concluding Observations Poland E/1999/22 para. 164.

providing information about the nature of the disease, modes of transmission and prevention techniques, including information on contraceptives.[384]

With regard to articles 7 and 8 of the Covenant (*i.e.* the right to work, fair conditions at work as well as the right to join and form trade unions and the right to strike), the Committee has paid special attention to the measures taken by the State to increase awareness among employers, judges of the labour courts and the police in order to guarantee the full implementation of these rights.[385] According to the Committee, the duty to promote is also essential in regard to the prohibition of discrimination against women, particularly for the full implementation of the prohibition of domestic violence. The Committee has urged States to organise public campaigns to raise awareness as regards the problem.[386]

Finally, it is relevant to mention that the Committee has paid particular attention to the duty to promote with regard to the right to education established in article 13 of the Covenant. The Committee has noted that human rights education, which is a component of the right to education, is itself a human right.[387] From the strong language used by the Committee in its Concluding Observations, it is possible to conclude that States Parties are required to take effective steps to ensure that human rights education is included in the curriculum of formal and non-formal education.[388] The Committee's approach in this regard is consistent with the approach of the Human Rights Committee which has also stated in its Concluding Observations that there is a duty to educate individuals as regards a culture of human rights.[389]

3.5 Concluding Comments on the use of the tripartite typology in the Concluding Observations

The tripartite typology is an analytical tool, which assists us to understand the complexities of reality and for that reason it is worth using. The Committee seems to have

---

384 See, for example, Concluding Observations Cameroon E/C.12/1999/11 para. 359; Concluding Observations Dominican Republic E/C.12/1997/10 para. 243; Concluding Observations Russian Federation E/1998/22 para. 127; and Concluding Observations Libyan Arab Jamahiriya E/C.12/1997/10 para. 192.

385 See, for example, Concluding Observations Paraguay E/1997/22 para. 87 and Concluding Observations Peru E/1998/22 para. 162.

386 See, for example, Concluding Observations Italy E/2001/22 para. 133; Concluding Observations Egypt E/2001/22 para. 177; and Concluding Observations Mongolia E/2001/22 para. 281.

387 According to the Committee 'human rights education is itself a human right'. Conclusions and decisions on future actions. Day of General Discussion on 'Human rights education and public information activities relating to the International Covenant on Economic, Social and Cultural Rights.' Eleventh session, 5 December 1994, E/1996/22, Chapter V, para. 324.

388 See, for example, Concluding Observations Australia E/2001/22 para. 400; Concluding Observations Iraq E/1998/22 para. 271; and Concluding Observations Ukraine E/1996/22 para. 276.

389 See, for example, HRC Concluding Observations Hungary CCPR/C/79/Add.22 para. 11 and Concluding Observations Ecuador CCPR/C/79/Add.92 para. 21.

understood this, and it started to explicitly apply the tripartite typology in the General Comments in 1999.

Unfortunately, the Committee has not used the terminology of the tripartite typology (respect/protect/fulfil) with great frequency in its Concluding Observations.[390] As analysed above, in the few cases that the Committee has explicitly referred to the tripartite typology, it has done so in broad terms and has usually only referred to the States' obligations relating to international financial institutions. The scant references that the Committee has made to the tripartite typology when examining States' reports is regrettable because it reflects a lack of consistency between the General Comments and the Concluding Observations. Nonetheless, most of the time it is apparent that the typology underpins the Committee's views in the Concluding Observations. It is therefore possible to arrive at a list of duties which can be derived from each level of obligation.

It would be appropriate if, in the future, the Committee began to expressly apply the terminology of the tripartite typology in its Concluding Observations. If the Committee explicitly used the typology in the Concluding Observations it would provide a better understanding of what States are required to do or refrain from doing in order to fully implement a given right and at the same time contribute to the consolidation of understanding of these concepts. This would assist and facilitate States in the implementation of the Covenant.

4 Concluding Comments

The analysis of the obligations imposed by human rights treaties from the point of view of different types or levels has constituted a great contribution by scholars to the understanding of the nature of State duties. This analysis has provided a new paradigm for examining the obligations imposed by all human rights.

This analytical tool has contributed enormously to the development of economic, social and cultural rights. By stressing that there are no sharp differences between human rights and demonstrating that the distinction between negative and positive rights is a simplification, it has reinforced the principle of the indivisibility of all human rights and has contributed to overcoming the misconception that economic, social and cultural rights are 'secondary' to civil and political rights.

The Committee demonstrated great perspicacity in adopting the tripartite typology in its General Comments. The application of this analytical tool has contributed to the further clarification of the normative content of the substantive rights of the Covenant. However, it would be appropriate if, in the future, the Committee should seek to conso-

390 Among the exceptional cases in which the Committee expressly refers to the tripartite typology in the Concluding Observations, see, for example, Concluding Observations Bulgaria E/2000/22 para. 236; Concluding Observations Argentina E/2000/22 para. 276; and Concluding Observations Dominican Republic E/19997/22 para. 236.

lidate its understanding of the typology and articulate its vision through the General Comments and Concluding Observations. In particular, it would be helpful for the Committee to apply the typology with greater consistency when considering States' reports.

Proposed by:	Duties to:				
Shue	Avoid depriving	Protect from deprivation	Aid deprived		
Eide	Respect	Protect	Facilitate	Fulfil	
Van Hoof	Respect	Protect	Ensure		Promote
Steiner & Alston	Respect	Protect/Prevent	Create institutional machinery	Provide Goods and services	Promote
The Committee	Respect	Protect	Fulfil		
			Facilitate	Provide	Promote

Figure 2: Approaches to typologies of State duties imposed by human rights treaties

PART THREE: OBLIGATIONS IMPOSED BY PART II OF THE COVENANT AT THE PRESENT STAGE OF INTERNATIONAL HUMAN RIGHTS LAW

Over the years, the Committee has provided a deeper understanding of the provisions contained in Part II of the Covenant. The aim of the Third Part of the study is to provide a systematic analysis of these provisions as they should be understood in the present stage of international law.

International human rights instruments are historical documents. This means that they were created at a certain time and that as instruments of social regulation they need to be interpreted according to prevailing social conditions. Only in so far as those who apply the instruments, such as judges, legislators, administrators, experts and private individuals, take into account changing realities will these instruments continue to be effective.

Part II of the Covenant contains articles 2 to 5 thereof. Articles 4 and 5 are analysed in Chapter VI together with a general survey of the obligations imposed by Part II. Chapter VII analyses article 2(1) ICESCR. This provision is of the utmost importance for understanding the obligations imposed by the Covenant and therefore it requires more in-depth examination. Chapter VIII analyses article 2(2), article 2(3) and article 3 ICESCR. These provisions refer to the principle of equality and non-discrimination and are therefore analysed together in the same Chapter.

In the following analysis, the meaning and scope of the obligations will be illustrated using the interpretation provided by the Committee in the Concluding Observations and General Comments. It must be stressed that the Concluding Observations quoted are meant to be illustrative as to what the Committee has said and they do not exhaust all instances in which the Committee may have expressed its opinion or ideas.

CHAPTER VI
GENERAL SURVEY OF PART II OBLIGATIONS

1 OBLIGATIONS IMPOSED BY PART II OF THE COVENANT

1.1 Introduction

In the previous chapters we have seen that the obligations imposed by each substantive right of the Covenant may be divided for analytical purposes into four levels: duties to respect, protect, fulfil and promote. We have stressed that to fully comply with a given substantive right contained in articles 6 to 15 of the ICESCR, States must satisfy all levels of obligations which are correlative to that right.

However, as mentioned in the introductory chapter, the obligations which are correlative to each of the substantive rights are not the only obligations imposed by the Covenant.[1] The text of the Covenant also contains a variety of obligations which are not correlative to any substantive right, although compliance therewith is fundamental for the proper implementation of the substantive rights.

To fully understand this, we should consider the structure of the Covenant. The provisions of the Covenant are divided into five Parts. Part I contains only one provision, article 1 which recognises the right of self-determination. Part II contains articles 2 to 5 which are general provisions applicable to all substantive rights contained in the Covenant. Part III contains the substantive rights of the Covenant in articles 6 to 15. Part IV (articles 16 to 23) establishes the supervisory system of the Covenant. Finally, Part V (articles 26 to 31) contains miscellaneous provisions, such as provisions on the ratification and entry into force of the treaty. The last-mentioned Part does not include States' duties.[2]

Based on the structure of the Covenant, we may divide the obligations it imposes into three categories: (1) Rights-based obligations imposed by Part III and Part I of the

1 See the Introduction, section 3.

2 Arguably, the only exception might be Article 28 ICESCR which establishes: 'The provision of the present Covenant shall extend to all parts of federal States without any limitation or exception.' However, this provision was envisaged by the drafters as a way to stress the validity of the Covenant in Federal States, rather than a State obligation. For further study see Nowak's analysis of article 50 ICCPR (Nowak, M.: *U.N. Covenant on Civil and Political Rights Commentary*, N.P. Engel Publisher, Kehl/Strasbourg/Arlington, (1993), pp. 636-638.

Covenant,[3] (2) General or basic obligations imposed by Part II, and (3) Procedural obligations imposed by Part IV.

The first group of obligations are those correlative to each substantive right of the Covenant (articles 6 to 15 ICESCR). These obligations are those that for analytical purposes, we may divide into the obligations to respect, protect, fulfil and promote. The obligations imposed by Part IV are related to the supervision process of the Covenant. The key obligation of this Part is the obligation to submit reports contained in article 16 ICESCR. These obligations are beyond the scope of the present study.

The obligations subject to our analysis here are those imposed by the provisions contained in Part II of the Covenant. Part II of the Covenant is composed of four articles: article 2 (general obligation clause), article 3 (duty to treat men and women equally in the enjoyment of rights), article 4 (general limitation clause) and article 5 (interpretation rules). As we will see, these provisions are essential for the implementation of the Covenant. Although these provisions do not directly concern the recognition of substantive rights, they prescribe the way in which States must behave in order to protect and guarantee the substantive rights contained in Part III. This being said, particular consideration should be given to article 2(2) and article 3 ICESCR. These two provisions may be seen as containing substantive rights to the extent that they provide individuals in general (article 2(2)) and women in particular (article 3) with a right to 'equal treatment.' However, as we will see, the fact that they were placed in Part II of the Covenant, rather than in Part III together with the substantive rights, suggests that rather than providing for an autonomous right of equality, they establish a general State obligation to give effect to the rights enshrined in the Covenant in a non-discriminatory way.

The obligations arising from Part II of the ICESCR are crucial for the implementation of the Covenant. While the most relevant of these are certainly the obligations imposed by article 2 ICESCR, all of the provisions contained in Part II are essential for the effective protection of economic, social and cultural rights. Unfortunately, despite their relevance, the provisions contained in Part II have not received the attention that they deserve.

For several years the provisions contained in Part II of the Covenant were neglected during the examination of States Parties' reports. The reporting cycle established by the ECOSOC in 1976 required States to submit reports in biannual stages. In the first stage States were to provide information on articles 6 to 9, the second stage covered articles 10 to 12 and the third stage articles 13 to 15 of the Covenant.[4] This scheme

3 As mentioned earlier, the duties imposed by the right to self-determination may also be considered as 'rights-based duties'. See Introduction, section 3.

4 ECOSOC Res. 1988 (LX) of 11 May 1976.

gave little opportunity to the supervisory bodies (first the Working Groups and then the Committee) to develop the normative content of the obligations arising from Part II.[5]

When the Committee began its sessions in 1987, it recognised the inadequacy of this procedure and recommended that ECOSOC should amend it. In 1988 ECOSOC changed the scheme,[6] establishing a global unified report covering all rights enumerated in the Covenant (the first report within two years of the entry into force of the Covenant and, thereafter, periodic reports at five-year intervals). However, it took some time before the transition to the new scheme was completed.[7]

The obligation to submit a single global report implies that States must report on articles 1 to 15 ICESCR and provide all the information necessary for the Committee to make a proper evaluation of compliance with the Covenant. Therefore, in contrast with the old reporting cycle, States are now required to provide information on the provisions contained in Part II of the Covenant, particularly the difficulties encountered in their implementation. However, in practice States do not tend to pay adequate attention to the articles contained in Part II of the Covenant. While States generally provide information on articles 2(2) (non-discrimination) and 3 (equal treatment of men and women),[8] that information has tended to be insufficient or not directly relevant for the proper evaluation of the extent to which they comply with these obligations. Furthermore, only a few States submit information regarding articles 4 and 5 of the Covenant.[9]

The lack of attention that States have tended to give to the provisions contained in Part II is in part due to the fact that the 'Revised Guidelines Regarding the Form and

5 In the 'General Guidelines regarding the form and contents of reports to be submitted by States Parties under articles 16 and 17 of the International Covenant on Economic, Social and Cultural Rights, in accordance with the programme established by Economic and Social Council Resolution 1988 (LX),' States were not required to provide information on articles 2 to 5 independently, rather they were merely required to 'give full attention to the matters dealt with in Part I and II of the Covenant' when reporting on the substantive rights covered by the reports. E/C.12/1987/2 of 24 December 1986, paras. 5, 32 and 52.

6 ECOSOC Res. 1988/4 of May 1988. UN doc. E/C.12/1989/4.

7 Although the Committee decided not to receive any further triennial reports after 1 January 1995 [E/1994/23 para. 363], for a certain period of time the Committee still considered reports from the old reporting circle.

8 See, for example, Third Periodic Report Portugal E/1994/104/Add.20, 22 May 1998; Fourth Periodic Report Ukraine E/C.12/4/Add.2, 21 March 2000; Fourth Periodic Report Germany E/C.12/4/Add3, 10 August 2000; and Fourth Periodic Report Sweden E/C.12/4/Add.4, 8 August 2000.

9 In many cases States' reports provide information on articles 2 and 3 and then jump to article 6. Nevertheless, there are exceptions. For example, the Third Periodic Report of Mexico deals with all articles contained in Part II of the Covenant (Arts. 2 to 6) [E/1994/104/Add.18 of 27 January 1998], although it does not provide appropriate or relevant information on each of them.

Contents of Reports'[10] require States to report on 'the general provisions of the Covenant,' but only contain questions on article 2 ICESCR. The Reporting Guidelines do not directly require information on articles 4 and 5, nor on article 3, despite its indisputable importance.[11]

The lack of attention to the provisions contained in Part II of the Covenant is undoubtedly a shortcoming on the part of the Guidelines. The decision not to expressly include articles 3, 4 and 5 in the Guidelines may have been viewed as being necessary in order to reach a compromise between different approaches presented in the Committee at the time when the Guidelines were drafted.[12] Nevertheless, it would have been desirable if the Committee had paid more attention in the Guidelines to the provisions contained in Part II.

The most relevant contribution of the Committee to the development of the normative content of the provisions of Part II is the landmark General Comment No. 3 of 1990, which is the Committee's most comprehensive analysis of a provision contained in Part II. However, the Committee seems to have neglected the importance of Part II provisions in its subsequent General Comments and has not addressed these provisions with sufficient attention. As a result, the Committee has lost important opportunities to clarify the normative content of Part II provisions.

Nonetheless, in spite of the deficiencies of the Guidelines and the lack of additional General Comments dealing with Part II provisions, so far the examination of States Parties' reports has provided the Committee with opportunities to develop the normative content of the provisions of Part II. Thus, over the years the Committee has developed a deeper understanding of the provisions contained in Part II of the Cove-

---

10 'Revised guidelines regarding the form and contents of reports to be submitted by States Parties under articles 16 and 17 of the International Covenant on Economic, Social and Cultural Rights.' UN doc. E/C.12/1991/1 of 17 June 1991, part A. [Hereinafter referred to as 'Reporting Guidelines' or 'Guidelines'].

11 Nonetheless, it is important to note that when dealing with many of the substantive rights, the Guidelines contain questions with regard to discrimination and equal treatment of men and women. For example, under Arts. 6 and 7 the Guidelines require information regarding non-discrimination and equal treatment of men and women [*e.g.* Guideline No. 6 Nos. 2 (a), 3(a), (b) and (c) and Art. 7 No. 2(c), 4(a)]. However, it would be desirable if the Guidelines directly addressed the issue of the unequal treatment of men and women under article 3. A general approach to the issue of equal treatment in the light of article 3 would provide a better opportunity to directly deal with the matter in a more comprehensive way. It is interesting to note that some Committee members have expressly noted that the omission of article 3 in the Reporting Guidelines is a shortcoming. See, for example, Ms. Jiménez Butragueño in E/C.12/2000/SR.15 para. 36.

12 During the drafting of the Guidelines there were basically two opposing approaches within the Committee. Some members were of the opinion that the Guidelines should include concise questions in order to enable States to provide brief reports while others considered it necessary to include lengthy questions in order to provide States with a clear picture of what was required. [See Alston, 1992, pp. 497-498]. The final decision seems to indicate that the Committee opted for a more precise set of guidelines albeit with significant shortcomings, such as the omission of articles 3, 4 and 5 of the ICESCR.

nant. However, we must recognise that there are still some uncertainties as to the scope and extent of the obligations imposed by the Covenant, particularly regarding article 2 ICESCR.

It would be appropriate for the Committee to pay more direct attention to these provisions, particularly through future General Comments. A clearer and better delineation of the obligations imposed by Part II of the Covenant will facilitate the implementation of the Covenant.

The present study attempts to provide practical guidance as to the scope and content of the obligations of Part II and to elucidate the minimum requirements with which a State must comply in order to fulfil the obligations contained therein. A detailed analysis of the meaning and scope of the obligations imposed by Part II ICESCR will enhance the protection of the substantive rights contained in the Covenant. Such an analysis may provide the tools for individuals and groups to formulate some of their economic and social claims in terms of non-compliance with State duties, thereby facilitating the work of the supervisory bodies.

The analysis of the Committee's work is the most obvious source for determining the current meaning and scope of the obligations imposed by the Covenant. Nevertheless, to the extent that it is pertinent, the work of other international bodies will also be mentioned. As previously discussed,[13] we must bear in mind that the Committee does not develop its views in a vacuum. On the contrary, it takes into account the developments achieved in human rights law by a variety of international actors, including the UN organs, specialised agencies, NGOs and in the academic literature. The work of all of these different actors provides what Mahoney has called 'the empirical evidence of the evolution'[14] that proves the existence of a generalised progress in the protection of economic, social and cultural rights. As the Committee has explicitly noted,[15] the developments achieved by other international actors are reflected in a 'contemporary interpretation' of the Covenant that States are required to respect.

When undertaking an analysis of the obligations imposed by Part II of the Covenant, it is important to bear in mind that the scope of the obligations that we identify might establish a lesser standard than one might expect or a standard which is lower than might be necessary for the protection of these rights in many parts of the world. But identifying the present standards may contribute to the work of human rights advocates by encouraging them to lobby for improvements in the protection of these rights. Moreover, as discussed, the special characteristics of human rights treaties require that interpretation should evolve with the times. Therefore, the scope of the obligations may differ from what was envisaged by the drafters, it is not static. The

13 See the analysis in Chapter II section 3.
14 Mahoney, 1990, p. 73.
15 See, for example, General Comment No. 13 para. 5.

meaning of the obligations will vary over the years and it is precisely for this reason that international human rights law is frequently described as being dynamic.

1.2 The question of the nature and nomenclature of obligations enshrined in Part II of the Covenant

It is beyond doubt that the provisions of Part II of the Covenant, as with Part II of ICCPR, are applicable in relation to all substantive rights. The provisions of Part II of the Covenant are undertakings of a general nature that States must fulfil in relation to each of the rights contained in articles 6 to 15 of the ICESCR.

In its General Comments, the Committee has tended to refer to the obligations imposed by Part II as 'general obligations.'[16] In General Comment Nos. 13 and 14, the Committee incorporated specific sections aimed at addressing 'general legal obligations' as a category of obligations separate from 'specific legal obligations.'[17] In general, this is a useful distinction although the Committee has not been sufficiently rigorous in its analysis. It has not clearly established the content of the two sections nor has it paid sufficient attention to all of the provisions contained in Part II of the Covenant.[18]

It would be desirable if the Committee were to further develop its analysis in future General Comments. The Committee could provide further clarity if, in future General Comments on substantive rights, it incorporated a detailed analysis of the obligations

---

16 See for example, General Comment No. 3 para. 1. Both General Comment No. 5 and No. 6 incorporate in their respective texts a specific heading: 'general obligations of States Parties.' General Comment No. 5 heading I paragraphs 8 to12 and General Comment No. 6 heading 4 paragraphs 16 to 19. The Human Rights Committee also seems to consider obligations imposed by Part II ICCPR as 'general obligations.' In fact, it calls obligations imposed by articles 2 and 5 'general undertakings by the States'. See, for example, A.M. on behalf of his wife v. Finland, Communication No. 398/1990, inadmissibility decision of 23 July 1992, para. 4.2 and M.G.B. and S.P. v. Trinidad and Tobago, Communication No. 268/1987, inadmissibility decision of 3 November 1989, para. 6.2.

17 In General Comment No. 13 the analysis of 'general legal obligations' is found in paragraphs 43 to 48 and the 'specific legal obligations' are analysed in paragraphs 49 to 57. In General Comment No. 14 the analysis of 'general legal obligations' is found in paragraphs 30 to 33 and the 'specific legal obligations' are analysed in paragraphs 34 to 37.

18 Part II provisions are analysed under 'general legal obligations' but also under another heading called 'special topics of broad application' in which the Committee has tended to mix the analysis of obligations under Part II provisions, such as Art. 2(2) (non-discrimination) and Art. 4 (limitations), with some other topics. Moreover, under the heading 'specific legal obligations' the Committee has tended to mix the analysis of correlative obligations (*e.g.* those examined under the 'tripartite typology') with obligations arising from reading Part II provisions in conjunction with the substantive rights (*e.g.* the obligation to monitor the rights and the obligation to assist and co-operate). From this author's perspective, these headings may cause confusion and it would be desirable if all Part II provisions were to be analysed under the same heading and not intertwined with others topics. Within the current structure of General Comments, one can lose sight of the fact that all provisions under Part II contain legal obligations of a general character applicable to each of the substantive rights contained in Part III.

arising from Part II provisions (articles 2 to 5) in conjunction with each specific substantive right under the heading 'general legal obligations'. Consequently, under the heading 'specific legal obligations,' it should analyse those obligations correlative to the substantive rights using the tripartite typology, but taking due care to avoid mixing the content of both sections.

The implementation of the Covenant would benefit if, in future, the Committee were to provide a careful explanation of the meaning of each Part II provision in conjunction with a substantive right. To provide this analysis the Committee may choose between employing the terminology used in General Comment Nos. 13 and 14 ('general obligations' and 'specific obligations'), while improving their content, or it could borrow the terminology used by scholars. For example, it might adopt the terminology used by Craven and employ the term 'basic obligations'[19] to describe the obligations imposed by Part II. It might also employ the terminology that has been used to describe the obligations imposed by Part II of the ICCPR[20] and to term them 'supporting guarantees.'[21]

An important issue relating to Part II which should be addressed by the Committee is the question of the independent or ancillary character of all the provisions contained in that Part of the Covenant. In other words, whether Part II provisions can be violated independently or if a simultaneous violation of a substantive right is necessary. The nature of Part II provisions has been thoroughly discussed with regard to the ICCPR. The Human Rights Committee, as well as scholars, seem to agree that the provisions contained in Part II ICCPR have an ancillary character. In other words, they consider that the obligations imposed by Part II ICCPR cannot be violated independently, and that violations can occur only in conjunction with a substantive right. However, at least in regard to article 2 ICCPR, there seem to be two different positions. According to Nowak, a violation of article 2 can occur only in conjunction with a substantive right. However, as he explains, the accessory character of article 2 does not mean that it can be violated only when some other provision of the Covenant has also been violated.[22]

---

19 As explained by Craven, 'the rights in Part III of the Covenant are universally governed by the terms of Part II (articles 2-5), which outlines the *basic obligations* undertaken by States in the implementation of the rights.' Craven, 1999, p. 107.

20 Part II of the ICCPR also contains arts. 2 to 5. Although article 2 of each Covenant has a different wording, they play the same role in establishing the nature of the obligations of their respective Covenant (the implication of the different wording is analysed in Chapter IV section 2.3). Articles 3 and 5 of each Covenant have almost the same wording, and both articles 4 may be seen as limitation clauses.

21 Joseph, S.; Schultz, J. and Castan, M.: *The International Covenant on Civil and Political Rights: cases, materials and commentary*, Oxford University Press, Oxford, (2000), pp. 7-9.

22 For a further analysis of the issue, see Nowak, *op. cit.* (note 2), pp. 34-36. To illustrate the point Nowak notes that 'Art. 6(2) does not prohibit the death penalty for the most serious crimes. As a result, a State Party may impose the death penalty for premeditated murder. If it sets this down in law for blacks only and not for whites, then article 6 alone has not been violated but rather the prohibition of discrimination in Art. 2(1) in conjunction with Art. 6.' (p. 35).

In contrast, Joseph *et al.* argue that all provisions contained in Part II of the ICESCR (articles 2 to 5, which they call 'supporting guarantees'), cannot be autonomously violated by a State Party. As they argue, 'violations cannot occur unless there is a *simultaneous violation* of a substantive right in Part III of the Covenant.'[23] This position seems to find support in some case law.[24]

With regard to the ICESCR, it is clear that as is the case with Part II of its sister Covenant, articles 2 to 5 have an accessory character in the sense that they are necessarily connected with the exercise of a substantive right contained in Part III (articles 6 to 15 ICESCR). However, it has not been clearly established by the Committee whether Part II provisions can be violated independently or if violations can only occur together with a simultaneous violation of a substantive right.[25] This is an important issue in light of the possible adoption of an optional protocol to the Covenant establishing a complaint procedure. In the debate on the content of such a protocol, the Committee has argued in favour of the application of the procedure to Part II of the Covenant and it would therefore be appropriate for the Committee to explicitly address this point.[26]

If this approach is adopted, complaints could be submitted for a violation of any of the rights contained in Part II of the Covenant (articles 2 to 5). Due to the dependent character of these provisions, it would be necessary for individuals to allege violations of these provisions in conjunction with one or several substantive rights such as article 2(2) (non-discrimination) or article 3 (equal treatment of men and women) in the enjoyment of, say, the right to housing or the right to the highest standard of health. Similarly, an alleged violation of article 4 (limitation clause), would necessarily be analysed in relation to restrictions imposed on the exercise of a substantive right

23 Joseph *et al.*, *op. cit.* (note 21), p. 8 (emphasis added).

24 See, for example, Lubicon Lake Band v. Canada, Communication No. 167/1984, views of 26 March 1990 and E.P. *et al.* v Colombia, Communication No. 318/1988, inadmissibility decision of 25 July 1990.

25 The Committee's approach is clear with regard to the non-discrimination provision. As we will see in Chapter VIII, a violation of article 2(2) or article 3 ICESCR does not require the simultaneous violation of a substantive right. See Chapter VIII section 2.1.

26 See, 'Report of the Committee to the Commission on Human Rights on a draft optional protocol for the consideration of communications concerning the non-compliance with the International Covenant on Economic, Social and Cultural Rights.' E/1997/22, Annex IV, paras. 24-31. In this report the Committee states that the complaint procedure should apply in relation not only to substantive rights (articles 6 to 15) but also to the articles contained in Part II of the Covenant. This 'comprehensive approach' in regard to rights that should be covered by the procedure seems to have found the greatest support since the beginning of the study on the adoption of a complaint procedure. However, there are still some doubts about the application of the procedure to article 1 ICESCR (right to self- determination). See, for example, the 'Draft Report of the Committee on Economic, Social and Cultural Rights to the Economic and Social Council in accordance with Economic and Social Council Resolution 1985/17 [E/C.12/1992/CRP.2/Add.3 paras. 68-78 of 10 December 1992]. This position is in line with the proposal by Mr. Alston in E/C.12/1991/WP.2 of 25 October 1991, E/C.12/1992/WP.9 of 27 November 1992 and E/C.12/1994/12 of 9 November 1994.

contained in Part III of the Covenant. However, from the present author's perspective, Nowak's approach is also valid as regards the ICESCR. A violation of Part II provisions does not necessarily presuppose a breach of a substantive right. Part II provisions can be violated even when a provision contained in Part III has not been violated independently.[27] For example, if a State Party imposes restrictions on the enjoyment of welfare benefits, *e.g.* by reducing food coupons which it gives to single mothers, the facts may show that there has not been a violation of article 11 itself, but rather that there has been a violation of article 4 in conjunction with article 11 ICESCR.[28]

2 Selected issues under Part II of the Covenant

2.1 Personal scope of the Covenant

Generally, under human rights instruments, rights are granted to 'everyone' and not only to nationals of States Parties. Therefore, in general, non-nationals also benefit from the rights guaranteed in human rights instruments.[29] Of course this general rule has some exceptions, as, for example, with regard to political participation.[30]

Exceptionally, some instruments for the protection of economic, social and cultural rights include limitations on the enjoyment of their rights by non-nationals. For example, in the European Social Charter, rights are guaranteed to nationals of the Contracting State and to foreigners 'only insofar as they are nationals of other Contracting parties lawfully resident or working regularly within the territory of the

27 The exception is article 5 ICESCR. See the analysis below in section 4 of the present Chapter.

28 See discussion in Chapter VIII, section 2.1.

29 This means, for example, that everyone under the jurisdiction of the State must be protected against torture or ill-treatment, or enjoys the freedom of religion or the right not to be arbitrarily killed.

30 The UDHR preamble states: 'Recognition of the inherent dignity and of the equal and inalienable rights of all members of the human family [...].'; Art. 1: 'All human beings are born free and equal in dignity and rights [...]'; Art. 2: 'Everyone is entitled to all the rights and freedoms set forth in this declaration, without distinction [...]'; and Art. 2 of the ICCPR states: 'Each State Party has to respect and to ensure *to all individuals within its territory and subject to its jurisdiction* the rights recognised in the Covenant' (emphasis added). Exceptionally some of the rights are expressly applicable to citizens as Art. 25 while article 13 applies only to aliens. See also: HRC's General Comment No. 15. The ACHR establishes in its Preamble: 'Recognising that the essential rights of man are not derived from one's being a national of a certain state, but are based upon attributes of the human personality [...]', and Art. 1 reads: 'To ensure to all persons subject to their jurisdiction the free and full exercise of those rights and freedoms, without discrimination [...]'. The ECHR establishes that the rights are granted to 'everyone within their jurisdiction' (Art. 1) with some limited exceptions such as articles 5 and 16. The AfCHR establishes in Art. 2 that, 'every individual shall be entitled to the enjoyment of the rights and freedoms [...] without distinction of any kind [...]'. Finally, we may note with regard to CERD, that Art. 1(2) can be viewed as a limitation; however, the supervising Committee has expressly referred to non-nationals in its jurisprudence and views. See CERD Recommendation XI (42) on non-nationals, para. 2.

Contracting party concerned.'[31] However, this type of general limitation clause *ratione personae* is the exception rather than the rule as, generally, instruments aimed at the protection of economic, social and cultural rights apply to everyone, without distinction between nationals and non-nationals.[32]

This general rule is applicable to the Covenant. Generally, the economic, social and cultural rights embodied in the Covenant apply to nationals and non-nationals of States Parties. The only exception appears in article 2(3) ICESCR, which establishes that '[d]eveloping countries, with due regard to human rights and their national economy may determine to what extent they would guarantee the economic rights recognised in the present Covenant to non-nationals.' This provision will be discussed at greater length below but it is important to note here that this is a very limited exception, applicable only to developing countries and merely in relation to economic rights.[33]

In sum, since the Covenant does not contain any limitation *ratione personae*, as in the case of the European Social Charter, it should be understood that the Covenant's rights apply to everyone, including non-nationals, under the jurisdiction of the State Party. Only developing States, under the conditions of article 2(3) ICESCR, may impose limitations on the enjoyment of some of the Covenant's rights by non-nationals.

Following the Committee's approach, we understand 'non-nationals' as being synonymous with 'non-citizens', meaning those foreigners who are not naturalised in the State Party concerned but who are *de jure* or *de facto* resident in the country. This means that the person is habitually present in the country legally (with a permanent residence permit or other type of permission to remain), or even if she/he is 'illegally' residing in the country. The Committee seems to exclude from the protection of the

31 See Appendix to the Social Charter and appendix to the Revised European Social Charter. Nevertheless, this principle has exceptions. For further analysis see, Gomien, D.; Harris, D. & Zwaak, L.: *Law and practice of the European Convention on Human Rights and the European Social Charter*, Council of Europe Publishing, Strasbourg, (1996), pp. 432-433.

32 For example, the CRC, which includes economic, social and cultural rights, applies to all children within the jurisdiction of the State Party (Art. 2). The CEDAW Optional Protocol also provides protection for the economic, social and cultural rights of all women under the jurisdiction of the State Party, without excluding non-nationals (see Art. 2 OP). According to CERD, States have an obligation to protect the economic, social and cultural rights contained therein without discrimination against non-citizens (Art. 1(2) and Art. 5). The Protocol of San Salvador applies to everyone under the jurisdiction of a State Party (Art. 1). The AfCH, which includes a wide range of economic, social and cultural rights also applies to 'everyone' without distinction. The same is established in the African Charter on the Rights and Welfare of the Child, which applies to 'every child.' The UNESCO Convention against Discrimination in Education requires States to give the same protection to nationals and non-nationals resident in their territory (Art. 3(c)). Similarly, some ILO Conventions aim specifically to protect foreigners, such as ILO Convention No. 118 (Convention concerning Equality of Treatment of Nationals and Non-Nationals in Social Security, adopted on June 28, 1962), or provide for the same treatment between national and foreign workers, such as ILO Convention No. 97 (Convention concerning Migration for Employment Revised 1949, adopted on July 1, 1949).

33 Limburg Principle No. 44.

Covenant all those aliens who are not resident (in a broad sense) in the State but merely visitors, such as tourists or persons on business visits.[34]

2.1.1 The Committee's approach in the General Comments

In the General Comments the Committee has clearly stated that the Covenant applies to *everyone* within the jurisdiction of a State Party.[35] Therefore, we should understand that 'everyone' includes non-nationals. However, in contrast with the detailed and systematic reference to non-nationals that others human rights treaty bodies make in their General Comments or Recommendations,[36] the issue of non-nationals has not been analysed in any detail by the Committee in its General Comments.

Only in General Comment No. 13 on the right to education (article 13 ICESCR) does the Committee directly refer to non-nationals and even then the reference is a brief one. Based on this General Comment, we may conclude that, according to the Committee, 'everyone' includes 'non-nationals,' 'irrespective of their legal status.'

In sum, taking into account that the Committee has repeatedly stressed that the Covenant applies to 'everyone within the jurisdiction of the State', and in a recent General Comment it has further clarified that 'everyone' includes 'non-nationals irrespective of their legal status', it is possible to conclude that on the basis of the General Comments the Committee holds the view that the Covenant applies to both nationals and non-nationals within the State Party concerned, notwithstanding the legality of the presence of the non-nationals within the State. However, as we will see, when examining States Parties' reports, the Committee is less rigorous in its approach and has applied different standards depending on the groups of non-nationals involved.

---

34 The Committee generally refers to those 'regularly present' in the territory of the State concerned 'regardless of their legal status'. See for example, General Comment No. 13 para. 34. In addition, see Concluding Observations Luxembourg E/1998/22 para. 388 (*foreigners residing in the State*); Concluding Observations Italy E/2000/22 para. 110 (*foreigners regularly present on the national territory)*; Concluding Observations Switzerland E/1999/22 para. 344 (*foreigners residing in the State)*; List of Issues Japan E/C.12/Q/JAP/1 para. 7 (*foreign residents)*; and List of Issues Iceland E/C.12/Q/ICE/1 para. 6 (*foreign residents).*

35 See, for example, General Comment No. 1 para. 3 (*all individuals within the jurisdiction)*; General Comment No. 8 para. 10 (*each individual living within its jurisdiction)*; General Comment No. 12 para. 14 (*every State is obliged to ensure for everyone under its jurisdiction*); General Comment No. 13 para. 52 (*for all those within its jurisdiction*); and General Comment No. 14 para. 12 (*to everyone [...] within the jurisdiction of the State Party]*. See in addition, General Comment No. 9 para. 9, General Comment No. 13 paras. 6 and 39 and General Comment No. 14 para. 51.

36 It has to be pointed out that the HRC and CERD Committees have addressed the rights of non-citizens through their General Comments and General Recommendations, respectively, in a much more detailed manner. See, for example, CERD Committee General Recommendation XI on non-citizens and Human Rights Committee General Comment No. 13 para. 13; No. 17 para. 5; No. 27 para. 4; and No. 28 para. 31. In particular, see General Comment No. 15 on the position of aliens under the Covenant.

2.1.2 The Committee's approach in the Concluding Observations

When considering States Parties' reports, the Committee pays special attention to the protection of the economic, social and cultural rights of non-nationals within the jurisdiction of States Parties to the Covenant. Nonetheless, although the Committee has clearly established in its General Comments that the Covenant applies to everyone under the jurisdiction of the State regardless of citizenship and whether or not they are legally present in the country, when examining State reports it is sometimes quite flexible in its approach. The Committee has been more or less rigorous depending on whether the non-national is legally in the country (legally resident), illegally present (undocumented) or whether the non-national belongs to a particular category, such as refugees or asylum seekers.

In the light of the Committee's flexible approach, it is necessary to analyse the treatment accorded to the different categories of non-nationals:

(a) *Foreign nationals 'legally' in the country concerned:*

In the light of the Committee's Concluding Observations, there can be no doubt that the Covenant applies fully to all foreign nationals legally residing in a State Party. According to the Committee, all individuals in this category must be accorded the treatment given to citizens with regard to the enjoyment of all of the Covenant's rights.[37]

The enjoyment of the Covenant's rights on the same footing as citizens is obvious in the case of foreigners who have a residence permit in the country concerned. Residents pay taxes and in most respects they are like citizens in the community where they live so there are no compelling reasons to deny them the enjoyment of economic, social and cultural rights. However, it is not absolutely clear from the Committee's work if this category (foreign nationals 'legally' in the country concerned), includes only those who have a 'residence permit'[38] or if it also includes those who are living legally within the State because they have been admitted to the State in accordance with the applicable immigration law but have only been granted temporary status, such as foreign students.[39]

---

37 Concluding Observations Switzerland E/1999/22 para. 344. In addition see List of Issues Switzerland E/C.12/Q/SWI/1 para. 5 of 22 December 1997.

38 While sometimes the Committee has merely referred to foreigners 'who are legally residing in the country' [*e.g.* List of Issues Switzerland E/C.12/Q/SWI/1 para. 5 of 22 December 1997], on at least one occasion it has referred to those with 'residence permits' [*i.e.* Concluding Observations Nigeria E/1999/22 para. 105].

39 To understand this point it might be of assistance to look to developments in Refugee Law relating to the terms 'lawfully staying' in and 'lawfully in' a State. This topic has been extensively analysed by Goodwin-Gill, G.: *The refugee in international law*, second paperback edition, Clarendon Press, Oxford, (1998), pp. 307 *et seq*. Although an in-depth analysis of this issue is beyond the scope of the present study, it is interesting to note that the UNHCR has interpreted the term 'lawful' in a wide sense, considering that it is that which is not prohibited and which must be assessed in accordance with prevailing national law and regulations; while the term 'stay' means 'something less than durable

While the Committee as a whole should clarify this point, it is clear that, at least for some Committee members, foreign nationals 'legally' in the country include not only those who have a 'residence permit', but also those who possess other types of authorisation to remain over the medium and long term, such as foreign students. When considering the report of Finland, for example, some Committee members expressed their concern about the fact that foreign students legally in the country were not covered by the social security system available to residents. This suggests that those who have an authorisation to remain in the country but who do not possess a 'residence permit', would enjoy the same rights as residents.[40]

(b) *'Illegal' foreigners residing in the country concerned:*
When a non-citizen is staying in the State Party illegally (because she/he has entered the country unlawfully or subsequent to legal entry has contravened the applicable immigration law), the Committee's approach is more sympathetic to States.

While the Committee requires States to treat foreigners 'legally' in the country as if they were citizens, in regard to 'illegal' foreigners it has applied a lower standard. Instead of requiring States to respect, protect and fulfil the rights of those illegally in the country, generally it merely requires States to respect and protect the principle of non-discrimination.

In other words, with regard to illegal aliens,[41] the Committee has merely required States (a) to refrain from denying them equal access to the available facilities. Therefore, if the State provides for some level of enjoyment of these rights (*e.g.* free primary education or emergency medical care), it must do so without discriminating against foreigners legally or illegally in the country. Thus, using the same example, States must provide illegal immigrants emergency medical care or primary education on the same footing as nationals.[42] (b) to protect them against discriminatory actions by law en-

---

residence, although clearly more than a transit stop.' See UNHCR IOM/FOM 60/88 'Note on Lawfully Staying.'

40 See, for example, Mr. Ahmed in E/C.12/1996/SR.37 paras. 37 and 39. While the Concluding Observations did not specifically include a reference to this difference in treatment, this could be because the Government representative explained that this issue was being examined by the Supreme Court in Finland [E/C.12/1996/SR.37 para. 40]. Nonetheless, the Committee's Concluding Observations contain recommendations referring to discrimination and cuts to the welfare system that would affect the specific issue of foreign students legally in the country. Concluding Observations Finland E/1997/22 paras. 306 and 316.

41 As we will see below, when it appears to the Committee that the 'illegal' foreigner is actually working in the country concerned, it applies a higher standard of protection and requires States to fully apply the Covenant.

42 Concluding Observations Austria E/1995/22 paras. 253 and 259. In General Comment No. 14 the Committee endorsed this position indicating that 'States are under the obligation to respect the right to health by, *inter alia*, refraining from denying or limiting equal access for all persons including prisoners or detainees, minorities, asylum seekers and *illegal immigrants* to preventive, curative and palliative health services.' (General Comment No. 14 para. 34, emphasis added).

forcement officials of third parties.[43] The Committee has been clear in stating that the principle of non-discrimination extends to everyone residing in the territory of a State Party, '*including non-nationals, and irrespective of their legal status*.'[44] This is not to say that States cannot establish any difference in treatment between citizens (including foreigners legally within the State), and illegal foreigners but, rather, that any differentiation must comply with the principle of non-discrimination (article 2(2) ICESCR). Hence, if the State is to distinguish between citizens and illegal foreigners in the enjoyment of the Covenant's rights, the differentiation must be reasonable, objective and with a legitimate aim (a purpose legitimate under the Covenant). In other words, those in a similar situation must be treated equally and the mere fact that a person is a non-citizen does not in itself allow for different treatment. Any unreasonable distinction between citizens and non-citizens will violate the Covenant.

The continuing concern of the Committee regarding the proper application of the principle of non-discrimination is reflected in its Lists of Issues, in the dialogue with State representatives, in the Concluding Observations and in the General Comments. In the List of Issues, for example, the Committee often requires information as to how the State applies the principle of non-discrimination (article 2(2)) to 'foreigners' without specifying any distinction based on their status, and this would therefore include those legally and illegally in the country.[45] In its Concluding Observations, the Committee has expressed regret when it finds that there is discrimination against 'foreigners,' clearly referring to both legal and illegal foreigners.[46]

The application of the principle of non-discrimination with regard to non-nationals will be further analysed in Chapter VIII. Here we merely wish to stress that the Committee has continuously and consistently stated that the principle of non-discrimination applies to non-citizens irrespective of their status (legally or illegally within the State Party concerned).

43 For example, Concluding Observations Spain E/C.12/1/Add.2 para. 17, Concluding Observations Ukraine E/C.12/1/Add.65 paras. 12 and 29 and Concluding Observations Republic of Korea E/1996/22 para. 82.

44 See, for example, General Comment No. 13 para. 34.

45 See, for example, Concluding Observations Japan E/C.12/1/Add.67 para. 61. In addition, List of Issues Denmark E/C.12/Q/DEN/1 para. 8 of 19 June 1998 ('Describe the judicial practice regarding the application in Denmark of the laws prohibiting discrimination against [...] foreigners') and List of Issues Italy E/C.12/Q/ITA/1 para. 6 of 21 May 1999 ('Please indicate what actions has been taken to curb manifestations of racism, xenophobia and ill-treatment of foreigners by the police officers and officials'). See also, List of Issues Georgia E/C.12/Q/GEO/1 para. 11 of 21 May 1999.

46 See, for example, Concluding Observations Finland E/C.12/2000/21 paras. 440 and 454, Concluding Observations Germany E/1999/22 para. 313 and Concluding Observations Sri Lanka E/1999/22 paras. 72 and 83.

(c) *Migrant workers:*
The Committee has not been very consistent in relation to the language it employs to refer to non-national workers. Sometimes it refers to them as 'migrant workers'[47] or 'foreign workers',[48] but without specifying their legal status, and sometimes it mentions their status by using the expression 'illegal workers.'[49]

In accordance with the International Convention on the Protection of the Rights of All Migrant Workers and Members of their Families, it is possible to define a 'migrant worker' as a non-national who is engaged or has been engaged in a remunerated activity, irrespective of whether she/he is 'legally' (documented) or 'illegally' (undocumented) in the country concerned.[50] Therefore, we may conclude that when the Committee refers solely to 'migrant workers' or 'foreigner workers' without specifying their status, it includes both those who are legally and illegally in the State concerned.

From the Concluding Observations, it appears that when the Committee has received information about foreign nationals working in a State Party, it has required that the State concerned fully apply the Covenant's rights to those workers, irrespective of their legal status in the country.[51] This approach is particularly important with regard to illegal workers who tend to be more exposed to abuses, such as sub-minimum wages, dangerous and unsafe working conditions and longer working hours. Due to their vulnerable situation they are in need of more rigorous protection.[52]

The Committee's concern regarding illegal workers was evident when it examined the working conditions of illegal Haitian workers in sugar cane plantations (the so-called *bateyes)* in the Dominican Republic. The Committee acknowledged that Haitian illegal workers, particularly female workers, were subject to exploitation and were deprived of their rights and access to social services.[53] Therefore, the Committee urged the State Party 'to take all necessary measures to ensure that Haitian illegal immigrants in the Dominican Republic *enjoy their economic, social and cultural rights fully and*

---

47 See, for example, Concluding Observations Norway E/1996/22 para. 210, List of Issues China E/C.12/Q/HKSAR/1 para. 5 of 25 May 2000 and List of Issues Cyprus E/C.12/Q/CYP/1 para. 13 of 23 May 1997.

48 See, for example, Concluding Observations Libyan Arab Jamahiriya E/1998/22 para. 185 and List of Issues China E/C.12/Q/HKSAR/1 para. 6 of 25 May 2000.

49 See, for example, Concluding Observations Spain E/C.12/1/Add.2 paras. 10 and 17 and Concluding Observations Germany E/C.12/1/Add.68 para. 20.

50 See Preamble and articles 2 and 5 of the International Convention on the Protection of the Rights of All Migrant Workers and Members of their Families (adopted by General Assembly Res. 45/158 of 18 December 1990).

51 See, for example, Concluding Observations Dominican Republic E/1997/22 para. 224; Concluding Observations Portugal [Macao] E/1997/22 para. 251; Concluding Observations Libyan Arab Jamahiriya E/1998/22 para. 185; and Concluding Observations Nigeria E/1999/22 para. 105.

52 The Committee specifically considers migrant workers as a disadvantaged group. See, Reporting Guidelines, article 11 paragraph 2(b)(I).

53 Preliminary Concluding Observations on the Second Periodic Report of the Dominican Republic E/1997/22 para. 224.

without discrimination.'[54] Furthermore, the Committee expressed the view that 'the regularisation of the situation of these illegal residents, through the delivery of residence permits or naturalisation, is necessary.'[55]

Similarly, when considering the initial report of Libyan Arab Jamahiriya, the Committee expressed concern about the working conditions of illegal foreign workers and recommended that 'the status and working conditions of foreign workers be improved without delay, and that these persons be treated with dignity and be enabled to benefit fully from the rights enshrined in the Covenant'.[56]

In sum, when facing a situation which involves 'illegal foreigners', the Committee has merely required States to respect the principle of non-discrimination. If illegal aliens are actually working in a State Party, the Committee has applied a stricter standard and required States to 'fully' apply the Covenant to these workers. The Committee has stressed, in particular, that foreign workers, irrespective of their status, must

54 Concluding Observations Dominican Republic E/1998/22 para. 233 (emphasis added).

55 Concluding Observations Dominican Republic E/1998/22 para. 233. It is interesting to note that the issue of the living conditions of the Haitian workers in the Dominican Republic is a good illustration of the indivisibility of all human rights. Both the HRC and CERD Committees have discussed the issue. The HRC in 1993 expressed its concern 'over the lack of protection afforded to Haitians living or working in the country from such serious human rights abuses as forced labour and cruel, inhuman or degrading treatment. The Committee expresses its concern over the fact that the protection of the fundamental human rights of foreigners is subject to reciprocity. The Committee also expresses its concern over the degrading living and working conditions of Haitian labourers and the tolerated practices that effectively restrict their freedom of movement. Although some progress has been made in improving their living and working conditions, particularly with regard to child labour, these remain at an unacceptably low level. Furthermore, while many Haitian workers have been prevented from leaving their place of work, there have also been incidents of mass expulsions from the country. In this regard, the Committee considers that Presidential Decree No. 233-91, which resulted in the mass deportation of Haitian workers under 16 and over 60 years of age, represents a serious violation of several articles of the Covenant.' Consequently, it recommended that 'the situation concerning the living and working conditions of Haitian labourers should be addressed as a matter of priority. The State Party should ensure the implementation of laws concerning labour standards, including adequate monitoring of working conditions. In this regard, the Committee emphasises the necessity of strengthening the capacity of the labour inspectorate to effectively monitor the working conditions of Haitian labourers, with a view to ending their slave-like exploitation. Child labourers in particular require a higher level of protection and the relevant international standards should be vigorously applied. There should also be more active enforcement, particularly in the 'export zones', of the exercise of trade union rights in conformity with article 22 of the Covenant. Additionally, Presidential Decree No. 233-91 should be abolished rather than merely suspended.' CCPR/C/79/Add.18 para. 9 of 5 May 1993. More recently, the CERD Committee stated: 'the Committee recommends that the State Party take urgent measures to ensure the enjoyment by persons of Haitian origin of their economic, social and cultural rights without discrimination. Efforts should be made, in particular, to improve their living conditions in the *bateyes* (shanty towns)', CERD/C/304/Add.74 para. 11, of 12 April 2001.

56 Concluding Observations Libyan Arab Jamahiriya E/1998/22 para. 190.

enjoy article 7 (safe and fair working conditions),[57] article 8 (the right to form and join trade unions),[58] and article 9 (social security)[59] on the same footing as nationals.

(d) *Refugees and asylum seekers:*
A refugee is a person who fulfils the criteria established in the 1951 Convention relating to the Status of Refugees[60] and its 1967 Protocol.[61] In other words, a refugee is a person who, 'owing to well-founded fear of being persecuted for reasons of race, religion, nationality, membership of a particular social group or political opinion, is outside the country of his nationality and is unable or, owing to such fear, is unwilling to avail himself of the protection of that country.'[62]

The term 'asylum seeker' may be defined as an alien who seeks the protection of the State by claiming refugee status within the meaning of article 1 of the 1951 Convention relating to the Status of Refugees, as amended by the 1967 Protocol.[63]

The application of the Covenant to refugees and asylum seekers is beyond doubt. Although they are non-nationals, the Committee has clearly established that the Covenant applies to refugees and asylum seekers alike.[64] This means that refugees and

57 See, for example, Concluding Observations Dominican Republic E/1997/22 para. 224; Concluding Observations Portugal [Macao] E/1997/22 para. 251; Concluding Observations Libyan Arab Jamahiriya E/1998/22 para. 185; Concluding Observations Nigeria E/1999/22 para. 105; Concluding Observations Jordan E/2001/22 para. 238; and Concluding Observations Republic of Korea E/C.12.1/Add.59 paras. 17 and 38.

58 For example, examining the Second Periodic Report of Senegal, the Committee expressed its concern that despite its earlier recommendations, foreign workers were still not permitted to form trade unions and called upon the State to repeal this prohibition. Concluding Observations Senegal E/C.12/1/Add.62 paras. 22 and 44. See also Concluding Observations Senegal E/1994/22 para. 224. In the same vein, Concluding Observations Jordan E/2001/22 para. 238. See, in addition, the approach of Mr. Texier in E/C.12/1996/SR.38 para. 5.

59 For example, the Concluding Observations of Portugal [Macao] which expressly state that, '[t]he Committee also urges the enactment of legislation on the right to social security so as to ensure full compliance with the requirements of the Covenant, and recommends that the State Party extend the coverage of social security to non-resident workers.' Concluding Observations Portugal [Macao] E/1997/22 para. 261. See, also Concluding Observations Mauritius E/1996/22 para. 238.

60 Adopted on 28 July 1951 by the United Nations Conference of Plenipotentiaries on the Status of Refugees and Stateless persons convened under General Assembly Res. 429 (V) of 14 December 1950. Hereinafter: CSR

61 Protocol Relating to the Status of Refugees of 31 January 1967.

62 Art. 1 CSR.

63 See, for example, Art. 1 of the 1990 Dublin Convention Determining the State Responsible for Examining Applications for Asylum lodged in one of the Member States of the European Communities.

64 The Committee accords to 'refugees' and 'asylum seekers' the same level of protection. This is clearly the correct approach given that the determination of refugee status has only a declaratory value. See paragraph 28 UNHCR Handbook on the Procedures and Criteria for Determining Refugee Status [hereinafter: UNHCR Handbook]: 'A person is a refugee within the meaning of the 1951 Convention as soon as he fulfils the criteria contained in the definition. This would necessarily occur prior to the time at which his refugee status is formally determined. Recognition of his refugee status does therefore

asylum seekers must enjoy the Covenant's rights on the same footing as citizens of the State concerned.[65] Moreover, according to the Committee, they are a special category of non-nationals and require special protective measures due to their vulnerability.[66]

Examining the Third Periodic Report of Italy, for example, the Committee urged the State 'to extend the subsidised health-care system to asylum-seekers without discrimination.'[67] In the same vein, considering the Third Periodic Report of Canada, the Committee expressed concern about the fact that loan programmes for post-secondary education were available to Canadian citizens and permanent residents but that asylum seekers and refugees were ineligible for these programmes. The Committee urged the Government to expand the programme to them and took the opportunity to state that the prohibition of discrimination on the basis of 'citizenship status' was prohibited under the Covenant.[68] Examining the initial report of Belgium, the Committee 'strongly urged' the State to fully ensure that asylum seekers and refugees were protected 'from any acts or laws which in any way result in discriminatory treatment within the housing sector.'[69]

As the Covenant is fully applicable to refugees and asylum seekers, States Parties must respect, protect and fulfil their rights. In this regard, the Committee has made clear that, notwithstanding the level of development of a country, States Parties must provide refugees and asylum seekers with basic social services, including health care and education for their children.[70] When a large influx of refugees creates problems for a country, the Committee has recognised this type of situation under 'factors or difficulties affecting the enjoyment of the Covenant', but has nonetheless stressed the necessity to apply the Covenant to groups of refugees.[71]

It is difficult to deny that asylum seekers and refugees are in an extremely vulnerable position and in need of greater protection than other foreigners in the country owing to the fact that their rights are more easily violated and that they may suffer

---

make him a refugee but declares him to be one. He does not become a refugee because of recognition, but is recognised because he is a refugee'.

65 See, for example, Concluding Observations Canada E/1999/22 para. 414; Concluding Observations Surinam E/1996/22 para. 162; and Concluding Observations United Kingdom of Great Britain and Northern Ireland [Hong Kong] E/1995/22 para. 291. In addition List of Issues Bolivia E/C 12/Q/BOL/1 para. 8 of 21 September 2000; List of Issues Australia E/C.12/Q/AUSTRAL/1 para. 10 of 23 May 2000; and List of Issues Bulgaria E/C.12/Q/BUL/1 para. 6 of 19 June 1998.

66 See, for example, Concluding Observations Germany E/1999/22 paras. 316 and 327; Concluding Observations Sweden E/1996/22 para. 137; and Concluding Observations Denmark E/2000/22 paras. 99 and 105.

67 Concluding Observations Italy E/2001/22 paras. 123 and 138.

68 Concluding Observations Canada E/1999/22 paras. 414 and 424.

69 Concluding Observations Belgium E/1995/22 para. 14.

70 See, for example, Concluding Observations Senegal E/C.12/1/Add.62 para. 54 and Concluding Observations Syrian Arab Republic E/C.12/1/Add.63 para. 23.

71 See, for example, Concluding Observations Azerbaijan E/C.12/1/Add.20 paras. 12, 17, 24 and 30 and Concluding Observations Kenya E/C.12/1993/6 para .5.

disproportionate harm.[72] The Maastricht Guidelines on Violations of Economic, Social and Cultural Rights expressly indicate that asylum seekers and refugees are among the groups that can suffer disproportionate harm as victims of violations of economic, social and cultural rights.[73]

Their particularly vulnerable position may explain why the Committee accords to refugees and asylum seekers a higher standard of protection when examining the reports of States Parties. The Committee places their level of protection higher than that accorded to 'migrant workers'. Generally, with regard to the latter, the Committee seems not to require the adoption of special protective measures.[74] A possible explanation for the different treatment accorded to foreign workers in comparison with asylum seekers and refugees might be found in the differences between the two categories that have been identified by UNHCR. In a nutshell, while both migrant workers and refugees are outside their country of origin, the key element in the definition of the status of a refugee is that she/he 'has a well-founded fear of persecution.' According to the UNHCR Handbook on the Procedures and Criteria for Determining Refugee Status, 'a migrant is a person who, for reasons other than those contained in the definition, voluntarily leaves his country in order to take up residence elsewhere. He may be moved by the desire for change or adventure, or by family or other reasons of a personal nature. If he is moved exclusively by economic considerations, he is an economic migrant and not a refugee.'[75] It is beyond the scope of this work to analyse the differences between a migrant worker and an asylum seeker.[76] However, it is important to note that, in practice, the distinction between economic migrants and asylum seekers may not be so easy to determine. Indeed, economic factors may be such as to make life

72 In fact, International law seems to recognise their special circumstances and accords them different treatment, for example, special protection is accorded to them under refugee law and human rights law with regard to the prohibition of expulsion or refoulement. See Art. 33 CSR, Art. 3 CAT, Art. 7 ICCPR, Art. 22(8) ACHR and Art. 3 ECHR. Additionally, see Art. 7 of the Declaration on the Human Rights of Individuals who are not Nationals of the Country in which they live [adopted by General Assembly Res. 40/144 of 13 December 1985] and Art. 3 of the Declaration of Territorial Asylum [adopted by General Assembly Res. 2312 (XXII) of 14 December 1967].

73 The Maastricht Guideline No. 20.

74 Exceptionally, the Committee has analysed the situation of migrant workers together with refugees and asylum seekers and required the adoption of protective measures in favour of all of them. For example, in the case of Denmark, the Committee 'urges the State Party to take all corrective measures to reduce the level of unemployment of young people, foreign nationals, immigrants and refugees.' Concluding Observations Denmark E/2000/22 para. 115.

75 UNHCR Handbook para. 62.

76 For an interesting analysis see: Hathaway, J.: *The law of refugee status*, Butterworths, Canada, (1991), pp. 116 *et seq.*

unbearable in the country of origin, and these conditions could be of such gravity as to amount to 'persecution' or to give rise to a 'well founded fear of persecution.'[77]

(e) *Stateless persons:*
According to the Convention Relating to the Status of Stateless Persons,[78] a 'stateless person' is a person who is not considered as a national by any State. The Committee considers that the Covenant applies fully to stateless persons and that they must therefore enjoy the pertinent rights on the same footing as citizens.[79] It should be noted that when States Parties have not ratified the 1961 Convention on the Reduction of Statelessness, the Committee recommends that they do so.[80]

(f) *The Roma population:*
When examining the enjoyment of the Covenant's rights by foreigners (non-citizens), the Committee has sometimes included the situation of the Roma.[81] From this author's perspective such an approach is appropriate when the Roma people move between different countries or when their citizenship is not recognised. However, it is important to bear in mind that, in a great majority of cases, the Roma possess the nationality of the State concerned. This is clear, for example, in the case of Italy, where, according to the Government, 80 percent of the Roma population in the country are Italian citizens.[82]

Therefore, when the Roma population in the country concerned are nationals of that State, it is beyond doubt that States are required to treat them as any other citizen, irrespective of their different national origin. When they are foreigners (non-citizens of the State concerned), the above-mentioned analysis of the treatment of non-nationals is applicable. However, two important remarks are necessary: first, national origin is an expressly prohibited ground for discrimination as laid down in article 2(2) ICESCR. Second, in those States in which the citizenship of the Roma is not recognised, it is important to recall the CERD Committee's General Recommendation that States

77 See UNHCR Handbook para. 63; Hathaway, *op. cit.* (note 75), pp. 116 *et seq.*. A good example is Gashi v. the Secretary of State for the Home Department in the Immigration Appeal Tribunal in the UK. Appeal No.HX/75478/95.

78 Adopted in New York on 28 September 1954, entered into force on 6 June 1960. United Nations Treaty Series No. 5158, vol. 360, p. 117.

79 See, for example, Concluding Observations Azerbaijan E/1998/22 para. 322 and Concluding Observations Syrian Arab Republic E/C.12/1/Add.63 para. 23. In addition, see, List of Issues Morocco E/C.12/Q/MOR/1 para. 5 of 25 May 2000 and List of Issues Kyrgyzstan E/C.12/Q/KYRG/1 para. 8 of 10 December 1999.

80 See, for example, Concluding Observations Italy E/2001/22 para. 128 and Concluding Observations Syrian Arab Republic E/C.12/1/Add.63 para. 32.

81 This approach is also followed in the study on 'The rights of non-citizens' prepared by the Special Rapporteur Mr. D. Weissbrodt in accordance with Sub-Commission decision 2000/103 of 1 August 2000. See E/CN.4/Sub.2/2001/20 and E/CN.4/Sub.2/2001/20 Add.1 of 6 June 2001.

82 See Mr. Moreno (Italy) in E/C.12/2000/SR.6 paras. 32 and 58.

Parties to the Convention 'ensure that legislation regarding citizenship and naturalisation does not discriminate against members of Roma communities.'[83] This is especially relevant when we consider that the great majority of the States Parties to the ICESCR are also bound by the CERD.[84]

In sum, to the extent that they are citizens of the State concerned, there would be no point in analysing the situation of the Roma at this point. Nonetheless, it is correct to treat them as a separate category when addressing the issue of the prohibition of discrimination. In fact, the Roma suffer from structural inequalities that require special attention to their rights in order to allow them to overcome this discrimination. In the present study the situation of the Roma is analysed more fully when dealing with the prohibition of discrimination in Chapter VIII.

2.1.3 Concluding comments

All of the rights contained in the Covenant apply to everyone under the jurisdiction of the State Party whether they are lawfully or unlawfully present. While the Committee has certainly stressed this principle on many occasions in its General Comments, it seems that when considering State reports, the Committee has not applied this principle in a strict manner. The degree of flexibility in the application of the principle depends on the different categories of non-nationals involved and on the rights at issue.

The application of the Covenant to those legally residing in the country is clear, as is its application to refugees, asylum seekers and Roma (non-citizens). Whilst all of the Covenant's rights should apply to illegal non-citizens residing in a State Party, the Committee has yet to clearly establish that this interpretation applies in all cases. Thus far, the exceptions have been those cases in which it has been apparent to the Committee that there are [illegal] workers who are being exploited in the State concerned. In such circumstances, the Committee has made it clear that the Covenant's rights apply and that States are required to take measures for their protection, including considering the possibility of granting legal residence to the workers involved.

The Committee also needs to adopt more clear and uniform terminology in its Concluding Observations when referring to foreigners in a State Party. While it sometimes specifically refers to illegal foreigners, on many occasions it is not clear if it refers to those foreigners legally residing in the country or if it also includes illegal foreigners. The use of clear language to refer to foreigners, both legal and illegal, would provide a higher degree of clarity to the Committee's analysis.

---

83 CERD Committee General Recommendation XXVII on discrimination against Roma.

84 The exceptions are those States Parties to the ICESCR which are not parties to the CERD, such as Angola, Benin, the Democratic People's Republic of Korea, the Dominican Republic, Paraguay, Thailand, Equatorial Guinea, Grenada, Guinea Bissau, Honduras, and Kenya. Of course, there would be few, if any, Roma in these States.

The Committee should be very strict in applying the Covenant to *everyone* within the jurisdiction of the State, including foreigners illegally residing in the country. The Committee has repeatedly stressed that the Covenant is a vehicle for the protection of vulnerable groups within society[85] and without any doubt the great majority of illegal immigrants fall within the most vulnerable groups. It would be appropriate for the Committee to clarity that illegals should enjoy all of the Covenant's rights. As Schachter notes, denying those rights to illegals 'is certainly contrary to the spirit of human rights, [and] contrary to the letter of the Covenant.'[86]

Finally, it should be mentioned that States can legitimately differentiate between citizens and non-citizens. However, as we will see, they must respect the principle of non-discrimination. The principle of non-discrimination is analysed in greater depth in Chapter VIII. Suffice it to note here that States Parties to the Covenant must provide information to the Committee regarding any difference in treatment between nationals and non-nationals and provide justification for those differences with reference to the Covenant.

2.2 Territorial scope of the ICESCR

In contrast to article 2 of its sister Covenant, which expressly provides that each State Party undertakes obligations in regard to all individuals '*within its territory and subject to its jurisdiction*', the ICESCR does not make any express reference to its territorial application.[87]

However, from the Committee's work it is clear that the territorial scope of the Covenant is the jurisdiction of the State Party. The Committee's draft optional protocol expressly establishes competence to receive communications from any individual or group '*subject to the jurisdiction'* of the State responsible for the presumed violation.[88] Thus, according to the draft, individuals or groups would be able to submit complaints even if they are not 'within the territory' of a State Party when filing the complaint or if the violation took place while they were outside the territory of that State.

It is clear from the work of the Committee and from the jurisprudence of other treaty bodies that the Covenant applies to all territories over which the State Party exercises control, even *de facto* control. The Committee has expressly interpreted the

85 See, for example, General Comment No. 1 para. 3; General Comment No. 3 para. 12; Concluding Observations Cyprus E/1999/22 para. 298; and Concluding Observations Germany E/1999/22 para. 327.
86 Schachter, O.: 'Protecting the world's exiles: the human rights of non-citizens.' In: *HRQ*, vol. 22, (2000), p. 285.
87 For an analysis of the scope of article 2(1) ICCPR with regard to this point see, Buergenthal, T.: 'To respect and to ensure: State obligations and permissible derogations.' In: *The International Bill of Rights*. Henkin, Louis (ed.), New York, Columbia University Press, (1981), pp. 73-77.
88 E/C.12/1996/6, Annex IV, para. 21 (emphasis added).

term 'jurisdiction' of the State as applying to all areas where a State Party maintains 'geographical, functional or personal jurisdiction.'[89]

2.2.1 The Committee's approach in the General Comments

Through its General Comments, the Committee has constantly stated that the Covenant applies to everyone 'within the jurisdiction' of the State.[90] In this regard it should be stressed that the Committee has opted for a more appropriate formulation than the one adopted in article 2(1) ICCPR which states 'within its territory *and* subject to its jurisdiction.' (Emphasis added). As scholars have noted, a literal interpretation of this expression may lead to absurd results.[91] However, through its jurisprudence,[92] the Human Rights Committee has clarified the meaning of these terms and taken an expansive view in light of the object and purpose of the Covenant.[93]

In its first General Comment, the Committee used the wording 'all individuals within its territory *or* under its jurisdiction.'[94] However since then it has generally used the expression 'within the jurisdiction' which is more appropriate in light of the object and purpose of the Covenant and in line with the American and European Conventions.

2.2.2 The Committee's approach in the Concluding Observations

The territorial scope of the Covenant has taken on special relevance in some situations in which it has been necessary for the Committee to clarify its normative significance. Two cases are particularly worth noting.

First, the Committee has clarified the territorial application of the Covenant when a State Party is in actual control of part of the territory of another State and is alleged to be violating the Covenant. When considering the initial report of Israel, the Committee needed to confront allegations of violations of the Covenant rights of Palestinians

89 Concluding Observations Israel E/1999/22 para. 232.

90 See, for example, General Comment No. 14 paras. 12 and 51; General Comment No. 13 paras. 6, 41 and 52; General Comment No. 9 para. 9; General Comment No. 8 para. 10; and General Comment No. 4 para. 13. In General Comment No. 12 the Committee uses a wording which is slightly different because it refers to everyone 'under its jurisdiction' (para. 14).

91 As Nowak explains, a literal interpretation would lead to absurd results, for example, that '[n]ationals of a State Party who are prevented from entering their mother country would be unable to rely on their right to enter under Art. 12(4) because they are not on the territory of the State concerned.' Nowak, *op. cit.* (note 2), p. 41.

92 See, for example, Lopez Burgos v. Uruguay, Communication No. 52/1979, views of 29 July 1981 and Celiberti de Casariego v. Uruguay, Communication No. 56/1979, views of 29 July 1981.

93 See, Buergenthal, *op. cit.* (note 86), pp. 73-77; Nowak, *op. cit.* (note 2), p. 41-43; and Harris & Joseph, 1995, pp. 3-4. In addition, see for example, Lopez Burgos v. Uruguay, *loc. cit.* (note 92) and Celiberti de Casariego v. Uruguay, *loc. cit.* (note 92).

94 General Comment No. 1 para. 3: 'A second objective is to ensure that the State Party monitors the actual situation with respect to each of the rights on a regular basis and is thus aware of the extent to which the various rights are, or are not, being enjoyed *by all individuals within its territory or under its jurisdiction.*' (Emphasis added).

in the occupied territories. However, while the State had provided information on the enjoyment of the Covenant's rights by Israeli settlers in the occupied territories, it had not provided any information about the enjoyment of the Covenant's rights by Palestinians there.[95] The argument of the Israeli authorities was that in the occupied territories of the West Bank and Gaza Strip, the Palestinian authorities had full jurisdiction in all matters covered by the Covenant, such as education and health. Therefore, according to the Israeli authorities, Israel was not responsible for the protection of Palestinians in the occupied territories.[96] However, the Committee noted that the State's obligations under the Covenant apply in 'all territories and populations under its *effective control.*'[97] Consequently, the Committee expressed regret that Israel did not provide adequate information in relation to the occupied territories, unambiguously noting that it is obliged to provide information on the enjoyment of the Covenant's rights with regard to *everyone* within the territory in which it exercises control.[98] The Committee stressed the applicability of the Covenant to all territories under Israel's jurisdiction by requesting that the State provide additional information on the realisation of economic, social and cultural rights in the occupied territories in order to complete the examination of the State Party's initial report.[99] In sum, from the Committee's work it is beyond doubt that States Parties are required to apply the Covenant within their territories and within the territory over which they have effective control.

It is interesting to note that the conclusions of the Committee in the case of Israel are in line with the approach followed by both the HRC and CERD Committee. These treaty bodies have not only stressed that Israel has the responsibilities to fully apply their respective instruments in the occupied territories,[100] but they have also discussed and expressed their concern about the socio-economic conditions within the State's jurisdiction. In this regard, for example, both Committees have discussed the living

95 Concluding Observations Israel E/1999/22 para. 234. It is important to mention that in the List of Issues, the Committee expressly required the Government of Israel to explain why the report did not include a discussion on the extent to which Palestinians living in the occupied territories enjoy their economic, social and cultural rights. List of Issues Israel E/C.12/Q/ISR/1 para. 1 of 10 June 1998.

96 See, for example, Mr. Blass (Israel) in E/C.12/1998/SR.31 para. 45.

97 Concluding Observations Israel E/1999/22 para. 234.

98 Concluding Observations Israel E/1999/22 para. 234.

99 Concluding Observations Israel E/1999/22 para. 258. The Government of Israel submitted additional information which was examined during the 26th extraordinary session of the Committee. However, the information did not address the enjoyment of the Covenant's rights in the occupied territories and the Committee again deplored this significant omission [Concluding Observations Israel E/C.12/1/Add.69].

100 See Concluding Observations Israel CCPR/C/79/Add.93 para. 10 and CERD Committee Concluding Observations Israel CERD/C/304/Add.45 para. 10.

conditions of Arabs and Bedouins, the access of Palestinians to land and water in the occupied territories and the right to housing.[101]

In a second relevant case, the Committee also explained the State's responsibility for the application of the Covenant in non-metropolitan territories (dependent territories). In contrast with article 34 of the European Social Charter which applies to non-metropolitan territories only if an express declaration is made,[102] the Covenant applies to all territories without requiring such a declaration. This was apparent when the Committee considered the Second Periodic Report of the Netherlands (the European part of the Kingdom). The State argued that 'the Government of the Netherlands is not responsible for the implementation of economic, social and cultural rights in Aruba and the Netherlands Antilles, given that Aruba and the Netherlands Antilles are equal parts of the Kingdom of the Netherlands and the Government of the Netherlands contributes every year 1.5 per cent of GNP to Aruba and the Netherlands Antilles.'[103] However, the Committee expressed concern regarding this statement and in its Concluding Observations 'urges the State Party to ensure that it complies fully with its obligations under the Covenant as they apply to Aruba and the Netherlands Antilles.'[104]

With regard to the territorial application of the Covenant, it is important to note that the Covenant does not require States Parties to protect individuals living abroad who are normally subject to their jurisdiction against the wrongful acts of a foreign State. However, the Committee has shown apprehension with regard to a strict interpretation of the Covenant's territorial application and this concern suggests a more protective approach in this regard. When considering the initial report of Sri Lanka, the Committee noted with concern that 'hundreds of thousands of Sri Lankan women [were] working abroad as domestic helpers, many of them underpaid and treated as virtual slaves.'[105] Certainly, according to the information received by the Committee, these women were subject to exploitation, but the violations had been committed abroad and attributed to another State.[106]

Generally, under the Covenant, States do not assume obligations to protect individuals against violations committed abroad by another State.[107] Nonetheless, in the case of Sri Lanka, the Committee seemed to apply a broad interpretation in considering that, under the Covenant, Sri Lankan authorities did have a role to play in the protection of

---

101 See Concluding Observations Israel CCPR/C/79/Add.93 paras. 12, 14 and 24. In addition see the statements by Ms. Evatt [Summary Record CCPR/C/SR.1675 paras. 76-78]. As to the CERD Committee, see Concluding Observations Israel CERD/C/304/Add.45 paras. 17 and 19.

102 Article 34 European Social Charter and Article L of the Revised European Social Charter.

103 Concluding Observations the Netherlands E/1999/22 para. 186.

104 Concluding Observations the Netherlands E/1999/22 para. 194.

105 Concluding Observations Sri Lanka E/1999/22 para. 77.

106 It is worth recalling here that there is a violation of the obligation to protect when a State fails to take the necessary measures to safeguard persons within its jurisdiction. Therefore, even when such women are exploited by third parties, the foreign State would be held responsible.

107 However, it may be possible to protect a national who is a victim abroad through diplomatic channels.

their nationals and it examined the State's 'internal responsibility' for the situation. Indeed, the Committee approached the national consequences of the emigration of these women by taking into account the welfare of the children they left behind. The Committee 'regrets that the Government has not made a serious effort to assess the negative impact of this phenomenon on children who are left in vulnerable and difficult circumstances without their mothers and to take appropriate remedial actions.'[108] Subsequently, the Committee acknowledged that it 'recognises that economic conditions provide a strong incentive for many adults to seek work abroad, but notes that any resulting separation of parents, and specially mothers, from their children can have significant negative consequences, especially for the children. The Committee recommends that a study be undertaken to shed more light on the issues involved and to provide a basis for more informed decision-making in such cases.'[109]

Moreover, in this case, the Committee seemed to suggest that the State retained some responsibility as to the fate of those women abroad due to its failure to take preventive measures. In this line of reasoning, the Concluding Observations note that 'the Committee strongly recommends that the Government undertake an assessment of the impact on children of the prolonged absence of their mothers working abroad with a view to educating Sri Lankan women in this regard, and to discourage women from leaving the country for employment abroad as domestic helpers, the conditions of which are often deplorable.'[110]

2.2.3 Concluding comments

There must be no doubt that the Covenant applies to *everyone within the jurisdiction* of the State Party. This is the interpretation consistently provided by the Committee in the examination of State Party reports as well as in its General Comments. In the light of the Committee's work, it is clear that 'within the jurisdiction' entails all territories in which the State Party exercises control, even *de facto* control. Consequently, States must provide information to the Committee on the enjoyment of the Covenant's rights by everyone within the territories under their control.

Bearing in mind the possible adoption of an optional protocol establishing a complaint procedure, it would be appropriate for the Committee to follow the relevant jurisprudence of the Human Rights Committee and the European Court of Human Rights in which they apply the territorial application of their respective instruments in the light of the object and purpose of human rights instruments. In this context, we note

108 Concluding Observations Sri Lanka E/1999/22 para. 77.

109 Concluding Observations Sri Lanka E/1999/22 para. 94. In the same vein, in the Concluding Observations Philippines in 1995, it was noted: '[w]hile the Committee recognises, in relation to the issue of Filipino overseas workers, that the Government cannot control such emigration, it believes that more can and should be done to inform and educate existing potential workers about the difficulties they might face abroad and about their rights.' Concluding Observations Philippines E/1996/22 para. 128.

110 Concluding Observations Sri Lanka E/1999/22 para. 91.

that, according to the Human Rights Committee, States Parties can be held accountable for violations of rights contained in the ICCPR which its agents commit in the territory of another State, either with the acquiescence of the Government of that State or without it.[111] Moreover, States Parties are responsible for the actions committed by their diplomatic representatives abroad.[112] And finally, as is apparent from the HRC jurisprudence, persons who have fled abroad are not prevented from submitting communications against the State where a violation is alleged to have taken place.[113]

With reference to the case law of the European Court of Human Rights, we recall here the case of Loizidou v. Turkey where the Court stressed that the concept of 'jurisdiction' is not restricted to the national territory of the State. The Court held that the responsibility of the State 'could also arise when as a consequence of military action – whether lawful or unlawful – it exercises effective control of an area outside its national territory. The obligation to secure, in such an area, the rights and freedoms set out in the Convention, derives from the fact of such control whether it be exercised directly, through its armed forces, or through a subordinate local administration.'[114]

Another important decision of the European Court which is of relevance in this context is the judgement in the case of Cyprus v. Turkey, where it held that 'the acquiescence or connivance of the authorities of a Contracting State in the acts of private individuals which violate the Convention rights of other individuals within its jurisdiction may engage that State's responsibility under the Convention.'[115] This approach would be appropriate to deal with violations of the Covenant's rights by third parties, such as those committed by transnational corporations.

3 General limitation clause (Article 4 ICESCR)

'The States Parties to the present Covenant recognise that, in the enjoyment of those rights provided by the State in conformity with the present Covenant, the State may subject such rights only to such limitations as are determined by law only in so far as this may be compatible with the nature of these rights and solely for the purpose of promoting the general welfare in a democratic society.'

---

111 See, for example, Lopez Burgos v. Uruguay, *loc. cit.* (note 92), para. 12.3 and Celiberti de Casariego v. Uruguay, *loc. cit.* (note 92), para. 10.3. In both cases the individual opinion of Mr. Tomuschat are essential for a proper understanding of the Committee's views.

112 See, for example, Mabel Pereira Montero v. Uruguay, Communication No. 106/1981, views of 31 March 1983 and Samuel Lichtensztejn v. Uruguay, Communication No. 77/1980, views of 31 March 1983.

113 See, for example, Antonio Viana Acosta v. Uruguay, Communication No. 110/1981, views of 29 March 1984 and Massiotti *et al.* v. Uruguay, Communication No. 25/1978, views of 26 July 1982.

114 Loizidou v. Turkey, Application No. 1531/89, Judgement on the merits of 28 November 1996, para. 52.

115 Cyprus v. Turkey, Application No. 25781/94, Judgement of 10 May 2001, para. 81.

This provision is similar to article 31(1) of the European Social Charter[116] and article 5 of the Protocol of San Salvador.[117] However, there are some differences of which we should take note. The limitation clauses of the ICESCR and the Protocol of San Salvador are both formulated in permissive terms. They permit States to impose restrictions, but only if they comply with the requirements set forth therein. In contrast, the limitation clause of the European Social Charter is formulated in negative terms and prohibits the imposition of restrictions on certain rights, except in specific circumstances.[118] This formulation has the advantage that it emphasises the exceptional character of such restrictions. However, as we will see, the limited scope of article 4 ICESCR clearly reflects its protective function and its limited application.

Another difference between article 4 ICESCR and article 31(1) ESC is that the European clause seems to allow more discretion to States to impose limitations on the enjoyment of rights. In fact, the range of justifications that can be invoked under article 4 ICESCR is limited. The ESC contains additional grounds on the basis of which States may restrict or limit rights, specifically *public interest, national security, public health* and *morals*. These grounds are not contained in article 4 ICESCR and therefore, in general, under the Covenant the States Parties are not allowed to impose limitations or restrictions on the Covenant's rights on the basis of such conditions.

However, it is important to note that article 4 ICESCR is a general clause applicable to all substantive rights contained in Part III of the Covenant. Moreover, article 8 ICESCR expressly allows restrictions to the enjoyment of the rights contained therein on the basis of specific grounds. For example, the right to form and join trade unions (article 8(1) ICESCR) allows States to impose restrictions in the interest of *national security* or *public order* or for *the protection of the rights and freedoms of others*.[119]

116 Article 31(1) ESC uses the following formulation: '[...] shall not be subject to any restrictions or limitations not specified [...], except such as are prescribed by law and are necessary in a democratic society for the protection of the rights and freedoms of others or for the protection of public interest, national security, public health, or morals.'
The second paragraph of the article adds, 'The restrictions permitted under this Charter to the rights and obligations set forth herein shall not be applied for any purpose other than that for which they have been prescribed.'

117 Article 5 Protocol of San Salvador states, 'The States Parties may establish restrictions and limitations on the enjoyment and exercise of the rights established herein by means of laws promulgated for the purpose of preserving the general welfare in a democratic society only to the extent that they are not incompatible with the purpose and reason underlying those rights.'

118 Article 31(1) ESC uses the following formulation: '[...] shall not be subject to any restrictions or limitations not specified [...], except such as are prescribed by law and are necessary in a democratic society for the protection of the rights and freedoms of others or for the protection of public interest, national security , public health, or morals.' The second paragraph of the article adds, 'the restrictions permitted under this Charter to the rights and obligations set forth herein shall not be applied for any purpose other than that for which they have been prescribed.'

119 See, for example, Art. 8(a) ICESCR. The same grounds for limitations are prescribed in regard to the right of trade unions to function freely (Art. 8(c) ICESCR) (emphasis added). For a comprehensive analysis of the meaning of these expressions see the Limburg Principles Nos. 59 to 69.

Although article 4 ICESCR authorises States to impose limitations on the enjoyment of the Covenant rights, the Committee has emphasised that article 4 'is primarily intended to protect the rights of individuals rather than to permit the imposition of limitations by States.'[120] Therefore, States wanting to impose limitations must interpret article 4 in a very restrictive manner and comply with all the protective safeguards contained therein.

Moreover, it seems that there are some Covenant rights that cannot be subject to restrictions. This is stressed by the Limburg Principles, which state that 'the article [article 4 ICESCR] was not meant to introduce limitations on rights affecting the subsistence or survival of the individual or integrity of the person.'[121]

It is important to stress here that the limitation clause of article 4 is not intended to deal with limitations required by inadequate resource availability.[122] As commentators have noted, from the *travaux préparatoires* it is clear that article 4 was seen by the drafters:

> 'As dealing with limitations other than those that could be imposed under article 2(1) on the grounds of limited resource availability. The debate over Article 4 thus focused on the need for measures to harmonise the relationship between enjoyment of particular rights and the legitimate interests of the community. The limitation clause was directed towards cases where rights might collide with one another and where the exigencies of state-administered socioeconomic welfare programs might necessitate limitations on the provisions of benefits or other entitlements; limitations different in kind from those already contained in Article 2(1).'[123]

The protective character of article 4 is reflected in its wording which contains numerous safeguards, such as 'determined by law,' 'compatible with the nature of these rights', 'solely for the purposes of promoting the general welfare,' and 'in a democratic society'. Because the meaning of these phrases has been developed extensively elsewhere,[124] only a brief discussion is necessary here.

(a) *Determined by law:*

This is a very important safeguard. According to the Limburg Principles, any law imposing restrictions has to comply with some formal, as well as substantive require-

---

120 General Comment No. 14 para. 28. See, also, General Comment No. 13 para. 42 and Limburg Principle No. 46.

121 Limburg Principle No. 47.

122 This point has been explained elsewhere. See the analysis in Alston, P. & Quinn, G.: 'The nature and scope of States parties' obligations under the International Covenant on Economic, Social and Cultural Rights.' In: *HRQ,* vol. 9 No. 2, (1987), pp. 194-197.

123 *Ibidem:* p. 194 (Footnote omitted).

124 See Limburg Principles Nos. 48-56; Dankwa, E.V.O & Flinterman, C.: 'Commentary by the rapporteurs on the nature and scope of States parties' obligations.' In: *HRQ*, vol. 9, (1987), pp. 143-145; and Alston & Quinn, *loc. cit.* (note 122), pp. 192-205.

ments. The formal requirements entail that the law must be a national law of general application, clear, accessible to everyone and in force at the time when the limitation is applied. Moreover, the law imposing the limitation must provide adequate safeguards and effective remedies against illegal or abusive imposition.[125]

As to the substantive requirements, the Limburg Principles state that 'laws imposing limitations on the exercise of economic, social and cultural rights shall not be arbitrary or unreasonable or discriminatory.'[126] These requirements provide significant additional protection to individuals and further restrict the discretion of States to impose limitations on the enjoyment of the Covenant's rights.

In other words, any restriction on the enjoyment of the rights set forth in the Covenant must have an objective and reasonable justification. Similarly, there must be a reasonable relationship between the aim for which the restriction is used and the measures taken.

The principle of non-discrimination will be analysed in further detail when we deal with article 2(2) ICESCR.[127] However, here it is important to note that States Parties cannot impose restrictions that positively affect one segment of society to the detriment of another without there being an objective and reasonable criterion for the differential treatment. This means, for example, that there is a violation of this principle if, in order to gentrify or develop an urban area for the benefit of the upper classes, the State imposes restrictions on poor people who are evicted from their homes in order to make way for the new development.[128] This example illustrates an infringement of the principle of non-discrimination and such actions can never be said to promote the 'general welfare in a democratic society' and therefore States must refrain from taking such measures.

(b) *Restriction must be compatible with the nature of these rights:*
As indicated in the Limburg Principles, this phrase requires that 'a limitation shall not be interpreted or applied so as to jeopardise the essence of the right concerned.'[129] States Parties have the burden of providing that a limitation is compatible with the 'nature' of a given right.

Before the Committee began functioning, some scholars had argued that this phrase suggested that, by virtue of their nature, some rights may be considered not to be

125 Limburg Principles Nos. 48, 50 and 51. See in addition, 'The Siracusa principles on the limitation and derogation provision in the International Covenant on Civil and Political Rights,' Principles Nos. 15-18, In: *The Review International Commission of Jurist*, No. 36, June (1986), pp. 47-56. The Siracusa Principles were adopted by a group of 31 distinguished experts in international law who met in Siracusa, Sicily in 1984.

126 Limburg Principle No. 49.

127 See the analysis of the principle of non-discrimination in Chapter VIII of the present study.

128 See General Comment No. 7 para. 5.

129 Limburg Principle No. 56.

subject to limitations. The example mentioned by scholars was the right to food.[130] The Committee has not clearly endorsed this interpretation, although there are reasons for viewing it as the correct approach. In fact, the prohibition on imposing restrictions on the right to food has been emphasised by some Committee members.[131]

From this author's perspective, a restriction on the enjoyment of a right would affect the very 'nature' (essence) of the right if it implies a *de facto* derogation of the right. For example, if, in order to have access to medical care, individuals need to fulfil an excessive number of requirements, it may be that an individual in a critical condition does not receive the necessary treatment on time and dies as a result. In such a case, the requirements meant that the individual was prevented from receiving the necessary treatment.

In the light of General Comment No. 14, it is possible to say that the minimum core content of the rights can never be subject to restrictions. Such restrictions are not compatible with the 'nature' of the right and would imply a *de facto* derogation from the right.[132]

> '47. In determining which actions or omissions amount to a violation of the right to health, it is important to distinguish the inability from the unwillingness of a State party to comply with its obligations under article 12. This follows from article 12(1), which speaks of the highest attainable standard of health, as well as from article 2(1) of the Covenant, which obliges each State party to take the necessary steps to the maximum of its available resources. A State which is unwilling to use the maximum of its available resources for the realization of the right to health is in violation of its obligations under article 12. If resource constraints render it impossible for a State to comply fully with its Covenant obligations, it has the burden of justifying that every effort has nevertheless been made to use all available resources at its disposal in order to satisfy, as a matter of priority, the obligations outlined above. It should be stressed, however, that a State party cannot, under any circumstances whatsoever, justify its non-compliance with the core obligations set out in paragraph 43 above, which are *non-derogable.*' (Emphasis added)

130 Dankwa & Flinterman, *loc. cit.* (note 123), pp. 143-144.

131 See, for example, Mr. Riedel E/C.12/1998/SR.32 para. 53.

132 As noted in the General Comment 'It should be stressed, however, that a State Party cannot, under any circumstances whatsoever, justify its non-compliance with the core obligations set out in paragraph 43 above which are non-derogable.' [General Comment No. 14 para. 47]. From this author's perspective, the Committee is not very clear on this point. The statement that the core obligations are 'non-derogable' might suggest that there are some other provisions under the Covenant which are susceptible to derogation. As we will see, due to the absence of a provision providing for derogation, none of the rights contained in the Covenant can be derogated from. This statement should be understood as indicating that the core content of the right cannot be subject to any restriction as restrictions are incompatible with the very nature of the right.

(c) *For the purposes of promoting the general welfare:*
This requirement 'shall be construed to mean furthering the well-being of the people as a whole.'[133] As explained by commentators, any limitation must be 'for and in the interest of the society as a whole.'[134] This requirement prevents States from invoking interests such as 'national security' or 'preservation of public order' to justify limitations on economic, social and cultural rights, except if they prove that they are 'genuinely synonymous' with 'general welfare.'[135]

The *travaux préparatoires* of the Covenant show that the requirement of 'general welfare in a democratic society' contained in article 4 ICESCR was adopted in order to further develop the protection of economic, social and cultural rights. In fact, the term 'democratic society' was introduced in order to replace terms such as 'morality' and 'public order' contained in article 29 UDHR (limitation provision). It was considered that the latter grounds were unrelated to the rights protected by the Covenant and that they could give rise to problems of interpretation.[136]

The fact that the restrictions permitted under article 4 cannot be applied for a purpose other than the promotion of general welfare in a democratic society implies an important additional limitation to the discretion of States Parties. Let us illustrate this with an example. Suppose that a State Party to the Covenant limits social welfare benefits previously provided to asylum seekers in its territory and argues that the measure is necessary to reduce economic incentives which attract 'bogus asylum claimants' (economic migrants making unfounded claims in order to receive the welfare entitlement available to asylum seekers), or to discourage those who have already lodged their claims from pursuing them.[137] In light of article 4, such measures may entail a violation of the Covenant. Although the purpose of such measures may be genuine and legitimate in the light of national immigration policies or the legitimate sovereign right of a government to combat illegal immigration, it does not allow governments to breach the international obligations assumed under the Covenant. Under article 4 ICESCR, immigration control and the eradication of abuses would not be a legitimate justification for restricting the rights set forth in the Covenant. Under the obligations assumed through the ICESCR, any restriction or limitation on the rights (in this example, the welfare benefits provided to asylum seekers), must be taken solely

133 Limburg Principle No. 52.

134 Dankwa & Flinterman, *loc. cit.* (note 124), p. 143.

135 See Alston & Quinn, *loc. cit.* (note 122), p. 202.

136 See, *Ibidem:* pp. 203-205 and Svensson-McCarthy, A.: *The international law of human rights and states of exception with special reference to the travaux préparatoires and case-law of the international monitoring organs*, Martinus Nijhoff Publishers, the Hague, (1998), pp. 159-161.

137 The example is particularly relevant when we take into account that in recent years there has been a decline in support for the institution of asylum in many countries (acknowledged by UNHCR EXCOM Annual Report 1999. UN doc. A/AC.96/923 of 14 September 1999, para. 3), and that the reasons cited here are often used as a justification by the States concerned.

with the purpose of promoting the 'general welfare' in a 'democratic society' and not for immigrations reasons.

In our example, the State can only restrict the Covenant rights if it has economic constraints and there is a demonstrable necessity to limit the enjoyment of these rights (*e.g.* by reducing or cutting social welfare benefits to asylum seekers). But even if the State is facing a real constriction of resources, diminishing or withdrawing welfare benefits must be the final resort and the restriction remains open to scrutiny by the Committee.[138] It will always be necessary for the Committee to examine whether or not the restrictive measures are truly required by economic circumstances. In sum, a State Party to the Covenant which seeks to legitimately prevent an inflow of asylum seekers with which it cannot objectively cope must find ways to do so that do not infringe international obligations under the Covenant.

(d) *In a democratic society:*
According to the Limburg Principles, 'while there is no single model of a democratic society, a society which recognises and respects the human rights set forth in the Charter of the United Nations and the Universal Declaration of Human Rights may be viewed as meeting this definition.'[139] As stated in the Principles, this expression must be interpreted as imposing a further restriction on the application of limitations.[140] Furthermore, the Principles establish that 'the burden is upon a State imposing limitations to demonstrate that the limitations do not impair the democratic functioning of the society.'[141]

The reference to a 'democratic society' has a decisive role to play in controlling the application of restrictions. In fact, the notion of a democratic society requires respect for the principle of 'proportionality' and therefore a balance must be struck between the purposes and the limitations imposed. The limitations imposed on the enjoyment of the Covenant's rights must be those that are strictly required by the exigencies of the situation. The harsher the restriction imposed by the State on the enjoyment of rights, the stronger the reasons required to justify it.

In this context, it is worth mentioning that the European Court of Human Rights has also held that the principle of proportionality is implicit in the concept of 'democratic society' contained in article 8 ECHR,

> '[...] enables the Court to balance all the relevant interests and factual circumstances, and also to take into account the intensity of the infringement as well as the question whether the essence of the right invoked has been infringed. The scale that the Court utilises seems to imply that the more far-reaching the infringement or the more essential the aspect of the

---

138 Alston & Quinn, *loc. cit.* (note 122), p. 181.
139 Limburg Principle No. 55.
140 Limburg Principle No. 53.
141 Limburg Principle No. 54. See, in addition, the Siracusa Principles Nos. 19 to 21.

right that has been interfered with, the more substantial or compelling the legitimate aims pursued must be.'[142]

With reference to the Covenant, the principle of proportionality entails that States must not impose restrictions that are disproportionate to the aim sought, for example, by restricting the movement of people with HIV/AIDS in order to control the HIV/AIDS pandemic.[143] The proportionality test is a strict one. When examining States Parties' reports, the Committee should employ it as a tool to determine compliance with the Covenant when States impose limits on the exercise of rights. In general, restrictions on the enjoyment of economic, social and cultural rights are harsh in nature and must be exceptional and properly justified.

In sum, any restriction on the enjoyment of the Covenant's rights must be legally established, non-discriminatory, proportional, compatible with the nature of the rights and designed to further the general welfare. As article 4 ICESCR is a general clause contained in Part II of the Covenant, every restriction upon the enjoyment of the Covenant's rights must meet the requirements of article 4. These requirements are very strict and are thus difficult to satisfy in most cases. The few cases that seem to justify restrictions are related to economic crises or natural disasters that require the reallocation of resources to deal with the damage. However, even in such events, resource scarcity does not relieve the State from the burden of complying with all obligations imposed by the Covenant. Even in the event of a decline in the resources caused by external factors, the State must comply with certain minimum obligations and give due priority to vulnerable social groups.[144] Moreover, States must respect the principle of non-discrimination. As Klerk notes,

> 'A declining economy is no justification for burdening only socially disadvantaged groups. No new discriminatory situations should be created; and even in a time of a declining economy states are obliged to end existing discriminatory practices. Nondiscrimination is not a favor that can be granted only in time of a growing economy.'[145]

It is important to mention here that any restrictions must be consistent with the State's other international obligations, as required by article 5 ICESCR.[146] Finally, it is also important to stress that the burden falls upon States Parties to prove that a limitation imposed upon the enjoyment of the Covenant's rights is legitimate. This is, of course,

142 Dijk, P. van & Hoof, G.J.H. van, 1998, p. 537.

143 See General Comment No. 14 para. 28.

144 As emphasised by the Maastricht Guidelines, 'resource scarcity does not relieve States of certain minimum obligations in respect of the implementation of economic, social and cultural rights,' Maastricht Guidelines No. 10. See also, General Comment No. 4 para. 11.

145 Klerk, 1987, p. 264.

146 The scope of article 5 will be dealt with in the next section.

a heavy burden of proof, but it is consistent with the strong protection provided by article 4.

3.1 The Committee's approach to article 4 ICESCR in the General Comments

Article 4 ICESCR may serve as an important tool to strengthen the protection of economic, social and cultural rights because it establishes significant safeguards against undue limitations to the enjoyment of the Covenant's rights. However, the Committee does not seem to fully recognise the relevance of this provision. Only in General Comment Nos. 13 and 14 has the Committee made brief references to article 4 ICESCR and even in these General Comments it does so without any in-depth analysis. Nevertheless, the brief references in the General Comments allow us to draw some conclusions as to the Committee's approach to the 'general limitation clause.'

Principally through its General Comments, the Committee has emphasised the protective character of article 4. As it has emphasised, 'the Covenant's limitations clause, article 4, is primarily intended to be protective of the rights of individuals rather than permissive of the imposition of limitations by the State.'[147] In line with the protective character of the provision, the Committee stresses that States Parties have the burden of justifying that the restrictions imposed on the exercise of the rights comply with 'each of the elements identified in article 4.'[148]

Furthermore, the Committee has noted that even when limitations are permitted, 'they should be of limited duration and subject to review.'[149] The Committee has explicitly stated that restrictions that are not in conformity with article 4 constitute a 'violation' of the Covenant.[150]

The Committee has been very explicit as to the importance of the principle of proportionality with regard to article 4 ICESCR.[151] Although the Committee has referred to the limitation clause almost solely in relation to the right to the highest standard of health, from the Committee's approach it is possible to conclude that the Committee considers that the principle of proportionality requires compliance with two additional principles that we may term 'suitability' and 'indispensability'. The principle of 'suitability' requires that any restrictive measures be appropriate for the achievement of the aims pursued.[152] The principle of 'indispensability' requires that the restrictions must not be more severe than is necessary for the attainment of the aim sought. As the

147 General Comment No. 13 para. 42 and General Comment No. 14 para. 28.

148 General Comment No. 13 para. 42 and General Comment No. 14 para. 28.

149 General Comment No. 14 para. 29.

150 General Comment No. 13 para. 59.

151 General Comment No. 14 para. 28.

152 General Comment No. 14 para. 28.

Committee explains, 'the least restrictive alternative must be adopted where several types of limitations are available.'[153]

Furthermore, and although it employs language that is rather weak, the Committee also emphasises in General Comment No. 14 that limitations should be of limited duration, and that they should be subject to review.[154]

3.2 The Committee's approach to article 4 ICESCR in the Concluding Observations

Considering State reports, the Committee has not dealt with the restrictions imposed on the enjoyment of the Covenant's rights in a consistent and straightforward manner.[155] Arguably, the lack of attention that the Committee has paid to article 4 is a consequence of the insufficient information that it receives. While it is clear that States Parties have the burden of justifying any restriction imposed on the enjoyment of the Covenant's rights they tend to provide little or no information on this issue. However, the Committee shares an important part of the responsibility for the inadequate information that it receives in regard to limitations imposed by the State on the enjoyment of the Covenant's rights. In fact, the 'Reporting Guidelines'[156] do not require States to provide information regarding article 4 and in the great majority of cases the Committee does not require such information from States either in the List of Issues prepared by the Committee's pre-sessional working group, or as follow-up measures. These omissions are regrettable.

Due to the inadequacy of the 'Reporting Guidelines', in most cases States do not include in their reports information on the limitations or restrictions imposed on the enjoyment of the Covenant's rights. Of the few States that do include such information, the data provided tends to be, at best, only indirectly relevant to the Covenant or appears to be irreconcilable with reality. For example, some States have included voluminous information under the heading 'article 4 ICESCR,' but refer principally to national procedures for imposing a state of emergency and the civil and political rights that may be suspended. However, they generally fail to describe exactly how economic, social and cultural rights may be affected.[157]

From the few State reports that incorporate relevant information regarding article 4, we may deduce that there is a high level of compliance with article 4 ICESCR. In

153 General Comment No. 14 para. 29.

154 General Comment No. 14 para. 29.

155 The exception is the approach to the restrictions imposed by States on the enjoyment of article 8 ICESCR. See the analysis below.

156 See note 10.

157 See, for example, Initial Report Nepal E/1990/5/Add.45 para. 88, Third Periodic Report Portugal E/1994/104/Add.20 para. 73-96 and Initial Report Peru E/1990/5/Add.29 paras. 114-122 and para. 153.

fact, States report (a) that they do not impose limitations on the enjoyment of economic, social and cultural rights,[158] and, (b) that the limitations imposed in their national legislation are compatible with the requirements set forth in article 4.[159] Unfortunately, in many cases such statements seem closer to fantasy than to reality. To illustrate this, we need only refer to the Second Periodic Report of the Dominican Republic which expressly noted that 'because of the intrinsic nature of the economic, social and cultural rights of the human person, it is difficult to conceive of any type of restrictions on them either in legislation or in practice.'[160] Similarly, the Second Report of Algeria stated that 'the measures taken under the state of emergency in no way affect the implementation of the International Covenant on Economic, Social and Cultural Rights. Algerian citizens have continued to exercise in full the rights recognised in the Covenant despite the havoc wrought and the crimes committed by terrorist criminals.'[161]

Despite the fact that States do not usually provide information on article 4 in their reports, the Committee does not generally use the List of Issues to require States to do so. The Committee has required information in relation to article 4 in the List of Issues in very few cases and has done so in very general terms.[162]

Rather than requesting information regarding article 4 (general limitation clause), the Committee has sometimes inquired about the limitations imposed in the exercise of a specific right. Again, such questions, except in the case of article 8, are very exceptional.[163] In the limited number of cases in which the Committee has required

---

158 Third Periodic Report Mexico E/1994/104/Add.18 para. 52. In this case, it is worth noting that the alternative Report presented by a group of NGOs highlighted a significant number of restrictions imposed by the Government (paras. 130-139). Unfortunately, the report presented these restrictions under the heading 'Article 5: restrictions upon the fundamental rights respected in Mexico', while the section refers principally to the contents of article 4 and not to article 5 ICESCR (Nonetheless, at the beginning of this section the alternative report made a reference to the State report that is correct, because it refers to para. 52 of the State report which relate to article 4 ICESCR). See also, the Second Periodic Report of the Dominican Republic [E/1990/6/Add.7 para. 32] and the Second Periodic Report of Morocco [E/1990/6/Add.20 para. 46].

159 See, for example, Second Periodic Report Venezuela which states, 'Venezuela fully recognises and complies with the provisions of the statement in article 4 of the Covenant.' E/1990/6/Add.19 para. 26. Along the same line, see for example, Initial Report of Egypt E/1990/5/Add.38 paras. 71-74; Initial Report China [Hong Kong] E/1990/5/Add.43 para. 39; Initial Report Zimbabwe E/1990/5/Add.28 paras. 12-13; Initial Report El Salvador E/1990/5/Add.25 para. 28; and Initial Report Guatemala E/1990/5/Add.24 para. 8.

160 Subsequently, the report states, 'The intrinsic nature of these rights has been fully understood by the Dominican State, which has not established any limitations on their enjoyment either in its constitutional principles or in positive law.' Second Periodic Report of the Dominican Republic E/1990/6/Add.7 para. 32.

161 Second Periodic Report Algeria E/1990/Add.26 para. 46.

162 See, for example, List of Issues Kyrgyzstan E/C.12/Q/KYRG/1 para. 12, of 10 December 1999 and List of Issues Portugal E/C.12/Q/POR/1 paras. 9-10, of 21 May 1999.

163 See, among the exceptions, the List of Issues issued in connection with the Third Periodic Report of Canada, where in regard to the right to health it was asked about 'any evidence of restrictions' in access to health care for the poor and what the Government was doing to remedy the situation. [List of Issues

information regarding limitations imposed on the exercise of a given substantive right in the List of Issues, it has done so because it has previously received information about the existence of undue restrictions. For example, in the List of Issues to be taken up in connection with the consideration of the Third Periodic Report of the Syrian Arab Republic, the Committee requested information regarding the limitations imposed on article 15 ICESCR because it had received an alternative report stating that there was a 'systematic limitation of Kurdish culture and of Kurds' possibilities to engage in cultural activities, such as the prohibition on speaking and publishing materials in the Kurdish language, and producing Kurdish music.' Due to this information, the Committee requested the State to provide additional information.

As mentioned, although the Committee generally does not require information on the limitations imposed on the enjoyment of rights, the exception is the analysis of limitations imposed by States under article 8 ICESCR, which are constantly addressed by the Committee.[164] Article 8 ICESCR allows restrictions on more grounds that those provided for in the general limitation clause of article 4 ICESCR[165] and this fact justifies that the Committee strictly monitors the application of such restrictions by States. However, the Committee should pay more attention to restrictions imposed by States Parties on the enjoyment of other rights as well.

During the consideration of a State's report, it has sometimes become apparent to the Committee that restrictions or limitations have been imposed on the enjoyment of the Covenant's rights. However, even in such situations, the Committee has not always applied article 4 ICESCR in a rigorous manner. An illustrative example is the examination of the Third Periodic Report of Canada. In this case, it was apparent that the State had placed restrictions or limitations on the enjoyment of the Covenant's rights.[166]

Canada E/C.12/Q/CAN/1 para. 54, of 10 June 1998]. Similarly, with regard to the report of Georgia, in relation to article 3, the Committee requested information about restrictions on women's work that the State had referred to in its report [List of Issues Georgia E/C.12/Q/GEO/1 para. 14, of 21 May 1999].

164 The Committee has analysed restrictions imposed on the enjoyment of article 8 in, for example, Concluding Observations Honduras E/C.12/1/Add.57 para. 18; Concluding Observations Jordan E/2001/22 paras. 240 and 254; Concluding Observations Kyrgyztan E/2001/22 para. 343; Concluding Observations Morocco E/2001/22 paras. 533 and 557; Concluding Observations Denmark E/2000/22 para. 110; Concluding Observations Germany E/C.12/1/Add.68 para. 22; and Concluding Observations Ukraine E/C.12/1/Add.65 para. 27. In some cases, the Committee clearly expressed the view that the restrictions imposed by the State constituted a 'violation' of article 8 ICESCR. See, for example, Concluding Observations Canada E/1999/22 para. 406; Concluding Observations Nigeria E/1999/22 paras. 111 and 130; and Concluding Observations United Kingdom of Great Britain and Northern Ireland E/1998/22 para. 294.

165 See the text accompanying note 119.

166 The restrictions imposed were apparent in the information provided by the State [Third Periodic Report Canada E/1994/104/Add.17 and reply to the List of Issues E/C.12/Q/CAN/1], as well as from the information provided by NGOs. In this regard, of particular relevance was the written statement submitted by the American Association of Jurists (Pan-Canadian section) and the *Ligue des droits et libertés du Québec* [E/C.12/1998/NGO/4, of 10 November 1998].

Exceptionally, the List of Issues addressed the question of limitations[167] and some Committee members took it up with the Government representative during the dialogue.[168]

The 'constructive dialogue' held with the Government representatives seemed to indicate that the Committee was sympathetic to the idea that if the State clearly shows the existence of budgetary difficulties it may be justified in imposing limitations, but it would need to provide proof in this respect.[169] Arguably, government representatives were able to prove the existence of some economic restrictions during the dialogue.

In the Concluding Observations on the Third Periodic Report of Canada, it was clearly stated that vulnerable groups within Canadian society had been affected by the restrictions or limitations imposed upon the enjoyment of the Covenant's rights.[170] However, the language employed by the Committee in the Concluding Observations was relatively weak, particularly if we compare it with the Committee's approach in its General Comments. The Committee seems to have accepted the Government's plea of resource scarcity as a justification for restrictions, and the Concluding Observations do not reflect the strong position held in General Comment No. 3 on vulnerable groups. According to General Comment No. 3, 'even in times of severe resources constraints whether caused by a process of adjustment, of economic recession, or by other factors *the vulnerable members of society can and indeed must be protected.*'[171] Although some Committee members emphasised this point during the dialogue, it was not subsequently incorporated in the Concluding Observations.[172]

What is even more striking is that the Committee seemed to have forgotten that the protective character of article 4 ICESCR places upon States the heavy burden of justifying that restrictions imposed on the exercise of the rights comply with each of

---

167 List of Issues Canada E/C.12/Q/CAN/1 paras. 16 to 22 and para. 56, of 10 June 1998.

168 See, for example, during the 47th meeting the statements by Mr. Pillay [E/C.12/1998/SR.47 paras. 16 and 31]; Mr. Ceausu [E/C.12/1998/SR.47 para. 26]; Ms. Jiménez Butragueño [E/C.12/1998/SR.47 para. 27]; Mr. Ahmed [E/C.12/1998/SR.47 para. 28]; Mr. Sadi [E/C.12/1998/SR.47 para. 46]; and Ms. Bonoan-Dandan [E/C.12/1998/SR.47 para. 49]. In addition, see the statements made in the following 48th session, by Mr. Pillay [E/C.12/1998/SR.48 paras. 3-4 and 31]; Mr. Ahmed [E/C.12/1998/SR.48 paras. 6-7]; and Mr. Sadi [E/C.12/1998/SR.48 para. 10].

169 Illustrative in this regard is the statement by Mr. Sadi who noted, 'Si el Comité puede hacerse una idea de los problemas económicos que tiene el país quizás comprenderá mejor por qué se han impuesto tantas restricciones a la población y por qué el Gobierno no puede hacer frente a las obligaciones que le incumben en virtud del Pacto.' E/C.12/1998/SR.48 para. 10.

170 See, for example, Concluding Observations Canada E/1999/22 paras. 386, 394 and 395.

171 General Comment No. 3 para. 12.

172 It is worth mentioning that during the dialogue with the Committee the position of some Committee members with regard to vulnerable groups was clear. They clearly stated that even in the event of economic restraints, vulnerable groups within Canadian society must continue to be protected. See, for example, Mr. Sadi in E/C.12/1998/SR.47 para. 46.

the elements identified in that article 4.[173] During the 'constructive dialogue' with the Committee, the Government representatives provided some arguments as to the reasons for such expenditure cuts[174] and the Committee was sympathetic to these arguments. Nonetheless, there were other relevant issues under article 4 ICESCR that were not directly addressed. For example, there was no discussion as to whether or not the limitations were 'compatible with the nature of the rights' or if their sole purpose was 'promoting the general welfare.' The Government did not provide any justification as to these points and the Committee did not directly address the issue.

Moreover, in the Concluding Observations, the Committee did not address other important issues relating to article 4 ICESCR which are now well settled. For example, that restrictions which are not in conformity with article 4 constitute a 'violation' of the Covenant[175] and that restrictions need to be appropriate for the achievement of the aims pursued and not more severe than necessary for the attainment of that aim.[176] In sum, when the Committee examined the Third Periodic Report of Canada it did not address in a direct manner the compatibility of the restrictions with each of the protective safeguards of article 4, nor it did it analyse whether the limitations imposed were strictly required by the exigencies of the situation.

An important issue to discuss in this context is the compatibility of restrictions imposed by States under structural adjustment programmes with the general limitation clause of article 4 ICESCR. When implementing structural adjustment policies, States Parties to the Covenant must take into account the Covenant as a whole, and particularly article 4 ICESCR, if the measures constitute restrictions on the enjoyment of the Covenant's rights.

The initial report of Honduras is an interesting starting point for an analysis of the problems raised by structural adjustment measures adopted by a State Party. With regard to article 4 ICESCR, the Government of Honduras expressly stated that Honduran legislation was compatible with the Covenant. However, subsequently it noted that, 'at the practical level the Government has taken a number of economic structural adjustment measures which have infringed or diminished in one way or another the rights recognised in the Covenant: the effect has been to further impoverish the already disadvantaged groups; this situation has occurred not only in Honduras but also in other countries of Latin America.'[177] According to the argument of the Government of Honduras, the State is not required to comply with article 4 ICESCR in regard to the structural adjustment measures implemented in the country. This approach suggests

173 This later became apparent in General Comment No. 13 para. 42 and General Comment No. 14 para. 28.

174 See, for example, Mr. Moher (Canada) in E/C.12/1998/SR.47 para. 34 and Mr. Mundie (Canada) in E/C.12/1998/SR.47 paras. 40-43.

175 General Comment No. 13 para. 59.

176 General Comment No. 14 paras. 28 and 29.

177 Initial Report Honduras E/1990/5/Add.40 para. 36.

that notwithstanding that structural adjustment measures may constitute restrictions on the enjoyment of the Covenant's rights, their adoption is beyond the control of the State.[178]

The Committee clearly noted that this approach was not in conformity with the Covenant. In the Concluding Observations, the Committee noted that the structural adjustment policies had 'negatively affected the enjoyment of economic, social and cultural rights by the population, and especially the vulnerable and marginalized groups of society.'[179] Moreover, rather than considering such measures as being beyond the responsibility of the State, it further 'strongly urged' Honduras 'to ensure that the Covenant is taken into account in the formulation and implementation of all policies concerning economic, social and cultural rights.'[180] The Committee also recommended that Honduras 'explicitly take the Covenant into account in relation to the policies, programmes and projects deriving from its Poverty Reduction Strategy paper, which forms part of the enhanced Highly Indebted Poor Countries Initiative.'[181]

It must be beyond doubt that, according to the Committee, States Parties have the duty to take into account the Covenant's rights in their negotiations with international financial institutions (*i.e.* IMF and the World Bank).[182] Therefore, Honduras, and in general all countries that may be in a similar situation, are required to take into consideration their obligations under the Covenant when negotiating plans and measures with international financial institutions. If the structural adjustment measures entail restrictions on the Covenant's rights, States are required to comply with each of safeguards of article 4 of the Covenant.[183] It is worth stressing that, according to General Comment No. 14, the failure of the State to take into account its legal obligations when entering into bilateral or multilateral agreements with other States or

---

178 This is relevant because other States have also tried to justify restrictions related to structural adjustment programmes. For example, when presenting its Third Periodic Report, Bulgaria noted that the economic recession related to structural adjustment programmes adopted in agreement with financial institutions had negatively affected its ability to comply with its obligations. The Committee was clear in its Concluding Observations that the State should 'evaluate the economic reform programmes with respect to their impact on poverty, and make efforts to adjust these programmes in such a way that they adequately respond to the social needs of the population [...].' Concluding Observations Bulgaria E/C.12/1999/11 paras. 221 and 236. See, also Concluding Observations Argentina E/C.12/1999/11 para. 258.

179 Concluding Observations Honduras E/C.12/1/Add.57 para. 10.

180 Concluding Observations Honduras E/C.12/1/Add.57 para. 30.

181 Concluding Observations Honduras E/C.12/1/Add.57 para. 36.

182 See, for example, Concluding Observations Bulgaria E/C.12/1999/11 para. 236; Concluding Observations Georgia E/C.12/1/Add.42 para. 22; Concluding Observations Morocco E/C.12/1/Add.55 para. 38; Concluding Observations Argentina E/C.12/1999/11 para. 276; Concluding Observations Cameroon E/C.12/1999/11 para. 352; and Concluding Observations Mexico E/C.12/1999/11 paras. 396 and 397.

183 The issue of structural adjustment policies is analysed under 'obligation to protect' [Chapter V section 3.3] and under section 3.2 of the present Chapter.

international organisations entails a 'violation' of the Covenant.[184] The position of the Committee in this regard may well be explained by the comments of a Committee member who noted during the drafting of the general comment that 'developing countries may be able to negotiate less strict conditions on loans from international financial institutions if they could argue that excessively strict conditions would prevent them from meeting the minimum requirements laid down by the Committee on Economic, Social and Cultural Rights for guaranteeing the right to health [...].'[185]

3.3 Concluding Comments on the Committee's approach to article 4 ICESCR

The restrictions or limitations imposed by States on the enjoyment of economic, social and cultural rights may have negative consequences for individuals and it is regrettable that the Committee has not paid greater attention to this issue. The Committee should strictly monitor States Parties' compliance with article 4 ICESCR, requiring them to comply with each of its requirements when imposing limitations on the enjoyment of the rights in question.

So far, the Committee has not given article 4 ICESCR the importance that is required to strengthen the implementation of the Covenant. The 'Reporting Guidelines' do not directly deal with article 4 and, as a consequence, States' reports generally do not give the Committee the opportunity to address the imposition of limitations. Even when it has become clear from the information received by the State or an NGO or from the facts revealed during the constructive dialogue that restrictions have been imposed, the Committee's response has been somewhat weak.

It would be advisable for the Committee to improve the quality of State reporting both by requiring information on limitations to the enjoyment of the rights in the List of Issues and by being more inquisitive with State representatives [186] when examining

---

184 According to General Comment No. 14: 'violations of the obligation to respect are those State actions, policies or laws that contravene the standards set out in article 12 of the Covenant and are likely to result in bodily harm, unnecessary morbidity and preventable mortality. Examples include [...] the failure of the State to take into account its legal obligations regarding the right to health when entering into bilateral or multilateral agreements with other States, international organisations and other entities, such as multinational corporations.' General Comment No. 14 para. 50.

185 Mr. Riedel in E/C.12/2000/SR.10 para. 24. Mr. Riedel was the Rapporteur for the drafting of the General Comment No. 14.

186 During the 'constructive dialogue' Committee members sometimes direct probing questions towards State representative in regard to limitations imposed on the enjoyment of the Covenant's rights but this interest is often not reflected in the Concluding Observations. With the exception of restrictions imposed on the rights contained in article 8 ICESCR, the Committee's Concluding Observations do not appropriately deal with the issue of limitations or restrictions.

the State report. In this regard, it would also be appropriate for the Committee to amend its Reporting Guidelines[187] so that more attention is given to article 4.[188]

The Committee should send States a clear message to the effect that article 4 must be interpreted and applied restrictively. The Committee could do so through more rigorous supervision of limitations on the enjoyment of the Covenant's rights. While it is true that the Committee does not always receive the information necessary to assess whether the State has or has not imposed limitations, the Committee members should play a more active role and request such information. Whenever there are grounds to believe that limitations may have been imposed, the Committee should require additional information.

When the existence of limitations becomes apparent, the Committee should require States to justify them and to prove that they have complied with each of the requirements contained in article 4. The supervision of any restrictions imposed on the enjoyment of the Covenant's rights should be made on a regular basis and Concluding Observations should contain direct and express mention of compliance with article 4 ICESCR.

3.4 The absence of a non-derogation provision

Article 4 of the Covenant refers to the possibility of imposing restrictions or limitations on the exercise of specific Covenant rights. However, it does not provide a general derogation clause, such as that provided for in article 4 of its sister Covenant, the ICCPR.

The lack of a derogation provision in the Covenant gives rise to important questions: Does the lack of a derogation provision mean that derogating from the rights set

---

187 See note 10.

188 It is interesting to note that the Human Rights Committee's guidelines are better designed for seeking such information because they contemplate the following important points,
'[…] C. General guidance for contents of all reports
C.1The articles and the Committee's general comments. The terms of the articles in Parts I, II and III of the Covenant must, together with general comments issued by the Committee on any such article, be taken into account in preparing the report. […]
D.2 Contents of the report […]
D.2.1A State Party should deal specifically with every article in Parts I, II and III of the Covenant; legal norms should be described, but that is not sufficient: the factual situation and the practical availability, effect and implementation of remedies for violation of Covenant rights should be explained and exemplified. […]
E.2 Periodic reports should be structured so as to follow the articles of the Covenant. If there is nothing new to report under any article it should be so stated.[…]
E.4 There may be circumstances where the following matters should be addressed, so as to elaborate a periodic report:
There may have occurred a fundamental change in the State Party's political and legal approach affecting Covenant […]'.

forth in the Covenant is prohibited in any circumstance whatsoever? Is the lack of a derogation provision an appropriate omission or is it a deficiency in the Covenant? To what extent is the Covenant applicable in emergency situations?

As a first step to answering these questions, it may be appropriate to examine other instruments aimed at the protection of economic, social and cultural rights and whether or not they contain derogation provisions. If we look to the regional instruments, we find that the European Social Charter contains a derogation clause in article 31 ESC.[189] This provision is similar to the derogation clause contained in the European Convention (article 15 ECHR). However, in contrast with article 15 of the European Convention, this provision of the Social Charter does not seem to have had any practical importance.[190]

Although the American Convention includes a derogation clause (article 27 ACHR), the Additional Protocol to the American Convention on Human Rights in the Area of Economic, Social and Cultural Rights ['Protocol of San Salvador'] does not contemplate the possibility of derogating from the rights set forth therein. In this case, it is reasonable to conclude that the drafters of the social instrument expressly omitted such a clause because the instrument was negotiated and adopted well after the ICESCR. The African Charter on Human and Peoples' Rights recognises a wide range of economic, social and cultural rights but does not contain a derogation provision.[191]

At the Universal level, the Convention on the Right of the Child, which protects civil and political as well as economic, social and cultural rights, does not envisage the possibility of derogating from the rights contained therein. The absence of a derogation provision in this instrument is especially significant given that it has achieved almost universal ratification.

Moreover, other international instruments for the protection of economic, social and cultural rights generally do not contemplate the possibility of derogation. This is the case, for example, with the numerous ILO Conventions that, with the exception of the 1930 'Convention concerning Forced or Compulsory Labour',[192] do not contain general

---

189 Article 30(1) of the ESC: 'In time of war or other public emergency threatening the life of the nation any Contracting Party may take measures derogating from its obligations under this Charter to the extent strictly required by the exigencies of the situation, provided that such measures are not inconsistent with its other obligations under international law.' See also Art. F (1) of the Revised European Social Charter.

190 See Gomien *et. al.*, *op. cit.* (note 31), p. 431.

191 However, the limitation clause contained in this Charter is so broad that it seems that there is no need for derogation. For further analysis see, Diop, M.: 'The African Charter on Human and Peoples' Rights and the inviolability of the fundamental rights.' In: *Non-Derogable rights and states of emergency.* Prémont, D; Stenersen, C. and Oseredczuk, I. (eds.) Association of International Consultants of Human Rights (CID), Brussels, (1996), pp. 421-428.

192 ILO Convention No. 29, adopted on June 28, 1930, entered into force on May 1, 1932. Article 2(2)(d) states, ' Nevertheless, for the purposes of this Convention, the term forced or compulsory labour shall not include [...] (d) any work or service exacted in cases of emergency, that is to say, in the event of war or of a calamity or threatened calamity, such as fire, flood, famine, earthquake, violent epidemic

provisions enabling derogation.[193] Similarly, there is no derogation clause in the UNESCO Convention Against Discrimination in Education nor in the Convention Relating to the Status of Refugees or the Convention Relating to the Status of Stateless Persons, which all contain provisions for the protection of important economic, social and cultural rights.

It can generally be said that instruments aimed at the protection of economic, social and cultural rights (with the exceptions mentioned), do not expressly allow States Parties to derogate from the rights in cases of public emergency. From this author's point of view, the lack of derogation provisions in this kind of instrument, and in the Covenant in particular, is an appropriate omission. Admittedly, as is correctly pointed out by Craven, the lack of a derogation provision in the Covenant gives rise to the possibility of some inconsistencies in relation to the application of the Covenant and other human rights instruments.[194] However, despite these potential inconsistencies, it is still possible to argue that the lack of a derogation provision is an appropriate omission in the Covenant because the very nature of economic, social and cultural rights does not allow for the kind of derogation contemplated in civil and political rights instruments.

It is important to bear in mind that the rationale for derogation provisions is to strike a balance between the sovereign right of a government to maintain peace and order during public emergencies, and the protection of the rights of the individual from abuse by the State.[195] Thus, under civil and political rights instruments, the State is allowed to suspend the exercise of some rights when necessary to deal with an emergency situation (*e.g.* derogation of the right to peaceful assembly), provided it complies with safeguards against any abuse of these derogation provisions. However, it seems difficult to imagine a circumstance in which derogation from the rights contained in the ICESCR would be necessary to maintain peace and order from the perspective of human rights law. For example, it is difficult to see how derogation from the right to food or the right to the enjoyment of the highest attainable standard of health would assist in resolving a conflict situation rather than worsening it. Perhaps the exception

---

or epizootic diseases, invasion by animal, insect or vegetable pests, and in general any circumstance that would endanger the existence or the well-being of the whole or part of the population.'

193 For a valuable analysis of the notion of public emergency in the international labour conventions see Svensson-McCarthy, *op. cit.* (note 136), pp. 326-366.

194 As he explains, 'a State may legitimately derogate from its obligation to ensure the right to join and form trade unions (Article 22 of the CCPR) by virtue of Article 4 of the CCPR, but may not do so under the terms of the CESCR.' Craven, *loc. cit.* (note 19), p. 111.

195 As Svensson-McCarthy notes in regard to article 4 ICCPR, 'it [...] follows clearly from the preparatory works that article 4 was intended to fulfil the two-fold purpose of providing the States Parties with adequate means of defending the imperilled existence of the nation, whilst at the same time guaranteeing the maximum protection of human rights, that is to say, the maximum strictly allowed by the conditions imposed by the severity of the exceptional crisis.' Svensson-McCarthy, *op. cit.* (note 136), p. 214.

might be derogation from the rights contained in article 8 ICESCR (the right to form and join trade unions and the right to strike). Nevertheless, as mentioned above, the State is allowed to place restrictions on the enjoyment of article 8 ICESCR if it is 'necessary in a democratic society in the interests of national security or public order or for the protection of the rights and freedoms of others.' Therefore this right does not seem to require a general derogation clause.

From this author's perspective, derogating from the Covenant's rights, with the exception mentioned, would be of little help in dealing with a threatening situation. Moreover, article 2(1) ICESCR and the general limitation clause of article 4 ICESCR are sufficiently flexible to allow for a balance to be struck between peace and order and the individual's rights in emergency situations.[196]

Without doubt, this is the approach adopted by the Committee. From the work of the Committee it is apparent that the Covenant fully applies in emergency situations such as war, internal conflict, internal disturbances or riots. For example, when considering the Third Periodic Report of Iraq, the Committee clearly noted that the Covenant was applicable despite the war with the Islamic Republic of Iran and the conflict following Iraq's invasion of Kuwait. The Committee even stated that the Covenant applied despite the international embargo against Iraq but did expressly acknowledge that the embargo has negatively affected a large section of the Iraqi population, particularly the most vulnerable groups of society.[197] According to the Committee, although all of these circumstances were indeed 'emergency situations' which had hampered the full implementation of economic, social and cultural rights, Iraq remained responsible for implementing the Covenant and under the obligation to take all appropriate measures to the maximum of its available resources.[198]

In another case of an 'emergency situation', the internal armed conflict in Guatemala, the Committee noted that the existence of armed conflict in the country for more than 30 years hampered the enjoyment of rights and that the implementation of the Covenant could not be ensured without the adequate implementation of the peace accords. However, it did not consider that such circumstances justified any derogation from the rights of the Covenant.[199] Moreover, when considering the report of Sri Lanka, the Committee recognised that the armed conflict between the Government and the Liberation Tigers of Tamil Eelam (LTTE) had hampered the enjoyment of the rights recognised in the Covenant. However, it was clear that the Covenant was still applicable and that the Government needed to take more action to fulfil its obligations.[200]

196 Alston & Quinn, *loc. cit.* (note 121), pp. 217 and 219.
197 Concluding Observations Iraq E/1998/22 para. 253.
198 Concluding Observations Iraq E/1998/22 paras. 254 and 269.
199 Concluding Observations Guatemala E/1997/22 para. 123.
200 Concluding Observations Sri Lanka E/1999/22 paras. 69 *et seq.*

The Committee does not only consider that the Covenant is fully applicable in emergency situations, it has also noted that recourse to derogation might worsen the emergency rather than remedy it. For example, when examining the Third Periodic Report of Colombia, the Committee considered that the frequent recourse to states of emergency had had adverse repercussions on the enjoyment of economic, social and cultural rights in Colombia.[201] In the case of Peru, the Committee went further, suggesting that in emergency situations, instead of derogating from the Covenant's rights as a way to maintain peace and public order, it would be more appropriate to extend the application of the Covenant's rights to the most vulnerable groups within society.[202] In the words of the Committee 'the introduction and implementation of much needed social justice measures, *i.e.* political, economic, and social reforms, are needed in order to break the vicious circle of violence and counter violence and to win over the indigenous population, the peasants and other underprivileged sectors of Peruvian society.'[203]

Based on the Committee's approach, it is possible to say that a State Party is not permitted to derogate from the rights contained in the Covenant in an emergency situation resulting from war or internal armed conflict. On the contrary, it seems that any *de facto* derogation from these rights in times of emergency is an undue restriction on the exercise of the Covenant's rights. When emergency situations threaten States Parties, the Committee takes note that the State is facing difficulties which impede the full implementation of the Covenant. Nonetheless, there can be no doubt that States remain responsible for implementing the Covenant and that they must take all adequate steps to the maximum of their available resources. In other words, while the Committee may often seem to be sympathetic to the difficulties faced by the State, if the State does not take sufficient measures to the maximum of its available resources, the Committee does not hesitate to express its concern.

In sum, the Committee's approach to emergency situations confirms that the Covenant applies in all circumstances and that it is not necessary to derogate from the rights contained therein in order to deal with an emergency situation. In effect, the Committee seems to view the flexibility of article 2(1) ('take steps to the maximum of available resources') and article 4 ICESCR (general limitation clause), as sufficient tools to counter crisis situations. Nevertheless, the lack of a derogation provision does not mean that States cannot lawfully suspend the exercise of the rights contained in Covenant.

Under the rules of general international law, States Parties to an international treaty may suspend the exercise of treaty provisions in the case of *force majeure.*[204] This means that although the Covenant does not contemplate a derogation provision and

201 Concluding Observations Colombia E/1996/22 para. 180.
202 Concluding Observations Peru E/1998/22 para. 141.
203 Concluding Observations Peru E/1998/22 para. 156.
204 See article 61 VCLT.

makes no express provision for the case of war or other public emergencies, in extreme crisis situations a State Party may refer to the notion of *force majeure* to attempt to justify not fully complying with the Covenant.

However, in order to justify non-compliance due to *force majeure,* under international law the State must have no alternative course of action other than non-compliance. This is well explained in the ILC Draft Articles on Responsibility of States for Internationally Wrongful Acts which state,

> 'The wrongfulness of an act of a State not in conformity with an international obligation of that State is precluded if the act is due to *force majeure,* that is the *occurrence of an irresistible force or of an unforeseen event, beyond the control of the State, making it materially impossible in the circumstances to perform the obligation.*'[205]

In the context of the Covenant, the impossibility rule implies that if a State Party suffers en extraordinary event such as war, internal armed conflict, natural disaster or an unforeseen economic crisis of great magnitude that makes it impossible to comply with the Covenant obligations, it may preclude the wrongfulness of the non-compliance with some of the Covenant's rights by virtue of *force majeure.*

The Maastricht Guidelines on violations of economic, social and cultural rights stress the importance of distinguishing inability to comply from unwillingness of the State to comply. A case of *force majeure* is by definition a situation of inability and therefore any action or omission by a State due to *force majeure* would not amount a violation of the Covenant.[206] However, there are strict conditions that State Parties must fulfil in order to justify the suspension measure due to *force majeure.*

1. As established in the ILC's definition of *force majeure*, it must be *materially impossible* for the State to comply with the Covenant. This means that the State does not have any course of action open to it other than non-compliance with the Covenant obligations. This is a stricter requirement than those contemplated in the derogation provisions of the human rights instruments. Under article 4 ICCPR, article 15 ECHR and article 27 ACHR, States are not required to prove that they are in a situation in which it is *materially impossible* to comply with the obligations and that they do not have any alternative course of action.[207] In accordance with the derogation provisions

205 Art. 23(1) Draft Articles on Responsibility of States for Internationally Wrongful Acts as adopted by the ILC at its fifty-fifth session on 9 August 2001 (emphasis added). See the text in: A/RES/56/83 of 12 December 2001. For a commentary of this provision by the Special Rapporteur Mr. James Crawford, see Crawford, James: *The International Law Commission's Articles on State Responsibility: Introduction, text and commentaries*, Cambridge University Press, Cambridge, 2002, pp.170-173.

206 The Maastricht Guideline No. 13.

207 In the 'Report of the meeting of experts on rights not subject to derogation during states of emergency and exceptional circumstances' held in Geneva in May 1995, the group of experts concluded, '[d]erogations set a lower threshold for absolving a State of responsibility for non-compliance with a

mentioned above, in the case of a public emergency, States are merely required to comply with the requirements establish therein, notwithstanding that there may be other ways to deal with the emergency situation at hand other than derogation.

In contrast, in order to be able to invoke to *force majeure* in order to preclude the wrongfulness of non-compliance, a State Party must demonstrate that it is materially impossible to proceed in any other manner than a course of action which is contrary to the Covenant. This means that they must show that every effort has been made to comply with the Covenant by using all available resources at their disposal in order to avoid the non-compliance, but that despite such efforts there is no other course of action than the non-observance of a Covenant obligation.[208]

2. If a State alleging *force majeure* proves that the 'irresistible force of circumstances' makes it materially impossible to comply with the obligations under the Covenant, it must also prove: (a) the causal relationship between the *force majeure* and the failure to comply, and (b) that it had not deliberately or by negligence contributed to the creation of the *force majeure.*[209]

3. Any State Party seeking to justify a restriction on the enjoyment of the Covenant due to *force majeure* must comply with the principle of good faith or *pacta sunt servanda*

---

treaty than impossibility [*force majeure*].' As an example, the report mentions the relevant case-law of the European Court of Human Rights and notes that, '[t]he type of emergency measures found to be valid in the Lawless v. Ireland [Application No. 332/57, Judgement of 7 April 1961] and Ireland v. the United Kingdom [Application No. 5310/71, Judgement of 13 December 1977] cases, for example, were not necessary in the sense of being the unavoidable result of *force majeure*. The suspected terrorists could have been left at large. Their detention was only necessary in the sense of the legal definition of necessity stated in Lawless: apt to overcome specific problems which form part of a grave imminent threat to the life of the nation, yet carefully selected to have a lesser impact on human rights than other possible alternatives. In this sense, derogation is not necessary because it is no longer materially possible to protect certain human rights; it is necessary in order to protect the nation, or the State, or the *ordre public*, without which there can be no protection of human rights. Derogation is, in the sense, preventive – although, of course, it is allowed only if the danger is both grave and imminent.' Prémont *et al.*, 1996, pp. 27-49 at para. 27.

208 The difference between the concept of 'public emergency' under human rights law and the concept of *force majeure* in general international law is clearly explained by Svensson-McCarthy. After indicating that the non-performance of international legal obligations 'must be due to some irresistible force of circumstances leaving no choice of action' she notes that, '[w]hilst this is […] a basic condition for the acceptance of the plea of *force majeure* in general international law, the crisis situations covered by the concept of public emergency in international human rights law do, generally speaking, in most cases, albeit not necessarily always, present the responsible authorities with a variety of means of how to manage the situations concerned. In other words, the human rights notion "public emergency" is consequently of a more intentional voluntary nature than the general international law concept "*force majeure*".' Svensson-McCarthy, *op. cit.* (note 136), p. 348.

209 *Ibidem*: p. 345.

(article 26 VCLT).[210] This means that in their assessment of both whether they are prevented from performing their obligations and the existence of any non-violatory course of action they must act in good faith, taking into account the general welfare of society. As explained by commentators, the burden of proof for demonstrating good faith falls upon States. As they note, '[a] State not capable of providing inability due to forces reasonably beyond its control, therefore, would be in violation of economic, social and cultural rights.'[211]

4. The specific object and purpose of the Covenant as a human rights treaty requires the adaptation of the general international law rule of *force majeure* to human rights standards. Due to the fact that the Covenant does not contain a derogation provision, it is reasonable to expect that, to the maximum extent possible, States should comply with standards not lower than those provided by the human rights instruments that do contemplate the possibility of derogation. In fact, it must be understood that *force majeure* is indeed a very extraordinary circumstance and it must be interpreted restrictively and in the light of the object and purpose of the Covenant.

This requirement is explained in the report of the meeting held by a group of experts on the 'non-derogable rights and states of emergency.'[212] As stated in the report,

> 'Human rights treaties protect a special kind of *ordre public*, rather than reciprocal interests of States. Consequently, some provisions of the international law of treaties are not well suited to application to human rights treaties. There may be sound policy reasons to interpret the rule of impossibility in a somewhat different way as applied to human rights treaties, and the common treaty provisions on derogation would be an appropriate source for elements which could be used in fashioning a special version of this rule.'[213]

In other words, if derogation from the rights set forth in the Covenant is to be permitted under the rules of general international law, such derogation should, to the maximum extent possible, comply with the standards of protection established by human rights treaties which establish the possibility for derogation.[214] In the light of the requirements

---

210 Article 26 VCLT and article 13 of the 1949 Draft Declaration on the Rights and Duties of States which provides, 'Every state has the duty to carry out in good faith its obligations arising from treaties and other sources of international law, and it may not invoke provisions in its constitutions or its laws as an excuse for failure to perform this duty.'

211 Dankwa *et al.*, 1998, pp. 24-25.

212 Report of the meeting of Experts on rights not subject to derogation during states of emergency and exceptional circumstances, Prémont *et al.*, *op. cit.* (note 135), para. 28.

213 *Ibidem*: pp. 27-46 at para. 28.

214 Svensson-McCarthy arrives at a similar conclusion in her study on emergency situations and the ILO Conventions, as she notes, 'if temporary suspensions or derogations are at all permitted under the international labour conventions, which do not even make express provision for the case of war or other public emergencies, the applicable principles should be the same or at least not less severe than with

set forth in human rights treaties which do envisage the possibility of derogation, States Parties should, at a minimum, comply with the following principles:[215]

Non-discrimination: The prohibition of discrimination is contained in article 4 ICCPR and article 27 ACHR. In the context of the Covenant, this principle requires that if it is materially impossible for a State to comply with some obligations under the Covenant, the State must comply with the principle of non-discrimination to the maximum extent possible during the crisis. This means that any difference in treatment must have an objective and reasonable justification, considering the circumstances of the case. For example, if an earthquake destroys all schools in a given area and during the emergency the State is able to provide primary education in temporary shelters only to half of the students normally enrolled, it would be a violation of the Covenant if it were to make the replacement programme available only to male students.

Proportionality: The duration and extent of the derogation due to *force majeure* should be limited to what is strictly required by the exigencies of the situation. States must avoid undue derogation both *ratione temporis* and *ratione personae*. In other words, the derogation must not continue beyond the period of time strictly required to deal with the crisis and it must affect as few individuals as possible. Using the example cited above, this means that if an earthquake destroys schools in a certain region and this obliges the State to suspend children's right to primary education in the area involved due to the lack of infrastructure, the State must not maintain the suspension beyond the reasonable period of time required to build new schools. The duty to avoid undue derogation *ratione personae* implies that the State must not suspend the right to primary education of children living in areas not affected by the earthquake. In other words, as Svensson-McCarthy notes, 'if the State persists in failing to fulfil its obliga-

---

respect to treaties which do foresee such possible events. This approach would appear to be more consistent with contemporary international law than a solution based on the reciprocal suspension of legal obligations.' Svensson-McCarthy, *op. cit.* (note 136), p. 329.

215 It is beyond the scope of the present study to analyse the requirement of the derogation clauses contained in civil and political instruments. The analysis will merely mention the most important of these requirements for the present study. For further analysis see, Svensson-McCarthy, *op. cit.* (note 136); Nowak, *op. cit.* (note 2), pp. 72-93; Buergenthal, *op. cit.* (note 87), pp. 78-86; Lockwood, B.; Finn, J. & Jubinsky, G.: 'Working paper for the Committee of experts on limitation provisions.' In: *HRQ*, vol. 7 No. 1, (1985), pp. 35-88; Hartman, J.: 'Working paper for the Committee of Experts on the article 4 derogation provision.' In: *HRQ*, vol. 7 No. 1, (1985), pp. 89-131; O'Donnell, J.: 'States of exception.' In: *The Review of the International Commission of Jurists*, vol. 21, December (1978), pp. 52-60; Loucaides, L.S.G.: 'Restrictions or limitations on the rights guaranteed by the European Convention on Human Rights.' In: *Essays on the developing law of human rights*, Martinus Nijhoff, Dordrecht/Boston/London, (1995), pp.179-218; Gomien *et al.*, *op. cit.* (note 31), pp. 209 *et seq.*; and Dijk P. van & Hoof G.J.H. van, *op. cit.* (note 142), 1998, pp. 730 *et seq.*

tions under international law after the termination of the *force majeure*, the State's conduct will become unlawful.'[216]

Take all necessary measures in order not to imperil compliance with obligations imposed by non-derogable rights: Under human rights instruments that allow for derogation, there are several rights which cannot be subject to restriction. If a State is in a situation in which it is materially impossible to comply with the Covenant requirements, it must take all the necessary measures to avoid non-compliance with the obligations imposed by the hard core of non-derogable rights under other human rights instruments.

In other words, even when a State Party is not responsible for the failure to comply with some economic, social and cultural rights due to *force majeure*, it must still comply with other international obligations of a non-derogable character such as those imposed by article 4(2) ICCPR, article 27(2) ACHR, article 15(2) ECHR and the 1949 Geneva Conventions and the two 1977 Additional Protocols.[217] This obligation is particularly important taking into account, for example, the non-derogable character of the right to life and its strong links with some of the Covenant rights, such as the right to food and the right to the highest attainable standard of health.

Only if the State complies with the above-mentioned requirements would it be justified in not complying with the rights contained in the Covenant. Nevertheless, it is worth mentioning that due to the flexibility of article 2(1), the limitation clause of article 4 ICESCR and the reservations to the enjoyment of some of the Covenant's rights submitted by some States Parties, there are very few cases in which States Parties will genuinely need to invoke *force majeure.*

It is worth noting, for example, that when examining State reports, the Committee has acknowledged the occurrence of natural disasters that have dramatically affected States.[218] Although it is clear that it takes into account these situations in its evaluation of the implementation of the Covenant and is more sympathetic to the State in its

216 Svensson-McCarthy, *op. cit.* (note 136), p. 345 (footnote omitted).

217 It is interesting to note that, by their very nature, the Geneva Conventions and the 1977 Protocols are designed to be applicable in exceptional circumstances and therefore admit no derogation. The protection of economic, social and cultural rights in armed conflict has been analysed in detail elsewhere, and is far beyond the scope of the present study. For an in-depth analysis see: Rosas, A. & Sandvik-Nylund, M.: 'Armed conflicts.' In: *Economic, social and cultural rights: a textbook*. Eide, A.; Krause, C. & Rosas, A. (eds.), Martinus Nijhoff, second revised edition, Dordrecht, (2001), pp. 407-421.

218 The Committee has addressed natural disasters such as an earthquake in Mexico [Concluding Observations Mexico E/2000/22 para. 375]; a hurricane in Honduras [Concluding Observations Honduras E/C.12/1/Add. 57 para. 10]; floods in Venezuela [Concluding Observations Venezuela E/C.12/1/Add.56 para. 7]; and a drought in Algeria [Concluding Observations Algeria E/1996/22 para. 289]. It is worth stressing that 'natural disasters' also include man-made disasters such as the Chernobyl nuclear disaster [*e.g.* Concluding Observations Belarus E/1997/22 para. 278].

Concluding Observations, it has not even acknowledged the possibility of derogation from the Covenant's obligations.[219]

Finally, it is worth stressing once again that the question of whether or not a situation gives rise to *force majeure* is not a question to be resolved solely by the State concerned. On the contrary, it is an issue that would affect the international obligations of the State Party and must be examined by the Committee as the supervisory body of the Covenant.[220] As the principle of impossibility is by its very nature only applicable in very exceptional circumstances, the Committee must be very strict whenever a State attempts to justify the non-performance of Covenant obligations due to *force majeure.*

4 The principles of interpretation contained in article 5 ICESCR

Article 5 of the Covenant contains two rules for the interpretation of the Covenant: (a) 'the prohibition of abuse of rights' (article 5(1)) and (b) 'the savings clause' (article 5(2)). This is the final provision of Part II of the Covenant. However, it appears that Nowak is correct in observing that 'systematically speaking' it would have been more appropriate to locate article 5 together with the provisions of the general character contained in Part IV of the Covenant.[221] In fact, in Part IV there are another two articles which refer to the interpretation of the Covenant (article 24 and article 25 ICESCR). Nonetheless, article 5 emphasises the protective character of the Covenant and the limited discretion of States Parties to impose limitations on the exercise of the Covenant's rights, and therefore it may be justifiable that it should be included in Part II of the Covenant immediately following article 4 ICESCR.

Article 5 of the Covenant has been analysed in detail elsewhere[222] but, unfortunately, the Committee has not developed the normative content of this provision any further because it has only referred to article 5 very exceptionally. Like article 4 ICESCR this provision is not included in the Guidelines and information about article 5 is almost never required in the List of Issues nor as a follow-up measure.[223]

---

219 See, for example, Concluding Observations Uruguay E/1995/22 para. 68; Concluding Observations Ukraine E/1996/22 paras. 257-258; Concluding Observations Algeria E/1996/22 para. 289; and Concluding Observations Mexico E/2000/22 paras. 374-375.

220 This is in line with the practice of the Committee of Experts of the ILO when examining States' arguments relating to public emergency. Svensson-McCarthy, *op. cit.* (note 136), pp. 341-342.

221 Although Nowak specifically refers to Art. 5 ICCPR and states that it would be better placed in Part V ICCPR (which is equivalent to Part IV ICESCR), the provisions are similar. As we will see, there are a few differences, basically with regard to the order of the phrases, but they do not alter its meaning.

222 Specifically in relation to article 5 ICESCR see, Limburg Principles Nos. 57 and 58 and Alston & Quinn, *loc. cit.* (122), pp. 206-209. As for article 5 ICCPR, which is similar to the one which is the subject of our study see, among others, Nowak, *op. cit.* (note 2), pp. 94-102 and Buergenthal, *op. cit.* (note 87), pp. 86-90.

223 There are some minor exceptions, such as List of Issues Kyrgyzstan E/C.12/Q/KYRG/1 para.13 of 10 December 1999.

Sometimes States do provide information with regard to article 5 ICESCR.[224] However, in most such cases, the information is not truly pertinent to the implementation of the Covenant, principally because States tend to refer to civil and political rather than economic, social and cultural rights.[225]

The Committee has not paid much attention to article 5 in its General Comments and, to July 2002, the only mention of article 5 was found in General Comment No. 14. However the reference is perhaps more closely related to the general limitation clause of article 4 ICESCR than to article 5 ICESCR.[226]

4.1 The prohibition of abuse of rights (article 5 paragraph 1)

> *'Nothing in the present Covenant may be interpreted as implying for any State, group or person any right to engage in any activity or to perform any act aimed at the destruction of any of the rights or freedoms recognised herein, or at their limitation to a greater extent than is provided for in the present Covenant.'*

This provision is in line with the general rule of interpretation that establishes that an international treaty must be interpreted in good faith and in the light of its object and purpose.[227] The purpose of article 5(1) is to make it impossible for States, individuals or groups to 'engage in any activity' or 'perform any act' *aimed* at (a) destroying the

224 See, for example, Dominican Republic E/1990/6/Add.7 paras. 32-34, of 15 March 1995; Second Periodic Report Venezuela E/1990/6/Add.19 paras. 26 and 29, of 8 January 1999; Initial Report Croatia E/1990/5/Add.46 paras. 45-47, of 21 August 2000; Initial Report Nepal E/1990/5/Add.45 25 paras. 89-90, of September 2000; Initial Report of China [Hong Kong] E/1990/5/Add.43 para. 40, of 20 September 1999; Initial Report Kyrgyzstan E/1990/5/Add.42 paras. 16-17, of 26 February 1999; and Initial Report Egypt E/1990/5/Add.38 para. 75, of 30 June 1998.

225 See for example, the lengthy explanation provided under the heading 'article 5' in the Initial Report of Peru E/1990/5/Add.29 paras. 123-173, of 16 June 1996. See also the Third Periodic Report Mexico E/1994/104/Add.18 paras. 53-54, of 27 January 1998 (as an example, the Report stated that the Government of Mexico had 'ratified' the Universal Declaration of Human Rights).

226 General Comment No. 14 refers to article 4 ICESCR in paragraph 28, which establishes that 'Issues of public health are sometimes used by States as grounds for limiting the exercise of other fundamental rights. The Committee wishes to emphasise that the Covenant's limitation clause, article 4, is primarily intended to protect the rights of individuals rather than to permit the imposition of limitations by States [...]. Such restrictions must be in accordance with the law, including international human rights standards, compatible with the nature of the rights protected by the Covenant, in the interest of legitimate aims pursued, and strictly necessary for the promotion of the general welfare in a democratic society.' Subsequently, in paragraph 29, the General Comment refers to article 5(1) ICESCR, indicating, 'In line with article 5(1), such limitations must be proportional, *e.g.* the least restrictive alternative must be adopted where several types of limitations are available. Even where such limitations on grounds of protecting public health are basically permitted, they should be of limited duration and subject to review. However, as was previously analysed, the principle of 'proportionality' is more related to article 4, than to the 'prohibition of abuse' contained in article 5(1) ICESCR.

227 Art. 31 VCLT. See the analysis in Chapter III section 2.3.

rights and freedoms set forth in the Covenant or (b) limiting them to a greater extent than is provided for therein.

It is worth stressing that this provision emphasises the importance of the 'aim' or 'purpose' of a given activity. As Buergenthal notes with regard to the equivalent and almost identical provision of the ICCPR, '[b]y focusing on the 'aim' of a given activity, article 5(1) calls for a scrutiny of motives and purposes and permits subjective elements to be taken into account [...].'[228]

As noted, this provision also precludes States from imposing limitations to a greater extent than is provided for by the Covenant. Article 5(1) forms an integral whole together with articles 4 (general limitations clause) and 8 ICESCR which authorises restrictions on the enjoyment of the rights.[229] No limitations to the Covenant's rights are allowed to a greater extent than is expressly provided for in these provisions.[230] Hence, limitations may only be imposed for the purposes envisaged in these provisions and there is no room for implied limitations. The Limburg Principles unambiguously endorse this interpretation in stating that 'Article 5(1) underlines the fact that there is no general, implied or residual right for a state to impose limitations beyond those which are specifically provided for in the law.'[231]

The prohibition of misuse by private Parties is contained in the reference to 'any group or person.' This provision prevents someone from relying on a Covenant right to misuse it for the purpose of promoting activities aimed at the destruction of the rights that the Covenant proclaims. This would be the case, for example, if there is evidence that in exercising the right to form and join trade unions (article 8 ICESCR), an individual pursues the elimination of other trade unions or advocates racial discrimination. If this is the case, the State Party may lawfully deny him/her the exercise of article 8 ICESCR. However, it is important to note that it would be a violation of the Covenant if the State deprived this person of the enjoyment of other rights contained in the Covenant.[232]

Finally, it is important to stress that the jurisprudence of the European Court of Human Rights relating to article 17 ECHR and that of the Human Rights Committee on article 5(1) ICCPR, make apparent the ancillary character of this provision.[233] In other words, a violation of article 5(1) will only occur in conjunction with the violation of another provision of the Covenant.

228 Buergenthal, *op. cit.* (note 87), p. 87.

229 *Idem.*

230 It is perhaps worth mentioning here once again that article 8 ICESCR establishes specific grounds for restrictions on the exercise of the rights to form and join trade unions and the right to strike.

231 Limburg Principles No. 57.

232 See Buergenthal, *op. cit.* (note 87), p. 89.

233 With regard to the article 17 ECHR see, Dijk P. van & Hoof, G.J.H. van, *op. cit.* (note 142), pp. 750-755 and Loucaides, *op. cit.* (note 216), pp. 208-212. Regarding article 5(1) ICCPR see, Nowak, *op. cit.* (note 2), pp. 94-100; Buergenthal, *op. cit.* (note 87), 1981, pp. 86-89; and O'Donnell, *op. cit.* (note 216), pp. 58-60.

4.2 The savings clause (article 5 paragraph 2)

> *'No restrictions upon or derogation from any of the fundamental human rights recognised or existing in any country in virtue of law, conventions, regulations or custom shall be admitted on the pretext that the present Covenant does not recognize them or that it recognizes them to a lesser extent.'*

This provision is also called 'the most favourable to the individual clause.' As Buergenthal notes, '[t]he purpose of this provision is to ensure that the Covenant is not used as a basis for denying or limiting other more favourable or more extensive human rights which individuals might otherwise enjoy or be entitled to, whether under international law or national law or practice.'[234] The notion that the provisions of the Covenant should be interpreted in the manner most favourable to the individual is also stressed in the Limburg Principles which state that,

> '[t]he purpose of article 5(2) is to ensure that no provision in the Covenant shall be interpreted to prejudice the provisions of domestic law or any bilateral or multilateral treaties, conventions or agreements which are already in force, or may come in force, under which more favourable treatment would be accorded to the persons protected. Neither shall article 5(2) be interpreted to restrict the exercise of any human right protected to a greater extent by national or international obligations accepted by the State Party.'[235]

As Nowak notes with regard to the identical clause in the ICCPR, the savings clause 'gives expression to the principle that the rights of the Covenant merely represent *minimum standards* and that the cumulation of various human rights conventions, domestic norms and customary international law may not be interpreted to the detriment of the individual.'[236]

The principle that the higher standard of protection must apply is also expressly recognised in article 5(2) ICCPR[237] and similar formulations are found in article 29(b)

234 Buergenthal, *op. cit.* (note 87), p. 88. Although the author refers to article 5(2) ICCPR, it is entirely pertinent in regard to article 5(2) ICESCR.

235 Limburg Principle No. 58.

236 Nowak, *op. cit.* (note 2), p. 95 (footnote omitted, emphasis in the original).

237 Arts. 5(2) ICESCR and 5(2) ICCPR differ slightly as to the order of the phrases, but the meaning is the same. Art. 5(2) ICCPR establishes, 'There shall be no restriction upon or derogation from any of the fundamental human rights recognised or existing in any State Party to the present Covenant pursuant to law, conventions, regulations or custom on the pretext that the present Covenant does not recognise such rights or that it recognises them to a lesser extent.'

ACHR[238] and article 53 of the ECHR.[239] In the latter two instruments there is no reference to 'custom.'[240] The Covenant emphasises the importance of the 'savings clause' by reiterating its underlying principle in its formulation of a series of substantive rights. This is the case, for example, when dealing with the right to form and join trade unions, the right of the trade unions to function freely and the right to strike (article 8 ICESCR). In this context it is worth stressing article 8(3) ICESCR which reads, '[n]othing in this article shall authorise States Parties to the International Labour Organisation Convention of 1948 concerning Freedom of Association and Protection of the Right to Organise to take legislative measures which would prejudice, or apply the law in such a manner as would prejudice, the guarantees provided for in that Convention.' This provision supplements article 5(2) ICESCR.

In general, the application of the 'most favourable to the individual clause' is of the utmost importance when a State Party to the Covenant has ratified other international instruments that accord protection to economic, social and cultural rights. Such instruments may protect everyone under the jurisdiction of the State (*e.g.* Protocol of San Salvador), or only a specific group (*e.g.* the Convention on the Status of Refugees which provides for the protection of some economic, social and cultural rights of refugees). When States are parties to more than one instrument concerning economic, social and cultural rights, the rights most favourable to the individual must prevail. Therefore, in those cases where other instruments recognise rights not covered by the Covenant (such as the right to property),[241] or the Covenant recognises them to a lesser extent (such as the right to a healthy environment),[242] States must comply with the higher standard of protection.

---

238 Art. 29(b) ACHR: 'No provision of this Convention shall be interpreted as: [...] Restricting the enjoyment or exercise of any right or freedom recognised by virtue of the laws of any State Party or by virtue of another convention to which one of the said states is a Party.'

239 Art. 53 ECHR: 'Safeguard for existing human rights. Nothing in this Convention shall be construed as limiting or derogating from any of the human rights and fundamental freedoms which may be ensured under the law of any High Contracting Party or under any other agreement to which it is a Party.' Before the entry into force of Protocol No. 11 this provision was article 60 ECHR.

240 Nonetheless Art. 29 (d) ACHR states that 'No provision of this Convention shall be interpreted as [...] excluding or limiting the effect that the American declaration of the Rights and Duties of Man and other international acts of the same nature may have.' Given that one of the principal 'effects' of international declarations such as the ADHR is precisely to contribute to the formation of customary law, arguably Art. 29 (d) should be construed as referring to custom. Reference to customary law may have an important role to play. As the Committee noted when examining the report of Israel, 'basic economic, social and cultural rights as part of the minimum standards of human rights are guaranteed under customary international law [...].' Concluding Observations Israel E/C.12/1/Add.69 para. 13.

241 The right to property is recognised by Art. 21 ACHR, Art. 14 AfCHR, Art. 13 CSR and to some extent by Art. 1 First Optional Protocol to the ECHR.

242 See, for example, article 11 Protocol of San Salvador.

This provision also plays an important role when another instrument contains more detailed regulations that take into account the specific necessities of the beneficiaries. To illustrate this, the Convention Relating to the Status of Refugees [CSR] protects some economic, social and cultural rights which are more precise than those contained in the Covenant, such as the provisions regarding the recognition of foreign school certificates, diplomas and degrees (articles 19 and 20 CSR), or the specific aspects of labour legislation and social security (article 24 CSR). For States Parties to both instruments, the broader scope of protection must apply.

4.3 Other interpretative provisions contained in the Covenant

As mentioned above, in addition to the interpretative principles contained in article 5, two additional provisions regarding interpretation are included in Part IV of the Covenant in articles 24 and 25 ICESCR, which are equivalent to articles 46 and 47 ICCPR respectively. Although these provisions are beyond the scope of the present study, it is worth recalling their contents here.

Article 24 ICESCR establishes:

> *'Nothing in the present Covenant shall be interpreted as impairing the provisions of the Charter of the United Nations and of the constitutions of the specialised agencies which define the respective responsibilities of the various organs of the United Nations and of the specialised agencies in regard to the matters dealt with in the present Covenant.'*[243]

Article 25 ICESCR sets out that:

> *Nothing in the present Covenant shall be interpreted as impairing the inherent right of all peoples to enjoy and utilise fully and freely their natural wealth and resources.*[244]

Although the drafters considered it necessary to expressly add these provisions, a proper interpretation of article 5 would arrive at the same result. In fact, the Limburg Principles expressly state that '[I]n addition, article 5 is intended to ensure that nothing in the Covenant shall be interpreted as impairing the inherent right of all peoples to enjoy and utilise fully and freely their natural wealth and resources.'[245]

---

243 See also article 46 ICCPR.
244 See also article 47 ICCPR.
245 Limburg Principle No. 57.

4.4 Concluding Comments on the Committee's approach to article 5 ICESCR

Article 5 ICESCR is a provision that has been little discussed in the context of the Covenant. Although the effects of the lack of attention to this provision are not as grave as in the case of the lack of attention to article 4 ICESCR, further attention to article 5 by the Committee would enhance the protection of the rights under the Covenant. This would be of particular importance in the event of the adoption of an optional protocol to the Covenant establishing a complaints procedure. The Committee's Draft Optional Protocol envisages the possibility of submitting complaints in case of a violation of article 5 ICESCR.[246] If this proposal is accepted, it would be appropriate for the Committee to take into account the jurisprudence of the European Court of Human Rights regarding article 17 ECHR and that of the Human Rights Committee regarding article 5 ICCPR. Such jurisprudence illustrates the important role that this kind of provision plays in the protection of individual rights.[247]

246 'Report of the Committee on Economic, Social and Cultural Rights to the Commission on Human Rights on a Draft Optional Protocol for the consideration of communications concerning non-compliance with the International Covenant on Economic, Social and Cultural Rights.' E/1997/22, Annex IV, para.25.

247 With regard to article 5 ICESCR see, for example, Lopez Burgos v. Uruguay, *loc.cit* (note 92), and Celiberti de Casariego v. Uruguay, *loc.cit* (note 92). In these cases, article 5(1) was viewed by the majority of the Committee as extending the Covenant's scope of application. However, it is important to examine the clarifying individual opinion of Mr. Tomuschat in both views. We also note that article 5(1) has, on occasion, been applied by the Human Rights Committee as a basis for declaring a Communication to be inadmissible. See, for example, M.A. v. Italy, Communication No. 117/1981, inadmissibility decision of 10 April 1984.

CHAPTER VII
ANALYSIS OF ARTICLE 2(1) OF THE ICESCR

Article 2

'Each State party to the present Covenant undertakes to take steps, individually and through international assistance and co-operation, especially economic and technical, to the maximum of its available resources, with a view to achieving progressively the full realisation of the rights recognised in the present Covenant by all appropriate means, including particularly the adoption of legislative measures.'

1 INTRODUCTION

This provision, and particularly the notion of 'progressive' realisation using 'available resources', have given rise to much uncertainty with regard to the nature and extent of the legal obligations imposed by the Covenant. Some scholars[1] and, especially, government representatives[2] have taken the view that this article and its phrase 'progressive realisation' is so vague as to amount to a 'programmatic right.' They have interpreted this provision as a mere 'aspiration', without creating a real obligation for States.

However, at the present stage of development of international human rights law, such interpretations are no longer tenable. According to the Committee, such interpretations not only go against developments in international law but also undermine the object and purpose of the Covenant, and are contrary to the intentions of its drafters.[3]

1 See, for example, Vierdag, E.W.: 'The legal nature of the rights granted by the International Covenant on Economic, Social and Cultural Rights'. In: *NYIL*, vol. IX (1978) pp. 69-105; Cranston, M.: *What are human rights*. The Bodley Head, London/Sydney/Toronto, (1973); and Bossuyt, M.: '*La distinction entre les droites civils et politiques et les droits economiques, sociaux et culturels.*' In: Revue des Droits de l'Homme (Human Rights Law Journal), vol. 8 No. 4, (1975), pp. 783-820.

2 Occasionally government representatives have held the view that the provisions of the Covenant constitute principles and programmatic objectives rather than legal obligations, and consequently that the provisions of the Covenant cannot be given legislative effect. See, for example, Concluding Observations Switzerland E/1999/22 para. 348; Concluding Observations the Netherlands E/1999/22 para. 177; and Concluding Observations the United Kingdom of Great Britain and Northern Ireland E/1998/22 para. 293. In the last mentioned case, the Committee found that the Government's position was 'disturbing' and generally the Committee has expressed its great regret with regard to these statements. The Committee has clearly expressed that it does not share this view and has recalled its position in General Comment No. 3.

3 See General Comment No. 3 para. 9 and Alston, 1995, p. 38.

As we will see, it is important not to overstate the principle of 'progressive realisation.' Although it is true that the sister Covenant, the ICCPR, does not use the term, as the Committee has noted consistently since one of its earliest General Comments, the principle of progressive realisation 'constitutes a recognition of the fact that full realisation of all economic, social and cultural rights will generally not be able to be achieved in a short period of time.'[4] The presumption that only civil and political rights impose obligations of an immediate nature while all economic, social and cultural rights impose obligations of a long-term character is an oversimplification.[5] Certainly, economic, social and cultural rights involve progressive realisation to a greater extent than civil and political rights. Nevertheless, it would be difficult to dispute that the full realisation of all human rights is a progressive undertaking. The *full* realisation of all human rights requires States to progressively develop policies and targets. Furthermore, as the Committee has noted, the phrase 'progressive realisation', 'must be read in the light of the overall objective, indeed the *raison d'être*, of the Covenant which is to establish clear obligations for States Parties in respect of the full realisation of the rights in question.'[6]

One commentator captured the essence of the problem when he noted that article 2(1) ICESCR is 'a fairly unsatisfactory article, with its convoluted phraseology in which clauses and sub-clauses are combined together in an almost intractable manner, making it virtually impossible to determine the precise nature of the obligations.'[7] Due to the fact that this provision is essential for the proper understanding of the legal obligations imposed by the Covenant, its intricacy has been an enormous obstacle to the implementation.

As the Committee notes, article 2(1) 'is of particular importance to a full understanding of the Covenant and must be seen as having a dynamic relationship with all of the other provisions. It describes the nature of the general legal obligations undertaken by States Parties to the Covenant.'[8]

While compliance with the principle of 'progressive realisation' depends on the availability of resources in each State Party, this provision also prescribes particular modes of conduct that are compulsory for all States Parties, regardless of their level of development. Therefore, while the 'progressive realisation' of economic, social and cultural rights is dependent on the specific circumstances of the State concerned, article 2(1) also imposes obligations that have the same content for all States Parties regardless of their level of development. These obligations considerably limit the discretion of States with regard to the implementation of the Covenant and require immediate implementation.

4 General Comment No. 3 para. 9.
5 See the analysis in Chapter IV.
6 General Comment No. 3 para. 9.
7 Craven, 1998, p. 151.
8 General Comment No. 3 para. 1.

The following analysis will identify the core obligations imposed by article 2(1). Before embarking on this analysis, it is important to note that while these obligations are discussed separately in order to highlight their specific features, they are intertwined and should be viewed as an organic whole.

2 The obligation to take steps and to devote the maximum of available resources

> 'Each State party to the present Covenant *undertakes to take steps*, […] *to the maximum of its available resources*'

States Parties are obliged to *take steps* to achieve progressively the full realisation of the rights recognised in the Covenant. This obligation is immediately applicable and is not subject to limitation.[9] Hence, it is not an obligation to take action in the future. States, regardless of their level of development, must take steps immediately to achieve the full realisation of the rights enshrined in the Covenant.

As noted by the Committee in General Comment No. 13,

> 'While the Covenant provides for progressive realisation and acknowledges the constraints due to the limits of available resources, it also imposes on States Parties various obligations which are of immediate effect. States Parties have immediate obligations in relation to the right to education, such as […] the obligation 'to take steps' (art. 2(1)) towards the full realisation of article 13. Such steps must be 'deliberate, concrete and targeted' towards the full realisation of the right to education.'[10]

As indicated, all provisions contained in Part II of the Covenant apply to all the substantive rights of the Covenant. Thus, States Parties must 'take steps' without delay to implement each of the rights enumerated in Part III. Furthermore, States must take steps which are 'deliberate, concrete and targeted' toward the full realisation of the rights.[11]

If a State has assumed the obligation of 'full realisation' of the Covenant rights to everyone within its jurisdiction, it has to take the necessary measures to get there and

9 See, for example, General Comment No. 3 para. 2, General Comment No. 13 para. 43 and General Comment No. 14 para. 30. See, in addition, Limburg Principle No. 16 which reads as follows: 'All States parties have an obligation to begin immediately to take steps toward full realisation of the rights contained in the Covenant.'

10 General Comment No. 13 para. 43.

11 See General Comment No. 3 para. 2.

hence this conclusion is logical and States cannot wait indefinitely to take steps.[12] They are obliged 'to move as expeditiously and effectively as possible' towards this goal.[13]

Even in a time of crisis, States Parties remain responsible for compliance with the obligation to take steps to the maximum of available resources, particularly for the protection of vulnerable groups within society. As the Committee notes,

> '[E]ven in times of severe resources constraints whether caused by a process of adjustment, economic recession, or by other factors the vulnerable members of society can and indeed must be protected by the adoption of relatively low-cost targeted programmes.'[14]

The Committee has stressed this obligation in strong terms through its Concluding Observations. For example, in the case of Iraq, the Committee noted that the sanctions against the country had had a negative effect, hampering the full implementation of some of the Covenant rights. Nonetheless, the Committee underlined that 'the State party remains responsible for implementing its obligations under the Covenant 'to the maximum of its available resources', in accordance with article 2, paragraph 1, of the Covenant.'[15] Further in the same Concluding Observations, it noted that 'while being aware that the embargo imposed on Iraq creates extremely difficult conditions with respect to the availability of food, medicines and medical articles, the Committee recommends that the Government take all necessary measures, to the maximum extent of its available resources, to address the needs of the population, and in particular those of the most vulnerable groups, such as children, the elderly and nursing mothers, in relation to article 12 of the Covenant.'[16] This approach is in line with General Comment No. 8 where the Committee notes that 'the imposition of sanctions does not in any way nullify or diminish the relevant obligations of that State party [the affected State].'[17] If, having ratified or acceded to the Covenant, a State Party remains passive and does not take any 'deliberate', 'concrete' and 'targeted' steps to achieve progressively the Covenant's rights, it would be in violation of the Covenant.

It is worth noting that this obligation also requires States to take an active role to prevent and protect individuals against violations of economic, social and cultural rights by private actors.[18] States Parties must take steps to ensure that private entities, including transnational corporations, do not deprive individuals of their rights. The passivity of a State in the face of a violation of rights by private entities may entail a violation of the Covenant. For example, in the case of the Russian Federation, the

12 Limburg Principle No. 21.
13 General Comment No. 3 para. 9.
14 General Comment No. 3 para. 12.
15 Concluding Observations Iraq E/1998/22 para. 253.
16 Concluding Observations Iraq E/1998/22 para. 281.
17 General Comment No. 8 para. 10.
18 See the analysis in Chapter V, section 3.3.

Committee stated that it was 'alarmed' at reports informing that the economic rights of indigenous peoples were being violated with impunity by oil and gas companies, and that the State had not taken steps to protect them from the exploitation. Therefore, the Committee recommended to the State 'that action be taken to protect the indigenous peoples from exploitation by oil and gas companies.'[19] Along the same lines, the Committee 'strongly urged' Honduras to take measures to protect workers negatively affected by the use of toxic substances by transnational banana and gold mining companies.[20]

The obligation to take steps is 'to the maximum of available resources.' The resources 'available' are not only the resources within a State, but also the resources available from the international community through 'international assistance and co-operation'. The obligations regarding international assistance and co-operation are analysed below in section 2.8. Here we will focus principally on the States' domestic resources.

The term 'to the maximum of its available resources' does not require a State to devote all the resources at its disposal nor, obviously, does it require a State to devote resources that it does not have in order to fulfil these rights. Nevertheless, it does impose limitations on a State's freedom to allocate resources.[21] The allocation of resources is not left to the complete discretion of a State and the Committee must supervise State compliance with this obligation.

The obligation to use the 'maximum available resources' also implies the duty to use the resources allocated in an effective and efficient manner and the prohibition of the diversion of resources devoted to Covenant-related issues. In this regard, the Committee stresses the importance of combating corruption that negatively affects the implementation of the rights.[22] In the case of Colombia, for example, the Committee noted with concern that funds allocated in the budget for social expenditure had not been fully used for that purpose and consequently considered that the Government 'should combat the practice of non-utilisation of budget items earmarked for social expenditure in the State's overall budget and ensure that such appropriations are used for the purposes for which they were budgeted'.[23]

In practice, the supervision of compliance by each State Party with the obligation to take steps to the maximum of its available resources gives rise to complex problems. However, the difficulties that the Committee might encounter in monitoring compliance do not detract from the fact that it is a legally binding obligation with which States Parties must comply in good faith.

resources

limits allocation of resources

19 Concluding Observations Russian Federation E/1998/22 paras. 100 and 116.
20 Concluding Observations Honduras E/C.12/1/Add.57 paras. 24 and 38.
21 Alston, 1984, p. 38.
22 See, for example, Concluding Observations Nigeria E/1999/22 paras. 97 and 119 and Concluding Observations Mexico E/2000/22 paras. 381 and 394.
23 Concluding Observations Colombia E/1996/22 para. 181.

2.1 Measuring State compliance with the obligation to devote the maximum available resources

Because States Parties have freely assumed the obligation to take steps 'to the maximum of their available resources', the Committee may supervise the allocation of resources by a State Party.

According to the Maastricht Guidelines on violations of economic, social and cultural rights, a State violates the Covenant if it does not devote the maximum of its available resources to the full realisation of the rights.[24] However, the supervision of compliance with this obligation is certainly very complex and this gives rise to legitimate concerns about the capability of the Committee to carry out this supervision effectively.[25]

In order to monitor the obligation of each State Party to devote the 'maximum' of its 'available resources', the Committee requires both highly technical information and expertise. An assessment of this obligation would require that the Committee clarify the basis for determining what constitutes 'available resources' for the purpose of the Covenant and, for example, if 'resources' only refers to financial resources or also other resources such as human and technological resources.[26] Once it has defined 'available resources' it would be required to calculate the 'maximum' of these resources available to a State Party at a given time. These kinds of assessments now seem to be beyond the real possibilities of the Committee. The Committee does not receive all of the necessary information as to the resources available in the States Parties from State reports. Moreover, the Committee members do not posses the highly technical expertise necessary to measure compliance with this obligation if it were to be measured using a mathematical calculation of all the resources available in the State Party concerned.

To overcome the difficulties in accurately measuring State compliance with the obligation to devote the 'maximum available resources', the Committee has developed a series of indicators. These indicators enable the Committee to measure compliance with this obligation by analysing accessible information, such as data on the percentage of the national budget allocated to specific areas such as health, education and defence.

The principal indicator employed by the Committee is a comparative analysis of the financial resources spent by the State in Covenant-related expenditures and non-related

24 Maastricht Guideline No. 15 (e) reads as follows: 'Violations of economic, social and cultural rights can also occur through the omission or failure of States to take necessary measures stemming from legal obligations. Examples of such violations include: [...] (e) The failure to utilise the maximum of available resources towards the full realisation of the Covenant.'

25 For a comprehensive analysis of this issue, see Robertson: 'Measuring state compliance with the obligation to devote the 'maximum available resources' to realising economic, social and cultural rights.' In: *HRQ* vol. 16, (1994), pp. 693-714.

26 Robertson, *loc. cit.* (note 25), p. 697.

items. If there have been significantly more funds allocated to non-related areas, such as military defence, than to Covenant-related expenditures such as health or education, the Committee considers this as an indicator of non-compliance.[27]

Another indicator used by the Committee is a comparison between the money spent by the State Party in the implementation of a specific Covenant right and that which is spent for the same item by other States with the same level of development. Thus, if the percentage of the national budget allocated by a State for education is considerably inferior to that devoted by another State with the same level of development, it is considered by the Committee as being indicative of the non-use of the maximum of available State resources. For example, when examining the Second Periodic Report of the Dominican Republic, the Committee noted with great concern that State expenditure on education and training as a proportion of total public spending was less than half the average in Latin America.[28]

The Committee also finds that violation of this obligation may be indicated when the State has not spent funds allocated to certain Covenant-related activities due to inefficient administration or corruption. For example, in the case of Colombia, the Committee found that the State's practice of 'non-utilisation' of budget items allocated to social expenditures was an indication of non-compliance with this obligation.[29]

While the Committee clearly relies on these indicators in order to measure States' compliance, it seems to recognise the limitations of its analysis by taking a cautious attitude in the Concluding Observations. For example, when examining the initial report of the Philippines, it stressed that 'in terms of the availability of resources, the Committee notes with concern that a greater proportion of the national budget is devoted to military spending than to housing, agriculture and health combined.'[30] Consequently, the Committee recommended to the State that 'consideration be given to increasing the proportion of the national budget' devoted to Covenant-related expenditures.[31]

In the Concluding Observations on the Second Periodic Report of the Republic of Korea, the Committee noted that 'the high level of defence expenditure is in contrast with the shrinking budget for key areas of economic, social and cultural rights.'[32] Moreover, it expressed that it was 'disturbed' by the fact that the 'portion of the government budget allocated to health, which is under 1 per cent, is low and declining.'[33] However, it does not directly address this issue in its recommendations.

27 See, for example, Concluding Observations Philippines E/1996/22 para. 121.
28 Concluding Observations Dominican Republic E/1997/22 para. 228.
29 Concluding Observations Colombia E/1996/22 para. 200.
30 Concluding Observations Philippines E/1996/22 para. 121.
31 Concluding Observations Philippines E/1996/22 para. 123.
32 Concluding Observations on the Second Periodic Report of Korea E/C.12/1/Add.59 para. 9.
33 *Ibidem*: para. 26.

When examining the initial report of Azerbaijan, the Committee expressed its concern about the high percentage of public expenditure devoted to the development of the oil industry in comparison with the funds devoted to enable individuals to be self-supporting. Thus, it recommended that the State 'encourage diversification of the economy in other industries and particularly local small and medium-scale enterprises, which are important for the means of livelihood of major segments of the population.'[34]

The Committee is well aware that different countries have different levels of resources and it takes their different circumstances into account when assessing compliance with this obligation. Indeed, when examining reports of developed states, the level of scrutiny is higher and the Committee is more demanding. For example, examining the reports of Korea, the Committee expressed that it was disturbed by the fact that only primary education was provided free of charge. According to the Committee, 'given the strength of the Korean economy it appears appropriate that free education should also be extended to the secondary and higher sectors.'[35] It further recommended that the State pay immediate attention to this problem.[36] In contrast, when examining the implementation of the Covenant in the Solomon Islands, the Committee acknowledged that 'the lack of financial resources due to the prevailing economic crisis in Solomon Islands leaves little scope to the State Party for providing adequate educational services.' Obviously, in this case it would not have been realistic to recommend that the State implement free secondary education and the Committee only focused on the implementation of compulsory primary education.[37]

The Committee seems to consider that the existence of serious problems with the implementation of a right in a developed State is sufficient to indicate that it has not devoted the maximum of its available resources. For example, when considering the Third Periodic Report of Canada, the Committee noted that there were a high number of homeless people living in that country. Consequently, it did not hesitate to manifest its grave concern that 'such a wealthy country […] has allowed the problem of homelessness and inadequate housing to grow to such proportions […]'.[38]

Nonetheless, even in the case of developing States, there are minimum standards with which States must comply and they therefore need to allocate the necessary resources. For example, examining the report of Cameroon, the Committee stated that there was an extremely low level of protection accorded to the right to education. It therefore 'urged' the State 'to allocate increased resources to education.'[39] In the case

---

34 Concluding Observations Azerbaijan E/1998/22 para. 345.

35 Concluding Observations Republic of Korea E/1996/22 para. 29. See in addition, the Concluding Observations on the Second Periodic Report E/C.12/1/Add.59 para. 29.

36 Concluding Observations Republic of Korea E/1996/22 para. 84.

37 Concluding Observations Solomon Islands (without report) E/2000/22 para. 206.

38 Concluding Observations Canada E/1999/22 para. 399.

39 Concluding Observations Cameroon E/2000/22 para. 357. See in addition, for example, Concluding Observations Colombia E/1996/22 para. 192.

of Uruguay, the Committee noted that 'the resources devoted to public health and education are inadequate,'[40] and recommended the State to take measures 'to increase the real salaries of teachers and nurses.'[41]

The indicators developed by the Committee to measure compliance with the obligation to devote the maximum of available resources need to be further improved. So far, these indicators have enabled the Committee only to make general statements and they tend to use rather weak language. Moreover, the Committee has not applied them in a consistent and strict manner to all States in the same circumstances. However, we should not forget that these indicators were developed by the Committee as a creative way to overcome the difficulties in assessing State compliance with this obligation. The Committee's work in this area has made it apparent that with appropriate information it *is* possible to supervise compliance with this obligation. Thus, for example, if an optional protocol establishing a complaint procedure is adopted, the Committee will be quite able to monitor compliance with the obligation to devote the maximum of available resources provided it has access to the relevant information.

3 The obligation to continuously improve conditions and the prohibition of taking deliberately retrogressive measures

> '[…] with a view to *achieving progressively the full realisation* of the rights recognised in the present Covenant'

According to its ordinary meaning, the term 'progressive' means 'making continuous forward movement.'[42] Thus, States Parties are required to continuously take steps forward in order to achieve the full realisation of the rights recognised in the Covenant. The idea of forward movement entails two complementary obligations:

I. The obligation to continuously improve conditions, and
II. The obligation to abstain from taking deliberately retrogressive measures except under specific circumstances

Non-compliance with either obligation would be a violation of the Covenant. Hence States may violate these article 2(1) obligations not only through actions (obligation II), but also through omissions (obligation I).

3.1 The obligation to continuously improve conditions

According to the Committee, States Parties have a 'specific and continuing obligation' to move as expeditiously and effectively as possible towards the full realisation of all

40 Concluding Observations Uruguay E/1999/22 para. 368.
41 Concluding Observations Uruguay E/1999/22 para. 378.
42 Oxford Student's Dictionary, Oxford University Press, second edition 1988.

substantive rights contained in the Covenant. As early as its General Comment No. 3, the Committee noted that article 2(1) imposes an obligation 'to move as expeditiously and effectively as possible' towards the full realisation of all economic, social and cultural rights.[43]

The requirement to continuously improve conditions is reiterated in article 11(1) regarding the right to adequate living conditions, including food, clothing and housing. According to this provision,

> 'The States Parties to the present Covenant recognize the right of everyone to an adequate standard of living for himself and his family, including adequate food, clothing and housing, and to the *continuos improvement of living conditions.'* (Emphasis added).

However, it is beyond doubt that the obligation to continuously improve conditions as required by article 2(1) ICESCR applies to all substantive rights contained in the Covenant. In fact, the Committee has expressly stated this with regard to article 12 ICESCR on the right to the highest attainable standard of health. As set forth in General Comment No. 14:

> 'States Parties have a specific and continuing obligation to move as expeditiously and effectively as possible towards the full realisation of article 12 of the Covenant.'[44]

The violation of human rights due to 'acts of omission' is well established in international law, not only in relation to economic, social and cultural rights,[45] but also to civil and political rights. As is clear from the European Court of Human Rights, when positive actions on the part of the State are necessary 'the State cannot simply remain passive.'[46]

43 General Comment No. 3 para. 9.

44 General Comment No. 14 para. 31.

45 See Maastricht Guidelines No. 15: 'violations through acts of omission'. In addition, see the examples of violations of the right to health through States' omission included in General Comment No. 14 para. 49.

46 Airey v. Ireland, Application No. 6289/73, Judgement of 9 October 1979, para. 25. The European Court has arrived at the same conclusion in other cases in which it has found a State obligation to take positive action. In this context, it is worth noting the case of McCann and others v. the United Kingdom [Application No. 18984/91, Judgement of 27 September 1995]. In this case, the Court found a violation of the right to life (article 2 ECHR) due to the State's passive behaviour. The State's omission was not to have prevented the victims (suspects of terrorist acts) from travelling into the territory under its jurisdiction as well as the failure to take appropriate care in the control and organisation of the arrest operation. [See para. 213]. Along the same lines, passive State behaviour has been found to violate other provisions. See, for example, the violation of article 8 ECHR found in López Ostra v. Spain [Application No. 16798/90, Judgement of 9 December 1994] and the violation of article 3 ECHR in the case of A. v. the United Kingdom [Application No. 25599/94, Judgement of 23 September 1998].

Harvey examined when State inaction would constitute a violation of the Covenant. As he pointed out more than a decade ago:

> 'If a State undertakes to implement policies that cause a clear deterioration in the protection hitherto afforded a right specified in the agreement, a complainant might argue that the State was violating its obligations for the progressive achievement of that right. Even if a State merely tolerated deterioration in conditions, its inaction might justify a claim that the State had not taken steps to the maximum of its available resources to realise the right. Reductions in government-financed social welfare benefits could give rise to claims of the first type, while intentional government inaction in the face of clear deterioration in certain indices of social well-being could give rise to claims of the second type. The legal theory advanced in both instances would be that the agreement imposes ratcheted obligations on State Parties to the agreement with respect to the listed rights. That is, State Parties may not be obligated to achieve any particular level of protection for the listed rights, but once having achieved a certain level, they may be obligated to maintain it.'[47]

If States Parties must take continuous steps forward toward the full realisation of the Covenant's rights, then the passivity of States in the case of a decline in the protection of these rights due to external circumstances may be considered a violation of the Covenant. States cannot tolerate a decline in the degree of protection afforded to a particular right without taking any action to try to redress or improve the situation. This obligation is particularly stringent in the case of vulnerable groups. States must actively take steps to protect vulnerable groups even in times of severe resource constraints.

The Committee has stressed this obligation when States Parties have remained passive in the face of a deterioration in the level of protection of rights due to, for example, an increase in HIV infection rates, an increase in sexual tourism in the country or a deterioration of the environment due to the exploitation of natural resources by third parties. According to the Committee, in such cases States are required to take steps to address the situation.

For example, when considering the implementation of the Covenant in the Solomon Islands, the Committee noted that there were threats to the natural environment caused by practices of deforestation and overfishing which affected the right to an adequate standard of living (article 11 ICESCR). It therefore recommended that the State take measures to prevent the excessive exploitation of the country's natural resources.[48] When examining the Third Periodic Report of the Russian Federation, the Committee expressed 'serious concern' about the increase in HIV infections and 'urged' the State to address the problem as a matter of the utmost importance. Therefore, it recommended to the State that it should undertake an 'information campaign which explains the nature of the disease, the modes of transmission, including sexual modes of

47 Harvey, 1987, p. 416.
48 Concluding Observations Solomon Islands E/2000/22 paras. 204 and 209.

transmission, and prevention techniques [to] be undertaken in the mass media. It also recommends that the State Party adopt laws and take all necessary measures to prevent discrimination against persons who are HIV positive.'[49] In the same vein, when examining the initial report of Honduras, the Committee expressed concern about 'the high incidence of HIV/AIDS in the State Party, which is among the highest in the region', and the inadequate information provided by the State Party to the population. Therefore, it 'urged' the State Party 'to undertake effective measures to address the high level of persons living with HIV/AIDS.'[50]

In the case of Sri Lanka, the Committee noted that it was 'deeply concerned' about the sexual exploitation of Sri Lankan children by foreign tourists. The Committee regretted that the State had not seriously addressed the problem and 'strongly recommended' that the State take steps to 'seek out those who are responsible for the sexual exploitation of children and to prosecute them to the full extent of the law.'[51]

The obligation to actively take continuous steps also applies in the opposite situation, when there is a considerable increase in the resources available. It is clear from the Concluding Observations that whatever the level of State development, if the level of resources improves, so must its level of commitment to economic, social and cultural rights. In fact, the Committee expects that the resources allocated to the realisation of these rights increases in a manner which is proportional to the global increase in resources.

When examining the report of El Salvador, for example, the Committee emphasised that 'the continued existence of such levels of poverty in a country experiencing constant economic growth is unjustifiable.'[52] In the case of Portugal, the Committee noted with concern that the increase in the minimum wage had not kept pace with economic growth and recommended that the Government seek to ensure a graduated increase in the minimum wage which took into account Portugal's economic growth.[53] Similarly, in the case of Mexico the Committee noted that the State had improved it's 'macroeconomic performance', creating 'an environment conducive to a more effective implementation of the rights under the Covenant.'[54] However, the Committee regretted that 'despite the positive growth of macroeconomic indicators in Mexico, especially the sharp decrease in the level of inflation, the National Wages Commission has not adjusted the minimum wage level upwards.' Moreover, noting the inadequacy of the minimum wages to obtain a basic food basket, the Committee explicitly stated that

49 Concluding Observations Russian Federation E/1998/22 paras. 113 and 126.
50 Concluding Observations Honduras E/C.12/1/Add.57 paras. 26 and 47.
51 Concluding Observations Sri Lanka E/1999/22 paras. 76 and 90.
52 Concluding Observations El Salvador E/1997/22 para. 58
53 Concluding Observations Portugal E/1996/22 paras. 95 and 98.
54 Concluding Observations Mexico E/2000/22 para. 365.

Mexico was 'in violation of article 7 paragraph (a) (ii) of the Covenant.'[55] The obligation to improve the conditions for the enjoyment of the Covenant's rights if available resources increase is again particularly important in regard to the protection of vulnerable groups. For example, examining the report of Canada, the Committee expressed its concern on account of the fact that 'during a time of strong economic growth and increasing affluence' the State had not taken measures to protect vulnerable groups within society 'from poverty and homelessness.'[56]

3.2 The prohibition of taking deliberately retrogressive measures

In 1990, analysing the scope of article 2(1) ICESCR the Committee noted,

> '[A]ny deliberately retrogressive measures [...] would require the most careful consideration and would need to be fully justified by reference to the totality of the rights provided for in the Covenant and in the context of the full use of the maximum available resources.'[57]

In order to understand the Committee's statement, it is important to analyse what constitutes a 'deliberately retrogressive measure'. The Committee has not provided a definition. However, some guidance is to be found in General Comment No. 4 which states,

> '[A] general decline in living and housing conditions, *directly attributable* to policy and legislative decisions by States Parties, and in the absence of accompanying compensatory measures, would be inconsistent with the obligations under the Covenant.'[58]

It is therefore possible to argue that a 'deliberate retrogressive measure' means any measure that implies a step back in the level of protection accorded to the rights contained in the Covenant which is the consequence of an intentional decision by the State. This may occur, for example, if a State Party:

(a) Adopts any legislation or policy with a direct or collateral negative effect on the enjoyment of the rights by individuals or if it introduces legislation which discriminate in the enjoyment of the Covenant rights.[59]

retrogr measures

55 Concluding Observations Mexico E/2000/22 para. 382. Article 7(a)(ii) recognises 'the right of everyone to the enjoyment of just and favourable conditions of work which ensure in particular [...] a decent living for themselves and their families in accordance with the provisions of the present Covenant.'
56 Concluding Observations Canada E/1999/22 para. 409.
57 General Comment No. 3 para. 9.
58 General Comment No. 4 para. 11. (Emphasis added).
59 See General Comment No. 13 para. 59.

(b) Abrogates any legislation or policy consistent with these rights unless obviously outdated or replaced with equally or more consistent laws or compensatory measures.[60]

(c) Makes an unjustified reduction in public expenditures devoted to implementing economic, social and cultural rights, in the absence of adequate compensatory measures aimed to protect the injured individuals.[61]

(d) Adopts regional measures for the protection of human rights, without integrating economic, social and cultural rights. The Committee expressly noted this when European countries were debating the draft Charter of Fundamental Rights of the European Union.[62]

Despite the Committee's position in General Comment No. 3, over the years the Committee has taken a rather flexible approach to the adoption of deliberately retrogressive measures by States Parties. For many years, with a few exceptions, the Committee did not strictly monitor the adoption of deliberately retrogressive measures adopted by States. The Committee does not systematically inquire as to the justification

60 According to the Maastricht Guidelines on Economic, Social and Cultural Rights, a violation of these rights occurs through an act of the State when it makes a 'formal removal or suspension of legislation necessary for the continued enjoyment of an economic, social and cultural right that is currently enjoyed.' Guideline No. 14 (a). See, also, General Comment No. 4 para. 11 and General Comment No. 12 para. 19.

61 For example, in the case of the Russian Federation, the Committee was very concerned about the curtailing of funds to modernise an out –of date water delivery system and recommended to the State that the system should be improved 'as a matter of priority.' [Concluding Observations Russian Federation E/1998/22 paras. 111 and 124]. In the case of Nigeria the Committee regretted the fact that the Government's social and health allocations were consistently being diminished and that it had introduced fees and charges which had not existed previously [Concluding Observations Nigeria E/1999/22 para. 124]. The Concluding Observations of Zimbabwe stated that 'the Committee expresses concern about cutbacks in education expenditure which result in non-compliance with article 13(2)(a) requiring free compulsory and universal primary education' [Concluding Observations Zimbabwe E/1998/22 para. 77].

62 The 'Statement of the Committee on Economic, Social and Cultural Rights to the Convention to draft a Charter of Fundamental Rights of the European Union' emphasises: 'the Committee, while wishing to express its fullest support for these proposals, would nevertheless like to point out that if economic and social rights were not to be integrated in the draft Charter on an equal footing with civil and political rights, such negative regional signals would be highly detrimental to the full realisation of all human rights at both the international and domestic levels, and *would have to be regarded as a retrogressive step contravening the existing obligations of member States of the European Union under the International Covenant on Economic, Social and Cultural Rights.* In such a case, the Committee might have to raise this issue when examining reports by States parties, as a violation of the obligation under article 2, paragraph 1, of the Covenant to 'achieving progressively the full realisation of the rights recognised' in that Covenant, i.e. taking measures geared to progressively realise and promote economic, social and cultural rights.' E/2001/22, Annex VIII, para. 4 (emphasis added).

for such measures by reference to the totality of the rights of the Covenant and the full use of all available resources and generally it does not include any reference to the adoption of retrogressive measures in the Concluding Observations.

Moreover, in the few situations where the Committee has analysed the existence of retrogressive measures it has not been sufficiently strict. For example, the Concluding Observations of Mauritius in 1994 state that 'the Committee is also concerned about the reintroduction of fees at the tertiary level of education, which *constitutes a deliberate retrogressive step.'*[63] However, the Committee included a very short section containing 'suggestions or recommendations' and, unfortunately, failed to mention the 'deliberate retrogressive measures adopted.' Arguably, the lack of further analysis in the case of Mauritius was the result of the Committee's examination of the situation in the absence of the State report. However, the Committee acted similarly when examining the Initial Report of Nigeria in 1998. In this case, the Committee regretted the fact that the authorities had reintroduced primary school fees in certain parts of the country and imposed hospital charges where they had not previously existed.[64] It also noted that university fees had dramatically increased the year before.[65] However, despite the existence of what were clearly retrogressive measures with respect to the right to education and the right to health and that some Committee members had clearly acknowledged this during the 'constructive dialogue' with government representatives,[66] the Committee did not include any further statement regarding this issue in the Concluding Observations.

In contrast, when examining the report of Germany, the Committee noted with concern that 'tuition fees for university education are increasing, despite the fact that article 13 of the Covenant calls for the progressive introduction of free higher education.'[67] Consequently, the Committee recommended that the State 'avoid increases in university tuition fees, in compliance with article 13 of the Covenant.'[68]

Most of the time, the lack of effective Committee supervision as regards the adoption of retrogressive measures is the result of the fact that it is difficult for the Committee to know whether or not a State has taken such measures. To enable the Committee to arrive at such a conclusion, it is necessary to undertake a very complex analysis and to consider a wide rage of information. An illustrative example is the examination of the Third Periodic Report of Canada. The Concluding Observations indicated that there had been retrogressive measures that principally affected vulnera-

63 Concluding Observations Mauritius E/1995/22 para. 181.

64 Concluding Observations Nigeria E/1999/22 para. 124.

65 Concluding Observations Nigeria E/1999/22 para. 126. As noted by a Committee member during the 'constructive dialogue', during the first quarter of 1997, the Government had introduced a policy establishing a 1,000 per cent increase in university fees. See Mr. Thapalia E/C.12/1998/SR.8 para. 59.

66 See, for example, Mr. Riedel in E/C.12/1998/SR.8 para. 62.

67 Concluding Observations Germany E/1999/22 para. 321.

68 Concluding Observations Germany E/1999/22 para. 336.

ble groups within Canadian society. However, it was not easy for the Committee to reach this conclusion. The Committee needed to resolve a complex issue: it was necessary to establish whether the 'Canada Assistance Plan' [CAP] which was replaced by the 'Canada Health and Social Transfer' [CHST] had established national standards for social welfare.

The Canadian Government argued that the CAP did not establish a specific level of financial assistance[69] and that if it had not established any standards, then the new system could not be considered as a retrogressive measure because it did not provoke a loss of standards. After a thorough examination, the Committee finally rejected the government's argument that there were no pre-existing standards, expressly noting that 'the CHST had eliminated the standards set forth by the CAP'.[70] However, the Committee was not strict enough in its Concluding Observations. Although the Committee noted that the replacement of the CAP with the CHST entailed a retrogressive measure which had had a range of adverse consequences for the enjoyment of the Covenant rights by disadvantaged groups in Canada,[71] it did not then directly indicate the incompatibility of the measures with the Covenant.

In general, it is possible to conclude that for many years the Committee did not seriously monitor the adoption of deliberately retrogressive measures by States Parties. This situation began to change after 1998 when the Maastricht Guidelines on Violations of Economic, Social and Cultural Rights clearly established that the adoption of any deliberately retrogressive measure that reduces the extent to which any economic, social and cultural rights are guaranteed, constitutes a violation of the Covenant.[72] Probably as a result of the influence of the Guidelines, when the Committee adopted the 'Outline for Drafting General Comments on Specific Rights of the International Covenant on Economic, Social and Cultural Rights' in November 1999, it included, among the issues to be considered in the drafting of future general comments, the adoption of 'retrogressive measures' under the section of 'violations.'[73]

---

69 See, for example, Mr. Mundie (Canada) in E/C.12/1998/SR.47 paras. 7 and 18 and Mr. Moher in (Canada) E/C.12/1998/SR.47 para. 34.

70 Concluding Observations Canada E/1999/22 para. 394.

71 Concluding Observations Canada E/1999/22 para. 394.

72 Guideline No. 14 reads as follows: 'violations of economic, social and cultural rights can occur through the direct action of States [...]. Examples of such violation include: [...] (e) the adoption of any deliberately retrogressive measure that reduces the extent to which any such rights are guaranteed. (g) the reduction or diversion of specific public expenditure, when such restriction or diversion results in the non-enjoyment of such rights and is not accompanied by adequate measures to ensure minimum subsistence rights for everyone.'

73 The Outline contains a 'checklist' of the issues that the Committee states should be included in future General Comments on substantive rights. See 'Outline for drafting general comments on specific rights of the international covenant on economic, social and cultural rights. ' E/2000/22, Annex IX, section V on 'violations.'

Consequently, General Comment No. 13 on 'the right to education' adopted by the Committee in December 1999 establishes,

> '45. There is a *strong presumption of impermissibility of any retrogressive measures* taken in relation to the right to education, as well as other rights enunciated in the Covenant. If any deliberately retrogressive measures are taken, the State party has *the burden of proving that they have been introduced after the most careful consideration of all alternatives and that they are fully justified by reference to the totality of the rights provided for in the Covenant and in the context of the full use of the State party's maximum available resources.'*

The importance of this statement becomes evident when we bear in mind that before General Comment No. 13, the Committee had not undertaken any systematic monitoring of the retrogressive measures adopted by States in the great majority of cases. Unfortunately, the Committee has yet to implement this approach in the examination of State reports.

In 2001, when examining the Fourth Periodic Report of Ukraine, the Committee noted with concern that 'the budgets allocated for education and scientific research have fallen sharply, leading to a deterioration in the quality of education.'[74] In this case, although the Committee recommended that the State 'take all necessary measures to allocate the required resources to implement effectively'[75] the right to education, it did not require the State to justify the measures under the standards set forth in the General Comment.

The statement concerning the presumption of the impermissibility of any retrogressive measure was repeated in General Comment No. 14 which was adopted in May 2000.[76] However, in this latter General Comment the Committee went even further than in its previous General Comments. General Comment No. 14 stated that:

> '32. As with all other rights in the Covenant, there is a strong presumption that *retrogressive measures* taken in relation to the right to health are not permissible. If any deliberately retrogressive measures are taken, the State party has the burden of proving that they have been introduced after the most careful consideration of all alternatives and that they are duly justified by reference to the totality of the rights provided for in the Covenant in the context of the full use of the State party's maximum available resources.'(Emphasis added).
> […]

---

74 Concluding Observations Ukraine E/C.12/1/Add.65 para. 17.

75 Concluding Observations Ukraine E/C.12/1/Add.65 para. 32.

76 General Comment No. 14 para. 32 reads as follows: 'As with all other rights in the Covenant, there is a *strong presumption* that retrogressive measures taken in relation to the right to health are *not permissible*. If any deliberately retrogressive measures are taken, the State Party has the burden of proving that they have been introduced after the *most careful consideration of all alternatives and that they are duly justified by reference to the totality of the rights provided for in the Covenant* in the context of the full use of the State Party's maximum available resources.' (Emphasis added).

'48. Violations of the right to health can occur through the direct action of States or other entities insufficiently regulated by States. The adoption of any retrogressive measures incompatible with the *core obligations* under the right to health, outlined in paragraph 43 above, constitutes a violation of the right to health.' (Emphasis added).

Reading both paragraphs together, we may conclude that retrogressive measures are *prima facie* incompatible with the Covenant and that States have the burden of proving their compatibility. The final assessment of a violation will come as a result of a comprehensive evaluation carry out by the Committee after considering every factor, such as a demonstrable limitation of resources and the respect of the Covenant as a whole, including the non-discrimination clauses and the limitation clause of article 4 ICESCR.

The obligation to 'progress' allows for exceptions in certain situations. However, as paragraph 48 of General Comment No. 14 suggests, a retrogressive measure may not affect the core content of the obligations imposed by a substantive right. In other words, there is a minimum level which must be respected if the State is to avoid violating the Covenant.

The 'core obligations' and the 'minimum core content' of each right are analysed below in this Chapter.[77] Here it is necessary to examine when it is justified for States Parties to take retrogressive measures or to fail to take steps towards the full realisation of the substantive rights in question.

The Committee has recognised that there are some circumstances, such as an economic crisis or a natural disaster, that require additional resources and in which the adoption of retrogressive measures or the omission to actively take steps to improve the conditions is unavoidable. According to the Committee, if the State encounters a situation in which the deterioration in the standard of development is inevitable even using the maximum available resources, the Committee takes these circumstances into account and adopts a flexible approach. However, this is not to say that in such circumstances States enjoy unlimited discretion and the Committee has clearly established that there are some limits on how States may handle such crisis situations.

vulnerable grps

It is beyond doubt that States must pay particular attention to vulnerable groups. If an economic recession or budgetary cuts to social welfare expenditures have had a particular impact on the most vulnerable groups, the Committee has not only expressed its regret, but has also reminded the States in question of the importance of the view expressed in General Comments No. 3[78] in which it stressed that

77 See section 7.

78 See, for example, Concluding Observations Spain E/1997/22 para. 101, Concluding Observations Philippines E/1996/22 para. 124 and Concluding Observations Solomon Islands E/2000/22 para. 206.

> 'Even in times of severe resource constraints whether caused by a process of adjustment, of economic recession or by other factors the vulnerable members of the society can and indeed must be protected by the adoption of relatively low-cost targeted programmes.'[79]

The Committee is very consistent in this approach. As it indicated in General Comment No. 4 on the right to adequate housing,

> 'The Committee is aware that external factors can affect the right to a continuous improvement of living conditions, and that in many States Parties overall living conditions declined during the 1980s. However, as noted by the Committee in its General Comment 2 [...], despite externally caused problems, the obligations under the Covenant continue to apply and are perhaps even more pertinent during times of economic contraction. It would thus appear to the Committee that a general decline in living and housing conditions, directly attributable to policy and legislative decisions by States Parties, and in the absence of accompanying compensatory measures, would be inconsistent with the obligations under the Covenant.'[80]

In examining States' reports, the Committee has taken into account a variety of circumstances on the basis of which it has taken a more relaxed approach. For example, when examining the reports of Eastern European countries, it has analysed the 'economic cost of transition' under 'factors and difficulties impeding the implementation of the Covenant' and on that basis has not been very strict in its approach.[81] Nonetheless, it has established some clear positions and made clear that there is a certain minimum standard that States must respect. For example, when examining the initial report of Azerbaijan, the Committee requested information on measures being taken or envisaged for the protection of vulnerable groups and recommended that the State address 'as a matter of utmost urgency the basic needs of the population, including safe drinking water, food, affordable housing and health care.'[82] In the case of Belarus, the Committee also emphasised that 'that any economic reform adopted should be undertaken in a manner that is consistent with protection of the economic and social rights of the poorer segments of society.'[83]

The Committee has also adopted a more flexible approach when States are recovering from armed conflict or natural disasters or when they have a considerable debt burden. An illustrative case is Honduras. When the Committee analysed its initial report, it noted that 'the efforts of the State party to comply with its obligations under

---

79 General Comment No. 3 para. 12.

80 General Comment No. 4 para. 11.

81 For example, Concluding Observations Ukraine E/1996/22 para. 258, Concluding Observations Belarus E/1997/22 paras. 276-277 and Concluding Observations Azerbaijan E/1998/22 paras. 326 and 354.

82 Concluding Observations Azerbaijan E/1998/22 paras. 340 and 354.

83 Observations Belarus E/1997/22 para. 288.

the Covenant are impeded by the fact that it is classified as a highly indebted poor country and that up to 40 per cent of its annual national budget is allocated to foreign debt servicing.'[84] Moreover, the Committee noted that the State suffered the consequence of an appalling natural disaster in 1998, hurricane Mitch, which aggravated the problems of poverty in the country.[85]

Examining the report of Croatia, the Committee recognised that 'Croatia is in a state of transition, recovering from armed conflict, which is causing complex socio-economic, political and other difficulties in the implementation of the rights provided for in the Covenant, including a breakdown of the social welfare system, acute levels of unemployment and extensive damage to the nation's physical infrastructure.' Due to these circumstances, the Committee was not overly severe with the State in its Concluding Observations, although it suggested that in some areas there had been a deterioration in the situation that was worse than should have been expected given the State's circumstances. The Committee did, however, express its concern about 'the deterioration in the general standard of living in the State Party, which has ensued in part from economic instability, high levels of unemployment, non-payment of salaries of many workers, the unrecovered pension payments made by Croatians prior to independence and the destruction during the war of vital infrastructure and settlements that have not yet been reconstructed.'[86]

In the case of Colombia, the Committee considered the fact that 'the recent economic recession along with certain aspects of the structural adjustment programmes and economic liberalization policies introduced by the State Party, have aggravated the negative effects on the enjoyment of economic, social and cultural rights by the population and in particular by the most disadvantaged and marginalized groups.' Due to these circumstances, the State had reduced subsidies for health care and these measures had particularly affected women and indigenous groups. The Committee expressed its concern about this reduction and 'urged' the State 'to allocate a higher percentage of its GDP to the health sector and to ensure that its system of subsidies does not discriminate against the most disadvantaged and marginalized groups.'[87]

When examining the Second Periodic Report of Jamaica, the Committee acknowledged that 'the consequences of the 1995-1996 financial crisis, inflation and the increasing cost of servicing a public debt that reached in excess of 140% of GDP in March 2000, have seriously affected the capacity of the State Party to implement the Covenant.' However, it expressed 'particular concern about the inadequate level in State expenditure on education, accompanied by a decline in the quality of education.

84 Concluding Observations Honduras E/C.12/1/Add.57 para. 9
85 Concluding Observations Honduras E/C.12/1/Add.57 para. 11.
86 Concluding Observations Croatia E/C.12/1/Add.73 paras. 7 and 18.
87 Concluding Observations Colombia E/C.12/1/Add.74 para. 31.

It is reported that recent State Party statistics show that 40% of children who complete primary education can 'neither read nor write.'[88]

From the analysis of the Committee's work, it is possible to conclude that a State Party seeking to justify a retrogressive measure or a failure to comply with the obligation to continuously improve conditions due to resource constraints must:

(a) Demonstrate that every effort has been made to use all resources at its disposal. This implies that the State not only has the burden of proving the lack of resources, but it must also prove that it has unsuccessfully sought to obtain international assistance. This has clearly been the approach taken by the Committee and it is also stressed by the Maastricht Guidelines.[89]

(b) Demonstrate that every effort has been made to use the resources at its disposal to satisfy, as a matter of priority, certain minimum obligations with respect to the implementation of the Covenant. This obligation is over and above that of justifying lack of resources.

(c) Demonstrate that particular attention has been paid to vulnerable groups within society and, in particular that it has taken measures to prevent or ameliorate the adverse consequences that vulnerable groups may suffer.[90]

(d) Rescind any restrictive measures taken to reduce Covenant-related expenses due to real constraints on resources and repair adverse effects on the population, in particular among vulnerable groups, once the resource constraints disappear and the economy recovers.[91]

(e) Take adequate measures to ensure that the reduction in resources does not result in the violation of the State Party's obligations under the Covenant[92] and in particular those of article 4 ICESCR. To the extent that a retrogressive measure places a limita-

88 Concluding Observations Jamaica E/C.12/1/Add.75 paras. 5 and 19.

89 See, for example, General Comment No. 3 para. 10 and General Comment No. 12 para. 17. Along the same lines, the Maastricht Guideline No. 13 states that 'a State Party claiming that it is unable to carry out its obligations for reasons beyond its control has the burden of proving that this is the case.'

90 The Committee noted with regard to Canada that 'since 1994, in addressing the budget deficits by slashing social expenditure, the State Party has not paid sufficient attention to the adverse consequences for the enjoyment of economic, social and cultural rights by the Canadian population as a whole, and by vulnerable groups in particular' [Concluding Observations Canada E/1999/22 para. 386]. See in addition, for example, Concluding Observations the Netherlands E/1999/22 para. 191.

91 See, for example, Concluding Observations the Netherlands E/1999/22 para. 176 and Concluding Observations Mexico E/C.12/1999/11 para. 382.

92 See, for example, Concluding Observations Finland E/1997/22 para. 316, Concluding Observations Philippines E/1996/22 para. 124 and Concluding Observations Sweden E/1996/22 para. 145.

tion on the rights, States must comply with the conditions set out in article 4 ICESCR, which stipulates:

> 'The States Parties to the present Covenant recognise that, in the enjoyment of those rights provided by the State in conformity with the present Covenant, the State may subject such rights only to such limitations as are determined by law only in so far as this may be compatible with the nature of these rights and solely for the purpose of promoting the general welfare in a democratic society.'

As an analysis of this provision is to be found in the previous chapter, it is not necessary to repeat it here.[93] However, it is important to stress that States bear the burden of proof and in most cases it is difficult to satisfy the requirements established in article 4 with regard to the imposition of limitations.

The lack of strict supervision as regards the adoption of retrogressive measures by States is a consequence of the fact that it is very difficult for the Committee to identify a retrogressive measure and it is even harder to evaluate whether or not it was justified in the light of article 4. Such an evaluation requires not only a high level of expertise, but also a good knowledge of the country situation. Nonetheless, it is important to stress that such supervision is feasible and at the national level domestic courts should (and indeed must) be able to monitor and supervise the adoption of retrogressive measures that affect the enjoyment of economic, social and cultural rights.

4 THE OBLIGATION TO ACCORD A DEGREE OF PRIORITY TO HUMAN RIGHTS IN THE ALLOCATION OF RESOURCES

> ' [...] with a view to *achieving progressively the full realisation* of the rights recognised in the present Covenant'

States have the sovereign right to decide where and how they allocate their resources. Due to material limitations, prioritisation is always necessary when States allocate resources. States are required to decide first which rights are to be implemented and which expenditures are the most compelling. By ratifying or acceding to the Covenant, States freely assume some obligations that imply limitations to their discretion. The question here is the extent to which the Covenant imposes limitations on the discretion of States Parties to allocate their resources.

According to the Limburg Principles,

93 General Comment No. 13 para. 42.

'28. In the use of the available resources due priority shall be given to the realization of rights recognized in the Covenant, mindful of the need to assure to everyone the satisfaction of subsistence requirements as well as the provision of essential services.'

Various commentators have also adopted this approach[94] which seems to be a necessary consequence of the obligation to take steps to achieve progressively the full realisation of the rights. If a State does not accord some degree of priority to the implementation of the Covenant's rights, it will hardly comply with the obligation under article 2(1) ICESCR and it would be very difficult for it to justify non-compliance with the Covenant's obligation. Therefore, a State Party wishing to comply with the obligations assumed under the Covenant must admit the existence of some limits to its sovereign discretion to decide where to allocate resources. Two important principles of international law support this conclusion. First, the Covenant is binding upon the States Parties and they must perform their obligations in good faith.[95] Second, States cannot invoke their internal law as a justification for the failure to perform the terms of a treaty.[96]

The obligation that States Parties must give a degree of priority to the implementation of the Covenant's rights or, to adopt the language of the Limburg principles, to give 'due priority' to them, provides us with guidance in assessing compliance with the Covenant. Take, for example, the case of a developing State which is Party to the Covenant where the authorities must decide whether to devote resources to building a new airport or to provide clean water to poor rural areas. Do the authorities of a developing State in the above situation violate the Covenant if they decide not to devote the money to Covenant-related expenditures?

This is certainly a complex issue. The duty to accord 'due priority' to the implementation of the Covenant's rights leaves with States a wide margin of discretion in deciding how to allocate available resources. In the example, the decision to build an airport is not *per se* a violation of the Covenant. It may be possible that in the long term, a new airport brings greater investment and taxes that place the State in a better position to comply with the Covenant's obligations. On the other hand, if in the long

94 This interpretation finds support in some academic writing, such as, Goodwin-Gill, S.: 'Obligations of conduct and result.' In: *The right to food.* Alston, P. & Tomaševski, K. (eds.), Martinus Nijhoff Publishers, Utrecht (1984), p. 116; Alston, op. cit. (note 21), p. 38; and Trubek, D.M.: 'Economic, social and cultural rights in the third world: human rights law and human needs programs.' In: *Human rights in international law: legal and policy issues.* Meron, Theodor (ed), Clarendon Press, Oxford, (1984), vol. 1, Chapter 6, pp. 214 *et seq.*. As Trubek notes, this obligation is also supported by the legislative history of the Covenant (p. 215).

95 Art. 26 Vienna Convention on the Law of Treaties 1969 'Every treaty in force is binding upon the parties to it and must be performed by them in good faith.'

96 Art. 27 Vienna Convention on the Law of Treaties 1969 'A Party may not invoke the provisions of its internal law as justification for its failure to perform a treaty [...].' In addition see Art. 13 of the Draft Declaration on Rights and Duties of States of 1949.

term it is proved that the principal advantage of the airport has been to facilitate tourist trips for the wealthy few, the policy would constitute a violation of the Covenant. But what if the decision was between buying new military aircraft or devoting the money to social expenditures in a country without any threat to its security? In sum, it is extremely difficult for an international monitoring body to supervise the obligation to give 'due priority' to the realisation of the rights recognised in the Covenant.

Therefore, the question here is not whether or not there is an obligation to give 'due priority' to the implementation of the Covenant over and above other goals but, rather, how to supervise this obligation and whether the Committee is able to do so. As has been noted by one Committee member, 'if States Parties appearing before the Committee were to be asked what their priorities were, the Committee should ask itself whether it had the expertise to judge those priorities and whether or not it was qualified to judge a Government's political choices. In a fully democratic society, which the Covenant was supposed to guarantee, how could the Committee challenge what the people demand?'[97]

While these concerns are legitimate, it should be stressed that the Committee's approach has not been to tell the State where to spend its money or what priorities to establish for resource allocation. Rather, the Committee's role has been to supervise whether or not a State Party is honouring its obligations 'to take steps to the maximum of its available resources' by giving some degree of priority to the implementation of the Covenant. However, the burden of proving the degree of priority given to the satisfaction of the rights lies with the State Party. Therefore, if a State argues that it has been unable to comply fully with its Covenant obligations due to resource constraints, it has the burden of proving that every effort has been made to use all available resources at its disposal in order to satisfy, 'as a matter of priority', the obligations set forth in the Covenant, particularly the satisfaction of the minimum essential level of each right.[98]

On occasion the Committee has recognised that the resources available to the State Party are limited and it has indicated which are the specific priorities where the State should allocate the limited resources at its disposal. For example, after examining the report of Colombia, the Committee suggested that the State give priority to improving the supply of low-cost housing for the benefit of the poorest sectors of society and to allocate resources to provide the entire population with drinking-water and sewerage services.[99] In the case of Bolivia, it recommended that the State Party give priority to education in its budget. While these are merely suggestions, the Committee's 'suggestions' as to the priorities for the allocation of resources employ more mandatory language when there is a high level of discrimination against women in the State

97 See Mr. Adekuoye in E/C.12/1995/SR.22 para. 50.

98 See General Comment No. 12 para. 17 and General Comment No. 14 para. 47. The notion of the 'minimum essential level' of each right is analysed below.

99 Concluding Observations Colombia E/1996/22 para. 200.

concerned. In such cases, the Committee has 'urged' the State Party to give priority to overcoming the inequality against women.[100]

The Committee has sometimes expressed satisfaction when a State Party has changed its previous policies and began to give priority to the satisfaction of these rights over other goals, such as military spending or public 'beautification' projects. For example, when examining the Second Periodic Report of the Dominican Republic, the Committee noted with satisfaction that the new government had started giving priority to housing projects rather than to ornamental public works, as its predecessor had done.[101]

Finally, it is worth stressing that the Covenant does not provide any rules for prioritising the allocation of resources to specific rights, nor has the Committee provided any concrete rules in this regard. In general, the Committee seems to analyse the issue of allocation of resources in a very broad and tentative manner. Although it is true that in general the Committee has paid more attention to the need for increased resources devoted to the right to adequate housing[102] and the right to education,[103] it does not follow that these rights should be given preference over others. Arguably, the attention that the Committee pays to these issues is a consequence of the fact that it has received more information about them.

5 The obligation to take 'all appropriate' measures towards the full implementation of the rights

'[...] *by all appropriate means*, including particularly the adoption of legislative measures.'

In general, the Covenant does not set out what measures the State must take in order to give effect to the rights contained therein, it merely requires States to do so 'by all

100 See, for example, Concluding Observations Zimbabwe E/1998/22 para. 80; Concluding Observations Georgia E/2001/22 para. 100; Concluding Observations Republic of Korea E/1996/22 para. 81; and Concluding Observations Iraq E/1995/22 para. 141. See in addition, the Committee's statement in regard to the fourth 'World Conference on Women: Action for Equality, Development and Peace.' E/1996/22, Annex VI.

101 Concluding Observations Dominican Republic E/1998/22 para. 206. See also, for example, Concluding Observations Honduras E/C.12/1/Add.57 para. 7.

102 The Committee has stressed 'the need for increased resources regarding the right to adequate housing' [Concluding Observations Dominican Republic E/1998/22 para. 240]. The Committee recommended that a State Party should 'devote a substantial proportion of its budget to creating conditions leading to more people being adequately housed, in accordance with General Comment No. 4' [Concluding Observations Azerbaijan E/1998/22 para. 351]. See also, Concluding Observations Nigeria E/1999/22 para. 136 and Concluding Observations Canada E/1999/22 para. 421.

103 See, for example, Concluding Observations Peru E/1998/22 para. 166; Concluding Observations Paraguay E/1997/22 para. 91; Concluding Observations Cameroon E/2000/22 para. 357; Concluding Observations Guinea E/1997/22 para. 208; and Concluding Observations Bolivia E/C.12/1/Add.60 para. 44.

appropriate means.' The 'appropriate means' may be, for example, legislative, judicial, administrative, financial, educational, or social measures.[104] As stressed by the Limburg Principles, the only limitation is that the means must be 'consistent with the nature of the rights in order to fulfil their obligations under the Covenant.'[105]

Each State Party has to devise its own measures, in accordance with its specific circumstances, including its financial resources, national legal system, population, geographic distribution of the population, natural resources and the existence of other international obligations.[106] This implies that each State must act with creativity and innovation to identify the appropriate means to implement each of the Covenant's rights. As two commentators have noted, appropriate means may be 'universally valid or relevant or may be quite specific to a particular culture or legal system.'[107]

It is important to stress that some of the substantive provisions contained in Part III of the Covenant spell out specific means by which the right concerned is to be achieved.[108] However, such specific means indicated in the substantive provisions are not exhaustive and they do not exclude the pursuit of other means.

States Parties do not enjoy unlimited discretion as to the adoption of means. Ultimately, It remains for the Committee to assess whether or not the means chosen by a State were indeed 'adequate'. For that reasons, States are required to indicate in their reports not only the measures that have been taken but also the basis on which they are considered to be the most 'appropriate' under the circumstances.[109] Although the expression 'by all appropriate means' is very general and vague, over the years the Committee has further clarified its meaning.

As the Committee notes,

> '[T]he Covenant adopts a broad and flexible approach which enables the particularities of the legal and administrative systems of each State, as well as other relevant considerations to be taken into account.'
>
> [...]
>
> 'But this flexibility coexists with the obligation upon each State party to use all the means at its disposal to give effect to the rights recognised in the Covenant. In this respect, the fundamental requirements of international human rights law must be borne in mind [...].'[110]

---

104 General Comment No. 3 para. 7

105 Limburg Principle No. 17.

106 General Comment No. 9 para. 1.

107 Steiner & Alston, 1996, p. 268.

108 See, for example, articles 6(2), 11(2), 12(2), 13(2) and 15(2) ICESCR.

109 General Comment No. 3 para. 4.

110 General Comment No. 9 paras. 1-2.

In the light of the Committee's Concluding Observations and General Comments, it is possible to conclude that the measures are 'appropriate' to the implementation of the Covenant when they respect certain principles, such as:

(1) *The measures must be 'reasonable', 'effective' and produce results compatible with the obligations under the Covenant:*

In the light of the Committee's work it is safe to say that States have the burden of proving that the measures taken are reasonable in light of their specific circumstances. In order to evaluate the 'reasonableness' of the measures taken, the Committee has taken into account the level of development of the State concerned. Thus, when it analyses the compliance with the Covenant by developed States, it requires that the measures lead to a higher standard of protection than in the case of developing States. This is clear, for example, in the Concluding Observations of the Republic of Korea, which state, 'the Committee is of the view that the Government, *in view of its economic resources,* has inadequately addressed the economic, social and cultural rights of the most marginalized members of society.'[111] The Committee needs to further elaborate the 'reasonableness' requirement of the measures. In this regard it would be desirable if it takes into account some relevant domestic jurisprudence.[112]

The measures should also be 'effective'. The Committee has not developed a clear test to assess the 'effectiveness' of the measures taken to implement the Covenant. However, in the light of the Concluding Observations we may deduce that measures are not effective when the State has not allocated the financial and human resources necessary for their implementation. For example, when examining the Third Periodic Report of the Russian Federation, the Committee found that despite the fact that the State had taken some measures to address a series of problems such as child labour and inadequate working conditions, the measures had been 'ineffective' because the State had not 'devoted sufficient funding' for their implementation.[113] In particular, the Committee noted the necessity that the State party increased the funding of the labour inspectorate as a manner to enforce the existing legal prohibition.[114]

The Committee has frequently assessed whether or not the measures have been 'effective' for achieving the required result. Thus, in the Concluding Observations it is not rare to find that the Committee considers that the measures taken by the State

111 Concluding Observations Republic of Korea E/1996/22 para. 78 (emphasis added).

112 In this context it is worth noting the judgement of the Constitutional Court of South Africa in the Grootboom case in which the Court developed a test of the 'reasonableness' of the measures to implement the right to adequate housing. [The Government of the Republic of South Africa v. Irene Grootboom, case CCT 11/00 decided on 4 October 2000, 2001 (1) SA 46 (CC) paras. 39-44]. Available at: http://www.concourt.gov.za/date2000.html (last visited July 2000).

113 Concluding Observations Russian Federation E/1998/22 para. 104.

114 Concluding Observations Russian Federation E/1998/22 para. 119.

concerned have been 'ineffective' or 'insufficient' to fulfil the obligations under the Covenant.[115]

Once it has found that measures have not been 'effective', the Committee has usually recommended in general terms that more effective measures be adopted.[116] Exceptionally, the Committee has specifically indicated which measures it considers to be effective for the implementation of a given right in the State concerned. For example, when examining the Second Periodic Report of the Dominican Republic, the Committee considered that the State was not ensuring the rights of the illegal Haitian migrants within the country. Therefore, it called upon the State 'to take all necessary measures' to ensure the enjoyment of all economic, social and cultural rights 'fully and without discrimination.' The Committee then went further by specifically indicated that the 'regularisation of the situation of these illegal residents, through the delivery of a residence permit or naturalisation' was the 'necessary' measure to achieve this end.[117]

When assessing whether or not the measures adopted by a State have been 'appropriate', the Committee has also taken into account the final result produced by the measures adopted. According to the Committee, the measures should produce results that are consistent with the full discharge of its obligations under the Covenant.[118] Therefore, States are required to devise a plan of action and to take into account the effect that a given measure may produce in the enjoyment of other Covenant's rights in order not to fail in the compliance of other obligations.

(2) *States must take into account the means which have proved to be the most effective in ensuring the protection of other human rights*:

As the Committee notes, '[w]here the means used to give effect to the Covenant on Economic, Social and Cultural Rights differ significantly from those used in relation to other human rights treaties, there should be a compelling justification for this, taking into account the fact that the formulations used in the Covenant are, to a considerable extent, comparable to those used in treaties dealing with civil and political rights.'[119]

The Committee recommends that States Parties accord equal treatment to both Covenants in terms of their domestic legal status and that if measures are taken to incorporate civil and political rights treaty obligations, consideration ought to be given to similar measures in relation to economic, social and cultural rights.[120] In the case of

---

115 See, for example, Concluding Observations Philippines E/1996/22 paras. 112 and 119; Concluding Observations Surinam E/1996/22 para. 158; Concluding Observations Georgia E/2001/22 para. 89; and Concluding Observations Iraq E/1998/22 para. 279.

116 See, for example, Concluding Observations Peru E/1998/22 para. 148.

117 Concluding Observations Dominican Republic E/1998/22 para. 233.

118 General Comment No. 9 para. 5.

119 General Comment No. 9 para. 7.

120 See, for example, Concluding Observations Switzerland E/1999/22 para. 365 and Concluding Observations Iceland E/2000/22 para. 84.

Switzerland, for example, the Committee recommended that 'the State party accord equal treatment to both the International Covenant on Civil and Political Rights and the International Covenant on Economic, Social and Cultural Rights in terms of their domestic legal status and that if measures are taken to incorporate civil and political rights treaty obligations consideration be given to similar measures in relation to economic, social and cultural rights.'[121]

In sum, the Covenant gives each State Party discretion to determine the 'appropriate means' to implement the Covenant provisions in accordance with their own circumstances and the particularities of their legal and administrative systems. Although the Committee has not expressly developed a general test for the assessment of the 'appropriateness' of the measures, it has became clear that States do not enjoy unlimited discretion in the selection of these means. The 'appropriateness' of the means chosen is subject to review by the Committee in its examination of States' reports and it is not rare that it has found that the measures adopted have not been 'appropriate'.

In the next section the focus is on three types of measures for the implementation of the Covenant. These types of measures are (1) legislative measures, (2) judicial and other 'appropriate' remedies, and (3) educational measures. Although there are many other 'appropriate' measures for the purposes of article 2(1) ICESCR, these three types of measures are those which have received the greatest degree of attention from the Committee to date.

5.1 Legislative measures

> '[...] by all appropriate means, including *particularly the adoption of legislative measures*.'

According to article 2(1), each State Party must decide what are 'appropriate means' for the implementation of the Covenant in the light of its particular circumstances. However, the Covenant clearly indicates a preference for the adoption of legislative measures.

A literal interpretation of the text of the Covenant and an examination of the drafters' intentions do not lead to the conclusion that States Parties are obliged to take legislative measures. However, interpreting the Covenant taking into account its specific object and purpose, in light of the present conditions and with a view to making the provision effective,[122] the Committee has noted that in some cases the adoption of legislative measures is compulsory.

Having said that, the first question to be resolved is whether or not there is a general obligation for States Parties to incorporate the Covenant in their domestic legal order. The Committee has directly addressed this issue and noted that,

121 Concluding Observations Switzerland E/1999/22 para. 365.

122 See Chapter III, Section 2.3.

> 'While the Covenant does not formally oblige States to incorporate its provisions in domestic law, such an approach is desirable. Direct incorporation avoids problems that might arise in the translation of treaty obligations into national law, and provides a basis for the direct invocation of the Covenant rights by individuals in national courts. For these reasons, the Committee strongly encourages formal adoption or incorporation of the Covenant in national law.'[123]

This approach would appear to be a compromise between the different views held by the Committee members. This was illustrated during the debate which took place on the day of general discussion on 'the interpretation and practical application of the obligations incumbent upon States Parties to the International Covenant on Economic, Social and Cultural Rights' held during the twelfth session in May 1995. The different positions of some Committee members were apparent during the debate. For example, Mr. Texier stressed that 'if States ratified the Covenant they had an obligation to introduce legislation to implement its provisions; the Committee should stand firmly behind that principle.'[124] In response to this view, Mr. Grissa commented that it was 'both inappropriate and undeniable for the Committee to encourage States to legislate in areas in which they would be powerless to act. The Committee's condemnation of a country for failing to legislate would be far less damaging to the country than the enactment of certain legislation.'[125] In reply, Mr. Texier 'expressed surprise that the Committee had never questioned the fact that the Covenant obliged States to enact legislation and that no State had ever reacted against that obligation, affirming instead the various rights which the Covenant promoted.'[126]

Before embarking on an analysis of when the Committee has considered that the adoption of legislative measures as 'indispensable', a brief review of the validity of the Covenant in the domestic legal order and the self-executing nature of the Covenant's provisions is required.[127]

---

123 General Comment No. 9 para. 8.

124 E/C.12/1995/SR.22 para. 32.

125 E/C.12/1995/SR.22 para. 36.

126 E/C.12/1995/SR.22 para. 47.

127 It is beyond the scope of the present study to address this topic in any detail. For a comprehensive review see, *inter alia*, Craven, M.: 'The domestic application of the International Covenant on Economic, Social and Cultural Rights.' In: *NILR*, vol. XL, (1993), pp. 367-404; Iwasawa, Y.: 'The doctrine of self-executing treaties in the United States: a critical analysis.' In: *VJIL*, vol. 26 No. 3, (1986), pp. 627-692; Schachter, O.: 'The obligation to implement the Covenant in domestic law.' In: *The International Bill of Rights*. Henkin, Louis (ed.), Columbia University Press, New York, (1981), pp. 311-331; Leary, V.: *The automatic incorporation of international labour conventions in municipal law*. The Graduate Institute of International Studies, University of Geneva, (1979); Conforti, B.: 'National courts and the international law of human rights'. In: *Enforcing international human rights in domestic courts*. Conforti, B. & Francioni, F. (eds.), Martinus Nijhoff, The Hague/Boston/London, (1997), pp. 3-14; and Scheinin, M.: 'Direct applicability of economic, social and cultural rights: a critique of the doctrine of self-executing treaties.' In: *Social rights as human rights: a European challenge*, Institute for Human Rights, Åbo Akademi University, Åbo, Finland, (1994), pp. 73-90.

5.1.1 The validity of the Covenant in the domestic legal system

The Committee has addressed this issue in General Comment No. 9 which sets forth that:

> '5. The Covenant does not stipulate the specific means by which it is to be implemented in the national legal order. And there is no provision obligating its comprehensive incorporation or requiring it to be accorded any specific type of status in national law. Although the precise method by which Covenant rights are given effect in national law is a matter for each State party to decide, the means used should be appropriate in the sense of producing results which are consistent with the full discharge of its obligations by the State party. The means chosen are also subject to review as part of the Committee's examination of the State party's compliance with its obligations under the Covenant.
>
> 6. An analysis of State practice with respect to the Covenant shows that States have used a variety of approaches. Some States have failed to do anything specific at all. Of those that have taken measures, some States have transformed the Covenant into domestic law by supplementing or amending existing legislation, without invoking the specific terms of the Covenant. Others have adopted or incorporated it into domestic law, so that its terms are retained intact and given formal validity in the national legal order. This has often been done by means of constitutional provisions according priority to the provisions of international human rights treaties over any inconsistent domestic laws. The approach of States to the Covenant depends significantly upon the approach adopted to treaties in general in the domestic legal order.'

The method by which treaties becomes national law is determined by the domestic legal order of the State concerned. Therefore, the domestic validity of the Covenant and its status (the rank or hierarchy of the Covenant in the domestic legal order), will depend on the system adopted by the State. In broad terms, we may say that in some States there is an automatic incorporation of treaty provisions once they have been ratified and published in the official gazette (*e.g.* France, Mexico and the Netherlands) while other States require the express legislative enactment of treaty provisions before they become domestic law (*e.g.* the United Kingdom, Commonwealth countries and Scandinavian countries).[128]

---

128 The variety of domestic methods for implementation is very rich. Scholars have classified them, for example, into *adoption, incorporation, transformation, passive transformation and reference.* Moreover, States may apply more than one of these methods. See, for example, Scheinin, M.: 'International human rights in national law.' In: *An introduction to the international protection of human rights: a textbook.* Hanski, Raija & Suksi, Markku (eds.), Institute for Human Rights, Åbo Akademi University, second revised edition, Åbo, Finland, (1999), pp. 417-428 and Dijk, P. van: 'Domestic status of human rights treaties and the attitude of the judiciary: the Dutch case.' In: *Progress in the spirit of human rights*, Nowak, M; Steurer, D. & Tretter, H. (eds.), Kehl am Rhein, N.P. Engel, (1988), pp. 631-649.

As noted by the Committee, the Covenant does not provide for any specific means by which it should be given domestic effect. Nonetheless, the Committee must determine if the means chosen by the State produce results which are compatible with the Covenant. Thus, the Committee requires that States must report whether the Covenant has been incorporated in domestic legislation and if the rights have been invoked before any domestic courts.[129] When the States have not incorporated the Covenant in domestic legislation and it has not been invoked before the courts, the Committee has expressed its regret.[130]

The Committee is particularly concerned with regard to States Parties in which there is no 'automatic incorporation' of international treaties in the domestic legal order. For example, when examining the Third Periodic Report of the United Kingdom, the Committee found it 'disturbing' that the position of the State Party was 'that provisions of the Covenant, with certain minor exceptions, constitute principles and programme objectives rather than legal obligations, and that consequently the provisions of the Covenant cannot be given legislative effect.'[131] Consequently, the Committee suggested that the State 'take appropriate steps to introduce the Covenant into legislation, so that the rights covered by the Covenant may be fully implemented. It is encouraged that the State Party has taken such action with respect to the European Convention on Human Rights and is of the view that it would be appropriate to give similar due regard to the obligations under the Covenant.'[132] When examining the Third Periodic Report of Australia, the Committee regretted that 'because the Covenant has not been entrenched as law in the domestic legal order, its provisions cannot be invoked before a court of law.' Consequently, the Committee 'strongly recommended' that the State 'incorporate the Covenant in its legislation, in order to ensure applicability of the provisions of the Covenant in the domestic courts.'[133]

In the case of Denmark, the Committee regretted that 'the Covenant has not been incorporated in domestic law' and noted that 'although the provisions of the Covenant may be directly invoked before the courts or referred to by the courts, there is no case law as yet. In this respect, the Committee expresses concern that lawyers and judges may not be sufficiently aware that the rights enshrined in the Covenant may be invoked

---

129 Such information is often required in the List of Issues [*e.g.* List of Issues Luxembourg E/C.12/Q/LUX/2 para. 1; Trinidad and Tobago E/C.12/Q/T&T/1 para. 1 and Colombia E/C.12/Q/COL/2 paras. 5 and 6]. During the dialogue with government representatives the topic is usually analysed again and sometimes the Committee will request very specific information. See, for example, the dialogue of the Committee with the representatives of Iceland E/C.12/1999/SR.4.

130 See, for example, Concluding Observations Peru E/1998/22 para. 142; Concluding Observations Iceland E/2000/22 para. 78; Concluding Observations the United Kingdom of Great Britain and Northern Ireland E/1998/22 para. 304; Concluding Observations Germany E/1999/22 para. 329; and Concluding Observations Zimbabwe E/1998/22 para. 70.

131 Concluding Observations United Kingdom of Great Britain and Northern Ireland E/1998/22 para. 293.

132 Concluding Observations United Kingdom of Great Britain and Northern Ireland E/1998/22 para. 304.

133 Concluding Observations Australia E/2001/22 paras. 379 and 389.

before the courts.'[134] Therefore, the Committee 'urged' the State 'to take appropriate steps to give full legal effect to the Covenant, so that the rights covered by it may be fully integrated into the legal system.'[135] Similarly, when examining the report of Sweden, the Committee regretted that the Covenant 'is not given full effect in the State Party's legal order and therefore cannot be directly invoked before courts.' Then, it 'urged' the State 'to take appropriate steps to give full effect to the Covenant in its legal system, so that the rights covered by it may be directly invoked before the courts.'[136]

Nonetheless, the Committee also expressed concern with regard to countries where there is automatic incorporation of the Covenant. For example, in the case of France, the Committee expressed concern that 'despite the constitutional provision (article 55) stipulating the primacy of international law over national law and the monistic principle adopted by the State Party incorporating international law in the domestic legal order, the Covenant and its provisions are not considered directly applicable by some courts of law (*e.g.* the *Conseil d'Etat)* resulting in a dearth of court decisions in which reference is made to the Covenant and its provisions.'[137]

The Committee's approach to the domestic validity of the Covenant is similar to that of the Maastricht Guidelines which set forth that

> 'The direct incorporation or application of international instruments recognising economic, social and cultural rights within the domestic legal order can significantly enhance the scope and effectiveness of remedial measures and should be encouraged in all cases.'[138]

5.1.2 Direct applicability of the Covenant (self-executing)

The term 'self-executing' treaties has been assigned different meanings and it now gives rise to some confusion.[139] The Committee uses the term 'self-executing' in General Comment No. 9 to refer to norms that are 'capable of being applied by courts without further elaboration.'[140] However, the Committee occasionally uses the term 'direct applicability' as synonymous with the term 'self-executing.' By doing so, the Committee creates confusion. It would be desirable if in the future the Committee were to opt for one of the two terms and it would be preferable for it to avoid the term 'self-executing.'[141]

---

134 Concluding Observations Denmark E/2000/22 para. 103.
135 Concluding Observations Denmark E/2000/22 para. 111.
136 Concluding Observations Sweden E/C.12/1/Add.70 paras. 15 and 27.
137 Concluding Observations France E/C.12/1/Add.72 para. 13.
138 Maastricht Guideline No. 26.
139 For an analysis of the different meanings of the doctrine of self-executing treaties, see Iwasawa, *loc. cit.* (note 131), pp. 635-642
140 General Comment No. 9 para. 10.
141 See, for example, Iwasawa, *loc. cit.* (note 131), p. 642 and Craven, *loc. cit.* (note 131), p. 378.

In order to avoid confusion, the following analysis uses the term 'direct applicability' instead of 'self-executing' when referring to provisions susceptible of application by judicial or administrative authorities without the need for further measures such as enacting legislation. It should be noted that 'direct applicability' differs from 'domestic validity.' As Iwasawa has pointed out, the domestic validity of a treaty is a prerequisite for its domestic applicability, but even if a treaty has validity in the domestic legal order it is not necessarily 'directly applicable.'[142]

At issue here is whether or not the Covenant's provisions are capable of being directly applicable by courts and administrative bodies. The Committee has directly addressed this issue noting that,

> '11. The Covenant does not negate the possibility that the rights it contains may be considered self-executing in systems where that option is provided for. Indeed, when it was being drafted, attempts to include a specific provision in the Covenant to the effect that it be considered 'non-self-executing' were strongly rejected. In most States, the determination of whether or not a treaty provision is self-executing will be a matter for the courts, not the executive or the legislature. In order to perform that function effectively, the relevant courts and tribunals must be made aware of the nature and implications of the Covenant and of the important role of judicial remedies in its implementation. Thus, for example, when Governments are involved in court proceedings, they should promote interpretations of domestic laws which give effect to their Covenant obligations. Similarly, judicial training should take full account of the justiciability of the Covenant. It is especially important to avoid any a priori assumption that the norms should be considered to be non-self-executing. In fact, many of them are stated in terms which are at least as clear and specific as those in other human rights treaties, the provisions of which are regularly deemed by courts to be self-executing.'

In a previous General Comment, the Committee had noted that,

> '[...] in addition, there are a number of other provisions in the International Covenant on Economic, Social and Cultural Rights, including articles 3, 7(a)(i), 8, 10(3), 13(2) (a), (3) and (4) and 15 (3) which would seem to be capable of immediate application by judicial and other organs in many national legal systems. Any suggestion that the provisions indicated are inherently non-self-executing would seem to be difficult to sustain.'[143]

In other words, the Committee recognises that the courts and administrative bodies of each State Party must decide whether or not a norm is 'directly applicable' and the criteria applied may vary depending on the State. However, the Committee has stressed that there is nothing 'inherent' in the Covenant's rights that would deny them 'direct applicability' in many national legal systems. As an example of the rights which would

142 Iwasawa, *loc. cit.* (note 131), p. 643.
143 General Comment No. 3 para. 5.

fulfil the criteria for 'direct applicability' in many legal system, the Committee has mentioned the obligation to ensure equal treatment for men and women (article 3); the obligation to ensure fair wages and equal remuneration for work of equal value without distinction of any kind (article 7(a)(i)); the right to form and join trade unions and the right to strike (article 8); the obligation to take measures for the protection of children and young persons without discrimination, the obligation to penalise by law the employment of children and young persons in harmful or dangerous work, and the duty to prohibit child labour (article 10(3)); the duty to provide compulsory primary education free of charge (article13 (2)(a)); the duty to respect the freedom of parents to choose the school of their children (article 13(3)); the freedom to establish and direct educational institutions (article 13(4)); and the freedom which is indispensable for scientific research and creative activity (article 15 (3)).

This list of provisions is merely exemplary and the Committee has stressed that there are many other provisions that are also susceptible to immediate application. As it has stated, many provisions of the Covenant are as clear and specific as provisions contained in other human rights treaties, such as the ICCPR, which are deemed to be directly applicable.[144] This assertion is of key importance if we bear in mind that, as Scheinin points out, 'the tendency to accept direct applicability in the case of economic, social and cultural rights to a lesser extent than in the case of civil and political rights is not a logical or normative consequence of the 'nature' of the rights belonging to these categories.'[145]

Nonetheless, as the Committee notes, in order to enhance the direct applicability of the Covenant's rights, judges and administrators need to be more aware of the precise meaning of the rights. Therefore, it has called upon Governments to promote the meaning of the provisions so as to ensure that these rights are consistently enforced in courts of law. Consequently, the Committee has recommended that States Parties provide training to judges, prosecutors, lawyers, social workers and others responsible for the implementation of the Covenant to ensure that the rights are invoked in the courts and are considered to be 'directly applicable'.[146]

When Government representatives have asserted that the Covenant rights are not directly applicable, the Committee has forcefully rejected these assertions. For example, after considering the initial report of Switzerland the Concluding Observations stated: 'the Committee disagrees with the position of the State Party that provisions of the Covenant constitute principles and programmatic objectives rather than legal

144 As the Committee noted 'it is especially important to avoid any a priori assumption that the norms should be considered to be non-self-executing. In fact, many of them are stated in terms which are at least as clear and specific as those in other human rights treaties, the provisions of which are regularly deemed by courts to be self-executing.' General Comment No. 9 para. 11.

145 Scheinin, *op. cit.* (note 131), p. 85.

146 See, for example, Concluding Observations Azerbaijan E/1998/22 para. 344, Concluding Observations France E/C.12/1/Add.72 para. 23 and Concluding Observations Denmark E/2000/22 para. 103.

obligations, and that consequently the provisions of the Covenant cannot be given legislative effect. The Committee does not share the view of the Swiss authorities and recalls that in its General Comment No. 3 (1990) on the nature of States Parties' obligations [...] it refers to a number of provisions in the Covenant, such as those of article 8 on the right to strike and those of article 13 on the right to education, which seem to be capable of immediate application within the judicial system. The Committee is of the view that any suggestion that the above-mentioned provisions are inherently non-self-executing seems to be difficult to sustain.'[147]

Similarly, when examining the Second Periodic Report of the Netherlands, the Committee rejected the argument of a State representative who asserted that 'for essentially technical reasons the Covenant is not directly applicable'.[148] The Committee stressed that 'at a minimum, certain provisions of the Covenant are potentially able to be directly applied both in law and in policy.'[149] Consequently, the Committee recommended that 'the Government reassess the extent to which the provisions of the Covenant might be given direct applicability within the Kingdom.'[150]

5.1.3 Indispensable legislative measures

Although States enjoy discretion as to the manner in which they satisfy the obligation to take steps, according to the Committee the adoption of legislative measures may sometimes be an 'indispensable' step in the process of implementation. The Committee has used this approach consistently since General Comment No. 3 and has further developed it in the Concluding Observations and General Comments.

General Comment No. 3 sets forth:

> '3. The means which should be used in order to satisfy the obligation to take steps are stated in article 2 (1) to be 'all appropriate means, including particularly the adoption of legislative measures'. The Committee recognizes that *in many instances legislation is highly desirable and in some cases may even be indispensable.* For example, it may be difficult to combat discrimination effectively in the absence of a sound legislative foundation for the necessary measures. In fields such as health, the protection of children and mothers, and education, as well as in respect of the matters dealt with in articles 6 to 9, legislation may also be an indispensable element for many purposes.' (Emphasis added).

Based on the language adopted by the Committee, it is possible to conclude that if States do not take legislative measures in some circumstances they would not be able

147 Concluding Observations Switzerland E/1999/22 para. 348.
148 Concluding Observations the Netherlands E/1999/22 para. 177.
149 Concluding Observations the Netherlands E/1999/22 para. 177.
150 Concluding Observations the Netherlands E/1999/22 para. 187.

to comply with the Covenant requirements. On the other hand, legislative measures on their own may not be sufficient to satisfy the obligations under the Covenant.[151]

The Committee explained this approach in General Comment No. 7 on forced evictions. In this General Comment, the Committee notes that the obligations of States Parties to the Covenant in relation to forced evictions 'are based on article 11(1), read in conjunction with other relevant provisions. In particular, article 2(1).'[152] Further, it stresses that,

> '9. Article 2(1) of the Covenant requires States Parties to use 'all appropriate means', including the adoption of legislative measures, to promote all the rights protected under the Covenant. Although the Committee has indicated in its General Comment No. 3 (1990) that such measures may not be indispensable in relation to all rights, it is clear that legislation against forced evictions is an essential basis upon which to build a system of effective protection.'[153]

The Committee continues by indicating which legislative measures are necessary to fully implement the prohibition of forced evictions. This statement suggests that although each State Party has the discretion to chose the means to implement the Covenant, the adoption of legislative measures will sometimes prove indispensable for the effective protection of a given right or a component thereof. The Committee has applied the same approach with regard to other rights.

Through its General Comment and Concluding Observations, the Committee has indicated when the adoption of legislative measures is essential for the effective protection of the substantive rights. In General Comment No. 3 the Committee noted that legislative measures 'may be indispensable' in order to provide effective protection in the following areas: (1) to combat discrimination; (2) in the field of health; (3) in the protection of children and mothers; (4) in the field of education; and (5) in respect of the matters dealt with in articles 6 to 9.[154] Certainly, this list is extremely broad and covers almost all of the substantive rights found the Covenant. Over the years, the Committee has provided more guidance on this and has further specified when legislative measures are 'indispensable' steps for the implementation of the Covenant. However, the Committee needs to be even more consistent and to further develop its approach.

While we do not pretend to analyse in detail the Committee's views on the necessity of legislative measures for the implementation of substantive rights, some examples from its approach in the Concluding Observations are necessary to illustrate the point. The focus will therefore be on those areas mentioned by General Comment No. 3

151 General Comment No. 3 paras. 3-4 and Limburg Principle No. 18.

152 General Comment No. 7 para. 8.

153 General Comment No. 7 para. 9.

154 General Comment No. 3 para. 3.

where legislative measure 'may be necessary,' and how the Committee has provided concrete examples of this obligation. Before analysing the Committee's approach in the Concluding Observations, it is worth noting that by 'legislative measures', the Committee seems to mean not only the requirement to enact a new legislative provision, but also the duty to reform, amend and repeal legislation which is manifestly inconsistent with the Covenant.[155]

a) *To combat discrimination*[156]

From the Concluding Observations it is possible to conclude that legislative measures constitute not merely 'appropriate' but, rather, 'indispensable' steps to combat *de jure* discrimination. In other words, States are obliged to repeal, amend or modify any discriminatory legislation. In particular, the Committee has stressed this approach in order to combat any legislative measures with discriminatory effect against women and children.[157] The Committee has been very strict in this regard and, for example, it has not hesitated to consider the failure to amend or repeal discriminatory legislation against children born out of wedlock as a 'violation' of the Covenant.[158]

This approach is also clear in the General Comments, in which the failure to repeal legislation which discriminates against individuals or groups in the field of education is considered a 'violation'.[159] In the same vein, it has required States to repeal discriminatory legislation against the right to adequate housing[160] and against the right to health.[161]

The Committee's approach finds support in the Limburg Principles and in the Maastricht Guidelines. According to the Limburg Principles, 'upon becoming a Party to the Covenant states shall eliminate *de jure* discrimination by abolishing without delay any discriminatory laws, regulations and practices [...] affecting the enjoyment of economic, social and cultural rights.'[162] In the same vein, the Maastricht Guidelines

155 See for example, Concluding Observations Republic of Korea E/1996/22 para. 80; Concluding Observations the Netherlands [Aruba] E/1999/22 para. 206; Concluding Observations Switzerland E/1999/22 para. 364; Concluding Observations Cyprus E/1999/22 para. 291; and Concluding Observations Philippines E/1996/22 para. 129. See in addition Limburg Principle No. 18.

156 The principle of non-discrimination in the Covenant is analysed in detail in Chapter VIII.

157 See for example, Concluding Observations Iraq E/1998/22 para. 274, Concluding Observations Belarus E/1997/22 para. 290 and Concluding Observations Cyprus E/1999/22 para. 291.

158 For example, Concluding Observations Sri Lanka E/1999/22 paras. 74 and 89; Concluding Observations Morocco E/2001/22 para. 558; Concluding Observations Uruguay E/1998/22 para. 377; Concluding Observations Algeria E/1996/22 para. 296; and Concluding Observations Japan E/C.12/1/Add.67 para. 41.

159 General Comment No. 13 para. 59.

160 General Comment No. 7 para. 9.

161 General Comment No. 4 para. 50.

162 Limburg Principle No. 37.

consider the existence of discriminatory legislation denying the enjoyment of rights to a particular individual or groups as violating the Covenant.[163]

Moreover, the Committee seems to consider the adoption of legislative measures to combat some forms of discrimination against women to be 'indispensable'. Such measures include legislation to prevent and prohibit sexual harassment in the workplace[164] and to penalise the practice of female genital mutilation[165] and domestic violence against women.[166]

Finally, it is important to note that, according to the Committee, legislative measures are sometimes required for the protection of vulnerable groups within society such as asylum seekers and refugees.[167] In this regard, the Committee has paid particular attention to the necessity of adopting anti-discrimination legislation to protect persons with disabilities.[168]

(b) *In fields such as health, the protection of children and mothers and education*

With regard to the right to the highest standard of health, the Committee has noted that legislative measures are indispensable, for example, to protect individuals against environmental degradation. In General Comment No. 14 the Committee stated that the failure 'to enact or enforce laws to prevent the pollution of water, air and soil by extractive and manufacturing industries' is a 'violation' of the Covenant.[169] This has very far-reaching consequences but, unfortunately, until recently the Committee did not

163 Maastricht Guideline No. 14 (b).

164 See, for example, Concluding Observations Cameroon E/2000/22 paras. 332 and 348; Concluding Observations Mongolia E/2001/22 para. 281; Concluding Observations Georgia E/2001/22 para. 89; Concluding Observations Poland E/1999/22 paras. 151 and 159; Concluding Observations Sri Lanka E/1999/22 para. 78; and Concluding Observations Iraq E/1998/22 para. 250.

165 See, for example, General Comment No. 14 para. 35; Concluding Observations Nigeria E/1999/22 para. 133; Concluding Observations Guinea E/1997/22 para. 207; and Concluding Observations Egypt E/2001/22 para. 155.

166 See, for example, Concluding Observations Georgia E/2001/22 para. 101; Concluding Observations Italy E/2001/22 para. 133; Concluding Observations Egypt E/2001/22 para. 177; Concluding Observations Republic of Congo E/2001/22 para. 202; Concluding Observations Mongolia E/2001/22 para. 281; Concluding Observations Cameroon E/2000/22 para. 348; Concluding Observations Nigeria E/1999/22 para. 133; and Concluding Observations Russian Federation E/1998/22 para. 118. It is well established that violence against women is a form of discrimination (See, *e.g.* CEDAW General Recommendation No. 19).

167 See, for example, Concluding Observations Azerbaijan E/C.12/1/Add.20 para. 54 and Concluding Observations Germany E/1999/22 para. 327.

168 This approach is evident in General Comment No. 5 on persons with disabilities [see, *e.g.* para. 16] as well as in the Concluding Observations. For example, examining the report of Georgia, the Committee noted that legislative provisions are required to ensure disabled persons access to the labour market E/2001/22 para. 86. In addition see, for example, Concluding Observations Georgia E/2001/22 paras. 86 and 99; Concluding Observations Egypt E/2001/22 para. 165; Concluding Observations Ireland E/2000/22 para. 149; and Concluding Observations Israel E/1999/22 para. 264.

169 General Comment No. 14 para. 51.

closely monitor compliance with this obligation when examining States' reports.[170] Fortunately, since the adoption of the General Comment it has adopted a more consistent approach. For example, in the case of Honduras, the Committee 'strongly recommended' that the State should implement existing legislative measures to avoid violations of environmental and labour laws by transnational companies. It also 'strongly urged' the State to adopt and implement legislative measures to protect workers against the use of toxic substances that caused damage to their health and to the environment.[171]

Scholarly writers have further developed when legislative measures are necessary to implement the right to health. For example, Toebes observes that legislative measures, among others, are required (a) in order to assure adequate access to health care provided by third parties; (b) to assure that adequate information on health care is provided by third parties; (c) to assure that access to family planning and pre- and post-natal care is provided by third parties; (d) to assure that adequate access to water and sanitation is provided by third parties; (e) for protection against environmental and industrial health infringements by third parties, particularly in the field of environmental health; and (f) for protection against traditional practices.[172] While the Committee comes close to this approach in General Comment No. 14,[173] it has yet to provide additional guidance as to when legislative measures are required to give effect to the right to health in its Concluding Observations.

In the field of the protection of mothers, the Committee has indicated the necessity to adopt legislative measures to protect the working conditions of pregnant women, particularly the prohibition of dismissal and adequate maternity benefits for pregnant women.[174] As for the protection of children, the Committee has stressed the necessity to adopt legislative measures to combat the sexual and labour exploitation of children.[175]

---

170 The Committee has examined environmental degradation in some States, although not with the frequency and the attention that one might expect. See, for example, Concluding Observations Russian Federation E/1998/22 paras. 100 and 124; Concluding Observations Solomon Islands E/2000/22 para. 204; Concluding Observations Nigeria E/1999/22 para. 123; Concluding Observations Azerbaijan E/1998/22 para. 331; and Concluding Observations Israel E/1999/22 para. 257.

171 Concluding Observations Honduras E/C.12/1/Add.57 paras. 24, 36 and 38.

172 Toebes, 1998, pp. 314-315.

173 See General Comment No. 14 paras. 35 and 51.

174 For example, Concluding Observations Bulgaria E/2000/22 paras. 227 and 242; Concluding Observations Mongolia E/2001/22 para. 281; Concluding Observations Mexico E/2000/22 paras. 383 and 399; Concluding Observations Cyprus E/1999/22 para. 292; Concluding Observations Switzerland E/1999/22 paras. 353 and 369; and Concluding Observations Dominican Republic E/1997/22 para. 233.

175 See, for example, Concluding Observations Philippines E/1996/22 para. 125; Concluding Observations Paraguay E/1997/22 para. 77; Concluding Observations Sri Lanka E/1999/22 para. 90; Concluding Observations Nigeria E/1999/22 para. 134; Concluding Observations Egypt E/2001/22 paras. 163 and 178; Concluding Observations Congo E/2001/22 para. 204; Concluding Observations Republic of Korea E/C.12/1/Add.59 para. 21; and Concluding Observations Senegal E/C.12.1/Add.62 para. 49.

Bearing in mind that with the exception of Somalia, all States Parties to the ICESCR are also parties to the Convention on the Rights of the Child [CRC],[176] in regard to the adoption of legislative measures which are 'indispensable' to protect children against labour exploitation, it is relevant to recall here article 32 CRC that requires States to take legislative measures, particularly to provide for a minimum age for admission to employment, the regulation of hours and conditions of employment and penalties or other sanctions to ensure compliance.

Finally, the Committee has not further elaborated upon when legislative measures are indispensable steps to implement the right through the Concluding Observations. Nonetheless, it has provided guidance in this respect in General Comment Nos. 11 and 13.

(c) *In respect of the matters dealt with in articles 6 to 9*

Through its Concluding Observations, the Committee has indicated that some elements of the right to work (article 6), the right to enjoy just and favourable conditions of work (article 7), the right to form and join trade unions, the right to strike (article 8) and the right to social security (article 9) must be implement by legislative measures. However, the Committee needs to fine-tune its approach.

With regard to articles 6 and 7, it is possible to conclude that, according to the Committee, some legislative measures are indispensable in order to implement the right to enjoy just and favourable conditions of work. This includes legislation regulating the prevention of accidents in the workplace, establishing adequate working hours and legal actions against employers who fail to comply[177] and legislation that provides for a minimum wage and its periodic adjustment.[178] In the light of the Concluding Observations, it is possible to conclude that States are required to take legislative measures to protect the freedom to form and join trade unions, the right to strike and the right to collective bargaining. Consequently, they must also repeal any limitation established by law to the freedom to join trade unions and the right to strike.[179] If the legislation of

176 Adopted by GA Res. 44/25 of 20 November 1989 and which entered into force 2 September 1990.

177 See, for example, Concluding Observations Italy E/2001/22 paras. 118 and 131; Concluding Observations United Kingdom of Great Britain and Northern Ireland [Hong Kong] E/1997/22 para. 342; Concluding Observations Republic of Korea E/1996/22 para. 75; Concluding Observations Surinam E/1996/22 para. 165; Concluding Observations Morocco E/2001/22 para. 556; Concluding Observations Cameroon E/2000/22 para. 331; Concluding Observations Mexico E/2000/22 para. 399; and Concluding Observations Russian Federation E/1998/22 para. 104.

178 For example, Concluding Observations Finland E/1997/22 para. 315; Concluding Observations Kyrgyzstan E/2001/22 para. 342; Concluding Observations Morocco E/2001/22 paras. 529 and 554; Concluding Observations Cameroon para. 333; Concluding Observations Sri Lanka E/1999/22 para. 90; Concluding Observations Canada E/1999/22 para. 407; and Concluding Observations Peru E/1999/22 para. 147.

179 See, for example, Concluding Observations Canada E/1999/22 para. 406; Concluding Observations Colombia E/1996/22 para. 188; Concluding Observations Republic of Korea E/1996/22 paras. 71 and 80; Concluding Observations Norway E/1996/22 para. 227; Concluding Observations Iraq E/1998/22

a State Party does not recognise the right to join a trade union, to bargain collectively and to strike, the Committee considers this to be a violation of article 8.[180] For example, the Concluding Observations of Luxembourg state that 'the Committee considers that failure to incorporate the right to strike in domestic law constitutes a breach of article 8 of the Covenant.'[181] The precise and consistent interpretation provided in regard to the necessity to adopt legislative measures to implement article 8 ICESCR is supported by the fact that this article is worded differently than the general wording of the Covenant. In fact, article 8 does not employ the general formula that States Parties 'recognise the rights of everyone,' but, rather, requires that they 'ensure' the right.[182]

Finally, regarding article 9, the Committee has been very general, without providing much assistance as to when it considers that legislative measures are required to give effect to this right. In referring to the right to social security, the Committee has merely made general statements, for example, urging the 'enactment of legislation on the right to social security so as to ensure full compliance with the requirements of the Covenant, and recommends that the State party extend the coverage of social security to non-resident workers.'[183] However, the Committee has not provided sufficient precision regarding the specific elements of those rights in which legislative measures are indispensable.

In sum, while it is safe to say that legislative measures are not indispensable in relation to all rights, in certain situations legislative measures are compulsory. The Committee has indicated some situations in which legislative measures are required to implement some rights or specific elements of them. However, it is important to bear in mind that States do not fulfil the obligation to take legislative measures by merely 'enacting' the legislation required. In order to comply with the obligation to 'adopt legislation', States are also compelled to effectively enforce the legislation. This is particularly relevant when there are customs or traditions rooted in society that negatively affect the enjoyment of the Covenant's rights. If a State Party adopts legislation

---

para. 349; Concluding Observations Uruguay E/1998/22 para. 276; Concluding Observations Kyrgysztan E/2001/22 para. 356; Concluding Observations the United Kingdom of Great Britain and Northern Ireland [Hong Kong] E/1997/22 para. 343; Concluding Observations Argentina E/2000/22 para. 279; and Concluding Observations Mauritius E/1996/22 para. 244.

180 In addition, see, for example, Concluding Observations Canada E/1999/22 para. 406; Concluding Observations Saint Vincent and the Grenadines E/1998/22 para. 426; Concluding Observations El Salvador E/1997/22 para. 167; and Concluding Observations the United Kingdom of Great Britain and Northern Ireland E/1998/22 para. 306.

181 Concluding Observations Luxembourg E/1998/22 para. 294.

182 The other exceptions to the general wording are article 2(2) where the undertaking is 'to guarantee', and article 3 ICESCR which also uses the wording 'to ensure.' Nevertheless, it is important to note that today these distinctions do not appear to be very important, because at the present stage of development of international law, the meaning of these different terms has become blurred. The Covenant has been interpreted as imposing certain duties, of an immediate nature, notwithstanding the progressive character attributable to its provisions.

183 Concluding Observations Portugal [Macao] E/1997/22 para. 263.

in accordance with the Covenant, but it is not implemented effectively due to customs or traditions, the State has then failed to comply with its obligations under the Covenant.[184]

Additionally, the aim and purpose of the legislation should be in accordance with the reality of its application. The Committee has repeatedly emphasised the necessity to enact legislation that addresses national conditions and has expressed its concern when there are gaps between the protection of rights in legislation and in practice. For example, the Committee expressed its concern in the case of the Dominican Republic where the legislation did not recognise common law marriages, while 60% of all marriages were of this nature.[185] When there are disparities between the aim and purpose of the legislation and the reality of its application, States are responsible for any such deficiency[186] and the Committee requires that 'energetic efforts' be undertaken to close the gap.[187] The requirement that legislation should be in accordance with the reality of its application is relevant in the context of social welfare benefits which must be provided at a realistic level.[188] Similarly, when legislation establishes a legal minimum wage, it must be sufficient to ensure a decent living for workers and their families.[189] The importance of this requirement has been continuously stressed by the Committee which has stated that in establishing the legal minimum wage governments should take into account economic growth and the inflation rate.[190] Specifically, States should increase the minimum wage if there has been economic growth and in the event of inflation, the minimum wage should be increased in order to maintain the purchasing power of workers.[191] When examining the report of Portugal, for example, the Commit-

---

184 See, for example, Concluding Observations Sri Lanka E/1999/22 para. 76, Concluding Observations Nigeria E/1999/22 para. 133 and Concluding Observations Egypt E/2001/22 para. 172.

185 Concluding Observations Dominican Republic E/1997/22 para. 233.

186 This is clear at the European level in the case of X and Y v. the Netherlands [Application No. 8978/80, Judgement of 26 March 1985, para. 40] where the Court held 'it is hardly deniable that the Netherlands authorities have a degree of responsibility resulting from the deficiency in the legislation which gave rise to the violation of article 8'.

187 See, for example, Concluding Observations Libyan Arab Jamahiriya E/1998/22 para. 189.

188 The Committee examined this issue in the case of Canada. The Committee recommended that 'federal, provincial and territorial governments address homelessness and inadequate housing as a national emergency by [...] increasing shelter allowances and social assistance rates to realistic levels [...].' Concluding Observations Canada E/1999/22 para. 421.

189 Article 7 ICESCR.

190 See, for example, Concluding Observations Peru E/1998/22 para. 147, Concluding Observations Finland E/1997/22 para. 315 and Concluding Observations Canada E/1999/22 para. 407.

191 In the Concluding Observations on the Third Periodic Report of Mexico, the Committee stated that it 'regrets that despite the positive growth of macroeconomic indicators in Mexico, especially the sharp decrease in the level of inflation, the National Minimum Wages Commission has not adjusted the minimum wage level upwards. At present, about five minimum wages are needed to obtain the officially set basic food basket, *in violation* of article 7, paragraph (*a*)(ii) of the Covenant and as reflected in national legislation (article 123, Title VI of the Constitution).' Concluding Observations Mexico E/2000/22 para. 382.

tee expressed concern regarding the fact that 'the increase in the minimum wage has not kept pace with economic growth in recent years and is concerned about a tendency for the minimum wage to depreciate.' Consequently the Committee recommended that 'the Government seek to ensure a gradual increase in the minimum wage, which should take account of Portugal's economic growth and the inflation rate, with the object of increasing the purchasing power of those living on the minimum wage.'[192] Finally, as the Committee has stressed, 'the adoption of legislative measures [...] is by no means exhaustive of the obligations of States Parties.'[193]

5.2 Judicial and other 'appropriate' remedies

> '[...] by all appropriate means, *including* particularly the adoption of legislative measures.'

As is evident from the text, legislative measures are not the only 'appropriate means' and there are other measures that may also be considered 'appropriate' for the purpose of article 2(1) ICESCR. According to the Committee, judicial and other remedies are among the measures that may be considered appropriate.[194]

In General Comment No. 9 on the domestic application of the Covenant, the Committee notes the 'broad and flexible approach' of article 2(1) ICESCR which requires States to give effect to the Covenant 'by all appropriate means.' However it also stresses,

> '2. But this flexibility coexists with the obligation upon each State party to use all the means at its disposal to give effect to the rights recognized in the Covenant. In this respect, the fundamental requirements of international human rights law must be borne in mind. Thus the Covenant norms must be recognized in appropriate ways within the domestic legal order, *appropriate means of redress, or remedies, must be available to any aggrieved individual or group,* and appropriate means of ensuring governmental accountability must be put in place.' (Emphasis added)

This approach finds support in the Limburg Principles, which set forth that:

> 'States Parties shall provide for effective remedies including, where appropriate, judicial remedies.'[195]

Furthermore, according to the Limburg Principles:

192 Concluding Observations Portugal E/1996/22 paras. 95 and 98.
193 General Comment No. 3 para. 4.
194 General Comment No. 3 para. 5 and General Comment No. 9 para. 9.
195 Limburg Principle No. 19.

> 'In reporting on legal steps taken to give effect to the Covenant, States Parties should not merely describe any relevant legislative provisions. They should specify, as appropriate, the judicial remedies, administrative procedures and other measures they have adopted for enforcing those rights and the practice under those remedies and procedures.'[196]

In some of the General Comments on specific substantive rights, the Committee has stressed the importance of judicial or other appropriate remedies, albeit with somewhat 'softer' language than in General Comment No. 9. As stressed by the Committee,

> 'Any person or group who is a victim of a violation of [the right to adequate food and the right to health] should have access to effective judicial or other appropriate remedies at both national and international levels. All victims of such violations are entitled to adequate reparation, which may take the form of restitution, compensation, satisfaction or guarantees of non-repetition.'[197]

However, as indicated by the Committee,

> 'A State party seeking to justify its failure to provide any domestic legal remedies for violations of economic, social and cultural rights would need to show either that such remedies are not 'appropriate means' within the terms of article 2, paragraph 1, of the International Covenant on Economic, Social and Cultural Rights or that, in view of the other means used, they are unnecessary. It will be difficult to show this and the Committee considers that, in many cases, the other means used could be rendered ineffective if they are not reinforced or complemented by judicial remedies.'[198]

Therefore, States Parties bear an onerous burden of proof and, as the Committee itself states, it will be difficult to justify the non-provision of judicial remedies.

5.2.1 Judicial remedies

It is traditionally argued that there are fundamental differences between civil and political rights and economic, social and cultural rights.[199] As a consequence of the alleged difference in nature between the two sets of rights, it is argued that civil and political rights are justiciable, whereas economic, social and cultural rights are not. Thus, according to this view, only violations of the former can be judged to have occurred, or to be occurring, by judicial or similar bodies. Generally, the gist of the argument is that economic, social and cultural rights are 'inherently' non-justiciable.[200] The Committee explicitly rejects this approach and stresses that judicial remedies for

---

196 Limburg Principle No. 78.
197 General Comment No. 12 para. 32 and General Comment No. 14 para. 59.
198 General Comment No. 9 para. 3.
199 See the analysis in Chapter IV section 2.2.
200 See Vierdag, *loc. cit.* (note 1), pp. 81-82.

the violation of Covenant rights may be established and that there is nothing in their nature that impedes it.[201] As it notes,

> 'While the general approach of each legal system needs to be taken into account, there is no Covenant right which could not, in the great majority of the systems, be considered to possess at least some significant justiciable dimensions. [...] The adoption of a rigid classification of economic, social and cultural rights, which put them by definition, beyond the reach of the courts would thus be arbitrary and incompatible with the principle that the two sets of human rights are indivisible and interdependent. It would also drastically curtail the capacity of the courts to protect the rights of the most vulnerable and disadvantaged groups of society.'[202]

The Committee's approach finds widespread support in scholarly writing. There seems to be agreement that economic, social and cultural rights are not 'inherently' non-justiciable.[203]

For our purposes, it is important to stress that while the Committee convincingly states that the Covenant rights are not intrinsically non-justiciable and judicial remedies for violations may be essential in some circumstances, it also seems to support the position that 'justiciability' is not an indispensable characteristic of 'rights'. In other words, the Committee's view appears to be that the Covenant's rights are not intrinsically non-justiciable but that, if in a given society and at a given time, these rights cannot be claimed before the courts, this fact does not diminish the character of Covenant rights as 'legal rights' which impose obligations upon States Parties.

In General Comment No. 3 from 1990 the Committee noted,

---

201 General Comment No. 9 para. 10.

202 *Idem.*

203 For studies on the issue of the justiciability of economic, social and cultural rights, see, for example: Scott, C. & Macklem, P.: 'Constitutional ropes of sand or justiciable guarantee? Social rights in a new South African constitution.' In: *University of Pennsylvania Law Review*, vol. 141, No.1, November (1992), pp. 1-148; Scott, C.: 'The interdependence and permeability of human rights norms: towards a partial fusion of the International Covenants on Human Rights.' In: *Osgoode Hall Law Journal,* vol. 27, Ottawa, Canada (1989), pp. 769-878; Leary, V.: 'The right to complaint: the right to health.' In: *The right to complain about economic, social and cultural rights*. Coomans, Fons & Hoof, G.J.H. van (eds.), Netherlands Institute of Human Rights, SIM Special No.18, Utrecht (1995*), pp. 87-102; Arambulo, K.: *Strengthening the supervision of the International Covenant on Economic, Social and Cultural Rights: theoretical and procedural aspects*, Intersentia, Antwerp, (1999); Addo, M.K.: 'Justiciability re-examined.' *Economic, social and cultural rights: progress and achievement*. Beddart, R. & Hill, D. (ed.), Macmillan, London, (1992), pp. 93-120; and Alston, P.: 'Establishing a right to petition under the Covenant on Economic, Social and Cultural Rights'. In: *Collected Courses of the Academy of European law. The protection of Human Rights in Europe,* vol. IV, Book 2. European University Institute, Florence (1993), p. 115-153.

> 'Among the measures which might be considered appropriate in addition to legislation, is the provision of judicial remedies with respect to rights which may, in accordance with the national legal system, be considered justiciable.'[204]

Hence according to General Comment No. 3, each State Party may decide when it is or is not appropriate to establish judicial remedies in accordance with its own circumstances. Eight years after this statement, the Committee issued a new General Comment to further develop the content of General Comment No. 3 and it adopted more rigorous language in respect of the requirement of judicial remedies. According to General Comment No. 9,

> 'There are some obligations, such as (but by no means limited to) those concerning non-discrimination, in relation to which the provision of some form of judicial remedy would seem *indispensable* in order to satisfy the requirements of the Covenant. In other words, *whenever a Covenant right cannot be made fully effective without some role for the judiciary, judicial remedies are necessary.*'[205] (Emphasis added).

This statement is of crucial importance as the Committee stresses that sometimes judicial remedies are not only 'appropriate' but 'indispensable' to comply with the Covenant. Therefore, if the State Party does not provide for judicial remedies, in some cases it will be in violation of the Covenant. Unfortunately, the Committee does not provide examples as to when judicial remedies are compulsory and it only provides a very broad interpretation. This begs the following question: when is the role of the judiciary essential to give effect to the rights enshrined in the Covenant?

In its Concluding Observations, the Committee has expressed regret when none of the provisions of the Covenant may be directly invoked by the Courts, considering such situations 'inconsistent' with the approach adopted in General Comment No. 3.[206] Aware of the fact that the guarantee of access to judicial remedies would be meaningless without a competent, impartial and independent tribunal, the Committee has expressly stated the importance of the independence of the judiciary as an 'essential instrument for the protection of economic, social and cultural rights.'[207] However, it does not provide further guidance as to when judicial remedies are 'indispensable' to satisfy the requirement of the Covenant. However, as noted above, it falls to States to prove that 'judicial remedies' are not 'appropriate' means in a given case.

---

204 General Comment No. 3 para. 5.

205 General Comment No. 9 para. 9.

206 See, for example, Concluding Observations the Netherlands E/1999/22 para. 200; Concluding Observations Germany E/1999/22 para. 312; Concluding Observations Cameroon E/2000/22 para. 325; Concluding Observations Armenia E/2000/22 para. 298; Concluding Observations Iceland E/2000/22 para. 78; and Concluding Observations Ireland E/2000/22 para. 131.

207 See, for example, Concluding Observations Tunisia E/2000/22 para. 176, Concluding Observations Azerbaijan E/1998/22 para. 332 and Concluding Observations Nigeria E/1999/22 para. 98.

Neither of these two General Comments provide further guidance as to when judicial remedies are indispensable with regard to specific rights. The Committee has gone furthest in establishing when judicial remedies are required in relation to the right to adequate housing. In General Comment No. 4, the Committee indicates some elements of the right that are susceptible to judicial review, but it does not take a clear-cut position regarding when those measures are 'indispensable.'[208]

Although the Committee needs to provide further guidance as to when judicial remedies are essential for full compliance with an obligation, it is also true that statements denying the justiciability of these rights have become more and more counterfactual. Increasingly, at the national level, individuals can bring claims when they allege a violation of some of these rights. The existence of national case law on the protection of these rights has been explicitly recognised by governments during the 'constructive dialogue' as well as in State reports.[209]

5.2.2 Other effective remedies

The obligation to provide remedies does not necessarily imply the obligation to provide 'judicial' remedies. There may also be other appropriate remedies. Although there are circumstances in which judicial remedies would be 'indispensable', there are other effective remedies. In addition to the possibility of claiming a violation of a right before a court, the Committee has also stressed that there are other techniques which are appropriate for promoting and protecting these rights. The Committee pays particular attention to the development of national human rights institutions, such as national human rights commissions and Ombudsperson institutions. In fact, the Committee dedicated General Comment No. 10 to stressing the important role that these kinds of institutions may play and it provides examples of the types of activities that these institutions can undertake to protect economic, social and cultural rights.[210] Therefore, the Committee has called upon States Parties to ensure that the mandates of these institutions include appropriate attention to economic, social and cultural rights.[211] The

208 General Comment No. 4 para. 17.

209 See, for example, Concluding Observations Iraq E/1998/22 para. 248, Concluding Observations Cyprus E/1999/22 para. 275 and Concluding Observations Switzerland E/1999/22 para. 342. See also, for example, Third Periodic Report Italy E/1994/104/Add.19 para. 1 and Third Periodic Report Mexico E/1994/104/Add.18 para. 553.

210 See General Comment No. 10. For a comprehensive analysis of the role of national human rights institutions in the protection of economic, social and cultural rights see, *inter alia*, Gomez, M.: 'Social economic rights and human rights Commissions'. In: *HRQ*, vol. 17 No. 1, (1995), pp. 155-169 and Wyrzykowski, M.: Social rights in the jurisprudence of the Commissioner for citizens' rights in Poland. In: *Social rights as human rights: a European challenge*, Institute for Human Rights, Åbo Akademi University, Åbo, Finland, (1994), pp. 251-273.

211 The Committee has called for this not only in General Comment No. 10, but also in relation to specific countries through the Concluding Observations, for example Concluding Observations Tunisia E/C.12/1999/11 para. 172.

Committee supervises this by requesting that States that have national human rights institutions include information on their mandates and activities in the State reports.[212]

When examining State reports, the Committee has noted with satisfaction when States have established such institutions and has encouraged States to do so. The Committee has also stressed that it is important that national human rights institutions enjoy a broad margin of independence. The Committee has placed particular emphasis on the necessity of transparency and independence for their effectiveness and has encouraged States to provide these institutions with mandates that include the review of complaints of violations of Covenant rights.[213]

The Committee has also noted the role that administrative proceedings may play. In the Committee's words,

> 'Administrative remedies will, in many cases, be adequate and those living within the jurisdiction of a State party have a legitimate expectation, based on the principle of good faith, that all administrative authorities will take account of the requirements of the Covenant in their decision-making. Any such administrative remedies should be accessible, affordable, timely and effective. An ultimate right of judicial appeal from administrative procedures of this type would also often be appropriate.'[214]

5.3 Information campaigns and educational programmes

The Committee has paid increasing attention to the requirement of undertaking public information campaigns and educational programmes as 'appropriate' measures to implement some of the Covenant's rights. This approach is stressed in General Comment No. 14 on the right to the highest standard of health. According to the Committee, 'the prevention, treatment and control of epidemic, endemic, occupational and other diseases requires the establishment of prevention and education programmes for behaviour-related health concerns such as sexually transmitted diseases, in particular HIV/AIDS, and those adversely affecting sexual and reproductive health, and the promotion of social determinants of good health, such as environmental safety, education, economic development and gender equity.'[215] The Committee also notes that the obligation to fulfil the right to health requires States to undertake 'health education, as well as information campaigns, in particular with respect to HIV/AIDS, sexual and reproductive health, traditional practices, domestic violence, the abuse of alcohol and

---

212 General Comment No. 10 para. 4.

213 See, for example, Concluding Observations Nigeria E/1999/22 para. 100; Concluding Observations Poland E/1999/22 para. 143; Concluding Observations Kyrgyzstan E/2001/22 para. 333; Concluding Observations Bulgaria E/2000/22 para. 216; Concluding Observations Tunisia E/2000/22 para. 164; and Concluding Observations Cameroon E/2000/22 para. 326.

214 General Comment No. 9 para. 9.

215 General Comment No. 14 para. 16.

the use of cigarettes, drugs and other harmful substances.'[216] The Committee states that a core obligation of the right to health is that States must 'provide education and access to information concerning the main health problems in the community, including methods of preventing and controlling them.'[217] The General Comment places particular emphasis on the requirement of public information campaigns and educational programmes as an essential measure for the realisation of women's right to health.[218]

Through the Concluding Observations, the Committee has stressed the importance of educational programmes to combat discrimination, particularly against women and for the realisation of the right to health. A review of the Concluding Observations indicates that the adoption of information campaigns and educational programmes is essential to prevent and combat discrimination against women, particularly domestic violence.[219]

Furthermore, through its Concluding Observations, the Committee has stressed the importance of measures to prevent and deal with problems of drug and alcohol abuse,[220] to protect women against the practice of female genital mutilation[221] and to provide information on contraceptives and reproductive health.[222]

6 The obligation to monitor the realisation of the rights and to devise strategies and programmes for their implementation

> 'Each State party to the present Covenant undertakes to *take steps*, [...] with a view to achieving progressively the full realisation of the rights recognised in the present Covenant'

Both the obligations to monitor the realisation of the rights and to devise strategies for their implementation are essential preconditions for compliance with article 2(1) ICESCR and they may be considered to be independent, 'implied' obligations. This is in fact the approach adopted by the Committee.

Over the years the Committee has clearly noted that in order to comply with the immediate obligation to 'take steps', States Parties to the Covenant are required to monitor the realisation of the rights in their jurisdiction and to devise strategies and programmes for their implementation. States cannot comply with the obligation to take

216 General Comment No. 14 para. 31.
217 General Comment No. 14 para. 44.
218 General Comment No. 14 para. 21.
219 See, for example, Concluding Observations Egypt E/2001/22 para. 177; Concluding Observations Jordan E/2001/22 para. 249; Concluding Observations Israel E/1999/22 para. 270; Concluding Observations Switzerland E/1999/22 para. 369; Concluding Observations Dominican Republic E/1998/22 para. 231; and Concluding Observations Iraq E/1998/22 para. 274.
220 See, for example, Concluding Observations Iceland E/2000/22 para. 86.
221 See, for example, Concluding Observations Cameroon E/2000/22 paras. 329 and 347.
222 See, for example, Concluding Observations Cameroon E/2000/22 para. 359 Concluding Observations Mexico E/2000/22 para. 405 and Concluding Observations Poland E/1999/22 para. 158.

steps that are 'deliberate, concrete and targeted as clear as possible'[223] without establishing a system for monitoring the nature and scope of the existing problems and the level of enjoyment of all economic, social and cultural rights by all individuals under their jurisdiction and to devise strategies and programmes to respond to the problems identified.[224] According to the Committee, these obligations are complementary and of an immediate nature.[225] Although compliance with many of the Covenant's obligations will depend on the availability of resources, the State needs first to determine the level of enjoyment of the rights set forth in the Covenant and then to devise a plan according to the necessities identified. If it is necessary, the State Party must request assistance to the Office of the UN High Commissioner for Human Rights to fully comply with this obligation.[226]

According to the Committee,

> 'The obligations to monitor the extent of the realization, or more especially of the non-realization, of economic, social and cultural rights, and to devise strategies and programmes for their promotion, are not in any way eliminated as a result of resource constraints.'[227]

In the fulfilment of these obligations, special attention should be given to 'any specific groups or subgroups, which appear to be particularly vulnerable or disadvantaged'.[228] Thus, States Parties should identify the needs of vulnerable and disadvantaged groups and attempt to find the most suitable approach to deal with their needs.[229]

In its General Comments, the Committee has emphasised the obligation to monitor and to devise a plan for the realisation of specific substantive rights. For example, in General Comment No. 12 on the right to adequate food it stresses,

> '31. States Parties shall develop and maintain mechanisms to monitor progress towards the realization of the right to adequate food for all, to identify the factors and difficulties affecting the degree of implementation of their obligations, and to facilitate the adoption of corrective legislation and administrative measures [...].'

General Comment No. 13 on the right to education sets forth that,

223 General Comment No. 3 para. 2.

224 See General Comment No. 1 para. 4, General Comment No. 3 para. 11 and General Comment No. 5 para. 13.

225 See, for example, General Comment No. 4 para. 13.

226 See, for example, Concluding Observations Sudan E/2001/22 para. 327 and Concluding Observations Georgia E/2001/22 para. 100.

227 General Comment No. 3 para. 11.

228 General Comment No. 1 para. 1

229 See, for example, General Comment No. 5 paras. 13-14 and General Comment No. 6 para. 5.

'They [States Parties] are also obliged to establish and maintain a transparent an effective system which monitors whether or not education is, in fact, directed to the educational objectives set out in article 13(1).'[230]

With regard to the right to the highest attainable standard of health, the Committee has been more specific, noting that,

'53. The most appropriate feasible measures to implement the right to health will vary significantly from one State to another. Every State has a margin of discretion in assessing which measures are most suitable to meet its specific circumstances. The Covenant, however, clearly imposes a duty on each State to take whatever steps are necessary to ensure that everyone has access to health facilities, goods and services so that they can enjoy, as soon as possible, the highest attainable standard of physical and mental health. This requires the adoption of a national strategy to ensure to all the enjoyment of the right to health, based on human rights principles which define the objectives of that strategy, and the formulation of policies and corresponding right to health indicators and benchmarks. The national health strategy should also identify the resources available to attain defined objectives, as well as the most cost-effective way of using those resources.'

Through its Concluding Observations, the Committee has stressed the same principle. After considering the initial report of Sudan, for example, the Committee 'urged' the State 'to devote adequate attention to identifying its most urgent problems and concerns about economic, social and cultural rights under the Covenant and to formulate these priorities in a comprehensive plan of action for human rights, in which the possible measures to be taken are categorized according to feasibility of realization in terms of time and resources.'[231]

6.1 Obligation to monitor the enjoyment of the Covenant rights

As the Committee states, regardless of their level of development, States Parties are obliged 'to ascertain, through regular monitoring, the nature and scope of the problems existing within the State [...]'.[232] This obligation must be implemented immediately after ratification or accession to the Covenant.[233] As the Committee point outs, 'diagnosis and knowledge of the existing situation' is the 'essential first step.'[234] States must give special priority to identify the level of enjoyment of these rights by vulnerable and

230 General Comment No. 13 para. 49.

231 Concluding Observations Sudan E/2001/22 para. 327.

232 General Comment No. 5 para. 13.

233 In General Comment No. 4, for example, the Committee notes 'effective monitoring of the situation with respect to housing is another *obligation of immediate effect*.' General Comment No. 4 para. 13.

234 General Comment No. 1 para. 3.

disadvantaged groups within society.[235] The rationale for monitoring the level of enjoyment of the rights is to enable States to identify deficiencies and prevailing difficulties, to evaluate any progress achieved and to provide a basis for devising priorities and strategies for future actions. As emphasised by the Committee after considering the Second Periodic Report of Korea, 'a human rights approach [...] must begin with a proper understanding of the actual situation in respect of each right, accurate identification of the most vulnerable groups, and the formulation of appropriate laws, programmes and policies.'[236]

According to the Maastricht Guidelines, 'the failure to monitor the realisation of economic, social and cultural rights, including the development of criteria for assessing compliance' constitutes a violation of the Covenant.[237] The importance of the use of indicators has been stressed by the Sub-Commission Special Rapporteur on the realisation of economic, social and cultural rights,[238] the report of the United Nations expert seminar on economic, social and cultural rights held in January 1993[239] and in the Vienna Declaration and Program of Action of the World Conference.[240] According to the Committee, States Parties should identify appropriate indicators and national benchmarks with regard to each of the substantive rights.[241]

Through its Concluding Observations, the Committee has also noted the importance of implementing an appropriate system for gathering information on the basis of indicators that are in accordance with criteria used by UN specialised agencies. It has also recommended that States Parties establish national benchmarks and elaborate disaggregated statistical data. It draws the attention of the Governments to the fact that inappropriate, outdated or insufficient data do not serve as a sound basis for government policy.[242] On issues such as domestic violence, child abuse, child pornography and prostitution, the Committee seems to be stricter with regard to the necessity of gathering information and providing statistical data. As the Committee has sometimes stressed, the lack of statistical data and other information with regard to these problems

235 See, for example, General Comment No.1 para. 3, General Comment No. 3 para. 12 and General Comment No. 4 para. 13.

236 Concluding Observations Republic of Korea E/C.12/1/Add.59 para. 34.

237 Maastricht Guideline No. 15 (f).

238 See E/CN.4.Sub.2/1990/19.

239 A/CONF.157/PC/73.

240 A/CONF.157/23, part II, para. 98.

241 See particularly, General Comment No. 14 paras. 57 and 58.

242 See, for example, Concluding Observations Mexico E/2000/22 para. 392; Concluding Observations Paraguay E/1997/22 para. 93; Concluding Observations Spain E/1997/22 para. 112; Concluding Observations Ukraine E/1996/22 para. 260; Concluding Observations Surinam E/1996/22 paras. 157 and 166; and Concluding Observations Norway E/1996/22 para. 210.

prevents both the authorities and the Committee from assessing their true gravity and extent.[243]

6.2 Obligation to devise and adopt a plan of action

The obligation to devise and adopt a plan of action is only expressly required by the text of the Covenant in relation to compulsory primary education (article 14 ICESCR). However, the Committee has made it clear that article 2(1) implies the obligation to develop and adopt a detailed plan of action for each of the rights enshrined in the Covenant.[244] This obligation is also of immediate effect[245] and it goes beyond the mere recommendation of the World Conference on Human Rights held in Vienna in 1993.[246]

When examining States' reports, the Committee has regretted when States have not established a comprehensive national plan of action and has urged them to do so. Recently, the Committee began to require States to annex a copy of the national plan of action to their periodic reports.[247] The Committee has noted the importance of involving civil society in general and the targeted groups in particular in the planning, implementation and evaluation process of national plans of action.[248] Thus, States should establish a system of consultation and participation. This is clear, for example, in the Concluding Observations of Mexico which set forth: 'the Committee urges the State Party to address the structural causes of poverty in Mexico and to adjust the social programmes accordingly. Furthermore, the Committee invites the State Party to involve closely the *civil society in general, and the target groups in particular, in the planning, implementation and evaluation* of these programmes.'[249]

---

243 See, for example, Concluding Observations Norway E/1996/22 para. 225; Concluding Observations Ukraine E/1996/22 para. 265; Concluding Observations Cyprus E/1999/22 para. 293; and Concluding Observations Algeria E/1996/22 para. 303.

244 General Comment No.1 para. 4.

245 See, for example, Concluding Observations Tunisia E/2000/22 para. 179. The obligation is to 'devise' a plan, it is not that the plan should be 'adopted' or submitted to the Committee immediately.

246 The World Conference held in Vienna in 1993 recommended that States 'consider the desirability of drawing up a national action plan identifying steps whereby that State would improve the promotion and protection of human rights.' A/CONF.157/23, Part II, para. 71.

247 See, for example, Concluding Observations Belgium E/2001/22 paras. 469 and 480; Concluding Observations Panama E/C.12/1/Add.64 paras. 10 and 28; Concluding Observations Nepal E/C.12.1/Add.66 para. 39; Concluding Observations Japan E/C.12/1/Add.67. para. 36; and Concluding Observations Republic of Korea E/C.12.1/Add.59 para. 44.

248 See, for example, General Comment No. 5 para.14; General Comment No. 6 para. 5; General Comment No. 12 para. 29; and General Comment No. 14 para. 54.

249 Concluding Observations Mexico E/2000/22 para. 393 (emphasis added). In this context it is interesting to note that in the statement adopted by the Committee on 'poverty and the International Covenant on Economic, Social and Cultural Rights' in May 4, 2001, it notes 'the right to participate is reflected in numerous international instruments, including the International Covenant on Economic Social and Cultural Rights [...]'. According to the Committee this is established in Art. 13(2) ICESCR.

In General Comment No. 14 the Committee sets out several requirements with which States must comply when establishing a plan of action. Although this General Comment refers specifically to the right to the highest attainable standard of health, these requirements also apply with regard to other substantive rights. Thus, it is possible to suggest that a plan of action for the implementation of the Covenant's rights should, as a minimum: (a) comply with the principle of non-discrimination; (b) respect the right of individuals and groups to participate in decision-making processes; (c) be based on the principles of accountability, transparency and independence of the judiciary; (d) include provisions on the targets to be achieved and the time-frame for their achievement, the means by which the benchmarks could be achieved, the intended collaboration with civil society, including experts, the private sector and international organisations; (e) designate those responsible for the implementation of the plan; and (f) establish possible recourse procedures.[250]

It is worth noting that in the report on the technical assistance mission to Panama, the Committee recommended that the State adopt a plan of action with the same kinds of requirements set forth in General Comments No. 14. Therefore, it would appear that these are the requirements with which all plans of action should comply.[251]

Finally, it is important to note that the Committee sometimes refers to the obligation to adopt a plan of action in relation to one specific substantive right[252] while on other occasions it mentions a comprehensive national plan.[253] Therefore, we might conclude that States Parties may comply with this obligation by establishing plans of action for each of the substantive rights contained in the Covenant, or by adopting one comprehensive national plan.

7 The obligation to ensure the minimum core level for each right

In 1990, in General Comment No. 3, the Committee set forth that:

> '10. On the basis of the extensive experience gained by the Committee, as well as by the body that preceded it, over a period of more than a decade of examining States Parties' reports the Committee is of the view that *a minimum core obligation* to ensure the satisfac-

---

250 General Comment No. 14 paras. 54-56.

251 Report on the technical assistance mission to Panama of the Committee on Economic, Social and Cultural Rights E/1996/22, Annex V, para. 79.

252 The Committee refers to the obligation to adopt a plan of action in reference to a substantive right in, for example, General Comment No. 14 para. 43; General Comment No. 4 para. 13; Concluding Observations Russian Federation E/1999/22 para. 123; Concluding Observations Azerbaijan E/1998/22 para. 352; and Concluding Observations Canada E/1999/22 para. 421.

253 See, for example, General Comment No. 1 para. 4; Concluding Observations Syrian Arab Republic E/C.12/1/Add.63 para. 27; Concluding Observations Panama E/C.12/1/Add.64 para. 26; Concluding Observations Nepal E/C.12/1/Add.66 para. 39; and Concluding Observations Republic of Korea E/C.12/1/Add.59 para. 44.

> tion of, at the very least, *minimum essential levels* of each of the rights is incumbent upon every State party. Thus, for example, a State party in which any significant number of individuals is deprived of essential foodstuffs, of essential primary health care, of basic shelter and housing, or of the most basic forms of education is, *prima facie*, failing to discharge its obligations under the Covenant. If the Covenant were to be read in such a way as not to establish such a minimum core obligation, it would be largely deprived of its raison d'être. By the same token, it must be noted that any assessment as to whether a State has discharged its minimum core obligation must also take account of resource constraints applying within the country concerned. Article 2 (1) obligates each State party to take the necessary steps 'to the maximum of its available resources'. In order for a State party to be able to attribute its failure to meet at least its minimum core obligations to a lack of available resources it must demonstrate that every effort has been made to use all resources that are at its disposition in an effort to satisfy, as a matter of priority, those minimum obligations.'[254] (Emphasis added).

This is of great significance although it is not altogether clear. To determine the implications of the statement, it is first necessary to clarify the concept of '*minimum core obligation*' and '*minimum essential level*' of each right. The Committee does not provide much guidance in defining these notions. Fortunately, the academic literature has further developed their meaning.[255] As Coomans notes, the 'minimum essential level' of each right is the 'essential elements without which a right loses its substantive significance as a human right.'[256] These elements constitute the 'minimum core content' of each right and the 'minimum core obligations' are those obligations necessary to satisfy these minimum essential levels.[257]

Therefore, each substantive right imposes upon States a variety of 'core obligations' that they are obliged to satisfy. These 'core obligations' correspond to the satisfaction of the essential level without which States will be in violation of the Covenant. Alston points out that the fact that each right has a 'minimum core content' 'would seem to

254 General Comment No. 3 para. 10.

255 For a comprehensive analysis of the 'minimum core content', see, *inter alia,* Örücü, E.: 'The core of rights and freedoms: the limit of limits.' In: *Human Rights: from rhetoric to reality*. Campbell, T.; Goldberg, D.; Mclean, S. & Mullen, T. (eds.), Blackwell, New York, (1986), pp. 37-59, Arambulo, *op. cit.* (note 207), pp. 130-145 and Alston, P.: 'Out of the abyss: the challenges of confronting the new UN Committee on Economic, Social and Cultural Rights.' In: *HRQ*, vol. 9, (1987), pp. 331-381. With regard to the minimum core content of specific substantive rights, see, *inter alia*, Leckie, 1995, pp. *108 et seq.* (right to adequate housing); Coomans, 1995, p. 17 (right to education); and Toebes, 1998, pp. 281 *et seq.* (right to health).

256 Coomans, *loc. cit.* (note 259), p. 17.

257 In 1987, Alston used the expression 'minimum core content' to identify the 'absolute minimum entitlement, in the absence of which a State party is to be considered to be in violation of its obligations'. Certain confusion seems to have been generated by the fact that the General Comment of 1990 uses the expression 'core obligation' to refer to the obligation corresponding to that minimum core content and 'minimum essential level' for the former definition. See Alston, *loc. cit.* (note 259), pp. 351-355.

be a logical implication of the use of the terminology of rights. In other words, there would be no justification for elevating a 'claim' to the status of a right (with all the connotations that concept is generally assumed to have) if its normative content could be so indeterminate as to allow for the possibility that the right holders possess no particular entitlement to anything. Each right must therefore give rise to an absolute minimum entitlement, in the absence of which a State Party is to be considered to be in violation of its obligations.'[258] As stressed by the Maastricht Guidelines 'such minimum core obligations apply irrespective of the availability of resources of the country concerned or any other factors and difficulties.'[259]

The failure to comply with the minimum essential level of each right is *prima facie* a violation of the Covenant and the burden of proof would then be on the State to justify such situations. In the Committee's words, 'in order for a State Party to be able to attribute its failure to meet at least its minimum core obligations to a lack of available resources it must demonstrate that every effort has been made to use all resources that are at its disposition in an effort to satisfy, as a matter of priority, those minimum obligations.'[260]

It is clear from the Committee's work that even when a State has privatised some public services it remains responsible for the satisfaction of a minimum essential level of each right. Privatisation does not relieve the State of its obligation to ensure that minimum essential levels of each right are enjoyed by individuals, particularly the most vulnerable and disadvantaged groups within society.[261]

Once it is established that States must guarantee a minimum essential level of each right, the question is to determine what constitutes the 'essential level' or 'core content' of each right. Over the years the Committee has struggled to identify the core content of each right, but has not met with much success. This is not to say that the Committee is to blame, because identifying the minimum entitlements without which a right loses its substance is a complex task and the results tend to be rather theoretical or abstract. For example, in general Comment No. 12 the Committee took a step forward and included the 'core content' of the right to adequate food:

> '8. The Committee considers that the *core content* of the right to adequate food implies:
> The availability of food in a quantity and quality sufficient to satisfy the dietary needs of individuals, free from adverse substances, and acceptable within a given culture;
> The accessibility of such food in ways that are sustainable and that do not interfere with the enjoyment of other human rights.' (Emphasis added).

---

258 *Ibidem:* pp. 352-353.

259 Maastricht Guidelines No. 9.

260 General Comment No. 3 para. 10. See also General Comment No. 14 para. 47.

261 See, for example, General Comment No. 14 para. 35; Concluding Observations Philippines E/1996/22 para. 120; Concluding Observations Peru E/1998/22 para. 161; and Concluding Observations Australia E/2001/22 para. 395.

Further on the Committee explains the meaning of the elements of the 'core content' identified.[262] Although this was an important step that required a significant level of analysis, it is still rather abstract. Due to the difficulties in determining the minimum essential level of each right, since General Comment No. 13 the Committee has opted for a more pragmatic approach. Instead of defining the 'core content' of the right, it has identified various obligations indispensable for ensuring a minimum essential level of that right.

Thus, with regard to the right to education, the Committee notes that,

> '57. In its General Comment 3, the Committee confirmed that States Parties have 'a minimum core obligation to ensure the satisfaction of, at the very least, minimum essential levels' of each of the rights enunciated in the Covenant, including 'the most basic forms of education'. In the context of article 13, this core includes an obligation: to ensure the right of access to public educational institutions and programmes on a non-discriminatory basis; to ensure that education conforms to the objectives set out in article 13(1); to provide primary education for all in accordance with article 13(2)(a); to adopt and implement a national educational strategy which includes provision for secondary, higher and fundamental education; and to ensure free choice of education without interference from the State or third parties, subject to conformity with 'minimum educational standards' (art. 13(3) and (4)).'[263]

In General Comment No. 14, the Committee expressly decided to follow the same approach and to indicate the 'core obligations' of the right to the highest standards of health.[264]

Thus, with regard to the right to the highest standard of health the General Comment sets forth that:

> 'In the Committee's view, these core obligations include at least the following obligations:
> (a) To ensure the right of access to health facilities, goods and services on a non-discriminatory basis, especially for vulnerable or marginalized groups;
> (b) To ensure access to the minimum essential food which is nutritionally adequate and safe, to ensure freedom from hunger to everyone;
> (c) To ensure access to basic shelter, housing and sanitation, and an adequate supply of safe and potable water;

262 General Comment No. 12 paras. 8-13.

263 General Comment No. 13 para. 57.

264 As commented by one member of the Committee, 'the idea of core content has been applied in General Comment No. 3; however, the Committee has struggled over how to incorporate it into General Comment No. 13 and has eventually taken the pragmatic approach of defining not the core content but the core obligations incumbent upon States Parties. The Committee has decided to recommend adopting the same approach in the general comment on the right to health.' Mr. Hunt in E/C.12/2000/SR.10 para. 27. Mr. Hunt was the rapporteur for the draft General Comment No. 13. See also the statement adopted by the Committee on 'poverty and the International Covenant on Economic, Social and Cultural Rights' on May 4, 2001, E/C.12/2001/10 paras. 15-18.

(d) To provide essential drugs, as from time to time defined under the WHO Action Programme on Essential Drugs;
(e) To ensure equitable distribution of all health facilities, goods and services;
(f) To adopt and implement a national public health strategy and plan of action, on the basis of epidemiological evidence, addressing the health concerns of the whole population; the strategy and plan of action shall be devised, and periodically reviewed, on the basis of a participatory and transparent process; they shall include methods, such as right to health indicators and benchmarks, by which progress can be closely monitored; the process by which the strategy and plan of action are devised, as well as their content, shall give particular attention to all vulnerable or marginalized groups.

44. The Committee also confirms that the following are obligations of comparable priority:
(a) To ensure reproductive, maternal (pre-natal as well as post-natal) and child health care;
(b) To provide immunization against the major infectious diseases occurring in the community;
(c) To take measures to prevent, treat and control epidemic and endemic diseases;
(d) To provide education and access to information concerning the main health problems in the community, including methods of preventing and controlling them;
(e) To provide appropriate training for health personnel, including education on health and human rights.'

The identification of the 'core obligations' of substantive rights has been an important step in the clarification of the normative content of the Covenant. However, much work needs to be done to further develop the core obligations to ensure the 'minimum essential level' of other substantive rights in the Covenant.

The Committee has stressed that States are obliged to comply with the core obligations even in situations of armed conflict, emergency and natural disaster. Moreover, after a State Party has ensured the core obligations of economic, social and cultural rights, 'it continues to have an obligation to move as expeditiously and effectively as possible towards the full realisation of all the rights in the Covenant.'[265]

In this context it is important to mention the 'minimum threshold approach.' [266]

---

265 Statement adopted by the Committee on 'poverty and the International Covenant on Economic, Social and Cultural Rights' on May 4, 2001. E/C.12/2001/10 para. 18. See in addition, Chapter VI, section 3.

266 The idea of the 'minimum threshold approach' was first introduced by Andreassen, Skålnes, Smith and Stokke in 1988 [Andreassen, B.; Skålnes, T.; Smith, A.G. & Stokke, H.: 'Human rights performance in developing countries: the case for a minimum threshold approach.' In: *Human rights in developing countries*. Akademisk Forllag, Copenhagen, (1988), pp. 333-356]. The same notion was further developed by Eide in 1989 [Eide, A.: 'Realisation of social and economic rights and the minimum threshold approach.' In: *HRLJ*, vol. 10 (1989*), pp. 35-51] and again by Andreassen, Smith and Stokke in 1992 [Andreassen, B.; Smith, A.; Stokke, H.: 'Compliance with economic and social human rights: realistic evaluations and monitoring in the light of immediate obligations.' In: *Human rights in perspective: a global assessment*. Eide and Hagtve (eds.), Blackwell, (1992), pp. 253-267 and Eide, A.: *Right to adequate food as a human right,* United Nations Publication, Sales No. E.89.XIV.2, New York, (1989), pp. 35-51.

The idea is to operationalise the abstract notion of 'minimum core content' of each right by means of country-specific thresholds measured by indicators such as nutrition, infant mortality and income. In a recent statement the Committee has indicated that 'when grouped together, the core obligations established an 'international minimum threshold'.[267] Therefore, it seems that the development of the 'core obligations' of each right would serve to identify the minimum threshold of the rights applicable to all States Parties.

8 Obligations regarding international assistance and co-operation

> 'Each State party to the present Covenant undertakes to take steps, individually and *through international assistance and co-operation, especially economic and technical* [...].'

The obligation for States Parties to take steps to the maximum of their available resources refers both to the resources existing within a country and those available from the international community though international co-operation and assistance.[268]

The principle of international co-operation among States is established in the United Nations Charter (articles 55 and 56) and has been subject to a number of subsequent developments.[269] The purpose of the reference to international assistance and co-operation in the Covenant is to emphasise that such co-operation must be oriented, as a matter of priority, to the realisation of all human rights.[270]

The following analysis focuses on the legal implications of the reference to international assistance and co-operation in article 2(1) ICESCR at the present stage of international human rights law. Due to the fact that the obligations in regard to international assistance and co-operation are different for wealthier States which are in a position to assist and for States which are recipients of such assistance and co-operation, the analysis will be divided between 'developed' and 'developing' States.

The Committee's work suggests that commitments in regard to international assistance and co-operation are closely linked with the obligations to comply with the 'core obligations' (obligations that ensure the minimum core content of each right). On the one hand, developed States are required to co-operate and assist developing States in fulfilling the core obligations. On the other hand, developing States are required to use the resources received from the international community to satisfy the core obligations

267 Statement adopted by the Committee on 'poverty and the International Covenant on Economic, Social and Cultural Rights' on May 4, 2001. E/C.12/2001/10 para. 16.

268 General Comment No. 3. para. 13.

269 See, for example, the Declaration on Principles of International Law concerning Friendly Relations and Co-operation Among States in accordance with the Charter of UN GA. Res. 2625 (XXV) and the Declaration on the Right to Development, adopted by General Assembly Res. 41/128 of 4 December 1986.

270 See Limburg Principles Nos. 29-34 and the commentaries by E.V.O. Dankwa and C. Flinterman [Dankwa & Flinterman, 1987, pp. 140-141].

as a matter of priority. As a Committee member notes, the core obligations and the obligations relating to international assistance and co-operation 'should be seen as two halves of a package.'[271] The Committee's approach on the necessity to look at these two obligations together is reflected in General Comment No.14 where the Committee identified the 'core obligations' of the right to the highest standards of health, and then added that:

> '45. For the avoidance of any doubt, the Committee wishes to emphasize that it is particularly incumbent on States Parties and other actors in a position to assist, to provide 'international assistance and cooperation, especially economic and technical' (29) which enable developing countries to fulfil their core and other obligations indicated in paragraphs 43 and 44 above.'

In addition to article 2(1) ICESCR, reference to international assistance and co-operation is also to be found in article 11 ICESCR. According to article 11(1), States Parties agree to 'take appropriate steps to ensure the realisation of this right [right of everyone to an adequate standard of living], recognising to this effect the essential importance of international co-operation based on free consent.' In article 11(2) States Parties, 'recognising the fundamental right of everyone to be free from hunger, shall take, individually and through international co-operation' the relevant measures enumerated in the provision. In light of the 'Revised Guidelines' regarding the form and contents of reports to be submitted by States Parties to the Committee, States are required to indicate the role of international assistance in the full realisation of each substantive right contained in the Covenant, except in the case of article 8 ICESCR.[272]

Although the present study focuses on the obligations of States Parties to the Covenant, we must bear in mind that, according to the Committee, the international community as a whole has a role to play. The Committee's approach may be considered to be summarised in the following statement:

> 'Where a State party is clearly lacking in the financial resources and/or expertise required [...] the international community has a clear obligation to assist.'[273]

---

271 Mr. Hunt in E/C.12/2000/SR.10 para. 27.

272 With regard to article 8 (the right to join and form trade unions and the right to strike), the Committee does not require States to indicate the role of international assistance for the full realisation of these rights. It seems that international assistance does not play any role in the full realisation of these rights. 'Revised general guidelines regarding the form and contents of reports to be submitted by States Parties under articles 16 and 17 of the International Covenant on Economic, Social and Cultural Rights.' UN doc. E/C.12/1991/1.

273 General Comment No. 11 para. 9.

8.1 Developed States

It is not easy to determine the implications of the reference to international assistance and co-operation with regard to developed States, understood as those States which are in a position to assist and co-operate with others. Before the Committee started to function, Alston and Quinn commented,

> '[O]n the basis of the preparatory work it is difficult, if not impossible, to sustain the argument that the commitment to international co-operation contained in the Covenant can accurately be characterised as a legally binding obligation upon any particular state to provide any particular form of assistance. It would, however, be unjustified to go further and suggest that the relevant commitment is meaningless. *In the context of a given right it may, according to the circumstances, be possible to identify obligations to co-operate internationally that would appear to be mandatory on the basis of the undertaking contained in Article 2(1) of the Covenant.*
> Moreover, policy trends and events in the general areas of international development co-operation subsequent to the adoption of the Covenant in 1966 may be such as to necessitate a reinterpretation of the meaning to be attributed today to Article 2(1).'[274]

In the nearly fifteen years that have passed since this statement was made, much water has passed under the bridge. Principally through the Committee's work, the legal implications of the commitment to international co-operation contained in article 2(1) have been further developed. Yet the obligations imposed by this provision are still not absolutely clear. The following will attempt to identify the present meaning of the provision.

In 1990, the Committee noted:

> '14. The Committee wishes to emphasize that in accordance with Articles 55 and 56 of the Charter of the United Nations, with well-established principles of international law, and with the provisions of the Covenant itself, *international cooperation for development and thus for the realization of economic, social and cultural rights is an obligation of all States.* It is particularly incumbent upon those States which are in a position to assist others in this regard. [...] It emphasizes that, in the absence of an active programme of international assistance and cooperation on the part of all those States that are in a position to undertake one, the full realization of economic, social and cultural rights will remain an unfulfilled aspiration in many countries.'[275]

---

274 Alston & Quinn, 1987, p. 191. (Emphasis added). This article was prepared by the authors for the symposium on the implementation of the International Covenant on Economic, Social and Cultural Rights held in Maastricht in June 1986. The participants at this symposium agreed on the Limburg Principles. As analysed in Chapter I, the Committee was established in 1985, but held its first session in March 1987. See Chapter I, section 2.

275 General Comment No. 3 para. 14. (Emphasis added).

The Committee refers only to an obligation to 'co-operate' but does not mention any duty to 'assist.' This apparent omission is explained by one commentator who points out that 'although there is clearly an obligation to co-operate internationally, it is not clear whether this means that wealthy States Parties are obliged to provide aid to assist in the realisation of the rights in other countries.'[276]

This does not mean that developed States have no obligations as a result of the reference to 'international assistance and co-operation' contained in article 2(1). In order to shed some light on the obligations for developed States to assist and co-operate it is useful to use the 'tripartite typology.'[277] It seems to be well established that as an analytical tool the 'tripartite typology' can be used to describe States' obligations at the national as well as international level.[278] In the light of the Committee's work, it is possible to conclude that the international obligations of developed States arising from article 2(1) ICESCR would be the following:

(1) *Obligation to respect*: Developed States are obliged to abstain from any policy that may impede or violate the full realisation of economic, social and cultural rights in other countries.[279] For example, in light of General Comment No. 2, it is possible to say that developed States must avoid involvement in projects which would result in large-scale evictions in another country.[280] Arguably, it also entails the duty to abstain from participating in decisions of inter-governmental bodies that might obstruct or hinder the realisation of these rights. When considering the report of Belgium, for example, 'the Committee encourages the Government of Belgium, as a member of international bodies, in particular IMF and the World Bank, to do all it can to ensure that the policies and decisions of those organisations are in conformity with the obligations of States Parties to the Covenant, in particular the obligations contained in article 2, paragraph 1, concerning international assistance and co-operation.'[281] Similar statements have

276 Craven, 1999, p. 108.

277 The tripartite typology is analysed in Chapter V. The tripartite typology, although in a different stage of its development, has been used to describe the international obligations by, *inter alia,* Alston and Craven. Alston has applied the tripartite typology as it was developed by Shue with regard to the obligation to assist under article 11 ICESCR [Alston, *op. cit.* (note 21), pp. 45-46]. Craven applied the well-established typology of respect, protect and fulfil, with regard to the obligation contained in article 2(1) ICESCR. [Craven, 1995, pp. 144-152].

278 The Committee itself applies the 'tripartite typology' to analyse international obligations. See, for example, General Comment No. 14 para. 39. In addition, see Concluding Observations Cameroon E/2000/22 para. 352, Concluding Observations Argentina E/2000/22 para. 276 and Concluding Observations Bulgaria E/2000/22 para. 236.

279 Clearly, this is the entire underpinning of General Comment No. 8.

280 General Comment No. 2 para. 6 and General Comment No. 4 para. 19.

281 Concluding Observations Belgium E/2001/22 para. 493.

been included by the Committee in the Concluding Observations on the reports of other developed States such as Italy,[282] Germany[283] and Japan.[284]

Furthermore, the Committee has made express reference to the international duty to respect in regard to the right to health, stating that 'to comply with their international obligation in relation to article 12, States Parties have to respect the enjoyment of the right to health in other countries [...]'[285] With this statement, the Committee goes beyond its General Comment on the right to food where it uses weaker language and indicates that 'States Parties should take steps to respect the enjoyment of the right to food in other countries.'[286] General Comment No. 14 also states that 'States Parties have an obligation to ensure that their actions as members of international organisations take due account of the right to health.'[287]

(2) *Obligation to protect*: The Committee has not consistently developed the international obligations implied by this level. It has directly referred to this type of obligation in regard to the right to health indicating that 'to comply with their international obligation in relation to article 12, States Parties have [...] to prevent third parties from violating the right in other countries, if they are able to influence these third parties by way of legal or political means, in accordance with the Charter of the United Nations and applicable international law.'[288] It is perfectly possible to consider that the same obligation will apply to all substantive rights contained in the Covenant.

(3) *Obligation to fulfil*: As interpreted by the Committee, developed States are not under a general obligation to facilitate and provide for the satisfaction of the Covenant's rights in other States. However, we have to recognise that General Comment No. 14 comes close to interpreting that there are such obligations with regard to the right to health. As it stresses therein, 'depending on the availability of resources, States should facilitate access to essential health facilities, goods and services in other countries, wherever possible and provide the necessary aid when required.'[289]

Despite the fact that the reference to international assistance and co-operation in article 2(1) has not been interpreted as imposing a general obligation to provide for the satisfaction of the rights, when examining the reports of developed States, the Committee has often recommended that each State 'review its budget allocations for interna-

282 Concluding Observations Italy E/2000/22 para. 126.
283 Concluding Observations Germany E/C.12/1/Add.68 para. 31.
284 Concluding Observations Japan E/C.12/1/Add.67 para. 37.
285 General Comment No. 14 para. 39.
286 General Comment No. 12 para. 36.
287 General Comment No. 12 para. 36.
288 General Comment No. 14 para. 39.
289 General Comment No. 14 para. 39.

tional co-operation with a view to increasing its contribution in accordance with the United Nations recommendation.'[290] The Committee has encouraged States to achieve the target of 0.7 percent of the GNP. For example, when examining the report of Japan, the Committee 'urged' the State 'to increase its efforts to provide international assistance to developing countries and to establish a time frame within which the internationally accepted goal of 0.7 per cent of GNP set by the United Nations will be achieved.'[291] When the percentage of GNP devoted to aid has decreased, the Committee has expressed its regret[292] and when States have complied with this target the Committee has commended them.[293]

Although there may not be a general international obligation for developed States to provide for the satisfaction of the Covenant rights in less wealthy countries, such an obligation seems to arise in the context of disaster relief and humanitarian assistance. According to General Comment No. 12,

> '38. States have a joint and individual responsibility, in accordance with the Charter of the United Nations, to cooperate in providing disaster relief and humanitarian assistance in times of emergency, including assistance to refugees and internally displaced persons. Each State should contribute to this task in accordance with its ability. The role of the World Food Programme (WFP) and the Office of the United Nations High Commissioner for Refugees (UNHCR), and increasingly that of UNICEF and FAO is of particular importance in this respect and should be strengthened. Priority in food aid should be given to the most vulnerable populations.'

In the same vein, General Comment No. 14 sets forth,

> '40. States Parties have a joint and individual responsibility, in accordance with the Charter of the United Nations and relevant resolutions of the United Nations General Assembly and of the World Health Assembly, to cooperate in providing disaster relief and humanitarian assistance in times of emergency, including assistance to refugees and internally displaced persons. Each State should contribute to this task to the maximum of its capacities. Priority in the provision of international medical aid, distribution and management of resources, such as safe and potable water, food and medical supplies, and financial aid should be given to the most vulnerable or marginalized groups of the population. Moreover, given that some diseases are easily transmissible beyond the frontiers of a State, the international community has a collective responsibility to address this problem. The economically developed States Parties have a special responsibility and interest to assist the poorer developing States in this regard.'

---

290 See, for example, Concluding Observations Finland E/2001/22 para. 449 and Concluding Observations Belgium E/2001/22 para. 492.

291 Concluding Observations Japan E/C.12/1/Add.67 para. 37.

292 Concluding Observations France E/C.12/1/Add.72 paras. 14 and 24.

293 Concluding Observations Sweden E/C.12/1/Add.70 para. 7.

8.2 Developing States

States Parties to the Covenant that do not possess the necessary resources for the full realisation of the rights set forth in the Covenant are obliged, according to article 2(1), to 'actively seek assistance' to ensure the enjoyment of economic, social and cultural rights by everyone in their territories.[294] Developing States in need of international assistance may request it from (i) wealthier States, (ii) UN Specialised Agencies, such as ILO, UNESCO, WHO, and FAO, or (iii) other inter-governmental or non-governmental organisations, including international financial institutions such as the World Bank, the IMF or the Inter-American Development Bank. The Committee has given particular encouragement to States to seek assistance from the Office of the High Commissioner on Human Rights. Developing States may require assistance for a variety of reasons such as to identify difficulties and to set priorities for future actions, to deal with specific problems, to directly implement a certain right or to be able to submit a comprehensive report to the Committee.[295]

According to the Committee, every effort should be made by States in need of international assistance to obtain it.[296] They should also identify in their reports any particular needs that they might have for technical assistance or development co-operation.[297]

Furthermore, in light of the Committee's work, we may conclude that developing States are not only obliged to 'seek assistance', but also to comply with some other obligations when they are actually receiving assistance. In this regard developing States would be required:

(1) To refrain from obstructing international organisations in their legitimate efforts to gain access to individuals under the jurisdiction of the State in order to assist them in the enjoyment of economic, social and cultural rights.[298]

294 See, for example, General Comment No. 4 para. 10; General Comment No. 5 para. 13; General Comment No. 6 para. 18; General Comment No. 11 para. 11; Concluding Observations Sri Lanka E/1999/22 para. 86; Concluding Observations Nigeria E/1999/22 para. 129; Concluding Observations Surinam E/1996/22 para. 166; Concluding Observations Armenia E/2000/22 para. 312; and Concluding Observations Jamaica E/C.12/add.75 para. 23. In addition, see Alston, *op. cit.* (note 21), p. 42 and Craven, *op. cit.* (note 280), p. 106.

295 See for example, Concluding Observations Surinam E/1996/22 para. 166 and Concluding Observations Guinea E/1997/22 para. 211.

296 See, for example, Concluding Observations Ukraine E/1996/22 para. 271.

297 General Comment No. 2 para. 10.

298 See, for example, Concluding Observations El Salvador E/1997/22 paras. 171 and 185 and Concluding Observations Mexico E/2000/22 para. 387. See, in addition, General Comment No. 12 para. 19.

(2) To utilise the assistance received in a way that will contribute to the realisation of the objectives and purposes of the Covenant, giving priority to the satisfaction of the minimum core obligations.[299]

(3) To establish mechanisms to ensure an effective use of the international assistance received, to facilitate the distribution of the assistance received, to ensure that the intended recipients receive the assistance provided and to implement an effective monitoring regime.[300]

(4) To give priority to the fulfilment of the needs of the most vulnerable and disadvantaged groups within society with the assistance received.[301]

Finally, it is worth noting that through the constructive dialogue and the Concluding Observations, the Committee has played a useful role in encouraging States to make use of available international technical assistance programmes to States in need of them.

9 Concluding Comments

Article 2(1) is an essential provision of the Covenant. It has a dynamic relationship with all substantive rights contained in the Covenant. Article 2(1) defines the nature of the obligations with which each State Party must comply in relation to each of the rights contained in articles 6 to 15 ICESCR. The wording of article 2(1) of the Covenant is certainly elusive and intricate, in particular due to the inclusion of the notions of 'progressive realisation' and 'maximum available resources' which have given rise to much uncertainty. Since its inception, the Committee has understood the necessity of clarifying the content of this provision. As early as 1990 (three years after the Committee's first session), the Committee adopted a General Comment on article 2(1) ICESCR in order to provide guidance and to eliminate some misconceptions about the meaning of this provision.

Over the years, through its Concluding Observations, the Committee has had the opportunity to apply General Comment No. 3 while examining State reports and has

299 The Committee has recommended that international co-operation be devoted to the goal of implementing of economic, social and cultural rights. See, for example, Concluding Observations Guatemala E/1997/22 para. 137, Concluding Observations Colombia E/1996/22 para. 202 and General Comment No. 14 para. 45.

300 See, for example, Concluding Observations Sri Lanka E/1999/22 para. 86; Concluding Observations Ukraine E/1996/22 para. 271; and Concluding Observations Colombia E/1996/22 para. 202. See, in addition, General Comment No. 4 para. 19.

301 See, for instance, Concluding Observations Sri Lanka E/1999/22 para. 86 and General Comment No. 12 para. 38.

provided guidance as to the meaning of the provision in specific circumstances. Moreover, the Committee has adopted additional General Comments in which it has further developed some of the elements contained in General Comment No. 3. Particularly relevant in this regard are General Comment No. 9 on the domestic application of the Covenant, and the comprehensive General Comment Nos. 13 and 14, which refer to specific substantive rights but also develop elements of article 2(1) ICESCR.

As a result of its systematic approach, the Committee has achieved a deeper understanding of the complex normative content of article 2(1). From the Committee's work, it is possible to discern several distinct legal obligations. These obligations constitute the 'hard core' of article 2(1) and they are characterised by the fact that they apply uniformly to all States Parties to the Covenant regardless, of their level of development. Thus, it is incumbent upon every State to comply with the obligations enumerated in the present chapter. These obligations are not contingent upon the availability of resources and they are of an immediate character.

The development by the Committee of the normative elements of article 2(1) constitutes a key contribution to the implementation of the Covenant. For all those called upon to apply the Covenant, this contribution provides an essential understanding of what State behaviours are compulsory under the Covenant. As such, this information is of fundamental importance for evaluating compliance with the Covenant. From the perspective of governments, the list of obligations analysed provides guidance as to the requirements which are of particular interest to the Committee. For judges, lawyers and human rights advocates, the obligations derived from article 2(1) may be used as a tool to assess the level of compliance with the Covenant.

However, despite the important contribution of the Committee in identifying the immediate obligations deriving from article 2(1) ICESCR, there remains much room for further development. The Committee needs to provide further guidance as to the scope of the obligations and clearly it must improve its methods of supervision as regards many of these obligations. If the Committee does not take steps to monitor the compliance with the obligations deriving from article 2(1) more strictly it could undermine its achievements in identifying the 'hard' components of this provision.

Chapter VIII
Obligations Deriving from the Principle of Equality and Non-Discrimination

Article 2

2. The States Parties to the present Covenant undertake to guarantee that the rights enunciated in the present Covenant will be exercised without discrimination of any kind as to race, colour, sex, language, religion, political or other opinion, national or social origin, property, birth or other status.

3. Developing countries, with due regard to human rights and their national economy, may determine to what extent they would guarantee the economic rights recognized in the present Covenant to non-nationals.

Article 3

The States Parties to the present Covenant undertake to ensure the equal rights of men and women to the enjoyment of all economic, social and cultural rights set forth in the present Covenant.

1 Introduction

The principle of non-discrimination[1] is contained in article 2(2) ICESCR which is a general non-discrimination clause applicable to the Covenant as a whole and is complemented by other provisions prohibiting discrimination on specific grounds. For

1 A detailed analysis of the principle of equality and non-discrimination is beyond the scope of the present study. The present analysis focuses on the principle of non-discrimination under the Covenant and the general approach of international law will only be addressed to the extent required in the present analysis. For a more comprehensive analysis of the principle of non-discrimination in international law, see *inter alia,* Vierdag, E.W.: *The concept of discrimination in international law: with special reference to human rights*. Nijhoff, (1973); Bayefsky, A.: 'The principle of equality or non-discrimination in international law.' In: *HRLJ*, vol. 11 No. 1-2, (1990) pp. 1-34; Loenen, T. & Rodrigues, P. (eds.): *Non-discrimination law: comparative perspectives*. Kluwer, The Hague, (1999); McKean, W.: Equality and discrimination under international law. Clarendon Press, Oxford, (1983); Dinstein, Y.: 'Discrimination and international human rights.' In: *Israel Yearbook on Human Rights*, vol. 15, (1985), pp. 11-27; Goldstein, S.: 'Reverse discrimination: reflections of a Jurist.' In: *Israel Yearbook on Human Rights*, vol. 15, (1985), pp. 28-42; Hannikainen, L. and Nykänen, E. (eds.): *New trends in discrimination law: International perspectives*. Publications of Turku Law School, vol. 3 No. 1, Turku, (1999); Ramcharan, B.G.: 'Equality and Nondiscrimination'. In: *The International Bill of Rights*. Henkin, L. (ed.), New York, Columbia University Press, (1981), pp. 246-269; and Fredman, Sandra (ed.): *Discrimination and human rights: the case of racism*. Oxford University Press, Oxford, (2001).

example, in Part II of the Covenant we find article 3 which prohibits discrimination between men and women in the enjoyment of all rights. Part III includes a prohibition of discrimination in the conditions of work for men and women and equal remuneration for work of equal value (article 7(a)(i)); prohibition of discrimination in promotion within employment (article 7(c)); a prohibition of any discrimination in the protection and assistance for all children and young persons (article 10(3)); and prohibition of discrimination in higher education (article 13).

Article 2(2) is contained in Part II of the Covenant and applies to all substantive rights contained in Part III (articles 6 to15). As we will see, the prohibited grounds for discrimination enumerated in article 2(2) are not exhaustive and discrimination on other grounds is also prohibited under this provision. Therefore, the additional provisions specifying prohibited grounds for discrimination in the exercise of specific rights may be deemed to reinforce the obligation.

The principle of non-discrimination in the Covenant is of the utmost importance for its application and the Committee itself has noted that the 'philosophy of the Covenant is based on the principle of non-discrimination and the idea of universality of human rights'.[2] Moreover, according to the Committee 'guarantees of equality and non-discrimination should be interpreted, to the greatest extent possible, in ways which facilitate the full protection of economic, social and cultural rights.'[3]

The present analysis will focus principally on the obligations of States Parties derived from article 2(2) and article 3 of the Covenant. Mention will also be made of article 2(3) ICESCR which should be considered to be a restrictive exception to the principle of non-discrimination contained in article 2(2) ICESCR.

2 The Meaning and Scope of the Non-Discrimination Provisions of the Covenant on Economic, Social and Cultural Rights

2.1 The scope of the non-discrimination provision

As is also the case with article 3 ICESCR, article 2(2) is not directed against discrimination in general but, rather, the provision is linked to the enjoyment of the substantive rights contained in Part III of the Covenant (articles 6 to 15 ICESCR). Therefore, the Covenant does not establish an autonomous right to be free from discrimination, it only prohibits discrimination in the exercise of the substantive rights it contains.

In the majority of cases, discrimination in the enjoyment of a substantive right will amount to a violation of article 2(2) and article 3 (in cases of gender discrimination) with a simultaneous violation of one or more substantive right(s). However, this is not necessarily so in all cases. It is possible that discrimination in the enjoyment of a

2 See, for example, Concluding Observations Algeria E/1996/22 para. 293.
3 General Comment No. 9 para. 15.

substantive right amounts to a violation of article 2(2) without it being a simultaneous violation of the substantive right. For example, if a State sets up a health care system to provide treatment for cancer free of charge, but smokers are not beneficiaries due to their propensity to develop cancer, it would be a violation of article 2(2) due to discrimination in the exercise of article 12 ICESCR, but would not entail a further violation of this substantive right. Furthermore, if in the example, the health care system is applied in order to benefit only men and not women, it would also be a violation of article 3 ICESCR.

The Committee expressly supports this approach in General Comment No. 13, when it explains that 'a State party has no obligation to fund institutions established in accordance with article 13(3) and (4); however, if a State elects to make a financial contribution to private educational institutions, it must do so without discrimination.'[4] Hence, if a State provides financial assistance to some schools but not to others, it may be in violation of article 2(2), but not necessarily of article 13 ICESCR.

Although article 2(2) is not a free-standing right and must be linked to the enjoyment of a substantive right, the analysis of the non-discrimination provision in the Concluding Observations suggests that the Committee's approach is close to that of the European Court in the sense that it is sufficient that the subject falls within the general scope of the substantive rights. Thus, although the Covenant does not recognise the right to property, the Committee has referred, for example, to discriminatory legislation which imposes limitations on property ownership by women or to restrictions regarding credit and access to land and property, because such restrictions affect the enjoyment by women of the right to work and the right to food.[5]

2.2 The meaning of 'discrimination'

As with the ICCPR, the Covenant neither defines the term 'discrimination' nor indicates what constitutes discrimination. However, as we will see, it is possible to refer to the definition of discrimination adopted by other international treaties.[6]

The principle of non-discrimination is of the utmost importance in international law. Prohibitions of discrimination are contained in, for example, the UN Charter (articles 1(3), 13(1)(b), 55(c) and 76), the Universal Declaration of Human Rights (articles 2 and 7), the ICCPR (articles 2(1) and 26) and the CRC (article 2). There are also some instruments specifically aimed at addressing only specific prohibited grounds for discrimination, such as CERD and CEDAW. There are other instruments aimed at

4 General Comment No. 13 para. 54.

5 See for example, Concluding Observations Senegal E/C.12/1/Add.62 para. 15 and Concluding Observations Cameroon E/1998/22 para. 327. In order to understand the link with the enjoyment of the right to food, see General Comment No. 12 para. 26.

6 This approach has been suggested by Alston [see Alston, 1987, p. 87] and it is adopted by the Human Rights Committee in its General Comment No. 18 [General Comment No. 18 para. 6].

addressing the prohibition of discrimination in the exercise of one or several rights, such as ILO Convention No.111[7] which refers to discrimination in the exercise of the right to work (employment and occupation), and the UNESCO Convention against Discrimination in Education.[8]

Of the international instruments mentioned, a definition of discrimination is included in article 1(1) CERD,[9] article 1 CEDAW,[10] article 1(1) ILO Convention No. 111,[11] and article 1(1) Convention against Discrimination in Education.[12] Among these various conceptions of 'discrimination', the Committee follows the definition contained in article 1(1) CERD. In fact, when the 'Reporting Guidelines'[13] refer to non-discrimination with regard to article 6, the Committee requires States to indicate in their reports:

> 'Whether there exist in your country any *distinctions, exclusions, restrictions or preferences*, be it in law or in administrative practices or in practical relationships, between persons or groups of persons, made on the basis of race, colour, sex, religion, political opinion, nationality or social origin, which have the effect of nullifying or impairing the recognition, enjoyment or exercise of equality of opportunity or treatment in employment or occupation. What steps are taken to eliminate such discrimination?'[14]

In the same vein, in General Comment No. 5 the Committee notes that,

---

7 Convention Concerning Discrimination in respect of Employment and Occupation, adopted on June 25, 1958.

8 Adopted on December 14, 1960.

9 CERD Art. 1(1) defines 'racial discrimination' as: 'any distinction, exclusion, restriction or preference based on race, colour, descent, or national or ethnic origin which has the purpose or effect of nullifying or impairing the recognition, enjoyment or exercise, on an equal footing, of human rights and fundamental freedoms in the political, economic, social, cultural or any other field of public life.'

10 CEDAW Art. 1(1) defines 'discrimination against women' as: 'any distinction, exclusion or restriction made on the basis of sex which has the effect or purpose of impairing or nullifying the recognition, enjoyment or exercise by women, irrespective of their marital status, on the basis of equality of men and women, of human rights and fundamental freedoms in the political, economic, social, cultural, civil or any other field.'

11 Art. 1(1) of ILO Convention No. 111, provides that discrimination includes: 'Any distinction, exclusion or preference made on the basis of race, colour, sex, religion, political opinion, national extraction or social origin, which has the effect of nullifying or impairing equality of opportunity or treatment in employment or occupation;[...].'

12 Art. 1(1) of the Convention against Discrimination in Education, provides that discrimination: 'includes any distinction, exclusion, limitation or preference which, being based on race, colour, sex, language, religion, political or other opinion, national or social origin, economic condition or birth, has the purpose or effect of nullifying or impairing equality of treatment in education [...].'

13 Revised General Guidelines Regarding the Form and Contents of Reports to be Submitted by States Parties under articles 16 and 17 of the International Covenant on Economic, Social and Cultural Rights. E/C.12/1991/1, 17 June 1991. ('Reporting Guidelines') Art. 6, General Comment No. 5 para. 15 and General Comment No. 12 para. 18.

14 E/C.12/1991/1 at Art. 6 para. 3. (Emphasis added).

> '[F]or the purposes of the Covenant, 'disability-based discrimination' may be defined as including any *distinction, exclusion, restriction or preference, or denial* of reasonable accommodation based on disability which has the effect of nullifying or impairing the recognition, enjoyment or exercise of economic, social or cultural rights.[...]'[15]

Therefore, it is possible to conclude that prohibited discrimination under the Covenant includes any *distinction, exclusion, restriction or preference* which is based on any ground such as race, colour, sex, language, religion, political or other opinion, national or social origin, property, birth or other status and which has the effect or purpose of impairing or nullifying the recognition, enjoyment or exercise by all persons, on an equal footing, of all of the rights contained in the Covenant. An explanation of the elements of the concept of 'discrimination' is required.

2.3 Distinctions, protective and affirmative action

During the *travaux préparatoires* of article 2(2) of the Covenant there was debate as to whether it was more appropriate to use of the term 'distinction' or 'discrimination.' The draft submitted by the Commission on Human Rights to the Third Committee of the General Assembly contained the word 'distinction' as did article 2 of the UDHR.[16] However, the Third Committee, acting on a proposal by the Italian, Argentinean and Mexican delegations, replaced the word 'distinction' with the term 'discrimination'. The aim of this substitution was to stress that there are some distinctions that may be justified.[17] As early as 1935, the Permanent Court of International Justice stressed that the principle of equality may require different treatment 'in order to attain a result which establishes an equilibrium between different situations.'[18]

Today, it is well established in international human rights law that not all distinctions in treatment constitute discrimination. This is summed up by the axiom 'persons who are equal should be treated equally and those who are different should be treated differently' ('in proportion to the inequality').[19] As indicated by the Human Rights Committee, 'the enjoyment of rights and freedoms on an equal footing [...] does not mean identical treatment in every instance.' Hence, there may be situations in which a different treatment is justified.

15 General Comment No. 5 para. 15. (Emphasis added).

16 Art. 2 paragraph 1 of the UDHR reads as follows: 'Everyone is entitled to all the rights and freedoms set forth in this Declaration, without distinction of any kind, such as race, colour, sex, language, religion, political or other opinion, national or social origin, property, birth or other status.' (Emphasis added).

17 For a more detailed analysis of the drafting history of article 2(2) ICESCR see Klerk, Y.: 'Working paper on article 2(2) and article 3 of the International Covenant on Economic, Social and Cultural Rights.' In: *HRQ*, vol. 9, (1987), pp. 250-273 and Ramcharan, *op. cit.* (note 1), pp. 258-259.

18 Minority Schools in Albania (1935) 3 *World Court Reports* 498 (Hudson ed.1938).

19 As added by Vierdag. See, Vierdag, *op. cit.* (note 1), p. 7.

Although not all differences in treatment are discriminatory, international law establishes some criteria for determining when a distinction amounts to discrimination. In a nutshell, it is possible to say that a distinction is compatible with the principle of equality when it has an objective and reasonable justification, pursues a legitimate aim under the Covenant and there is a reasonable relationship of proportionality between the means employed and the aim sought to be realised.[20] These requirements have been stressed by some of the major human rights supervisory bodies. For example, in the words of the Human Rights Committee,

> 'Not every differentiation of treatment will constitute discrimination, if the criteria for such differentiation are reasonable and objective and if the aim is to achieve a purpose which is legitimate under the Covenant.'[21]

As the European Court of Human Rights has stated:

> 'According to the Court's established case-law, a distinction is discriminatory if it 'has no objective and reasonable justification', that is, if it does not pursue a 'legitimate aim' or if there is not a 'reasonable relationship of proportionality' between the means employed and the aim sought to be realised.'[22]

In the same vein, the Inter-American Court of Human Rights has held that,

> 'Accordingly, no discrimination exists if the difference in treatment has a legitimate purpose and if it does not lead to situations which are contrary to justice, to reason or to the nature of things. It follows that there would be no discrimination in differences in treatment of individuals by a state when the classifications selected are based on substantial factual differences and there exists a reasonable relationship of proportionality between these differences and the aims of the legal rule under review. These aims may not be unjust or

20 See, for example, Dijk, P. van & Hoof, G.J.H. van: *Theory and practice of the European Convention on Human Rights*, Kluwer Law International, The Hague, third edition, (1998), p. 719; Bayefky, loc. cit. (note 1) pp. 11-18; and Craven, M.: *The International Covenant on Economic, Social and Cultural Rights: a perspective on its development*, Clarendon Press, Oxford, Paperback edition, with corrections, (1998), p. 163.

21 General Comment No. 18 para. 13. See, in addition, Shirin Aumeeruddy Cziffra and 19 other Mauritian women v. Mauritius, Communication No. 35/1978 para. 9(2); Alain Lestourneaud v. France, Communication No. 861/1999, inadmissibility decision of 3 November 1999 para. 4(2); Miroslav Blazek, George A. Hartman and George Krizek v. Czech Republic, Communication No. 857/1999, views of 12 July 2001, para. 5(6); and M. Schmitz-de Jong v. the Netherlands, Communication No. 855/1999, views of 16 July 2001, para. 7(2). With regard to the application of this principle by other UN treaty bodies, see, for example, CERD General Recommendation XIV on article 1, paragraph 1, contained in UN doc. A/48/18.

22 Marckx v. Belgium, Application No. 6833/74, Judgement of 13 June 1979, para. 33.

unreasonable, that is, they may not be arbitrary, capricious, despotic or in conflict with the essential oneness and dignity of humankind.'[23]

Thus, differences in treatment (distinction, exclusion, restriction or preference) that comply with the criteria mentioned above are not discriminatory and do not infringe article 2(2) ICESCR. Furthermore, there are some preferential treatments which may not be considered to be discrimination, such as the special treatment aimed at protecting some types of persons, for example pregnant women[24] or disabled persons.[25] In such cases the purpose of the preferential treatment is to remedy inequalities which are inherent in the situation.[26] Similarly, affirmative action, defined as measures necessary 'to diminish or eliminate conditions which cause or help to perpetuate discrimination'[27] aimed to benefit historically disadvantaged groups within society, such as blacks in the USA, must not be considered as 'discrimination'.[28]

The Committee has not expressly stated in a General Comment that distinctions made on the basis of objective and reasonable criteria do not amount to discrimination. However, from its work it is apparent that it does apply these criteria. For example, when examining the report of Japan, it noted,

> 'The Committee requests the State party to take note of its position that the principle of non-discrimination, as laid down in article 2 (2) of the Covenant, is an absolute principle and can be subject to no exception, *unless the distinction is based on objective criteria.*'[29]

---

23 I/A Court HR Advisory Opinion No. 4 'Proposed amendments to the naturalization provisions of the Constitution of Costa Rica', OC-4/84 of January 19, 1984, para. 57.

24 See, for example, according to Art. 4(2) CEDAW: 'Adoption by States Parties of special measures, including those measures contained in the present Convention, aimed at protecting maternity shall not be considered discriminatory.'

25 See, for example, Art. 4 ILO Convention No. 159 concerning vocational rehabilitation and employment (disabled persons) [adopted in 1983], which states '[…] special positive measures aimed at effective equality of opportunity and treatment between disabled workers and other workers shall not be regarded as discriminating against other workers.'

26 As Dinstein notes in regard to pregnant women 'of course, the state of maternity in the individual instance is temporary. But as long as the human species survives, maternity cases will endure'. Dinstein, *loc. cit.* (note 1), p. 15.

27 See General Comment No. 18 para. 10.

28 For example, according to Art. 1(4) CERD, 'Special measures taken for the sole purpose of securing adequate advancement of certain racial or ethnic groups or individuals requiring such protection as may be necessary in order to ensure such groups or individuals equal enjoyment or exercise of human rights and fundamental freedoms shall not be deemed racial discrimination, provided however, that such measures do not, as a consequence, lead to the maintenance of separate rights for different racial groups and that they shall not be continued after the objectives for which they were taken have been achieved.'

29 Concluding Observations Japan E/C.12/1/Add.67 para. 39. (Emphasis added).

Similarly, in the Concluding Observations on the initial report of Croatia it was stated that,

> 'The Committee expresses particular concern that the granting of citizenship under the Law on Croatian Citizenship (1991) has not been governed by *fair and objective* non-discriminatory criteria based on pre-war residence and connections to Croatia, and as a result has *heavily favoured* ethnic Croats.'[30]

In general, the Committee has stressed the applicability of the principle of non-discrimination when it is apparent that the distinction has been unreasonable. However, it does not generally note that it has arrived at this conclusion by applying the well-established criteria mentioned above.[31]

In the Covenant there is no special provision requiring affirmative action or special protective measures but it is clear that, according to the Committee, in some circumstances the principle of non-discrimination requires States to take affirmative action or protective measures to prevent or compensate for structural disadvantages. These measures entail special preferences which should not be considered discriminatory because they are aimed to address structural disadvantages or to protect particularly vulnerable groups, encouraging equal enjoyment of human rights.[32]

In contrast with its sister Committee, the Human Rights Committee, the Committee has not provided a definition on the concept of affirmative action.[33] However, it is

---

30 Concluding Observations Croatia E/C.12/1/Add.73 para 11. (Emphasis added).

31 From this author's perspective it is not necessary to expressly provide the reasoning when the arbitrariness of the distinction is evident (as has been the case for most of the distinctions supervised by the Committee). This has also been the approach of the Human Rights Committee when deciding upon some individual complaints. In some difficult cases, the Human Rights Committee has expressly stated that the distinction made by the State has been 'unjustified' or 'not reasonable or objective.' However, in other cases, it has merely mentioned that there been a violation of the principle of non-discrimination. For example, in the case of Graciela Alto del Avellanal v. Peru, the HRC concluded that the Peruvian law which gave husbands the exclusive right to represent matrimonial property and to initiate legal procedures on behalf of the communal property of the married couple constituted discrimination. In this case, the distinction was so evident that the Committee did not need to recall the criteria in its view. It merely noted, 'With regard to discrimination on the ground of sex the Committee notes further that under article 3 of the Covenant State Parties undertake 'to ensure the equal right of men and women to the enjoyment of all civil and political rights set forth in the present Covenant' and that article 26 provides that all persons are equal before the law and are entitled to the equal protection of the law. The Committee finds that the facts before it reveal that the application of article 168 of the Peruvian Civil Code to the author resulted in denying her equality before the courts and constituted discrimination on the ground of sex.' [Communication No. 202/1986, views of 28 October 1988, para. 10.2].

32 For a comprehensive analysis on 'affirmative actions, see 'The concept and practice of affirmative action'. Preliminary report submitted by Mr. Marc Bossuyt, Special Rapporteur in accordance with Sub-Commission resolution 1998/5. E/CN.4/Sub.2/2000/11.

33 Through its General Comments, the Human Rights Committee often refers to the requirement of the adoption of affirmative action and it has adopted a definition in General Comment No. 18 para 10, which reads as follow: 'The Committee also wishes to point out that the principle of equality some-

possible to conclude that it considers the adoption of affirmative action necessary under the same circumstances as the Human Rights Committee. For example, when it examined the report of Guatemala, the Committee recommended that 'all legislative and other reforms take into account the need to promote and *reverse* the devastating effects of discrimination against the indigenous population, in particular through *affirmative action*.'[34]

Affirmative actions are aimed at the removal of obstacles to the advancement of vulnerable groups such as women, minorities, indigenous peoples, refugees and disabled persons and are of temporary character, meaning that they must not continue after their objectives have been achieved. The Committee has expressly indicated this characteristic when referring to the necessity of affirmative action in regard to the right to education. In General Comment No. 13 the Committee notes that:

> 'The adoption of temporary special measures intended to bring about de facto equality for men and women and for disadvantaged groups is not a violation of the right to non-discrimination with regard to education, so long as such measures do not lead to the maintenance of unequal or separate standards for different groups, and provided they are not continued after the objectives for which they were taken have been achieved.'[35]

While this statement specifically addressed the right to education, it clearly represents the general approach of the Committee.[36] Nonetheless, we may note that this statement is broad and it does not distinguish between protective and affirmative action. Protective action (*e.g.* aimed at the protection of pregnant women or disabled persons) and affirmative action (designed to benefit structurally or historically disadvantaged groups) must be distinguished. While the benefits for the former apply irrespective of time limits, affirmative action measures are essentially temporary. The latter measures must not continue after their objectives of equality have been achieved. Nevertheless, it is important to bear in mind that some groups of persons may be beneficiaries of both

---

times requires States parties to take *affirmative action* in order to diminish or eliminate conditions which cause or help to perpetuate discrimination prohibited by the Covenant. For example, in a State where the general conditions of a certain part of the population prevent or impair their enjoyment of human rights, the State should take specific action to correct those conditions. Such action may involve granting for a time to the part of the population concerned certain preferential treatment in specific matters as compared with the rest of the population. However, as long as such action is needed to correct discrimination in fact, it is a case of legitimate differentiation under the Covenant.' (Emphasis added.)

34 Concluding Observations Guatemala E/1997/22 para 140.

35 General Comment No. 13 para. 32.

36 This statement is supported by the fact that the Committee decided to present General Comment Nos. 13 and 11 as a contribution to the World Conference against racism, racial discrimination, xenophobia and related intolerance. This approach clearly suggests that the Committee considers that these General Comments reflect its general approach to discrimination. See A/CONF.189/PC.1/14 of February 29, 2000.

kinds of measures. For example, in the case of women, certain 'affirmative actions' are necessary to ensure equal enjoyment of their rights (*e.g.* to ensure equal access to employment), and such measures must end once that aim has been achieved. But there are also certain protective measures in favour of women which are not designed to end, such as the protective measures against trafficking or special protection afforded to pregnant women.

Despite the progress made during recent years in clarifying the obligation of affirmative action under the Covenant, the Committee should elucidate its scope with further precision. As Craven notes, affirmative actions might take the form of (a) specific benefits to disadvantaged groups, such as advice, training, housing or food or (b) quota systems in public employment, education or employment training.[37] Until now the Committee has only made general statements. For example, in regard to the quota systems, it has suggested that they are necessary, but without any further explanation.[38] Certainly, the Committee needs to be more precise in regard to the form that affirmative action should take.

In sum, when examining States' reports, the Committee applies the general criteria under international law. However, it would be advisable for the Committee to expressly set out the standard of scrutiny that it uses and apply it in a consistent and strict manner. By doing so, the Committee would further limit the margin of discretion of States parties in assessing whether or not, and to what extent, a given situation justifies a difference in treatment.

2.4 Direct and indirect discrimination

In the definition of the term 'discrimination' in the international instruments, we find that discriminatory intent is not a necessary element. This is clear from the phrase 'which has the purpose *or the effect* of nullifying or impairing the equality of treatment.[39] Hence, it is the final result that matters, regardless of the intention of the act. The Committee has clearly stated that article 2(2) implies a prohibition of both kinds of discrimination. In General Comment No. 5, for example, the Committee merely referred to the 'effect' of the distinction, exclusion or preference.[40] Similarly, in General Comment No. 12 the Committee sets forth that,

37 Craven, 1995, pp.186-187.

38 For example, when examining the report of Israel 'the Committee notes with regret that more than 72 per cent of persons with disabilities are unemployed. The new Law of Equality for People with Disabilities 1998 has not set any *quota* for the employment of such persons.' Concluding Observations Israel E/1999/22 para 241(emphasis added).

39 See Art. 1 CERD, Art. 1 CEDAW and Art. 1 UNESCO Convention against Discrimination in Education.

40 General Comment No. 5 para. 15.

> 'Any discrimination in access to food, as well as to means and entitlements for its procurement, on the grounds of race, colour, sex, language, age, religion, political or other opinion, national or social origin, property, birth or other status *with the purpose or effect* of nullifying or impairing the equal enjoyment or exercise of economic, social and cultural rights constitutes a violation of the Covenant.'[41]

Despite the clear approach adopted in these General Comments, the Committee has not been very consistent in its supervision of 'indirect' discrimination. In the examination of State Reports, the issue of indirect discrimination has been analysed by the Committee only rarely. Nonetheless, in this regard it is worth mentioning the case of Belgium. The Committee considered that despite the fact that a Belgian law concerning cohabitants in the unemployment regime was to be applied uniformly to men and women, it had disproportionately negative consequences for women.[42] In this case the Committee expressed concern at the discriminatory effects of legislation, even when Government Representatives have expressly stated before the Committee that the legislation was not intended to be discriminatory.

As we will see, the approach adopted by the Committee when examining the report of Belgium was in line with that of the CERD Committee. The CERD Committee has stated that 'in seeking whether an action has an effect contrary to the Convention, it will look to see whether that action has an unjustifiable disparate impact upon a group [...]'.[43]

It would be desirable for the Committee to begin to apply the principle of indirect discrimination with greater frequency when examining State reports. It should pay greater attention to the possible adverse impact of legislation and State actions on particular groups. It is therefore essential that the Committee receive information on the 'effect' of a given law, policy or practice. In this regard, sources other than the State might play an important role in providing the Committee with the necessary information.

2.5 Discrimination by private actors

In contrast with other international instruments, such as CERD and CEDAW, the Covenant does not expressly require States to take actions to prevent and combat discrimination committed by third persons[44] and the *travaux préparatoires* are not clear

41 General Comment No. 12 para. 18. (Emphasis added.)
42 See the analysis below, in the text accompanying note 138.
43 CERD General Recommendation XIV para. 2
44 Art. 2(d) CERD reads as follows: 'Each State party shall prohibit and bring to an end, by all appropriate means, including legislation as required by circumstances, racial discrimination by any persons, groups or organisation.' In the same vein, Art. 2 (e) CEDAW requires States 'to take all appropriate measures to eliminate discrimination against women by any person, organisation or enterprise.'

in this respect.[45] However, in light of the Committee's work it is possible to conclude that article 2(2) requires States Parties to prohibit private persons and bodies from practising discrimination.[46] In this regard, the Committee has placed particular emphasis on compliance with the principle of non-discrimination in the private sector, in relation to racist and xenophobic behaviour and domestic violence.[47]

In General Comment No. 5, for example, the Committee states,

> 'Given the increasing commitment of Governments around the world to market-based policies, it is appropriate in that context to emphasize certain aspects of States parties' obligations. *One is the need to ensure that not only the public sphere, but also the private sphere, are, within appropriate limits, subject to regulation to ensure the equitable treatment of persons* with disabilities. In a context in which arrangements for the provision of public services are increasingly being privatized and in which the free market is being relied on to an ever greater extent, it is essential that private employers, private suppliers of goods and services, and other non-public entities be subject to both non-discrimination and equality norms in relation to persons with disabilities. In circumstances where such protection does not extend beyond the public domain, the ability of persons with disabilities to participate in the mainstream of community activities and to realize their full potential as active members of society will be severely and often arbitrarily constrained. This is not to imply that legislative measures will always be the most effective means of seeking to eliminate discrimination within the private sphere. Thus, for example, the Standard Rules place particular emphasis on the need for States to "take action to raise awareness in society about persons with disabilities, their rights, their needs, their potential and their contribution".'[48]

While this General Comment specifically refers to 'persons with disabilities', it is possible to conclude that it applies to all kinds of vulnerable and disadvantaged groups within society. When examining States' reports, the Committee has usually supervised the steps taken by States to prevent racial and xenophobic discrimination by third parties.[49]

---

45 Klerk, *loc. cit.* (note 17), pp. 266-267.

46 This topic has been further developed above in Chapter V, section 3.3.

47 While the Committee has consistently emphasised the duty to protect against discrimination by private actors, there are some areas of discrimination in the private sphere to which the Committee has not given proper attention. For example, it has not addressed the need to promote and take positive measures to provide support to enterprises owned by victims of discrimination by, for example, providing credit facilities and training [See Durban Declaration and Programme of Action, available at: http://www.unhchr.ch/html/racism/Durban.htm (last visited July 2002)]. Note that the problem of domestic violence is analysed independently in section 4.4.

48 General Comment No. 5 para. 11 (emphasis added, footnote omitted). See in addition, General Comment No. 14 para. 26.

49 See, for example, Concluding Observations China [Hong Kong] E/C.12/1/Add.58 para. 15. Concluding Observations Panama E/C.12.1/Add.64 para. 12, and Concluding Observations Croatia E/C.12/1/Add.73 para. 9. See, in addition, List of Issues Finland E/C.12/Q/FIN/2 para. 8 and List of Issues Sweden E/C.12/Q/SWE/2 para. 8.

From the Committee's approach in General Comments and Concluding Observations, we must conclude that States are obliged to regulate behaviour within the community in order to prevent and protect against violation of economic, social and cultural rights by third parties. As we will see, in order to do so, in some cases States must take legislative measures to penalise some forms of conduct and carry out educational programmes and campaigns.[50]

3 ARTICLE 2(2): NON-DISCRIMINATION

> 'The States Parties to the Present Covenant undertake to guarantee that the rights enunciated in the present Covenant will be exercised without discrimination of any kind as to race, colour, sex, language, religion, political or other opinion, national or social origin, property, birth or other status.'

3.1 Grounds covered by the provision

Article 2(2) of the Covenant enumerates ten grounds of prohibited discrimination: (a) race, (2) colour, (3) sex, (4) language, (5) religion, (6) political or other opinion, (7) national or social origin, (8) property, (9) birth, and (10) 'other status'.

The grounds enumerated in article 2(2) are merely illustrative and not exhaustive.[51] The term 'or other status' has an open-ended meaning. This is clearly the interpretation given by the Committee in its Concluding Observations as well as in the General Comments. Indeed, when examining the issue of whether discrimination on the grounds of disability or age was prohibited by the Covenant, it concluded that 'other status' 'clearly applied' to discrimination on grounds not expressly contained in article 2(2) ICESCR.[52] On the other hand, the Committee has analysed additional grounds as being 'suspect' or prima facie illegitimate.

Through its General Comments the Committee has paid particular attention to the following grounds:

(a) *Disability: According to the Committee in its General Comment No. 5,*

> '5. The Covenant does not refer explicitly to persons with disabilities. Nevertheless, the Universal Declaration of Human Rights recognizes that all human beings are born free and equal in dignity and rights and, since the Covenant's provisions apply fully to all members of society, persons with disabilities are clearly entitled to the full range of rights recognized in the Covenant [...]. Moreover, the requirement contained in article 2(2) of the Covenant

---

50 See, for example, Concluding Observations Portugal E/2001/22 para. 420.

51 See Klerk, *loc. cit.* (note 17), p. 253; Craven, *op. cit.* (note 20), pp. 153 *et seq.;* and Limburg Principle No. 36. This seems to be the majority position of the academic writers as well as the interpretation adopted by the Committee. For another opinion see Bayefsky, *loc. cit.* (note 1), p. 5.

52 See, General Comment No. 5 para. 5 and General Comment No. 6 paras. 10 and 11.

that the rights 'enunciated [...] will be exercised without discrimination of any kind' based on certain specified grounds 'or other status' clearly applies to discrimination on the grounds of disability.'

(b) *Age: The Committee states in General Comment No. 6 that,*

'11. Another important issue is whether discrimination on the basis of age is prohibited by the Covenant. Neither the Covenant nor the Universal Declaration of Human Rights refers explicitly to age as one of the prohibited grounds. Rather than being seen as an intentional exclusion, this omission is probably best explained by the fact that, when these instruments were adopted, the problem of demographic ageing was not as evident or as pressing as it is now.

12. This is not determinative of the matter, however, since the prohibition of discrimination on the grounds of 'other status' could be interpreted as applying to age.'

Of the General Comments issued up to July 2002, only Nos. 5 and 6 are aimed specifically at addressing the enjoyment of the Covenant rights by a single vulnerable group, clearly establishing the prohibition of discrimination against them. However, in other General Comments the Committee has also dealt with grounds which are considered illegitimate that are not expressly contained in article 2(2). For example, in General Comment No. 14, the Committee notes that by virtue of article 2(2) and article 3 ICESCR the Covenant prohibits any discrimination on the basis of 'race, colour, sex, language, religion, political or other opinion, national or social origin, property, birth, *physical and mental disability, health status (including HIV/AIDS), sexual orientation and civil, political, social or other status [...].*'[53]

General Comment No. 13 also refers to other suspected grounds for discrimination, albeit not as directly and straightforwardly as in General Comment No. 14. For example, it expressly states that the 'everyone' includes 'non-nationals.' In the Committee's words:

'The Committee [...] confirms that the principle of non-discrimination extends to all persons of school age residing in the territory of a State party, *including non-nationals, and irrespective of their legal status.*'[54]

The Committee has made the same observation specifically with regard to the right to educational freedom (article 13(4) ICESCR).[55] In this General Comment, the Committee also notes that in light of General Comment No. 5 and General Comment No. 6,

53 General Comment No. 14 para. 18. (Emphasis added).
54 General Comment No. 13 para. 34.
55 General Comment No. 13 para. 30.

disability and age are suspected grounds for discrimination.[56] Furthermore, when referring to technical and vocational education it includes among the vulnerable groups which must be the target of this type of education: 'children of migrant workers, refugees and persons with disabilities.'[57] By doing so the Committee suggests that preferential treatment in favour of these groups are not to be considered discriminatory.[58]

In the light of the Concluding Observations, it is also clear that the prohibited grounds for discrimination are not limited to those indicated in article 2(2).[59] Through its Concluding Observations the Committee has paid particular attention to distinctions on the grounds of sexual orientation, disability, health status and nationality. For example, the Committee has expressed concern when States discriminate on the ground of sexual orientation and in instances when States have not prohibited discrimination on the basis of sexual orientation in their national legal systems, the Committee has 'urged' them to do so.[60] In line with its General Comments, when considering States' reports, the Committee has supervised discrimination on the grounds of age and disability.[61] With regard to the prohibition of discrimination on the basis of health status, in the Concluding Observations the Committee has referred almost exclusively to discrimination against persons who are HIV-positive or who suffer from AIDS.[62] In this regard, the Committee has 'urged' States Parties 'to ensure' that their 'law, regulations and practices in relation to HIV/AIDS are non-discriminatory'.[63]

Article 2(2) refers to 'national origin' as a prohibited ground for discrimination and not to 'nationality' and it is unclear whether or not the term 'national origin' applies to non-nationals.[64] However, this point is no longer of great relevance due to the fact

56 General Comment No. 13 para. 35.

57 General Comment No. 13 para. 16.

58 See General Comment 13 para. 32.

59 For example, when examining the report of Ukraine, the Committee noted, 'The Committee recommends that the State Party strengthen the provisions in its legal order with respect to the prohibition of discrimination in accordance with article 2(2) of the Covenant, *in particular* on the ground of race, colour, sex, language, religion, political or other opinion, national or social origin, property, birth or other status.' Concluding Observations Ukraine E/C.12/1/Add.65 para. 22. See, also, Concluding Observations Jordan E/2001/22 para. 234.

60 See, for example, List of Issues China E/C.12/Q/HKSAR/1 para.4 of 25 May 2000 and Concluding Observations China [Hong Kong] E/C.12/1/Add.58 para. 15. The Committee has also commended States when they include in their national legal systems the prohibition of discrimination based on sexual orientation. In addition, see Concluding Observations Sweden E/C.12/1/Add.70 para. 8 and Concluding Observations Ireland E/2000/22 para. 127.

61 See, for example, Concluding Observations Senegal E/C.12/1/Add.62 para. 17; Concluding Observations Japan E/C.12/1/Add.67 para. 25; Concluding Observations Ireland E/2000/22 paras. 127 and 142; Concluding Observations Canada E/1999/22 para. 421; Concluding Observations Saint Vincent and the Grenadines E/1998/22 para. 422; and Concluding Observations Croatia E/C.12/1/Add.73 para. 12.

62 See, for example, Concluding Observations Russian Federation E/1998/22 para. 126.

63 See, for example, Concluding Observations Algeria E/C.12/1/Add.71 para. 39 and Concluding Observations Egypt E/2001/22 para. 180.

64 See the analysis in Craven, *op. cit.* (note 20), pp. 172-174.

that the Committee's work indicates that 'nationality' is also a suspected ground. The Committee has clearly stated that the Covenant applies to everyone under the jurisdiction of the State Party.[65] This is not to say that all distinctions between nationals and non-nationals are prohibited under the Covenant but, rather, that distinctions must comply with the principle of non-discrimination and hence any distinction in treatment imposed by the State between nationals and non-nationals must be reasonable, objective, proportional and with a legitimate aim.[66] There are some distinctions between nationals and non-nationals that may be considered legitimate. For example, if a foreigner and a national of a State Party are in different situations in relation to contributions to the social security scheme, they may be treated differently. However, it would be a violation of the principle of non-discrimination if they were in analogous circumstances for the purposes of enjoyment of social security but were treated differently.[67]

Some restrictions may also be permitted with regard to the exercise of the right to work.[68] Factors such as, national security or the requirements necessary to perform a job may in some cases justify distinctions between nationals and non-nationals. This is the approach, for example, of some ILO Conventions which allow for some distinctions on the basis of the inherent requirements of a particular job[69] or due to the State's interests.[70] These include, for example, restrictions on employment in certain higher civil service posts or posts bearing some relation to the security of the State.

The ultimate responsibility for determining whether any difference in treatment between nationals and non-nationals amounts to discrimination lies with the Committee.[71] States wishing to differentiate between nationals and non-nationals have the burden of proof in demonstrating that the distinction, exclusion or restriction does not

65 See the analysis in Chapter VI section 2.1.

66 See section 2.2.

67 The Committee has suggested this approach when it considered the initial report of Nigeria. The Committee noted that many foreign workers with residence permits who had 'participated in and contributed to the social security system' had been expelled by the State without receiving adequate compensation for their social security contributions. Concluding Observations Nigeria E/1999/22 para. 105.

68 As Craven commented with regard to the principle of non-discrimination between nationals and non-nationals in the exercise of the right to work (article 6 ICESCR), the mere fact that the United Kingdom and France considered it necessary to enter, respectively, a reservation to and an interpretative declaration on Art. 6, in order not to preclude impositions of restrictions in the access of non-nationals to employment, appear to be confirmation of the requirement of equality imposed by Art. 6 regarding national and non-nationals. See Craven, *op. cit.* (note 20), p. 215.

69 Article 1(2) of ILO Convention No. 111 establishes, 'Any distinction, exclusion or preference in respect of a particular job based on the inherent requirements thereof shall not be deemed to be discrimination.'

70 ILO Convention No. 143 Concerning Migrations and Abusive Conditions and thePromotion of Equality of Opportunity and Treatment of Migrant Workers [Adopted in June 24, 1975], establishes in article 14(e) that, 'A member may restrict access to limited categories of employment or functions where this is necessary in the interests of the State'.

71 See the analysis in Chapter VI section 2.1.

entail discriminatory treatment. In recent years the Committee has increasingly devoted more attention to supervising the enjoyment of economic, social and cultural rights by non-nationals without discrimination. The Committee has paid particular attention to the enjoyment by non-nationals of article 7 (safe and fair working conditions),[72] article 8 (the right to form and join trade unions),[73] article 9 (social security)[74] and article 13 (the right to education).[75] Finally, it must be stressed that even when some distinctions between nationals and non-nationals may be reasonable, States Parties must not discriminate against any particular nationality.[76]

3.2 The immediate character of the obligation of non-discrimination

On several occasions the Committee has stressed that the Covenant imposes various obligations which are of immediate effect and has specifically stressed in many General Comments and Concluding Observations that the duty of States Parties to guarantee the exercise of the relevant rights without discrimination is of immediate effect.[77] As stated in General Comment No. 11:

---

72 See, for example, Concluding Observations Dominican Republic E/1997/22 para. 224; Concluding Observations Portugal [Macao] E/1997/22 para. 251; Concluding Observations Libyan Arab Jamahiriya E/1998/22 para. 185; Concluding Observations Nigeria E/1999/22 para. 105; Concluding Observations Jordan E/2001/22 para. 238; and Concluding Observations Republic of Korea E/C.12.1/Add.59 paras. 17 and 38.

73 For example, when examining the Second Periodic Report of Senegal, the Committee expressed its concern that despite its earlier recommendations, foreign workers were still not permitted to form trade unions and called upon the State to repeal this prohibition. Concluding Observations Senegal E/C.12/1/Add.62 paras. 22 and 44 and Concluding Observations Senegal E/1994/22 para. 224. In the same vein, Concluding Observations Jordan E/2001/22 para. 238. See, in addition, the approach of Mr. Texier in E/C.12/1996/SR.38 para. 5.

74 For example, the Concluding Observations of Portugal [Macao] expressly state that, '[t]he Committee also urges the enactment of legislation on the right to social security so as to ensure full compliance with the requirements of the Covenant, and recommends that the State Party extend the coverage of social security to non-resident workers.' Concluding Observations Portugal [Macao] E/1997/22 para. 261. See also, Concluding Observations Mauritius E/1996/22 para. 238.

75 See for example, Concluding Observations Canada E/1999/22 para. 414, Concluding Observations Germany E/1999/22 para. 327 and Concluding Observations Azerbaijan E/1998/22 para. 324. See, in addition, List of Issues Switzerland E/C.12/Q/SWI/1 para. 3, List of Issues Ireland E/C.12/Q/IRE/1 para. 11 and List of Issues Bulgaria E/C.12.Q/BUL/1 para. 6.

76 This approach is particularly evident when the Committee supervises distinctions drawn by some European States between European Union citizens and foreigners of other nationalities. See, for example, List of Issues France E/C.12/Q/FRA/1 para. 6 and Concluding Observations Iceland E/200/22 para. 72. In addition see CERD General Recommendation XI on non-citizens.

77 See General Comment No. 3 para. 1; General Comment No. 11 para. 10; General Comment No. 13 paras. 31 and 43; and General Comment No. 14 para. 30. Through its Concluding Observations the Committee has also stressed the immediate character of the non-discrimination provision. See for example, Concluding Observations Japan E/C.12/1/Add.67 para. 12; Concluding Observations Yugoslavia E/2001/22 para. 496; and Concluding Observations Zimbabwe E/1998/22 para. 79.

> 'The prohibition against discrimination enshrined in article 2 (2) of the Covenant is subject to neither progressive realization nor the availability of resources; it applies fully and immediately [...].'[78]

Scholars have also stressed that obligations stemming from the prohibition of discrimination in article 2(2) ICESCR must be implemented fully and immediately. According to Limburg Principle No. 22: 'Some obligations under the Covenant require immediate implementation in full by all States Parties, such as the prohibition of discrimination in article 2(2) of the Covenant.' Furthermore, principle No. 35 states, 'Article 2(2) calls for immediate application and involves an explicit guarantee on behalf of the States Parties.'

This interpretation finds support in the specific wording used in articles 2(2) and 3 of the Covenant and in their position within the Covenant.[79] Article 2(2) uses the term 'guarantee' and article 3 uses the term 'ensure' which have been considered as imposing obligations of an immediate nature.[80] Moreover, as Klerk argues, articles 2(2) and 3 are not subordinate to the principle of progressive realisation contained in article 2(1) as this principle is only applicable to the substantive rights contained in Part III.[81]

Although States must implement the prohibition of discrimination without delay upon becoming party to the Covenant, it is important to recognise that there are in fact distinctions in the enjoyment of economic, social and cultural rights and it necessarily takes time to abolish them. Therefore, the immediate character of the principle of non-discrimination must be understood to require States to comply immediately with some obligations [82] such as abstention from enforcing any discriminatory practices and the

78 General Comment No. 13 para. 31.

79 For the debate during the drafting of the Covenant see, *inter alia*, E/CN.4/SR.274 (1952), A/C.3/L.1054 and Add. I, (1952) and A/C.3/SR.1206 (1962).

80 See, for example, Alston, P. & Quinn, G.: 'The nature and scope of States parties' obligations under the International Covenant on Economic, Social and Cultural Rights.' In: *HRQ,* vol. 9, No. 2, (1987), pp.184-186 and Alston, P.: 'The International Covenant on Economic, Social and Cultural Rights.' In: *Manual on human rights reporting under six major international human rights instruments*, United Nations, second edition, Geneva, UN doc. GV.E.97.0.16, (1997), p. 89.

81 According to Klerk, the principle of gradual application does not apply to article 2(2) and Art. 3 because, 'Articles 2 and 5 indicate how the substantive right recognised in the Covenant should be realised. These rights are enumerated in Part III (Articles 6 to 15). So, when Article 2(1) speaks of the 'full realisation of the rights recognised in the present Covenant' it applies to these substantive rights. It does not apply, however, to the other articles that indicate the way in which the provisions in Part III should be applied. The provisions in Part II are on a par, none is subordinate to any of the others.' Klerk, *loc. cit.* (note 17), p. 261.

82 See, for example, General Comment No. 14 para. 34 and General Comment No. 13 para. 39. The analysis of the immediate obligations derived from the principle of non-discrimination is provided below in section 3.3.

treatment of all individuals without discrimination. Similarly, States Parties must take immediate steps to eliminate *de facto* discrimination as soon as possible.[83]

This is well explained by the Limburg Principles which set forth that,

> '37. Upon becoming a party to the Covenant states shall eliminate *de jure* discrimination by abolishing without delay any discriminatory laws, regulations and practices (including acts of omission as well as commission) affecting the enjoyment of economic, social and cultural rights.
>
> 38 *De facto* discrimination occurring as a result of the unequal enjoyment of economic, social and cultural rights, on account of a lack of resources or otherwise, should be brought to an end as speedily as possible.'

In sum, it is possible to conclude that the principle of non-discrimination requires States to comply immediately, without delay, with some obligations derived from the principle of non-discrimination. Such obligations include the duty to take immediate steps to eliminate any *de facto* discrimination in the enjoyment of economic, social and cultural rights.

3.3 Obligations deriving from the principle of non-discrimination

The Committee refers to the principle of non-discrimination in its General Comments and when examining State reports it actively monitors States' compliance with the non-discrimination provision. In the light of the Committee's work, it is possible to conclude that while, in general, States have discretion as to the means for the implementation of the Covenant, some measures are indispensable in order to comply with the principle of non-discrimination.

The following analysis will identify the obligations imposed by article 2(2) ICESCR. It is important to stress that while these obligations are discussed separately in order to highlight their specific features, they are interrelated and should be viewed as forming an organic whole.

(a) *To abstain from denying or limiting equal access for all persons to the enjoyment of the rights*

This is a duty from the first type or level of State obligations: the duty to respect each of the substantive rights contained in the Covenant. This duty was stressed by the Committee in General Comment No. 14 on the right to the highest attainable standard of health,

83 See for example, General Comment No. 13 para. 37 and Concluding Observations United Kingdom of Great Britain and Northern Ireland E/1998/22 para. 307.

'34. In particular, States are under the obligation to respect the right to health by, *inter alia*, refraining from denying or limiting equal access for all persons, including prisoners or detainees, minorities, asylum seekers and illegal immigrants, to preventive, curative and palliative health services; abstaining from enforcing discriminatory practices as a State policy; and abstaining from imposing discriminatory practices relating to women's health status and needs.[...].'

The Committee has also stressed this obligation with regard to other substantive rights, for example in General Comment No. 13 the Committee notes that,

'Educational institutions and programmes have to be accessible to everyone, without discrimination, within the jurisdiction of the State party.'[84]

In general, upon becoming a party to the Covenant, States must refrain from implementing any practice or policy with a discriminatory impact in the enjoyment of the substantive rights.

(b) *To review national legislation in order to assess the existence of any discriminatory impact and to repeal or amend legislation that it is found to be discriminatory*

In light of the Committee's Concluding Observations, it is possible to conclude that States Parties are required to undertake a comprehensive review in order to assess if their legislation and administrative rules and practices are discriminatory or have any discriminatory impact.[85] As it is the effect and not the intention of the legislation that matters, a review carried out *in abstracto* without taking into account the effect of legislation, rules and practices is not sufficient to comply with this requirement. Hence, States must carefully examine the effect that the implementation of any legislation, procedures or practice actually has on the enjoyment of these rights. They must proceed to comply with this obligation on their own initiative after the entry into force of the Covenant and thereafter on a regular basis. If a review indicates that the legislation or practices have or may have a discriminatory impact, the State in question must repeal, abolish or amend them.[86] For example, as stressed by the Committee in General Comment No. 13, violations of the right to education include the 'failure to repeal legislation which discriminates against individuals or groups, on any of the prohibited grounds, in the field of education.'[87]

84 General Comment No. 13 para. 6. See in addition, paras. 31-37.

85 See, for example, General Comment No. 1 para. 2. In addition, see, for example, Concluding Observations Denmark E/2000/22 para. 113, Concluding Observations Croatia E/C.12/1/Add.73 para. 20 and Concluding Observations Egypt E/2001/22 para. 175.

86 See, for example, General Comment No. 5 para. 13 and General Comment No. 13 para. 59.

87 General Comment No. 13 para. 59.

The ultimate determination as to whether or not the legislation has a discriminatory effect remains the responsibility of the Committee. Hence, after considering a State report the Committee may call upon the State to 'reassess' certain legislation or practices found to have a discriminatory impact[88] and require the State to repeal, abolish or amend them if it appears that they are discriminatory.[89]

The Committee has given special attention to the obligation to repeal or amend any legislation which discriminates against children born out of wedlock, in particular in relation to the curtailment of their inheritance and nationality rights.[90] For example, when examining the report of Sri Lanka, the Committee noted that legislation that discriminated against children born out of wedlock 'violated' the Covenant.[91] The Committee has also stressed the necessity to repeal any discriminatory provision against persons with disabilities.[92]

(c) *To take legislative measures to combat discrimination*
As indicated by the Committee in General Comment No. 3,

> 'The Committee recognizes that in many instances legislation is highly desirable and in some cases may even be indispensable. For example, it may be difficult to combat discrimination effectively in the absence of a sound legislative foundation for the necessary measures.'[93]

In General Comment No. 5, the Committee stresses that, 'in order to remedy past and present discrimination, and to deter future discrimination, comprehensive anti-discrimination legislation in relation to disability would seem to be indispensable in virtually all States Parties.'[94] In general, as analysed above, it is well established that legislative measures are compulsory for the implementation of the principle of non-discrimination.[95] Hence, although there are a number of means that States *may* take to combat discrimination, it is clear that they *must* take legislative measures.

---

88 See, for example, Concluding Observations Cameroon E/2000/22 para. 327, Concluding Observations Sri Lanka E/1999/22 para. 74 and Concluding Observations Israel E/1999/22 para. 239.

89 In addition, see for example, Concluding Observations Denmark E/2000/22 para. 113; Concluding Observations Poland E/1999/22 para. 160; Concluding Observations Aruba E/1999/22 para. 206; and Concluding Observations Cyprus E/1999/22 para. 291.

90 See, for example, Concluding Observations Japan E/C.12/1/Add.67 para. 14 and Concluding Observations Morocco E/2001/22 paras. 534 and 558.

91 Concluding Observations Sri Lanka E/1999/22 para. 74. The Committee has stated that the concept of 'illegitimate children' is 'unacceptable in a modern society' [Concluding Observations Japan E/C.12/1/Add.67 para. 41].

92 See, for example, General Comment No. 5 para. 13 and Concluding Observations Japan E/C.12/1/Add.67 para. 52.

93 General Comment No. 3 para. 3.

94 General Comment No. 5 para.16.

95 See the analysis in Chapter VII section 5.1.3.

This approach finds support in the Concluding Observations, in which the Committee has further clarified when legislative measures are indispensable. The Committee has devoted particular attention to the necessity to adopt legislation to protect again and to prevent discrimination on the grounds of age,[96] disability,[97] gender,[98] health status (HIV/AIDS infected people)[99] and race.[100]

In some cases, the legislative measure that States are required to take are of a criminal nature. States are required to penalise certain discriminatory behaviours that may adversely affect the enjoyment of economic, social and cultural rights by some vulnerable or disadvantaged groups. For example, in the light of the Committee's work it seems that States Parties are required to penalize acts of racial discrimination by public officials and private persons.[101] When examining the Report of China (Hong Kong Special Administrative Region), the Committee noted that 'the failure by HKSAR to prohibit race discrimination in the private sector constitutes a breach of its obligations under article 2 of the Covenant.'[102]

In some circumstances the Committee has been very specific in indicating the legislative measures required. For example, after considering the report of the Dominican Republic, the Committee indicated with some precision those legislative measures that it considered necessary to combat the general problem of discrimination against persons of Haitian origin. As it noted, 'it thus appears necessary to adopt clear legislation on nationality which would provide legal security to persons of Haitian origin born in the Dominican Republic.[103]

(d) *To take special protective measures and affirmative action for the benefit of vulnerable and disadvantaged groups*

The principle of non-discrimination under the Covenant requires States to take positive measures or affirmative action in order to ensure to vulnerable and disadvantaged

96 See, for example, General Comment No. 6 para. 18 and Concluding Observations Mongolia E/2001/22 para. 263.

97 See, for example, Concluding Observations Mongolia E/2001/22 para. 263, Concluding Observations Finland E/2001/22 para. 433 and Concluding Observations Ireland E/2000/22 para. 149.

98 See section 4.

99 States must prevent all discriminatory measures against infected persons especially through the adoption of legislative measures. See, for example, Concluding Observations Russian Federation E/1998/22 para. 126; Concluding Observations Algeria E/C.12/1/Add.71 para. 39; and Concluding Observations Egypt E/2001/22 para. 180.

100 See, for example, Concluding Observations Dominican Republic E/1998/22 para. 230.

101 See, for example, Concluding Observations Dominican Republic E/1998/22 para. 230; Concluding Observations Spain E/1997/22 para. 111; Concluding Observations Belgium E/2001/22 para. 483; Concluding Observations China [Hong Kong] E/C.12/1/Add.58 para. 15; and Concluding Observations Ukraine E/C.12/1/Add.65 para. 22. See in addition, CERD General Recommendation XV on article 4 of the Convention. UN doc. A/48/18 para. 3.

102 Concluding Observations China [Hong Kong] E/C.12/1/Add.58 para. 30.

103 Concluding Observations Dominican Republic E/1998/22 para. 225.

groups equal enjoyment of the Covenant's rights.[104] The aim of these measures is to improve the situation of the targeted group so as to place them in equal situations with other more privileged groups. These measures cannot be considered 'discrimination' under the Covenant. This is expressly provided by the Committee which has stated that,

> 'Because appropriate measures need to be taken to undo existing discrimination and to establish equitable opportunities such actions should not be considered discriminatory in the sense of article 2(2) of the International Covenant on Economic, Social and Cultural Rights as long as they are based on the principle of equality and are employed only to the extent necessary to achieve that objective.'[105]

In General Comment No. 13 the Committee again stressed this principle, indicating that,

> '32. The adoption of temporary special measures intended to bring about de facto equality for men and women and for disadvantaged groups is not a violation of the right to non-discrimination with regard to education, so long as such measures do not lead to the maintenance of unequal or separate standards for different groups, and provided they are not continued after the objectives for which they were taken have been achieved.'

Affirmative action measures (those aimed at diminishing or eliminating conditions which cause or help to perpetuate discrimination) must end once the aim has been achieved. They are necessarily of a temporary nature.[106] As clearly stated by the Limburg Principles:

> 'Special measures taken for the sole purpose of securing adequate advancement of certain groups or individuals requiring such protection as may be necessary in order to ensure to such groups or individuals equal enjoyment of economic, social and cultural rights shall not be deemed discrimination, provided, however, that such measures do not, as a consequence, lead to the maintenance of separate rights for different groups and that such measures shall not be continued after their intended objectives have been achieved.'[107]

At present, it seems clear that the Committee interprets the principle of non-discrimination so as to require the adoption of special measures or programmes in order to ensure the equal enjoyment of rights to some vulnerable and disadvantaged groups. When the comprehensive study carried out by Craven was first published in 1995, he commented,

---

104 The equal enjoyment of rights has been considered as a 'basic concern' of the Covenant. Dankwa & Flinterman, 1987, p. 142.

105 General Comment No. 5 para. 18. While the Committee was referring to disability-based discrimination, bearing in mind the approach of the Committee in its Concluding Observations, this principle may be considered to be of general application.

106 General Comment No. 18 para. 10.

107 Limburg Principle No. 39.

> 'Even if the *travaux préparatoires* do recognise the legitimacy of affirmative action, there is little indication outside the scope of article 3 that such positive measures are in fact required. [...] The Committee has directed a number of questions towards affirmative action especially as regards people with physical disabilities and ethnic or racial minorities. In doing so it seems to accept the legitimacy of such action even if there has been a residual concern over its ultimate purpose. Nevertheless, it has not explicitly recognised the obligatory nature of affirmative action. It could be argued that the Committee implicitly recognises such an obligation through its requirement that States concentrate upon the situation of vulnerable and disadvantaged groups in society, but this is nevertheless a matter that ideally should be made clear in a future General Comment.'[108]

However, following the publication of Craven's study, the Committee took important steps which require us to reassess these assertions. Up to June 1994, when Craven's study was completed, the Committee had concluded only four General Comments.[109] However, it was precisely in General Comment No. 5, that the Committee adopted the most relevant statement with regard to affirmative action.[110] In General Comment No. 5 the Committee notes,

> 'The obligation in the case of such a vulnerable and disadvantaged group [persons with disabilities] is to take positive action to reduce structural disadvantages and to give appropriate preferential treatment to people with disabilities in order to achieve the objectives of full participation and equality within society for all persons with disabilities.'[111]

In the same vein, the requirement of affirmative action has been stressed by the Committee in other General Comments adopted after the mentioned study was published.[112] Thus, in General Comment No. 13 the Committee notes that,

> '32. The adoption of temporary special measures intended to bring about de facto equality for men and women and for disadvantaged groups is not a violation of the right to non-discrimination with regard to education, so long as such measures do not lead to the maintenance of unequal or separate standards for different groups, and provided they are not continued after the objectives for which they were taken have been achieved.'

Again, it is possible to conclude that although this statement relates specifically to the right to education, it must be beyond doubt that it is generally applicable. In its Concluding Observations, the Committee has also interpreted the non-discrimination principle as requiring affirmative and protective measures. For example, when consid-

108 Craven, *op. cit.* (note 20), p. 186 (footnotes omitted).
109 Craven, *op. cit.* (note 20), p. 5.
110 General Comment No. 5 was adopted in the Committee's eleventh session on December 9, 1994.
111 General Comment No. 5 para. 9.
112 See, for example, General Comment No. 6 para. 13, General Comment No. 12 para. 13 and General Comment No. 13 paras. 16(e), 26 and 47.

ering the report of Portugal (Macao) the Committee urged 'the Portuguese Administration to take affirmative steps to facilitate the integration of persons of Chinese origin into the placement programme of the civil service.'[113]

The Committee has paid special attention to the necessity for affirmative action for the benefit of women, [114] immigrants,[115] ethnic minorities,[116] refugees and asylum seekers,[117] Roma[118] and indigenous populations.[119] These measures are aimed at redressing imbalances or eliminating conditions which are incompatible with the Covenant and which have developed due to structural inequalities. As mentioned, this type of measure intended to redress imbalances must be ended once the aim has been achieved.

The Committee has also stressed the necessity to take measures to protect certain groups, such as pregnant women,[120] persons with disabilities,[121] and older persons[122] in order to ensure that they enjoy economic, social and cultural rights on an equal footing with other individuals. These groups may suffer a disproportionate impact in the enjoyment of economic, social and cultural rights if the State does not take positive

---

113 Concluding Observations Portugal [Macao] E/1997/22 para. 261.

114 See section 4.3.

115 See, for example, Concluding Observations Sweden E/C.12/1/Add.70 para. 29.

116 See, for example, General Comment No.13 para. 32; Concluding Observations Syrian Arab Republic E/C.12/1/Add.63 paras. 30 and 45; Concluding Observations Ukraine E/C.12/1/Add.65 para. 12; Concluding Observations Nepal E/C.12.1/Add.66 para. 46; Concluding Observations Japan E/C.12/1/Add.67 para. 40; and Concluding Observations Croatia E/C.12/1/Add.73 paras. 10 and 21. Examining the report of France, the Committee expressly stressed the necessity to adopt special measures of protection in favour of minority groups by noting that 'equality before the law is not always adequate to ensure the equal enjoyment of human rights, and in particular economic, social and cultural rights, by certain minority groups in a country.' Concluding Observations France E/C.12/1/Add.72 para. 15.

117 An illustrative example is the case of Italy, where the Committee 'urged' the State 'to extend the subsidised health care system to asylum seekers.' Concluding Observations Italy E/2001/22 para. 138. See in addition, for example, Concluding Observations Syrian Arab Republic E/C.12/1/Add.63 para. 32.

118 See, for example, Concluding Observations Germany E/1999/22 para. 317; Concluding Observations Romania E/1995/22 paras. 94 and 97; Concluding Observations Italy E/2001/22 para. 129; and Concluding Observations Bulgaria E/2000/22 para. 223. It is important to stress that the increased interest that the Committee has expressed with regard to the discrimination against Roma populations is in line with the work of other treaty bodies, such as the CERD Committee. See CERD General Recommendation XXVII on 'Discrimination against Roma'.

119 See for example, Concluding Observations Guatemala E/1997/22 para. 140; Concluding Observations Paraguay E/1997/22 para. 83; Concluding Observations Honduras E/C.12/1/Add.57 paras. 14 and 33; Concluding Observations Bolivia E/C.12/1/Add.60 para. 30; and Concluding Observations Panama E/C.12/1/Add.64 para. 12.

120 See for example, Concluding Observations Switzerland E/1999/22 para. 369 and Concluding Observations Bulgaria E/2000/22 paras. 227 and 242.

121 See, for example, Concluding Observations Portugal [Macao] E/1997/22 para. 254, Concluding Observations Georgia E/2001/22 paras. 86 and 99 and Concluding Observations Ireland E/2000/22 para. 149.

122 See, for example, General Comment No. 6 para. 10 and Concluding Observations Bulgaria E/2000/22 para. 238.

measures to protect them. States are required to design programmes to address their specific circumstances in order to ensure the equal enjoyment of the Covenant's rights. The positive measures for groups in need of protection should be of unlimited duration.

Generally, when positive measures or affirmative action are required, the Committee does not give precise guidance as to what form of measures States should adopt. It seems that the form of the measures taken falls within the discretion allowed to States to choose the means to implement the Covenant.

4 Article 3: Equal rights of men and women

'States parties to the present Covenant undertake to ensure the equal right of men and women to the enjoyment of all economic, social and cultural rights set forth in the present Covenant'

4.1 The necessity to reaffirm article 2(2) on the ground of sex

During the drafting of the Covenant there was debate as to whether or not to include this provision which is common to both Covenants. According to some government representatives, this provision was redundant inasmuch as article 2(2) ICESCR already established the prohibition of discrimination on the ground of sex. As expressed by some delegates, the inclusion of provisions relating to women alone would only weaken the general prohibition of discrimination contained in article 2 of each Covenant and would provoke confusion as to the meaning and application of these provisions. On the other hand, the majority held the opinion that it was important to retain article 3 in each Covenant as it was argued that article 3 did not merely state the principle of equality between the sexes but obligated States to make equality effective in reality. It was said that articles 3 of each Covenant enshrined a principle of elementary justice which was denied even in most developed countries.[123]

Even today the arguments presented in favour of retaining article 3 remain relevant. Although article 2(2) prohibits gender-based discrimination, the additional and more specific requirement that article 3 imposes are hardly superfluous. Despite the fact that there are numerous international legal instruments that emphasise the prohibition of sex discrimination,[124] in general women still do not enjoy human rights as fully as men do.[125]

---

123 See Bossuyt, 1987, pp. 75-78.

124 See, for example, Art. 1(3) UN Charter, Art. 3 ICCPR and CEDAW. In addition, see the commitment to ensure the equal status of women in respect of all human rights in the World Conference on Human Rights held in Vienna in 1993.

125 A good explanation of the necessity to stress the principle of equality between the sexes is provided in the Preamble of CEDAW, adopted in 1981, and Recommendation No. R (85) 2 on legal protection against sex discrimination, adopted by the Committee of Ministers on 5 February 1985, at the 380th meeting of the Ministers' Deputies.

The unequal enjoyment of human rights by both sexes is even greater in the case of economic, social and cultural rights. The economic contribution of women within the family and within society as a whole is not sufficiently recognised. In many parts of the world, socio-cultural stereotypes limit the role of women to the domestic sphere and consider their role as less relevant than other roles in society. In many countries women still do not have access to education or to the means of production, such as land ownership, on an equal basis with men. Additionally, often in the context of special situations of deprivation, women tend to be 'doubly victimised', whether due to the fact that they live in rural, agricultural societies,[126] as members of a particular racial or ethnic group,[127] due to disability[128] or because they are elderly persons.[129]

In sum, the prevalence and severity of sex-based discrimination justifies the special treatment afforded to this illegal ground of discrimination. By establishing a provision specifically against gender discrimination, the Covenant stresses the importance of taking effective measures to combat it. The Committee itself has also paid particular attention to the problem of sex discrimination, considering that the economic, social and cultural rights of women is a 'critical area of concern.'[130] Moreover, the Committee has stressed that 'the Covenant is predicated on the principles of absolute non-discrimination against women and their full enjoyment of all the rights enjoyed by men.'[131]

126 See Art. 14 CEDAW.

127 See CERD General Recommendation XXV on gender-related dimensions of racial discrimination. HRI/GEN/1/Rev.5, pp. 194-195.

128 The Committee expressly addressed the double victimization of disabled women in General Comment No. 5 by stating, 'Persons with disabilities are sometimes treated as genderless human beings. As a result, the double discrimination suffered by women with disabilities is often neglected. Despite frequent calls by the international community for particular emphasis to be placed upon their situation, very few efforts have been undertaken during the Decade. The neglect of women with disabilities is mentioned several times in the report of the Secretary-General on the implementation of the World Programme of Action. The Committee therefore urges States Parties to address the situation of women with disabilities, with high priority being given in future to the implementation of economic, social and cultural rights-related programmes.' General Comment No. 5 para. 19 (footnotes omitted).

129 In General Comment No. 6 the Committee notes that, 'In accordance with article 3 of the Covenant, by which States Parties undertake 'to ensure the equal right of men and women to the enjoyment of all economic, social and cultural rights', the Committee considers that States Parties should pay particular attention to older women who, because they have spent all or part of their lives caring for their families without engaging in a remunerated activity entitling them to an old-age pension, and who are also not entitled to a widow's pension, are often in critical situations.' General Comment No. 6 para. 20. See also Lack, D.: 'Human Rights and the disadvantaged' in *HRLJ,* vol. 10 No. 1-2, (1989), p. 54.

130 Statement of the Committee at the twelfth session, held on May 17, 1995. E/1996/22, Annex VI, para. 9. The Committee also gives particular attention to the topic in the Concluding Observations.

131 Concluding Observations Libyan Arab Jamahiriya E/1998/22 para. 182.

4.2 The Committee's supervision of article 3

In order to assess whether or not a State Party is complying with the equal treatment provision of article 3, when considering States' reports, the Committee has analysed the existence of legislation with the purpose or the effect of discriminating against women. However, the Committee has been particularly concerned with what occurs in practice. The Committee supervises whether women are effectively enjoying economic, social and cultural rights on an equal footing with men.

In order to assess women's enjoyment of economic, social and cultural rights in practice, the Committee analyses indicators such as the gender balance in high- and low-wage groups in the work force, comparative unemployment rates and illiteracy rates.[132] Thus, for example, in the case of Ukraine, the Committee expressed concern regarding the fact that most low-paid workers and 80 per cent of the unemployed were women. The same occurred in the case of Poland where women earned, on average, only 70 per cent of the wages earned by men, despite their generally high level of education. When considering the report of Sweden, the Committee noted with concern that, on average, women earned only 83 percent of men's salaries.[133] Due to the importance for the Committee to analyse what occurs in practice rather than to examine only legislative texts, it has required that States submit information on the enjoyment of rights by women in practice.[134]

It is on the basis of an objective assessment of conditions in the country that the Committee forms its views. This is clear, for example, in the Concluding Observations of the United Kingdom of Great Britain and Northern Ireland, where the Committee noted that 'despite the elaborate machinery and legislation for protection against discrimination, there continues to exist to a significant degree de facto discrimination against women [...]. The Committee notes that women continue to occupy a significantly lower percentage of managerial positions, particularly in the private sector and a disproportionate percentage of lower paid jobs and part-time work.'[135] In the same vein, after considering the report of Japan, the Committee expressed concern that in that country women working in enterprises were employed primarily in clerical services and had no opportunity of promotion to the professional ranks.[136]

---

132 See, for example, Concluding Observations Jamaica E/C.12/1/Add.75 para. 9, Concluding Observations Sudan E/2001/22 para. 315 and Concluding Observations Guinea E/1997/22 para. 208.

133 Concluding Observations Ukraine E/C.12/1/Add.65 para. 10, Concluding Observations Poland E/1999/22 para. 152 and Concluding Observations Sweden E/C.12/1/Add.70 para. 19.

134 This is apparent in the 'Reporting Guidelines.' See, for example, paras. 9(a), 15(c), 17(a), 37(a) and 60(a).

135 Concluding Observations United Kingdom of Great Britain and Northern Ireland E/1998/22 para. 295.

136 Concluding Observations Japan E/C.12/1/Add.67 para. 17.

The Committee has also analysed some forms of 'indirect discrimination' against women. In other words, it has taken into account when the effect of a given law produces a discriminatory effect on them regardless of the intention of the State. For example, when examining the Second Periodic Report of Belgium, the Committee acknowledged that a law regarding cohabitants in the unemployment insurance regime had a disproportionate impact on women (the majority of persons in the cohabitant category falling under that law were women). Although the government expressly indicated that the regulation had not been drawn up with this intention,[137] it was important for the Committee to analyse the effects rather than the purpose of the law. Consequently, it urged the State to review the law 'in order to eliminate its indirect discriminatory impact on women.'[138] The Committee's approach in this case is consistent with the prohibition of indirect discrimination against women which has been adopted by other international bodies.[139]

4.3 Obligations deriving from article 3

States Parties have limited discretion with regard to the implementation of article 3 ICESCR. All the obligations imposed by the principle of non-discrimination contained in article 2(2) are also applicable when the discrimination is on the basis of sex. However, due to the importance that the Committee has attributed to the principle of equality between the sexes, it has further developed many of the obligations specifically in relation to article 3 ICESCR.

In the following analysis, some of the obligations derived from the principle of non-discrimination will be addressed taking into account the specific aspects developed by the Committee in relation to sex discrimination.

(a) *The obligation to adopt legislation to prohibit all forms of gender-based discrimination*

The Committee has stressed that legislative provisions are sometimes indispensable in order to protect the rights of women against violations by third parties. The Committee has placed particular emphasis on the necessity to take legislative measures to protect women against discrimination in the workplace and to ensure the enjoyment, without discrimination, of the right to work (article 6) and just and favourable conditions of work, including equal pay for work of equal value (article 7). In this regard, the Committee has stressed the necessity to adopt legislation to protect women against discrimination in access to employment, in their promotion at work, to ensure the

137 Mr. Vandamme (Belgium) in E/C.12/2000/SR.65 para. 8.

138 Concluding Observations Belgium E/2001/22 para. 484.

139 See, for example, the approach of the European Court of Justice with regard to indirect sex discrimination in: Bilka-Kaufhaus GmbH v. Karin Weber Von Hartz, case No. 170/84, 13 May 1986 and Rinner-Kühn v. FWW Spezial-Gebäudereinigung GmbH, case No. 171/88, 13 July 1989.

provision of maternal benefits[140] and to discourage the discriminatory dismissal of pregnant women.[141] The Committee has also stressed the obligation to penalise sexual harassment in the workplace,[142] as well as domestic violence.[143] In addition to the requirement of adopting legislative measures to address such problems, the Committee has also suggested that article 3 requires States Parties to incorporate a gender equality perspective in the existing legislation.[144]

(b) *The obligation to repeal legislative provisions with a discriminatory effect on the equal rights of men and women*

When the Committee has identified the existence of legislative provisions which impose restrictions on the enjoyment of economic, social and cultural rights by women, it has required that they be repealed or amended. It has paid particular attention to restrictions on the acquisition and transmission of nationality, in the field of inheritance, limitations of women's access to means of production (such as limitations on acquiring and securing land, property and housing or laws denying credit and bankruptcy) and differences in the marriage regime (*i.e.* more severe punishment of women for adultery, difference in divorce law, unilateral repudiation by the husband).[145]

When examining the report of Cameroon, for example, the Committee stated that it was 'deeply concerned that the Government of Cameroon has not yet embarked on the necessary law reform to repeal laws which maintain the unequal legal status of women, particularly in aspects of the Civil Code and the Commercial Code relating to, *inter alia*, the right to own property and the laws regarding credit and bankruptcy, which restrict women's access to the means of production. They are in *flagrant violation* of the non-discrimination and equal treatment provisions of the Covenant

140 For example, Concluding Observations Switzerland E/1999/22 para. 369, Concluding Observations Suriname E/1996/22 paras. 158 and 164 and Concluding Observations Bulgaria E/2000/22 paras. 227 and 242.

141 See, for example, Concluding Observations Senegal E/C.12.1/Add.62 para. 40; Concluding Observations Mongolia E/2001/22 para. 281; Concluding Observations Mexico E/2000/22 para. 399; and Concluding Observations Bulgaria E/200/22 paras. 227 and 242.

142 See for example, Concluding Observations Mongolia E/2001/22 para. 281. Concluding Observations Dominican Republic E/1998/22 para. 231 and Concluding Observations Poland E/1999/22 para. 159.

143 See the analysis in section 4.4.

144 See, for example, Concluding Observations Syrian Arab Republic E/C.12/1/Add.63 para. 31 and Concluding Observations Japan E/C.12/1/Add.67 para. 42.

145 See, for example, Concluding Observations Morocco E/2001/22 para. 551; Concluding Observations Poland E/1999/22 para. 160; Concluding Observations Senegal E/C.12/1/Add.62 paras. 15 and 38; Concluding Observations Syrian Arab Republic E/C.12/1/Add.63 para. 14; Concluding Observations Nepal E/C.12.1/Add.66 para. 17; Concluding Observations Egypt E/2001/22 para. 175; Concluding Observations Republic of Congo E/2001/22 para. 202; Concluding Observations Jordan E/2001/22 para. 234; Concluding Observations Sudan E/2001/22 para. 321; Concluding Observations Surinam E/1996/22 para. 164; and Concluding Observations Iraq E/1998/22 para. 274.

[…]'.[146] In the case of Morocco, the Committee 'urges' the State 'to amend existing legislation that institutionalises discrimination against women, such as provisions of family, inheritance and personal status law, with a view to strengthening the legal status of women.'[147]

It is important to stress here that the existence of legislative measures imposing restrictions upon women with regard to, for example, the right to inheritance, the right to own property and in access to credit, directly affects the enjoyment of some economic, social and cultural rights by women. As the Committee explained in relation to the implementation of the right to adequate food at the national level:

> 'The strategy should give particular attention to the need to prevent discrimination in access to food or resources for food. This should include: guarantees of full and equal access to economic resources, particularly for women, including the right to inheritance and the ownership of land and other property, credit, natural resources and appropriate technology; measures to respect and protect self-employment and work which provides a remuneration ensuring a decent living for wage earners and their families (as stipulated in article 7(a)(ii) of the Covenant); maintaining registries on rights in land (including forests).'[148]

The UN Commission and Sub-Commission have also tackled this issue. They have adopted several resolutions urging governments to amend and repeal laws and policies pertaining to land, property and housing 'which deny women security of tenure and equal access and rights to land, property and housing.'[149]

(c) *The obligation to take steps for the eradication of any custom or traditional practices that constitute de facto discrimination against women including the penalisation of some behaviours*

In many countries there are social practices such as polygamy, arranged marriages, forced marriages of widows with a late husband's brother and female genital mutilation that perpetuate an unequal treatment of women.[150] According to the Committee, such practices are not compatible with article 3 of the Covenant. For example, after considering the report of Zimbabwe, the Committee noted that 'despite the Government's stated policy of *de jure* equality of men and women, the Committee views the situation of women in Zimbabwean society, particularly in rural districts, as very unsatisfactory. It is concerned about de facto discrimination against women, attributable to traditional

146 Concluding Observations Cameroon E/2000/22 para. 326. (Emphasis added).

147 Concluding Observations Morocco E/C.12/1/Add.55 para. 40.

148 General Comment No. 12 para. 26.

149 See for example, Sub-Commission Res. 1998/15 [in: E/CN.4/Sub.2/res/1998/15] and Commission on Human Rights Res. 2000/13 [in: E/CN.4/res/2000/13]. Also Commission on the Status of Women, Res. 42/1 of March 13, 1998.

150 The problem of female genital mutilation is addressed below in this Chapter under the topic of 'domestic violence' in section 4.4.

practices such as arranged marriages of children and forced marriages of widows with a late husband's brother. *Such practices are incompatible with article 3 of the Covenant.*'[151]

In order to combat traditional practices that violate the economic, social and cultural rights of women, the Committee has required States to take all appropriate measures to combat such practices and beliefs. The Committee has suggested that the penalisation of practices that adversely affect the economic, social and cultural rights of women are sometimes indispensable. The Committee has also stressed the necessity of undertaking promotional campaigns and programmes and to introduce specific policies to improve women's access to education.[152]

4.4 Obligation to combat domestic violence

Over the years, the Committee has paid increased attention to the problem of domestic violence against women. Domestic violence is a form of discrimination and due to its importance in the work of the Committee, it will be analysed separately. The phenomenon of violence against women may be analysed under the prohibition of discrimination in general or specifically under the obligation to ensure equal treatment for men and women.

As indicated in the UN Declaration on the Elimination of Violence against Women, 'violence against women is a manifestation of historically unequal power relations between men and women, which have led to domination over and discrimination against women by men and to the prevention of the full advancement of women.'[153] Along the same lines, the Committee on the Elimination of Discrimination against Women has noted that, 'gender-based violence is a form of discrimination that seriously inhibits women's ability to enjoy rights and freedoms on a basis of equality with men.'[154]

As has been indicated, 'domestic violence' includes:

---

151 Concluding Observations Zimbabwe E/1998/22 para. 73. (Emphasis added).

152 See, for example, Concluding Observations Zimbabwe E/1998/22 para. 80; Concluding Observations Cameroon E/2000/22 para. 347; Concluding Observations Mongolia E/2001/22 para. 281; Concluding Observations Surinam E/1996/22 para. 164; Concluding Observations Iraq E/1998/22 para. 274; and Concluding Observations Switzerland E/1999/22 para. 369. See, in addition, CEDAW General Recommendation No. 3 on education and public information campaigns [UN doc. A/42/38].

153 The UN Declarations on the Elimination of Violence against Women, General Assembly Res. 48/104 contained in UN doc. A/48/49 of December 1993.

154 CEDAW General Recommendation No. 19 para.1 [UN doc. A/47/38 30/01/92]. It is worth noting that on the basis of the CEDAW Protocol, the CEDAW Committee may take action to protect individual victims of domestic violence.

> 'Violence against women and girls by an intimate partner, including a cohabiting partner, and by other family members, whether this violence occurs within or beyond the confines of homes.[…] The term 'domestic' here refers to the types of relationships involved rather than the place where the violent act occurs.'[155]

According to the UNICEF study on 'Domestic violence against women and girls', violence against women defined in this manner includes physical abuse, sexual abuse and rape in an intimate relationship, psychological and emotional abuse, femicide,[156] sexual abuse of girl children and adolescents, forced prostitution, sex-selective abortions, female infanticide and differential access to food and medical care and traditional and cultural practices affecting the health and lives of women.[157] This inclusive approach fits with the manner in which the Committee has dealt with the problem of domestic violence. The Committee has accorded considerable importance to the phenomenon of violence against women and it supervises the occurrence within States Parties of all of the phenomena mentioned above. This has been especially true in recent years and the Committee has analysed the topic at length when examining States' reports.

The Committee has sometimes considered violence against women in conjunction with violence against children and some State reports have addressed the topic of violence against women and children together.[158] This approach may be justified on practical as well as more juridical grounds. In practical terms, violence against women may have an impact on children (especially within the family environment), and at the very least it would constitute psychological violence against children. From a juridical point of view, both cases refer to violence in the private sphere and the State is responsible where it has not taken the necessary actions to protect those at risk. Furthermore, from the point of view of the ICESCR, when the Committee deals with both kinds of violence together, the underlying rationale is the obligation of States to protect women and children, as required by article 10 (protection of the family, mothers and children) and article 12 (the right to enjoy the highest standards of health). Due to the fact that it may be difficult to argue that domestic violence against children is a form of

155 Kapoor Sushma: 'Domestic violence against women and girls', UNICEF Innocenti Research Centre, Digest No. 6, Florence, June 2000, p. 2. Available at: http://www.unicef-icdc.org/publications/index.html (last visited July 2002).

156 This term is understood as the murder of women by their batterers. 'Domestic violence against women and girls', *Ibidem*: p. 6.

157 'Domestic violence against women and girls', *Ibidem*: pp. 4-7.

158 See, for example, Concluding Observations Iraq E/1998/22 para. 238, Fourth Periodic Report of Germany E/C.12/4/Add.3 paras. 143 *et seq.* (of August 10, 2000) and Third Periodic Report of Canada E/1994/104/Add.17 paras. 235 *et seq.* (of 20 January1998).

discrimination,[159] the following approach will focus on domestic violence against women and female children.

The phenomenon of domestic violence clearly shows the interdependency of all economic, social and cultural rights. When there is no State response to the phenomenon of domestic violence, there would be a violation of article 2(2) (prohibition of discrimination on the ground of sex) and article 3 (equal treatment for men and women) together with a violation of article 12 (right to enjoy the highest standard of health) and it may also indicate a simultaneous violation of another substantive right such as article 10 (protection of the family, mothers and children and young persons).

As the Committee noted in the Concluding Observations on Cyprus, '[t]he Committee expresses its serious concern at the incidence of domestic violence against women and children in Cypriot society. The continuation of this situation calls into question whether the State Party has made its best efforts to comply with its obligation under articles 10 and 12 of the Covenant. In particular the Government appears to have failed to adopt an adequate prevention policy, to enforce fully the existing legislative measures to combat violence in the family and to assist victims of such violence.'[160] The problem of domestic violence may also be closely related with the enjoyment of other rights such as, for example, the right to adequate housing (article 11 ICESCR). When examining the report of Canada, the Committee noted that 'the significant reduction in provincial social assistance programmes, the availability of affordable and appropriate housing and widespread discrimination with respect to housing create obstacles to women escaping domestic violence.'[161]

Through the Concluding Observations it is possible to conclude that according to the Committee, States must prevent and protect women against discrimination in the form of domestic violence through specific measures. This has become clear in the most recent Concluding Observations such as that issued following the examination of the report of Mongolia, which noted,

> 'The Committee calls on the State party to enforce efficiently in practice labour legislation prohibiting discrimination against women in employment, such as prohibition of the dismissal of pregnant women and the criminalization of sexual harassment. The Committee urges the State party to organize public campaigns to raise awareness about domestic violence, to criminalize spousal rape and to provide victims with shelters and adequate remedies.'[162]

---

159 For example, the European Court of Human Rights has found that violence against children in the domestic sphere (violence by the stepfather against a child), amounted to inhuman or degrading treatment (violation article 3 ECHR), due to the failure of the Government to provide adequate protection for the child. Case of A v. United Kingdom, Application No. 255599/94, Judgement of 23 September 1998.

160 Concluding Observations Cyprus E/1999/22 para. 287.

161 Concluding Observations Canada E/1999/22 para. 403.

162 Concluding Observations Mongolia E/2001/22 para. 281.

From the work of the Committee the following specified measures seem to be compulsory for States Parties in order to prevent and combat domestic violence:

(1) The duty to pay due attention to the phenomenon of domestic violence, undertaking in-depth studies and analysis particularly aimed at examining the situation within society and to devise targeted strategies to best protect and ensure the economic, social and cultural rights of the population affected by domestic violence.[163]

The Committee has indicated that in order to comply with this obligation it is important that States collect statistical data and other relevant information. The lack of this information prevents both the Committee and the Government itself from assessing the real extent of the problems and thus hinders efforts to address them efficiently.[164]

(2) To adopt an appropriate preventive policy that includes the necessary legal measures, particularly penalising the practice of domestic violence including marital rape.[165] The State is also required to undertake educational programmes to combat such practices.[166]

(3) The Committee suggests that in cases of domestic violence it is necessary for the State to provide for judicial remedies and to establish mechanisms to provide support and assistance to victims.

In General Comment No. 9 the Committee notes that:

> 'There are some obligations, such as (but by no means limited to) those concerning non-discrimination, in relation to which the provision of some form of judicial remedy would seem indispensable in order to satisfy the requirements of the Covenant.'[167]

---

163 The Committee has expressed serious concern regarding the continuing problem of violence against women and the insufficient attention paid by Governmental institutions. See, for example, Concluding Observations Ukraine E/1996/22 para. 263; Concluding Observations Mauritius E/1996/22 para. 245; Concluding Observations Dominican Republic E/1997/22 para. 231; Concluding Observations Uruguay E/1998/22 para. 372; and Concluding Observations Sweden E/1996/22 para. 146.

164 See, for example, Concluding Observations Azerbaijan E/1998/22 para. 335; Concluding Observations Sweden E/1996/22 para. 146; Concluding Observations Mauritius E/1996/22 para. 240; and Concluding Observations Switzerland E/1999/22 para. 357.

165 See, for example, Concluding Observations Mongolia E/2001/22 para. 281; Concluding Observations Uruguay E/1998/22 para. 272; Concluding Observations Surinam E/1996/22 para. 164; and Concluding Observations Cameroon E/2000/22 para. 346.

166 See, for example, Concluding Observations Dominican Republic E/1998/22 paras. 231 and 274, Concluding Observations Colombia E/1996/22 para. 196 and Concluding Observations Mongolia E/2001/22 para. 281.

167 General Comment No. 9 para. 9.

The Committee has not systematically established when judicial remedies are indispensable, and it is not absolutely clear when they are required to satisfy the principle of non-discrimination. The exception is with regard to domestic violence. When dealing with this type of discrimination, the Committee has suggested that the existence of judicial remedies for women are indispensable. According to the Committee, specific programmes should be put in place in order to receive complaints, to investigate instances of abuse and to bring the perpetrators to justice. Moreover, according to the Committee, States are required to provide assistance to women who are victims of such violence.[168]

5 Article 2(3): Non-nationals in developing countries

> *'Developing countries, with due regard to human rights and their national economy may determine to what extent they would guarantee the economic rights recognised in the present Covenant to non-nationals.'*

As a general rule, all economic, social and cultural rights embodied in the Covenant apply equally to everyone under the jurisdiction of the State Party[169] and the prohibition of discrimination contained in article 2(2) also protects non-nationals. Thus, article 2(3) ICESCR appears to be the only exception to the principle of non-discrimination.[170] However, this provision is very limited in scope and its correct interpretation requires a consideration of its drafting history. The provision was designed to deal with a very specific problem and it has clear limitations.

According to the *travaux préparatoires,* the inclusion of this provision was proposed by the delegate of Indonesia in order to protect the rights of the nationals of former colonies which had recently gained independence at the time of drafting in which there were powerful economic groups of non-nationals in control of important sectors of the economy. Thus, the aim of the provision was to entitle 'developing countries' to limit the extent to which they were obliged to allow elite groups of non-nationals to enjoy economic rights as a method by which to gain or maintain control over their weak economies. As stressed by the Limburg Principles, the term 'developing countries' in this provision means 'those countries which have gained indepen-

168 For example, Concluding Observations Jordan E/2001/22 para. 250; Concluding Observations Mongolia E/2001/22 para. 281; Concluding Observations Poland E/1999/22 para. 159; Concluding Observations Zimbabwe E/1998/22 para. 80; Concluding Observations Russian Federation E/1998/22 para. 118; Concluding Observations Dominican Republic E/1998/22 para. 274; and Concluding Observations Iraq E/1998/22 para. 274. See also CEDAW General Recommendation No. 12 para. 3. UN doc. A/44/38.

169 See the analysis of the territorial application of the Covenant in Chapter VI section 2.2.

170 For a comprehensive review of article 2(3) see Dankwa, E.V.O.: 'Working paper on article 2(3) of the International Covenant on Economic, Social and Cultural rights.' In: *HRQ*, vol. 9 (1987), pp. 230-249. In the present study the focus is placed on the Committee's approach to the provision.

dence and which fall within the appropriate United Nations classifications of developing countries.'[171]

The provision only entitles such countries to determine 'to what extent they would guarantee economic rights' to non-nationals. Thus, States may not limit *all* rights, but merely 'economic rights.' The Covenant does not define which are the 'economic rights' and it is not very clear to which rights the term refers. As one commentator notes,

> 'The right to work in Article 6 is the clearest example of such a right [economic right], although it can also be considered a social right. 'Just and favourable conditions of work' as specified under article 7 also seems to be an economic right. Similarly, 'improved material conditions' for teaching staff in Article 13(2)(e) may be classified under economic rights. Because the rights to form and join a trade union and to strike (Article 8(a) and (b) respectively) are closely connected with employment, they may be considered economic rights, but they also may be classified as political rights. It appears that economic rights, in the context of the Covenant, are rights that enable a person to earn a living or that relate to that process.'[172]

The Committee has not dealt with this provision in its Concluding Observations nor in its General Comments. In accordance with the general principle of human rights law that exceptions must be interpreted narrowly and in the light of the object and purpose of the Covenant, the exception in article 2(3) should be interpreted narrowly.[173] In general, it is easy to agree with Craven when he points out that this provision is not currently relevant because no developing State has sought to invoke it.[174]

6 An integrated approach to non-discrimination

Although a thorough analysis of the so-called 'integrated approach' is beyond the scope of the present study,[175] it is important to mention, however briefly, that although the discrimination clause in the Covenant is not subject to an international complaints procedure, at the international level discrimination in the enjoyment of the rights laid down in the Covenant may be challenged under article 26 of the ICCPR. Article 26 ICESCR is of a free standing nature and its application is not confined to the rights contained in the ICCPR.

---

171 Limburg Principle No. 44.

172 Dankwa, *loc. cit.* (note 170), p. 240. (Footnote omitted).

173 Limburg Principle No. 42.

174 See Craven, 1997, p. 108. Moreover, some developing countries freely exclude this option. For example, the AfCHR awarded the right to work (essentially an economic right that developing States are excused from granting to non-nationals) to everyone without limitation to nationals (Art.15 AfCHR).

175 See Chapter II section 2.2.

According to the Human Rights Committee's General Comment No. 18,

> 'Article 26 provides that all persons are equal before the law and are entitled to equal protection of the law without discrimination, and that the law shall guarantee to all persons equal and effective protections against discrimination on any of the enumerated grounds.'[176]

The grounds enumerated in article 26 are not exhaustive. In fact, the wording used is the following: 'such as, race, colour, sex, language, religion, political or other opinion, national or social origin, property, birth or other status'. The use of the words 'such as' indicates that it is not intended to be a complete list while the phrase 'or other status' makes it clear that it is illustrative. The importance of article 26 ICCPR arises when there is a legislative provision or a State action or omission with a discriminatory impact on the enjoyment of the economic, social and cultural rights. As the HRC has noted,

> 'When legislation is adopted by a State party, it must comply with the requirement of article 26 that its content should not be discriminatory. In other words, the application of the principle of non-discrimination contained in article 26 is not limited to those rights which are provided for in the Covenant.'[177]

Certainly, the HRC has applied article 26 in relation to the enjoyment of economic, social and cultural rights in many cases.[178] Among these cases it is important to highlight the landmark case of Zwam de Vries v. the Netherlands. In this case the State concerned argued that article 26 overlaps with the provision of article 2(2) of the ICESCR. Therefore, its argument stated that if article 2(2) (non-discrimination clause) and article 9 (right to social security) of the ICESCR were not justiciable within that Covenant (in the sense that they were not subject to the same kind of petition procedure as available under the ICCPR), then they should not be rendered justiciable by means of an interpretation which imports them into article 26 of the ICCPR. By refusing to accept this argument, the HRC implicitly rejected the notion that what is protected within the ICESCR cannot be protected by the ICCPR. On the contrary, the Committee held that 'the provisions of article 2 of the ICESCR do not detract from the full application of article 26 of the ICCPR.'[179]

---

176 See HRC General Comment No. 18 para. 12.

177 See HRC General Comment No. 18 para. 12.

178 See, for example recent cases such as, Dietmar Pauger v. Austria, Communication No. 716/1996, views of 25 March 1999 and Johannes Vos v. the Netherlands, Communication No. 786/1997, views of 29 August 1999. Other relevant jurisprudence: Hendrika S. Vos v. the Netherlands, Communication No. 218/1986, views of 29 March 1989; Broeks v. the Netherlands, Communication No. 172/1984, views of 9 April 1987; Danning v. the Netherlands, Communication No. 180/1984, views of 9 April 1987; and Ibrahima Gueye *et al.* v. France, Communication No. 196/1985, views of 3 April 1989.

179 Zwaam de Vries v. the Netherlands, Communication No. 182/1984, views of 9 April 1987, para. 12.1.

Therefore, legislative measures envisaging any unreasonable distinction between individuals under the jurisdiction of a State Party in the enjoyment of the economic, social and cultural rights set forth in the Covenant constitute a violation of article 26 ICCPR and if a State has ratified the First Optional Protocol to the ICCOPR, a victim of discrimination has a right to submit a complaint to the HRC. The important aspects of the application of article 26 ICCPR should be noted here.

First, according to article 26 ICCPR, States Parties are obliged to establish judicial remedies in the case of discrimination occurring in the public and even in the private sphere. As the HRC has noted,

> 'The Committee observes that under articles 2 and 26 of the Covenant the State party is under an obligation to ensure that all individuals within its territory and subject to its jurisdiction are free from discrimination, and consequently the courts of States Parties are under an obligation to protect individuals against discrimination, whether this occurs within the public sphere or among private parties in the quasi-public sector of, for example, employment [...].'[180]

The application of article 26 has served to protect individuals from discrimination in the enjoyment of a variety of economic, social and cultural rights. Of the numerous examples, we may recall here Arieh Hollis Waldman v. Canada, in which the HRC stated that 'the Covenant does not oblige States Parties to fund schools which are established on a religious basis. However, if a State party chooses to provide public funding to religious schools, it should make this funding available without discrimination'.[181] In Garcia Pons v. Spain, it was stated that 'although the right to social security is not protected, as such, in the International Covenant on Civil and Political Rights, issues under the Covenant may nonetheless arise if the principle of equality contained in articles 14 and 26 of the Covenant is violated.'[182][183]

Finally, it is also important to note that in the application of the principle of non-discrimination in article 2(2) and article 3, States must respect their other international obligations. For States Parties to the ICESCR which are also party to the CEDAW,[184] many obligations with regard to socio-economic issues acquire greater precision. Such is the case, for example, with State obligations in fields such as education (article 10

180 Franz Nahlik v. Austria, Communication No. 608/1995, views of 22 July 1996, para. 8.2.

181 Arieh Hollis Waldman v. Canada, Communication No. 694/1996, views of 5 November 1996, para. 10.6.

182 García Pons v. Spain, Communication No. 454/1991, views of 30 October 1995, para. 9.3.

183 For a comprehensive analysis on how and to what extent the right to social security has become justiciable through the prohibition of discrimination, see: Krause, C. and Scheinin, M.: 'The right not to be discriminated against: the case of social security.' In: *The jurisprudence of human rights law: a comparative perspective*. Orlin, T.S., Rosas, A. and Scheinin, M. (eds.), Institute for Human Rights, Åbo Akademi University, Åbo, Finland, (2000), pp. 253-286.

184 Adopted on December 18, 1979 and which entered into force on September 3, 1981.

CEDAW), employment (article 11 CEDAW), in the field of health care (article 12 CEDAW), areas of economic and social life (article 13 CEDAW) and in matters relating to marriage and family relations (article 16 CEDAW).

7 Concluding Comments

From the analysis of the Committee's work, particularly General Comment No. 5 (on persons with disabilities), Nos. 11 and 13 (on the right to education) and No. 14 (on the right to the highest attainable standard of health), as well as the Concluding Observations, it is clear that the Committee applies the general international principle of equality and non-discrimination. Specifically, the Committee permits restrictions based on objective and reasonable criteria and with a legitimate aim under the Covenant. It has also noted that temporary special measures intended to bring about equality for vulnerable and disadvantaged groups do not constitute violations of the right to non-discrimination 'so long as such measures do not lead to the maintenance of unequal or separate standards for different groups and provided they are not continued after the objectives for which they were taken have been achieved.'[185]

The Committee has stressed the obligation of States Parties to protect individuals against discrimination committed by private individuals and has even required the criminalisation of some form of behaviour to discourage individuals from discriminating in the enjoyment of economic, social and cultural rights. It has also monitored the existence of 'indirect' discrimination because, according to the Committee, the intention of the State is of little importance as discrimination exists when a distinction, exclusion or preference has the 'purpose or the effect' of nullifying or impairing enjoyment of the Covenant's rights. The Committee not only supervises the existence of discriminatory legislation or practices but also examines situations of *de facto* discrimination. In such cases, the Committee requires States to take immediate steps to redress the imbalance. As a result of the Committee's work, it is clear that the grounds enumerated in article 2(2) ICESCR are not exhaustive. The Committee supervises differential treatment on grounds not enumerated in article 2(2) and it has expressly referred to a number of other suspected grounds, such as age, disability, health conditions and nationality.

Although it is clear that the Committee applies the general principle of equality and non-discrimination, it is indispensable that it addresses article 2(2) and article 3 ICESCR in a General Comment. While there are indications that over the years the Committee has considered the importance of adopting a specific General Comment

185 General Comment No. 13 para. 32.

referring to the principle of equality and non-discrimination and that some research has been done in this area, the Committee has yet to take any action.[186]

The quality of the Concluding Observations is uneven with regard to non-discrimination. While some are clear and in accordance with the general international rules on non-discrimination, in others there is a lack of consistency and the international rules are not rigorously applied. A clear interpretation of the principle of equality and non-discrimination in a General Comment would serve as a guideline that would permit both greater consistency and quality in the Concluding Observations and it would undoubtedly strengthen the application of the Covenant.

The prohibition of discrimination is a cross cutting issue of concern to different UN human rights instruments, such as CERD, ICCPR, CEDAW and CRC and the prohibition of discrimination has also been addressed by the Sub-Commission on the Promotion and Protection of Human Rights in its standard setting instruments. The Committee is in an advantageous position which enables it to act as catalyst for the different approaches (such as women, children and minorities and migrants) As most forms of discrimination particularly affect the enjoyment of economic, social and cultural rights, the Committee should assume its responsibility to analyse the non-discrimination provision, taking into account the work of other UN bodies.

186 It is striking that General Comment No. 3 on article 2(1) adopted in 1990 expressly notes that a separate General Comment on non-discrimination was to be considered in the Committee's sixth session [General Comment No. 3 para. 1].

CHAPTER IX
SUMMARY AND CONCLUDING OBSERVATIONS

1 SUMMARY

During recent decades, levels of global wealth have grown at an impressive rate but at the same time inequalities in wealth distribution and the gap between the rich and the poor have also increased significantly. While some people take the enjoyment of comforts made available by technological advances for granted and consume goods and services at a rate unimaginable even just a few decades ago, for the majority of humanity all this seems unattainable and many persons die of hunger or curable diseases, do not have shelter, access to education or basic sanitation facilities. Undoubtedly this raises questions on the moral plane, but it is also a juridical problem. This study has attempted to show that at least the 145 States Parties to the International Covenant on Economic, Social and Cultural Rights [ICESCR] bear significant obligations with regard to the fulfilment of these rights.

The study has emphasised the dynamic character of international law and the evolution of rights. As is generally recognised, human rights are not static but, rather, they evolve over time in order to adapt to new circumstances and to strengthen the protection of individuals. This is also true of economic, social and cultural rights. In the decades since the Covenant entered into force, the mechanisms for the protection of economic, social and cultural rights have significantly increased in number and improved their methods of work and additional duties have been imposed upon States under economic, social and cultural rights treaties.

It is indisputable that the ICESCR has benefited from this evolution. The increased attention to economic, social and cultural rights has significantly benefited the protection afforded by the Covenant. As a result, the normative content of the Covenant is now not only more precise, but the scope of the obligations imposed has also been expanded, providing broader protection to individuals and limiting the discretion of States Parties.

Over the years a wide range of international and national actors involved in the implementation of the Covenant have contributed to the development of a clearer understanding of many of the obligations it imposes. The Committee on Economic, Social and Cultural Rights has played a pre-eminent role in this process and acted as a catalyst.

Chapter I of the study has examined the Committee's origins and its working methods, emphasising that the Committee has used its working methods to further develop the normative content of the Covenant. The Committee has used the General Comments and Concluding Observations in a creative and innovative manner to provide further guidance as to the normative content of the Covenant.

Chapter II demonstrated that the Committee does not interpret the Covenant in a vacuum. It provided a broad picture of the developments in the field of economic, social and cultural rights and showed how these developments have contributed to the process of clarifying the normative content of the obligations imposed by the Covenant. The Chapter provides examples on how the Committee has interpreted the Covenant in light of the developments achieved in the field of economic, social and cultural rights as well as international human rights law in general.

Chapter III set out the rules of interpretation of international human rights norms, emphasising that the specific object and purpose of human rights treaties (the protection of the human person), requires that they be interpreted in a manner which makes the rights effective in the light of prevailing circumstances. This Chapter also included an analysis of the 'legitimacy' of the Committee's interpretation of the Covenant. 'Legitimacy' is understood as a bundle of factors that bring pressure upon States to comply with the Committee's interpretation. The study identifies eight factors or indicators of legitimacy: (a) the independence and expertise of Committee members; (b) diversity of membership; (c) continuity and coherence; (d) predictability; (e) efficiency; (f) objectivity; (g) reasonableness and practicability; and (h) support by other international bodies. On the basis of an examination of each of these factors, the study concludes that the Committee enjoys an acceptable degree of legitimacy, although it still needs to improve its status in several respects.

The analysis provided in Chapters I, II and II revealed that over the years the Committee has developed an increasing confidence in its work. It has adopted stricter Concluding Observations and more sophisticated and precise General Comments. In doing so it has deterred non-compliance and deepened the understanding of the obligations imposed by the Covenant. In line with the general principles of treaty interpretation, when interpreting the Covenant the Committee has attempted to make its provisions fully effective in the light of prevailing circumstances. In this manner the Committee has extended the protection afforded by the Covenant while at the same time enhancing its effectiveness.

Part Two of the study, which includes Chapters IV and V, analysed the nature of the obligations imposed by the Covenant. As a preliminary analysis, Chapter IV examined the alleged difference in nature between civil and political rights on the one hand and economic, social and cultural rights on the other on the basis of the arguments advanced by those who were in favour of the adoption of two separate instruments, one for each category of human rights.

The analysis was intended to demonstrate that the manner in which the jurisprudence under the two Covenants has evolved now renders untenable the arguments which were advanced during the time of the drafting. At this stage the study concluded that all human rights impose a variety of obligations which may be different in nature. Hence, the difference 'in nature' exists between obligations rather than between rights. To illustrate the argument, the study upheld the idea that all human rights impose a '*continuum of a variety of duties*' or a '*spectrum of a variety of duties*.' At one end of the spectrum there are obligations of non-interference by States and towards the other end we find obligations requiring positive action on the part of States.

A specific duty may be located anywhere along the spectrum, regardless of the category from which it springs (civil and political or economic, social and cultural rights). The degree of State involvement, the degree of precision in delineation of the obligations as well as the resources necessary to comply with a duty do not depend on the Covenant from which the correlative right emerges but, rather, on the specific type of duty in question. In order to be effective at a given time and in a given situation a single right may impose a series of duties. The duties tend to be different in nature.

The study demonstrated this point by examining the jurisprudence on the right to life of the major international human rights supervisory bodies: the European Court of Human Rights, the Inter-American Court of Human Rights and the Human Rights Committee. Although the right to life is traditionally considered to impose only negative obligations, over the years this right has been interpreted as requiring States to comply with a broad range of obligations. Each of these obligations is of a different nature and may require negative State behaviours as well as positive behaviours. Such positive obligations allow States a broad margin of discretion, they require the expenditure of considerable resources, and are less precise than the mere prohibition of arbitrarily depriving someone of the right to life. They are not only implicit in the text, but also vaguely formulated by supervisory bodies. Nevertheless, they can be, and indeed are, subject to scrutiny by judicial and quasi-judicial organs. The existence of positive obligations is apparent not only in relation to the right to life, but also in other civil and political rights, such as the prohibition of torture and other forms of ill-treatment, the right to privacy and the right of peaceful assembly. It is now clearly established that purely negative duties would not provide effective protection for the individual and therefore interpretations that posit only negative duties would not be compatible with the object and purpose of a human rights treaty.

The study concluded at this point that the content of the obligations, that is, the form that they take and the way in which they impose their requirements upon States, are similar with regard to both categories of human rights. This is not to say that they are identical, however. If we analyse the rights as imposing a spectrum of obligations with the most negative obligation at the one end and the most positive at the other, it would be fair to say that, in general, civil and political rights tend to be interpreted as requiring less intervention by States (obligations closer to the negative component), and that economic, social and cultural rights tend to be interpreted as imposing obligations closer to the positive component of the spectrum. Nevertheless, such differences are not due to the 'nature' of the rights. They merely demonstrate a tendency which has been remarkably influenced by the international mechanisms for implementation and, in particular, the absence of an individual complaints procedure to further develop the normative content of economic, social and cultural rights.

Moreover, the fact that these positive obligations are subject to judicial scrutiny renders the arguments against the justiciability of economic, social and cultural rights untenable.

Important contributions to the understanding of the nature of the obligations imposed by the Covenant have been made by academic writers through the development of typologies of States duties. The typologies are analytical tools to examine the obligations imposed by each right and classify these obligations in different types or levels. The typologies were examined in Chapter V of the study.

Chapter V first examined the development of the typology in academic writing, comparing the advantages and shortcomings of each of the proposals. It then proceeded to examine the Committee's application of the so-called 'tripartite typology.' Under this typology all human rights are viewed as imposing three levels of State obligations: obligations to respect, protect and fulfil. Finally, on the basis of the Committee's approach to the 'tripartite typology' in its General Comments, the study provided concrete examples of the duties imposed by each level of State obligations in the light of the Committee's Concluding Observations.

Part Three of the study focused on the obligations imposed by the provisions contained in Part II of the Covenant. Part II of the Covenant is composed of four articles: article 2(1) (general obligation clause), article 2(2) (non-discrimination provision), article 2(3) (restrictive limitation on the enjoyment of the rights by non-nationals), article 3 (duty to treat men and women equally in the enjoyment of rights), article 4 (general limitation clause) and article 5 (interpretation rules). The provisions of Part II have a dynamic relationship with all of the substantive rights contained in the Covenant. Part II imposes obligations with which States Parties must comply with regard to each of the substantive rights contained in Part III of the Covenant (articles 6 to 15 ICESCR.) They prescribe the way in which States must behave in order to protect and guarantee the substantive rights contained in articles 6 to 15 of the ICESCR.

The study considers that it is important to focus on the obligations imposed by Part II provisions as an appropriate way to reinforce the accountability of States and to facilitate the supervision of the Covenant. A clear understanding of the meaning and scope of these obligations is considered necessary to enhance the protection of the substantive rights. Therefore, the study has provided practical guidance as to the scope and content of the obligations contained in Part II of the Covenant and elucidated the minimum requirements with which a State must comply in order to fulfil these obligations.

The analysis of this Part began with a general survey of the provisions contained in Part II of the Covenant. First, it referred to the nature of the provisions contained in

Part II. It concluded that articles 2 to 5 have an accessory character in the sense that they are necessarily connected with the exercise of a substantive right contained in Part III (articles 6 to 15 ICESCR). However, it is argued that, in general, a violation of Part II provisions does not necessarily entail a breach of a substantive right. Part II provisions can be violated even when a provision contained in Part III has not been violated.

Second, on the basis of the Committee's General Comments and Concluding Observations, Part III of the study addressed the personal and territorial scope of the Covenant. As to the personal scope, it is concluded that all of the rights contained in the Covenant apply to everyone under the jurisdiction of the State Party, whether lawfully or unlawfully present. The study showed that although the Committee has certainly stressed this principle on many occasions in its General Comments, when considering States Parties' reports the Committee has not applied it in a strict manner. The degree of flexibility in the application of the principle depends on the different categories of non-nationals involved and on the rights at issue.

As to the territorial application of the Covenant, the study concluded that there can be no doubt that the Covenant applies to *everyone within the jurisdiction* of the State Party. This is the interpretation consistently provided by the Committee in the examination of State Party reports as well as in its General Comments. In the light of the Committee's work, it is clear that 'within the jurisdiction' entails all territories in which the State Party exercises control, even *de facto* control. Consequently, States must provide information to the Committee on the enjoyment of the Covenant's rights by everyone within the territories under their control.

Chapter VI included a detailed analysis of articles 4 and 5 of the ICESCR. Article 4 contains a general limitation clause. This provision is of a protective nature and establishes several requirements with which States must comply when imposing limitations or restrictions on the enjoyment of the rights of the Covenant. After analysing these requirements, it was observed that although restrictions or limitations imposed by States on the enjoyment of economic, social and cultural rights may have negative consequences for individuals, it is regrettable that the Committee has not paid greater attention to this issue. It was considered that the Committee should strictly monitor whether States Parties comply with article 4 ICESCR.

While article 4 of the Covenant refers to the possibility of imposing restrictions or limitations on the exercise of specific Covenant rights, it does not provide a general derogation clause, such as that provided in article 4 of its sister Covenant, the ICCPR. The study analysed the consequences of the absence of a derogation provision. On the basis of the Committee's approach, it was concluded that the Covenant applies in all circumstances and that it is not necessary to derogate from the rights contained therein in order to deal with an emergency situation. It was argued that the Committee views the flexibility of article 2(1) ('take steps to the maximum of available resources'), and article 4 ICESCR (general limitation clause), as sufficient tools to face situations of crisis. Nevertheless, the lack of a derogation provision does not mean that States cannot lawfully suspend the exercise of the rights contained in the Covenant. The study analysed in detail such situations and the necessary requirements with which States must comply for a suspension under the rules of general international law.

Chapter VI also analysed article 5 of the Covenant. Article 5 contains two rules for the interpretation of the Covenant: (a) 'the prohibition of abuse of rights' (article 5(1)) and (b) 'the savings clause' (article 5(2)). The analysis demonstrated that these provisions have been little discussed in the context of the Committee and that further attention to article 5 by the Committee would enhance the protection of the rights contained in the Covenant.

Chapter VII analysed article 2(1) of the Covenant. Article 2(1) is an essential provision that defines the nature of the obligations with which each State Party must comply in relation to each of the rights contained in articles 6 to 15 ICESCR. The wording of article 2(1) of the Covenant is certainly elusive and intricate, in particular due to the inclusion of the notions of 'progressive realisation' and 'maximum available resources' which have given rise to much uncertainty.

From the Committee's work, it is possible to discern several distinct legal obligations arising from article 2(1). While compliance with the principle of 'progressive realisation' depends on the availability of resources in each State Party, it is argued that this provision also prescribes particular modes of conduct that are compulsory for all States Parties regardless of their level of development. As set out in Chapter VII, these obligations are the following:

(a) The obligation to take steps and to devote the maximum of available resources;
(b) The obligation to continuously improve conditions and the prohibition of taking deliberately retrogressive measures;
(c) The obligation to accord a degree of priority to human rights in the allocation of resources;
(d) The obligation to take 'all appropriate' measures towards the full implementation of the rights;
(e) The obligation to monitor the realisation of the rights and to devise strategies and programmes for their implementation;
(f) The obligation to ensure the minimum core level of each right; and
(g) The obligations regarding international assistance and co-operation.

These obligations constitute the 'hard core' of article 2(1) and they are characterised by the fact that they apply uniformly to all States Parties to the Covenant, regardless of their level of development. These obligations are not contingent upon the availability of resources and they are of an immediate character. These obligations considerably limit the discretion of States with regard to the implementation of the Covenant and require immediate implementation.

Finally, Chapter VIII analysed articles 2(2), article 2(3) and article 3 ICESCR. These provisions refer to the principle of equality and non-discrimination and are therefore analysed together in the same Chapter. The analysis shows that the Committee has applied the general international principle of equality and non-discrimination. Specifically, the Committee has permitted restrictions based on objective and reasonable criteria and with a legitimate aim under the Covenant. It has considered that temporary special measures intended to bring about equality for vulnerable and disadvantaged groups do not constitute violations of the principle of non-discrimination. It was also observed that the Committee has stressed the obligation of States Parties to protect individuals against discrimination committed by private individuals and has even required the criminalisation of some forms of behaviour in order to discourage individuals from discriminating in the enjoyment of economic, social and cultural rights. The Committee has also monitored the existence of 'indirect' discrimination, considering that the intention of the State is of little importance as discrimination exists when a distinction, exclusion or preference has the 'purpose or the effect' of nullifying or impairing the enjoyment of the Covenant's rights.

As a result of the Committee's work, it is clear that the grounds enumerated in article 2(2) ICESCR are not exhaustive. The Committee has supervised differential treatment on grounds not enumerated in article 2(2) and it has expressly referred to a number of other suspected grounds, such as age, disability, health conditions and nationality.

It is stressed by the study that the development by the Committee of the normative elements of Part II provisions constitutes a key contribution to the implementation of the Covenant. For all those called upon to apply the Covenant, this contribution provides an essential understanding of what State behaviours is compulsory under the Covenant. From the perspective of governments, the list of obligations analysed provides guidance as to the requirements which are of particular interest to the Committee. For judges, lawyers and human rights advocates, the obligations derived from Part II may be used as tools by which to assess the level of State compliance with the Covenant. However, despite the important contribution of the Committee in identifying the immediate obligations derived from Part II, there remains a great deal of room for development. The Committee needs to provide additional guidance as to the scope of the obligations and, clearly, it must improve its methods for supervising compliance with many of the obligations analysed.

2 The Time for an 'Obligations Approach'

Over the years, the determination of the normative content of the Covenant has been hindered due to a number of factors. The most significant obstacles include the complexities of article 2(1) of the Covenant and the weakness of the supervisory system which is based exclusively on State reporting. It is well known that the examination of individual cases by judicial or quasi-judicial bodies facilitates the process of clarifying the content and scope of a given norm. Thus, the absence of a complaints procedure for the supervision of the Covenant has made the clarification process an even more difficult task.

To overcome the difficulties in assessing compliance with the intricate text of article 2(1) ICESCR, scholars have developed the so-called 'violations approach'. By identifying the normative content of the provisions contained in Part II (articles 2 to 5 ICESCR) of the Covenant, the study has attempted to demonstrated that nowadays it is possible to complement the 'violations approach' by taking into account the precise obligations imposed by the Covenant as developed in the work of the Committee.

Since the time of the Covenant's entry into force in 1976, Part II provisions have acquired a clearer meaning. Today it is apparent that they impose important limitations on States' discretion when implementing the rights of the Covenant. As mentioned above, the obligations identified in the study are compulsory for all States Parties to the Covenant, regardless of their level of development. They may be considered as the 'minimum core content' of Part II of the Covenant.

Identifying the scope of the obligations imposed by the Covenant is essential for determining whether or not the State has failed to comply with those obligations. States Parties can only be held accountable if the obligations that they have assumed are clear. At the same time, all bodies called upon to apply the Covenant must be aware of the content and scope of the obligations in order to ensure State compliance. Thus, the analysis of the State's obligations is the appropriate means to reinforce the accountability of States and to facilitate the supervision of the Covenant.

The study has identified and analysed the series of obligations imposed by the provisions contained in Part II of the Covenant at the present stage of development of international law. An analysis of this type may provoke two distinct but opposing reactions. For some, the scope and content of the obligations of Part II provisions as they have been identified in the present study might be considered to be too limited or restrictive. It may well be believed that the Covenant imposes more far-reaching obligations upon States Parties. Others may consider that the obligations identified in the preceding chapters impose an excessive burden upon States Parties and that they go beyond what is provided for in the treaty's text. In response to both points of view it is important to stress that the present study has attempted to identify the normative content of Part II of the Covenant at the present stage of international human rights law and that we must recognise the dynamic character of international law. Those who believe that the Covenant imposes (or should impose) stricter obligations should keep in mind that in addition to identifying the level of protection afforded today, we have an important responsibility to advocate for further developments and to raise the standards of protection. The dynamic character of international law implies that the specific object and purpose of the Covenant (the protection of the inherent dignity of human beings) compels an interpretation that renders that protection effective in present day conditions. This is particularly important in regard to the international obligations to assist and co-operate in the implementation of the Covenant. An improvement in the implementation of the Covenant around the globe makes it indispensable that developed States assume greater international responsibility with regard to less advantaged States.

3 A FUTURE OPTIONAL PROTOCOL TO THE COVENANT AND THE OBLIGATIONS APPROACH

In recent years we have witnessed important steps towards the adoption of an optional protocol establishing a complaints procedure for the Covenant. During the early discussions regarding the adoption of an optional protocol, some commentators argued that it was premature to adopt such an instrument. It was considered essential to further develop the normative content of the Covenant before proceeding to adopt an individual complaints procedure.[1] The present study demonstrated that these arguments against the adoption of an optional protocol are no longer tenable. Such arguments are insensitive to the developments achieved in the clarification of the normative content of the Covenant during recent years. The current level of understanding of the normative content of the Covenant is such that it could be suitably reinforced through the adoption of a complaints procedure. Furthermore, greater in-depth examination of the scope and meaning of the obligations imposed by the Covenant compels us to advocate for such a procedure. The examination of individual cases though a petitions procedure is the necessary next step for further clarifying the normative content of the Covenant.

Within the framework of the draft optional protocol prepared by the Committee, individuals would be able to submit communications in the case of a failure to comply with the provisions contained in Part II.[2] With two exceptions,[3] States Parties that have submitted comments on the report of the Committee on a draft optional protocol[4] have not rejected the proposal.[5] If a protocol establishing a complaints procedure is adopted and the Committee's proposal as to the articles covered is accepted, individuals would be able to lodge complaints alleging violations of the provisions contained in Part II of the Covenant.

1 See in the Introduction note 20.

2 The Committee's draft submitted to the Commission on Human Rights in 1996 proposes the possibility of lodging complaints for a violation of articles 1 to 15 of the ICESCR. [E/CN.4/1997/105].

3 The exceptions are Canada [E/CN.4/1998/84/Add.1, of 16 March 1998] and Sweden. According to the latter State, 'the Government of Sweden remains unconvinced, however, that the suggested draft optional protocol presents an optimal way forward in strengthening the international mechanisms needed to contribute to the universal realisation of economic, social and cultural rights.' [E/CN.4/2001/62/Add.1, of 20 March 2001].

4 See Commission on Human Rights Resolutions 1999/25 and 2000/9, of 17 April 2000.

5 See, for example, E/CN.4/2000/49, of 14 January 2000 and E/CN.4/2001/62/Add.1, of 20 March 2001.

When an individual is faced with violation of economic, social and cultural rights and is contemplating the possibility of recourse to a quasi-judicial organ, he/she must bear in mind the content and scope of the international legal obligations of the State concerned. As the obligations contained in Part II apply with regard to all substantive rights, it is thus necessary to examine the Committee's understanding of these norms.

4 Future Improvements for the Normative Clarification of the Covenant

This study is intended to contribute to the enhancement of the normative content of the Covenant, particularly of the provisions of Part II. It is premised on the understanding that a clearer normative content of the Covenant would enhance its implementation and international supervision. In addition to the recommendation for the adoption of an optional protocol, the study includes several modest proposals for a further clarification of the normative content of the Covenant.

The study shows that the Committee has consistently incorporated the tripartite typology of State obligations in its General Comments but recommends that the Committee also seek to apply systematically the typology in its Concluding Observations. If the Committee were to expressly employ the typology in the Concluding Observations it would provide a better understanding of what State actions and omissions are required to implement the Covenant fully.

The study in addition expresses that it would be appropriate for the Committee to adopt General Comments on issues concerning the implementation of the provisions of Part II. Specifically, it is desirable for the Committee to adopt a General Comment on the general limitation clause of article 4 ICESCR; it is furthermore of utmost importance for the Committee to issue a General Comment on non-discrimination and equal treatment (articles 2(2) and 3 of the Covenant). Given the increasing size and complexity of migratory movements around the world, the Committee should also further clarify its approach to the enjoyment of Covenant rights by non-nationals (article 2(3) of the Covenant).

It would be appropriate for the Committee to modify its 'Reporting Guidelines' so that they fully address the provisions of Part II which at present are not adequately reflected therein. This would facilitate the work of the Committee in monitoring their compliance. Until now, the information received from States Parties with regard to the provisions contained in Part II has generally been poor and has not permitted adequate supervision by the Committee.

The Committee should, moreover, pay greater attention to the provisions of Part II when considering State reports. The Committee has not been consistent in supervising the application of Part II obligations and this is reflected in its Concluding Observations. The Committee has sometimes demonstrated great creativity in overcoming obstacles to supervising compliance with the obligations imposed by Part II provisions, but on occasion its observations have been poor and have not been consistent with well established supervisory standards. If the Committee were to monitor the obligations imposed by Part II of the Covenant with greater rigour, it would thus enhance the implementation of the Covenant and the enjoyment of economic, social and cultural rights by individuals.

In the context of a changing international environment, the Committee should also take greater account of new obstacles to the effective protection of economic, social and cultural rights. Among such obstacles we may recall here the strong tendency toward an unfettered market economy and privatisation processes,[6] structural adjustment programmes, the foreign debt of developing countries and the enormous inequalities in wealth distribution.[7] Globalisation has changed the international context dramatically, and many of its consequences need to be considered within the framework of the Covenant.[8] As discussed, during recent years the Committee has taken some steps to address some of these obstacles by examining the work of the World Bank, the IMF and multinational corporations in its General Comments and Concluding Observations. However, the enormous impact of the activities of these bodies on the enjoyment of economic, social and cultural rights by individuals requires that the Committee devise

6 It should be noted that the existence of the State as a provider was presumably what the drafters had in mind. However, nowadays, States have been substituted in many aspects by the market as the main providers. This issue was well summed up by Craven in a single paragraph, 'It is often presumed [...] that the principal dimension of the rights is in their legitimisation of claims against the State for the provision of certain social benefits whether in housing, social security, food, employment, health care or education. Indeed, it is entirely probable, that during the drafting of the Covenant, States had in mind the establishment of large centralised systems for the provision of these various public goods. Fifty years later, however, such a vision does not appear consonant with the current economy orthodoxy that demands tight control over public expenditure, and invites the privatisation of public services and the substitution of State control by market forces. Nor is it entirely consonant with the reality in many countries in which the main providers of education, housing and food, are not States, but rather communities or individuals themselves.' Craven, 1997, p. 107.

7 For an analysis of these barriers to the enjoyment of economic, social and cultural rights, see, for example, the final report of the Special Rapporteurs Mr. D. Türk on 'The realisation of economic, social and cultural rights', specially Part II: 'Ongoing Barriers: The main challenges of our time'. E/CN.4/Sub.2/1992/16 paras. 38-138, of 3 July 1992; Mr. J. Bengoa on 'The relationship between the enjoyment of human rights, in particular economic, social and cultural rights and income distribution', E/CN.4/Sub.2/1997/9, of 30 June 1997; and Mr. J. Oloka Onyango and Ms. Deepika Udagama on 'Globalisation and its impact on the full enjoyment of human rights,' E/CN.4/Sub.2/2000/13, of 15 June 2000. In addition see, *El derecho a la equidad: ética y mundialización social*. Terre des Hommes, Icaria, Barcelona, (1997). In particular the contributions of A. Teitelbaum, 'El problema de la impunidad. Las violaciones de los derechos económicos, sociales y culturales', pp. 117-154; B. Simma, 'Mecanismo, jurisprudencia y perspectivas del Pacto Internacional de Derechos Económicos, Sociales y Culturales', pp. 155-170 and P. Texier, 'Las misiones de asistencia técnica del Comité de Derechos Económicos, Sociales y Culturales', pp. 171-175.

8 The importance of this issue has been specifically addressed by the Committee. Indeed, it devoted a day of general discussion to the issue of 'Globalisation and its impact on the enjoyment of economic, social and cultural rights' during its eighteenth session in 1998. E/1999/22, Chapter V, paras. 436-461.

creative ways to supervise and enforce compliance with the Covenant by these institutions. In this regard, the Committee should put more effort into the supervision of State compliance with duties to prevent and protect individuals from the detrimental impact of the activities of these increasingly important international actors on their enjoyment of economic, social and cultural rights. The efficacy of the Committee *vis a vis* the increasing impact of transnational corporations will depend on its creativity in adapting its working methods and its approach to address the effects of the operations of these corporations on the enjoyment of the Covenant's rights.

The present study has been based principally on the work of the Committee itself; several additional recommendations are therefore appropriate with regard to its General Comments and Concluding Observations. While the General Comments generally reflect the serious commitment of the Committee to interpret the Covenant in light of relevant developments in international human rights law, their quality has been rather uneven. Some Concluding Observations do not reflect the Committee's approach taken in the General Comments and some have even gone against long-standing positions of the Committee. In order to clarify further the normative content of the Covenant, it would be desirable if the Committee were to be more rigorous as regards the final outcome of the examination of State reports. It is regrettable that on occasion, important issues raised during the 'constructive dialogue' with Government representatives are not taken into account in the Concluding Observations. It has also occurred that some issues included under 'principal subjects of concern' are not reflected in the 'suggestions and recommendations' made by the Committee. As a result, the Committee has lost important opportunities to provide guidance as to the normative content of the Covenant and to share the experience that it has developed over the years.

Despite the limited facilities for the Committee, it is still possible for it to improve its supervisory function. The Committee is an expert body and its Concluding Observations should better reflect this. It must reduce the speculative character of some of its Concluding Observations by adopting strict, precise conclusions. Although there have been important developments over the years, many recent Concluding Observations lack precision and they are not formulated using compelling language. To the extent that the Concluding Observations are formulated in more precise terms, the greater their impact would be at the national level.

To achieve higher quality in the Concluding Observations, the Committee should begin by setting the direction for and maintaining control over the 'constructive dialogue' with State representatives. It should set the tone by not allowing generalities and abstraction in the dialogue, maintaining a focused discussion that addresses tangible issues. Given the limitations on the Committee's work, it would also be appropriate for it to strengthen co-ordination and co-operation with other UN treaty monitoring bodies and UN specialised agencies.

In recent years the Committee has adopted detailed General Comments which have benefited from the input of a variety of different actors in the drafting process (*i.e.*

General Comments Nos. 12, 13 and 14). The results of this approach are evident in the lengthy General Comments which are generally of good quality but which contain some inconsistencies. On occasion it seems that the Committee has attempted to incorporate a wide variety of views without fully processing their content or undertaking serious analysis of their consistency. Although these recent General Comments may be considered to be an important contribution to the clarification process of the normative content of the Covenant, to some extent they lack the path-breaking, innovative content of some of the early General Comments.

Finally, it is relevant to note that the support that the Committee receives from the Secretariat is of utmost importance for its work. While it is possible to recognise that there have been some further improvements over the years, there is still much room for improvement. The Committee will only be in a position to improve the quality of its work if it is supported by a professional and expert Secretariat which is able to carry out research, undertake good offices with States Parties, develop and maintain a good working relations with NGOs and Specialised Agencies and develop expertise on the real problems faced by States Parties to the Covenant.

5 Future Challenges to the Protection of Economic, Social and Cultural Rights

Over the years, the Committee as well as some NGOs have undertaken enormous efforts to ensure that the Covenant is recognised as a key human rights instrument which is binding upon States. In large part due to the work of the Committee, the Covenant is no longer neglected and has emerged as an important tool for the international protection of economic, social and cultural rights. However, much of its potential remains unexploited. Certainly, to fulfil the potential of the Covenant, the Committee will need to further improve its working methods. However, the Committee should not be considered as the only actor in this battle. Civil society, including academic institutions, international lawyers, NGOs, trade unions, and individuals have an important role to play. In this regard, it is important to stress the significant role that academic institutions and NGOs can play in the promotion of the Covenant and of the work of the Committee. Only to the extent that individuals at the national level are aware that States are bound by international obligations in the field of economic, social and cultural rights will they be able to press their governments for change.

The implementation of economic, social and cultural rights at the domestic level requires the empowerment of individuals. Individuals must be aware of the existence of the State's obligations and the public informed of the Committee's views on the State's level of compliance. Certainly this is not an easy task and, at a minimum, it requires committed NGOs, with the necessary expertise and resources to do training and capacity building at the domestic level. In specific terms, it would be important for NGOs already committed to working on economic, social and cultural rights to enhance their promotional activities of the normative component of the Covenant as well as of the Committee's Concluding Observations and General Comments. Additionally, human rights NGOs which principally focus on the implementation of others rights must recognise the principle of the indivisibility of all human rights and put it into practice by integrating their approaches.

Academic institutions should also assume their responsibility in relation to the promotion of human rights in general and economic, social and cultural rights in particular. It is necessary that they overcome the increasingly outmoded view that considers human rights as a minor branch of international law; universities should dedicate greater resources to the study of this subject. Views would change if graduate students from different legal and non-legal disciplines were to receive some human rights education, with particular emphasis on the indivisibility of all human rights.

States must fully assume their responsibilities. States parties to the Covenant must comply with the obligation to submit reports and to implement the Committee's Concluding Observations. The Committee described the different objectives served by the preparation and submission of reports by States in its first General Comment, but States need to take these objectives more fully into account and further improve the quality of the reports as well as make efforts to submit them on time. In addition, States should endeavour to send well-prepared delegations to conduct the dialogue with the Committee. States should ensure that following the constructive dialogue, all those involved in the preparation of the reports, the legislative branch and all administrative authorities relevant for the enforcement of the Covenant are informed of the Committee's Concluding Observations.

States should make serious efforts to comply with their obligation to promote the Covenant among judges, lawyers, members of the legislature, administrative officials, groups of professionals, members of national human rights institutions, public policy decision-makers, municipal and regional government employees, among others. Public employees concerned must be aware of the content of the Covenant and the different methods of implementation. In the same vein, States should promote social participation in the design of strategies and programmes for the Covenant's implementation.

States should also incorporate the provisions of the Covenant in domestic law. As the Committee notes, direct incorporation provides a basis for the invocation of the Covenant in domestic courts.[9] Nonetheless, it is important to take into account that the domestic application of the Covenant should not be limited to judicial enforcement. There are numerous other means to implement the Covenant but the success of such measures will necessary require co-ordinated efforts of all branches of the State.

Governments should take heed of the arguments in favour of the adoption of an optional protocol establishing an individual complaint procedure. While there is a growing movement in favour of the adoption of such a protocol, it is imperative that

9 See General Comment No. 10 para. 8.

States which support the idea of a complaints procedure undertake a concerted effort together with international civil society to encourage and facilitate the drafting and eventual adoption of an optional protocol and its subsequent ratification by the greatest number of States possible.

Finally, States which have not yet ratified the Covenant should consider doing so in order to demonstrate a minimum degree of commitment to improving the well-being of the individuals under their jurisdiction. This is particularly true of the United States of America which remains the most significant non-party. However, while it is certainly regrettable that this 'hyper-power' has consistently refused to become party to the Covenant, and has therefore deprived its own nationals of international protection of their economic, social and cultural rights and recourse to an international supervisory mechanism, it should be emphasised that this has not overshadowed the consistent endorsement of these rights by the rest of the World community.

SELECTED BIBLIOGRAPHY

ADDO, MICHAEL K.: Justiciability re-examined. In: *Economic, social and cultural rights: progress and achievement.* Beddart, R. & Hill, D. (ed.), Macmillan, London, (1992), pp. 93-120.

ALSTON, PHILIP & QUINN, GERARD: The nature and scope of States parties' obligations under the International Covenant on Economic, Social and Cultural Rights. In: *Human Rights Quarterly,* vol. 9 No. 2, (1987), pp. 156-229.

ALSTON, PHILIP & SIMMA BRUNO: First session of the UN Committee on Economic, Social and Cultural Rights. In: *American Journal of International Law,* vol. 81 No. 3, July (1987), pp. 747-756.

ALSTON, PHILIP & SIMMA BRUNO: Second session of the UN Committee on Economic, Social and Cultural Rights. In: *American Journal of International Law,* vol. 82 No. 3, July (1988), pp. 603-615.

ALSTON, PHILIP & CRAWFORD, JAMES (eds.): *The future of UN human rights treaty monitoring*, Cambridge University Press, Cambridge, (2000).

ALSTON, PHILIP: International law and human right to food. In: *The right to food.* Alston, P. & Tomaševski, K. (eds.), Martinus Nijhoff Publishers, Utrecht, (1984), pp. 9-69.

ALSTON, PHILIP: International law and the right to food. In: *Food as a human right.* Eide, A.; Eide Barth W.; Goonatilake, S.; Gussow, J. & Omawale (eds.), United Nations University, Tokyo, (1984*), pp. 162-174.

ALSTON, PHILIP: Out of the abyss: the challenges of confronting the new UN Committee on Economic, Social and Cultural Rights. In: *Human Rights Quarterly*, vol. 9, (1987), pp. 332-381.

ALSTON, PHILIP: U.S. ratification of the Covenant on Economic, Social and Cultural Rights: the need for an entirely new strategy. In: *American Journal International Law*, vol. 84, (1990), pp. 365-392.

ALSTON PHILIP: Implementing economic, social and cultural rights: the functions of reporting obligations. In: *Bulletin of Human Rights*, No. 89/1, New York, (1990*), pp. 5-11.

ALSTON, PHILIP: No right to complain about being poor: the need for an optional protocol to the economic rights Covenant. In: *The future of human rights protection in a changing world: fifty years since the four freedoms address. Essays in honour of Torkel Opsahl.* Eide, A. & Helgesen, J. (eds.), Norwegian University Press, Oslo, (1991), pp. 79-100.

ALSTON, PHILIP: The Committee on Economic, Social and Cultural Rights. In: *The United Nations and human rights: a critical appraisal.* Alston P. (ed.), Clarendon Press, Oxford, (1992), pp. 473-508.

ALSTON, PHILIP: The legal framework of the Convention on the Right of the Child. In: *Bulletin of Human Rights*, No. 91/2, United Nations Publications, New York, (1992*), pp. 1-5.

ALSTON, PHILIP: Establishing a right to petition under the Covenant on Economic, Social and Cultural rights. In: *Collected Courses of the Academy of European Law: the protection of human rights in Europe.* Academy of European Law, Kluwer Law International, vol. IV, Book 2, The Hague, (1993), pp. 107-152.

ALSTON, PHILIP: Economic and social rights. In: *Human rights: an agenda for the next century.* Henkin, L. & Hargrove, J. (eds.), American Society International Law, Studies in Trasnational Legal Policy No. 26, Washington, (1994), pp. 137-166.

Selected Bibliography

ALSTON, PHILIP: The interplay between rights: denial and neglect. In: *Human rights: the new consensus*, Regency Press, (1994*), pp. 111-186.

ALSTON, PHILIP: Draft optional protocol providing for the consideration of communications, E/C.12/1994/12, report submitted to the Committee on Economic, Social and Cultural Rights. In: *The right to complain about economic, social and cultural rights*. Coomans, F. & Hoof, G.J.H. van (eds.), SIM Special No. 18, Utrecht, (1995), pp. 179-198.

ALSTON, PHILIP: The International Covenant on Economic, Social and Cultural Rights. In: *Manual on human rights reporting under six major international human rights instruments*, United Nations, second edition, Geneva, UN Doc. GV.E.97.0.16, (1997), pp. 65-169.

ALSTON, PHILIP: Making economic and social rights count: a strategy for the future. In: *The Political Quarterly Publishing*, (1997*), pp. 188-1995.

ALSTON, PHILIP: What's in a name: does it really matter if development policies refers to goals, ideals or human rights? In: *Human rights in development co-operation*. Helmich, H. (ed.), SIM Special No. 22, Utrecht, (1998), pp. 95-106.

ANDREASSEN, BÅRD-ANDERS; SKÅLNES, TOR; SMITH, ALAN G. & STOKKE, HUGO: Human rights performance in developing countries: the case for a minimum threshold approach. In: *Human rights in developing countries*. Akademisk Forlag, Copenhagen, (1988), pp. 333-356.

ANDREASSEN, BÅRD-ANDERS, SMITH, ALAN G. & STOKKE, HUGO: Compliance with economic and social human rights: realistic evaluations and monitoring in the light of immediate obligations. In: *Human rights in perspective: a global assessment*. Eide, A. & Hagtvet, B. (eds.), Blackwell, Oxford, (1993), pp. 253-267.

ANNAN, KOFI A.: Strengthening United Nations actions in the field of human rights: prospects and priorities. In: *Harvard Human Rights Journal*, vol. 10, Spring (1997), pp. 1-10.

APODACA, CLAIR: Measuring women's economic and social rights achievements. In: *Human Rights Quarterly*, vol. 20, (1998), pp. 139-172.

ARAMBULO, KITTY: *Strengthening the supervision of the International Covenant on Economic, Social and Cultural Rights: theoretical and procedural aspects*, Intersentia, Antwerp, (1999).

BAEHR, PETER; FLINTERMAN, CEES & SENDERS, MIGNON (eds.): *Innovation and inspiration: fifty years of the Universal Declaration of Human Rights*, Royal Netherlands Academy of Arts and Sciences, Amsterdam, (1990).

BAYEFSKY, ANNE F.: The principle of equality or non-discrimination in International Law. In: *Human Rights Law Journal,* vol. 11 Nos. 1-2, (1990), pp. 1-34.

BAYEFSKY, ANNE F. (ed.): *The human rights treaty system in the 21st Century*, Kluwer Law International, The Hague, (2000).

BEDDART, RALPH & HILL, DILYS (eds.): *Economic, social and cultural rights: progress and achievement*, Macmillan, London, (1992).

BEETHAM, DAVID: What future for economic and social rights? In: *Political Studies,* Special Issue, (1995), pp. 41-60.

BEETHAM, DAVID: Democracy and human rights: civil, political, economic, social and cultural. In: *Human rights: new dimensions and challenges. UNESCO manual on human rights.* Symonides, J. (ed.), Ashgate/Dartmouth/United Kingdom, (1998), pp. 71-97.

BERENSTEIN, ALEXANDRE: Economic and social rights: their inclusion in the European Convention on Human Rights, problems of formulation and interpretation. In: *Human Rights Law Journal,* vol. 2 Nos. 3-4, (1981), pp. 257-280.

BERNHARDT, R.: Thoughts on the interpretation of human rights treaties. In: *Protecting human rights: the European dimension: studies in honour of Gérard J. Wiarda.* Matscher, F. & Petzold, H. (eds.), Carl Heymanns, Köln, (1988), pp. 65-72.

BOEREFIJN, INEKE: *The reporting procedure under the Covenant on Civil and Political Rights: practice and procedure of the Human Rights Committee*, Intersentia, Antwerp, (1999).

BOEREFIJN, INEKE: Follow-up of the views of the United Nations treaty bodies. In: *The executions of Strasbourg and Geneva human rights decisions in the national legal order*, Kluwer, The Netherlands, (1999), pp. 101-112.

BOEREFIJN, INEKE; BROUWER MARJOLEIN & FAKHREDDINE, REEM (eds.): *Linking and learning in the field of economic, social and cultural rights*, Netherlands Institute for Human Rights, SIM Special No. 27, Utrecht, (2001).

BOS, MAARTEN: Theory and practice of treaty interpretation. In: *Netherlands International Law Review*, vol. XXVI (1980), pp. 3-38 and vol. XXVII (1980), pp. 135-170.

BOSSUYT, MARC: La distinction entre les droites civils et politiques et les droits economiques, sociaux et culturels. In: *Revue des Droits de l'Homme* (Human Rights Law Journal), vol. 8 No. 4, (1975), pp. 783-820.

BOSSUYT, MARC: *Guide to the 'travaux préparatoires' of the International Covenant on Civil and Political Rights*, Martinus Nijhoff Publisher, Dordrecht, (1987).

BOSSUYT, MARC: International human rights systems: strengths and weaknesses. In: *Human rights in the twenty-first century: a global challenge.* Mahoney, K. & Mahoney, P. (eds.), Martinus Nijhoff Publishers, Dordrecht, (1993), pp. 47-55.

BOULESBAA, AHCENE: The nature of the obligations incurred by States under article 2 of the UN Convention against Torture. In: *Human Rights Quarterly*, vol. 12, (1990), pp. 53-93.

BOVEN, THEO C. VAN; FLINTERMAN, CEES & WESTENDORP, INGRID (eds.): *The Maastricht guidelines on violations of economic, social and cultural rights*, Netherlands Institute for Human Rights, SIM Special No. 20, Utrecht, (1998).

BROWNLIE, IAN: *Principles of public international law*, Oxford University Press, fifth edition, Oxford, (1998).

BUEREN, GERALDINE VAN: Alleviating poverty through the constitutional court. In: *South African Journal of Human Rights*, vol. 15, (1999), pp. 52-74.

BUERGENTHAL, THOMAS & SHELTON, DINAH: *Protecting human rights in the Americas: cases and material*, Engel, Kehl am Rhein, fourth revised edition, (1995).

BUERGENTHAL, THOMAS: To respect and to ensure: State obligations and permissible derogations. In: *The International Bill of Rights.* Henkin, L. (ed.), Columbia University Press, New York, (1981), pp. 72-91.

BUERGENTHAL, THOMAS: *International human rights in a nutshell*, West Publishing, St. Paul, Minnesota, second edition, (1995).

BUERGENTHAL, THOMAS: The evolution of international human rights. In: *Héctor Gros Espiell amicorum liber*, Bruylant, Brussels, vol. I, (1997), pp. 123-147.

BUHL, DANA & BLYBERG, ANN (eds.): *Ripple in still water: reflections by activists on local and national level work on economic, social and cultural rights*, International Human Rights Internship Program, Washington D.C., (1997).

BYRNES, ANDREW & CONNORS, JANE: Enforcing the human rights of women: a complaints procedure for the women's Convention? In: *Brooklyn Journal of International Law*, vol. XXI No. 3, (1996), pp. 679-798.

CANÇADO TRINDADE, ANTONIO: The current state of international implementation of human rights. In: *Hague Yearbook of International Law*, vol. 3, (1990), pp. 1-29.

CAPOTORTI, FRANCESCO: The International measures of implementation included in the covenants on human rights. In: *International protection of human rights.* Eide, A. & Schou, A. (eds.), Proceedings of the Seventh Nobel Symposium, Oslo, September 25-27, 1967, Interscience Publishers, Stockholm, (1968), pp. 131-138.

CASSESE, ANTONIO: Can the notion of inhuman and degrading treatment be applied to socio-economic conditions? In: *European Journal of International Law*, vol. 2, (1991), pp. 141-145.

CASTERMANS-HOLLEMAN, MONIQUE: The protection of economic, social and cultural rights within the UN framework. In: *Netherlands International Law Review,* vol. XLII, (1995), pp. 353-373.

CASTERMANS-HOLLEMAN, MONIQUE; HOOF, FRIED VAN & SMITH JACQUELINE: *The role of the nation-state in the 21st century: human rights, international organisations and foreign policy: essays in honour of Peter Baehr*, Kluwer, The Hague, (1998).

CHAPMAN, AUDREY: A 'violations approach' for monitoring the International Covenant on Economic, Social and Cultural Rights. In: *Human Rights Quarterly,* vol. 18 No. 1, (1996), pp. 23-63.

CHAPMAN, AUDREY: Violations of the right to health. In: *The Maastricht guidelines on violations of economic, social and cultural rights*. Boven, T.C. van; Flinterman, C. & Westendorp, I. (eds.), Netherlands Institute of Human Rights, SIM Special No. 20, Utrecht, (1998), pp. 87-112.

CHOLEWINSKI, RYSZARD: State duty towards ethnic minorities: positive or negative? In: *Human Rights Quarterly*, vol. 10, (1998), pp. 344-371.

CLAPHAM, ANDREW: *Human rights in the private sphere*, Clarendon Press, Oxford, (1993).

CLARK, TOM & NIESSEN, JAN: Equality rights and non-citizens in Europe and America: the promise, the practice and some remaining issues. In: *Netherlands Quarterly of Human Rights*, vol. 14 No. 3, (1996), pp. 245-275.

COMBRINCK, HELENE: Positive State duties to protect women from violence: recent South African developments. In: *Human Rights Quarterly*, vol. 20, (1998), pp. 666-690.

CONFORTI, BENEDETTO: National courts and the international law of human rights. In: *Enforcing international human rights in domestic courts*. Conforti, B. & Francioni, F. (eds.), Martinus Nijhoff Publishers, The Hague/Boston/London, (1997), pp. 3-14.

COOK, REBECCA J.: Accountability in international law for violations of women's rights by non-State actors. In: *Reconceiving reality: women and international law*. Dallmeyer, D.G. (ed.), Studies in Transnational Legal Policy No. 25, American Society of International Law, Washington D.C., (1993), pp. 93-142.

COOMANS, FONS & GALENKAMP, MARLIES: *Economic, social and cultural rights and collective rights*, Netherlands Institute of Human Rights, SIM Special No. 16, Utrecht, (1995*).

COOMANS, FONS & HOOF, G.J.H VAN (eds.): *The right to complain about economic, social and cultural rights*, Netherlands Institute of Human Rights, SIM Special No. 18, Utrecht, (1995**).

COOMANS, FONS: Clarifying the core elements of the right to education. In: *The right to complain about economic, social and cultural rights*. Coomans, F. & Hoof, G.J.H. van (eds.), Netherlands Institute of Human Rights, SIM Special, No. 18, Utrecht, (1995***), pp. 11-26.

COOMANS, FONS: Identifying violations of the right to education. In: *The Maastricht guidelines on violations of economic, social and cultural rights*. Boven, T.C. van; Flinterman, C. & Westendorp, I. (eds.), Netherlands Institute of Human Rights, SIM Special No. 20, Utrecht, (1998), pp. 125-146.

COOMANS, FONS: Follow-up action to State reporting on human rights: procedure and practice of the Committee on the Rights of the Child and the Committee on Economic, Social and Cultural Rights. In: *Rendering justice to the vulnerable: liber amicorum in honour of Theo van Boven.* Coomans, F.; Grünfeld, F.; Westendorp, I. & Willems, J. (eds), Kluwer Law International, The Hague, (2000), pp. 83-98.

COOMANS, FONS; GRÜNFELD, FRED; WESTENDORP, INGRID & WILLEMS, JAN (eds.): *Rendering justice to the vulnerable: liber amicorum in honour of Theo van Boven*, Kluwer Law International, The Hague, (2000).

CRANSTON, MAURICE: *What are human rights?* The Bodley Head, London/Sydney/Toronto, (1973).

CRAVEN, MATTHEW & DOMMEN, CAROLINE: Making room for substance: fifth session of the Committee on Economic, Social and Cultural Rights. In: *Netherlands Quarterly of Human Rights*, vol. No. 1, (1991), pp. 83-95.

CRAVEN, MATTHEW: The domestic application of the International Covenant on Economic, Social and Cultural Rights. In: *Netherlands International Law Review*, vol. XL (1993), pp. 367-404.

CRAVEN, MATTHEW: Towards an unofficial petition procedure: a review on the role of the UN Committee on Economic, Social and Cultural Rights. In: *Social Rights as Human Rights: a European challenge.* Drzewicki, K.; Krause, C. & Rosas, A. (eds.), Institute for Human Rights, Åbo Akademi University, Åbo, Finland, (1994), pp. 91-113.

CRAVEN, MATTHEW: *The International Covenant on Economic, Social and Cultural Rights: a perspective on its development*, Clarendon Press, Oxford, (1995).

CRAVEN, MATTHEW: The International Covenant on Economic, Social and Cultural Rights. In: *An Introduction to the international protection of human rights: a textbook.* Hanski, R. & Suksi, M. (eds.), Institute for Human Rights, Åbo Akademi University, Åbo, Finland (1997), pp. 99-118.

CRAVEN, MATTHEW: *The International Covenant on Economic, Social and Cultural Rights: a perspective on its development*, Clarendon Press, Oxford, Paperback edition with corrections, (1998).

CRAVEN, MATTHEW: The protection of economic, social and cultural rights in the Inter-American system of human rights. In: *The Inter-American system of human rights.* Harris, D. and Livingstone, S. (eds.), Clarendon Press, Oxford, (1998*).

CRAVEN, MATTHEW: The International Covenant on Economic, Social and Cultural Rights. In: *An introduction to the international protection of human rights: a textbook: second revised edition.* Hanski, R. & Suksi, M. (eds.), Institute for Human Rights, Åbo Akademi University, Åbo, Finland (1999), pp. 101-123.

CRAVEN, MATTHEW: Legal differentiation and the concept of human rights treaty in international law. In: *European Journal of International Law*, vol. 11 (2000), pp. 489-519.

CRAWFORD, JAMES: Revising the draft articles on state responsibility. In *European Journal of International Law*, No. 10 vol. 2, (1999), pp. 435-460.

DANKWA, E.V.O & FLINTERMAN, CEES: Commentary by the rapporteurs on the nature and scope of States parties' obligations. In: *Human Rights Quarterly*, vol. 9, (1987), pp. 136-146.

DANKWA, E.V.O; FLINTERMAN, CEES & LECKIE, SCOTT: Commentary on the Maastricht Guidelines on Violations of Economic, Social and Cultural Rights. In: *The Maastricht guidelines on violations of economic, social and cultural rights.* Boven, T.C. van; Flinterman, C. & Westendorp, I. (eds.), Netherlands Institute of Human Rights, SIM Special No. 20, Utrecht, (1998), pp. 13-34.

DANKWA, E.V.O; FLINTERMAN, CEES & LECKIE, SCOTT: Commentary on the Maastricht Guidelines on Violations of Economic, Social and Cultural Rights. In: *Human Rights Quarterly*, vol. 20, (1998*), pp. 705-730.

DANKWA, E.V.O.: Working paper on article 2(3) of the International Covenant on Economic, Social and Cultural rights. In: *Human Rights Quarterly*, vol .9 (1987), pp. 230-249.

DIAS, CLARENCE & PAUL, JAMES: Developing the human right to food as a legal resource for the rural poor: some strategies for NGOs. In: *The right to food.* Alston, P. & Tomaševski, K. (eds.), Martinus Nijhoff Publishers, Utrecht (1984), pp. 203-214.

DIENG, ADAMA (ed.): *Economic, social and cultural rights and the role of lawyers: special issue, The Review of the International Commission of Jurists* No. 55, Geneva, (1995).

DIJK, PIETER VAN & HOOF, G.J.H. VAN: *Theory and practice of the European Convention on Human Rights*, Kluwer Law International, The Hague, third edition, (1998).

DIJK, PIETER VAN: The interpretation of 'civil rights and obligations' by the European Court of Human Rights- one more step to take. In: *Protecting human rights: the European dimension: studies in honour of Gérard J. Wiarda*. Matscher, F. & Petzold, H. (eds.), Carl Heymanns, Köln, (1988), pp. 131-144.

DIJK, PIETER VAN: Domestic status of human rights treaties and the attitude of the judiciary: the Dutch case. In: *Progress in the spirit of human rights*. Nowak, M.; Steurer, D. & Tretter, H. (eds.), N.P. Engel, Kehl am Rhein, (1988*), pp. 631-649.

DIJK, PIETER VAN: A common standard of achievement: about universal validity and uniform interpretation of international human rights norms. In: *Netherlands Quarterly of Human Rights*, vol. 13 No. 2, (1995), pp. 105-121.

DIJK, PIETER VAN: 'Positive obligations' implied in the European Convention on Human Rights: are the States still the 'masters' of the Convention? In: *The role of the nation-State in the 21st century. Human rights, international organisations and foreign policy: essays in honour of Peter Baehr.* Castermans-Holleman, M.; Hoof, G.J.H. van & Smith, J. (eds.), Kluwer Law International, The Hague, (1998), pp. 17-33.

DIMITRIJEVIC, VOJIN: The monitoring of human rights and the prevention of human rights violations through reporting procedures. In: *Monitoring human rights in Europe: comparing international procedures and mechanims*. Bloed, A.; Leicht, L.; Nowak, M. & Rosas, A. (eds.), Kluwer Law International, The Netherlands, (1993), pp. 1-24.

DINSTEIN, YORAM: Discrimination and international human rights. In: *Israel Yearbook on Human Rights*, vol. 15, (1985), pp. 11-27.

DIOP, M.: The African Charter on Human and Peoples' Rights and the inviolability of the fundamental rights. In: *Non-Derogable rights and states of emergency*. Prémont, D.; Stenersen, C. & Oseredczuk, I. (eds.), Association of International Consultants of Human Rights (CID), Brussels, (1996), pp. 421-428.

DONG, EDWARD: UN human rights covenants become law: so what? In: *American Society of International Law*, 70 annual meeting, (1976), pp. 97-105.

DONNELLY, JACK: *International Human Rights*, Westview, second edition, Oxford, (1998).

DRZEWICKI, KRZYSZTOF; KRAUSE, CATARINA & ROSAS, ALLAN (eds.): *Social rights as human rights: a European challenge*, Institute for Human Rights, Åbo Akademi University, Åbo, Finland, (1994).

DUPUY, PIERRE-MARIE: Reviewing the difficulties of codification: on Ago's classification of obligations of means and obligations of result in relation to state responsibility. In: *European Journal of International Law*, No. 10 vol. 2, (1999), pp. 371-385.

EIDE, ASBJØRN & SCHOU, AUGUST (eds.): *International protection of human rights: proceedings of the Seventh Nobel Symposium*, Interscience Publishers, Stockholm, (1968).

EIDE, ASBJØRN & HELGESEN, JAN (eds.): *The future of human rights protection in a changing world: fifty years since the four freedoms address: essays in honour of Torkel Opsahl*, Norwegian University Press, Oslo, (1991).

EIDE, ASBJØRN: The international human rights system. In: *Food as a human right*. Eide, A.; Eide Barth W.; Goonatilake, S.; Gussow, J. & Omawale (eds.), United Nations University, Tokyo, (1984), pp. 152-161.

EIDE, ASBJØRN: *Right to adequate food as a human right*, United Nations Publication, Sales No. E.89.XIV.2, New York, (1989).

EIDE, ASBJØRN: Realisation of social and economic rights and the minimum threshold approach. In: *Human Rights Law Journal,* vol. 10, (1989*), pp. 35-51.

EIDE, ASBJØRN: Realisation of social and economic rights – the minimum threshold approach. In: *The Review of the International Commission of Jurists*, No. 43, (1989**), pp. 40-52.

EIDE, ASBJØRN: The four freedoms and human rights in the New International Order. In: *The future of human rights protection in a changing world: fifty years since the four freedoms address: essays in Honour of Torkel Opsahl.* Eide, A. & Helgesen, J. (eds.), Norwegian University Press, Oslo, (1991), pp. 1-8.

EIDE, ASBJØRN: Future protection of economic and social rights in Europe. In: *Monitoring human rights in Europe: comparing international procedures and mechanisms.* Bloed, A.; Leicht, L.; Nowak, M. & Rosas, A. (eds.), Martinus Nijhoff Publishers, Dordrecht, (1993), pp. 187-219.

EIDE, ASBJØRN: Economic, social and cultural rights as human rights. In: *Economic, social and cultural rights: a textbook.* Eide, A.; Krause, C. & Rosas, A. (eds.), Martinus Nijhoff Publishers, Dordrecht, (1995), pp. 21-40.

EIDE, ASBJØRN: The right to an adequate standard of living including the right to food. In: *Economic, social and cultural rights: a textbook.* Eide, A.; Krause, C. & Rosas, A. (eds.), Martinus Nijhoff Publishers, first edition, Dordrecht, (1995*), pp. 89-106.

EIDE, ASBJØRN: Freedom from want: taking economic and social rights seriously. In: *Reflections on the Universal Declaration of Human Rights: a fiftieth anniversary anthology.* Heijden, B. van der & Tahzib-Lie, B. (eds.), Martinus Nijhoff Publishers, The Hague/Boston/London, (1998), pp. 121-129.

EIDE, ASBJØRN: Universalization of human rights versus globalisation of economic power. In: *Rendering justice to the vulnerable: liber amicorum in honour of Theo van Boven.* Coomans, F.; Grünfeld, F.; Westendorp, I. & Willems, J. (eds.), Kluwer Law International, The Hague, (2000), pp. 99-120.

EIDE, ASBJØRN: Economic, social and cultural rights as human rights. In: *Economic, social and cultural rights: a textbook.* Eide, A.; Krause, C. & Rosas, A. (eds.), Martinus Nijhoff Publishers, second revised edition, Dordrecht, (2001), pp. 9-28.

EIDE, ASBJØRN; KRAUSE, CATARINA & ROSAS, ALLAN (eds.): *Economic, social and cultural rights: a textbook*, Martinus Nijhoff Publishers, second revised edition, Dordrecht, (2001).

EVANS, TONY: *US hegemony and the project of universal human rights*, St. Martin's Press, New York, (1996).

FALK, RICHARD: On treaty interpretation and the New Haven approach: achievements and prospects. In: *Virginia Journal of International Law*, vol. 8 No. 2, (1968), pp. 323-355.

FERGUSON, CLARENCE CLYDE: The United Nations human rights covenants: problems of ratification and implementation. In: *American Society of International Law,* 62 Annual Meeting, (1968), pp. 83-123.

FLINTERMAN, CEES: The protection of economic, social and cultural rights and the European Convention on Human Rights. In: *The dynamics of the protection of human rights in Europe: essays in honour of Henry G. Schermers.* Lawson, R. & Blois, M. de (eds.), Martinus Nijhoff Publishers, Dordrecht, vol. III, (1994), pp. 165-174.

FORREST F.; SCHNABLY, S.; SLYE, R.; WILSON, R.; FALK, R.; SIMON, J. & KOREN, E.: *International human rights law and practice: cases, treaties and materials*, Kluwer Law International, The Hague/London/Boston, (1997).

FRANCK, THOMAS M.: *The power of legitimacy among nations*, Oxford University Press, New York, Oxford, (1990).

FREDMAN, SANDRA (ed.): *Discrimination and human rights: the case of racism*, Oxford University Press, Oxford, (2001).

FREEMAN, MICHAEL D.A.: *Lloyd's Introduction to jurisprudence*, Sweet & Maxwell, London, (1994).

GAAY FORTMAN, BAS DE & KLEIN GOLDEWIJK, BERMA: *Where needs meet rights: economic, social and cultural rights in a new perspective*, World Council of Churches, Geneva, (1999).

GALLIGAN, BRIAN & SAMPFORD, CHARLES (eds.): *Rethinking human rights*, Federation Press, Sydney, (1997).

GINSBERG, MITCHELL & LESSER, LEONARD: Current development in economic and social rights: a United State perspectives. In: *Human Rights Law Journal*, vol. 2, (1981), pp. 237-256.

GOLDSTEIN, STEPHEN: Reverse discrimination: reflections of a jurist. In: *Israel Yearbook on Human Rights*, vol. 15, (1985), pp. 28-42.

GOLSONG, HERIBERT: Interpreting the European Convention on Human Rights beyond the confines of the Vienna Convention on the Law of Treaties? In: *The European system for the protection of human rights.* Macdonald, R. St.J.; Matscher, F. & Petzold, H. (eds.), Martinus Nijhoff Publishers, The Netherlands, (1993), pp. 147-162.

GOMEZ, MARIO: Social economic rights and human rights Commissions. In: *Human Rights Quarterly*, vol. 17 No. 1, (1995), pp. 155-169.

GOMIEN, DONNA; HARRIS, DAVID & ZWAAK, LEO: *Law and practice of the European Convention on Human Rights and the European Social Charter*, Council of Europe Publishing, Strasbourg, (1996).

GOMIEN, DONNA (ed.): *Broadening the frontiers of human rights: essays in honour of Asbjørn Eide*, Scandinavian University Press, Oslo, (1993).

GOODWIN-GILL, GUY S.: Obligations of conduct and result. In: *The right to food*. Alston, P. & Tomaševski, K. (eds.), Martinus Nijhoff Publishers, Utrecht (1984), pp. 111-118.

GOODWIN-GIL, GUY S.: *The refugee in international law*, second paperback edition, Clarendon Press, Oxford, (1998).

GORDON, LEONID: Socio-economic human rights: content, specifics, significance for Russia. In: *Social Sciences Quarterly Review*, vol. XXVIII No. 4, (1997), pp. 6-17.

GUTTO, SHADRACK B.O.: Beyond justiciability: challenges of implementing/enforcing socio-economic rights in South Africa. In: *Buffalo Human Rights Law Review*, vol. 4, (2000), pp. 79-102.

HANNIKAINEN LAURI AND NYKÄNEN EEVA (eds.): *New trends in discrimination law: international perspectives*, Publications of Turku Law School, vol. 3 No. 1, Turku/Åbo, Finland, (1999).

HANNUM, HURST: Human Rights. In: *The United Nations and international law*. Joyner, C. (ed.), co-publication of the American Society of International Law and Cambridge University Press, (1997), pp. 131-154.

HANSKI, RAIJA & SUKSI, MARKKU (eds.): *An introduction to the international protection of human Rights: a textbook*, Institute for Human Rights, Åbo Akademi University, Turku/Åbo, Finland (1997).

HANSKI, RAIJA & SUKSI, MARKKU (eds.): *An introduction to the international protection of human rights: a textbook*, Institute for Human Rights, Åbo Akademi University, second revised edition, Turku/Åbo, Finland, (1999).

HARRIS, D.; O'BOYLE, M. & WARBRICK, C.: *Law of the European Convention on Human Rights*, Butterworths, London, (1995)

HARRIS, DAVID & JOSEPH, SARAH: *The International Covenant on Civil and Political Rights and United Kingdom Law*, Clarendon Press, Oxford, (1995).

HARRIS, D.J.: *Cases and materials on International Law*, Sweet & Maxwell, fifth edition, London, (1998).

HARRIS, DAVID: Commentary by the rapporteur on the considerations of States parties' reports and international co-operation. In: *Human Rights Quarterly,* vol. 9, (1987), pp. 147-155.

HART, H.L.A: *The concept of law*, Clarendon Law Series, second edition, Oxford, (1994).

HARTMAN, JOAN: Working paper for the Committee of Experts on the article 4 derogation provision. In: *Human Rights Quarterly*, vol. 7 No. 1, (1985), pp. 89-131.

HARVEY, PHILIP: Monitoring mechanisms for international agreements respecting economic and social human rights. In: *Yale Journal of International Law*, vol. 12 No. 2, (1987), pp. 396-420.
HASSAN, PARVEZ: The International Covenants on Human Rights: an approach to interpretation. In: *Buffalo Law Review*, vol. 19 No. 3, spring (1970), pp. 35-50.
HATHAWAY, JAMES: *The law of refugee status*, Butterworths, Canada, (1991).
HEIJDEN, BAREND VAN DER & TAHZIB-LIE, BAHIA (eds.): *Reflections on the Universal Declaration of Human Rights: a fiftieth anniversary anthology*, Martinus Nijhoff Publishers, The Hague, (1998).
HENKIN, LOUIS; NEUMAN, GERALD; ORENTLICHER, DIANE & LEEBRON, DAVID: *Human rights*, Foundation Press, New York, (1999).
HENKIN, LOUIS (ed.): *The International Bill of Rights: the Covenant on Civil and Political Rights*, Columbia University Press, New York, (1981).
HENKIN, LOUIS: Economic-social rights as 'rights': a United States perspective. In: *Human Rights Law Journal*, vol. 2, (1981), pp. 223-236.
HERINGA, AALT WILLEM: Art. 26 CCPR and social security: recent Dutch cases invalidating discriminatory social security laws. In: *SIM Newsletter*, vol. 1, (1998), pp. 19-26.
HIGGINS, ROSALYN: The United Nations: still a force for peace. In: *The Modern Law Review,* vol. 52 No. 1, (1989), pp. 1-21.
HIGGINS, ROSALYN: Some thoughts on the implementation of human rights. In: *Bulletin of Human Rights* No. 89/1, New York, (1990), pp. 60-66.
HIGGINS, ROSALYN: *Problems and process: international law and how we use it*, Clarendon Press, first edition reprinted, Oxford, (1998).
HIGGINS, ROSALYN: International law in a changing international system. In: *Cambridge Law Journal*, vol. 58 No. 1, (1999), pp. 78-95.
HIRSCHT, RAN: 'Negative' rights vs. 'positive' entitlements: a comparative study of judicial interpretations of rights in an emerging neo-liberal economic order. In: *Human Rights Quarterly*, vol. 22 (2000), pp. 1060-1098.
HOOF, G.J.H. VAN: *Rethinking the sources of international law*, Kluwer Law and Taxation Publishers, Deventer, The Netherlands, (1983).
HOOF, G.J.H. VAN: Legal nature of economic, social and cultural rights: a rebuttal of some traditional views. In: *The right to food.* Alston, P. & Tomaševski, K. (eds.), Martinus Nijhoff Publishers, Utrecht, (1984), pp. 97-110.
HOOF, G.J.H. VAN: Explanatory note on the Utrecht draft optional protocol to the International Covenant on Economic, Social and Cultural Rights. In: *The right to complain about economic, social and cultural rights.* Coomans, F. & Hoof, G.J.H. van (eds.), Netherlands Institute of Human Rights, SIM Special No.18, Utrecht, (1995), pp. 147-178.
HOWARD, RHODA: The full-belly thesis: should economic rights take priority over civil and political rights? Evidence from Sub-Saharan Africa. In: *Human Rights Quarterly,* vol. 5, (1983), pp. 467-490.
HUMPHREY, JOHN P.: *Human Rights & the United Nations: a great adventure*, Transnational Publishers, New York, (1984).
HUNT, PAUL: *Reclaiming social rights: international and comparative perspectives*, Dartmouth, Aldershot, (1996).
IWASAWA, YUJI: The doctrine of self-executing treaties in the United States: a critical analysis. In: *Virginia Journal of International Law*, vol. 26 No. 3, (1986), pp. 627-692.
JACK, DANIEL: Human Rights and the disadvantaged. In: *Human Rights Law Journal*, vol.10 Nos. 1-2, (1989), pp. 53-60.

JASPERS, TEUN: The challenging struggle for fundamental social rights. In: *The role of the nation-state in the 21st century. Human rights, international organisations and foreign policy: essays in honour of Peter Baehr*. Castermans-Holleman, M.; Hoof G.J.H. van & Smith, J. (eds.), Kluwer Law International, The Hague (1998), pp. 79-90.

JASUDOWICZ, TADEUSZ: The legal character of social rights from the perspective of international law as a whole. In: *Social rights as human rights: a European challenge*. Institute for Human Rights, Åbo Akademi University, Åbo, Finland (1994), pp. 23-42.

JHABVALA, FARROKH: On human rights and the socio-economic context. In: *Netherlands International Law Review*, vol. XXXI, (1984), pp. 149-182.

JHABVALA, FARROKH: The practice of the Covenant's Human Rights Committee 1976-1982: review of State party reports. In: *Human Rights Quarterly*, vol. 6 No. 1, (1984*), pp. 81-106.

JHABVALA, FARROKH: Letter to the editor. In: *Human Rights Quarterly*, vol. 7, (1985), pp. 242-243.

JOCHNICK, CHRIS: Confronting the impunity of non-State actors: new fields for the promotion of human rights. In: *Human Rights Quarterly*, vol. 21, (1999), pp. 56-79.

JOSEPH, SARAH; SCHULTZ, JENNY & CASTAN, MELISSA: *The International Covenant on Civil and Political Rights: cases, materials and commentary*, Oxford University Press, Oxford, (2000).

KLEIN, ECKART (ed.): *The monitoring system of human rights treaty obligations*, Verlag, Berlin, (1998).

KLEIN, ECKART: The duty to protect and to ensure human rights under the International Covenant on Civil and Political Rights. Unpublished document on file with the author, (1999), pp. 295-322.

KLERK, YVONNE: Working paper on article 2(2) and article 3 of the International Covenant on Economic, Social and Cultural Rights. In: *Human Rights Quarterly*, vol. 9, (1987), pp. 250-273.

KRAUSE, CATARINA & SCHEININ MARTIN: The right not to be discriminated against: the case of social security. In: *The jurisprudence of human rights law: a comparative interpretative approach*. Orlin, T.S.; Rosas, A. & Scheinin, M. (eds.), Institute for Human Rights, Åbo Akademi University, Åbo, Finland, (2000), pp. 253-286.

KÜNNEMANN, ROLF: A coherent approach to human rights. In: *Human Rights Quarterly*, vol. 17, (1995), pp. 323-342.

KÜNNEMANN, ROLF: Violations of the right to food. In: *The Maastricht guidelines on violations of economic, social and cultural rights*. Boven, T.C. van; Flinterman, C. & Westendorp, I. (eds.), Netherlands Institute of Human Rights, SIM Special No. 20, Utrecht, (1998), pp. 165-190.

LAWRENCE BARSH, RUSSEL: Measuring human rights: problems of methodology and purpose. In: *Human Rights Quarterly*, vol. 15, (1993), pp. 87-121.

LAWSON, RICK & BLOIS, MATTHIJS DE (eds.): *The dynamics of the protection of human rights in Europe: essays in honour of Henry G. Schermers*, Martinus Nijhoff Publishers, Dordrecht, (1994).

LEARY, VIRGINIA: *The automatic incorporation of international labour conventions in municipal law*, The Graduate Institute of International Studies, University of Geneva, (1979).

LEARY, VIRGINIA: Lessons from the experience of the International Labour Organisation. In: *The United Nations and human rights: a critical appraisal*. Alston, P. (ed.), Clarendon Press, Oxford, (1992), pp. 580-619.

LEARY, VIRGINIA: The right to complaint: the right to health. In: *The right to complain about economic, social and cultural rights*. Coomans, F. & Hoof, G.J.H. van (eds.), Netherlands Institute of Human Rights, SIM Special No. 18, Utrecht, (1995), pp. 87-102.

LEARY, VIRGINIA: Justiciability and beyond, complaints procedures and the right to health. In: *Economic, Social and Cultural Rights and the role of Lawyers: special issue, The Review of the International Commission of Jurists* No. 55, Geneva, (1995*), pp. 105-122.

LEARY, VIRGINIA: A violation approach to the right to work (labour rights). In: *The Maastricht guidelines on violations of economic, social and cultural rights*. Boven, T.C. van; Flinterman, C. & Westendorp, I. (eds.), Netherlands Institute of Human Rights, SIM Special No. 20, Utrecht, (1998), pp. 113-123.

LECKIE, SCOTT: The UN Committee on Economic, Social and Cultural Rights and the rights to adequate housing: towards an appropriate approach. In: *Human Rights Quarterly*, vol. 11 No. 4, (1989), pp. 522-560.

LECKIE, SCOTT: An overview and appraisal of the fifth session of the UN Committee on Economic, Social and Cultural Rights. In: *Human Rights Quarterly*, vol. 13, (1991), pp. 545-572.

LECKIE, SCOTT: From infancy to adulthood: UN Committee on Economic, Social and Cultural Rights and the right to adequate housing. In: *Human Rights Tribune*, vol. 1 No. 3, (1992), pp. 10-11.

LECKIE, SCOTT: The right to housing. In: *Economic, social and cultural rights: a textbook.* Eide, A.; Krause, C. & Rosas, A. (eds.), Martinus Nijhoff Publishers, Dordrecht, (1995), pp. 107-124.

LECKIE, SCOTT: Another step towards indivisibility: identifying the key features of violations of economic, social and cultural rights. In: *Human Rights Quarterly,* vol. 20 No. 1, (1998), pp. 81-124.

LECKIE, SCOTT: The Committee on Economic, Social and Cultural Rights: Catalyst for change in a system needing reform. In: *The future of UN human rights treaty monitoring*, Alston, P. & Crawford, J. (eds.), Cambridge University Press, Cambridge, (2000), pp. 129-144.

LIEBENBERG, SANDRA: The protection of economic and social rights in domestic legal systems. In: *Economic, social and cultural rights: a textbook.* Eide, A.; Krause, C. & Rosas, A. (eds.), Martinus Nijhoff Publishers, second revised edition, Dordrecht, (2001), pp. 55-84.

LOCKWOOD, B.; FINN, J. & JUBINSKY, G.: Working paper for the Committee of experts on limitation provisions. In: *Human Rights Quarterly*, vol. 7 No. 1, (1985), pp. 35-88.

LOENEN, TITIA & RODRIGUES, PETER (eds.): *Non-discrimination law: comparative perspectives*, Kluwer Law International, The Hague, (1999).

LOENEN, TITIA: Rethinking sex equality as a human right. In: *Netherlands Quarterly of Human Rights*, vol. 3, (1994), pp. 253-270.

LOUCAIDES, LOUKIS G.: Restrictions or limitations on the rights guaranteed by the European Convention on Human Rights. In: *Essays on the developing law of human rights*, Martinus Nijhoff Publishers, Dordrecht/Boston/London, (1995), pp. 179-218.

MAHONEY, KATHLEEN E. & MAHONEY, PAUL (eds.): *Human Rights in the twenty-first century: a global challenge*, Martinus Nijhoff Publishers, Dordrecht, (1993).

MAHONEY, PAUL: Judicial activism and judicial self-restraint in the European Court of Human Rights: two sides of the same coin. In: *Human Rights Law Journal,* vol. 11 Nos. 1-2, (1990), pp. 57-88.

MARSHALL, GEOFFREY: Justiciability. In: *Oxford essays in jurisprudence*. Guest, A.G. (ed.), Oxford University Press, Oxford, (1961), pp. 265-288.

MARTIN, DAVID: The Limburg Principles turn ten: an impact assessment. In: *The Maastricht guidelines on violations of economic, social and cultural rights*. Boven, T.C. van; Flinterman, C. & Westendorp, I. (eds.), Netherlands Institute of Human Rights, SIM Special No. 20, Utrecht, (1998), pp. 191-205.

MATAS, DAVID: Economic, social and cultural rights and the role of lawyers: North American perspectives. In: *Economic, social and cultural rights and the role of lawyers: special issue, The Review of the International Commission of Jurist No. 55*, Geneva, (1995), pp. 123-140.

MATSCHER, FRANZ (ed.): *The implementation of economic and social rights: national, international and comparative aspects*, NP Engel Verlag, Kehl am Rhein/Strasbourg/Arlington, (1991).

McBRIDE, JEREMY: Protecting life: a positive obligation to help. In: *Bulletin des droits de'Homme,* No. 9, (2000), pp. 56-66.

McCHESNEY, ALLAN: Promoting the general welfare in a democratic society: balancing human rights and development. In: *Netherlands International Law Review*, vol. XXVII, (1980), pp. 283-334.

McCORQUODALE, ROBERT: Self-determination: a human rights approach. In: *International and Comparative Law Quarterly,* vol. 43, October (1994), pp. 857-885.

McGOLDRICK, DOMINIC: *The Human Rights Committee*, Clarendon Press, Oxford, (1994).

McGOLDRICK, DOMINIC: Sustainable development and human rights: an integrated conceptions. In: *International and Comparative Law Quarterly,* vol. 45, October (1996), pp. 796-818.

McKEAN, WARWICK: *Equality and discrimination under international law*, Clarendon Press, Oxford, (1983).

MERON, THEODOR: *Human rights and humanitarian norms as customary law*, Oxford University Press, Oxford, (1989).

MERRILLS, J.G.: The effectiveness principle. In: *The development of international law by the European Court of Human Rights*, Manchester University Press, New York, (1988), Chapter V, pp. 89-112.

MILNER, WESLEY; POE, STEVEN & LEBLANG, DAVID: Security rights, subsistence rights, and liberties: a theoretical survey of the empirical landscape. In: *Human Rights Quarterly*, vol. 21, (1999), pp. 403-443

MOELLENDORF, DARREL: Reasoning about resources: Soobramoney and the future of socio-economic claims. In: *South African Journal of Human Rights*, vol. 14, (1998), pp. 327-333.

MORPHET, SALLY: Economic, social and cultural rights: the development of governments' views, 1941-88. In: *Economic, social and cultural rights: progress and achievement*. Beddart, R. & Hill, D. (ed.), Macmillan, London, (1992), pp. 74-92.

MOWER, GLEN A.: *International cooperation for social justice: global and regional protection of economic social rights,* Greenwood Press, Westport, Connecticut/London, England, (1985).

NEWMAN, FRANK & WEISSBRODT, DAVID: *International human rights: law, policy and process,* Anderson Publishing, second edition, Cincinnati Ohio, (1996).

NOWAK, MANFRED: The effectiveness of the International Covenant on Civil and Political Rights: stocktaking after the first eleven sessions of the Human Rights Committee. In: *Human Rights Law Journal*, vol. 1 Nos.1-4, (1980), pp. 136-170.

NOWAK, MANFRED: The right to education: its meaning, significance and limitations. In: *Netherlands Quarterly of Human Rights*, vol. 4, (1991), pp. 418-425.

NOWAK, MANFRED: *U.N. Covenant on Civil and Political Rights Commentary*, N.P. Engel Publisher, Kehl am Rhein/Strasbourg/Arlington, (1993).

NOWAK, MANFRED: The right to education. In: *Economic, social and cultural rights: a textbook.* Eide, A.; Krause, C. & Rosas, A. (eds.), Martinus Nijhoff Publishers, Dordrecht, (1995), pp. 189-212.

O' CONNOR, J.F.: *Good faith in international law*, Dartmouth, Aldershot, (1991).

O' DONNELL, J.: States of exception. In: *The Review of the International Commission of Jurists*, vol. 21, (1978), pp. 52-60.

O' FLAHERTY, MICHAEL & HEFFERNAN, LIZ: *International Covenant on Civil and Political Rights: international human rights law in Ireland*, Brehon Publishing, Dublin, (1995).

O' FLAHERTY, MICHAEL: *Human rights and the UN practice before the treaty bodies*, Sweet & Maxwell, United Kingdom, (1996).

O'REGAN, KATE: Introducing socio-economic rights. In: *Economic and Social Rights in South Africa [ESR Review]*, vol. 1 No. 4, (1999), pp. 71-72.

OLOKA-ONYANGO, JOE: Beyond the rhetoric: reinvigorating the struggle for economic and social rights in Africa. In: *California Western International Law Journal,* vol. 26 No. 1, (1995), pp. 1-74.

OLOKA-ONYANGO, JOE: Some reflections on the framework of economic social and cultural rights in Africa. In: *Economic, social and cultural rights and the role of Lawyers: special issue, The Review of the International Commission of Jurists* No. 55, Geneva, (1995*), pp. 167-194.

ÖRÜCÜ, E.: The core of rights and freedoms: the limit of limits. In: *Human rights: from rhetoric to reality,* Campbell, T.; Goldberg, D.; Mclean, S. & Mullen, T. (eds.), Blackwell, New York, (1986), pp. 37-59.

PEASE, KELLY-KATE: Economic globalisation and American society. In: *The United States and human rights: looking inward and outward.* Forsythe, D. (ed.), University of Nebraska Press, Lincoln, (2000), pp. 31-51.

PECES-BARBA MARTINEZ, GREGORIO: Reflections on economic, social and cultural rights. In: *Human Rights Law Journal,* vol. 2, (1981), pp. 281-294.

PELLOMPÄÄ, MATTI: Economic, social and cultural rights. In: *The European system for the protection of human rights.* Macdonald, R. St.J.; Matscher, F. & Petzold, H. (eds.), Martinus Nijhoff Publishers, The Netherlands, (1993), pp. 855-874.

PETTIT, PHILIP: Can the welfare State take rights seriously? In: *Law, rights and the welfare State.* Sampford, C.J.G. & Galligan, D.J. (eds.), Croom Helm, London/Sydney/Wolfeboro, New Hampshire (1986), pp. 67-85.

PLANT, RAYMOND: A defence of welfare rights. In: *Economic, social and cultural rights: progress and achievement.* Beddart, R. & Hill, D. (ed.), Macmillan, London, (1992), pp. 22-46.

PLANT, RAYMOND: Needs, agency and rights. In: *Law, rights and the welfare State.* Sampford, C.J.G. & Galligan, D.J. (eds.), Croom Helm, London/Sydney/Wolfeboro, New Hampshire (1986), pp. 23-48.

PLANT, ROGER: The right to food and agrarian systems: law and practice in Latin America. In: *The right to food.* Alston, P. & Tomaševski, K. (eds.), Martinus Nijhoff Publishers, Utrecht (1984), pp. 187-202.

POCAR, FAUSTO: Legal value of the Human Rights Committee's views. In: *Canadian Human Rights Yearbook* (1991-1992), pp. 119-123.

PREBENSEN, SØREN: Evolutive interpretation of the European Convention on Human Rights. In: *Protecting human rights: the European perspective: studies in memory of Rolv Ryssdal.* Mahoney, P.; Matsher, F.; Petzold, H. & Wildhaber, L. (eds.), Verlag, Köln/Berlin/Bonn/München, (2000), pp. 1123-1137.

PRÉMONT, D; STENERSEN, C. & OSEREDCZUK, I. (eds.): *Non-derogable rights and states of emergency,* Association of International Consultants of Human Rights (CID), Brussels, (1996).

RAMCHARAN, B.G.: Equality and non-discrimination. In: *The International Bill of Rights.* Henkin, L. (ed.), Columbia University Press, New York, (1981), pp. 246-269.

RAMCHARAN, B.G.: The right to life. In: *Netherlands International Law Review,* vol. 30 No. 3, (1983), pp. 279-329.

RAMCHARAN, B.G.: The concept and dimensions of the right to life. In: *The right to life in international law.* Ramcharan, B.G. (ed.), Martinus Nijhoff Publishers, Dordrecht, (1985), pp. 1-32.

RAMCHARAN, B.G.: State responsibility for violations of human rights treaties. In: *Contemporary problems of international law: essays in honour of Georg Schwarzenberger on his eightieth birthday.* Cheng B. & Brown, E.D. (eds.), Steven & son, London, (1988), pp. 242-261.

RIEDEL, EIBE: The examination of state reports. In: *The monitoring system of human rights treaty obligations.* Klein, E. (ed.), Verlag, Berlin, (1998), pp. 95-106.

ROBERTSON, A.H. & MERRILLS, J.G.: *Human rights in the world*, Manchester University Press, Fourth edition, Manchester, (1996).

ROBERTSON, A.H.: The implementation system: international measures. In: *The International Bill of Rights*. Henkin, L. (ed.), Columbia University Press, New York, (1981), pp. 332-369.

ROBERTSON, BERNARD: *Economic, social and cultural rights: time for a reappraisal*, New Zealand Business Roundtable, New Zealand, September (1997).

ROBERTSON, ROBERT E.: Measuring state compliance with the obligation to devote the "maximum available resources" to realising economic, social and cultural rights. In: *Human Rights Quarterly*, vol. 16, (1994), pp. 693-714.

RODLEY, NIGEL: Can armed opposition groups violate human rights? In: *Human rights in the twenty-first century: a global challenge*. Mahoney, K. & Mahoney, P. (eds.), Martinus Nijhoff Publishers, Dordrecht, (1993), pp. 297-318.

RODLEY, NIGEL: Conceptual problems in the protection of minorities: international legal developments. In: *Human Rights Quarterly*, vol. 17 No. 1, (1995), pp. 48-71.

RODLEY, NIGEL: *The treatment of prisoners under international law*, Clarendon Press, second edition, Oxford, (1999).

ROSAS, ALLAN & SANDVIK-NYLUND, MONIKA: Armed Conflicts. In: *Economic, social and cultural rights: a textbook*. Eide, A.; Krause, C. & Rosas, A. (eds.), Martinus Nijhoff Publishers, second revised edition, Dordrecht, (2001), pp. 407-421.

ROSAS, ALLAN: The implementation of economic and social rights: Nordic legal system. In: *The implementation of economic and social rights: national, international and comparative aspects*. Matscher, F. (ed.), NP Engel Verlag, Kehl am Rhein/Strasbourg/Arlington, (1991), pp. 223-236.

RUSSO, CARLO: La justiciabilité des droits économiques et sociaux. In: *Collected Courses of the Academy of European Law*, vol. III, Book 2, Kluwer Law International, The Hague, (1992), pp. 207-235.

RYSSDAL, ROLV: The protection of social and economic rights and the European Convention on Human Rights and Fundamental Freedoms. In: *The implementation of economic and social rights: national, international and comparative aspects*. Matscher, F. (ed.), NP Engel Verlag, Kehl am Rhein/Strasbourg/Arlington, (1991), pp. 1-4.

SADURSKI, WOJCIECH: Economic, rights and basic needs. In: *Law, rights and the welfare State*. Sampford, C.J.G. & Galligan, D.J. (eds.), Croom Helm, London/Sydney/Wolfeboro, New Hampshire, (1986), pp. 49-66.

SAMPFORD, C.J.G. & GALLIGAN, D.J. (eds.): *Law, rights and the welfare State*, Croom Helm, London/Sydney/Wolfeboro, New Hampshire, (1986).

SAMPFORD, CHARLES: The dimensions of rights and their statutory protection. In: *Law, rights and the welfare State*. Sampford, C.J.G. & Galligan, D.J. (eds.), Croom Helm, London/Sydney/Wolfeboro, New Hampshire, (1986), pp. 171-199.

SAMPFORD, CHARLES: The four dimensions of rights. In: *Rethinking human rights*. Galligan, B. & Sampford, C.J.G. (eds.), Federation Press, Sydney, (1997), pp. 50-71.

SCHACHTER, OSCAR: Protecting the world's exiles: the human rights of non-citizens. In: *Human Rights Quarterly*, vol. 22, (2000), pp. 280-297.

SCHACHTER, OSCAR: The obligation of the parties to give effect to the Covenant on Civil and Political Rights. In: *American Journal of International Law*, vol. 73, (1979), pp. 462- 465.

SCHACHTER, OSCAR: The obligation to implement the Covenant in domestic law. In: *The International Bill of Rights*. Henkin, L. (ed.), Columbia University Press, New York, (1981), pp. 311-331.

SCHACHTER, OSCAR: Towards a theory of international obligation. In: *Virginia Journal of International Law*, vol. 8 No. 2, (1968), pp. 300-322.

SCHEININ, MARTIN: Direct applicability of economic, social and cultural rights: a critique of the doctrine of self-executing treaties. In: *Social rights as human rights: a European challenge*, Institute for Human Rights, Åbo Akademi University, Åbo, Finland, (1994), pp. 73-90.

SCHEININ, MARTIN: Economic and social rights as legal rights. In: *Economic, social and cultural rights: a textbook.* Eide, A.; Krause, C. & Rosas, A. (eds.), Martinus Nijhoff Publishers, Dordrecht, first edition, (1995), pp. 41-62.

SCHEININ, MARTIN: International mechanisms and procedures for implementation. In: *An introduction to the international protection of human rights: a textbook.* Hanski, R. & Suksi, M. (eds.), Institute for Human Rights, Åbo Akademi University, Åbo, Finland (1997), pp. 355-378.

SCHEININ, MARTIN: Women's economic and social rights as human rights. In: *New trends in discrimination law: international perspectives*. Hannikainen, L. & Nykänen, E. (eds.), Publications of Turku Law School, vol. 3 No. 1, Turku, (1999), pp. 1-28.

SCHEININ, MARTIN: International human rights in national law. In: *An introduction to the international protection of human rights: a textbook.* Hanski, R. & Suksi, M. (eds.), Institute for Human Rights, Åbo Akademi University, second revised edition, Åbo, Finland (1999*), pp. 417-428.

SCHEININ, MARTIN: The right to enjoy a distinct culture: indigenous and competing uses of land. In: *The jurisprudence of human rights law: a comparative interpretative approach.* Orlin, T.S.; Rosas, A. & Scheinin, M. (eds.), Institute for Human Rights, Åbo Akademi University, Åbo, Finland (2000), pp. 159-222.

SCHEININ, MARTIN: Economic and social rights as legal rights. In: *Economic, social and cultural rights: a textbook.* Eide, A.; Krause, C. & Rosas, A. (eds.), Martinus Nijhoff Publishers, second revised edition, Dordrecht, (2001), pp. 29-54.

SCHMIDT, MARKUS: Treaty-based human rights complaints procedures in the UN: remedy or mirage for victims of human rights violations? In: *Human Rights/Droits del l'Homme,* No. 2, (1998), pp. 13-18.

SCHULKIN, JAY & KLEINDORFER, PAUL: Equity decisions: economic development and environmental prudence. In: *Human Rights Quarterly*, vol. 17 No. 2, (1995), pp. 382-397.

SCHWARZENBERGER, GEORG: Myths and realities of treaty interpretation. In: *Virginia Journal of International Law,* vol. 9 No. 1, (1968), pp. 1-19.

SCHWELB, EGON: Entry into force of the International Covenants on Human Rights and the Optional Protocol to the International Covenant on Civil and Political Rights. In: *American Journal of International Law*, vol. 70 No. 3, (1976), pp. 511-519.

SCHWELB, EGON: Some aspects of the International Covenants on Human Rights of December 1966. In: *International protection of human rights: proceedings of the seventh Nobel Symposium.* Eide, A. & Schou, A. (eds.), Interscience Publishers, Stockholm, (1968), pp. 103-130.

SCHWELB, EGON: The nature of the obligations of the States Parties to the International Covenant on Civil and Political Rights. In: *René Cassin amicorum discipulorumque liber*, Pédone, Paris, vol. I, (1969), pp. 301-324.

SCOTT, CRAIG & MACKLEM, PATRICK: Constitutional ropes of sand or justiciable guarantee? Social rights in a new South African Constitution. In: *University of Pennsylvania Law Review*, vol. 141 No. 1, (1992), pp. 1-148.

SCOTT, CRAIG: The interdependence and permeability of human rights norms: towards a partial fusion of the International Covenants on Human Rights. In: *Osgoode Hall Law Journal,* vol. 27, Ottawa, Canada (1989), pp. 769-878.

SCOTT, CRAIG: Reaching beyond (without abandoning) the category of 'economic, social and cultural rights.' In: *Human Rights Quarterly*, vol. 21, (1999), pp. 633-660.

SCOTT, CRAIG: Bodies of knowledge: a diversity promotion role for the UN High Commissioner for Human Rights. In: *The future of UN human rights treaty monitoring*. Alston, P. & Crawford, J. (eds.), Cambridge University Press, Cambridge, (2000), pp. 403-438.

SEIBERT-FOHR, ANJA: The role of the reporting system in respect of the development of human rights treaties' application. In: *The monitoring system of human rights treaty obligations*. Klein, E. (ed.), Verlag, Berlin, (1998), pp. 111-120.

SEN, AMARTYA: The right not to be hungry. In: *The right to food*. Alston, P. & Tomaševski, K. (eds.), Martinus Nijhoff Publishers, Utrecht, (1984), pp. 69-82.

SEN, AMARTYA: Human rights and economic achievement. In: *The East Asian challenge for human rights*. Bauer, J.R. & Bell, D.A. (eds.), Cambridge University Press, Cambridge, (1999), pp. 88-99.

SHELTON, DINAH: State practice on reservations to human rights treaties. In: *Canadian Human Rights Yearbook*, vol. 1, (1983), pp. 205-234.

SHELTON, DINAH: State responsibility for covert and indirect forms of violence. In: *Human rights in the twenty-first century: a global challenge*. Mahoney, K. & Mahoney, P. (eds.), Martinus Nijhoff Publishers, Dordrecht, (1993), pp. 265-276.

SHELTON, DINAH (ed.): *Commitment and compliance: the role of non-binding norms in the international legal system*, Oxford University Press, Oxford (2000).

SHUE, HENRY: *Basic rights: subsistence, affluence and U.S. foreign policy*, Princeton University Press, first edition, New Jersey, (1980).

SHUE, HENRY: *Basic rights: subsistence, affluence and U.S. foreign policy*, Princeton University Press, second edition, New Jersey, (1996).

SHUE, HENRY: The interdependence of duties. In: *The right to food*. Alston, P. & Tomaševski, K. (eds.), Martinus Nijhoff Publishers, Utrecht, (1984), pp. 83-96.

SIEGHART, PAUL: *The international law of human rights*, Clarendon Press, Oxford, (1983).

SIMMA BRUNO: The examination of state reports: International Covenant on Economic, Social and Cultural rights. In: *The monitoring system of human rights treaty obligations*. Klein, E. (ed.), Verlag, Berlin, (1998), pp. 31-48.

SIMMA, BRUNO: International human rights and general international law: a comparative analysis. In: *Collected Courses of the Academy of European Law*, vol. IV, Book 2, Kluwer Law International, The Netherlands, (1995), pp. 153-236.

SIMMA, BRUNO: The examination of State reports: International Covenant on Economic, Social and Cultural Rights. In: *The monitoring system of human rights treaty obligations*. Klein, E. (ed.), Colloquium Potsdam, 22/23 November 1996, Verlag, Berlin, (1998), pp. 31-48.

SIMMA, BRUNO: The implementation of the International Covenant on Economic, Social and Cultural Rights. In: *The implementation of economic and social rights: national, international and comparative aspects*. Matscher, F. (ed.), N.P. Engel Verlag, Kehl am Rhein/Strasbourg/Arlington, (1991), pp. 75-94.

SKOGLY, SIGRUN I.: Economic and social human rights, private actors and international obligations. In: *Human rights standards and the responsibility of transnational corporations*. Addo, M.K. (ed.), Kluwer Law International, The Hague, (1999), pp. 239-258.

SKOGLY, SIGRUN I.: *From human capital to human rights: the human rights obligations of the World Bank and the International Monetary Fund*. Dissertation presented to the University of Oslo, Faculty of Law for completion of the Degree of Doctor in Law. Unpublished edition, May, (2000).

STAMMERS, NEIL: A critique of social approaches to human rights. In: *Human Rights Quarterly*, vol. 17 No. 3, (1995), pp. 488-508.

STEINER, HENRY & ALSTON, PHILIP: Economic and social rights. In: *International human rights in context: law, politics, morals*, Clarendon Press, first edition, Oxford, (1996).

STEINER, HENRY & ALSTON, PHILIP: *International Human Rights in context: law, politics, morals*, Oxford University Press, second edition, Oxford, (2000).

STEINER, HENRY: Social rights and economic development: converging discourses? In: *Buffalo Human Rights Law Review,* vol. 4, (1998), pp. 25-42.

SVENSSON-McCARTHY, ANNA-LENA: *The international law of human rights and states of exception with special reference to the travaux préparatoires and case-law of the international monitoring organs*, Martinus Nijhoff Publishers, The Hague, (1998).

TOEBES, BRIGIT C.A.: *The right to health as a human right in international law*. Intersentia, Antwerp, (1998).

TOEBES, BRIGIT C.A.: Towards an improved understanding of the international human right to health. In: *Human Rights Quarterly,* vol. 21, (1999), pp. 661-679.

TOMAŠEVSKI, KATERINA: Human rights indicators: the right to food as a test case. In: *The right to food.* Alston, P. & Tomaševski, K. (eds.), Martinus Nijhoff Publishers, Utrecht, (1984), pp. 135-168.

TOMAŠEVSKI, KATERINA: Defining violations of the right to food. In: *The right to complain about economic, social and cultural rights.* Coomans, F. & Hoof, G.J.H. van (eds.), Netherlands Institute of Human Rights, SIM Special No. 18, Utrecht, (1995), pp. 35-76.

TOMAŠEVSKI, KATERINA: Health rights. In: *Economic, social and cultural rights: a textbook.* Eide, A.; Krause, C. & Rosas, A. (eds.), Martinus Nijhoff Publishers, Dordrecht, (1995*), pp. 125-142.

TOMAŠEVSKI, KATERINA: Justiciability of economic, social and cultural rights. In: *Economic, social and cultural rights and the role of lawyers: special issue, The Review of the International Commission of Jurist, No. 55*, Geneva, (1995**), pp. 203-218.

TOMUSCHAT, CHRISTIAN: What is a 'breach' of the European Convention on Human Rights? In: *The dynamics of the protection of human rights in Europe: essays in honour of Henry G. Schermers.* Lawson, R. & Blois, M. de (eds.), Martinus Nijhoff Publishers, Dordrecht, vol. III, (1994), pp. 315-335.

TRUBEK, DAVID M.: Economic, social and cultural rights in the third world: human rights law and human needs programs. In: *Human rights in international law: legal and policy issues.* Meron, T. (ed.), Clarendon Press, Oxford, vol. I, Chapter 6, (1984), pp. 205-271.

TÜRK, DANILO: The United Nations and the realization of economic, social and cultural rights. In: *The implementation of economic and social rights: national, international and comparative aspects.* Matscher, F. (ed.), NP Engel Verlag, Kehl am Rhein/Strasbourg/Arlington, vol. III, (1991), pp. 95-122.

TÜRK, DANILO: The future protection of economic, social and cultural rights: a Yugoslavian perspective. In: *Perspectives of an All-European system of human rights protection: the role of the Council of Europe, the CSCE, and the European Communities.* Kedzia, Z.; Korula, A. & Nowak, M., NP Engel Verlag, Kehl am Rhein/Strasbourg/Arlington, vol. I, (1991), pp. 319-325.

VASAK, KAREL (ed.): *The international dimensions of human rights*, UNESCO, Paris, (1992).

VIERDAG, E.W.: Some remarks about special features of human rights treaties. In: *Netherlands Yearbook of International Law,* vol. XXV, (1994), pp. 119-142.

VIERDAG, E.W.: *The concept of discrimination in international law: with special reference to human rights*, Martinus Nijhoff Publishers, (1973).

VIERDAG, E.W: The legal nature of the rights granted by the International Covenant on Economic, Social and Cultural Rights. In: *Netherlands Yearbook of International Law,* vol. IX, (1978), pp. 69-105.

VILJANEN, VELI-PEKKA: Abstention or involvement? The nature of State obligations under different categories of rights. In: *Social rights as human rights: a European challenge*, Institute for Human Rights, Åbo Akademi University, Åbo, Finland, (1994), pp. 43-66.

WEISSBRODT, DAVID: A new United Nations mechanism for encouraging the ratification of human rights treaties. In: *American Journal of International Law*, vol. 76 No. 2, (1982), pp. 418-429.

WELLMAN, CARL: *An approach to rights: studies in the philosophy of law and morals*, Kluwer Academic Publishers, Dordrecht, (1997).

WELLMAN, CARL: Solidarity, the individual and human rights. In: *Human Rights Quarterly*, vol. 22, (2000), pp. 639-657.

WESTENDORP, INGRID: The feasibility of a violations approach of women's economic, social and cultural rights. In: *The Maastricht guidelines on violations of economic, social and cultural rights*. Boven, T.C. van; Flinterman, C. & Westendorp, I. (eds.), Netherlands Institute of Human Rights, SIM Special No. 20, Utrecht, (1998), pp. 147-163.

WESTERVEEN, GERT: Towards a system for supervising States' compliance with the right to food. In: *The right to food.* Alston, P. & Tomaševski, K. (eds.), Martinus Nijhoff Publishers, Utrecht (1984), pp. 119-134.

WESTON, BURNS H.: US ratification of the International Covenant on Economic, Social and Cultural Rights: with or without qualifications. In: *US ratification of the human rights treaties: with or without reservations?* Lillich, R. (ed.), University Press of Virginia, Charlottesville, (1981), pp. 68-72.

WIERVSZEWSKI, ROMAN: some comments concerning the concept of economic and social rights. In: *Social rights as human rights: a European challenge*, Institute for Human Rights, Åbo Akademi University, Åbo, Finland (1994), pp. 67-72.

WYRZYKOWSKI, MIROSTAW: Social rights in the jurisprudence of the Commissioner for citizens' rights in Poland. In: *Social rights as human rights: a European challenge*, Institute for Human Rights, Åbo Akademi University, Åbo, Finland, (1994), pp. 251-274.

YOKOTA, YOZO: Reflections on the future of economic, social and cultural rights. In: *The future of international human rights.* Weston, B.H. & Marks, S.P. (eds. & contribs.), Transnational Publishers, Ardsley/New York, (1999), pp. 201-223.

Selected Spanish Bibliography

ABRAMOVICH VÍCTOR & COURTIS, CHRISTIAN: Hacia la exigibilidad de los derechos económicos, sociales y culturales. Estándares internacionales y criterios de aplicación ante los tribunales locales. In: *La aplicación de los tratados sobre derechos humanos por los tribunales locales*. Abregú, M. & Courtis, C. (eds.), Centro de Estudios Legales y Sociales, Buenos Aires, Argentina, (1997), pp. 283-350.

ALEXY, ROBERT: *Teoría de los derechos fundamentales*, Centro de Estudios Constitucionales, Madrid, (1993).

AÑON, MARÍA JOSÉ: *Necesidades y derechos: un ensayo de fundamentación,* Centro de Estudios Constitucionales, Madrid, (1994).

BERLIN, ISAIAH: *Cuatro ensayos sobre la libertad*, Alianza, Madrid, (1988).

BOBBIO, NORBERTO: *El Tiempo de los derechos*, Editorial Sistema, Madrid, (1991).

CARRILLO SALCEDO, J.A.: *Soberanía de los estados y derechos humanos en el derecho internacional contemporáneo*, Tecnos, Madrid, (1995).

CASCAJO CASTRO, JOSÉ LUIS: *La tutela constitucional de los derechos sociales*, Centro de Estudios Constitucionales, Cuadernos y Debates No. 5, Madrid, (1988).

CASSESE, ANTONIO: *Los derechos humanos en el mundo contemporáneo*, Ariel, Barcelona, (1993).

CHUECA SANCHO, ANGEL: Los derechos humanos protegidos en la Convención Americana de San José de 1969. In: *Revista Española de Derecho Internacional*, vol. XXXII, Nos. 1-3, Madrid, (1980), pp. 33-78.

CONTRERAS PELÁEZ, FRANCISCO: *Derechos sociales: teoría e ideología*, Tecnos, Madrid, (1994).

DIEZ DE VELASCO, MANUEL: *Las organizaciones internacionales*, Tecnos, ninth edition, Madrid, (1995).

DIEZ DE VELASCO, MANUEL & SOBRINO HEREDIA, J.M.: La política social internacional. In: *Garantía internacional de los derechos sociales*, Ministerio de Asuntos Sociales, Madrid, (1990).

EIDE, ASBJØRN: *El Derecho a una alimentación adecuada como derecho Humano*, Naciones Unidas, serie de estudios No. 1, sales No. S.89.XIV.2, New York, (1989).

FERNÁNDEZ, EUSEBIO: *Teoría de la Justicia y derechos humanos*, Editorial Debate, Madrid, (1984).

GARZÓN VALDÉS, ERNESTO: Necesidades básicas, deseos legítimos y legitimidad política en la concepción de Mario Bunge. In: *Derecho, ética y política*, Centro de Estudios Constitucionales, Madrid, (1993), pp. 417-435.

FAÚNDEZ LEDESMA, H.: *El sistema interamericano de protección de los derechos humanos*, Inter-American Institute for Human Rights, Costa Rica, (1996).

MARIÑO MENÉNDEZ, FERNANDO: *Derecho internacional público: parte general*, Trotta, Madrid, second edition, (1995).

MARIÑO MENÉNDEZ, FERNANDO (ed.): *Balance y perspectivas de Naciones Unidas en el cincuentenario de su creación*, Universidad Carlos III de Madrid, Boletín Oficial del Estado, Madrid, (1996).

MARIÑO MENÉNDEZ, FERNANDO & FERNÁNDEZ LIESA, CARLOS (eds.): *El desarrollo y la cooperación internacional*, Universidad Carlos III de Madrid, Boletín Oficial del Estado, Madrid, (1997).

MARTI DE VESES, C.: El proceso de positivación de los derechos económicos, sociales y culturales en el derecho internacional. In: *Anuario de Derechos Humanos,* No. 3, (1985), pp. 175-220.

MIGNONE, EMILIO F.: Los derechos económicos, sociales y culturales en las constituciones políticas de los países del cono sur. In: *Estudios básicos de derechos humanos*, Inter-American Institute for Human Rights, vol. V, Costa Rica, (1996).

ORDOÑEZ, JAIME & VELAZQUEZ ENRIQUE: *Derechos económicos y desarrollo en America Latina*, Inter-American Institute for Human Rights, San Jose, Costa Rica, (1991).

PASTOR RIDRUEJO, JOSE ANTONIO: *Curso de derecho internacional público y organizaciones internacionales*, Tecnos, fifth edition, Madrid, (1994).

PECES-BARBA MARTINEZ, GREGORIO: *Curso de derechos fundamentales: teoría general*, Universidad Carlos III de Madrid, Boletín Oficial del Estado, Madrid, (1995).

PECES-BARBA, GREGORIO: Sobre el puesto de la historia en el concepto de los derechos fundamentales. In: *Anuario de Derechos Humanos*, No. 4, Universidad Complutense, Madrid, (1986-1987), pp. 219-258.

PECES-BARBA, GREGORIO: *Tránsito a la modernidad y derechos fundamentales*, Mezquita, Madrid, (1982).

PEREZ LUÑO, ANTONIO E.: *Derechos humanos, estado de derecho y constitución*, Tecnos, fifth edition, Madrid, (1995).

PRIETO SANCHÍS, LUIS: Los derechos sociales y el principio de igualdad sustancial. In: *Revista del Centro de Estudios Constitucionales*, No. 22, Madrid, (1995), pp. 9-57.

RAWLS, JOHN: *Teoría de la justicia*, Fondo de Cultura Económica, Madrid, (1978).

SAUCA, J.M. (ed.): *Problemas actuales de los derechos fundamentales*, Universidad Carlos III, Boletín Oficial del Estado, Madrid, (1994).

SEN, AMARTYA: *Nuevo exámen de la desigualdad*, Alianza, Madrid, (1995).

SIMMA, BRUNO: Mecanismo, jurisprudencia y perspectivas del pacto internacional de derechos económicos, sociales y culturales. In: *El Derecho a la equidad. ética y mundialización social,* Icaria, Barcelona, (1997), pp. 151-170.

SQUELLA, AGUSTÍN: *Estudios sobre derechos humanos*, Edeval, Valparaiso, (1991).

TEITELBAUM, ALEJANDRO: El problema de la impunidad: las violaciones de los derechos económicos, sociales y culturales. In: *El Derecho a la equidad: ética y mundialización social*, Icaria, Barcelona, (1997), pp. 117-154.

TEXIER, PHILIPPE: Las misiones de asistencia técnica del Comité de Derechos Económicos, Sociales y Culturales. In: *El Derecho a la equidad: ética y mundialización social*, Icaria, Barcelona, (1997), pp. 171-176.

VILLÁN DURÁN, CARLOS: *Curso de derecho internacional de los derechos humanos,* International Institute for Human Rights, Strasbourg, (1995).

VILLÁN DURAN, CARLOS: *La protección de los derechos humanos en el sistema de las Naciones Unidas y de sus organismos especializados*, International Institute for Human Rights, Strasbourg, (1997).

Selected Documents

General Comments adopted by the Committee on Economic, Social and Cultural Rights

http://www.unhchr.ch/tbs/doc.nsf
Compilation of General Comments and General Recommendations Adopted by Human Rights Treaty Bodies. UN Doc HRI/GEN/1/Rev.5
Third session (1989)
General Comment No. 1 - Reporting by States parties.
Fourth session (1990)
General Comment No. 2 - International technical assistance measures (art. 22 of the Covenant).
Fifth session (1990)
General Comment No. 3 - The nature of States parties' obligations (art. 2, para. 1, of the Covenant).
Sixth session (1991)
General Comment No. 4 - The right to adequate housing (art. 11 (1) of the Covenant).
Eleventh session (1994)
General Comment No. 5 - Persons with disabilities.
Thirteenth session (1995)
General Comment No. 6 - The economic, social and cultural rights of older persons.
Sixteenth session (1997)
General Comment No. 7 - The right to adequate housing (art. 11 (1) of the Covenant): forced evictions.
Seventeenth session (1997)
General Comment No. 8 - The relationship between economic sanctions and respect for economic, social and cultural rights.
Nineteenth session (1998)
General Comment No. 9 - The domestic application of the Covenant.
General Comment No. 10 - The role of national human rights institutions in the protection of economic, social and cultural rights.
Twentieth session (1999)
General Comment No. 11 - Plans of action for primary education (art. 14).
General Comment No. 12 - The right to adequate food (art. 11).
Twenty-first session (1999)
General Comment No. 13 - The right to education (art. 13).
Twenty-second session (2000)
General Comment No. 14 - The right to the highest attainable standard of health (art. 12).

Selected General Comments adopted by the Human Rights Committee

Thirteenth session (1981)
General Comment No. 3 - Article 2. Implementation at the national level.
General Comment No. 4 - Article 3. Equality between sexes.

Sixteenth session (1982)
General Comment No. 6 - Article 6. The right to life
General Comment No. 7 - Article 7.
General Comment No. 9 - Article 10.
Twenty-first session (1984)
General Comment No. 12 - Article 1.
Twenty-third session (1984)
General Comment No. 14 - Article 6.
Twenty-seventh session (1986)
General Comment No. 15 - The position of aliens under the Covenant.
Thirty-seventh session (1989)
General Comment No. 18 - Non-discrimination.
Thirty-ninth session (1990)
General Comment No. 19 - Article 23. Protection of the family, the right to marriage and equality of the spouses.
Forty-fourth session (1992)
General Comment No. 20 - Article 7. Replaces General Comment No. 7 concerning prohibition of torture and cruel treatment or punishment.
General Comment No. 21 - Article 10. Replaces General Comment No. 9 concerning humane treatment of persons deprived of liberty.
Forty-eighth session (1993)
General Comment No. 22 - Article 18.
Fiftieth session (1994)
General Comment No. 23 - Article 27. The rights of minorities.
Fifty-second session (1994)
General Comment No. 24 - General Comment on issues relating to reservations made upon ratification or accession to the Covenant or the Optional Protocols thereto, or in relation to declarations under article 41 of the Covenant
Sixty-eighth session (2000)
General Comment No. 28 - Article 3. Equality of rights between men and women.

Selected General Recommendations adopted by the Committee on the Elimination of Racial Discrimination

Fifth session (1972)
General Recommendation I - States parties' obligations (art. 4 of the Convention).
General Recommendation II - States parties' obligations.
Thirty-second session (1985)
General Recommendation VII - Implementation of article 4 of the Convention.
Thirty-eighth session (1990)
General Recommendation VIII - Interpretation and application of article 1, paragraphs 1 and 4, of the Convention.
Forty-second session (1993)
General Recommendation XI - Non-citizens.
Fifty-sixth session (2000)
General Recommendation XXV - Gender-related dimensions of racial discrimination.
Fifty-seventh session (2000)
General Recommendation XXVII - Discrimination against Roma.

Selected General Recommendations adopted by the Committee on the Elimination of Discrimination against Women

Sixth session (1987)
General Recommendation No. 3 - Education and public information campaigns.
Seventh session (1988)
General Recommendation No. 5 - Temporary special measures.
General Recommendation No. 6 - Effective national machinery and publicity.
Eighth session (1989)
General Recommendation No. 12 - Violence against women.
General Recommendation No. 13 - Equal remuneration for work of equal value.
Ninth session (1990)
General Recommendation No. 14 - Female circumcision.
General Recommendation No. 15 - Avoidance of discrimination against women in national strategies for the prevention and control of acquired immunodeficiency syndrome (AIDS).
Tenth session (1991)
General Recommendation No. 18 - Disabled women.
Eleventh session (1992)
General Recommendation No. 19 - Violence against women.
Thirteenth session (1994)
General Recommendation No. 21 - Equality in marriage and family relations.

Selected reports of UN Sub-Commission on the Promotion and Protection of Human Rights' Special Rapporteurs

Bengoa, J.: 'The relationship between the enjoyment of human rights, in particular economic, social and cultural rights and income distribution.' E/CN.4/Sub.2/1997/9, of 30 June 1997.
Eide, A.: 'Report on the right to adequate food as a human rights.' E/CN.4/Sub.2/1987/23, of 7 July 1987.
Guissé, H.: 'Second interim report on the question of the impunity of perpetrators of human rights violations'. E/CN.4/Sub.2/1996/15, of 3 July 1996.
Sachar, R: 'The right to adequate housing'. E/CN.4/Sub.2/1993/15, of 22 June 1993 and E/CN.4/Sub.2/1995/12, of 12 July 1995 [final report].
Türk, D: 'The realisation of economic, social and cultural rights.' E/CN.4/Sub.2/1992/16, of 3 July 1992.

Selected Documents of the Committee on Economic, Social and Cultural Rights

Revised Guidelines Regarding the Form and Contents of Reports to be Submitted by States Parties Under article 16 and 17 of the International Covenant on Economic, Social and Cultural Rights. ECOSOC, Official Records, 1992, Supplement No. 3. UN Doc. E/1992/23.

Selected ILO Conventions

http://ilolex.ilo.ch:1567/english/convdisp1.htm
Convention No. 182: Convention concerning the Prohibition and Immediate Action for the Elimination of the Worst Forms of Child Labour
Convention No. 169: Convention concerning Indigenous and Tribal Peoples in Independent Countries

Selection of other Documents

The Limburg Principles on the Implementation of the International Covenant on Economic, Social and Cultural Rights. In: *Human Rights Quarterly,* vol. 9 No. 2 (1987), pp. 122-146.

The Maastricht Guidelines on Violations of Economic, Social and Cultural Rights. In: *The Maastricht Guidelines on Violations of Economic, Social and Cultural Rights*. Boven, Theo C. van; Flinterman, Cees & Westendorp, Ingrid (eds.), *SIM Special* No. 20, Utrecht, (1998), pp. 1-12.

The Quito Declaration on the Enforcement and Realisation of Economic, Social and Cultural Rights in Latin America and the Caribbean. In: Yale Human Rights and Development Law Journal, vol. 2, (1999) at. 5. Available at: *http://diana.law.yale.edu/yhrdlj/index_enhanced.htm*

The Siracusa Principles on the Limitation and Derogation Provisions in the International Covenant on Civil and Political Rights. In: *The Review International Commission of Jurist*, No. 36, June (1986), pp. 47-56.

Bangalore Declaration and Plan of Action. In: *Economic, social and cultural rights and the role of lawyers: special issue, The Review of the International Commission of Jurists* No. 55, Geneva, (1995).

NJCM Commentary: Dutch section of the International Commission of Jurist: *Commentary Concerning the Strengthening of Respect for Economic, Social and Cultural Rights, (1994).*

Standard Minimum Rules for the Treatment of Prisoners, approved by the ECOSOC by Resolutions 663 C (XXIV) of 31 July 1957 and 2076 (LXII) of 13 May 1977.

Body of Principles for the Protection of All Persons under Any Form of Detention or Imprisonment, adopted by General Assembly Resolution 43/173 of 9 December 1988.

Code of Conduct for Law Enforcement Officials, adopted by General Assembly Resolution 34/169 of 17 December 1979.

Principles of Medical Ethics relevant to the Role of Health Personnel, particularly Physicians, in the Protection of Prisoners and Detainees against Torture and Other Cruel, Inhuman or Degrading Treatment or Punishment, adopted by General Assembly Resolution 37/194 of 18 December 1982.

TABLE OF CASES

Human Rights Committee

African Commission on Human and Peoples' Rights

European Court of Human Rights

European Commission on Human Rights

Inter-American Court of Human Rights

Inter-American Commission of Human Rights

International Tribunal for the Former Yugoslavia

Committee of Ministers under the European Social Charter

European Court of Justice

National cases

Table of Advisory Opinions

International Court of Justice

Inter-American Court of Human Rights

INDEX

SCHOOL OF HUMAN RIGHTS RESEARCH SERIES

The School of Human Rights Research is a joint effort by human rights researchers in the Netherlands. Its central research theme is the nature and meaning of international standards in the field of human rights, their application and promotion in the national legal order, their interplay with national standards, and the international supervision of such application. The School of Human Rights Research Series only includes English titles that contribute to a better understanding of the different aspects of human rights.

Published titles within the Series:

1 Brigit C.A. Toebes, *The Right to Health as a Human Right in International Law*
ISBN 90-5095-057-4

2 Ineke Boerefijn, *The Reporting Procedure under the Covenant on Civil and Political Rights. Practice and Procedures of the Human Rights Committee*
ISBN 90-5095-074-4

3 Kitty Arambulo, *Strengthening the Supervision of the International Covenant on Economic, Social and Cultural Rights. Theoretical and Procedural Aspects*
ISBN 90-5095-058-2

4 Marlies Glasius, *Foreign Policy on Human Rights. Its Influence on Indonesia under Soeharto*
ISBN 90-5095-089-2

5 Cornelis D. de Jong, *The Freedom of Thought, Conscience and Religion or Belief in the United Nations (1946-1992)*
ISBN 90-5095-137-6

6 Heleen Bosma, *Freedom of Expression in England and under the ECHR: in Search of a Common Ground. A Foundation for the Application of the Human Rights Act 1998 in English Law*
ISBN 90-5095-136-8

7 Mielle Bulterman, *Human Rights in the External Relations of the European Union*
ISBN 90-5095-164-3

8 Esther M. van den Berg, *The Influence of Domestic NGOs on Dutch Human Rights Policy. Case Studies on South Africa,Namibia, Indonesia and East Timor*
ISBN 90-5095-159-7

9. Ian Seiderman, *Hierarchy in International Law: the Human Rights Dimension*
ISBN 90-5095-165-1

10. Anna Meijknecht, *Towards International Personality: the Position of Minorities and Indigenous Peoples in International Law*
ISBN 90-5095-166-X

11. Mohamed Eltayeb, *A Human Rights Approach to Combating Religious Persecution. Cases from Pakistan, Saudi Arabia and Sudan*
ISBN 90-5095-170-8

12. Machteld Boot, *Genocide, Crimes Against Humanity, War Crimes: Nullum Crimen Sine Lege and the Subject Matter Jurisdiction of the International Criminal Court*
ISBN 90-5095-216-X

13. Corinne Packer, *Using Human Rights to Change Tradition. Traditional Practices Harmful to Women's Reproductive Health in sub-Saharan Africa*
ISBN 90-5095-226-7

14. Theo R.G. van Banning, *The Human Right to Property*
ISBN 90-5095-203-8

15. Yvonne M. Donders, *Towards a Right to Cultural Identity?*
ISBN 90-5095-238-0

16. Göran K. Sluiter, *International Criminal Adjudication and the Collection of Evidence: Obligations of States*
ISBN 90-5095-227-5

17. Nicola Jägers, *Corporate Human Rights Obligations: in Search of Accountability*
ISBN 90-5095-240-2